The American Society of International Law
STUDIES IN FOREIGN INVESTMENT
AND
ECONOMIC DEVELOPMENT

Previously published
Foreign Enterprise in India: Laws and Policies by Matthew J. Kust
Foreign Enterprise in Colombia: Laws and Policies
by Seymour W. Wurfel
Foreign Enterprise in Nigeria: Laws and Policies by Paul O. Proehl
Foreign Enterprise in Mexico: Laws and Policies by Harry K. Wright

FOREIGN ENTERPRISE
IN JAPAN

Laws and Policies

FOREIGN ENTERPRISE IN JAPAN

Laws and Policies

---

by DAN FENNO HENDERSON

The University of North Carolina Press
Chapel Hill

Copyright © 1973 by
The University of North Carolina Press
All rights reserved
Manufactured in the United States of America
ISBN 0-8078-1210-2
Library of Congress Catalog Card Number 72-87493

Library of Congress Cataloging in Publication Data

Henderson, Dan Fenno, 1921–
    Foreign enterprise in Japan.

    (The American Society of International Law. Studies
in foreign investment and economic development)
        Bibliography: p.
        1. Business enterprises, Foreign—Japan.
2. Investments, Foreign—Law and legislation—Japan.
I. Title.   II. Series: Studies in foreign investment
and economic development.
Law   346'.52'092   72-87493
ISBN 0-8078-1210-2

For Louis S. *and* Louis D.

Foreword

Dan Fenno Henderson's unique study of *Foreign Enterprise in Japan* is the fifth and last of a series of studies, commissioned by the American Society of International Law, of the legal environment for foreign investment in selected countries. Earlier monographs on India, Colombia, Nigeria, and Mexico also were published by The University of North Carolina Press.

The aim of the series is to describe and analyze the legal institutions and practices that govern the participation of foreign capital and technology in economic development through thorough consideration of the experience of five key countries. Three are "developing"—a term that in the cases of India, Colombia, and Nigeria truly imports forward motion. A fourth, Mexico, has been developing at an especially notable rate. The fifth, Japan, is a phenomenon of economic upsurge all its own.

The factors that affect foreign private investment are not, or may not be, primarily "legal." Yet important policies of an economic, social, and ideological nature are often crystallized in legal form. The adequacy or inadequacy of the legal framework for investment may markedly influence the potential foreign investor in his decision to invest or not to invest. The possibilities and lack of possibilities for investment may in vital measure be governed by the laws in force. Moreover, the practice of governments in dealing with foreign investment is part of the raw material of international law; it is of great importance in the shaping of a law that has its impact upon, and reflects the impact of, the policies of governments, corporations, and lending institutions, national and international.

The committee of the Society that planned the series was under the chairmanship of the Honorable John R. Stevenson, then of the firm of Sullivan & Cromwell in New York, now the Legal Adviser of the U.S.

Department of State. Mr. Stevenson; Professor Covey T. Oliver, University of Pennsylvania Law School (who has served, *inter alia,* as U.S. Ambassador to Colombia and Assistant Secretary of State for Inter-American Affairs); Professor Myres S. McDougal, Yale Law School; Lester Nurick, Deputy General Counsel of the International Bank for Reconstruction and Development; and Walter Sterling Surrey of the firm of Surrey, Karasik, and Morse of Washington, D.C., assisted by the Society's staff, drew up the "guidelines" that have served as a general outline of contents for each book in the series.

In this series of country studies, each author has been assisted by an interdisciplinary advisory committee. Those who have counseled Professor Henderson, who is Professor of Law at the University of Washington School of Law, are: James L. Anderson of the Illinois Bar; Robert Barnett of the Asia Society; Thomas L. Blakemore, Jr., in legal practice in Tokyo; Carl J. Bradshaw, Vice President and Director of the International Division of Oak Electro-Netics Corporation; John Christensen, in practice in Tokyo; Mr. Yasuhiro Fujita, in practice in Tokyo; Miss Eleanor M. Hadley of Washington, D.C.; Eric H. Hager of the New York Bar; Professor Richard W. Jennings, University of California; Eugene H. Lee, in practice in Tokyo; Toshio Miyatake, also a Tokyo practitioner; Professor Hugh T. Patrick, Yale University; Richard W. Rabinowitz of the Tokyo Bar; Professor Henry Rosovsky, Harvard University; Professor Warren L. Shattuck, University of Washington School of Law; Peter Solbert of the New York Bar; and Griffith Way of the Bar of the State of Washington.

Neither the Society nor the advisory group bears responsibility for the views expressed in this book. Professor Henderson has had the benefit of a diversity of views and has formed his own. The Society is very pleased to have contributed to the preparation of a truly exceptional and timely work whose quality will, it is believed, attract wide appreciation.

On the Society's behalf, I wish to thank Professor Henderson, the members of the planning and advisory groups, and The University of North Carolina Press. May I also record the Society's profound and continuing appreciation to the Ford Foundation, whose generosity has supported this and so many other Society endeavors.

Stephen M. Schwebel
Executive Vice President
American Society of International Law

Washington, D.C.
March 1973

Preface

Throughout the 1960s and early 1970s, foreign enterprise in Japan was caught up in the worldwide controversy, largely articulated through OECD, over Japan's "insular internationalism"—a policy of allegedly trading and investing internationally (particularly in the U.S.), while maintaining insular restrictions domestically. Insularity is now subsiding, but while the debate was going on, understandably the issues were viewed differently, because of different perspectives, by the several participants—international organizations, the Japanese government, Japanese business, foreign governments, and foreign business, even in the later stages Japanese consumers. My preferences are for reciprocally free trade and investment underwritten, however imperfectly, by something like IMF, GATT, OECD, or other treaties, and I have approached the policy portions of this study from that perspective up to 1973.

After 1971, the treaty problems of capital liberalization in Japan had largely merged with the much broader problems of the world economy calling for changes in currency, capital, and trade structures to accommodate the increasing comparative strength of Japan and Europe. These were issues for economic diplomacy at the highest level, where relative national influence could be used to leaven unviable rigidities of the past, both national and international. Continued bilateral bickering at the legal and business level showed little promise, because real solutions would be diplomatic, multilateral, and necessarily premised on the obsolescence of the imaginary globally hard dollar as well as the old-styled *pax Americana*. Economic diplomacy was also forcing the U.S. by 1971 to protect her national interest, when encountering nationalism abroad; unilateral adherence to free trade or investment without reciprocity was becoming too costly. Instead of reacting piecemeal with new U.S. barriers invoked by weakness rather than strength, the U.S. was seeking a new structuring based on a flexibly adjustable reciprocity, and this new economic policy was having a major impact on Japan and its attitudes toward foreign enterprises, as I have tried to document within. There is still, however, a sharp contrast between Japanese attitudes toward foreign business entries into Japan, and the active solicitation of Japanese investment into the U.S. by delegations from the various states.

Rapid Japanese changes have delayed this book too long; I have continually felt entrapped by a hope to treat an overly broad subject in depth, while being regularly outdated by the dynamics of Japanese growth. But the discomforts of a prolonged gestation are relieved somewhat by realizing now that the book will appear finally at a time when it can close out an epoch in Japanese growth and point the way to another. An additional bonus, gradually accruing, has been much help from others. In 1963, monographic support was scarce for many of the topics covered by the guidelines of this series, but by 1972 the literature on Japan was becoming more adequate in support of a synoptic overview of the Japanese environment for foreigners. I have benefited much from these recent writers in both Japanese and English as is clear enough, I trust, from the notes and bibliography appended. I feel a similar kind of gratitude-in-general toward all the many Japanese with whom I have worked and learned both there and here, whether in government, business, or academics; some of the benefits of Japan's success achieved through such individual's vitality and dedication inevitably rubs off, even on the foreign observer.

In addition to my primary debts to the American Society of International Law and all members of the Advisory Committee, I wish to thank H. C. L. Merillat, Lehan K. Tunks, and Carl Bradshaw for their encouragement and help at the inception, and Stephen M. Schwebel and Warren L. Shattuck for their constant support in later stages.

Among Japanese lawyers, I have the greatest debt to Teisuke Akamatsu, Yasuhiro Fujita and Toshio Miyatake for their help over several years in one way or another. Also Akira Fukami and Moriyasu Michino helped on parts of the manuscript and bibliography at the final stage. My master's degree students on the U.S. side have all been helpful indirectly, but Griffith Way, Eugene H. Lee, James L. Anderson, John O. Haley, Yoshihiko Ito, and Donald Swisher deserve special mention. The views and errors herein are, of course, still mine.

During the processing of several drafts and preparing the manuscript for press, Takika Lee has assisted throughout with Japanese-language materials in Seattle, and Kinko Doyama has been most helpful in obtaining source materials in Tokyo and checking some English and Japanese citation styles. I have also been fortunate in having extraordinary secretaries. I wish to thank Setsuko Satō for the calligraphy and Ethel Edwards, Joan Short, Alice Thome, and June Votaw for their hard work and good cheer.

Dan Fenno Henderson

Seattle, Washington
1 June 1973

Contents

List of Abbreviations

AAA	American Arbitration Association
ACCJ	American Chamber of Commerce in Japan
AML	Anti-Monopoly Law
	(*Shiteki dokusen no kinshihō oyobi kōsei torihiki no kakuho ni kansuru hōritsu*)
CC	Civil Code
	(*Mimpō*)
CCP	Code of Civil Procedure
	(*Minji Soshōhō*)
Com. Code	Commercial Code
	(*Shōhō*)
Chūritsu Rōren	Federation of Independent Unions
CIF	Cost insurance and freight
Dist. Ct.	District Court
	(Post-WW II: *Chihō saibansho*)
Dōmei	Japanese Confederation of Labor
DSP	Democratic Socialist Party
	(*Minshū Shakaitō*)
EHS	*Eibun hōreisha*
	(Publishers of laws and ordinances in English)
FAA	Federal Arbitration Act (U.S.)
FCF	Foreign controlled firm
FCN	Treaty of Friendship, Commerce and Navigation
FECL	Foreign Exchange Control Law
	(*Gaikoku kawase oyobi gaikoku bōeki kanrihō*)
FEO	Federation of Economic Organizations
	(*Kenzai Dantai Rengōkai*)
FIC	Foreign Investment Council
	(*Gaishi Shingikai*)

FIL   Foreign Investment Law
              (*Gaishi ni kansuru hōritsu*)
FRF   Foreign Related Firm
              (*Gaishi-kei kigyō*)
FTC   Fair Trade Commission
              (*Kōsei Torihiki Iinkai*)
GATT   General Agreement on Tariffs and Trade
GNP   Gross National Product
Gr. Ct. Cass. Great Court of Cassation
              (Pre-WW II highest court: *Daishin'in*)
HCS   Higher Civil Servant
High Ct.   High Court
              (Post-WW II: *Kōtō saibansho*)
IMF   International Monetary Fund
JAIL   Japanese Annual of International Law
JCAA   Japanese Commercial Arbitration Association
              (*Kokusai Chūsai Kyōkai*)
JCED   Japan Committee for Economic Development
              (*Keizai Dōyūkai*)
JCP   Japan Communist Party
              (*Nihon Kyōsantō*)
JERC   Japanese Economic Research Center
              (*Nihon Keizai Kenkyūjo*)
JFEA   Japanese Federation of Employers' Association
              (*Nihon Keieisha Dantai Remmei*)
JSP   Japan Socialist Party
              (*Nihon Shakaitō*)
Kakyū minshū *Kakyū saibansho minji saiban reishū*
              (Lower court [*chihō saibansho*] civil case reports)
Keidanren   *Keizai Dantai Rengokai*
              (Federation of Economic Organizations)
Keishū   *Saikō saibansho keiji hanreishū*
              (Japanese Supreme Court Criminal Case Report)
Kōsai minshū *Kōtō saibansho minji hanreishū*
              (High Court [*Kōtō saibansho*] civil case reports)
K.K.   *Kabushiki kaisha*
              (Stock corporation)
LDP   Liberal Democratic Party
              (*Jiyū Minshūtō*)
LRAL   Labor Relations Adjustment Law
              (*Rōdō kankei chōseihō*)

LSL	Labor Standards Law (*Rōdō kijunhō*)
LUL	Labor Union Law (*Rōdō kumiaihō*)
Minroku	*Daishin'in minji hanketsuroku* (Great Court of Cassation Civil Case Reports)
Minshū	*Saikō saibansho minji hanreishū* (Japanese Supreme Court Civil Case Reports)
MITI	Ministry of International Trade and Industry (*Tsūshō Sangyōshō*)
MNC	Multinational Corporations
MOF	Ministry of Finance (Ōkurashō)
Nissho	*Nihon Shōkō Kaigisho* (Japan Chamber of Commerce)
OECD	Organization for Economic Cooperation and Development
Sanken	*Sangyō Mondai Kenkyūkai* ("Council on Industrial Policy")
SCAP	Supreme Command Allied Powers
Sōhyō	*Nihon Rōdō Kumiai Sō-hyōgi-kai* (Japanese General Council of Labor Unions)
Sup. Ct. G.B.	Supreme Court, Grand Bench (*Saikō Saibansho, Daihōtei:* Postwar highest court: all fifteen justices)
Tōdai	*Tōkyō Daigaku* (Tokyo University)
UCC	Uniform Commercial Code (U.S.)

PART ONE

Introduction: The Scale of Foreign Investments

I

Role of Foreign Enterprise: Past and Present

This book deals with the present-day posture and environmental problems of foreign enterprise in Japan against the broader backdrop of incipient economic internationalism. At the turn of the decade (1970), Japan needed to change her economic policy and official attitudes toward the outside world because of her postwar internal growth and consequent increasing impact on the world economy, and also because of changing and conflicting national attitudes abroad concerning foreign direct investment in the development process generally and toward the multinational corporations (MNC) specifically.[1]

By 1970 when Japan began to amass large foreign reserves, major conflicting claims—foreign versus domestic—were competing for funds in the Japanese political arena. The business elite and power-oriented nationalists were seeking funds to tie up foreign raw material sources and to promote Japanese multinational firms abroad, while some intellectuals, consumer groups, and labor (the opposition in general) were demanding pollution control, social security, public works, housing, research, better education, and an improved distribution system; these latter groups were insisting that resources had been committed excessively to plant and export promotion in the late 1960s, only to produce overcapacity, dumping, and enterprise nationalism abroad. And the statistics show in fact that between 1955 and 1965 the ratio of "social capital" to gross national product, already low, declined further from 1.02 to .87 and has never recovered.

Furthermore Japan's own peculiar past experiences with foreigners (including her successes in westernizing) have had an abiding influence on her postwar management of foreign business entries, just as these experiences have created, understandably, a kind of business nationalism

3

and insularity that are now difficult to overcome in shifting to a role more supportive of a free-world economy so obviously essential to Japanese interests in the 1970s. Yet the success of Japanese efforts to shift away from simple enterprise nationalism in favor of internationalism has become all the more critical because of the diminished capacity of the dollar to underwrite even the imperfect world economy of the past two decades and because of nascent regionalism developing in Europe.

We must, therefore, begin a story of present foreign enterprise in Japan with some attention to Japan's experience to date; to current Japanese policies and terminology concerning foreign investments; and also to the changing role everywhere of private foreign business abroad. Recent Japanese policy pronouncements from both government and business indicate an encouraging comprehension of these broader problems and a dedication to their solution.

Terms of Reference

When we orient a country study of this sort to the broader context of postwar, free-world economic development, it is clear that on the developed or developing spectrum, howsoever those terms may be defined, Japan had rehabilitated her war-torn industries and had surely achieved a "developed" status by most criteria during the 1960s.[2] By 1970 there were even those who described her as an emerging superstate and an incipient postindustrial society.[3] On the other hand, if we focus on Japan's inefficient distribution system and her "industrial dualism," one might still say in the early 1970s that Japan is "developed" in the heavy industrial sector and "developing" in the small and medium industries. Be that as it may, as early as 1964 the shift to a "developed" nation status was symbolized by her entry, then perhaps a bit prematurely (see Chapter VII), into the Organization for Economic Cooperation and Development (OECD) and her change from Art. 14 to Art. 8 status in the International Monetary Fund (IMF). In 1973, of all criteria, Japan's continuing dependence to some degree on outside technology and her frequently mentioned "economic dualism" (see Chapter III) are perhaps her weakest features in the "developed" nation profile. Certainly the lower strata of the "dualism" are still developing. As to technology, the date on which Japan may reach an equilibrium, wherein she is able to develop and sell as much new technology as she buys, is difficult to estimate now, though I would not expect it to be long, because of the very high priority now given to achieving technological independence in the 1970s.

Japan's expenditure for research and development has increased about 25 percent annually since 1965, amounting to about $4 billion in 1971, of which 73 percent was private funds and 27 percent government money. This $4 billion was 1.6 percent of the GNP as compared with 2.8 percent (or about $30 billion) for the U.S. or 2.4 percent for England. The rate of increase is, however, impressive, and the Japanese awareness of its importance is every day evident in the daily press and journals.[4]

Definitely, technological dependence has influenced, more than anything, Japanese foreign capital entries in the past. We can see these influences in the following summary of Japanese policies pursued between 1950 and 1970:

1. The Japanese government has had a scale of priorities for development, administered, until 1972 at least, by the most restrictive controls in the world, among major nations, for managing foreign entries;

2. Induction of selected foreign technology has been essential and encouraged, subject to official review of licensing contract terms such as duration, royalty rates, license-back, and export limits;

3. Debt financing (bonds or straight loans) was sometimes selectively sought, but only at favorable interest rates; and after 1970 Japan's own capital supply and interest rates were such that foreign capital was unattractive generally;

4. In debt financing, Japanese government borrowing (*e.g.*, initially from the World Bank) has been preferred over private borrowing abroad;

5. Japan has avoided foreign private equity capital, whenever possible;

6. Where foreign equity capital has been inducted, Japan has preferred "portfolio" over "direct investments"—"portfolio investment" meaning purchases of stock on the Japanese stock exchange without intending to participate in management; and "direct investment" meaning purchase of corporate shares sufficient to participate in management or control of a business enterprise—usually involving a manufacturing; service or sales facility; recently (1972) even foreign portfolio investments were limited to keep foreign currency reserves down;

7. Japan has permitted direct investment only when it seemed necessary in order to obtain certain essential foreign technology not available by mere licensing contracts;

8. In direct investments, Japan has favored joint-venture corporations (*i.e.,* both foreign and Japanese shareholding in a Japanese operating company);

9. As a rule, only minority interests were allowed for foreigners in

manufacturing joint ventures, the major exceptions being ventures continuing from prewar days or "yen-based" companies, or, since the 1967 liberalization, industries in which foreigners had no interest or capacity to compete;

10. Up to July 1963, of the few foreign-controlled Japanese companies approved, most were acquired without Japanese official approval by establishing "yen-based companies" (*i.e.*, foreign-owned Japanese corporations established without government approvals [*ninka*] conferring foreign-exchange guarantees for repatriation); this possibility was foreclosed by Japanese announcements in July of 1963.

At this point it is necessary to emphasize that the foregoing is only a capsule summary of policies as they have appeared in operation; no attempt, in short compass, can be made here to evaluate them in an objective sense, since their impact has different meanings for different interests (*e.g.*, Japanese bureaucracy, Japanese industry, Japanese consumers, international legal institutions, foreign business, and foreign governments). In the main, however, they seem to have served Japan well until about 1972.

Basically, these policies still represent the official Japanese attitudes toward foreign capital in Japan, in my opinion, even after six years of liberalization up through the latest phase, 1 May 1973.

Whereas between 1950 and 1972 Japanese policies against foreign majority interests were noticeably more restrictive than those of most major countries, the recent trend, especially in developing nations, favoring minority or 50–50 joint ventures as a preferable form of private direct investments is bringing international practice closer to the restrictions that Japan has consistently imposed since World War II, indeed throughout the last century. Japan, however, in its own overseas investments has not generally observed the growing preferences in host countries for minority joint ventures. We shall also see (Chapter VII) that these policies have posed serious legal and diplomatic problems between Japan and advanced nations in recent years, flowing from their alleged conflicts with the growing spirit of a single, free-world economy underwritten legally by GATT, IMF, OECD, and bilateral commercial treaties. But since 1970, growing regional solidarity in Europe and heightening tension over preferences and nontariff barriers have caused serious challenges to economic unity of the so-called free world and a strengthening of restrictions and counter-restrictions in short-sighted moves toward protection of national interests everywhere. After 1970 Japanese officialdom began to shift to a truly liberal position in trade matters because of her export strength and in the face of resistance to her market penetrations and dumping abroad, but unfortunately many counter-restrictions had already begun to build up in the U.S.

In investment, Japanese official practice resulted in several special usages worth noting at the outset. First, though licensing of technology is not commonly thought to be an "investment" elsewhere, the major Japanese investment statute, the Foreign Investment Law (1950; hereafter FIL),[5] has covered long-term licensing of patents or other industrial property as well as foreign-capital movements; both have been subjected to prior governmental approval (*ninka*). This statutory blending of industrial property imports with foreign-capital entries emphasizes the primacy, in past Japanese official thinking, of technological borrowings (*gijutsu dōnyū*). Indeed foreign "capital," it has been suggested, meant, to the Japanese, foreign technology. This flows from the Japanese determination to avoid major foreign equities and management participation in any existing Japanese firms (for policy toward new firms see Chapter VI), except where they are inextricably tied to essential patents or know-how. Needless to say this policy has posed problems for Japanese legal commitments under the U.S.-Japanese Treaty of Friendship, Commerce and Navigation (FCN Treaty), and under the OECD Codes. The Japanese statistics and official surveys also distinguish several types of direct investment:[6]

1. Purely foreign companies (*jun gaishi kaisha*): Japanese companies, the shares of which are wholly owned by foreign interests.

2. Joint-venture companies (*gōben gaisha*): Newly established Japanese companies, the shares of which are divided so that foreigners hold at least a certain minimum, frequently set at 15 or 20 percent for statistical convenience.

3. Existing companies with foreign capital introduced (*gaishi dōnyū kaisha*): Existing Japanese companies that have transferred a block of shares to a foreign enterprise; often the foreigner's share ratio is low, and almost always the foreigner obtains his shares in connection with a technological tie-up. This category does not include cases in which a Japanese company establishes a separate subsidiary and then transfers part of the shares to a foreigner; this is treated as a joint venture (see above).

4. All firms falling in 1, 2, and 3 above are often referred to as foreign-capital-related enterprises (*gaishi kei kigyō*) in Japanese sources.

5. Yen-based companies: Japanese corporations established before July 1963 by foreigners without foreign-exchange guarantees or Japanese governmental approvals for foreign-exchange repatriation of income or capital.

6. Foreign branches are, analytically, direct investment, but the Japanese regulations have treated foreign branches separately (see Chapter VI).

7. Small and medium enterprises (*chūshō kigyō*): This term is variously used, but sometimes precisely in official planning and in Japanese regulatory law. For example, in manufacturing it has meant companies capitalized up to 50,000,000 yen and with up to 300 employees; in commercial enterprises it sometimes means capital up to 10 million yen and up to 50 employees.

These various terms will be useful in grasping quantitatively the role of postwar foreign enterprise in present-day Japan (see p. 18).

Japanese Experiences with Foreign Enterprise before 1945

Japan was discovered for the Western world in 1543 by Portuguese,[7] blown off course by storms that took them to the southern island of Tanegashima off Kyūshū. Immediately, the Japanese became fascinated with the firearms and other western goods aboard the Portuguese ship, and as became typical later, they, rather than continually importing guns, soon learned to copy these firearms[8]—thereafter called "Tanegashima"—which greatly influenced later Japanese warfare and power relations.

During the following 430 years, Japanese experience with western business may be divided into four major phases:

1. Portuguese and Chinese (1542–1640);

2. The Dutch (and Chinese) monopoly during the Tokugawa seclusion (1640–1853);

3. Open trading, with the American share of growing importance (1854–1940); and

4. The postwar phase, wherein Japan has gradually become a major force in the free-world economy (1950–72).

The Portuguese and Dutch Trader

The early experience included no foreign manufacturing, of course, nor did it even include resident traders until the early 1600s when a handful of Dutch and English established their depots or "factories" at Hirado[9] and Nagasaki. Trade in the sixteenth century was a mere trickle, generally limited to one ship (*"carrack"*) commissioned by the Portuguese as a monopoly out of Goa and Macao and trading with the then largely independent daimyo of Kyushu. Characteristic of the trade was the close relationship between the traders and Christian missionaries, particularly Jesuits. With several daimyo vying to get the annual ship to call at their ports, the missionaries attempted, with only partial success, to direct the trading ship to those daimyo who were willing to encourage the baptism of their people. It takes little imagination to appreciate the romance and intense Japanese interest drawn by the western curiosities brought to Japan for the first time. Perhaps Japanese zest for Portuguese imports accounts in part for the Jesuits' early success in baptizing enough Japanese, even several daimyo,[10] to cause some shogunal anxiety, though the concern sprang more from political squabbling than from religious scruples.

Only after 1600 did the Spanish, Dutch, and English participate actively in this trade, which covered various goods but mostly consisted of Chinese silk for Japanese silver. Since Ming China (1367–1644) forbade direct Chinese trade with Japan, the foreigners became the indirect source of much of the Chinese, as well as some European, wares keenly sought by upperclass Japanese. Even more importantly, for its impact on later Japanese attitudes toward foreigners, the Japanese did not then venture extensively abroad; instead western traders brought the goods to Japan and sold them in Japan, lending support to religious activities that in turn embroiled the foreigners in political intrigues. By Tokugawa times, these involvements led to an abiding official distaste for most westerners generally, and Christianity was banned completely, first by Hideyoshi Toyotomi in 1587, followed by the ultimate expulsion of all Spaniards in 1624, all Portuguese in 1639, and a final ban on all missionaries and on foreign businessmen, except the Chinese and the Dutch, both of whom were rigidly confined to separate tiny depots in Nagasaki harbor by 1640.

The "southern barbarian" screens (*namban byōbu*)[11] of this period depict well the high interest in things foreign aroused by these first western traders in Japan. Conversely the early westerners developed a fascination for the Japanese, whom they often found so different as to be quite incomprehensible. The many fascinating strands of these original encounters with foreigners cannot be followed farther here, but significantly for us these first interminglings of vastly different people added up, despite a great deal of mutual admiration, to a residue of distrust leading to the extraordinary self-imposed isolation of Japan from the outside world for over two hundred years.

During the exclusion period (1640–1853), the Dutch trade was virtually the only contact with the Western world, and it was here that the Japanese learned to manage foreign traders; every aspect of their lives and activity was regulated including the volume of trade, averaging only a couple of ships a year during the eighteenth century. The Japanese people were much interested in their captive Dutch guests as the extensive sales of wood-block prints of Dejima and the Dutch ships will testify.[12] The Dutch representatives who remained on the tiny island Dejima at Nagasaki between ships were required to make annual trips of homage to Edo, like a daimyo,[13] but the Dutch were otherwise closely confined, and the general populace had almost no contact with them or, of course, with any other foreigner except the Chinese. In addition, the government forbade Japanese to leave Japan,[14] and the ultimate price of political intermeddling was a censorship of Christianity carried to the point of rejecting even Chinese books with so much as a stray mention of Christ.[15] Arai Hakuseki is supposed to have said of it: "There is danger in hunting wolves with tigers."[16] Suspected converts were forced to tread on Christian symbols (*fumie*); and for two entire centuries after the last foreign missionary left, public bulletin boards (*kōsatsu*) were continuously posted, repaired, and maintained at important crossroads in Japan, offering rewards for the apprehension of Christians.[17]

It is difficult to exaggerate the importance of the residual official repugnance to foreign visitors built up during the so-called "Christian Century" (1542–1640). On the positive side, the resultant isolation (1640–1853) produced a rich and distinctive culture, a tenacious sociality, and also a strong sense of cohesion amongst the already homogenous Japanese. These qualities have had lingering effects of critical importance, for, though Japanese hosts nowadays typically delight a visiting foreigner with graciousness to a "guest," it is fair to say, candidly, that the Japanese, as a people, have little capacity, even today, to absorb foreigners within their community; or conversely perhaps we should say that foreigners have little capacity to be absorbed amongst the Japanese, so vast are the differences in personality, customs, and culture underlying the gracious mannerisms of the tea house and, recently, of the golf course.[18] But let us emphasize that these observations, in this short compass, while important in understanding Japanese attitudes toward foreign business in Japan, must necessarily fall short of explaining causes or assessing faults.

After the Meiji Restoration (1868–1940)

If the Portuguese period produced an official Japanese sense of revulsion against foreign doctrinaire religionists and intermeddling traders, and if the Dutch period produced a sense of complacent ethnocentricity, the intrusions of American Commodore Perry in 1853 were probably as much as anything a frightening experience; the art of the day, the contemporary wood-block prints[19] depicting the long-nosed barbarians,[20] tell most vividly this story of dreadful misgiving. As far as early foreign traders were concerned, the apprehensions soon proved justified. During the first year of the new commercial treaties (1859), the foreign traders exploited the lopsided Tokugawa gold-silver ratio (1:5, as opposed to 1:16 in Shanghai) by buying up and exporting enough cheap gold to embarrass the Shogunate, though it may have also sparked foreign interest in other, more useful trade.[21] Even Alcock, the British diplomat in Edo, censured these foreign speculative abuses.[22] By 1860 the ratio, of necessity, shifted to match conditions in the outside world.

But soon, by internal pressures, the Tokugawa officialdom was thrown into chaos; within 15 years of Perry's arrival, the Shogunate, entrenched for over 250 years, was overthrown (1868) by a coalition of outside *samurai* bearing the banner of the cloistered Emperor, who moved from Kyoto to Edo and, renaming the city Tokyo, established a new central government there.

The new Imperial government inherited (1868) the overbearing western extraterritorial regimes[23] of the earlier treaties, and only after thirty years of struggle were these foreign indignities relinquished by the United States, Britain, France, Holland, and Russia, subjecting foreigners at last to Japanese law. Still it was another decade before Japan could freely mold its economy by way of adjustable protectionist policies, because the Tariff Convention of 1899 fixed the tariffs for the next decade. Also, when all is said and done, extraterritoriality, despite justifiable Japanese repugnance, was a prerequisite to minimal foreign participation in the beginning years, when the resident foreign experts were of critical importance to modernization.

Significantly, the Meiji government, in attempting to westernize and still maintain Japanese national integrity, positively discouraged foreign ownership of industry in Japan. True, there were early minor exceptions such as the Takashima Coal Mine (Saga), developed as a joint venture with British capital;[24] and two shipyards were developed in Osaka by foreigners before 1872. However, in order to rid Japan of even these few enterprises, the Japanese government soon purchased all foreign facilities, including even a German model farm in Hokkaido.[25] Also in 1872 the new government forbade local entities to borrow any more abroad and repaid all of the foreign indebtedness of some twenty-eight daimyo to avoid the risks of foreign controls possibly accruing from defaults.

Thereafter, foreign business in Japan, with very few exceptions until after World War I, consisted simply of traders, shipping, and some banking. Traders were, in fact, fairly numerous and indispensable to Japan's new trade,[26] for Japanese firms with the skills and capacities to trade directly abroad were not to appear until much later.[27] Indeed by the time of the Meiji restoration (1868), eighty-five foreign traders had already set up business in Yokohama;[28] the first American firm is said to have been Messrs. Reed and Dougherty, which went into business in 1855, only two years after Perry.

After the Sino-Japanese war (1894–95), the overall policy against foreign loans was relaxed some. Public borrowing of foreign capital, but not direct investment, was welcomed—that is, the Japanese government borrowed on government credit and funneled funds through the Industrial Bank of Japan to private borrowers, thus pursuing a public-directed development plan emphasizing basic industries. Coupled with hired foreign experts[29] and imported models or technology, often obtained by study abroad or imported specimens[30] rather than purchase by the licensing technique of today, this public borrowing from abroad (and later by selected private Japanese public utilities corporations) enabled Japan to plan its capital uses and also to control the economy in general and to maintain Japanese control of manufacturing by private enterprise particularly. This early policy was furthered by two fortunate events:

1. A profitable Sino-Japanese war (1895) resulting in reparations payments from the Chinese amounting to 364 million yen (231.5 million taels; 38 million sterling), against a total Japanese war expense of only 200 million yen;[31]

2. A profitable role in World War I, leading to extensive buying by her allies, after Japan entered on the Allied side.

This latter international sales windfall enabled the major Japanese trading firms, unique institutions about which we will have more to say in Chapter IV, to increase their role to substantial dominance in Japanese external commercial relations and to reduce the scope of activities of foreign traders in Japan after World War I.[32] Still, up to World War II, foreign traders performed a significant function of developing new export markets for Japanese manufactured products abroad[33] at the same time that direct foreign investment began to increase. Japan had a favorable trade balance with the United States in the 1930s similar to the situation since 1966.

Thus, by the end of World War I, Japan had not only maintained virtually 100 percent control of her manufacturing, and within fifty years had regained control of her trade, banking, and shipping, but had actually for the first time become a net capital exporter while avoiding substantial direct foreign investment accompanied by risks of managerial powers exercised by alien business. Perhaps part of the Japanese success in avoiding foreigners in industry was because of the misgivings of foreigners themselves. In any event, the hiring of foreign technicians in addition to Japanese government borrowing abroad had thus proved to be a viable method of industrialization up to 1920, and later it became again the pattern, adaptable by analogy, after World War II for importing alien techniques without alien control. This is in contrast to the Chinese experience in which foreign interests introduced western industrial technology by obtaining major control over commerce, banking, and shipping, as well as manufacturing and even railroads.

Between World War I and World War II

What was the extent of direct foreign investment introduced into Japan between World War I and the end of World War II (1945)? As noted, relatively minor beginnings of direct foreign investment occurred soon after Japan stabilized its credit by going on the gold standard 1 October 1897, and a few ventures existed briefly even before. Some of the more enduring of the pre-World War I relationships were, for example: Babcock and Wilson (majority interest) with Mitsui forming Tokyo Babcock in 1908 to make water-tube boilers; the tie-up in 1919 between Tokyo Shibaura and General Electric Corporation (U.S.); the Armstrong-Vickers (Britain) investment (45 percent) in Nippon Steel Manufacturing Company (Nippon Seiko); and Dunlop (Far Eastern) Rubber Company, which was exclusively foreign capital.[34]

Soon after World War I, several other important and enduring direct tie-ups occurred. Japan Electric (est. 1899) began manufacturing under a Western Electric license; Mitsubishi Electric Machinery Company began technological cooperation with Westinghouse Electric International in 1923; also in 1923 Fuji Electrical Machinery Company (Furukawa Zaibatsu) joined up with Siemens of Germany; and in 1931 Sumitomo Metal Company began working with Canada Aluminum Company. Also, as early as 1905 General Electric acquired Tokyo Electric Company, a small manufacturer of electric lamps, which by 1936 had become the leading maker of lamps, and by then Mitsui had acquired an interest in it. Other specific American operations were: Nippon Ford Automobile Company (1925), Nippon General Motors (1926), and Nippon Victor Phonograph Record Company, all from the U.S. Three quarters of all Japanese automobile production up to 1936 was American, mostly by assembling of imported engines and parts. The percentage would have been even larger except for direct limitations imposed by a law of 1935 providing for licensing to control auto makers.[35]

Though not exhaustive, the tabulation on page 15 covers major foreign direct investments in Japan as of January 1931.[36]

A comprehensive postwar survey[37] showed twenty-nine foreign enterprises of pre-World War II vintage still operating in Japan in 1969. These older operations were predominately European (seventeen), and fifteen have persisted only as minor promotional or sales businesses. A few, however, have become important postwar foreign-related concerns, including Shell Sekiyu, Mitsubishi Sekiyu (with Tidewater Oil Co. connections), Nihon IBM, Nihon National Cash Register, Yokohama Gomu (rubber), Sumitomo Gomu (formerly Dunlop Rubber), Teikoku Sanso (oxygen), Nestlé Nihon, and Tōyō Otis Elevators. Yamatake-Honeywell also has prewar roots. Several major electrical equipment manufacturers developed from prewar foreign technological and financial tie-ups, but they have now become relatively independent since World War II, with only minor, nonmanagerial influence from abroad. Those include: Tokyo Shibaura Denki (electric), Mitsubishi Denki, Sumitomo Denki, Fuji Denki, Nihon Denki, and Nihon Ita-garasu (plate glass).

As alternatives to direct foreign investment, the Japanese government allowed borrowing from abroad during two main periods (1899–1913 and 1924–30). These borrowings were largely for support of the Russo-Japanese war and for rebuilding after the 1923 earthquake, rather than for industrial innovation.[38] Several private bond issues abroad, mostly by electric power concerns, were also allowed in Paris and London in the 1920s, but this exceptional private borrowing abroad dribbled down again to nothing by 1931. The level of gross foreign indebtedness reached about 2 billion yen in 1914 and 2.3 billion in 1932.[39] Generally we can say that before World War II the Japanese maintained throughout a policy of minimal borrowing from abroad, a policy caused by fear of what might happen to control of Japanese industry if it were unable to pay such debts; also this doubtless accounts in part for an impeccable Japanese record of repayment. Fortunately, a well-developed banking system evolved early inside Japan (see below p. 130), thus facilitating domestic capital formation based on the extraordinary capacities of the Japanese people to save.

A century of experience makes it abundantly clear that Japan resolved at an early date to avoid foreign business controls at any price, and the policy has been relentlessly pursued to date, despite increasing international frictions recently caused by this restrictive stance in the

Foreign Direct Investments in Japan
January 1931

Nationality	No. Firms	Type of Industry	Total Cap.	Foreign Cap.
I. Foreign Branches				
American	15	Oil 1, electric 1, machinery 9, movie 2, confectionery 1, silk 1		
British	5	Electric 1, machinery 2, paint 1, beverage 1		
German	5	Electric 1, machinery 4		
Swiss	2	Machinery 1, electric 1		
Czech	1	Machinery 1		
Luxembourg	1	Machinery 1		
II. Japanese Subsidiaries				
(a) Wholly Owned			in Yen	in Yen
American	6	Electric 2, auto 2, machinery 1, records 1	18,000,000	
British	5	Rubber 1, oil 1, machinery 1, beverage 1, pharmaceuticals 1	38,450,000	
German	2	Beverage 1, sensitized paper 1	520,000	
(b) Joint Foreign-Japanese: Majority owned and foreign-management control				
American	6	Records 5, rubber 1	22,050,000	15,995,000
British	2	Auto 1, machinery 1	2,550,000	2,000,000
German	2	Machinery 2		338,000
(c) Joint Foreign-Japanese: Japanese management control				
American	9	Electric 6, gas 1, glass 1, rayon 1	100,700,000	21,595,000
British	9	Iron 2, iron products 1, cotton yarn 3, meriyasu 1, ice 1, celluloid 1	88,600,000	9,377,000
German	8	Electric 2, machinery 1, rayon 2, cotton 2, wool 1	29,285,000	9,377,000
Chinese	2	Wool 1, cotton 1	41,000,000	158,000
Swedish	1	Matches 1	6,600,000	3,400,000
French	1	Chemicals 1		
Others	6		39,760,000	364,000

face of aspirations to create the so-called "free-world economy" that in concept implies free capital movement. With the opening of the 1970s, larger segments of Japanese business and government had gained confidence in Japanese competitiveness, and relaxed some of the barriers. Especially during 1970 and 1971, the rate of foreign entries has quickened noticeably, with 118 (mostly minority interests) approved in only nine months (1 July 1970 to March 1971). This rise in the rate of foreign investments reflects both Japanese awareness of the need reciprocally to internationalize for Japan's own benefit and also the heightening foreign interest in the growing Japanese market. Still foreigners have but a tiny portion of the market (1.5 percent) measured by total sales of business in the nation.

Foreigners, as persons, have not so far been absorbed (or are not absorbable) into Japanese life in any significant numbers because of cultural differences. Of interest here are the figures showing foreign residents from various western nations in Japan as of 1970:[40]

Nationality	Number
U.S.	18,198
United Kingdom	2,856
West Germany	2,286
Canada	1,558
	24,898

Though the figures above include all western nations with more than 1,000 residents in Japan, for special reasons Asian nations (*e.g.,* Korea with 607,315 and China with 50,816) contribute the larger part of the 697,504 total foreigners in Japan in 1970. The Caucasians number less than 30,000, and there are practically no blacks.

Also no more than 2,303 persons of western nationality (*i.e.,* excluding 54,271 Koreans and 5,580 Chinese) became naturalized Japanese citizens in the past quarter century (1945–70).

By nationality the figures show:[41]

Brazil	922	(mostly nisei)
U.S.	767	(mostly nisei)
Canada	122	(mostly nisei)
Others	492	(may include some Asians)

For comparative purposes, it is interesting to note that in 1970 there were 4,247,000 aliens in the U.S. of whom about 2 percent (82,000) were Japanese; and 1,828 Japanese became naturalized citizens in the single year 1970.[42]

Foreign Investment in Japan 1945–1971

One measure of the importance of foreign investments in postwar Japan is the care with which official statistics on entry of foreign capital and technology are tallied up, published through the popular media, and avidly read in the business world. The record from 1950 through 1971 shows the following:[43]

Type of Foreign Investment	Dollar Amounts	
Loans (mostly World Bank loans)	7,655,457,000	
Stock*	8,508,507,000	
Portfolio stock purchases		7,261,670,000
Direct investment (with management participation)		851,591,000
Corporate bonds	830,569,000	
Beneficiary certificates	10,577,000	
Foreign bond issues	1,378,846,000	
*TOTAL	18,384,000,000	
Technological assistance contracts	9,870 (number of individual licenses)	

Actually the total U.S. direct investment in Japan has a book value of $1.7 billion for 1970;[44] in other words the validated investment figures ($851 million) given above (for all countries) is low because it does not cover current increased book value, or branch and yen-based investments. It is significant that during the 1950–71 period the qualitatively important direct investments, our main concern in this study, amounted to about 6 percent of all foreign equity investments in Japan. Furthermore, there were in 1968 only 51 foreign-controlled firms (50 percent or more) of any scope ($278,000, or 100 million yen) out of 660 so-called "foreign-related firms" (15 percent or more) in Japan.

Even as compared with the prewar estimates ($125,000,000; 1935), the 1970 cumulative U.S. total (about $1.7 billion) is in real terms

*These totals do not balance because nonconsequential items were not listed.

hardly a significant increase, when discounted for inflation and then considered as a percentage of gross national product. The $1.7 billion represents but 2 percent of U.S. direct investment abroad. As we shall see (p. 21 below), these foreign equities are also mostly minority interests in essentially Japanese operations, whereas in the 1930s there were relatively more foreign-controlled operations. Also, by fiscal 1972 (March 1972 to March 1973), Japan was investing five times as much abroad ($860 million) as she was allowing into Japan as direct investments ($165 million), as shown in the Mainichi newspaper, 30 April 1973. Of these direct investments 65 percent were majority controlled by the Japanese. In fact, Japanese official approvals were required for ventures without majority control for the Japanese party until 8 June 1972.[45]

Scope and Quality of Direct Investment (1945–1973)

Historical Phases of Postwar Direct Investment

The movement of foreign enterprises into Japan has occurred in four distinct phases in the postwar period: 1945–55; 1955–63 (abolition of the yen-based company); 1964–67; 1967–73 (liberalization). Since 1971, formal restrictions have been lifted on most industries (exceptions: agriculture, real estate, computers, petrochemical, nuclear, space, armaments, aircraft, public utilities, mining), but only for up to 50 percent foreign equities in the fields of real interest to foreigners and most significantly in new companies only. In existing companies foreigners were still (in 1972) limited to less than 25 percent of the total shares, unless by special screening an approval for more could be obtained (e.g., General Motors' 33 percent of Isuzu).

During the 1945–55 period the weakness of the Japanese economy and payment balances discouraged most foreign business, unless there were government guarantees of foreign exchange for later repatriation of income and principle. Most investments then were in the very basic oil, chemical, and metal industries, and at this point foreign funds, as well as technology, were critical in rebuilding those industries. Some major corporations involved in this phase were Nihon Sekiyu Seisei (Caltex), Koa Sekiyu (Caltex), Tōa Nenryo Kōgyō (Standard Vacuum), Showa Sekiyu (Shell), Asahi-Dow, Mitsubishi-Monsanto Kasei, Nihon Zeon, and Nihon Light Metals. These companies are still among the most influential foreign enterprises in Japan today.

From 1956 to 1963 was the era of the "yen-based company," running parallel with validated foreign entries, which, however, were held to a minimum by official Japanese policy during this period. Often the yen-based companies were the result of foreigners' desires to control their operations being so strong that they would rather forego government foreign-exchange guarantees for repatriation than submit to the accompanying official restrictions always exacted for such privileges. Then, too, many yen-based projects, because they catered only to the consumer market, would not have received validation even for a minority interest. This period also saw the first entries of foreign firms on a validated basis in food, textile, paper-pulp, and other consumer goods in addition to continued activity in the oils, chemicals, and machinery. For example, the following major enterprises were established during this period: Mitsui Polychemical, Showa Neoprene, Nihon Unicar (Union Carbide), Sumitomo-3M, Caterpillar-Mitsubishi, Shin-Nihon Musen, Kyokutō Sekiyu, Furukawa Aluminum, Jujo-Kimberly, and Sanyo-Scott. By 1960 the technology accompanying these basic industries became the foundation of Japan's critical switch to heavy goods in her export thrust, and her lessening emphasis on light, labor-intensive exports, which were thereafter gradually strengthening in Taiwan, Korea, Hong Kong, and other less-developed countries.

The "yen-based company" was prohibited by official announcements[46] in July of 1963 at the beginning of capital "liberalization" and Japan's OECD membership (1964). Its prior importance to foreign interests can be appreciated, however, by noting that from a group of only thirty wholly owned, foreign manufacturing enterprises of any scope, twenty-nine were originally yen-based.[47] Indeed, the yen-based company was virtually the only technique whereby foreigners could establish wholly owned operations in Japan, because to date the Japanese government has refused to approve wholly owned manufacturing companies under the FIL, with precious few exceptions, all of minor importance. Even under the new rules, each industrial category that has been liberalized to 100 percent has generally proved to be an industry already impenetrable by foreigners for business or other reasons so that official restrictions have become no longer in fact operative in each case before they have been formally removed.

From 1964 to 1967, the immediate result of the 1964 "liberalization" (on joining OECD) was in fact an increase of restrictions and a decrease in foreign entries into Japan, temporarily at least; and purely foreign companies were virtually forbidden, after the abolition of the yen-based company, until 1967.

From 1967 to 1973, the liberalization program gradually unfolded (see Chapter VII), and in a wider variety of industries the Japanese government began to grant validations for minority or 50–50 interests in Japan, including a large number of small and medium-sized sales companies, as well as a continued flow of manufacturing joint ventures started by influential foreign corporations. Texas Instrument, Toshiba-Ampex, Iwaki Glass, Komatsu International, Hoechst Japan, and Toppan Moore Business Forms were added during this period. Prevention of foreign control in enterprises was still a major goal, however, in all industries of foreign interest.

Of all "foreign-related firms" that were operating in Japan by 1973, more than 80 percent were established after 1960, and the pace has noticeably quickened again since 1970. There were 217 new firms (99 manufacturing and 118 sales or service firms) in 1971 and 351 (165 manufacturing and 186 sales or service firms) in 1972. However, nearly all of them were of minor scale (average $500,000 capital). The number of technological assistance contracts approved annually has also increased sharply (1971, 1,546 contracts; 1972, 1,916 contracts), showing the effect of substantial liberalization, especially since July 1972.

Finally, on 1 May 1973, the "100 percent liberalization" became effective. The government in announcing this new liberalization, some twenty-one months after the "fourth round" in 1971, stressed that it had abandoned the "fifty percent principle" and introduced the principle of 100 percent foreign ownership in both new and established Japanese enterprises (when agreed to by the latter's management). There were, however, five important "industries" excepted and seventeen other critical ones to be liberalized on delayed schedules up to 1976.

Scope of Direct Investment (1972)

Leaving aside, for the moment, foreign branches as a form of direct investment, there were 862 "foreign-related" enterprises (20 percent or more shares held by foreigners) in Japan by 1971, and over 1,000 by 1972.[48] Some of these are the remains of 316 yen-based companies, established before further yen incorporations were forbidden in 1963. About 240 of the 316 still respond to MITI's annual survey and some 75 of the yen enterprises have since acquired a validated status for capital increases. In the 1971 MITI survey, 776 (91 percent) "foreign-related firms" (hereafter FRF) responded, including indifferently large or small, sales or manufacturing, wholly owned, controlled by majority, 50–50, or only minority interest (20 percent to 49 percent), and yen-based or validated. Of the total 776 (yen-based and validated) companies, 220 were wholly foreign owned (95 percent or more), but most all of those are minor purchasing or sales or promotional subsidiaries. Adding the foreign majorities (more than 50 percent), the total of "foreign-controlled firms" (hereafter FCF) was 277; of the FRF remaining (499), there were 232 companies in which the foreign and Japanese interests were split 50–50, and 267 minorities. Only 277 of the total 776 are of substantial scale (*i.e.,* over 100 million yen; $278,000 capital at 360 yen to $1); and as we shall see, of these larger companies relatively few fall within the group of 277 FCF.

Qualitative Profile of Foreign Enterprise (1970)

To assist in grasping the overall significance of foreign enterprise in Japan, several raw statistical classifications are available at the end of the book (Appendix I) in Tables 1 to 8 showing, respectively, the overall distribution of some foreign-related firms by (1) type of business, (2) kind of interest (*i.e.,* purely foreign, joint venture, etc.), (3) share ratios, (4) size of capital, (5) number of employees, (6) dates of establishment, (7) combined type-share ratio by industry, and (8) combined type-capital scale by industry.[49]

But we need to extract, from the detailed data, answers to more significant questions, which arise in four broad areas. First, from among the gross category entitled "foreign-related firms" (FRF) in the Japanese statistics, how many are really "foreign" (*i.e.,* foreign-controlled firms, FCF)? What is the scope of operations of the foreign-controlled enterprises in terms of employees and capital? Second, what is the share of FCF's in overall Japanese business in terms of sales, profit and growth? Third, what impact have FRF had on Japanese labor and management practices and on the economy in terms of technological innovation, foreign trade, and balance of payments? Fourth, what are the characteristics (nationality, size, and organizational techniques) of the foreign, parent enterprises?

Weight of Truly "Foreign" Enterprises

To begin with, a major problem of definition arises out of the Japanese government's threshold validation (*ninka*) policy that limits foreign shareholdings to 50 percent or less in all situations attractive to foreigners throughout the postwar period, even after liberalization began (1967). Rather than determining corporate nationality by the usual method (*i.e.,* majority holdings), the Japanese reports and media, in discussing direct investment, tend to treat as "foreign" any firm with foreign interests of 20 percent (15 percent in some special studies) or more, despite the fact that foreigners make no important decisions in such minority ventures. For example, sales relationships, pricing (especially with parents), production programs, investment expansion, and cartel shares have all been determined largely for the convenience of the Japanese parent and its business complex (*keiretsu* and/or trade association), in the background of which has been the unseen (but much felt) "administrative guidance" flowing constantly from the government ministries. Of course, these critical matters in turn affect where the profits go. In short, the disposition in Japan to call any firm "foreign" that has only slight foreign content (15 percent) does tell us something important about past Japanese attitudes toward foreigners, but it tells us little about the foreigners' actual role in Japanese business. On the level of international policy, the Japanese have some good nationalistic reasons, besides xenophobia, for keeping foreign business in a low posture, and from a national viewpoint many of them are quite understandable in context, but that is a matter for later treatment (Chapter VII). What we first need to know is how much foreign business there really is.

Foreign-Controlled Firms

So, to quantify the really foreign business in Japan, the first step is to select out the FCF from the hundreds of firms that the Japanese statistics treat as "foreign-related enterprises"[50] without further seeking out the foreign-controlled firms. Then, secondly, it is necessary to sift from the FCF those with any size before we can grasp the significance of foreign enterprise in Japan from the welter of insignificant statistical detail.

In 1971, there were 277 FCF (51 to 100 percent), with only 11 percent of the FRF sales. These 277 firms included only 72 manufacturing firms; the rest (205) are purchasing and sales (146) and "others" (59, mainly services); the latter two categories were predominantly small in scale during the 1950–70 period because of the constricted opportunities for foreign firms to import into Japan, given the tight import controls then prevailing. Many sales and service firms were started as small businesses on a yen basis, often by individual entrepreneurs from diverse countries.[51] In the future, direct sales efforts may offer better opportunities for foreigners, if they are permitted (foreign chain stores are still limited to eleven units in 1973). For example, there were in 1971 at least 21 foreign-controlled sales firms in Japan with moderate capital (over 100 million yen; $278,000); the eight largest are capitalized at over $1 million. The prime examples of sales successes, frequently cited, are Coca-Cola and Nestlé (instant coffee), both of which have done well by direct approaches to the consumer market, backed up by strong trademarks and products difficult for Japanese firms to match. Esso, Shell, and Mobil in the oils and Olivetti, Remington-Univac, and Hoechst in machinery are also successful examples in direct consumer sales.

Scale of the Foreign-Controlled Subsidiaries (51–100 Percent)

Only 11 percent of all FRF sales in Japan (1969) were by FCF.[52] Also, among some 72 manufacturing FCF established by 1972, many are very small. In fact, only 26 of them have even moderate equity capital (100 million yen; $278,000); only 12 have over one million dollars in equity capital. Thus, in all Japan, including both sales (21) and manufacturing (26) firms, there are only some 47 sizable FCF, and only one of the seven really large (10 billion yen; $27.8 million) foreign-related firms (Shell, Esso, Mobil, Asahi Dow, IBM Japan, Caterpillar-Mitsubishi, and Nihon Light Metals) is majority owned— IBM Japan (99 percent). Besides the oils, manufacturing FRF (not FCF) tend to be of large scale in nonferrous metals, rubber, and paper, and small in food, drugs, metal goods, and precision instruments.

By industrial type, the FCF are found most predominantly among the smaller companies entering Japan later, for example in foods (twelve FCF out of eighteen FRF companies) and drugs. Among the earlier and larger heavy industrial entrants (oil refining, textiles, chemicals, machinery, nonferrous metals, metal goods, and rubber), the foreign interest is generally less than 50 percent.

To pursue this winnowing process a step further, we can judge the scope of these foreign-related enterprises, overall, by checking the sizes of their labor forces. Overall in 1969 the FRF labor force was 0.5 percent of the Japanese total, and 1.2 percent of total manufacturing labor. Here we do not have a more meaningful breakdown showing labor in FCF as such, but in the entire group of FRF, there are only 38 with over 1,000 employees and only 90 with over 300 employees. It is doubtful that more than half a dozen of these are also FCF, though one FCF (IBM) has about 10,000 employees. Indeed, one tally[53] shows 78 percent of all employees of 519 companies are in firms in which foreigners have 50 percent or less interest, and 87 percent of the employees are in the 90 companies with over 300 employees each. Besides the oil companies, the larger manufacturing FRF (with 1,000 employees or more) are: in general machinery, Fuji-Xerox, Caterpillar-Mitsubishi, Shinko-Pfaudler; in transportation equipment, Tōyō-Otis Elevator, Nihon Jido Kensokki, Aishin-Warner; in electrical equipment, IBM, Yamatake-Honeywell, Matsushita Denshi; and in other fields, National Cash Register, Sumitomo-3M, and Mitsubishi-Monsanto. In nonmanufacturing FRF with more than 1,000 employees are: Nihon Univac, Hoechst-Japan, and Nihon Olivetti.[54]

Foreign Branch Operations

Besides the foreign subsidiaries incorporated in Japan, there is considerable business done by foreign enterprises in Japan through branch offices (and some plants) registered in Japan. Though statistics covering branch funding before 1963 (new rules; Chapter VI) are not available, the 1963–70 data on foreign branches can be summarized as follows:

Kind of Activity	Number of Branches	Percentage of All Foreign Branches	Capital in Millions $US	Percentage of Total Capital
Sales and trade	148	45.4	48.5	43.7
Services	131	40.2	40.5	36.4
Manufacturing	20	6.1	7.3	6.6
Others	27	8.3	14.8	13.3
TOTAL	326	100.0	111.1	100.0

Foreign branch offices are not controlled under the FIL, but rather a prior report is required when the branch is established (by registering, Commercial Code, Art. 479) and approval under the FECL is required before the parent can transfer funds or technology to the branch in Japan, and similarly approvals are required to pay earnings to the parent abroad (see Chapter VI). This approval system has been restrictive, and few sizable manufacturing or even sales operations have been conducted by branch operation. In 1971 there were 542 remittance approvals (not new branches) to bring in funds for foreign branches in Japan amounting to $19.6 million; in 1972 there were 523 approvals for a total of $20.1 million for all Japanese branches.

Change in Foreign Shares of Individual Joint Ventures

Over the whole postwar period, foreign stockholding ratios have decreased somewhat per company, presumably by failure to pay in the foreign enterprisers' prorated amount of capital increases. For example, all of the foreign enterprises (about 29 in all) established before World War II had average foreign holdings of 71 percent at the time of incorporation, but the ratio had decreased to 45.2 percent by June 1967.

Interests established between 1946 and 1955 averaged 41.9 percent and had decreased slightly to 40.5 percent by June 1967. A slight decrease is also noticeable in the corporations established after 1956 as well.[55]

Also several firms that once were substantially foreign have now dropped below the 15 percent level; for example, Toshiba, Nihon Denki, Babcock-Hitachi, and Mitsubishi-Bonneru. On the other hand, some foreign majority interests have increased; for example, Hōnen Ribā (Unilever, 70 percent), Nichiro-Heinz (80.3 percent), Simmons Bed (100 percent), and Nihon Eiga Kikai (Bell and Howell, 75 percent). They seem to have increased because of disputes, weaknesses of the capital, technology, or management of the Japanese partners.

In sum, then, it is safe to say that there are only a half dozen large FCF manufacturing firms and under fifty FCF (including manufacturing as well as sales and services) that are even medium-sized. It seems important to stress the paucity of foreign-controlled firms so as to counteract impressions conveyed throughout the 1960s and early 1970s by periodic semiofficial lists of hundreds of "foreign-related" firms. Coupled with nervous mass-media treatment, the "foreign take-over" may have appeared to some Japanese to be present reality, or at least an imminently pending disaster.[56]

Comparative Business Performance (Sales, Profits, and Growth)

Total sales of all FRF in manufacturing, as a percentage of sales of all Japanese manufacturers, give an even better standard for measuring the role of foreign operations in Japan; in June 1971, that figure was about 3 percent. All-foreign business (not just manufacturing) was 1.5 percent of all-Japanese business, and FCF sales were but 11 percent of FRF sales (1.5 percent of the Japanese total).

The foreign share is, of course, higher in some fields than others, although, as the figures below show, it does not exceed 20 percent in any field except oil refining, which is occupied by FRF, not FCF, and not yet (1972) liberalized:[57]

Product	Percentage of Japan Total
Foods	1.2
Chemicals	4.9
Drugs	8.3
Oils	57.2
Rubbers	16.4
Nonferrous metals	5.7
General machinery	6.1
Electrical machinery	3.4

Also, among FRF themselves, about 40 percent are sales firms and 60 percent manufacturing. Large firms dominate performance; in 1969, the largest 126 firms[58] (FRF and FCF) had 77 percent of sales and 85 percent of profits after taxes. About 60 percent of the sales of FRF were made in only three industries, where there are virtually no foreign-controlled companies (oil, chemicals, and general machinery):

FRF Sales by Industrial Groups (1970)

Industry	Percentage of Foreign Total
Oils	34.5 (42% of all foreign manufacturing)
Chemicals	16.7
General machinery	15.7
Electrical machinery	13.2
Rubber	5.9
Nonferrous metals	6.9
Food	1.2

Sales growth in 1971 for major manufacturing was 19.1 percent, somewhat better than all Japanese manufacturing with 12.7 percent. Sales of wholly owned foreign manufacturing increased even more, but this was distorted by the extraordinary performance of Coca-Cola, IBM, and Nestlé. By types of industries, FRF sales ratios increased for foods and drugs and decreased in rubber goods and oils.

Profitability

In 1966 only 75 percent of the FRF showed a profit, and 25 percent (ninety-four companies) showed a loss. But then many FRF were too new to be in full operation. Overall, major foreign enterprise profits were about 3.5 percent of sales in 1971, and 4.1 percent for manufacturing alone, which is a little higher than the overall Japanese average (3 percent). The foreign share of total Japanese profits is 3.2 percent of overall industries, and 4.9 percent of manufacturing profits (as compared to only 1.5 and 3 percent respectively of total Japanese sales), showing that foreign firms are overall somewhat more profitable than domestic manufacturing, as might be expected considering they are only validated in innovative lines for their technology.

Foreign enterprise profits are higher in some types of industries than others: for example, higher in foods, drugs, electrical machinery, and chemicals than their Japanese counterparts or the overall FRF average, but lower in rubber, general machinery, and nonferrous metals than either the FRF or Japanese averages in the same industries. The following figures on FRF profits after tax as a percentage of total equity capital in the several industries are impressive:[59]

Industry	Average FRF Profit after Tax as Percentage of Equity (1969)
Metal products	25.1
General machinery	24.6
Textiles	19.5
Pulp and paper	14.6
Chemicals	14.0
Oils and coal	11.4
Rubber	8.0
Nonferrous metals	5.8

Looking closer at certain lines, foods and drugs had the highest profit rate of 10 percent of sales, explained largely by strong brands and the introduction of entirely new products (*e.g.,* Taito-Pfizer). As noted, Nestlé and Coca-Cola (also recently McDonald's and Colonel Sanders) have reaped remarkable Japanese profits from the mass consumers' market, but foreign enterprises making general machinery with a profit of 3 to 4 percent were below the average for Japanese machinery makers. Foreign rubber goods firms (mostly tires) are less profitable perhaps because they are small compared to Japanese Bridgestone Company (50 percent of the market). Aluminum ingots have proved to be fairly profitable, but by 1966 the extrusion industry was not yet profitable in Japan, because of the heavy initial equipment costs. The FCF (majorities) tend to be the most profitable, and the 50–50 joint ventures the least profitable. Appendix V shows the profitability of the top foreign firms based on income tax reports.

Cost factors are different than for comparable Japanese firms. Japanese personnel and interest costs are higher, and depreciation costs lower than that for foreign enterprises in Japan, because foreign enterprises are operating with higher concentrations of capital per worker and less borrowed capital. Of the 70 percent of foreign enterprises which were profitable between 1963 and 1966, only about half declared dividends, presumably because many were new and preferred to hold the surpluses in the corporation to build up capital surplus and the other reserves.

Exports and Imports Performance

In the 1963–66 period, foreign enterprises as an aggregate had a red trade balance, importing considerably more than they exported, though the balance is improving. In 1966, for example, FRF exports were 3.17 percent of the Japan total, while imports were 15 percent, compared to FRF total sales of 3.3 percent of Japan's total. The FRF trade deficit has been reduced since 1968 and, too, FRF operations have been validated by the government only (1) in fields where raw material imports are high (*e.g.,* oil, aluminum, etc.), or (2) to create substitutes for imports and allow Japan to get the benefit of the value added by processing, in effect important, only raw material more cheaply than the finished product could be brought in.

Other characteristics of the FRF export performance in Japan are:[60]

1. A strong tendency to export, if at all, to parents abroad; but chemicals, rubber, general machinery, and electrical machinery tend to export to all areas, while foods, drugs, and oil go primarily to other Asian buyers.

2. Overall, Asia is by far the major export area for foreign enterprises in Japan, largely because two-thirds of all foreign parent firms have confined the Japanese venture's exports to the Asian region, often by the joint-venture agreements.

3. Manufacturing FRF export about 7.3 percent of their total sales, and the highest export ratios are found in rubber goods (16.9 percent), electrical equipment (13.2 percent), general machinery (9.1 percent), and chemicals (9 percent). Certain companies have especially high export records; for example, Toshiba Rayovac, Matsushita Denkō Kōgyō, Shin-Nihon Musen, Nihon Unicar, and Mitsui Polychemical (polyethelyne).

4. Whereas only 1.9 percent was exported to foreign parents, Japanese FRF subsidiaries sold 11.3 percent of all goods to their Japanese parents. Sales to Japanese parents were high in drugs (37.3 percent), nonferrous metals (36.2 percent), and electrical industries (25.7 percent) and oil (16 percent).

Impact of FRF on Japanese Practices (Labor, Management, Etc.)

The foreign influence in the field of technology has been an immense factor in the rehabilitation of the entire Japanese modern industrial sector in the 1945–70 period. Equally obvious, however, is the fact that Japan has accepted foreign equity and managerial participation only where it was a necessary condition for obtaining essential technology from abroad. Even then, Japanese have distrusted FRF as a solution to Japanese technological deficiencies, because the FRF, allegedly, becomes permanently reliant upon foreign research and innovation,[61] whereas the mere Japanese licensee will strive to produce his own technology, knowing his foreign source is short-termed. Be that as it may, foreign influence, based on minority holdings, has been minimal in corporate decision-making. Such influence as there was has been concentrated in the field of management of technology and related fields.

Management

In FRF, only about 20 percent (260 out of 1310) of the regular managers (*jōkin,* ranked as section chief or above) were foreigners, and these few foreigners were concentrated in advertising, promotion, technology, and quality control. Acquisition of parts and raw material in certain industries (*e.g.,* drugs, oils, and foods) also falls within the foreign parents' control through personnel in Japan, only because the exclusive sources are abroad. In addition, ad hoc missions (*hi-jōkin*) are sometimes carried out by foreign executives on short assignments. The Japanese partner usually controls overall planning, personnel matters, finances, government compliance, and production.

Several different organizational patterns have been used by foreign parents to participate in the management of their Japanese ventures. Yet only 37 percent (out of some 454 FRF) have had any regular foreign executives at all in Japan, 63 percent relying entirely on a Japanese management staff.

The first pattern of participation is where the FRF maintains only a liaison officer in the Japanese venture, a pattern generally followed in wholly owned or majority-controlled ventures, especially after they have begun to operate smoothly. Second, in 50–50 companies, it is common for the foreign parent to appoint a chairman of the board for the Japanese subsidiary, and for the Japanese to appoint the president and division chiefs, with occasionally United States advisors also at the division level. Third, some foreign enterprises maintain in Tokyo an independent "Far Eastern Office," besides their Japanese venture, and the Far East manager participates in high policy decisions with the joint-venture president, who is Japanese. Fourth, in some wholly owned joint ventures, a responsible executive will be appointed by the parent, who in turn appoints subordinates from various nationalities as best suited to the job.

In general, foreign managerial participation in FRF is limited to technology, product promotion, and the like, and even FCF tend to leave management largely to the Japanese.

Labor Practices

FRF hire only 0.5 percent (178,000) of the Japanese labor force in all kinds of Japanese enterprises, and only 1.2 percent (152,000) in manufacturing.[62] Taken as a whole, FRF have tended to leave personnel management to their Japanese colleagues and follow the Japanese customs, as might be expected, where some 80 percent of the FRF employees work in firms where the foreign share is a minority. Besides, Japanese executive personnel policies favoring (1) lifelong hiring of generalists starting fresh out of the schools and (2) escalator-like status promotion by seniority are so strong that most foreign firms are obliged to comply.[63]

There are, however, some distinguishing features of FRF employment practices, prevailing most consistently where foreigners have at least 50–50 shareholding ratios. The major differences are: first, foreign enterprises hire only 40 percent of employees as new graduates, 14 to 17 percent from parent companies, and 43 to 46 percent from other companies. This latter "raiding" practice is contrary to long-standing Japanese custom because of the lifetime employment policy. Second, working hours tend to be shorter in the foreign-related enterprises, averaging forty-two hours per week as opposed to an average of forty-five hours in purely Japanese companies, and 7 percent of foreign enterprises, as opposed to only 2 percent for Japanese companies, have five-day instead of the standard Japanese six-day week. But, both of the latter foreign deviations from traditional Japanese practices may well become the norm in the future. Third, foreign enterprises also tend to pay higher wages, including higher starting wages; their average annual wage is thus 739,000 yen (about $2,050), compared with a Japanese annual wage varying between 670,000 yen, 596,000 yen, and 564,000 yen, decreasing with the size of the companies' labor force.[64] Fourth, FRF have less involvement with unions and labor disputes, mostly because, as seen above, the bulk of the foreign firms are of petty scale. Thus, 67.6 percent of all foreign enterprises have no union at all, but those few foreign enterprises with one thousand or more personnel are 87 percent unionized. Likewise, only 13 percent of all foreign enterprises have had labor disputes since 1962, compared to 42.2 percent in Japanese enterprises. However, 50 percent of foreign firms with over one thousand employees have had such disputes. The infrequency of labor disputes among foreign enterprises may be attributable to the fact that, unlike in Japanese enterprises, the upper-strata personnel (plant foremen and white collar) have not joined unions.

Characteristics of the Parent Firms Abroad

Nationality

The nationality distribution of the FRF's parent firms, as tabulated below, shows that nearly two-thirds are from the U.S. Indeed, eighty-three out of the top two hundred U.S. firms (from *Fortune*'s list, May 1972) have Japanese subsidiaries (20 percent plus), about thirty others have shares of less than 20 percent, and several others have branches.

Country		*Number of Companies*	
United States	477	(but several Swiss, Panamanian, Liechtenstein, and Canadian companies were predominantly American and should be added here)	
European	222		
		a. Swiss:	55
		b. German: 46	(I. G. Farben)
		c. English: 42	(including Shell and Unilever)
		d. French:	21
		e. Others:	58
Canadian	18		

World Enterprise Trend

Besides the 83 manufacturing firms from the *Fortune* list of the 200 top U.S. firms with subsidiaries (20 percent or more) in Japan, 16 world enterprises from the top 100 firms outside the U.S. (*Fortune*'s list)—reduced to 81 by excluding the 19 Japanese firms on the list—also have Japanese subsidiaries of 20 percent or more. These 99 world enterprises in manufacturing have a total of 129 manufacturing subsidiaries (out of a total FRF of 469), and in addition they have 22 of the total 288 sales FRF. These 151 firms established by world enterprises (FRF) have 62.5 percent of the gross sales of all FRF in Japan, though, if oil is excluded, it becomes 28.2 percent (remember that FCF have but 11 percent of FRF sales in Japan). The strength of this "world enterprise" movement in 12 types of Japanese industries can be seen in Appendix IV. The top 10 firms have been selected and ranked, world-wide, in 12 types of industries; then a check was made to determine how many of the 10 firms in each industry had a Japan operation. The results can be summarized as follows:

Industrial Types	Number of Firms (out of 10) with Japan Operation
1. Oils, chemicals, pharmaceuticals, electrical equipment, foods	6 to 8
2. Rubber goods, nonferrous metals, general machinery, ceramics	3 to 5
3. Textiles, paper and pulp	1 to 2
4. Iron and steel, transport equipment	None

Furthermore, in 1968, only forty-four of these foreign firms in Japan (11 percent) had only a Japan operation, besides their home business. The rest have at least one more operation in a third country. Also, there are at least forty-two major foreign parents with two or more subsidiaries in Japan. Especially in foods, rubber goods, and nonferrous metals, internationalized production by world enterprises, as well as internationalized sales programs, has become the norm.

Technique of Organization in World Enterprises

With the world enterprises, four different patterns for investing abroad occur frequently in Japan:

1. Investment through a specially established international (often foreign) subsidiary, *e.g.,* Coca-Cola Export (U.S.) and Nihon Coca-Cola; Caterpillar International (Swiss) and Caterpillar-Mitsubishi; Dow International (Swiss) and Asahi-Dow; IBM World Trade Corporation and Nihon-IBM;

2. Others set up a basic domestic subsidiary at the center and make investments in related areas (for example, Mobil Petroleum and Shell Oil);

3. Investment directly by the core company into a separate joint venture for each product line or division. Examples of this technique are

I. E. DuPont with ventures with Showa Denko, Mitsui Sekiyu Kagaku Kōgyō, and Tōyō Rayon. Also Borg-Warner, Celanese, Chemetron, Dow-Corning, FMC, and W. R. Grace use this form;

4. Investments, for manufacturing, through one joint-venture company per product, but selling and importing through a wholly owned sales company (for example, Bayer, General Electric, American Cyanamide, Sperry-Rand, and Motorola).

Another major characteristic of the joint ventures in Japan has been the numerous involvements of Japan's own world trading companies (Mitsubishi Shōji, Mitsui Bussan, Marubeni-Iida, C. Itoh & Co., etc.) because their offices have become virtually the "commercial embassy" for Japanese business in all major countries abroad (see Chapter IV). In joint ventures, the trading companies have often supplied the introductions and balance of control capital.

The Future of Foreign Enterprise in Japan

The future of foreign enterprises in Japan cannot be fully appreciated without considering also the on-going free-world internationalization of production by multinational companies and Japan's aspirations to participate therein[65] against the background of basic trade, investment, and currency adjustments proceeding throughout the world in the early 1970s and noticeably accelerating after the "Nixon Shock" of late 1971. We may feel rather confident that Japan, because of her need for international markets and raw-material sources, will maintain a cautious liberalizing course, and in fact peel off gradually the FIL restrictions as required by foreign pressures and as it becomes clear that liberalization will not entail the disasters so often predicted by segments of the press.[66] Overall the sales of FRF have grown (26 percent) faster than the Japanese average (24 percent), but not enough to cause alarm.[67] Still, the government will preserve a firm control of the economy and business.

Lacking the legal restrictions of the past twenty years, future foreign enterprise may increase somewhat in Japan, as exemplified by the recent General Motors–Isuzu, Ford–Tōyō Kōgyō, and Mitsubishi-Chrysler joint-venture projects in the auto industry, but note that Ford–Tōyō Kōgyō talks aborted. One major impediment will be the Japanese business community itself, which is tightly organized into trade associations and often into legal or "guidance" cartels with an intense nationalistic stance regarding internal resources, output quotas, and market shares. These associations of domestic competitors are skeptical of foreigners, and their resistance is enhanced further by traditional sales (and other) relationships informally maintained and elusive to outsiders. Another impediment to foreign growth is that, as noted earlier, the Japanese government will likely continue to supervise all industries (after FIL liberalization) by a second "line of defense," cartel regulations, and also by informal administrative guidance. The latter is elusive to foreign countermeasures, and sometimes in foreign quarters has seemed to be quite discriminatory against foreign enterprise; the same thing has been said of the trade associations in their important areas of self-regulation.[68] So the disappearance of direct official restrictions on foreign entry will probably coincide with the emergence of other obstacles from the industrial associations and indirectly from the government, because it, of course, regulates the cartels. Also, it was clear enough by the early 1970s, presumably, that Japanese "liberalization" had been only partial and on a leisurely schedule to coincide with "domestic fortification" efforts.[69] Even the fifth-round liberalization effective 1 May 1973 (with 100 percent foreign ownership approved in principle, subject to "exceptions") seems consistent with this approach, because of the selective and critical exceptions covering most competitive foreign industries.

In assessing the potentials of foreign enterprise in Japan, the affirmative factors seem to be the following. First, the growth of the world enterprise is strengthening, perhaps because the United States base of most of them[70] has a shrinking profit margin and has antitrust policies restricting further domestic concentrations in many cases; world enterprises also get a boost from the European Economic Community, as well as from new technology and communications making centrally rationalized management of far-flung super-corporations feasible and impressively efficient in competition. All of these factors tend to elevate the importance of global firms, which by definition will be interested in a country as globally important as Japan. Second, global firms have already recognized the rather ideal conditions (save for the restrictive governmental policies) for direct investment in Japan: Japan, even at a reduced 6 percent (1971), still has a higher long-term growth potential than most advanced nations; mass media for brand development; convenience as an Asian basing point; and remarkable political stability throughout the postwar period.

Finally, the Japanese have come to realize, from foreign criticism verging on open hostility, that, if they are to participate in the global economy, Japan must surely in fact liberalize, thus granting access to Japan for access to other countries for her firms. This realization comes not only from her more recent aspiration to launch her own multinational companies but also from her critical dependence on free worldwide markets for both her purchase of raw materials and her sale of exports in order to perpetuate her vital import-export cycle. More recently even the economies of importing foods and light manufactured products are becoming well accepted in Japan. These factors, clarified in the crucibles of severe foreign criticism, have recently created a fundamentally different official stance, at least at the top level.[71] The old autarchic preference plus excessive export pressures and a revised version of infant industry protection at home may still persist, but the direct and efficient threshold legal barriers are seen correctly now as leading only to protectionism abroad and jeopardizing Japan's access to resources and critical markets abroad. For example, by the rules of economic advantage, Japan should be importing more light goods and agricultural products possibly in exchange for more of her textiles exported to the U.S., but instead, disadvantageous protectionism prevails on both sides.[72] To avoid such problems, Japanese, U.S., and other officials must move toward a cautious attempt to mitigate the hardships of adjustments and to liberalize.

Thus the future Japanese problems will be of the same kind faced by all nations in attempting to preserve national autonomy or "sovereignty" in politics against the growing internationalization of production and distribution that is increasingly dominated by private corporations with neutral or multinational stances regarding labor, capital, and materials and motivated basically by the economics of production and exchange— and not by local jobs, defense requirements, or "national interests."[73] Whatever balance may be struck by other nations regarding this shared dilemma, one would suspect, based on a long record of experience, that Japan would maintain by one means or another a firm control on foreign entry and on Japanese industry.

PART TWO

The General Environment for Foreign Enterprise

II

The Political Climate

Introduction

Three years has been suggested as a period required for the present-day foreign representative to learn his job in a Tokyo joint venture, and it has been estimated that four out of five fail regardless of preparation.[1] The reason is that communications problems for the transpacific interpolator are perhaps the most trying in the entire business world. It is trite to continually be saying that Japan is different and difficult, but it is essential to realize that competence in things Japanese requires a specialist's career dedication, not a generalist's briefing. Just as the manager in Japan runs the risk of "going native," the short-time inspector from the home office regularly commits errors of understanding and judgment, frequently creating for the Tokyo-based representative his most serious problems. Though usually well meaning, these "*sukiyaki* experts" oversimplify (*e.g.,* "just like Italy or France, etc. etc.") the Tokyo man's very particular problems, deprecate his subtle long-term achievements, and create erroneous impressions at home, leaving the Tokyo representative without a real hearing—alone, overworked, and over there. The root of the problem is the utter inadequacy of the business letter as a vehicle of cross-cultural communication. Or, even more fundamentally, perhaps the monolingual head office may not realize that cross-cultural communication is going on, admittedly with much enervating transpacific static and loss of message.

By the same token, the entire Japanese environment for business cannot be capsulized in chapter-sized, academic pills explaining why some "go native" or curing the legal or business generalists of the blithe penchant for oversimplifying Japan. Rather, Part II seeks only to convey the essential information and generalizations from recent literature and to present, topically, those major features of the Japanese scene—political, economic, and commercial—which need to be explored further by those who linger long enough to appreciate the subtleties of one of the most refined, distinctive, and integrated societies in world history.

Japan has had a stable government favorable to domestic business during two decades of postwar politics, and there is no doubt that Japan's center of gravity is in the polity not the economy—a source of puzzlement for Japan's numerous economic determinists of various Marxist stripe in academia and opposition politics. It is essential, therefore, for foreign business to have a basic grasp of the peculiar relations between business and politicians as well as the underlying political process, which are introduced in this chapter. Of course, the high performance of the economy is the major attraction for foreign business, and the characteristics of the economy, its resources, size, growth, and structure are outlined in Chapter III. Finally, in Chapter IV, general features of Japanese labor, business structure, and operations are set forth, with an attempt to draw together from all of the information in Part II a glimpse of the highly integrated workings of the political economy in response to government planning and institutional manipulation. This elemental building block (politics, economy, labor, business) approach is used because of the difficulties of presenting interstitially to non-specialists what seems to be an irreducible bulk of essential information that forms the critical context in which foreigners have had to launch their artificially frail enterprises—artificially frail because of the official stricture placed upon them at the threshold.

Political Stability

Japan has the oldest reigning dynasty in the world today, but when the new constitution became effective (1947), the Imperial position was reduced to only symbolic significance in Japanese government. Formalities aside, this is a role that had in fact obtained for centuries, a role that had often shielded the Imperial household in the past from the risks of political maneuverings; thus, in a sense, the Emperor's present posture explains why the Japanese state embodied in the Imperial concept has had such remarkable formal stability and longevity.

Stability has also been characteristic of the underlying real-power balance between the political parties during the past twenty years, but ironically, this too is a stability existing only on the surface. Beneath there is an extreme polarity between the ruling party and the leftist opposition, and there is vigorous factionalism within both major parties

—the Liberal Democratic (Jiyū Minshu-tō) and the Japan Socialist (Shakaitō) parties, hereafter LDP and JSP respectively. By far the most cohesive organization is found in the Japanese Communist party (hereafter JCP), and in the December 1972 election, the JCP also showed an increase protest voter support, capturing thirty-eight seats in the Diet (491).

Historical Résumé

While the Japanese Imperial dynasty emerged from mythology at an unknown date, probably during the second century A.D., historical knowledge of Japanese institutions began in the sixth, seventh, and eighth centuries when the Japanese imported from China a written language, Buddhism, and sophisticated legal institutions based on T'ang models. Then beginning about 900 A.D., the Chinese-styled central Imperial government in Kyoto lost most of its power to a new cluster of local power centers, indigenous in origin but interestingly analogous to the feudalism of the Western world. The "feudal" period in all of its phases spanned roughly a millenium (900–1868), during which time the local regimes were held together by the Emperor at the center, more or less, and a succession of hereditary military lords (*shōgun*). These began with the Kamakura Shogunate (1185–1333 A.D.); then the Muromachi Shogunate (1333–1447), which faded away completely in the sixteenth century and was not replaced again until 1603; then the Tokugawa Shogunate (1603–1868) was established, lasting until Japan was opened to the modern world beginning with Commodore Perry's visit in 1853.

The Tokugawa regime is important as the incubator for a peculiar traditional and familial collectivism (in the family, the village, and the inchoate "nation") and an accompanying unique individual psychology shaped by these groups, which even to this day condition in a determinative way the Japanese individual's attitudes toward his company, his government, and society. Thus, many astute analysts of recent Japanese political development and modernization typically start with some base concepts of "tradition" (Tokugawa) and "modern" and then trace Japanese development along a scale between them,[2] in an effort to explain what is palpably different in a society of predominantly modern appearance.

Even though in my view "modernization" as used in such inquiries need not necessarily imply democratic political values,[3] Japan has in fact not only modernized by other criteria, such as increasing her GNP and per capita income, but has also steadily moved, again in her own peculiar way, toward more universalistic values and a wider popular participation in government; admittedly a critical step in democratization was externally sponsored by the Supreme Command Allied Powers (SCAP) in 1945. Still the result continuing to unfold is a "democracy" essentially made in Japan with its own distinctive emphasis on harmony, consensus, and compromise, and basically distrustful of majoritarianism as such.[4]

The important events in the past century of political evolution were: the arrival of Perry (1853), which opened Japan to the Western world and ended her extraordinary seclusion (1640–1853); the Meiji restoration (1868), which ushered in the new centralized Imperial government complete with Western education, bureaucracy, and positive law, which for the first time was applied uniformly throughout Japan; the Meiji Constitution (1889), promulgated in response to pressures for wider popular participation; and universal manhood suffrage (Taishō Democracy) of 1925. Continuity was broken between 1932 and 1945 when competitive political parties went defunct under military rule, but defeat followed by the Allied occupation (1945–52) brought the present constitution (1947), which is liberal, democratic, and if foreign inspired, at least Japanese in execution. Such a brief enumeration of events in Japan's fascinating political history may at least remind us of Japan's continuous uses of her own past, mixed with foreign importations, to build her future with a remarkable lack of either revolutionary violence or virulent xenophobia. But we must now turn to the present structure and process of postwar Japanese democracy.

Governmental Structure

The underlying premises of the Constitution of 1947 are popular sovereignty with universal suffrage (including for the first time the franchise for women), a parliamentary-styled, two-house Diet with a responsible prime minister and Cabinet, and a more modern "Bill of Rights" than the U.S., backed up by new powers of judicial review somewhat similar to that of the United States Supreme Court. The constitution has become, during the past two decades, a "legally justiciable" constitution, as compared with the prewar "political" constitution.[5] For the Japanese Supreme Court has developed civil rights concepts in the case law and also its own right to protect them by declaring legislative and executive acts unconstitutional.[6] Indeed, the *Sakagami*[7] (1951) and *Nakamura*[8] (1962) cases have already held legislative acts to be unconstitutional; thus postwar Japan has now produced its counterpart of *Marbury* v. *Madison* (1803) in the U.S.[9]

The sovereign people act through their local groups, parties, and Diet composed of two houses—the House of Representatives (491), and the House of Councillors (250), the latter subordinate in case of conflict between the houses on basic issues. The prime minister is elected by the Diet and appoints his Cabinet, though the really critical election, in fact, has been the election of the president of the ruling LDP, who then becomes prime minister; the Cabinet, appointed by the prime minister, may be overthrown by a lack of confidence in the Diet; and the Diet may be dissolved by the prime minster to determine at the polls a conflict between the Diet and the Cabinet.[10]

Finally, the famous "peace clause" (Art. 9) deserves mention because of its renunciation of war and consequent importance to international relations; it is virtually unique in the world's constitutions. Understandably, the "peace clause" is highly controversial in Japan at the level of political interpretation: the ruling LDP has maintained, by enunciation of the so-called "Yoshida Doctrine," that certain limited self-defense forces are constitutional; the leftist opposition (especially the Japan Socialist party and the Communist party) has maintained that the "Self-Defense Force" and the U.S.–Japanese Security Treaty are unconstitutional. In two Supreme Court decisions the Socialists have tried to raise constitutional issues concerning the validity of the defense force and treaty before the Supreme Court, but the court has avoided the issue by invoking the "case or controversy" doctrine[11] and the "political question" doctrine[12] respectively. Thus, despite the "Peace Constitution," the validity of the U.S. Security Treaty and Japan's Self-Defense Force has been left for decision of the political branch of government, namely, the Diet, controlled by pro-American conservatives consolidated in the ruling LDP since 1955.

So, for twenty years, Japan has had great stability and continuity of policy, but, coexisting with it, extreme right-left polarity between the LDP and its Socialist opposition, both in turn fraught with extreme factionalism within their respective camps. The LDP factions seem to be held together not so much by a positive set of principles as by the pragmatic requirement of maintaining power against the challenge of the left, and the left is even less cohesive, having already splintered into several parties and factions.

Voting Trends

During the 1960s, the Liberal Democratic party gradually lost its majority of the popular vote (47.6 percent, 1970 and 46.9, 1972), though because of careful manipulation of candidates in each multimember district it has maintained an absolute majority (280; 1972) of the 491 seats in the important lower house.[13] Being to a significant degree rurally based, the LDP has, no doubt, lost some popular votes because of dramatic demographic shifts toward the city, which may also explain important leftist municipal victories (*e.g.,* in recent urban elections such as for the governorships of Kyoto and Tokyo). Thus, Japanese politics display, beneath the frozen surface of LDP rule, certain trends of considerable potential interest to foreign investors and business interests in general, and a coalition government drawn from the present leftist opposition is not impossible in the coming decade.

The 1969 election produced the following relative strengths in the important lower house:

Party	*Popular Vote*	*Per-centage*	*Seats H/R*	*Per-centage*
Liberal Democratic party	22,381,000	47.6	288	59
Japan Socialist party	10,074,000	21.5	90	18.5
Democratic Socialist party	3,636,000	7.7	31	6.4
Kōmeitō	5,124,000	10.9	47	9.7
Communist party	3,199,000	6.8	14	3
Independents (12 later joined the LDP)	2,492,000	5.3	16	3.3

The election in December 1972 provided a loss (20) for the LDP and a gain for the JSP (28) and JCP (24):

Party	*Seats (H/R)*
LDP	280
JSP	118
JCP	38
Kōmeitō	29
DSP	19
Independents	7
TOTAL	491

For the Japan Socialist party (JSP), the leading opposition, the 1969 results were the worst electoral disaster since the leftist merger in 1955. The JSP had had 145 seats in 1960, 144 seats in 1963, and 140 seats in 1967, but dropped to 90 in 1969. At the same time, emerging third parties (Clean Government party, Kōmeitō; and in 1972 the Japanese

Communist party) have grown so that the combined opposition parties have maintained more than one-third of the seats, thus preventing a long-standing plan of the Liberal Democrats to amend the new constitution (which requires a two-thirds Diet vote) to make it conform more closely to traditional institutions of the past. Paradoxically, the Socialists and allies, neutralist[14] in foreign policy, are still able, election after election, to defend the American-sponsored constitution.[15]

The Political Process

Prewar Parties

Under the earlier Meiji Constitution (1889), actual power was wielded by an oligarchy, whose spokesmen were drawn from five well-defined power groups: the military, the bureaucracy, the business clique (*zaibatsu*), the landlords and peerage, and a derivative group of politicians working through the old Diet, which did not control the prime minister directly as it does now.[16] All parts of the oligarchy had a somewhat independent voice in hammering out joint policies, later pronounced by the Emperor. The oligarchic balance was not entirely stable; for example, for a brief period in the 1920s, the politicians backed by *zaibatsu* gained in strength to the point where the prime ministers were selected amongst parliamentary statesmen in the Diet, a facet of the so-called "Taishō Democracy" (1912–25).[17] Prewar party politics in this phase were centered around Tokyo and two shallow parliamentary parties (the Seiyūkai and Minseitō) operating in the Diet.

The importance of the Seiyūkai dated from 1900 when the drafter of the Meiji Constitution, Hirobumi Ito, later turned to it for Diet support, but the party was sustained thereafter primarily by business led by the Mitsui *zaibatsu*. The Minseitō traces back to Shigenobu Ōkuma and his Kaishintō party, but came to be the Mitsubishi party up to the military takeover in the 1930s. For example, two prime ministers from the Minseitō, Takaaki Katō and Kijurō Shidehara, were sons-in-law of the founder of Mitsubishi, Yatarō Iwasaki, who himself supported Okuma.[18] Finally, the military became dominant in the 1930s, and until the end of World War II, other elements of the oligarchy were subordinate, including the parties. Despite its democratic shortcomings and the debacle of World War II, the Meiji Constitution served as the framework for significant achievements during the first seventy years of modern Japan, and in 1945 much of value remained upon which to build a strong and peaceful nation.

Present-Day Political Parties

The role of elected politicians in the Diet is now vastly different from their predecessors' situation. Formally, the new constitution pronounces the Diet the highest organ of state power;[19] the Diet not only makes the law, it elects the prime minister; and he and his Cabinet are responsible question is: which bureaucracy, business or government? (See below, to the Diet. This new supremacy is shared by "judicial supremacy" enunciated in Article 81 of the constitution, and actual supremacy, some would say, is still in the elitist bureaucracy. Perhaps the most significant question is: which bureaucracy, business or government? (See below, p. 55.)

Be that as it may, the new posture of the Diet, and its individual members, has unquestionably been nurturing a new kind of politician, a new kind of political party, and new relations between the ruling triumvirate—politicians, bureaucrats, and businessmen. The transition has been slow, and the system still retains much of the old and is still evolving with party-business-bureaucracy relationships quite different from those of the past.

In the transition now under way, all are dedicated to democracy, but it is still a special Japanese kind of "demorcracy." With pervasive rankings still a paramount social condition, there is no "equality" for lower ranks (except, significantly, equality to be heard); without alternation of parties in power (for nearly twenty-five years), there is no functioning bipartisanism, except again the important opportunity to be heard. The post-World War II "democracy" is then essentially a recognition of the right of all to be considered in consensus decision-making. Nor is this simply an ideal; in fact decisions are normally by consensus. Incessant meetings, discussions, and communications, much of it generated by private groups and the opposition, insures that all segments understand (if they do not embrace) the decision before it is made. "Democracy" is, perhaps, more than anything else, a popular rejection or negative reaction to the past authoritarian, "feudal" pattern of unilateral decisions in the prewar days. But, as I see it, socially and psychologically the Japanese understanding of "democracy" does not yet legitimate majoritarianism or equality in the classical liberal sense, however much these westernisms may be codified into the constitutional structure.

As noted, the major parties in 1972 are the LDP (280), JSP (118), JCP (38), Kōmeitō (29), and DSP (19). Leading up to this position, after initial postwar confusion, Japanese political parties first aligned in 1950 into a ruling conservative group and a leftist opposition arrangement somewhat like a polarized two-party system, with little in the middle. The system was, functionally, lopsided in favor of the ruling

conservatives and without alternation of power, except briefly (1947–
49) when a centrist coalition, organized by the Socialist party and led
by Tetsu Katayama, formed a cabinet that gave Japan its first Socialist
(and incidentally, first Christian) prime minister. Katayama had troubles
immediately, and a former bureaucrat, Ashida, fell heir to a similar
coalition that lasted only until 1949.

Except for this short interlude, the conservative parties have been
solidly in power in the Diet during the entire postwar period. For a
brief few years (1955–59), a two-party system seemed to operate effectively, when both the conservative and socialist groups came together
in 1955 to form the Liberal Democratic party (LDP) and Japanese
Socialist party (JSP) respectively. The Liberal Democratic party has
managed to hold itself together and has strengthened its internal organization considerably, but the opposition has splintered.

First, the Socialist party, comprised of the incipiently revolutionary
left wing and the more democratic right wing, lost part of the right wing
in 1960 when the Suehiro Nishio group broke away and formed the
Democratic Socialist party (DSP). The DSP increased its modest
strength in the Diet from an original seventeen in 1960 to thirty-one
in the 1969 election. More importantly, the Nichiren Buddhist organization called the Sōka Gakkai has sponsored a new party, the Kōmeitō,
which gained steadily, winning 47 seats in the 1969 election, then lost
ground in 1972. The sharp disagreement among all opposition parties,
including the Japanese Communist party (JCP) with 38 seats (1972),
is strong enough to lead one to suspect that a possible coalition amongst
them would be highly volatile, even if together they were to obtain a
majority of Diet seats in accordance with gradual trends in the popular
vote. Their importance as critics and opposition is, of course, crucial if
parliamentary government is to have any meaning in a regime without
alternation of power decade after decade.[20]

The Platforms and Support Groups for the Parties

Liberal Democratic Party

The ruling LDP is, as we shall see later, an alliance of some eight to
ten factions or "parties" within the party.[21] Also, the LDP is having
some difficulty in overcoming its prewar origins and becoming more
than a Tokyo coterie of parliamentary politicians by enlisting membership among the people and in localities outside Tokyo. By origins, the
LDP Diet members may be broken up into two distinct groups: the

"politicians," who have made their names through the electoral process, and a postwar group of "former bureaucrats" or business officials, who, on reaching retirement—usually at the early age of about fifty-five— enter politics and exploit their prior official connections with Japanese business. Thus, the reciprocal support among business, the bureaucracy, and the politicians is the core of the postwar ruling LDP.

The party stands for a kind of Japanese business competition within a peculiarly guided "free enterprise" system (see below, p. 144), insuring close cooperation and many personnel interchanges at the top among business, government, and party. The LDP finds it expedient to date to be pro-American in foreign policy and supports the security arrangements between the United States and Japan; at the same time it tries to leave the way open for business with the U.S.S.R., Communist China, and Taiwan by attempting, with only partial success, to separate economics and politics.[22] The LDP program is pragmatic: it strives to maintain its power, promote economic prosperity, enhance national prestige, and provide for the public welfare. An initial reactionary aspect of the program was its support, more active under the Kishi regime than since, for a revision of the Japanese Constitution to revert back to institutional patterns less democratic and more congenial to prewar models. This goal was thwarted in the 1950s by the Socialists and seems to be in fact unrealizable in the near future, though it is still part of the LDP program. An amendment project, *per se,* is not alarming, for surely there is some room for improvement of the present constitution, but just what amounts to "improvement" will probably remain controversial enough to thwart any change in the near future.[23]

Japan Socialist Party

The Japan Socialist party is a class party for "workers"; only parts of it have been able to decide between a radical revolutionary and, alternatively, a parliamentary stance,[24] and it is difficult to tell whether its permanent opposition status is the cause of its doctrinaire program or vice-versa; during the continuing and peaceful economic and social progress achieved under the LDP, it has been difficult for the opposition to offer a plausible alternative. Intellectual and elitist in its origins, the JSP is highly ideological in its general approach, especially in the left wing, and its active membership is mostly white collar. Ironically, though the JSP draws the highest vote of all the opposition parties, it is probably weaker in membership and regional organization outside Tokyo than either the JCP or the Kōmeitō. Thus, the JSP is seriously dependent on labor organizations and the leadership of Japan's largest Federation of Labor Unions (Sōhyō), which has about 45 percent of the entire organized labor force in Japan, totaling just under ten million. In rural areas, small farmers have responded little to JSP positions and though small businesses ("urban peasants") have often been dissatisfied with the LDP–Big Business "establishment," less than one-third have supported the JSP.

In foreign policy, the JSP has fostered what it calls "neutralism," meaning opposition to the U.S. military bases in Japan, to the U.S.–Japanese Security Treaty, and recently a pro-Communist Chinese posture. This leftist kind of "peace without defense" has not been very plausible to the Japanese majority but, as noted, has caused the JSP to support the present "peace" constitution against amendment. Of course, the JSP also advocates nationalization of industries, and it has wavered but tends now to favor the Red Chinese over the Soviets in the Sino-Soviet split. Factionalism[25] within the JSP has been even more disruptive than in the LDP: (1) the right wing is rather centrist in outlook and more mildly socialistic; (2) though the mainstream has three elements, it strives more to come to grips with realities of Japan; and (3) the left wing is still doctrinaire and doubtfully committed to the liberal democratic process. A major debate has grown out of these disparate factions as to whether the JSP should now try to be a cross-stratal national party or a class party for workers. The doctrinaire Sōhyō left-wing forces have created obstacles to attainment of middle-class and small-business support required to satisfy the desire of mainstream and right-wing elements for a national party.[26] The problem is the more critical, because continually being out of power perpetuates evidences of political immaturity in the party's failure to come to grips with reality and also sustains the cohesive intellectual particularism of its origins around important personalities.

Clean Government Party (Kōmeitō)

The Kōmeitō, born only in 1964 as a political arm of the Sōka Gakkai, a sect of Nichiren (*Seishū*) Buddhism, has emphasized nationalism and decried corruption of the ruling LDP. With a messianic zeal and flair for organization, its recent phenomenal growth (250,000 members) and success in electing most of its few candidates has attracted much attention up to 1972 when it lost ground at the polls. Capitalizing on a solid grass-roots organization derived from the Sōka Gakkai, the Kōmeitō appeals to the urban, insecure,[27] lower-income group, giving them a satisfying in-group identity. Also, despite its intolerant religious concern for all mankind symbolized by the term "one worldism" (blander in English than the Japanese—*chikyū minzoku shugi*), the Kōmeitō has actually campaigned on more practical issues than any of the leftist opposition except the JCP. In foreign policy, the party has opposed nuclear weaponry, the U.S.–Japanese Security Treaty, and U.S. bases in Japan and has favored an independent posture, U.S. withdrawal from Vietnam, and "one-China" (*i.e.,* the People's Republic of China); domestically it has opposed constitutional revision and LDP corruption and favored a variety of practical issues such as large personal tax exemption for low income groups.[28]

The 1969 advance (forty-seven seats) made it the third largest party, though some observers predicted that it could go little farther without making a fundamental readjustment between its religious and political posture, which was done, formally at least, in 1970, but still the party lost eighteen seats at the polls in 1972. This was partly because the Sōka Gakkai's militant conversion technique (*shakubuku*) and other forms of aggressiveness caused some public alarm, culminating in widespread criticism in 1970, after it tried to suppress a book by Professor (Meiji University) Hirotatsu Fujiwara, *I Denounce Sōka Gakkai.*

Japanese Communist Party

The Japanese Communist party is well organized, with 280,000 members and a substantial publication program. In the past, however, the JCP has been tainted, even more than the Socialist party, by foreign influence and issues and several ideological schisms, wavering between some sort of Japanese or neutral posture and support of the Soviets or the Communist Chinese. Now it is regarded as singularly pro-Soviet and hostile to pro-China factions but pursuing a "lovable" line within Japan with a focus on practical, local problems, which seems to be paying off.[29]

The leftist students' movement, important to Communists world-wide, is split in Japan, with great hostility between Chinese supporters and Soviet sympathizers, who now dominate the JCP. Because of the split in forces and nonacceptance by the Chinese of its neutralist position, thought to favor the USSR, the JCP has not been, until its upswing in 1972, a significant factor in Japanese national elections, drawing less than 10 percent of the national vote. In urban municipal elections, however, it has been and will continue to be a potent force to contend with, and whether it will continue the gains of 1972 may well depend on the plausibility of its new parliamentarianism as perceived by the electorate, or the performance of the LDP.

In sum, Japanese party activity has been dominated by the ruling LDP and its predecessors for most of the twenty-five years since World War II. A two-party arrangement emerged in 1955, but the opposition has since splintered, and there is general agreement that the LDP is likely to continue its absolute Diet majority in the near future or, even if it does not, that a new group is unlikely to last very long. The latest election seems to confirm this judgment that the "one-and-a-half party system" will continue. One need hardly observe that such an institutional context poses important problems for the viability of democratic values. Also obvious is the uncertainty inherent in major demographic changes and the small but continuing decline in LDP popular vote, coupled with the risks endemic to the multimember district system, in which payoff depends heavily on delicate party decisions as to the number of candidates it should run per district in order to maximize its victories without squandering votes.

Nevertheless, the bargaining and delaying tactics of the Socialists in the Diet have achieved some useful concessions over the years. Indeed, on several important occasions nonparliamentary tactics, even fisticuffs, have been effective to obtain compromises or withdrawals of certain controversial legislation, perhaps indicating a general tendency in Japan to strive for some sort of consensus and to rarely use raw majority power. A well-known example of leftist negative tactics was the forced cancellation of President Eisenhower's visit to Japan in 1960.[30] More encouraging has been the fact of a remarkably free press and other liberties, accompanied by a higher voluntary turnout at the polls (72 percent in 1972) than is achieved consistently in the United States, though the Japanese urban turnout is much lower than in the rural areas.

The Ruling Party

Nonetheless, for foreign businessmen, it is an important fact that the most significant competition for national power has been between LDP faction leaders; in fact this rivalry for the LDP presidency is a reason for the factions, giving them a legitimate function in governance, for the president of the ruling party becomes the prime minister.[31] Also, some of the most bitterly fought contests for Diet seats also occur between two or more LDP candidates within the same multimember districts. This of course breeds divisiveness and is a major obstacle to cohesion within the ruling party and significant to any of the opposition parties that might challenge it for a majority. These parties have been favored by the system to date and as yet know little of the political difficulties of capturing several seats in the same district, which is necessary to gain a majority in the Diet.

Since the LDP seems, for the time at least, entrenched in power, and since much of the most meaningful politicking does occur within the party, some understanding of the inner workings is essential.[32]

Shallow Membership Focused in Tokyo

Some characteristics of the LDP are shared with other Japanese parties as well. For example, Japanese political parties generally are not yet mass parties and generally do not have extensive membership in the countryside outside Tokyo, though the LDP has much voter (nonmember) support in the rural areas. The LDP is said to have about 1,950,-000 members (January 1966), but dues-paying members seem to be about 50,000 and among active members the high percent of former bureaucrats with Tokyo University educational background is remarkable.[33] The Socialist party has about 50,000 members and the Communist party about 280,000. The Kōmeitō has 250,000 members, but its strength is in the superlative underlying organization of the parent Sōka Gakkai of 15,000,000 members. The shallow membership of Japanese parties is explained probably by the fact that, as before the war, parties are still little more than groups of Dietmen with their respective supporters from business, organized labor, and other groups. Local allegiance is only meaningful when marshaled around a faction leader or an individual Dietman.

Factions

All Japanese political parties are characterized by factionalism within the party.[34] Particularly in the LDP, factionalism has an important function,[35] though it is typically and continuously decried by the newspapers and even by the party leadership. That function, after the conservative merger in 1955, has been to assist in electing a party president for a two-year term; each candidate for that top office must, of course, have some organizational base for his candidacy within the party; for that reason each important leader has his own faction. Factions are also reinforced by the medium-sized (three to five), multimember electoral districts. Most such districts have several Liberal Democratic candidates, each hoping to get one of the three to five seats, which go to the candidates with the highest pluralities. Since party financing is inadequate, and since no one faction could usually expect to get more than one candidate elected per district, the factions tend to fund and support different candidates, thus making some of these races among the LDP candidates themselves the most competitive. As noted, though, the multi-member district has the effect of giving more Diet representation to the opposition than a system of single-member districts would, but not quite as much as the left might get from purely proportional representatives.

Recently in the LDP there are from eight to ten constantly shifting factions. For example, the leading factions[36] in 1970 were Satō-Tanaka (61), Ohira (43), Miki (41), Fukuda (36), and Nakasone (34). Factions have their own leaders, financial backers, and headquarters offices, and some of them seem to have certain political characteristics, though they could hardly be called platforms. For example, the Satō faction drew heavily from former bureaucrats, while the former Ono faction was made up largely of prior politicians; the Murakami faction was largely former businessmen. The Fukuda faction is reputed to be the most conservative, and the Matsumura faction was said to be the most liberal. Each faction has its own group of business supporters who contribute to its coffers, quite apart from business contributions to the party as such. Indeed, the ability to raise money from business interests may be the single most important qualification of a faction chief in the LDP.

Individual Support Groups (Kōenkai)

Besides the party and the faction, individual Diet members solicit funds for their own support group, a postwar phenomenon called the *kōenkai* within a Diet member's district. These groups have arisen by confluence of the local needs of Dietmen for an assured core of votes and the needs of Japanese villages and other communities for representation and protection, after the land-owning gentry who had served that purpose were wiped out by occupation land reformers. Thus, most *kōenkai* draw votes strongly from a small grass-roots area, such as the village where the candidate was born. A *kōenkai* so organized may be called a vertical support group, whereas support from the entire area of the electoral district may be called a horizontal support group, but these latter are rare, and whether, in the course of modernizing, a concern for issues will turn Japanese political organization in that direction is an interesting question. Yasuhiro Nakasone is an avant-garde faction leader with such a support group.

Bearing in mind the prewar parliamentary antecedents of the LDP, the factions and their organizations geared to raise their own funds and to capture the party presidency, and bearing in mind also the individual's *kōenkai,* it is clear that much traditional, particularistic local behavior is underlying the present-day organization, thus keeping the party, as such, rather weak at the top.[37] Thayer[38] finds some evidence that the party as such is strengthening since 1960 through its Peoples' Organization for collecting funds and through its careful use of the party endorsement, which has drawn increasing recognition from local politicians and other external pressures.[39]

In summary, both the party system as a whole and the separate parties (LDP, JSP, DSP, Kōmeitō, and JCP) within it are vastly different from their counterparts in the United States or elsewhere, reflecting the underlying traditional political culture and behavior of the Japanese. The system is not multiparty, two-party, or one-party, though functionally it has two-party aspects, since the ruling LDP is offset against a rather consistent, doctrinaire left with a community of interest only in opposition. None of the parties has a mass membership base, and except for the JCP none of the parties is factionless or cohesively organized, though the basis of the groupings differs: in the case of the Liberal Democratic party it is along lines of pragmatic personal support; and in the Socialist party it is personal too, but with more ideology.

Quite apart from the very real intraparty and interparty political competition, the fact is that Japan is as nearly as humanly possible now conducted as an administrative state, wherein the alliance of the LDP, the bureaucracy, and business, by their best light, plan and administer the resources of the nation for national progress and public welfare. They proceed with only minimal concessions, as required by forceful Diet tactics, to their ideological opponents, and the elitist, inner core of some four hundred Tokyo-based LDP members wields virtually all of the policy-determining power with local activity limited largely to the elite educating the rural types, rather than seeking significant grass-roots input. We must remember, though, that the governing regime has cause to be nervous as the LDP popular vote declines (only 46.9 percent; 1972); also the elitist core of the regime is comprised of three parts, requiring much coordination and interplay:

1. The LDP;
2. A skilled and dedicated bureaucracy;
3. Organized business.

Indeed, business officialdom might almost be regarded as but a coordinate wing of the overall bureaucracy that blends imperceptibly with politics at the top. This is because the modern business elite are but managers, not owners as were the *zaibatsu,* and generally have the same education and values as the bureaucratic managers in government.

The interdependent workings of the three parts of the Japanese "establishment" have been aptly likened to the game of paper-scissors-rocks (*jankempon*): the bureaucratic paper covers business; politicians, like scissors, can cut through the paper; but business funding, solid as a rock, has obvious impact on the politicians. Such a relationship among business, the bureaucracy, and the LDP is the real key to Japan's phenomenal postwar performance. It therefore behooves those interested in Japanese business particularly to look somewhat closer at the relationship between business and the Liberal Democratic party, leaving until Chapter VI the workings of the bureaucracy in promoting Japanese business interests, especially abroad.

Business in Politics

Nowhere has Coolidge's aphorism to the effect that government's business is business been more apt than in Japan since 1945. There are several compelling reason for this:[40] first, Japan has long since reached a point in its industrial development in a qualitative sense where she must literally, in order to get essential raw materials and fuels, "trade or perish"; second, being reduced until recently to secondary status in military and diplomatic circles, after defeat in World War II, Japan has sought nationalistic fulfillment—something peculiarly important to Japanese—in the competition of world business; third, postwar land reform and rapid urbanization, plus lack of competitiveness of her farm products in world markets, have also reduced the importance of rural politics centered around the prewar landlords, leaving as successors to the old oligarchy only the bureaucracy, the new business elite, and the Liberal Democratic politicians (duly solicitous to rural power bases) to pursue their mutual goals. And indeed they do. Roughly 20 percent of the national budget of 1967 went into industrial subsidies (coal, small enterprises, shipping, etc.). (See p. 154) It is said that 90 percent of the government's work, in the law-making bodies, the ministries, and the administrative agencies, is concerned with problems of trade, business, and industry; even diplomacy tends to be a means to economic ends. This is understandable when international economic viability is an imperative, and it is especially understandable since the Japanese government, from the Meiji period onward, has always played a symbiotic role with big business. New requirements of housing, environmental protection, industrial zoning, growing suburbia, super highways, modernized transport, new port facilities, and other essentials of the highly industrialized, mass-consumer society have only served to enhance this close relationship dating from the beginnings of Japan's modernization. But recently the intensity of these public welfare needs is finally giving the thrust of the Japanese government-business alliance a new direction in 1973.[41]

Yet much of the Japanese intraparty political process of today draws heavily from the past and is culturally peculiar to Japan, making it difficult for outsiders to see its workings clearly through the formal foreign-looking structures of party and parliament. This is especially true of the inner workings of business circles with the LDP, the workings of the LDP with the bureaucracy, and the workings of bureaucracy with business. Yanaga[42] notes that Prime Minister Ikeda, in a candid moment, expressed an important point when he likened the prime minister to the captain of the ship and the business community to the compass, the implication being that business does point the direction, and if anything gets off course, the captain is held responsible and may be replaced.

In a sense, then, the party has been expected to convert economic power into political power, and when the business supporters are not satisfied with the conversion, Cabinets have soon fallen. For example, Yoshida (1954), Hatoyama (1956), Kishi (1960), and Satō (1972) were all forced to step aside when business had collectively determined that they were no longer useful. Likewise, it was the business circles that induced the Liberal Democratic party to push Ikeda to the fore in 1960 and later to announce Satō as his successor in 1964, this time without even the usual election to the LDP presidency. It has also been well documented that business, frightened by the possibilities of a Socialist or even Communist influenced government, literally required the conservative parties to merge into a unified Liberal Democratic party in 1955. Before we examine the methods by which this critical interaction between business and politics takes place, it is important first to be clear as to what we mean by "the business circles."

Zaikai (Not Zaibatsu)

Business circles (*zaikai*), as they affect politics, are a rather specific group of people. They are talented, articulate activists with a shared background typically from the law departments of key universities in Tokyo, especially Tokyo University. The "business" they represent primarily is big business, reducible to a core of about a hundred mammoth firms. More importantly, it is organized big business, acting as organized business, through the following five major business associations:

1. The Federation of Economic Organizations (FEO; Keizai Dantai Rengokai; Keidanren)
2. Japanese Committee for Economic Development (JCED; Nihon Keizai Dōyūkai; Dōyūkai)
3. Japanese Federation of Employers' Associations (JFEA; Nihon Keieisha Dantai Remmei; Nikkeiren)
4. The Japan Chamber of Commerce (Nihon Shōkō Kaigisho; Nisshō)
5. "Council on Industrial Policy" (Sangyō Mondai Kenkyūkai; Sanken)

The FEO represents about 750 major individual companies and significantly about 100 national associations of businesses, but its leading characteristic is that it speaks for big business, and the president, Uemura Kōgorō, has often been called the prime minister of Japan's "invisible government."

The JCED is known, since World War II, as a talented group of progressive and socially minded businessmen numbering about 1,500 individuals. They have gained a reputation as being the intellectuals of big business, and collectively they are influential in clarifying issues and recommending policies.

The JFEA handles with a united front management's strategies toward organized labor; JFEA is also said to be decisive in designating a man to become the minister of labor in case of Cabinet changes. Its membership is about the same as the FEO.

The Japan Chamber of Commerce, though it has a very broad membership, is often considered to speak also for smaller industry.

Sanken was only founded in 1966 by twenty of the most powerful men in Japanese business.[43] Arising out of a need felt in the JCED for a powerful and maneuverable group, Sanken has become an action-oriented group of individuals with enormous power unencumbered by size, procedures, and organization. For example, it was instrumental in the Yawata-Fuji steel merger, in liberalization of automobile investments, U.S.-Japanese trade talks, and now one of its main action programs is pollution control.

Besides the five major business organizations mentioned above, certain dynamic business leaders, usually presidents or chairmen of major industrial or financial corporations, wield considerable influence either individually or through intimate clubs that characteristically meet with well-chosen politicians and bureaucrats in traditionally styled teahouses.

A rare few of these are founders of major postwar corporations such as Matsushita Kōnosuke, Idemitsu Sazō, and Ishibashi Shōjirō.

These "business circles," as presently organized to make themselves felt in the postwar political arena, are quite different from the prewar *zaibatsu* that were controlled by family holding companies. Postwar business pressure may be even more focused than before World War II because almost all business now supports but one party (LDP). Even some 60 percent of medium and small business (*chūshō kigyō*) seems to support the LDP, despite alleged "second-class treatment." But there is competition by businesses for favors from the several factions. Also, just after 1945, by placing the proceeds from the sale of holding-company shares in the hands of the government, business became concentrated even further, since government was able to control this critical source of capital and use it, preferentially through the Japan Development Bank, to build up the "big four" (electricity, steel, coal, and shipbuilding). In 1972 new priorities for the Japan Development Bank were set by Cabinet decision to include atomic energy, shipping, technology (especially computers), distribution system, pollution, ocean resources, and others.[44] These subsidized industries thus strengthened become focused through organized representatives for the purpose of influencing government policy. In another sense, the business community is more uniform and politically focused, for now most spokesmen are no longer owners; they are practically all professional managers with shared training and public outlooks, and with the same general demands from politics; namely, favorable environmental control for the effective formation and operation of private enterprises (but with special Japanese characteristics and relationship with employees and government). Whereas, before the war, there was a two-party split betwen the Seiyukai and the Minseitō supported by Mitsui and Mitsubishi interests respectively, today all big business is uniformly supporting a single party, the ruling Liberal Democratic party.

Methods of Liaison

Business influences political policy in two fundamental ways. The first is money. By massive contributions to the Liberal Democratic party,[45] to its various factions,[46] and to individual Diet members, big business is able to virtually manipulate public power by staffing the Cabinet with friends. In 1960 there were 143 companies that contributed one million yen or more to political organizations. For a while (1955–61), business devised a separate organ (Keizai Saiken Kondankai,

KSK), administered by staff of the Federation of Economic Organizations (Keidanren), for the purpose of assessing corporations by size of capital and sales and pooling the funds to be used to support primarily the LDP.[47] "Socialist critics point out that the Conservative party exists to serve private monopoly by conducting elections and forming governments with the money furnished by big business. The government, in return, through its tax, fiscal, investment, loan, and labor policies favorable to big business, makes it possible for big business to realize the large profits from which the political contributions come that are used for winning elections."[48]

No little consternation was caused in political circles, including the Socialists, when the Tokyo District Court ruled in 1963 that gifts to the LDP made from funds of Yawata Steel Corporation by its officers were illegal.[49] The decision was based on the private-law theory that such political contribution was *ultra vires* and beyond the proper purpose of a corporation organized for profit. The decision was overruled on appeal in 1965 by the Tokyo High Court, which decision was affirmed by the Supreme Court in 1970.[50] Actually, some businessmen seem to have favored the lower court's ban on corporate gifts, because they would prefer to be allowed to contribute as individuals only, or through their clubs or associations, rather than by corporate gifts under pressure.[51]

Second, business exerts its influences through direct participation as Diet members, as members of government commissions (*shingikai*), as members of working committees of the Liberal Democratic party, and through very extensive committees and research programs of the aforementioned well-staffed business associations. As opposed to the U.S. Congress, which is heavily manned by lawyers, the Japanese House of Representatives is usually over one-third businessmen who have successfully run for the Diet. In addition, through other channels there are massive communications daily on all fronts among business, the LDP, and official government organs discussing, revising, and determining policies relating to business behind the scene and in formal sessions.

All of this activity would be seriously misunderstood if it were regarded as the kind of lobbying found, for example, in the United States. Japanese business is too much a part of the establishment—the ruling party and its governments—to be reduced to "lobbying"; it works from within the political party and from within government circles.

Political party contributions insure that a majority of friends are elected. As noted, between 1955 and 1961, an organ called the Keizai Saiken Kondankai, headed by Uemura Kōgorō (then vice chairman of FEO, now chairman), collected money and donated approximately

$10,716,000 (3,858,068,000 yen) to political parties with the hope of averting some of the past criticisms implying wrongdoings between business and government. The LDP received 95.3 percent of all of these funds. Most of the remainder (2.7 percent) went to the Socialist party as a hedge and as insurance against Communists.[52] In addition, of course, huge sums from individual companies are also distributed to the leading faction chiefs and individual Diet members. By the very nature of things, these funds cannot be accurately measured, especially because it is generally assumed that only a part of the funds are reported through the Agency of Autonomy (Jijichō), as required by law. One would suppose that, at the faction level, much of the money is spent for specific objectives of individual companies as opposed to donations for benefit of business circles in general, which usually goes to the party as such. Of course payments for specific governmental favors are illegal bribery,[53] and periodically rumors of bribery circulate in Tokyo, such as the shipping company scandal in early 1953 in which the arrest of Eisaku Satō (then transportation minister), elected 29 October 1970 for a fourth term as president of the LDP, is said to have been prevented only by intervention of the minister of justice, who ordered the procurators to desist.

Much of the top-level liaison between business and politics is well served by the ethnocentric, elitist, and bureaucratic nature of the LDP itself. The party, its factions, and the leaders in each are dependent upon highly personal, particularistic relationships with supporters based on school groupings (*gakubatsu*), family pedigrees (*kenami*) or marriage alliances (*keibatsu*), bureaucratic groupings (*kambatsu*), common birthplace (*kyōdōbatsu*), and the like. These small intimate circles often have their superior-inferior lines drawn in accordance with *oyabun-kobun* ("parent-child") relations well-defined in Japanese tradition. Such personal relationships, not only within the political parties and factions, but also within business circles and between the two, tend to create an interwoven group of business and governmental elites of similar outlook who communicate easily on a warm personal level. This is why intimate conversations at favorite teahouses instead of forensics at public meetings is the Japanese political style and the usual setting for high-level policy determinations. This way, the formalisms of government function smoothly in public, since all has been previously decided in private, except for disturbances occasionally introduced by the desperate Socialist opposition. It has been well said that the history of the Conservative party and the fortunes of the teahouses are but two wheels on the same cart.[54]

Major politicians all have their own groups of business leaders organized into clubs. These selective groups meet regularly to advise the leader and later support the positions taken. Prime Minister Eisaku Satō had a number of such clubs, for example, the Chōei Society, comprised of presidents of first-line companies who meet monthly for informal chats with the prime minister.[55]

From watching the flow of money, it would be easy to conclude that business has an absolute grip on the Liberal Democratic party, but actually the decision-making process is so diffuse, and the business interests so pluralistic, that such a conclusion is a bit too facile, especially because the nonpolitical bureaucracy is also a balancing factor in the triumvirate. More will be said about the interplay of bureaucracy, business, and political parties in Chapter VI, but it is important to remember here that, in the postwar period, top bureaucrats often retire and run for the Diet. They constitute 27 percent of LDP Diet members, compared to local politicians 22 percent, businessmen 18 percent, and journalists 7 percent.[56] This is partly because under the new constitution (1947), unlike prior practice, they cannot reach their ultimate goal of Cabinet membership without going into politics.

If the party's role is to translate the economic power of business into governmental power, it is important to remember that the bureaucracy also acts as the "subcontractors" in this process. The typical Cabinet minister must rely on the bureaucracy's expertise, and he does so to an extraordinary degree, because of the rapid turnover of cabinets and because of the remarkably shallow turnover of bureaucratic personnel within the ministries based on patronage when cabinets change.

Another strand in this seamless web is, as previously noted, the very low retirement age (fifty to fifty-five), when top bureaucrats begin in their final, but still vigorous, years to seek post-retirement jobs with business corporations or in a support group within business for a candidacy for the Diet. With such aspirations, retiring bureaucrats have, of course, a disposition to please business. Consequently, the bureaucracy, though it may try to be independent, actually caters to business, within legal limits, because of self-interest and because of similar training and natural empathy with their opposite numbers in business. So, though there has been a long tradition in past Japanese officialdom of looking down on nonofficials (*kanson-mimpi*), top business officials and top government officials nowadays are often easy political allies in support of the Liberal Democratic party. The kind of "tail-chasing" involved in the relationships of the parts within the broader establishment (bureaucracy, business, and the LDP) leads to politicization of the bureaucracy and, at the same time, the bureaucratization of politics by retired officials running for the Diet. Both processes, of course, go a long way toward explaining the one-and-a-half-party system in Japan.

Yanaga has emphasized that no such complex mixture of concentrated power exists in the U.S. as is found in Tokyo today:

> It is as if Washington, D.C., New York, Chicago, Philadelphia, Pittsburgh, Boston, and Detroit were rolled into one.
>
> Such a concentration of power is unknown in the United States. To create an analogous situation, it would be necessary to locate the head offices of America's hundred largest corporations in Washington, D.C., together with their presidents, board chairmen, and directors, many of whom would be related by marriage not only to each other, but to influential political leaders and government administrators. Furthermore, these top-level executives would, for the most part, claim the same alma mater, belong to the same country clubs, have ready access to government offices, maintain daily contact with government officials by phone or over the luncheon table, enjoy intimate relations with influential senators and congressmen, and also serve on government advisory bodies and administrative commissions.[57]

Furthermore, one must always remember that the Japanese establishment functions most effectively in the "tea-house setting" and that much in politics will escape the foreign observer if he focuses too much on the party organization or the constitutional framework of the Cabinet and Diet. Still, it is the constitutionally validated position of the Socialists and other opposition parties which makes them effective and which, more than anything else, holds the Liberal Democratic party together.

III

The Scope and Dynamics
of the Japanese Economy

Much of the postwar foreign business interest in Japan can be explained simply by the geography of emerging multinational corporations striving for global coverage in an imperfect free-world economy in which bilateral trade alone is not enough;[1] major Japanese corporations are now planning similar global expansion.[2] Coupled with this business incentive to enter Japan was the legal presumption, particularly among Americans, that they were entitled to operate in Japan, based on an instinct for free enterprise underwritten by postwar U.S. policy, and vested in national treatment provisions of the United States–Japanese Treaty of Friendship, Commerce, and Navigation.[3] Resisting these liberal and expansive thrusts by foreigners, Japanese officialdom has been pursuing predetermined, nationalistic goals restricting entry into the Japanese economy and aiming for a new world stature in heavy industry, which has required intricate manipulation of both the traditional and the modern social, political, and economic processes in which officialdom saw little place for foreign management. This attitude toward foreign management control has existed persistently in Japan from Perry, or even Dejima (see Chapter I). Japanese official ambitions have included not only rapid growth but also major structural changes in the economy, and these overall aspects must not be overlooked in the foreigners' scrutiny of details in their own industries. We shall be concerned in this chapter first with Japan's domestic resources and the dimensions and growth of the Japanese economy. Secondly we shall examine the growth of a mass-consumer market and the major structural shifts toward heavy industry, toward the knowledge industry, toward quality production, toward a basic reapportionment of the primary, secondary, and tertiary sectors, and in general toward the so-called three "I's"—innovation, integration, and internationalization. These, of course, are all taking place against a background of lingering "economic dualism," and the newer "industrial dualism" on the domestic scene, and the lingering mercantilism in Japan's international economic policies. In the final section of this chapter, we shall survey Japanese trade relations and future outlook for integration into the world economy.

Domestic Resources

Awareness of the poverty of Japanese raw-material resources is essential to any real comprehension of her rather special business structuring and governmental controls.

But, in the 1970s, resource problems must not be exaggerated. Japan's resource scarcity is a qualitative thing, for, paradoxically, in quantitative terms the ratio of Japanese imports to gross national product has still not reached its level of the 1930s, and even compared to other nations it is now the lowest in the free world, with the exception of the U.S. Furthermore, it is predicted that such quantitative import dependence will further decline to 1975. Another point often overlooked is that, in the present relatively open free-world economy, Japan's lack of domestic raw materials can be an advantage in the sense that she can procure them on a shrinking globe from whomsoever may offer them on a long-term reliable basis at the lowest price, without compulsions to develop her own, which might be less economical. To exploit such advantages unfolding with the internationalization of business, Japan has a major asset in her world-leading shipbuilding industry and a prime resource in her long coast line with many excellent deep-water ports, to which her huge tankers and ore carriers can deliver raw materials at increasingly low freight rates. Because of these several factors, in fact, world raw-material prices of Japan's imports have steadily gone down since 1950, as the export price index has gone up, though raw materials were trending upward in 1972.[4] But there is growing criticism of Japanese extractive development and export of raw-materials resources from poorer countries without minimal processing there—sometimes embarrassingly called neocolonialism. Often, too, Japanese buying is cartelized to prevent competition among her corporate buyers to the detriment of overseas sellers who are often highly competitive.

Japan's chief domestic resource is her people. In the 1970s her population, just over one hundred million, is one-half that of the U.S., and double that of the U.K. and West Germany. A comparatively highly trained and literate population is only a flick of the TV or radio switch away from the standardizing pulses of modern commercialism.[5] A highly effective and competitive educational system, beginning at age three with pressures from Japan's millions of anxious "education mamas" (*kyōiku mama*), performs a vital function in the national economy, for hierarchy imposed early in life by academic performance (meritocracy)[6] is pervasively characteristic of both the business and government bureaucracies. With only the first nine years (primary and middle school) compulsory, still by 1971, 84 percent proceeded through the higher school (*kōtō-gakkō*) of three years, and nearly 25 percent (as opposed to prewar 5 percent) proceeded on to the universities.[7] The four-year universities (about four hundred in all) are themselves informally ranked in the minds of employers, with Tokyo and Kyoto Universities ranked over the regional public universities, and public universities generally ranked over private universities; the "old Imperial universities" are ranked over the "new universities," and all public and all private universities are both ranked amongst themselves, thus supporting the ubiquitous hierarchy of Japanese society in general. Within the universities, the law departments and, to a lesser extent, economics and business are the matrix of power, though the law graduates only "major" in law and do not usually study beyond the four-year Bachelor of Arts degree; nor do most of the "law graduates (BA)" ever intend to qualify as practicing professional lawyers (*bengoshi*) as they do in the U.S. (see Chapter V). Tokyo (11 million) with 12 percent of the entire nation's population is the place where virtually all major financial and governmental decisions are made, especially in international business. Therefore public, and even the best private, universities (*e.g.,* Waseda and Keio) in Tokyo have come to outrank nearly all schools outside of Tokyo (Kyoto University excepted) in recent years.

Competition for college entrance is fierce, especially among applicants to the top universities, and rightly so, since entrance practically insures graduation and also a top managerial career later in Japanese business or government. Much pressure is thus placed on the Japanese universities as human classifiers. But, to date—despite serious defects and consequent protest—entrance and performance testing have been sufficiently fair and accurate, it seems, to produce results plausible enough to legitimate the university entrance examination as the classifier between managerial and clerical and between white- and blue-collar personnel types and to select out the elite from all Japan. Since the recent university turmoil culminating in 1969, however, many have appropriately questioned the quality of university education, and most thoughtful observers agree that the Japanese university is seriously underfinanced and that its structure, administration, and methods are outmoded.[8] Particularly criticized is the fact that 200 of Japan's four-year colleges (with 650,000 pupils, 72 percent) are private. These are inadequately financed, almost entirely on private funds, largely tuition, because great private wealth of the magnitude found in the origins of U.S. foundations and private colleges has not been available in postwar Japan. The private burden of higher education resting on parents of the students is highly exceptional among advanced countries, and most critics feel that it is essential for the Japanese government to begin now to somehow provide financing for the private institutions; others insist that sound meritocracy requires discriminating allocations of resources and the severe grading of students and of universities themselves. Quality of education has, nonetheless, been a real problem with a high student-faculty ratio of 32 to 1 in the private universities as compared to 8 to 1 in the public universities.[9] Americans will remember that most of the major universities in the U.S. are now public, and even the few major private universities of prestige are now operating to a major extent on public funding programs or quasi-public funding from foundations sponsored by tax exemptions. A major portion of Japanese higher education, the private universities, have no such succor.

While one may also admire the qualities of self-discipline and achievement found in abundance among the Japanese people as individuals, their prime distinguishing quality is in their sociality and loyalty to their respective groups (company, university, region, or nation), and the consequent social intensity of Japanese energy and effort, which consistently seems to add up to more than the sum of the parts in their corporate endeavor.[10] This extraordinary dedication to group or national goals, coupled with a six-day week, is undoubtedly the key to high Japanese economic performance, so fatuously dubbed a "miracle" in journalistic prattling throughout the 1960s. More will be said about this in connection with the Japanese labor market and labor-industrial relations (Chapter IV). These qualities produced a large per-hour cost advantage for Japan (1970: Japan $.96 per-hour; U.S.: $3.36).

Here, in discussing Japanese resources, however, we must emphasize that at least the Japanese labor supply has proven not to be inexhaustible, and one of the trends is for wages to outstrip productivity gains since 1968.[11] Since 1969 Japan has had a labor storage of sorts, after nearly a century of movement from farm to factory, creating what seemed for many years to be an inexhaustible, elastic supply of cheap labor for government-nurtured large urban enterprises. Even during the first decade after World War II, the labor force increased 15 percent, while population increased only 10 percent. Happily the increase occurred in the younger, low-wage group, thus furnishing manpower at the lowest rung of the ladder, reducing labor costs at a critical period in Japan's rehabilitation. Since the early sixties, however, younger men have been remaining in education beyond the compulsory nine years and entering higher schools and universities in larger percentages[12] (*e.g.,* middle school graduates entering the labor force: 760,000 in 1963 and 420,000 in 1970; and higher school: 970,000 in 1966 and 670,000 in 1970), so that the graduates from middle school and high school ready for blue-collar and clerical hiring have become more critically scarce with each ensuing year, forcing small- and medium-sized employers to raise wages and thus reduce the differential that has always existed between their starting wage rates and those of larger industries. Also declining are the differentials between blue- and white-collar wages and between starting wages for graduates (age twenty-two) and wages for the forty- and fifty-year-olds.[13]

Just how this shortage will run its course and affect labor costs and the industrial structure (dualism) is of critical importance to both domestic and foreign enterprises and to Japanese competitiveness in world markets. Like nearly everything else in Japan, part of the picture is the institutionally contrived nature of the so-called "shortage." Actually, and perhaps inevitably while modernizing, much underemployment and inefficiency of labor still remain in the small and medium enterprise sector, and particularly in the entire distribution system, but hiring the underemployed away from current employers in mid-career has always been industrial taboo because it disturbs the symmetry and vested interest of life-long personnel hierarchies in all major corporations. Routinely, major Japanese firms had always confined their hiring to new and cheap graduates just out of school at the bottom rung of the pay scale and for life (*shūshin koyō*). They then moved up inexorably by seniority (*nenkō joretsu*) in the same firm until retirement, significantly at the latest by age fifty-five, except a handful of major officers (*jūyaku*). The overall impact of this pervasive and peculiar system has been a remarkable lack of mobility of laborers and managers, until age fifty-five at least, in the large modern enterprises, though interfirm mobility is increasing now.[14] Today's pressure for workers in the modern sector is thus not easily satisfied from the multitude of underemployed in the small and medium sector. It is only in this peculiar Japanese sense that there is a labor shortage in Japan yet.

Land and Agriculture

Deprived of her colonies (mainly Korea, Taiwan, and Sakhalin), Japan's postwar territory does not serve her as well as her people. The territory (143,000 square miles) is slightly smaller than California (say 4 percent of the U.S.) and only about 18 percent of it is arable. Yet, by constantly improved tillage and uneconomic subsidies, Japanese farmers have made Japan 80 percent self-sufficient in food, and entirely self-sufficient in its chief staple, rice. But self-sufficiency comes at a high price: the governmentally pegged price for Japanese rice in 1972 was double that of the world market. Japan is the world's largest producer of fish and other marine products, but even though 80 percent of her territory is mountains and forest land, she produces roughly only one-half of her timber requirements. Postwar Japanese eating and living habits are rapidly assimilating certain western features;[15] young Japanese males (fifteen-year-olds) are larger than their ancestors (4'11¾" in 1900; 5'3" in 1960), and their life expectancy has increased a remarkable twenty years.[16] Thus, based on developing living styles and the doctrine of comparative advantages, more of Japan's food should be imported in the future, and indeed imports have been increasing recently.[17]

Raw Materials for Industry

Despite her quantitatively low ratio of imports to GNP, Japan has indeed an extraordinary *qualitative* dependence on imports for her most basic industrial raw materials, such as ores, fuels, and timber. Future estimates indicate that the situation will worsen, as may be seen from the following figures:[18]

Materials	Percentage Imported 1968	Percentage Imported 1975 (Estimated)
Copper	73.4	92.9
Lead	56.5	55.6
Zinc	53.8	63.6
Aluminum	100	100
Nickel	100	100
Iron Ore	84.7	90
Oil	99.5	99.7
Natural Gas	0	73.6
Uranium	100	100
Logs and Lumber	46.7	49.58

Obviously, a country that attains a major ranking in heavy industries, which Japan has done between 1952 and 1970, with such meager raw resources available domestically to sustain it, must live with high anxieties concerning freedom of trade, access to foreign raw-material sources, and foreign friendliness generally. Viewed qualitatively, no major country in the world is so dependent on the outside world; none of the postwar heavy industries in Japan has a substantial local source for the raw materials essential to start the first wheel turning. The ratio of raw-material imports to all-Japan imports is declining, however, with gradual liberalization of trade.[19] Further discussion of this topic will be deferred until the end of this chapter, but here is a point to remember: Japan's dependence has been largely accrued during the last twenty-five years as a result of governmental planning for the heavy industrial complex in Japan competitive with the U.S. and western Europe. Officially imposed import restrictions and officially approved purchasing cartels to prevent free competition among Japanese buyers in the world markets,[20] as well as "dumping"[21] in world export markets in recessionary periods, have caused tensions recently because of the inconsistency of a high international dependence coupled with what most foreigners feel to be an over-nationalistic policy in world trade.[22] The solution will require more long-term contracts wherein Japanese industries absorb more of the fluctuations in the raw-materials market in exchange for secure supplies. This will entail joint development with people at the raw-material sources and fair, reliable dealing at every turn.

Size of the Japanese Economy

The size and dynamism of the Japanese economy have been a major attraction to foreign enterprise, and predictions for the 1970s are favorable, perhaps even a bit euphoric.[23] For the economic indicators have become methods of scoring in Japan's national goal to surpass the west. Like a bathing beauty, that creature of the media, "the Japanese miracle," has its "three measurements"[24] (growth rate, GNP, and per capita income), which are carefully tallied and regularly reported, not just in Japan but worldwide. In the 1950s and 1960s, emphasis was on the rate of growth, but as output began to compare favorably with western nations, the gross size of the economy has been emphasized. Now, because of its superiority as a measure of human welfare, per capita income is getting the publicity as Japan, reputedly now in eighth place with $1840 per person, surpasses year by year more and more of the western European nations.

The accomplishment through 1971 can be shown in easily remembered rounded figures as follows:[25]

Population	105,000,000,000
Gross National Product	$242,000,000,000
National Income per Capita	$1,840
Exports	(almost) $ 28,000,000,000 (10%)

The table on page 72 shows the score to date in competition with the U.S., U.S.S.R., West Germany, U.K., and Mainland China.[26]

Growth Rate: Recent Projections to 1975

The 1975 projection of Japan's economic trends and dimensions are even more interesting to the foreign enterpriser, not only because of the indicated growth, but also because of the continuing qualitative changes foreseen.[27]

The projection for 1975 is:

Population	110 million
Gross national product	440 billion
Exports	41.8 billion
Imports	29.2 billion
Trade balance	12.6 billion
Overall balance	4.7 billion
Per capita GNP	$3,981 (U.S. $6,245)

In 1970, none of the several Japanese research institutes predicted a GNP growth rate of less than 10 percent (except the Sanwa Bank at 9.3 percent), and the Japan Economic Research Center of Tokyo, after weighing all factors, set the likely rate at 12.4 percent for the 1970–75 period, assuming favorable official policy and international cooperation. Western specialists on the Japanese economy also expect high growth in the 1970s but slower than the 1960s, and fiscal 1971 (6 percent) and 1972 (8.5 percent) rates of growth seem to be closer to such judgment thus far. No matter whether western experts (predicting between 7–8 percent annual growth)[28] or Japanese authorities (predicting between 9–13 percent) may turn out to be closer to the truth as its unfolds to 1975, all agree that high performance is a near certainty, though much depends, as in the past, on governmental policy and international cooperation.

Without forgetting that progressions unilineally up are not a law-of-nature and that there is evidence in 1972 of a slowdown, it is worth noting that Japanese estimates, of late, have regularly proven too low. To assist, however, in evaluating the 1970–75 quantitative projections of the Japanese economy, it is important to understand first the past growth rates and trends and their significance to future business growth.

Japanese Economic Growth Rates and GNP

Recent studies[29] of Japanese economic growth have reminded us that the high growth rate is not entirely a postwar phenomenon in Japan, for prewar growth averaged over 4 percent annually from 1878 to 1940, with critical gains at the rate of 2.6 percent annually in traditional agriculture, enabling industrialism to gain momentum before 1900. Still, after World War II, growth has been phenomenal, averaging 9 percent in the 1950s and 10 percent in the 1960s; even the lowest annual rate (3.3 percent in 1957–58) was a bit higher than the average growth rate of the U.S. economy throughout the 1950s.[30] From 1965 to 1970, the upward thrust strengthened to produce an annual rate of 13.3 percent, thrilling even further Japan's worldwide constituency of GNP watchers,[31] while her gross production surpassed the French, English, and finally the West Germans, leaving only the U.S.S.R. and the U.S. to be "conquered."

Per capita GNP is more meaningful than GNP as such, because of population differences (*i.e.,* the Japanese population is just short of double that of the United Kingdom or West Germany, and only half that of the U.S.). In fiscal 1971, Japan's per capita income of $1840, making it eighth place in the world, was slightly behind the U.K. ($2,025), West Germany ($2,850) the U.S. ($4,782), and several smaller countries such as Sweden, Denmark, Switzerland, and Canada.[32] In 1972 Japan's per capita income rose to about $2,400 by new exchange rates (308 yen to $1.00).

But, two caveats about Japanese per capita GNP are in order even after the revaluation (308 yen to $1) of 1971:

1. There is a large differential in wages received for roughly the same work in the large and small industrial sectors so that the per capita income figures gloss over a major inequality in living standards.

2. Japanese living habits and consumption scale also are sufficiently different to make international comparisons in money somewhat less meaningful, even as the exchange rate became more realistic at roughly 260 yen to $1.00.

Table of Significant National Figures

(1969, except as noted; values in dollars in all financial statistics)

Nation	Population	Gross National Product	National Per Capita Income	Annual Imports	Annual Exports
U.S.A.	203,216,000[P]	$932,300,000,000	$4,588	$36,052,000,000[P]	$37,314,000,000[P1]
U.S.S.R.	241,748,000[N2]	(1968) $611,050,000,000[N3]	(1968) $2,547[A4]	$10,327,000,000[S]	$11,660,000,000[S]
West Germany	60,842,000[S]	$151,000,000,000[S5]	$2,481	$24,933,000,000[S6]	$29,052,000,000[S]
U.K.	55,534,000[S]	$92,680,800,000[M7]	$1,669	$19,975,680,000[M8]	$17,611,200,000[M9]
Japan	102,650,000[J]	$170,000,000,000[D]	$1,641[I]	$15,024,000,000[S]	$15,990,000,000[S10]
Mainland China	1970 forecast[11] 814,000,000[B]	1970 forecast $170,000,000,000[B12]	1970 est. $105[13]	1967 est. $2,094,000,000[C]	$2,250,000,000[S14]

SOURCES:
A. Joint Economic Committee (U.S.), *Soviet Economic Performance, 1966–67.*
B. Joint Economic Committee (U.S.), *An Economic Profile of Modern China.*
C. Institute of Political Research (Taiwan), *Handbook of Chinese Communist Affairs;* some data from *Shin Chūgoku nenkan* ("New China Yearbook"), Japan, 1967.
D. *Japan Economic Journal.*

I. International Monetary Fund, *International Financial Statistics*, May 1970.

J. Bureau of Statistics, Office of the Prime Minister, *Monthly Statistics of Japan*, Feb. 1970.

M. Central Statistical Office (London), *Monthly Digest of Statistics*, Apr. 1970.

N. Izdateistvo Statistika (Moscow), *Narodnoe Hozjaistvo SSSR v. 1968 g*

P. *Economic Report of the President* (Washington), Feb. 1970.

S. *U.N. Monthly Bulletin of Statistics*, May, June 1970.

1. Source S: $37,978,000,000, excluding foreign aid and including military aid.

2. Census, 1 Jan. 1970. Source S estimate, 240,333,000.

3. "Gross Public Product," 550,000,000,000 rubles; Source S shows $270,084,000,000 Net Material Product, which differs from GNP by excluding value of services and including turnover taxes, in 1968; Source A estimates 1966 GNP at $357 billions; *Soviet News* (21 Apr. 1970) states that 1970 production increased 7.5% over 1969.

4. Same limitations as given in Note 3; Source A estimates $1532 per capita income in 1966; radio broadcast, 23 July 1970, stated current figure is "$133 per month" (= $1596 annually).

5. DM 599,600,000,000.

6. Excludes trade with East Germany.

7. 38,617,000,000 pounds; Source S shows 42,340,000,000 pounds ($101,616,000,000).

8. Source S: 8,352,300,000 pounds ($20,045,520,000).

9. Source S: 7,032,100,000 pounds ($16,877,040,000).

10. *Japan Report*: $16,044,000,000; *World Almanac*, 1970: $12,973,000,000.

11. 1 of 4 possible forecasts; Source C estimate (1967) is 773 million; Source S estimate: 740 million.

12. 1 of 4 possible forecasts; Source C estimate (1967), is $125,440,000,000.

13. Source B: $75 (1965).

14. Includes Mongolia, North Korea, North Vietnam; Source I (1964) estimates for mainland China only, $1,500,000,000 exports and $1,200,000,000 imports.

Leading Industries (1970–1975)

Highest growth in the 1970–75 period is expected in the so-called leisure, knowledge, and housing industries. As high as 47 percent (from 34 percent in 1960) of the GNP is expected from these areas. Thus, consumer market forces will be more important at least in international trade than they were in the 1950s, or even in the 1960s, when government policy emphasized producers with relatively little attention to consumers. Nonetheless, most households already have an electric washer, refrigerator, and TV—somewhat irreverently known to the Japanese as the Three Treasures (*sanshu no jingi*); that is, the sword, the mirror, and the jewel, symbols of the highest significance in Imperial Shinto rites. Current household goals have shifted[33] to the three C's (Car, Cooler, and Color TV), and with the growing gap in earnings, some can now even aspire to the five C's, adding Central Heating and a Cottage-in-the-Country. Significantly, however, the high excitement over property acquisition of a decade ago has already crested out,[34] though it is still strong. Family trips, as opposed to the company outing, are growing, as are plans for the first trip abroad in some families.

The leisure boom has happily brought the Japanese through the grubby *pachinko* (sort of pin-ball) phase and *chambara* (sword play) movie binge into the bowling, skiing, and boating era of recreation. So, leisure, knowledge (books, education, computers), and housing are said to be the high opportunity industries of the seventies in the consumer field.

Still, plant and equipment investment remains a key to growth, as in the past decade, and one prognosis expects it to increase 16.4 percent annually to at least 1975. This figure is admittedly most difficult to predict because of the 1960–65 record with 9.6 percent, but it jumped to 23.5 percent for the 1965–70 period. So the question becomes which of the two rates of the 1960s is likely to be the most accurate measure of the future.[35] The 1970–71 figures suggest that the rate of increase in private capital outlay is likely to be much lower and that achievement of growth predictions will depend more on governmental capital outlay for public facilities, pollution control, and the like.

Global Comparisons (1975)

In global terms, Japan's 1975 share of world GNP, as projected by JERC (probably over-optimistic), will be 12.3 percent ($440 billion) of a world total of $3,580 billion, compared with a share of only 6.5 percent in 1970. Japan's per capita GNP in 1975 of $4,150 will be larger than that of West Germany or the U.K., and sixth in the world (after the U.S., Canada, Switzerland, Sweden, and Denmark). Also, exports will increase 17.4 percent annually, compared to 8.6 percent for world trade generally. This will bring Japanese exports to $41.8 billion and imports to $29.2 billion, thus a favorable trade balance of 12.6 billion and an overall balance of payments of 4.7 billion in the black by 1975. These high growth prospects, whether realized entirely or not, are likely to sustain a vigorous foreign interest in the Japanese markets in the near future, as it has in the past. No better evidence of the oft-mentioned "difference" between Japan and other nonwestern countries can be found than her embarrassing habit of over-achieving against the targets in her economic plans.

Structural Changes and Trends (1965–75)

The sheer volume of Japanese economic expansion should not, however, be allowed to obscure even more important qualitative and structural changes as the economy continues to evolve in response to governmental planning and entrepreneurial energy.

The first significant shift is found in the changed proportions of the primary, secondary, and tertiary sectors:[36]

Sector	1965 Production	1965 Employees	1970 Production	1970 Employees	1975 Production	1975 Employees
Primary (Agriculture, Fisheries, & Forestry)	10%	25.6%	7%	18.2%	5%	12.6%
Secondary (Manufacturing & Construction)	40%	31.6%	42%	34.7%	44%	37.2%
Tertiary (Services, etc.)	50%	42.8%	51%	47.1%	51%	50.2%

Particularly notable is the "advanced" distribution of the labor force; as the primary sector shrinks, the manufacturing and services industries grow in response to the "mass consumer society," resulting in 50 percent of labor in the tertiary (services) sector by 1975.

The second important shift has been from labor-intensive industries competitive with Asian countries to capital-intensive, heavy industry (steel, chemicals and machinery) competitive with the U.S. and Europe.[37] This policy, begun before 1950, has been doggedly pursued with gov-

ernmental tax and credit preferences to assist the heavy modern enterprises. For example, with crucial funds initially derived from SCAP's
deconcentration program (*i.e.,* capital levy and the *zaibatsu* families'
stock sales), the Japan Development Bank (Nihon Kaihatsu Ginkō)
made 75 percent of its loans, amounting to 2.6 billion dollars up to
1964,[38] to the selected "big four" (steel, coal, electricity, and marine
transportation). Likewise, the "city banks" have loaned largely to modern heavy industry at lower interest rates (*e.g.,* in 1957, 8 to 8.5 percent) while small firms in light manufacturing normally borrow from
credit associations and mutual banks at higher rates (*e.g.,* in 1957,
10.75 to 12.43 percent).[39] A novel trend in the early months of 1972
was the growing city bank loans to smaller enterprises because of a lack
of demand for credit by their usual borrowers—the big, modern firms.

A third change is occurring as "soft" industries are gaining over the
maturing hard industries dominant in the 1960s; in the 1970s the action
will be in the so-called "three S's" (soft, system, and specialization),
as a world division of production and automation and computerization
continues to advance.

A fourth shift in the economy is just getting under way as a result of
recent Cabinet policy. A major effort and public spending program are
aimed at upgrading Japan's neglected public facilities—environment,
roads, ports, housing, and social welfare programs.

A fifth change is a narrowing of the differentials of Japanese "dualism" (see below). These shifts are beginning to forebode important
structural transformation, sparked by the first labor shortage in Japanese
industrial history briefly noted above. The starting wage differential,
whereby traditional, small, or dependent firms have paid less to hire
the left-overs from each annual crop of young graduates, has narrowed
drastically, because the scarcity of these graduates is the "labor shortage"; and significant organizational changes are emerging from the
malaise of small-firm bankruptcies, take-overs, and mergers, particularly
in the marginal subcontracting and distribution segment of the "lower
deck."[40] But these can be comprehended only after some background
concerning dualism itself.

Dualism: Economic and Industrial

Rural-Urban Dualism

Just as "factionalism" has been an embarrassing blemish on the Japanese body politic, "dualism" has been an economic disease deplored by
government and industry alike throughout the postwar period and even

before. In broadest terms "dualism" refers to a double-decked economic structure characteristic of modernizing economies[41] and comprised of a layer of new, large, well-paid modern producers and an underlying layer of small, financially weak, traditional producers.

Historically, what might be called "economic dualism" (as distinguished from industrial dualism) existed in Japan between traditional agriculture and modern industry, wherein agriculture, low paid as it was, was still able, by achieving probably the world's highest increases in productivity during the late nineteenth century, to increase output so as to release an abundant supply of cheap labor to the emerging factories in the cities. This type of "economic dualism" is now on the wane as agricultural workers dropped precipitously from nearly 40 percent of the work force in 1955 to an estimated 12 percent in 1975; also, artificially high official rice prices, double those in the world market, have raised the farmers' earnings to equal city averages. No longer an object of pity, nor a source of cheap labor, the Japanese farmers are now criticized for their subsidized affluence by both the urban Japanese who are hit by high food prices and foreigners who are denied a market by governmental protectionism.[42]

Traditional-Western Dualism

In the past, another kind of dualism[43]—that between the large, modern western-styled industries and the persisting small traditional crafts (also somewhat modernized over time)—has also performed a vital function in Japan's industrialization; that function has been to supply most of the people's basic consumer needs by use of existing productive skills and facilities; thus, new facilities were freed for the critical capital buildup for modernization. Japan has thus avoided in large part what some development economists have called the "demonstration effect"; namely, a tendency of people in developing countries to emulate western living styles, thus creating consumer demands, which in turn preempt modern productive facilities and drain off personal savings from the capital formation process necessary to a buildup in heavy industries. In Japan, supported by the strong ethnocentric preferences of consumers (*e.g.,* wooden clogs [*geta*], bean curds [*tōfu*], and straw mats [*tatami*] instead of shoes, cornflakes, and rugs respectively), the tiny existing traditional industries have been able until recently to take much of the pressure for consumer goods off the modern sector.[44]

Modern Industrial Dualism

But currently the most virulent dualism of interest to foreign enter-prisers is within the modern manufacturing sector. Too, some rural-urban and traditional-western dualism of the types that carried most of the weight of capitalizing the modern sector until about 1955 still remain, but the major problem now is the new "industrial dualism" that has crept into and permeated most of the modern manufacturing sector itself. This dualism is not peculiar to Japan;[45] it is found generally in developing countries; and, of course, large and small industries coexist in advanced countries too. The problem is that Japan, now an estab-lished member in the "advanced club," retains an immense "lower deck," with an enormous wage and productivity gap between her two tiers of industry.[46] In 1969, 50 percent (1964: 53.2 percent) of all manufacturing employees, as compared to 27 percent in the U.S., were employed in firms with fewer than 100 employees. In retailing and other distribution, the small enterprise share (79 percent) is even higher, contributing to a seriously inefficient sales system. Specifically, more than 26 percent of the industrial labor force is in distribution as com-pared, for example, with only 14 percent in the U.K.[47] Much of this "inefficiency," however, is explained by the habits of the Japanese house-wife (shopping daily within walking distance, partly as a social occa-sion to get out of the house), which can be catered to only by a host of tiny neighborhood retailers, who are in turn serviced by a complex hierarchy of intermediate wholesalers. Thus, changes are likely to be slow because of the difficulty in changing a routine to which housewives are enamored for their own reasons, unless something like "women's lib" can be effectively enlisted to break down such habits in the interest of efficiency and emancipation, which can be plausibly argued.

These special problems in distribution underscore the fact that it is a bit insensitive to speak of "the" medium and small enterprise problem, because there are several such problems depending on whether we are discussing manufacturing, distribution, services, or agriculture, or, even more specifically, depending on what industry is being discussed. The special problem in manufacturing arises from subcontracting practices whereby large firms control the output and prices of small firms that manufacture components often for a single domineering customer. The problem is not the size and diversity of the small-scale sector in Japan, but the dependence and consequent wage gap between the two tiers in the industrial structure for roughly equivalent work. The gap is much wider at each step-up in size of the manufacturer than in the U.S.,

France, West Germany, or Great Britain.[48] In 1969 the wage differential
in Japan was very great, as the following wage figures show:[49]

Enterprises Classified by Scale of Work Force	Cash Annual Wage per Employee
"Small and Medium"	
4 to 9 employees	334,000 yen (1968)
10 to 29 "	475,000 yen (1968)
30 to 99 "	594,000 yen
100 to 299 "	646,000 yen
"Large"	
300 to 999 "	747,000 yen
1,000 or more "	916,000 yen

But note that Shinohara shows that the differentials had already narrowed considerably in Japan by 1965 (*e.g.,* scale of 100–199 employees
was paying 70 percent and 50–99 was paying 66.3 percent).[50] This is
in contrast to increasing differentials in the 1950s.[51] The small firms
were losing more men to large firms by changes in employment and
were having more difficulty hiring the skilled labor and new middle and
high school graduates each year.[52] Also, small-firm workers put in longer
hours with higher risks of injury. Thus the small firms' labor problems
were still acute, though the wage differentials have been decreasing from
pressures caused by the overall labor shortage.[53] The 1969 figures indicate that fundamental shifts are being made now. Figures on cash wages
only (as distinguished from total labor costs, including cash wages,
goods, and services) show that manufacturing firms with under thirty
employees paid only 61.9 percent of the salary paid by large firms (500
or more), but medium firms (100–499) paid 80 percent in 1969.[54]

Similarly, productivity differentials widen in Japan as plant size decreases. For example, productivity in plants of 10–19 workers was only
29 percent of the productivity found in large Japanese plants (100+),
whereas in Britain, productivity for plants of that size was 90 percent
of the large ones. Thus "dualism," as a malady to be overcome by
development, does not refer so much to the fact that a strata of small
firms exists, or employs a large portion of the total work force, or
produces a major portion of GNP; it refers, rather, to the fact that
workers in small enterprises earn much lower wages and contribute much
less per worker to the national product, allegedly because of official discrimination, mainly in financing.

This then is not only a labor or a social problem; it is a potential political problem concerning basic economic policy. The question is how to deal with over half of the working populace who are said, by critics of the government, to be "second-class citizens." This argument puts the fault on the Liberal Democratic party, pointing out that a policy to favor heavy industries and large firms by preferences in taxes, scarce credit, subsidies, and priorities in importing western technology has deliberately created a second-class labor market (of unskilled and older retired personnel) with low wages, low technological level, weak finances, low productivity, and excessive competition, which adds up to a lower deck in the entire industrial structure which is not up to international standards and not fairly treated by domestic administration.[55]

The government, on the other hand, argues with some plausibility that even the lower sector has been able to enjoy a higher standard of living than would have been possible without the government's heavy emphasis on developing the large-scale industrial sector and that, in any event, the development of the modern sector was a necessary first step and better than any alternatives suggested. Outsiders have difficulty arbitrating these issues,[56] but all foreign observers on the Japanese scene must try to understand the dynamics of dualism, because significant changes are in process. However, these can be more adequately treated after discussing business structure and regulation in the next chapter.

Some Reasons for "High" Growth

Basically Japan's growth is the achievement of the Japanese people, the six-day week, and the nine- or ten-hour day. In part, though, Japanese economic dynamism[57] can be ascribed to astute governmental vision that sets the goals high and methodically blueprinted the way to attain them, and the governmental planning has been supported by an increasingly sophisticated gathering, analysis, and use of information and statistics. The planning reports and white papers rank high in their class, and officials producing them deserve high marks for generally knowing precisely, in quantitative terms, what the economy has done and is doing. Equally important is the vitality of Japanese entrepreneurs and the remarkable sociopolitical integration in Japan, which is almost uniquely effective for marshaling national energies in today's world.

Official Guidance

Take first the government's blueprint. Though SCAP (1945–52) was sometimes ambivalent in the immediate postwar period, it was clear enough by 1948 that the rehabilitation of Japanese industry was necessary both for Japanese well-being and as a strategic counterbalance in Asia. And, based on an analysis of "comparative economic advantages" in the year 1948, Japanese industrial plans might have emphasized labor-intensive goods such as toys and Christmas tree bulbs. Instead, with a strong but then low-keyed nationalism, the conservative government opted, from the very beginning of recovery efforts, to continue the aborted efforts of the 1930s to build a heavy industrial complex, competitive with major industrial countries of the west.[58] As noted, through the Japan Development Bank and other credit facilities, 75 percent of government funds up to 1964 were invested in the "Big Four" (steel, coal, electric power, and ships). Now they are equally concentrated on knowledge-intensive industries—atomic energy, ocean development, aircraft, foreign raw-material control, and the like.

There was more than economics involved in the developmental policy; the heavy industrial achievement of the past twenty years must be explained in part as a political drive for international economic stature in a new postwar world in which Japan had lost influence in military and diplomatic circles. The result has been an "enterprise nationalism" abroad, which by 1970 is but the individual corporate expression of a broader economic nationalism based in Tokyo. "The chief competition is foreign" is another way to express the unity of thinking in government and business alike, which has produced a formidable mutuality of efforts in dealings abroad and an enviable record of competitive success. The unity of state policy and business enterprise has rendered Japanese business dealings abroad something akin to "state trading" and has drawn the foreign criticism that Japan has failed to observe the liberal rules of the game—like playing baseball with ten men on the team. This phenomenon should not be overemphasized as something sinister or hostile, especially just now (1973) when Japanese commitments to internationalism are growing. On the other hand, Japanese economic nationalism is real enough to require realistic measures to deal with it.[59]

Social Integration

The second most basic explanation for Japanese growth has been the remarkable capacity of the Japanese people for purposive sociality and harmonious role-playing in domestic production. Put another way, Japan is not only effectively directed by official policy and unified nationalistically in dealing with outsiders but it is socially organized to support formal government in comprehensive and orderly domestic groupings (enterprises, industrial federations, business associations, cartels, etc.), within which nearly all members have a high degree of commitment to mutual goals and, significantly, an extraordinary understanding thereof, perhaps because of the peculiar Japanese consensus mode of decision-making.[60] While change is everywhere evident, still many of these organizational patterns, decision-making processes, and general attitudes toward fellow Japanese and Japan in general have traditional roots in Japan's past.[61] They are particularistic, comfortable, and wear well after long use; therefore, they require little of the surface kind of formalism of latter-day law and bureaucracy. For example, Japanese business does not need anything as overt and crude as a "buy America act"; to "buy Japan," whenever possible, is as natural to the industrial elite as to breathe, though the mass of consumers do have a taste for foreign products. These behavioral patterns, based on tradition for teamwork and adapted to modern uses, are the kinds of phenomena best isolated for comparison by foreign sociologists and anthropologists, who fortunately are now getting much work done in English.[62]

Constructive Competition

Another source of Japanese energy is subtle and paradoxical; it is the intense competition between loyalty groups within Japanese society. It springs, apparently, from a traditional form of competition—performance oriented and constructive—exemplified by rivalry in Edo times between daimyo domains, different villages, disciples of independent Confucianists, commercial houses, and the like. In modern Japan such rivalry exists among companies, governmental departments, and even universities in ways quite perplexing to non-Japanese, but essentially it is a drive to exalt or to vindicate one's name or one's group in a larger national context.

One aspect of the competitiveness among business firms is the concern with each firm's "market share" or status in the officially recognized business hierarchy, wherein, for example, Mitsubishi Shoji or Mitsui Bussan, being once ranked number one or number two in sales among Japanese trading firms, have a public status to maintain which demands the utmost from the entire staff to maximize sales, even at the expense of profit! However elusive this aspect of Japanese business is to the foreigner, its effect on growth cannot be overlooked. Nor should foreigners overlook the fact that competitiveness, be the stakes ever so high, is tempered for the good of Japan as enunciated by regulation or most often by informal administrative guidance or trade association understandings. Patriotism in the pragmatic sense is very much alive and effective in Japan.

High Capital Formation

Vision and supportive social organization have been the basis of Japanese growth in the broadest sense, but expansion has required also an immense amount of capital since 1945. Indeed, no factor in Japanese growth is quite so impressive as the Japanese capacity for well-focused domestic capital formation.[63] The ratio of gross investment to gross national expenditures increased from 22 percent in 1946 to an unbelievable 42 percent in 1961, averaging 33 percent from 1953 to 1960; prewar rates had never exceeded 23 percent. At the same time, of course, personal consumption as a portion of gross national expenditures declined from 70 percent in 1946 to 53 percent in 1962. This capacity for capital formation amounting to one-third of gross national product surpassed all western nations and even the regimented U.S.S.R.[64] Significantly, Japanese capital formation is largely generated on a "voluntary" basis within the context of "free enterprise," although the degrees of "freedom" and "volition" involved have both evoked scholarly controversy, as noted below.

The division of Japanese capital formation between the public and private sector, and between individual and corporate segments of the latter, may be shown comparatively as follows:[65]

Country	Public	Private A & B	Individual A	Corporate B
Japan	30%	70%	51%	19%
Korea	71%	29%	6%	23%
U.S.	19%	81%	47%	34%

Clearly the key to Japan's phenomenal capital formation has been household savings,[66] though governmental investment is also substantial. Furthermore, the ordinary laborer's household in Japan saves at almost the same ratio of his total pay, on the average, as all households. It has been suggested that this laborer's savings rate largely explains Japan's highest rank among nations in savings. Particularly remarkable is the constancy of Japanese savings in the face of a 6 percent annual rise in consumer prices since 1960. In corporate savings, another Japanese peculiarity, arising in part from the aforementioned status competition, is the tendency to invest even without reference to demonstrable demand in order to maintain the firm's "market share," often leading to the so-called "over-investment," excess capacity," "excessive competition," and "profitless prosperity," wherein great production and sales volume are generated with little profit. There are other good reasons for this phenomenon, such as the desire to meet fixed costs of high debt financing and of maintaining a full staff for the benefit of the permanent labor force and their families; thus shareholders' interests are rather secondary by short-term analysis. In fact, the "extravagant" use of bank-based debt is part of Japanese corporate strategy to avoid dividend compulsions and obtain tax deductions for the interest paid instead.

Household Savings

If Japanese household savings is the key to capital formation and growth, what then is the key to such extraordinary personal saving? A study of thirty-eight countries has shown that Japanese save the highest portion of net national product in the world. For example, Japan compares with five western countries as follows:

Japan	25%
Finland	20%
Germany	20%
Netherlands	20%
U.K.	10.1%
U.S.	9.6%

Even more impressive is Japanese household savings as a percentage of disposable income:

Japan	16.5%
Germany	13.5%
U.S.	6%

The following factors are important in the pattern of Japanese saving:

1. There are many reasons to explain the high postwar personal savings. One is that in the decade of the 1960s wages increased 11.8 percent every year, so that if spending patterns lagged, as many suppose they did, savings may have been easier.

2. Second, Japan's peculiar method of paying wages by "bonus" also encourages savings. The bonus (paid semiannually) amounts to roughly 25 percent of total wages. Some bonus is actually an obligation and not a gratuity left to managerial discretion although the exact amount is adjustable to company's performance during the period. With this system, the Japanese have become accustomed to live on their regular wages and save their bonuses.

3. As noted earlier (in connection with the demonstration effect),

the Japanese have clung to their unique, traditional food, clothing, and household furnishings in preference to more expensive western consumer goods. When the desire for western household appliances did catch on, the Japanese tended to reverse the buying order that was "normal" in developing nations and saved to purchase durables (television, washer, refrigerator) rather than increasing food and clothing purchases, since they preferred their already available, traditional staples.

4. Japan has largely lacked an installment consumer credit system until recently, so that Japanese tended to save their bonus payments until they could pay cash for expensive, durable items, the purchase of which stimulated the advancing industries at each stage.

5. Traditional Japanese frugality has been mentioned as a partial explanation for savings, and Blumenthal[67] has confirmed that larger savings are found in the "traditional" prefectures (*i.e.,* the presumably more "traditional" rural areas, as opposed to the cities).

6. Also Japanese save, to some extent no doubt, because they must, their social security system at the governmental level (contrast private corporate welfare) being grossly inadequate.

The foregoing characteristics not only go a long way to explaining Japanese capital formation based on exceptionally high capacities for personal savings but also provide important clues about marketing and sales promotion in Japan. Japanese household-budget analyses show that middle-level families save to make money (*i.e.,* to go into business or buy shares).

Corporate Savings

The corporate portion of private savings was greatly enhanced by the fact that the labor productivity increased at a higher rate than wages; between 1953 and 1962 productivity increased 222 percent, whereas wages increased only 175 percent, meaning higher profit potentials, thus a higher capacity for corporate savings. Since 1968 the situation has reversed and wages are increasing faster than productivity now, with ominous signs for future corporate saving.

Channeling and Control of Savings

For overall planning and promotion of industrial growth, the way in which Japanese households save is also critical: roughly 41 percent (1967) of household savings were placed in bank time-deposits, and 14.1 percent in cash; the rest was insurance, pensions, and the like. Recently (1971–72) Japanese savers have found bank deposits less attractive, because of the remarkable drop in interest rates just as inflation was rising, and these shifts away from bank deposits explain to some extent the doubling of stock market prices in 1972 and the steep rise in land prices.[68] But, to 1971 at least, this funneling of massive personal savings through the banking system in turn controlled by governmental monetary policy has provided a major leverage for official control and management of the economy during the past two decades. Though governmentally planned and guided, Japanese economic growth flows largely from private enterprise financed by capital derived from a mass base of disciplined popular behavior. Thus, it may well be that the explanation of the "Japan miracle" is no more complicated than the story of the ant and the grasshopper.

Benign Occupation Policy

Other ingredients of Japan's high-growth formula were a favorable international climate and considerable good fortune. One fortunate happenstance was the extraordinarily benign postsurrender treatment of Japan during the Allied occupation (1945–52), at least after 1947. Besides roughly $2 billion worth of mostly U.S. aid in the early years, it has been asserted[69] that the deconcentration policy carried out by SCAP stimulated growth by creating intense oligopolistic rivalry among all of Japan's major companies; their major thrust was for market positions, prompting ever more investment in plant capacity. Secondly, splitting the *zaibatsu* trading companies, which previously dominated foreign business contacts, stimulated freer and more diverse trade channels; this enabled wider diffusion of technology not entirely limited to the major *zaibatsu* of prewar times. And then, finally, the deconcentration gave rise to a new entrepreneurial class, replacing the old *bantō* subservience to the prewar holding companies.

War Windfalls: Korea and Vietnam

Like its war profits of the Sino-Japanese war (1895) and World War I (1920), a second stroke of luck was the windfall that Japanese industry received from both the Korean and Vietnam efforts (1968: $500 million). Especially, the U.S. spending in Japan during the Korean War (1950–53) was a critical boost (about $4 billion) at an important point in Japanese industrial recovery; conversely, of course, it was beneficial to the U.S., under the circumstances, to have these Japanese supply sources. Fortunate also was the fact that ever since Japan committed herself to a major heavy industrial complex dependent on imports for the bulk of her raw materials, the raw-material, free-world import price index (though since 1970 increasing) declined to 84 percent of the 1955 level, whereas Japanese export prices had declined to only 94.6 percent by 1964. At the same time, world trade has steadily increased, and Japan's share thereof has increased even faster without major recriminations, though grumbling is now increasing as some quarters feel that Japan is playing the game with too much nationalistic verve.[70]

Relief from Defense Expenses

Fortuitously finding herself under the U.S. defense umbrella, Japan has been spared the high costs of military spending burdening all other major nations with which she competes. The U.S. spent 9.8 percent of GNP ($367 per capita; 44 percent of the federal budget) on defense in 1968 and 7.8 percent in 1970, while Japan spent .84 percent of GNP in 1969 ($13 per capita; 7.73 percent of the national budget [1967]).[71]

Catching-up and the Technological Windfall

Also not to be overlooked in explaining the postwar high growth rate is the "opportunity of backwardness": Japanese growth started from a very depressed point in 1946 (1946 GNP = ⅐ GNP of 1941) because of the war devastation. A related explanation for high growth, the catching-up theory,[72] argues that Japan had already acquired the capacity for higher output and that she had not regained prewar levels until 1953, or levels which would have been reached at normal prewar growth rates, but for her defeat, until 1963. This argument is useful to explain the growth rate (10.8 percent) between 1946 and 1954, but it is not a sufficient explanation after 1954 because her growth rate has continued to accelerate ever more dramatically after 1963. Nonetheless, some of the growth was in fact "catching up," and a corollary is that, after 1945, Japan had access to a vast backlog of advanced western technology at bargain prices ($3 billion from 1950 to 1970).[73] Virtually all of the modern sector was rebuilt on imported techniques and know-how (⅔ of it American), and significantly, this technology has cost Japan considerably less by the licensing route than it cost the foreign licensors abroad in research and development expenses, not to mention savings over what it might have cost Japan to discover the technology at home, if indeed it were feasible at all under the circumstances of the times. For example, in 1970 the U.S. spent 3.4 percent of GNP, the U.S.S.R., 2.7 percent, the U.K., 2.3 percent, France 1.6

percent, West Germany 1.4. percent, and Japan (1969) 1.6 percent of GNP on research and development. Royalty costs to Japan have been $95 million in 1960, $166 million in 1965, and $506 million in 1970, but Japan was also earning $69 million from royalty payable to Japanese licensors by 1970. Governmental spending on research (about $5 billion) has been particularly low as compared with Europe and the U.S., but it has increased 13 percent annually since 1967, and it is expected that the government will spend $13 billion annually by 1975 with 23 percent increases thereafter until about 4 percent of GNP is committed to research and development. By now, though, Japan has skimmed the cream of accumulated foreign technology at cheap prices.

Low-Level Government Spending

Two further factors enhance the role of the private sector and the capacity for private investment. First is the very low proportion of gross national expenditures represented by government purchases. In Japan between 1952 and 1967 it was roughly 9 percent, as opposed to 21 percent in the U.S. Taxation is therefore also comparatively low in Japan: 6.7 percent of her personal income expenditures (1962: U.S. 17.5 percent; U.K. 16 percent; France 18.7 percent; West Germany 21.4 percent, and Sweden 25.6 percent). Again, however, the cost of government is sharply rising as Japan is forced to rectify deficiency in social capital, welfare, resources development, education, research, and environmental protection. Indeed the 1973 budget shows a spending increase of 25 percent, the largest since World War II.[74]

Housing Parsimony

Second, the OECD study of 1962 shows that only 8 percent of fixed capital investment (2.5 percent of GNP) was devoted to Japanese housing, whereas in other OECD countries for that year, housing was 25 percent of fixed capital and 4.5 percent of GNP. So, much the same way she avoids "unproductive" military investment, Japan also avoids "unproductive" housing costs. It has also been said that when Japanese were allowed some freedom to travel abroad in 1965, for the first time in thirty years, it was not because of Japanese governmental concern for popular freedom but because of OECD pressure to abolish restrictions inconsistent with free-world concepts.[75]

In ending a summary of Japanese growth and the causes behind it, it seems appropriate also to mention that the Japanese government has been operating on a "sound balanced budget" concept, whereby public debt has been kept at a minimum, and the populace has been spared the public burden of high interest costs. For example, in 1967 the expense of the national debt was only 2.33 percent (U.S.: 6 percent) of the budget.

Japan and the World Economy

Japan's basic industrial operations are interwoven into the fabric of the free-world economy perhaps more than any other major nation.[76] Since 1945 her industry has been largely rejuvenated by imported technology; in the early postwar phase, her industry operated on foreign capital including GARIOA and other aid funds to the extent of about $2 billion (1945–50). Her plants operate from day to day on raw materials imported across thousands of miles of ocean—*e.g.,* iron ore from India and Australia; coking coal from British Columbia in Canada and the Atlantic coast of the U.S.; oil from Kuwait and Sumatra; timber from the northwestern U.S.; and pulp from Alaska. Nor has industrial rehabilitation led to more independence. Indeed, the calculated shift from labor-intensive to heavy industries (metals and chemicals) accomplished in the past two decades has rendered Japan more dependent on the world economy, not only for raw materials and fuels, but also for export markets to an increasing degree. Especially during periods of Japanese recession as experienced in 1971–72, excessive exporting and even dumping become necessary to alleviate problems of overcapacity thus exposed by slackening domestic demand and exaggerated by the fixed-cost nature of Japanese labor and capital supply. In this section we will review certain features of Japan's current international posture.

Imports

Though her prewar share of world trade had not been regained until 1963, Japan quadrupled her trade in the 1960s, reaching the volume in 1970 of the U.S. in 1960. The situation in 1970 and the prognosis for 1975 may be seen below:[77]

	1970 (billion)	1975 (billion)
Imports	$18.5	$29.2
Exports	$19.8	$42
Share of World Trade	6%	10.4%

We have noted already the irony in the fact that imports as a percentage of GNP are lower (9.2 percent; 1969) than in the prewar period (1936; 23.1 percent) and, comparatively, Japan's import-GNP ratio is the lowest among major nations (West Germany 14.3 percent; Britain 18.6 percent; Italy 14.5 percent), excepting the U.S. (3.3. percent; 1967), and it is still declining. Despite this position, however, the essential fact is that by 1970, 60 percent of Japanese imports were critical ores and fuels without which the new heavy industrial complex could not turn a wheel. It is in this qualitative sense that Japanese dependence on imports is higher than any major country in the world. Including even the smaller advanced countries, only the Netherlands has a higher raw-material imports-GNP ratio than Japan at 7.9 percent and 5.6 percent respectively. This is, of course, no disadvantage, if free access to world supplies continues, but the point is that Japan's physical dependence makes her vulnerable to political decisions made elsewhere.

Food accounts for 15 percent of Japanese imports, leaving manufactured goods and all other products occupying only 25 percent. In sum, Japan has become the world's leading purchaser of foreign raw materials; as an important processing and manufacturing depot, Japan operates on foreign raw materials and caters of necessity to world markets for disposal of a large part of its finished product, though it is Japan's own domestic consumer's market that has sparked her rapid growth.[78]

The recent Japanese reductions of import restrictions and tariff reductions in 1972 has not produced reduced prices to Japanese consumers; instead the middlemen seem to be pocketing the profit, according to newspaper accounts at the end of the year. The government has tried to remedy the situation by withdrawing entry protection to Japanese distributors with trademarks covering foreign goods. This entry protection, exemplified by the famous "Parker pen case," was effected by the customs official's not allowing direct sales of genuine trademarked goods in Japan to bypass the exclusive distributor. In 1970, the Osaka District Court decided that exclusive distributors were not entitled to such trademark protection.[79] Since then, bars to entry have not been enforced by the Japanese customs office in an attempt to get foreign consumer items to flow in at prices lowered by revaluation and tariff concessions. The Japanese FTC has been investigating to find out why import prices have not gone down after the revaluation.

Exports

Heavy industrial products now occupy nearly 70 percent of all Japanese exports, though the "heavy export" category in her official statistics includes such things as cameras, binoculars, and watches. Ironically,

Japan is now a net importer of silk which, along with tea, was the export "work-horse" used to balance her payments in the Meiji period. Furthermore, other labor-intensive items are under competitive pressure from Korea, Taiwan, and Hong Kong to the point where the Japanese traders, known world-wide as "transistor salesmen" but a few years ago, are now being sold transistors by their Asian neighbors, or Japan is moving her own plants to those countries by direct investment in some instances.

A breakdown of Japanese exports by country shows a significant shift in the 1960s away from the southeast Asian markets that were assiduously promoted in the 1950s.[80] Instead, Japan's trade is now concentrated in the advanced nations, reflecting the shift to heavy industrial exports. In rounded figures, Japanese exports go as follows:

	Percentage in 1970	Percentage in 1975
U.S.	32	31.1
Southeast Asia	30	27.7
Western Europe	12	12.6
Oceana & South Africa	5	5.1
Latin America	5.3	5.4
Canada	3	3.2
Others	17.2	14.9

After the "Nixon shock" of August 1971, the Japanese government has come to realize, it seems, that it can no longer expect to increase exports without importing in return from the U.S. markets. As a consequence, strong efforts are now under way to develop other markets again in Southeast Asia, China and Europe.

The Japanese product shift has been dramatic and portends a different international role from the 1970s onward. Until recently, Japan has been a "marginal supplier" of many of her new products. That is, the strength of her domestic demand and certain structural factors are said to have caused Japanese exports to be largely "supply oriented."[81] According to this interpretation, Japanese postwar growth has been stimulated largely by industrial competition catering to domestic (not export) demand, because of the status orientation of firms in the hierarchies within each individual Japanese industry and the relatively good opportunities for profit in the protected, "hot-house" atmosphere of the domestic economy. But the same artificial domestic controls (allocation of import licenses, easy credit, and other governmental favors granted according to each firm's existing "market share") created "excessive status-competition" (rather than business competition for profit) among the emerging oligopolistic firms, causing overexpansion of plants simply to maintain each firm's domestic "market share." Also the drive for optimal scale to meet foreign competitors after liberalization has also aggravated this problem of over-capacity. This line of analysis concludes that during recessions new plants have had to keep running, even at a loss, so long as they could defray peculiarly Japanese fixed costs for labor and bank interest, if an export market could be found in which to dump them.[82]

Export upsurges have thus occurred during Japanese domestic recessions (e.g. 1971–72), because of excess plant capacity developed during investment booms. Hence Japanese export booms (e.g. 1972 trade surplus of $8 billion; $4 billion surplus from the U.S.), ironically, may be a sign of a down cycle and also of maladjustment of productive capacities rather than a national achievement. For example, under a headline entitled "Japan Auto Exports Hit New High Mark,"[83] we learn: "The sharp improvement was due to efforts of auto makers to boost exports to make up for dull domestic sales due to pressure of the year-long money squeeze." Thus the government's role in applying a tight money policy may amount to forced dumping, just as its pumping of funds into new plant capacities and export incentives may mean a flooding of the world markets.[84]

This phenomenon of the 1960s and early '70s may be a transitory problem which will decline hereafter because of a number of new factors at work. First is the shift to heavy industries, with capacity permanently geared to (and dependent upon) export markets so that the thrust to sell abroad is no longer directly geared to temporary sluggishness of the home market. Whether the new export market can be developed and relied upon will depend on continuation of free policies in world trade and Japanese willingness to import for balance. Secondly, Japan is entering a period of overseas direct investment herself,[85] which typically has become for other investor nations a substitute for trade, to some degree at least. For example, in the experience of the U.S., manufactured sales of foreign manufacturing subsidiaries are in 1970 estimated at about $77 billion as opposed to $30 billion of manufactured exports from the U.S. But, this statistical picture of trade replaced by foreign subsidiaries' production abroad is an oversimplification, for in many cases foreign manufacturing may become a substitute for past trade, which would have been otherwise lost, or a method of insuring exports from parent to foreign subsidiaries—to mention but a few factors in this complex situation.[86]

Dependence on Foreign Technology

Japan has depended on importation of foreign technology for the rehabilitation of her existing industries after World War II and for the establishment of some entirely new ones.[87] In two-thirds of all licensing agreements since 1945, the U.S. has furnished the technology; West Germany, the United Kingdom, and Switzerland have also been important sources. Royalty costs to Japan, at $95 million in 1960, growing to $240 million in 1967 and $506 million in 1970[88] (and overall 1950–70 only $3 billion), have been much less than the cost would have been to produce the same massive backlog of technology on her own. So, actually, it is dependence rather than forecasts of increased royalties which has inspired Japan to reach for a higher degree of future creativity in her own governmental and private research. Plans include increasing the outlay at an annual rate of 25 percent throughout the decade (1965–75), because her allocation of only 1.6 percent of GNP is behind that of the U.S. with 3.4 percent, the United Kingdom with 2.3 percent, and West Germany with 2 percent.[89]

It remains to be seen, of course, to what extent additional funds can extricate Japan from a technologically dependent posture or produce her share, at least, of the ongoing innovations in the modern industrial world. There is, however, growing evidence of innovative Japanese technology, shown by royalties received from her own foreign licensing. For example, between 1950 and 1970, Japan received $226 million in royalties against $2,581 million paid out.[90] Thus, technology exports were 9.3 percent of her technology imports during this period, and it seems that the imports were increasing faster than exports by the latest figures.[91] Another recent phenomenon is a reluctance of foreign firms with key patent rights to license Japanese competitors; a well-known example was Zenith's preference not to license under its TV patents covering the "black matrix formula."

Many Japanese exports of technology went to developing countries:

Importers of Japanese Technology

	Cases	Royalties Paid
Developing	273 (52%)	44%
Advanced	232 (44%)	45%
Communists	21 (4%)	11%

By country, though, the U.S. was the leading importer (1965–1969):

Importers of Japanese Technology (1965–1969, May)

Country	Cases	Payment (Percentage of Total Paid Abroad)
U.S.	96	17
Taiwan	66	11
Korea	49	10
India	35	7
England	29	5
Italy	21	10
West Germany	20	2
U.S.S.R.	12	9

But, even though Japanese technology moved abroad with increasing volume, Japan had surely by 1970 skimmed the cream from the technology accumulated abroad during her wartime isolation, and the cost of moving forward in the 1970s to higher levels of technical creativity will doubtless be significantly higher, as shown by her outlay of nearly $4 billion (1.63 percent of GNP) for research and development in 1970 alone.

Foreign Capital in Japan

Japan by 1970 had become a young capital-exporting nation with direct investments abroad increasing 31 percent annually between 1966 and 1972. Indeed, by 1972 Japanese direct investment abroad stood at $4.2 billion, more than double the incoming direct investment which had been permitted in Japan. But Japan prefers to compare this figure, not with foreign investment allowed into Japan, but with U.S. direct investment abroad, $78 billion (1970), and expects her total abroad to reach $28 billion by 1980. On the basis of book value, Japanese direct investments in North America (mostly sales offices) were 912 million (1972), and U.S. direct investments were less than that in Japan.[92] This has come about by a combination of increasingly heavy capital exports during the 1966–72 period and a continuing refusal to liberalize foreign direct investment in areas of real interest to foreigners. The latter strictures are consistent with a century of policy to expand without aid of direct foreign investment, to borrow from abroad only when absolutely necessary (only at favorable rates of interest), and always favoring public-to-public borrowing or issuance of Japanese government bonds. Hence, foreign private capital (as distinguished from technology and public aid) has not been critical in Japanese growth after 1950, though it has been appreciable. From 1950 to 1971, validations of foreign capital entries totaled slightly over $18 billion (see p. 17), of which $7.6 billion was for loans and bonds, $7.2 billion portfolio (entries, not net), and only $851 million direct investment entries (not net; book value about $3 billion).

Japanese Investments Abroad

Regarding capital movements, the most significant prospects for the 1970s are in Japan's outward investments that have been developing at a brisk rate since 1965, apparently in part to assist in reducing reserves ($19 billion 1973), which were growing from 1969 to 1973 at a rate high enough to embarrass the Japanese government because of its own restrictions on imports and inward investment. The trade balance is predicted to be favorable in the magnitude of $12 billion annually in 1975, with an overall balance in the black of $4.7 billion showing a capital export balance of $2.6 billion. Already in 1970, the excess of Japan's capital exports over inward investment was $938 million.[93]

From 1951 to 1971, a total of $3.6 billion in direct investments (compared to under $.85 billion direct investment in Japan) has been approved for disbursement outside Japan, and the major portion has flowed out of Japan since 1968 at a rate of increase of 30 percent per annum.[94] Also important are the loans that Japanese have made to foreign raw-material sources to enable them to develop mines and transport facilities, with long-term output commitments in exchange for the loans.

Balance of Payments

By 1971, Japan's foreign-exchange reserves had exceeded $5 billion with a substantially higher content of gold. By 1973, the reserves reached a phenomenal $19 billion. This may be explained, in part, by the shift to heavy industries and the fact that export markets may no longer be regarded as simply marginal demand for supply-oriented selling abroad to relieve excess plant capacity in the cyclical trough. The recent predictions are that Japanese exports will increase up to 1975 at a rate of 17.4 percent annually, roughly double the rate of world trade expansion. The favorable trade balance is expected by some Japanese economists to increase from $5 billion in 1970 to $12.6 billion in 1975, though such a balance would seem unwise for amicable international relations, unless the Japanese markets were completely unrestricted.

A substantial trade balance, which in turn will produce an overall favorable balance, even though net outward capital movements and consistent adverse balances on invisibles reduce it some, will give the Japanese economic planners for the first time funds with which to promote stable export markets backed up with warehousing, after-service, integrated sales organizations, and financing of buyers. Also, long-term investment opportunities abroad, previously constricted by adverse balance of payments and consequent fluctuations of sales volume and tight money policies, causing in turn cyclical business growth, can be considered by Japanese planners. For example, import liberalization seems desirable as a method of decreasing inflation: even more investment abroad will be possible; and foreign aid (1971, $2 billion; 0.23 percent of GNP) should increase to the goal already set by the Japanese at 1 percent of GNP; also the quality of Japanese aid may improve to allay foreign criticism that it is too self-interested.[95] In addition, at home Japan's social security system, social capital (roads, ports, water, and sewage facilities), pollution prevention, and low-quality private universities may be improved, along with a massive effort to produce Japan's share of technological innovations. These are all parts of the program announced in June 1971 by the Japanese government in its unsuccessful eight-point plan to counter pressures for revaluation, and its new seven-point plan of May 1972, which too failed with the currency changes of February 1973.

In sum then, Japan, at the turn of the decade, was in the black and at a stage of her development in relation to the free-world economy wherein she could play a more influential and confident role, but because of the calculated dependence of her new industrial structure on massive imports of fuel and raw materials and on export markets for her new heavy industrial products, she is increasingly tied to the international economy. Thus, the rosy prognosis found in the Japanese reports and forecasts reflected above can be realized only with a favorable climate abroad. In the 1970s, the goal will of necessity be the so-called three "I's": Integration (of Japanese production with world markets and integration of her two tiers of domestic dualism); Internationalization (of her aspirant multinational corporations as well as her governmental aid and defense posture);[96] and Innovation (required by absorption of foreign technology to the international level). Efforts in these directions up to 1973 have failed to alleviate the foreign pressures caused by Japanese neo-mercantilism. Henceforth more attention to the impact abroad must be given in planning Japanese export and investment programs.

IV

The Japanese
Business Environment

In no other major country in modern times have foreign enterprises had to take into account such different and effective habits of thinking and acting as in Japan. Foreign understanding of these different thought processes and behavioral patterns in Japan, derived from the interplay of an isolated, nonwestern tradition and her own developmental modes and timing, must precede effective business operations there.[1]

This is not to say that business with the Japanese must be unpleasant or unprofitable. On the contrary, the Japanese are, if different, highly civilized, commercially effective, delightfully courteous, instinctively aesthetic, and incomparably hospitable to outsiders, as outsiders. Such amenities and the enviable industrial performance, plus the western appearances of plants and executive offices, are however, deceptive; one must make a double effort to probe beneath the surface for Japanese thought processes explaining special personal and entrepreneurial behavior, and at the same time, one must be sensitive to the constant changes engulfing Japanese society, making a stationary cross-sectional view as risky as the surface appearances. This chapter is of necessity an impressionistic, broad-brushed sketch of (1) worker psychology and labor law, (2) features of the firm (kaisha), (3) something of supracorporate business organization, and (4) government-business relations and antitrust, below the level of politics discussed in Chapter II. All of these topics are as subtle as they are essential to foreign enterprisers; especially in the fields of labor law and antitrust, American lawyers must beware of deceptive surface likenesses to the "mother" law.

At the outset, three threshold caveats are in order concerning (1) the ineptitude of the English language, (2) quality and rate of change, and

(3) diversity persisting through the change, because all three aspects substantially blur and condition all simplistic generalizations inherent in an exercise of this scope.[2]

For example, terms such as "competition," "private industry," or "free enterprise," commonly used in discussions of Japanese business, conjure up in the minds of the readers in English quite different images from existing realities of Japanese business, as we shall see. "Collusive rivalry," "semiprivate industry," "quasi-public enterprise," respectively, might be more apt expressions, precisely because their western referents are unclear.

Another problem with English-language literature (as the medium between foreigners and the Japanese) is that most of it is written by the Japanese, because few foreigners can write about Japan, because they read no Japanese. The Japanese presentations are "simplified, sanitized, and tactfully slanted for what is assumed to be a relatively ignorant and insensitive" audience. Like "baby food" it scarcely nourishes a mature understanding, to borrow a *bon mot* from former Ambassador Reischauer.[3]

Also, rapid and constant change on the postwar Japanese scene makes the problem of understanding modern Japan, in metaphor, one of hunting a running rabbit not a sitting bird. At the most fundamental level of individual personality, the qualities of past generations will be diluted in the next wave of Japanese youth.[4] Also postwar Japanese social change during rapid industrial growth raises tough questions of the highest theoretical, as well as practical, interest. For a common western, casuistic assumption[5] that industrialization implies unilinear progress, propelled largely by labor-market forces and collective bargaining, from particularistic, simple society (Japanese?) to our rational, universalistic industrialism (also dehumanized, standardized, atomistic, individualistic), presumably shared by all in the end, may turn out—indeed, to some degree, likely will turn out—to be inappropriate as our own as well as Japanese industrialization further unfolds, and we begin to see more of our own problems and Japanese potential. Perhaps Japan's peculiar tradition-based hierarchical familism (or mutations of it) found in her current industrial-relations regime will in fact prove more usefully "modern" than our parochial, unilinear interpretation would lead one to suspect, simply because "familism" may fill the motivational gap between the poles (management and labor) inherent in western liberal individualism. If so, the Japanese way surely will not be without its own further adaptations, and the supreme test is in the offing as Japan finally undertakes, in the realities of the world economy, the transition

required by her carefully planned heavy industrial complex dependent
on a quick turnaround from (1) world raw-material sources, (2)
through the Japanese factory, and (3) back to world markets. Japanese
familism has heretofore ended at the water's edge, and henceforth, as
seen in Chapter III above, the challenge to her own self-interest will be
to contain latent nationalism within bounds consistent with her new
international economic requirements.

Diversity too, is rich and apparent in Japan, and one cannot talk
about all of Japanese industry, firms, managers, or employees in one
breath. For example, we have seen in reviewing industrial dualism that
Japanese business has two parts, each still quantitatively of nearly equal
importance in the Japanese GNP, but each with its own structural and
organizational qualities. Hereafter, in discussing "the worker," "the
firm," and "supracorporate organization," we will be primarily concerned
with insights into practices of the large modern sector, because of its
immediate importance to foreign enterprise and because of the official
hope (beginning to be justified) that much of the least privileged of the
lower tier will wither away. But with half of manufacturing and even
more of the tertiary sector (services and distribution) still on its
shoulders, small business cannot be overlooked, especially when foreigners address themselves increasingly to problems of Japanese marketing.

The Japanese Worker

In the western sense, the large Japanese company ideally has no
"employees" and no "industrial-relations" problems involving its "regular" labor force (*honkō*), though it does have an "enterprise union"
(see below).[6] Instead of employees, the Japanese firm has management
members and worker members; typically these "regular members" join
the large firms and the "company" union for life, and the firm is run
almost as much for them as by them,[7] of which we will also have more
to say later. Odd though all this may seem to the outsider, these cozy
familial features are highly congruent with Japanese culture to date.[8]

Unfortunately, unique cultural features that early interact with and
nurture the young Japanese personality are of very low visibility to most
foreign visitors and even to many monolingual resident businessmen.
Besides the mountainous language barrier,[9] there are several other reasons why monolingual short-time foreigners misunderstand. First, the
Japanese personality matures in the home and school, before the "member" reaches the business world, of course. Second, the usual foreigner

knows little of the home and school, because he is seldom invited to a Japanese house (as opposed to a restaurant), and he has little reason to investigate the lower schools, which are critical.[10] Third, most Japanese, precisely because of their osmotic way of perceiving the world, are unable to stand apart from it and explain their "natural" surroundings to the foreigner,[11] and, too, the same Japanese personality makes him a good listener and the foreigner, also for cultural reasons, does most of the talking. Fourth, the foreigner is always an "outsider" (*gaijin*), and there is an entirely different set of "diplomatic" relations for "us Japanese" (*ware ware Nihonjin*) to apply to a *gaijin,* as formal and fixed as a charming minuet and, by the same token, yielding little man-to-man understanding. Finally, facile familiarity with certain physical delights of Japanese culture (for example *tatami* rooms, hot baths, name-cards, and raw fish) may be mistaken by the novice for understanding the "people"; for this aspect of the culture is delightful, and foreign visitors readily adapt to *sukiyaki*-on-the-floor and graduate in a few days to *sashimi,* which by then they may order authoritatively as *maguro* (tuna) or even *toro* (choice oily cut) and forget entirely that it ever was "raw fish." All the while, the foreigner is dining with Japanese colleagues whose familial and hierarchic values are concealed by the isolating pattern appropriate to the minuet.[12]

What, then, are the essentials of the Japanese personality?[13] For foreign comprehension, the essential psychological fact is that, typically, the Japanese are not individualistic, and certainly not extroverted or self-assertive; the key values are (1) loyalty to the group and (2) achievement for the group, hence submersion in the group. Since "insiders" and "outsiders" have no group encompassing both, their relations proceed by "diplomacy" appropriate to friendly but outside outsiders, who can never really understand "us Japanese."

Though he is not self-assertive, neither is a Japanese a paragon of self-abnegation, for he sees his personal achievements as coming *pro rata* from group success, and experientially they have in ample measure. The group is thought to afford the member his opportunity for constitutive fulfillment through service to it. Needless to say, in western terms this situational nationalism sounds a bit Hegelian, but these values are modern adaptations of indigenous Confucianistic thought and contrast sharply with western individualism based on self-assertiveness, equality, and universalism.[14]

Such personality traits, of course, interact with, and find their supports in, Japanese social institutions, including the firm itself. But the Japanese personality begins at birth and is initially shaped in the hierarchical family where distinctive ways of child-rearing prevail—distinctive because of the intimate Japanese living habits. Also the standardizing cooperative attitudes of the rural village in the demanding rice cycle (now rapidly changing) and the resultant socializing tendencies are further developed in the school ("second village") and the peer group —all of which provide little individual privacy. The milieu affects profoundly the individual perception of self and world: some have even said the Japanese learns not by our subject-object (observer-observed) approach but by osmosis, by taking everything into a sensitive organic continuum that he is quite incapable of transcending as an independent observer.[15]

In brief, the social institutions supporting the Japanese personality have two chief structural tendencies: (1) familism and (2) hierarchy based first on merit and later on age.[16] The ubiquitous name-cards (*meishi*), tediously (and humorously to the westerner) ranking all individuals from janitor on up in the daily routine of Japanese business, are the commonest manifestations of the pervasive hierarchical cast of the Japanese mind. The emotive personality trait of respect for, and reliance on, superiors and elders[17] makes hierarchy much more comfortable to the Japanese than to a westerner obsessed with counterpoised ideas of authority and abstract equality.

Various modern adaptations of hierarchical familism persist as the individual progresses from family to school to firm. In the school the hierarchical allocation of status is based not on age or sex, as in the traditional Confucianistic family, but on merit demonstrated objectively by passing exams, significantly at the point of *entry* to each group. This is crucial to Japanese psychology because it permits competition for status to be concentrated formally (actually infighting abounds) against "outsiders" and preserves the integrity of the "family," where status must be objectively fixed if all is to function with harmony (*wa*). This permits a kind of familism (a certain in-group solidarity) to develop within the school among the elite who have passed and, similarly, after passing more entrance tests, within the firm at a later date.

As noted (Chapter III), all major firms also have their ranking within their industries, and for all of the top firms, there is also an elite channel for recruiting executive personnel leading from preferred lower schools (sometimes even down to kindergarten) to a few prestigious universities, mostly in Tokyo (Tokyo, Hitotsubashi, Keio, Waseda, and Kyoto University). Though unofficial, rankings are attached to all universities, and these rankings have critical weight in hiring by key governmental ministries (Finance, MITI, Bank of Japan) and the large business firms that are similarly ranked. Once a man is admitted into the firm for life, after passing the exams and interviews, the same familial loyalties develop toward it, but the intrafirm criterion of formal status is again shifted, this time away from personal competition to an objective criterion—age. Accordingly status promotion is, typically, by strict seniority for the thirty-odd years of a normal career to age fifty-five, and the company is therefore comprised of a hierarchy of age statuses, from the newest and lowest to the oldest and highest. Note, however, that major firms also have an "elite channel" toward top positions so that sometimes, even by their initial assignment in the firm, managerial newcomers think they can tell their chances for promotion throughout their future careers.

Even after he enters a firm, the elite university man still maintains the familial loyalty to his school and classmates, even those outside his firm, who make up an intimate network of contacts mutually promoting each other's careers throughout life. In hiring a young graduate, the firm takes this into account and seeks a graduate with promising classmates (*i.e.,* from a prestigious university), knowing that all will advance abreast to important positions in their respective businesses and governmental bureaucracies and be mutually useful to each other in due course. Similarly the candidate for membership in a firm is most concerned himself about the quality, already ascribed, of the people he is joining as evidenced by the firm's size and status in its industry.

Significantly, the Japanese competition for school entry is responsible for social mobility between generations roughly equal to that in the U.S., despite a very different value system. Equally significant is the fact that the first job decision typically ends an individual's social mobility; thus opportunity for social mobility is confined to childhood through adolescence.[18]

By the time he becomes a "member," our typical Japanese salaryman has realized his values of loyalty and achievement in irrevocably concrete ways: besides his family of birth, he has familial commitments to school and to the firm, in both of which he has already earned an irreversible, life-long hierarchical status based on merit (school record). For life, he is thus socialized and committed in a network of particularistic relationships, which makes it quite inconceivable from his standpoint that he should act, or be expected to act, as a "free individual," even for high reward proffered.[19] Even to a foreigner it should be clear, he supposes, that the logical consequence of his total commitment to his "group" (insiders) means great social distance between himself and outsiders, and here one must remember that, because there is national familism as well, the farthest "out" are the non-Japanese.

Whatever changes the distant future may bring, it seems certain that these Japanese personal qualities will continue to be normative at least, and, in fact, dominant in the modern industrial sector for the next decade or more; they are too deeply imbedded in the existing minds and institutions to disappear completely in a few years. As opined earlier, it would seem that some Japanese ways will persist in that they represent a useful balance in relations between individuals and productive institutions; though tradition based, they are functionally "modern," more so than some persisting friction-producing features of the Anglo-American industrial relations regimes. Not only because of increasing affluence but also because of economic pressures for flexibility and efficiency, there will be important personality changes toward a less security-conscious and more individualistic Japanese type, but the change will be readily perceptible only between generations as affluence and changes from the extended-rural to the nuclear-urban family continue to influence the attitude of youngsters. Also important changes are already in process in the labor market, and the resultant employment trends interacting with personality will ultimately foretell some shifts in intrafirm relations but not much in the short run of a decade.

The Japanese Firm

A product of its own history and milieu, the Japanese firm (*kaisha*) has been congenial to the psychology and interpersonal relations described above. Unlike the west, where industrial enterprise was "the brain child of entrepreneurs" and where labor, along with capital and raw materials, was a mere factor of production, in Japan the industrial firm was created first in the early Meiji period as a public enterprise necessary for the survival of the new Japan recently exposed to the ravages of the outside world.[20] The national slogan was "rich country, strong army" (*fukoku kyōhei*), and the "riches" were to be gained by modern industrial enterprise, simply added on top without disturbing the underlying traditional economy. The government was a major factor, both in directly establishing such enterprises (sold later to private operators) and also in providing capital (bonds) to many fledgling entrepreneurs from the *samurai* class, the payment being in government bonds in lieu of rice stipends in the egalitarian reforms dismantling feudal vestiges. The mentality of these *samurai* entrepreneurs[21] was highly infused with national honor and public consciousness, as well as, paradoxically, a disdain for commerce and money—one reason that industry is still more prestigious than merchandising, and production men honored over salesmen in Japan today, though I suspect this attitude is due for change before long. With industrialization in Meiji times (1868) an urgent national policy, these elite and patriotic entrepreneurs were motivated more by national duty than by business profit, and these historical characteristics of the Japanese firm—(1) the overriding separateness of modern industry from the tiny traditional shops and cottage industry and (2) the public nature of the modern sector's urgent national purpose—are still with us today, though the goal is now "to surpass the west," or in unstated form "to be bigger than the U.S."

Besides its national mission, "private enterprise" became even more of a social welfare institution in Japan because of the devastation of World War II and the peculiar twist of postwar Japanese unionism; firms were expected to provide basic sustenance for as many destitute workers as possible. Later this role proliferated into the several unusual employment practices promoted by elitist enterprise unions (discussed below), and further social welfare services, elsewhere assumed by government, became necessities of corporate operation as self-protection by the entire work force against inflation and high taxation.

Besides its public and social functions, the Japanese firm has retained an overall familial tone, which, as noted above, permits much less cleavage between "management" and "labor" than that typically found in the western analogue. The unions and their local leadership are within the firm, identifying much more with the firm's interests than with anything so abstract as the "laboring class" or even fellow craftsmen. Hence, despite leftish leadership in the federations at the national level, the enterprise union at the firm level acts in the interests of the firm, as well they might because typically all worker members have lifetime commitments to the firm—in other words it is *their* firm. There are nonmembers (temporary workers and subcontractors), but their sad status seems to be rationalized as an evil necessary to protect the life employment of the "members."[22]

Management Practices

Understandably the "industrial family" approach to business accounts for a number of management practices in the Japanese firm not found to the same degree in the west. We will describe several of these in three major areas: employment, organization, and decision-making.

Employment practices / In the large modern firm, there are five major employment policies[23] supportive of the "industrial family": (1) discriminatory uses of three kinds of blue-collar workers—lifetime, temporary, and subcontracted; (2) life employment (*shūshin koyō*) for all management, and some clerical and blue-collar workers as well, in large industries; (3) seniority promotions (*nenkō joretsu*); (4) an elaborate system of allowances and fringe benefits; and (5) diffuse involvement of management in the personal life of the worker members. The last three policies apply mainly to the life employees, where they exist.

1. Along with subcontracting, temporary and external employees, though not used at management levels, are important parts of the overall blue-collar employment system in major Japanese manufacturing firms, as a safety cushion by which the fixed cost of the life employment scheme is maintained for the more favored permanent members. Too often in western literature, the life employment system has been highlighted as the exotic core of the Japanese system, with only parenthetical treatment of this equally important if less savory aspect of the overall system.[24] Life employment is the ideal, but it is not realized in even half of the male blue-collar labor force and it is even less meaningful in the case of female workers. The rate of temporary employment varies with particular industries; in the early 1960s it was about 12 percent overall, but it has been declining recently. In shipbuilding, without considering the effects of subcontracting, temporary workers account for over 30 percent of the blue-collar labor force. With the tightening of the labor supply in recently years, however, temporary workers have become both scarce and expensive, foretelling important changes in the next decade, though just how this adjustment will be made is a difficult and controversial question connected more broadly with the ultimate fate of industrial dualism and the life employment system, both of which are weakening at present.

For management positions, however, the life employment system may be expected to remain substantially intact in large firms for some time to come, though even in management there is some lateral movement (*yoko suberi*) to affiliated companies and some intake of retiring government officials (*ama kudari*). Also mid-career hiring (*chūto saiyō*), though more common for engineers (*gijutsu-kei*), is increasing for managers (*jimu-kei*) in special growth situations.

2. The life employment and seniority promotion systems are special, normative, and mutually reinforcing features of the Japanese personnel system. It is said that, ideally, the industrial family, rather than temporarily "hiring a hand," engages the whole man for life, and after World War II this system was extended to some blue-collar as well as white-collar workers. The intake of life members is, of course, limited to young graduates beginning their careers just out of the schools. His-

torically graduates from middle school (fifteen-year-olds) joined the blue-collar (*kōin*) ranks, whereas high school and university graduates began work in a higher white-collar status (*shokuin*). Now, more youth continue on to higher education so that the number of young (and cheap) blue-collar members joining after middle school has sharply diminished (85 percent went into higher school in 1972), and with the increase of production skills the blue-collar–white-collar distinction itself is becoming blurred, especially in capital-intensive industries.

We are concerned here only with the higher class of personnel, the managers in their several stages of development. For them, recruitment practices reflect the gravity of a decision for life.[25] The firm normally asks its preferred university to recommend several candidates; the university, wishing to be asked again to be a source of executives, takes its responsibility seriously and is very selective with nominations; professors' judgments loom large. A special company exam is then given to all nominees, followed by interviews, and for management candidates, a final decision often comes from the president of the company himself. As noted, there is a clear division between technical (*gijutsu-kei*) and administrative (*jimu-kei*), and for the administrative personnel the emphasis is on generalists not experts; the lifetime commitment forces all participants to be concerned with the applicant's politics, congeniality, integrity, and character; conversely, little attention is given to special job competency because the new member will be with the company for life and can be adequately trained to benefit the company over his entire career.

3. Seniority promotion means intake at the lowest positions and automatic advancement in status and pay (historically 5 to 8 percent a year) by age. But there are "elite channels" to top positions, and promotion to these positions, as distinguished from pay promotion, is often more selective. As for pay, though, all entering in the same year normally get equal pay raises regardless of performance or position, unless a man seriously misbehaves.

This system began to stabilize in Japanese firms after 1910 when the gang bosses (*oyabun*), who had theretofore supplied factory labor (often part-time farmers, *dekasegi*) on contract, were hired into the firms, and in turn brought along their host of laborers (*kobun*), already ranked by length of service for the boss. Two aspects of the seniority promotion system are important: first, in lifetime employment, advancement can occur only within the company; advancing between companies is taboo. Second, abrasive competition within the industrial family is avoided somewhat by the objective promotion criteria—age and length of service. But job classification and pay according to job-and-capability are displacing the seniority system in more and more Japanese companies.[26]

4. An elaborate system of allowances and fringe benefits, also an outgrowth of the familial pattern, is a fourth feature of Japanese personnel practice. The main allowances include (1) lump-sum retirement allowances (*e.g.,* one month's salary per year of service) and (2) bonuses—semiannual "seasonal allowances" (*kimatsu teate*)[27]—varying with firm prosperity but typically totaling three to four months' basic salary per year (perhaps 30 percent of annual base salary). Besides these mandatory allowances (actually deferred salary, but with some leeway for management as to amount), fringe benefits total about 14 percent of total labor costs and include family allowances, housing, commuter costs, overtime, outings, loans, discount purchases, and the like. Eschewing details, total labor cost (*i.e.,* adding all allowances and all fringe benefits to basic salaries) amounts to about 180 percent of basic annual salary.[28] Thus the firm must furnish very substantial welfare services for its members, which in the west would typically be provided by public social-security programs; if provided by the western employer, it would be regarded in industrial relations as paternalistic in a pejorative sense. Understandably, Japanese employees in unpaternalistic foreign firms sometimes complain of a "suffocating rationality" and "dryness" about the firms' attitudes toward them. Recent strong trends to cut fringe benefits (*e.g.,* housing) and to shift the retirement pay to a pension system are signs of a more flexible work force in the future.

5. Personal involvement of management in the workers' "private affairs" is a fifth feature of the Japanese personnel practices, which contrasts sharply with the work-for-pay, pay-for-work, eight-to-five attitudes of the American employment relationship, with a sharp division between work and private life.[29] Marriages, funerals, and educational and career decisions are all matters in which a Japanese "member" expects, and even wants, the participation of his work superiors. Firms often maintain reception and funeral facilities, and the officers act as go-betweens (*nakōdo*) in marriage arrangements and counselors in time of personal crisis. The absence of any sharp distinction between the workshop and private life is also shown by the fact that employees seldom are in a hurry to leave the offices at quitting time; their tie to the firm is actually one of interest and status, not contract, and it has been said that the workshop has preference, even over the family, that the enterprise is "the fundamental home."[30]

What are the merits of these peculiar Japanese practices? Enough has been said, presumably, to underscore their congruence with the traditional culture, and only a moment's reflection will show that such congruence has been essential and effective to date. But, what about the future efficiency of such a cozy firm in the changing modern world of competitive business? And, are not underlying conditions also changing?

Several advantages are apparent, but by far the most important is the high motivation generated by the worker's knowing that success in his entire career will come only if his firm succeeds and by knowing that his own advancement depends on managing well his long-term relationship with his present fellow workers. This tight social compulsion, in fact, has produced reliable and dedicated performance. Second, the "permanent" employee can be trained early at low wages in skills specifically useful to his firm for decades to come, without loss from his moving to another competing firm. Third, Japanese employees, interested in the efficiency of *their* firm, do not resist innovation or automation, as workers sometimes do elsewhere, though this argument facilely assumes enough growth so that employees not needed after automation can be used elsewhere in the same firm.[31] Fourth, further flexibility is achieved because jobs must be assigned to employees, rather than employees to jobs, because the workers cannot be fired. Rigidity of personnel substitutes for rigidity of job specifications and ossifying union rules impersonalizing (rationalizing) specific work. Fifth, life employment plus seniority promotion initially favors the new "glamour" industries. This is because the rapid worker intake is almost exclusively at the lowest pay scale (*i.e.,* for young graduates) and the full cost of the life and seniority systems is not felt even *pro rata* for thirty-odd years when today's young are beginning to retire after annual increments each year in the interim, not to mention the yearly base-up raise negotiated by the unions. In the early years of a new "growth firm," the burden of seniority on cash flow is absent—the high wages of the seniors and the lump-sum settlements on retirement are not yet falling due and will not be in full force for a decade or more.

These are, in accrual accounting, deferred costs, like the semi-annual bonuses and salary payment monthly. The lump-sum retirement, as deferred salary, means that the funds are available for use of the firm until payment is due. As another aspect of "participative employment," these pay methods give the worker an important role in capital formation, especially while the new firm's workers are predominantly young. For example, in 1961, 46 percent of all manufacturing employees were under twenty-four years of age.

The system has its disadvantages too. Life employment means in effect that labor costs are fixed costs; permanent workers cannot be laid off during a business slump. A second disadvantage is the reverse of the benefit mentioned above: deferred labor costs may be concealed by inadequate accounting reserves in new growth firms, or presently adequate reserves may be eroded away by inflation (about 7 percent, consumer price index, in 1970). Conversely, firms with aging labor forces will experience increasing costs for the same work. The entire cost effect of this deferred system, and especially tendencies to change it, are indeed difficult to divine now, but certainly one possibility is a substantial dilution of seniority rights being "bought" now by the young in accepting low initial pay and expecting a higher rate decades later.

A critical point that we must remember is that, though congruent with tradition, the life-employment system in Japan is young; it has become established in most present-day firms only during the last twenty years, though there were beginnings of it in the interwar period. Few firms have a full age spread in their work force and, therefore, practically all are using funds from nonrecurring deferred labor cost. In a new setting of increasing international competition and constant innovation, it is fair to question whether fixed-cost labor is feasible at all without continued dramatic growth. Even during a growth period, is it feasible once a firm has aged sufficiently to acquire the costs of a full hierarchy of age groups on the payroll, some leaving annually with handsome retirement checks? This may depend on the cheapness of the hiring-in rate and the proportion of temporary workers, both factors having been rapidly eroding in recent years. It may turn out that Japanese firms have bought youthful loyalty with a long-term promise to be only partially performed in the future.

Quite apart from whether it will last, life employment has a limited coverage even now. It is, indeed, the "normative" practice throughout all strata of Japanese business, but the ideal is realized more in big modern firms than in small firms, more for white-collar than blue-collar workers, and more for males than females. In small firms there is normally much emotive familism, and life employment is the ideal, but it is not often financially feasible for such firms. Also, small firms themselves have lives quite often shorter than the employees; there were 9,206 bankruptcies among the small- and medium-sized firms in 1971.[32] Exit from the corporate work forces is high among the blue collars even in large firms[33]; in fact the percentage is said to be roughly one-half that of the U.S., partly explaining (or explained by) an enormous self-employed group in Japan (24 percent).[34]

We shall see in the next section that these strikingly different personnel practices affect the organization, and the decision-making process as well, at the management level in large Japanese firms.

Management Organization / Besides its legal structuring, management organization has two functions: to organize people and to organize work.[35] Unlike U.S. organizations emphasizing work and job specifications, the Japanese emphasis is on the people and character. The workshop is said to be an industrial *Gemeinschraft*,[36] and as Confucius said, "If interpersonal relations are right, the work will get done; and if the work gets done, universalistic legalisms are largely irrelevant."[37] Let us look at the Japanese firm's ordering of people and work, and then at the legalities,[38] though this order of things is rather the opposite of the American approach.

Concerning management personnel, there are five basic organizational principles in the Japanese firm of special comparative interest to foreigners.[39] First, the basic unit is not an individual position but a cluster of people with joint managerial responsibilities; these collectivities themselves form a pyramid with subsections (*kakari*) and sections (*ka*) comprising divisions (*bu*), each with its own top representative reporting to the next highest echelon up to top management (*i.e.,* the board of directors). As a corporate symbol, the president usually is the only *individual officer* who shows on the organization chart. But the more characteristic point is that also the functions of the section itself, and especially of the people within each section, are ill-defined and responsibilities are diffuse. This is another aspect of the rule: people are not assigned to jobs, but jobs are assumed by people, as occasion requires. Where motivation to work is supplied by identity with the firm's interest, the assumption is that there is less need for specific definitions of who does what for precisely how much.

Second, rather than manning the organization, the Japanese firm to some extent organizes for the men, and not infrequently sections are created simply because a man has reached the stage in his career when he should be a section chief. To a remarkable degree the firm is organized by personal hierarchy rather than function. There are few people labeled as specialists in Japanese firms, and this lack of universalistic specialties lessens potential mobility and reinforces life employment by binding a man to his firm.

Third, the personnel division in the firm is much larger and has more authority and much more control over the recruitment, placement, promotions, separations, and transfers of individual members than is the case, for example, in the U.S. In U.S. business, line officers typically control such decisions, with personnel managers only rendering staff assistance, whereas in Japan the personnel division shares the responsibilities with the line divisions. This difference is caused, again, by the lack of job specifications, defined goals, authority, and functional distribution of responsbility to various levels and divisions so that typically a given managerial employee will move in sequence from job to job under the general career guidance of the personnel department. This is why a Japanese, asked what he does, always specifies only his firm, whereas foreigners and some Japanese in foreign firms specify their job —sales, finance, production, etc.

A fourth principle is that the unit chief (*chō*) is rated not for his leadership so much as for the "followership" that he can induce—a forthright Japanese recognition of the truism that all authority leans heavily upon its acceptance or that real authority is the power to make decisions that do, in fact, guide the behavior of others.

Fifth, since all could hardly be so idyllic, divisions are found between exclusive informal cliques (*habatsu*) that are organized under senior officers, who act as parent figures (*oyabun*) and influence, in the manner of miniscule political parties, work assignments and the like, sometimes causing serious personal frictions.

In sum, general firm organization emphasizes people in a rigid hierarchy of personal statuses based on age with little formal delegation of authority, while work is typically organized by sections (clusters of officers) with little definition of responsibility, interpersonally or even intersectionally. In such a centralized system, all projects are authorized on an *ad hoc* basis from the top down and emphasis is on generalists rather than specialists and on line function to the exclusion of staff.

On the merits, the organization surely fits traditional Japanese familism and negates individualism, which needs specialties and work definition to extricate the individual from diffuse total absorption by group goals and to save him some private life. Such organization also makes for collective flexibility and emotive effectiveness in crises; it, in fact, maximizes communication through the peculiar decision-making process, *ringi-sei* (see below).

As for demerits, the rigid personal statuses coupled with diffuse work responsibility force the "real politics" in the firm to descend to informal cliques,[40] organized for personal gains along lines (*e.g.,* school ties) rationally irrelevant to firm objectives.

Another related disadvantage causing unproductive friction is that, as is so true between outsiders and insiders in Japanese society generally, the large firm's sections communicate too little laterally.[41] As firms become more complex, the emphasis on line to the exclusion of staff will require more and more adjustment, and bureaucratic inertia may come to outweigh familial loyalties. Already we hear much of "my home-ism" or "privatization"—recent verbal monstrosities used to express the new tendency of Japanese "members" to forsake the *kaisha* for wife, family, or personal pleasures. To the firm this is an unwelcome reverse movement from "industrial family" back to the natural family!

Law imposes a corporate framework on the firm and in almost all cases the firm is legally organized as a joint stock corporation (*kabushiki kaisha*), though the Commercial Code does little more than define powers of "top management," for reasons to be mentioned later.[42] Although originally modeled after the German corporation law, the Japanese corporate law (Commercial Code Book II) was revised in 1952 by a large infusion of American law, largely from Illinois (see Chapter V). Besides strengthening individual shareholders' rights and remedies,[43] the revised code puts the board elected by shareholders firmly in charge of business policy.[44] In addition, the corporation is legally represented in executive matters by a representative director (*daihyō torishimariyaku*) elected by the board,[45] and upon registration with the official commercial registry, he binds the corporation in dealing with third parties. The board may delegate powers to the representative directors or others and may make detailed rules for administering the firm.

The only other corporate officer provided for directly in the code is the "auditor" (*kansayaku*),[46] modeled after the German *Aufsichsrat*. In Germany the *Aufsichsrat* has strong supervisory powers over accounting and personal performance of top management. There is no strict American equivalent for such a position, although outside CPA's perform some of his accounting functions. In Japan, the German form only is followed. Actually, the position has often become a sinecure for deserving senior employees. In publicly held corporations listed on the stock exchanges, auditing by CPA's (*kōnin kaikeishi*) is required since 1948 by the Securities Exchange Law (*Shōken torihiki-hō*). The "auditor" is neither an accounting expert, nor, though formally elected by them, is he beholden to shareholders, because in publicly held corporations, shareholder meetings are dominated by top management holding the requisite proxies, as they generally are elsewhere. Major reforms of the "auditor's" position are now being considered in Japanese governmental and academic circles.[47] One experienced "chartered accountant of international repute" has said: "Japan, too, is experiencing a historical period in which industrial responsibility and commercial practices have far outrun prudent accounting practices."[48]

Actual management power in the Japanese firm is quite different from the legal forms sketched above. Typically a firm has a chairman of the board (*kaichō*), a president (*shachō*), a vice-president (*fuku-shachō*), and one or more executive (chief) directors (*semmu-torishimariyaku*), and several managing directors (*jōmu-torishimariyaku*).[49] These in turn usually make up a management committee (*jōmukai*), which meets perhaps once a week to determine policy and actually runs the company. None of these positions of operative power are, however, legally required in the Commercial Code but are instead ordinarily authorized in rules, analogous to by-laws, provided by the board of directors, or simply by arrangement developed in company customs. Generally, the president is in fact the chief executive and also legally a representative director. Sometimes the board chairman is also an active executive, and, if so, this would usually show by his registration as a representative director.

With actual policy determination typically residing in the smaller group (the management committee), the board of directors has severe limitations as a governing body in Japan.[50]

In a large modern company, the board is usually comprised of fifteen to twenty individuals, most of whom are not included in the *jōmukai*. These men are actually selected favorites of senior executives, who hold the proxies required to see that they are elected by the stockholders. In virtually all cases these junior directors are selected from within the company at the division-chief level. Typically there are no outsiders on the board, except as found in *keiretsu* exchanges. It is not only an elite, closed group drawn from within the company but also coextensive with top management, because, as noted, each director is also a busy operational officer in charge of a division or plant. Such a board nurtures solidarity and assures collectively an intimate inside knowledge over the entire range of corporate operations.

Weaknesses are equally obvious. First, typically a coterie of senior officers dominates the company, and the junior officers, deferential to those who appoint them, cannot be depended upon to exercise critical judgment in a crisis. Second, each of the board members is too busy with his specific operations within the firm to develop a company-wide outlook. And third, the absence of outsiders deprives management of a detached point of view, as well as depriving the shareholders of an outsider's check on the other director-officers' performance.

Solutions to both legal and functional problems of organization are being sought and experimented with in Japan. The generalist-specialist relationship is becoming more of a problem, as more staff (in proportion to line) personnel are required. The president's room (*shachō-shitsu*) in some firms has become a shop for staff experts and overall planners. Some experiments have placed staff experts at the same rank as senior line officers, which most Japanese still find rather humorous.[51]

Other experiments are being made, for example, with efficiency payments (*nōritsu-kyū*) to overcome "my home-ism," believed to spring in part from size and in part from the unfairness of equal pay for unequal work under the *nenkō joretsu* system. The Japanese are also trying what Americans call "divisional" management (*jigyōbu-sei*) and "profit centers" for certain products in an attempt to get better managerial control and to adapt the organization for measuring unit performance. During transition the old structural tendencies inevitably overlap the new rather than instantly disappearing. Overall, though, it is apparent that aggressive managers in advanced large firms realize that some older practices have been outgrown by sheer scale and technological change and that management must give more attention to planning, rational organization, specialities, and definition of responsibility, perhaps supplemented by task forces and special projects to make up for the older flexibility thus lost.

Decision-making in the Japanese firm (ringi-sei) / The firm's decision-making, typically, follows a pattern called "reverential inquiry" (*ringi-sei,* hereafter simply *ringi* system), which reflects the familial notions embedded in business organization and employment practices, as well as in Japanese society generally.[52] It is a unique institution substituting awkwardly for planning, mixing staff and line function, accomplishing decentralized involvement in a highly centralized formal structure, and resembling somewhat latter-day "participatory democracy." Typically the *ringi* system involves the following steps:

1. A low-level official confronted with an operational problem requiring an executive decision drafts, or has his colleagues draft, a recommendation (*ringi-sho*); this draft often gives one-sided supporting data —and often little data at all—without explaining alternatives.

2. It is then circulated to all interested sections of the company horizontally and vertically to collect approvals, hence the term "government by seals;" it is wryly said that, if some officer disapproves, the most he can usually do is put his seal of approval on it upside down.[53]

3. The *ringi* papers work their way up to the president for decision.

Although the underlings have the initiative in this system, and responsibility is dispersed as noted above, they must submit everything for approval of superiors where formal authority still resides.

This traditional system is said to have been borrowed from consensus decision-making in the old Tokugawa extended family or house,[54] which had a high degree of centralization of formal authority but decentralization of task performance, with the gap bridged in operations by consensus achieved through *ringi*. Thus, *ringi-sei* decision-making complements Japanese hierarchical organization and rigid centralized authority. Also the *ringi* system is a ponderous substitute for staff jobs, which are usually not separately manned in Japan.

In small groups, much can be said for the system because it achieves a high degree of communication, consensus, and coordination, and at the same time it distributes responsibility for action throughout the organization as *ringi* papers collect seals during the rounds of approval until the president, in ultimate authority, gives it the formally final but actually perfunctory stamp of validity.[55] The system also clearly squares with the realistic insight that authority to give orders can affect behavior only in a climate congenial to order acceptance, insured in the *ringi-sei* by the fact that interested managers have already approved in advance.

In large complex groups, however, the problems in the *ringi* system are manifold. It is slow and cumbersome; responsibility is dispersed and strong leadership and control are impossible. Also it does not permit a thorough review of alternatives as required in good planning so that actually communication during the process may be of a rather low quality. The *ad hoc* lowly origins of the *ringi* papers call for decisions on intuitive and piecemeal bases, as and when problems are encountered in operations at the lowest level, and all too often they are accepted rather uncritically on the way up.

In fact, the system is changing in large firms to provide a stronger role for top management with a supporting expert staff, long-term planning, precise budgeting, and even some formal delegation of authority. Some firms have discounted *ringi*-for-information and limited severely the levels canvassed when *ringi* is used. Several important firms (*e.g.,* Teijin, Asahi Chemical, Hokuriku Power, and Nippon Light Metals) have even taken the ultimate step and abolished the system, reportedly with good results.[56] These new trends are heralded as a change from management by seals to management by goals. Still, much can be said, especially in small firms, for the old-fashioned organization and decision-making backed by compliance of well-informed, loyal participants, rather than impersonal management controls external to the actors.

A review of the Japanese managerial system, life-employment practice, and organization may overemphasize its peculiarities in a rapidly changing Japan. Innovations, as shown by experiences abroad to be clearly required by large scale, advancing technology and increasing complexity, are being tried and those of merit are being incorporated into Japan's managerial system. One of the major needs is staff support and this requires specialists who must be trained. It would seem, then, that the absence of a professional curriculum in the universities must soon be remedied.

The Enterprise Union

Virtually all large modern Japanese firms have been unionized since 1945 as a result of SCAP's policy in favor of "industrial democracy," implemented by American-style legislation and conferring for the first time in Japanese history the rights to organize, bargain, and strike.[57] On the other hand, up to 1971 only a small portion of the small and medium enterprises (e.g., 3 percent of firms with twenty-nine employees or less) have been unionized. Still, never in history anywhere has there been such explosive union growth—from zero to 56 percent of all salaried workers between 1945 and 1949. After some decline from the 1949 peak, overall union membership stood in 1969 at about 28 percent (11 million) of all nonagricultural workers, a rate equal to that of the U.S. and only slightly less than Britain.

Collective bargaining (dantai kōshō) in the way it is done in the U.S. has not, however, kept pace with unionization but this is not to say that the Japanese way of "consultation" is not as good or better. Civil servants and other employees of public corporations and public utilities, amounting to about 30 percent of the unionized labor force,[58] are precluded from striking so that the bargaining potential in Japan is about 7 million employees of which an estimated 80 percent are covered by written collective agreements (dantai kyōyaku).[59] Japanese collective bargaining agreements are very simplistic, usually little more than recognition of the unions' rights, and not in a legal sense "contracts" that could be useful in day-to-day working relations in the Japanese factory or in settling disputes in the courts. Day-to-day relations are governed more by the employment regulations (shūgyō kisoku) to be discussed below.

In spite of its impressive postwar unionization record, Japanese labor has been less successful in American-style bargaining and also less successful as measured by the SCAP goal of "industrial democracy." This was because Japanese unionism foresook to some extent the "laboring class" and became an elitist device, captured by the "industrial family" in the form of the "enterprise union" (kigyō-betsu kumiai).

The enterprise union is not a "company union" (meaning management instigated), but its membership is limited to permanent workers in the same company; thus a closed-shop agreement is virtually unknown though union-shop clauses are very common. Some have said this kind of enterprise union does not function as a "union" at all, but rather as a labor consulting committee to work out problems between management and worker representatives as they arise regarding plant and payroll.

In any event, the enterprise union has an elitist color to it which manifests itself in three ways particularly. First, the enterprise unions exist mainly in large firms. The reason for little unionization in small firms is also simple: small firms are so unstable and operate on such thin margins that a union, if there were one, could do little more than throw most such marginal hosts into bankruptcy. Second, even in the large firm, the enterprise union accepts as members only life employees from the same firm. Temporary and external workers are excluded entirely from union membership, though some attempts are being made by enterprise unions to organize, separately, the labor force in affiliated companies, presumably to prevent work leakage by excessive subcontracting if the subcontracting or subsidiary firms' wages get too low.[60] Third, the "enterprise union" is controlled by its leaders[61] with little democratic participation by the membership, and, though not "company unions" in the western sense, the Japanese "enterprise union" shows much concern for firm success and deference to its officers.

These peculiarities can hardly be understood now without reviewing briefly just how this all came about. First, dire need after World War II created strong worker demands for guaranteed subsistence from the firm; this preoccupation with survival quickly revived the life employment and seniority systems, which had gained a foothold in the interwar period, but then mostly for upper-level staff only (*shokuin*). The postwar "enterprise union," soon representing all permanent employees, blue-collar and white-collar alike, then demanded life employment for all, excluding only supervisory personnel as required by the new American-style law. From this experience, the postwar "enterprise union" was born and proliferated to give Japanese unionism its most extraordinary characteristic and to dull the edge of the "national labor movement" that had been envisaged by SCAP, as well as the "rise of the laboring class" envisaged by the leftists.

The unions' inclusion of white-collar as well as blue-collar members reinforced hierarchical familism and prevented the usual western labor-management horizontal split flowing from union-management equality.

Especially this was true because white-collar members came rather naturally (in Japanese psychology) to dominate most enterprise unions and confer with management with minimal referral of policy problems to the membership. Also interference by broader craft, industrial, or national bargaining units was not tolerated because such "outsiders" might impair the firm's performance and jeopardize the inside unionists' lifetime interests in the firm.

Seen historically, then, Japanese firms have had too many social functions, too much national purpose, and too many overtones of the extended family to host an industrial-relations regime at the enterprise level characterized by either the usual western stand-off between management and labor or by politicking for the Marxist "laboring class." At the same time, in terms of short-time, Gomper-like goals, unionism has not done all it could in postwar Japan. The labor share has been remarkably low during the period of rapid growth, and wage increases have lagged behind rises in productivity,[62] a trend that recently has been reversed, from 1968 onward. On balance, though, the need for national capital formation and the results achieved from it for labor will fully justify the withholding of wages, whether voluntary and deliberate or not. And, be that as it may, the enterprise union has added much to industrial relations; its very presence reminds management that, unless workers' interests are attended to, the union may succumb to the ever-present and strident calls of national leftist labor leaders, who are constantly seeking to drive a wedge between the enterprise unions and management at the firm level. This very real threat introduces the problems of radicalism at the national level in the postwar Japanese labor movement.

There has been a confluence of Marxist ideology as well as American legalism into the mainstream of postwar Japanese labor familism—with highly novel results—which was not expected by SCAP. And, although they have been mutually reinforcing in unexpected ways, these three divergent sources have flowed, generally, at rather separate levels and in separate channels: familism through the enterprise union; Marxism through the national labor centers, mostly the Sōhyō; and American legalisms in the dispute settlement process, ironically, only when Marxists are successful in subverting the enterprise union procedures. Some minimal acquaintance with this subtle situation is essential.

To Japanese familism, SCAP's "industrial democracy" was a disquieting challenge. It was a direct affront to Japanese values in general—authority and hierarchy, subservience and loyalty, overall collectivistic harmony. Seen more concretely, the contractual universalism underlying western employment relations tends to connect with the labor market by job specifications and union work rules, in turn encouraging work mobility, individualism, and a lessening of group solidarity. We have already described the accommodation that eventuated from this clash of new and old values to produce a synthesis in the "enterprise union."

To Marxists the new labor laws were seen as an unprecedented legalized opportunity for "class struggle." But, as noted, the enterprise unionists had much less expansive goals—the security of privileged permanent workers within their specific enterprise. Also the bulk of the union membership had their feet so firmly planted on the ground that the Marxist ideologists were literally kicked upstairs to manipulate the national federations such as the old Sambetsu and the present Sōhyō as a political power base. For the same reasons these federations, in their various transformations, were deliberately isolated from bargaining within each firm, which bargaining was monopolized by the enterprise union.

Still, in mid-1971 over two-thirds of the enterprise unions are affiliated loosely with one or the other of the three major national federations (perhaps better called confederations): Sōhyō (4.2 million); Dōmei (2.1 million) and Chūritsu Rōren (1.3 million), but all three federations are alike in that their officers are treated as "outsiders" and are not permitted by their constituent enterprise unions to bargain collectively. Since 1965, however, the national federations have actively promoted the rather effective "spring offensive" (*shuntō*) for the annual "base-up" wage increases and also for semiannual bonuses. This rather practical movement has been useful to the enterprise unions in their specific negotiations for annual raises required to keep pace with inflation, and, indeed, this phenomenon may usher in a new phase in local-national unionism.[63]

Otherwise the federations are mainly concerned with politics. Sōhyō's public employee membership (about two-thirds of its total), which is excluded by law from striking,[64] explains in part the fact that Sōhyō is the main antigovernment Marxist force and the chief support for the leading opposition, the Socialist party. On the other hand, Dōmei, though with a smaller membership overall, represents the largest private industrial labor force, and it is the leading supporter of the more moderate opposition, the Democratic Socialist party. The Chūritsu Rōren is a loose confederation of so-called "neutral" unions that are bent on avoiding Marxist radicalism.

For the past twenty-five years, the maneuvering of various leftist splinter groups, including the Communist party, in a national unionist movement launched by American law is an interesting happenstance.[65] Particularly the leadership (not necessarily the membership) of the important Japan Teachers' Union (Nihon Kyōshokuin Kumiai) in years past has been avowedly revolutionary and dedicated to overthrow the conservative government.[66] Having lost at the ballot box, this resolute disposition to resort to "struggle" activity has won the Teachers' Union the nickname of the "red-crested white heron" (tanchō-zuru). Also, Sōhyō's habitual return to left-wing radicalism has been checked only by occasional desertions of its more sensible members. In recent years, and especially after the leftist excesses in the universities which crested in 1969 and were followed by public disapproval shown in the 1969 election, the national labor leaders show welcomed signs of moderating and focusing on more concrete economic goals for wage earners. Yet extreme leftist predilections at the national level are worth emphasizing here because the same kind of extreme leftist militancy has brightly colored the practical applications of the new American-style legislation in the adjustment of Japanese labor disputes.

The New Labor Laws / Japan's experience with labor legislation has been unique, for, in most advanced countries, labor law has ordinarily been the result rather than the cause of organized labor activity. But when SCAP-sponsored laws were adopted in Japan beginning in 1946, they triggered the remarkable labor movement, described above, virtually from scratch. "Literally in a matter of moments the labor relations law began to function, without the softening effect of tradition, without sophisticated understanding on the part of those responsible for its application, and, indeed, without an initial comprehension of the very words in which the new laws were couched."[67] So, although the peculiarities of the traditional Japanese firm and the harshness of an alien Marxist ideology were major factors in molding the unionism that ensued, still the movement cannot be fully understood without keeping in mind "the volcanic recency of this branch of Japanese law" derived from American models.

The story of postwar Japanese labor laws must begin with the Constitution, Art. 28, which provides for labor rights specifically: "The rights of workers to organize and to bargain and act collectively are guaranteed."

Such an express constitutional guarantee, strategically placed in Chapter III on "Rights and Duties of the People," is a strong underpinning for the Japanese labor movement. But it has also become a point of departure for the major split between labor lawyers in Japan into two camps—non-Marxist and Marxist, which here simply refers to those who regard labor law as just another tool in the inevitable class struggle rather than a framework for adjustment and cooperation.[68] In fact, Marxist labor-law scholars, who incidentally account for a major portion of the scholarly literature (all the more important because judicial precedent is yet scarce), have exploited fully this unqualified language of Art. 28, despite the fact that, by now in justiciable (as opposed to polemical) constitutional law, it is a rare individual right that need not be weighed against the rights of others (*i.e.,* the public interest), even though the judicial weighing is not easy nor the outcome always predictable.[69] The Marxist "absolute right" doctrine, used on occasion to rationalize forceful actions, is supported textually by the fact that some other provisions in the constitution (Chapter III) provide specifically for the balancing of private rights with the "public welfare" (*e.g.,* Art. 22 [1] and Art. 29), meaning, they say, that the absence of such provisions indicates the absence of any limitations on the exercise of rights conferred in Art. 28. In addition to the "inevitable balancing" counterargument, there is strong argument that the constitutional rights of Art. 28 are appropriately defined by the later labor legislation (see below) and that Art. 28 is not now directly applicable, except to test such legislation.[70]

Still, some lower court decisions have leaned in the Marxist direction, as we shall see. On the other hand, the Japanese Supreme Court has rejected these extreme interpretations, but unfortunately it takes time to accumulate an adequate body of precedent, and many significant issues remain undecided by the highest court. In those areas, foreigners who become involved in a labor confrontation will not be able to avoid legal assertions *à la Marx* served up by unionist lawyers.

Even before the constitution was drafted, the Labor Union Law[71] (hereafter LUL), passed in December 1945, was modeled after the American Wagner Act,[72] although it is said to have also drawn from proposals already made in the Japanese Diet as early as the 1920s. The new LUL granted to Japanese workers for the first time the right to organize, bargain collectively, and strike, and also the law set up labor relations commissions at the national and prefectural levels to administer the law and hear complaints of "unfair labor practices,"[73] which, unlike American law, are available only against employers, and the possibility of "unfair labor practices" on the part of labor are nowhere mentioned in the statute.

In September 1946, the Labor Relations Adjustment Law[74] (hereafter LRAL) aimed at adjusting labor disputes within the framework of the LUL and spelled out the functions of the labor relations commissions. Public employees were important because telecommunications, tobacco, salt, and camphor are public monopolies. Many railways, radio and TV stations, and some other enterprises are government owned, and certain public utilities are covered by special labor laws.[75] A third major law was enacted in April 1947 entitled the Labor Standards Law[76] (LSL); it provided minimum standards for nonunion as well as union labor. The foregoing three major laws (*rōdō sampō*) were supplemented by additional enactments including a law to regulate recruiting practices, especially to avoid the abuses of traditional "bossism" and brokerage practices.[77] Finally, in August 1947, the Ministry of Labor was established.

Though the foregoing laws have elicited one of the most dramatic labor movements in recent history, as has been noted, the same movement was manned in important ways by leftist radicals; over two thousand of them, aggrieved and disgruntled, were released from prisons by the occupation forces in 1945. As we have seen, the accommodation finally worked out between American labor-law concepts and Marxist radicalism has been a bifurcated union structure, extreme polarity in confrontations, and a dual labor-law literature. In the union structure the politically oriented national federations have become a leftist political base, and the "enterprise union" has monopolized collective bargaining.

In the present times of intensive worldwide "incomes policy" debate, the competing theories regarding proper government-labor-industry relations raise tough questions for all nations. There are the alleged ossifying effects of mature trade unionism as seen, for example, in Great Britain, causing, some would say, reduced international competitiveness plus incurable cost-push inflation. Understandably, some Japanese might well wonder whether in the coming "postindustrial economy" the old American-styled industrial-relation regime, which lines labor up against management in a minimally controlled but continual test of strength causing cost-push inflation, is not seriously time-bound and counterproductive as well as unfair to consumers, of whom "organized labor" is no longer even 50 percent. These are all real issues relating to the Japanese version of the Wagner Act, which cannot be arbitrated here, but the very least that can be said is that the facile infusion of an "improved" version of American legislation from the 1930s into an entirely different cultural environment of defeated Japan in the late 1940s produced results within a year or two quite unforeseen and unwanted by most of the "legislators." Intially, radicalism was the main winner in the interplay of Marxists with the American-style liberality in the collective bargaining and dispute settlement processes underwritten by the new labor laws. McArthur finally stepped in to prevent a general strike in 1948 when, at the height of its hunger and despair, the Japanese populace could ill afford a work stoppage. Recently (1968) the U.S., with twice the labor force, suffered an annual loss of 49 million man-days as compared with Japan's 2.8 million (*i.e.*, per capita, about 8.5 times).[78]

Some further specific attention to the Marxist influence on application of the "law" is required, not only because the yield was initially some rather exotic practices in the name of law, but also because the sorely needed judicial interpretation has taken time, and predictability as to judicial application of the laws still remains in large measure unsatisfactory though the practice is settling down more each year. Furthermore, for large foreign enterprises, the unsatisfactory legal processes[79] may be invoked more often because their foreign elements can cause tension, destroying the docility of the "enterprise union."

Looking to specific practices rationalized initially by Marxist lawyers as proper under the LUL and the LRAL, three "legal" interpretations will serve as warnings against complacent assumptions that the judicial gloss from the U.S. "mother law" is a useful guide in the Japanese context.

The first example is "factory occupation" by the worker and particularly the unusual radical doctrine "production control" (*seisan kanri*). "Factory occupation" is distinguished from *seisan kanri* because workers simply take over the plant and expel management but do not usurp management functions, whereas under *seisan kanri* action, management functions are also performed, including operating the factory and, in extreme instances, disposing of property to pay wages or to directly satisfy disputed claims. The Supreme Court has explicitly declared *seisan kanri* contrary to the constitution, Art. 29, protecting private property.[80] Nonetheless, a majority of labor-law scholars and several of the lower courts have upheld this unusual practice though now the Supreme Court decision is the law. In disputes involving simple "factory occupation" (without usurping management functions), the courts have often avoided a holding on its legality.

A second labor action with surprising "legal" consequences, as defined by the unions and their scholarly advocates,[81] is picketing. In Japan, unions have not limited proper picketing to acts done for informational purposes; instead they have in the name of the law and the constitution used picketing to prevent, by "might" or threat, workers willing to work from entering the plant. For example, one common technique is linking arms and not allowing anyone to pass through. The legal issue stems from interpretations of LUL, Art. 1 (2) (proviso), which protects labor from criminal liability for "appropriate action" under the LUL, "provided, however, that in no case shall the use of violence be construed an appropriate act of a labor union." This seems clear enough in intent and not too difficult to apply to arm-linking pickets, and the quoted language has been construed to outlaw threats of violence by pickets.[82] Still a substantial segment of the legal community has espoused a "might theory" that distinguishes passive exclusion by linking arms, which they say is legal, and forceful acts of commission, which are not. The Supreme Court has been consistently negative to the "might theory," though in holding to the principle that only peaceful means of persuasion are appropriate, all circumstances must be taken into account.[83] In the height of the fray, such a principle gives little guidance, and tendencies of the courts to absolve defendants of criminal liability for forceful acts led Japanese workers to think that mass picketing is entirely legal.[84]

Third, the lockout (*sangyōsho heisa*) as an appropriate means to counterunion activity is recognized as an "act of dispute" (*sōgi kōi*) by Japanese law[85] but with its own peculiar radical twist in past union practice,[86] according to which a lockout may not be effected by a Japanese employer by simply announcing that operations will cease and notifying the workers to absent the plant. In criminal law, the laborer is not criminally liable for refusing to leave and retaining possession of his work place, because it is argued that he remains an employee during a lockout or a strike; some argue he is also entitled to pay during a strike. Otherwise, they say, his constitutional right under Art. 28 is violated.[87] To effect a lockout, then, the employer must effectively lock the door and prevent the laborers from entering. Especially where laborers are always in the plant on multiple shifts, or where management simply lacks the strength or adequate locks, a lockout becomes physically impossible and, therefore, legally ineffectual. It has been said that a more open invitation to violence would be hard to imagine. Yet this "effective measure" theory was nonetheless espoused in one district court case[88] though the trend is running against it now.[89] Even so, there is a tendency to be lenient to overexuberant strikers even when violent. For example, failure to find theft against workers taking the employer's vehicles, though legally sound when rationalized with a finding of "no intent," still leaves the employer wronged and, in a practical sense, without a remedy.[90]

The foregoing sample can only stimulate a taste for the legal posturing by labor leaders and lawyers in Japan *à la Marx*. Continuing ambiguities in the substantive law are inevitable until the Supreme Court has time to build up a body of precedent. This makes the scholarly treatises prominent in the applications of the "law," which in turn are often a leftish gloss as described above.

But lest these ideological skirmishings be drawn out of perspective, it is important to remember that actually most enterprise unions work closely with management—indeed too closely, many observers feel. In the usual Japanese company, legal techniques are not so important in handling labor issues. For, within the enterprise, union organization corresponds roughly to the structure of the firm (*i.e.*, vertical and hierarchical), and most issues are handled by daily liaison between union and firm officials on all levels of plant and office. It is only when this mediating process breaks down completely, admittedly seldom in the usual large Japanese firm, that the legal inadequacies of the system become painfully apparent in a hostile confrontation.

One inadequacy in a time of crisis is the lack of a contractual conception of Japanese industrial relations, because of the closer, more diffuse familial employment relationship.[91] The "labor agreement" (*rōdō kyōyaku*), for example, is often barely more than a brief statement recognizing the union's legitimacy and right to bargain and pledging cooperation with virtually no specification of working rules or arbitration that would anticipate problems of the work routine.[92]

One reason that detailed collective bargaining contracts are usually not found in Japanese industrial relations is that the LSL of 1947 requires any employer with more than ten regular workers to establish "rules of employment" (*shugyō kisoku*) containing considerable detail as to pay, hours, and other working conditions.[93] LSL Art. 89 requires that the rules of employment include provisions on the (1) beginning and ending of the work day; (2) recesses, holidays, vacations; (3) shift changes; (4) compensation; (5) accounting; (6) promotions; and (7) age for retirement. If the company has arrangements for retirement allowances, minimal wages, bonuses; or requirements that workers provide food, tools, or other materials; or rules regarding safety and sanitation, accident and illness, or discipline or awards; or, finally, any other rules applicable to the workers, they too must be included in the "rules of employment." Art. 89(2) provides that separate rules may be made, if the employer so desires, concerning safety, wages, sanitation, accident, compensation and relief from illness, wages, or other matters.

Since the law gives the employer more control in making rules of employment than in a collective bargaining agreement, the rules have often displaced detailed provisions in collective bargaining contracts governing the workshop. In order to establish rules of employment, the employer draws them up and then refers them to the labor union, if there is one, or a workers' representative, whose opinion concerning them is reduced to writing, and the rules, with that opinion, must be filed with the Ministry of Labor, chief of the Labor Standards Inspection Office.[94]

Even though the workers' representative does not approve the rules of employment, they are still effective insofar as they do not violate law or provisions of a collective bargaining contract. But, of course, if serious disagreements existed, presumably the union would consider collective action under the LUL to protect the workers in order to obtain desired changes. The use of rules established under the LSL, which are more convenient for the employer,[95] can reduce the meaning of collective bargaining, though some more detailed contracts are now being drawn up. Still, in case of a confrontation, there are virtually no provisions for mediation or arbitration by a third party (other than the Labor Commission) in most Japanese collective-bargaining agreements.[96] Furthermore, in Japanese enterprise unionism, labor and management are both accustomed to warmth and harmony in intrafirm relationships, and consequently they find it very difficult to discuss a contested issue on a rational basis supported by data in lieu of the usual emotive *gemeinschaft* posture. For that purpose, the LRAL has provided the labor relations commissions that are to be brought into such crises; but they, too, tend to apply compromising (rather than contractual) techniques familiar to the Japanese culture.

When a serious management-labor confrontation has occurred regarding "unfair labor practice" of the employer, however, the union often takes to the courts, which, unlike American law, is an option conferred by interpretation of the procedural law[97] without need "to exhaust administrative remedies." The union is usually the moving party, because management does not have the benefit of "unfair labor practices" that are specified in the law and applicable to the union. Indeed, irreconcilable labor leaders favor the court action over labor commission action, because the provisional injunctions available are more effective. They have usually resulted in reinstatement plus back pay without a full decision on the merits, whereas commission actions are slower and less satisfactory. The most frequently mentioned problems with the labor relations commissions' proceedings are delay, caused by over-reliance on writing, too little control over witnesses and relevance of evidence because of the prevailing adversary approach, multiple hearings, delays in setting hearings, *written* instead of oral closing statements, and lack of tailored remedies, so that in discharge cases the decree is for all (reinstatement with back pay) or nothing.[98]

In summary it is important to reemphasize that, overall, the enterprise union has in the past made infrequent use of legal bargaining procedures and resultant contractual dispute settlement procedures, because both management and labor have mutual interests in the avoidance of work stoppage for the success of the firm. It is also fair to say that, Marxist prattling to the contrary, management has not regarded labor as a commodity or mere cost factor and has been concerned about the welfare of the employees. On the other hand, if a dispute does become aggravated and a Marxist-led union strikes and begins factory occupation or picketing action, both the substantive and procedural law in their present development will prove rather unsatisfactory to employers, a fact to be kept in mind by foreigners, especially American, who, though in a sense authors of these laws, will find their workings rather surprising.

There are two causes for concern regarding labor relations in the future. First, Japanese labor demands in the past have been held to levels consistent with firm success, because of life employment and labor's interest in the firm. However, one may surmise that management's ability to satisfy labor's demands has been relatively easy during the extraordinary growth in productivity[99] experienced in the past couple of decades. A test of industrial relations of a different sort may be in the offing, heralded by the recent wage increases in excess of productivity since 1968. Needless to say, such a trend, which has now continued for four years,[100] could raise issues a great deal more difficult than those in the early sixties when a 10 to 15 percent annual "base up" could be offered to labor and still not match productive gain to be received for the price.

The other development is equally thorny, if not so obvious. For blue-collar workers (managers apart), the life-employment system with annual seniority increases (in addition to the "base up") may be in jeopardy if starting wages for high school graduates are annually increased more than the seniority increment for present senior staff and if slack cannot be taken up by hiring temporary employees, also increasingly harder to find. This will not only dilute the life-employment system for blue collars, the rationale for which is being thus eroded away, but also an immobile enterprise labor force could become hungrier and less docile to handle at just the time when international economic relations may begin to stiffen. Only the future will provide the extent of these contingencies and the solution for them.

Supracorporate Business Organization

Like personal relations within the firm, the large modern enterprisers' relations with outside competitors and affiliates in Japan are organized, controlled, and hierarchical,[101] reflecting the governing fact that, since Meiji, modern industry has been an instrument of national policy. Each industry has its ranking by market shares, its "big three" or "big ten"; it has its trade association and cartels leading up to Keidanren, and even MITI might be included at the apex since much governmental action turns on a firm's ranking. Of course, all major countries have a ranking for firms and have industry-wide associations, but in Japan government favors are generally commensurate with the ranking.

As noted in Chapter III, the main feature of the overall business hierarchy is the horizontal split between the giants at the apex and the microbes at the base, which populate respectively the modern and traditional strata of the dualistic pyramid. There are, for example, about 825,605 corporations, reflecting a per capita rate of business incorporation roughly the same as that in the U.S.,[102] but only 1,099 had capital of over one billion yen (about $2.8 million), and these 1,099 corporations together had 60 percent of the entire corporate capital and 34 percent of all corporate sales in Japan. In fact, the top one hundred corporations have 33 percent of all corporate capital in Japan.[103] The underlying realities disclose a massive, post-World War II incorporation trend (*hōjin nari*), covering literally hundreds of thousands of tiny businesses, with countervailing bankruptcies at the rate of about ten thousand per year.[104] Small family retailers, cottage-type industry, and the like incorporate, with father as president and his wife and relatives as directors, using, nonetheless, the ponderous stock corporation (*kabushiki kaisha*) designed for large publicly held businesses but presumably chosen to reap benefits in terms of accounting, tax, and public image. Particularly the old-fashioned, inefficient, multitiered distribution system tends to perpetrate extreme atomization at the base of the corporate structure.[105]

The big business world is highly oligopolistic (*i.e.,* markets dominated by four to eight firms) and quite exclusive by now (though less so than prewar) because the Japanese government's national industrial plan has shaped oligopolistic markets in most products; only a few selected firms were allowed preferential financing, foreign exchange, and the critical foreign technology needed to build Japanese capacity in each line. As a consequence, the foreign enterpriser is normally concerned with the several hundred large corporations listed on one of the two sections of the Tokyo Stock Exchange. In all, there were 1,244 listed corporations in 1969; 687 in the First Section (1 billion yen [$2,780,000] capital required), and 557 in the Second Section (100 million yen [$278,000] capital). The Tokyo Stock Exchange, incidentally, accounted for 71 percent of all stock turnover in 1968 (daily average: 155,000,000 shares).

By world standards also, these modern Japanese giants are impressive. Based on sales, *Fortune*'s 1972 list (for 1971 business results of the 300 largest industrial firms in the world outside of the U.S.) included 75 Japanese firms, considerably ahead of the next country, Britain, with 64.[106] By U.S. standards, there are 147 Japanese firms with sales higher than the $176,000,000 for the lowest U.S. firm on *Fortune*'s 1972 list (showing 1971 sales results for the 500 largest U.S. industrial firms)—one for every three and one-half firms of that scale in the United States.[107] The lowest sales for the 500 largest Japanese industrial firms is $26,000,000, but the correlation is not perfect because Japanese firms do not ordinarily use consolidated accounting, and their congeries of subsidiaries are substantial.[108]

Especially the top one hundred Japanese industrial firms are powerful national institutions, wedded to correspondingly strong banking, trading, insurance, and shipping companies, forming an elite core of Japanese business that is governmentally nurtured to make them competitive in international markets. In 1971, there were sixteen Japanese firms (Nihon Steel, Toyota Motors, Nissan Motors, Hitachi, Matsushita Electric Industries, Mitsubishi Heavy Industries, Nippon Kokan, Tokyo Shibaura Electric, Nippon Oil, Sumitomo Metal Industries, Mitsubishi Electric, Kawasaki Steel, Ishikawajima-Harima, Kirin Brewery, Kobe Steel, and Honda Motors) with sales in excess of $1 billion, compared to the U.S. with 127 such billionaires in 1971. A study in 1971 turned up the remarkable fact that the top 100 companies (in terms of capital) also control another 2,818 firms, and altogether the capital of these parents and subsidiaries is nearly 40 percent of the nation's industrial capital, not to mention their capital in 4,794 other corporations in which these one hundred corporations hold 10 percent or more of the shares.[109]

Reflecting its Meiji origins, the "industrial family," now hosting the postwar enterprise union described above, has continued to be more nationalistic and welfare-minded than private corporations in the U.S. or Europe, and also modern Japanese firms have grouped themselves for pursuit of these broader purposes. So, to deal with a Japanese firm without knowing its collateral commitments to affiliates and even to competitors can be very poor business.

There are two kinds of supracorporate groupings. First, most firms have joined into families of firms (*keiretsu,* literally "alignment") wherein their mutual bank rations out scarce investment capital. We must emphasize that these *keiretsu* families (or "industrial families") are not family-controlled firms like the prewar *zaibatsu*. The new organizational principle is confederacy using the "one-set" technique,[110] which means that typically each *keiretsu* tries to nurture one major firm in each kind of industry (an oil company, a trading company, an electrical machinery company, a mining company, etc.), so that there is a whole cross-industrial spread fostering much horizontal and vertical business within a group complex, but little competition intramurally.

The second kind of supracorporate grouping, besides the *keiretsu,* is the industry-wide association, which organizes producers (competitors) in each industry for daily governmental liaison and cooperative action including cartels on a national scale.[111] Especially in international business, numerous legalized Japanese cartels function through these associations, to be described below.

Both types of supracorporate organizations are remarkably elaborated in Japan to serve group or national purposes transcending the capacities of individual firms. Basically, the *keiretsu,* embracing no competitors, is like a headless conglomerate (*i.e.,* without common ownership to tie it together at the top). On the other hand, the trade associations and cartels bring together all competitive producers in a given industry for governmental and industrial planning—also for investment allocations, orderly marketing, prevention of "excess competition," and recently to fortify against "foreign invasions." The essentials of both of these high-level types of organization will be discussed below; they are so important to operations that no Japanese firm would embark on an important venture without consulting the government, the bank, the trade association, and perhaps the *keiretsu* presidents' meeting (see below). And, such factors affect, sometimes definitively, market shares that foreigners may participate in by joint venture or alliance. Certainly no foreign firm should venture into the Japanese business world without exploring the specifics of these supracorporate systems that condition the ambience of his would-be Japanese associates.

Banking keiretsu

Basically, there are also three types of families of firms (*keiretsu*) that foreigners need to understand in order to identify their immediate corporate associates in the supracorporate structure of Japanese business today. The first type is the traditional *keiretsu,* derived from past *zaibatsu* experience; the second is the more loosely structured banking *keiretsu (kin'yu keiretsu)*; and the third is the enterprise *keiretsu (kigyō keiretsu)*.

The traditional *keiretsu,* though far removed from the prewar combines and not properly called a *zaibatsu* today, includes the three groups of firms with prewar *zaibatsu* ties—Mitsubishi, Mitsui, and Sumitomo. Even the successors of the former Yasuda Zaibatsu have some similar residual ties in the Fuji bank group, but for my purposes I will treat the more cohesive and exclusive Mitsubishi, Mitsui, and Sumitomo groups as a separate category, because there does seem to be considerably more structure and coordination in these *"zaibatsu*-derived" *keiretsu,* presumably in part because of past personal connections. Each group has its bank and trading company that play important functions; each group has its Presidents' Club for liaison, cooperation, and sometimes joint action on a voluntary basis (see Appendix VII). Except for the fact that they manage to get much closer coordination and mutual financing and shareholding, many features of these *zaibatsu*-derived *keiretsu* are found in the banking *keiretsu* (below). Joint funding of new ventures (such as atomic fuel, research and knowledge projects, and ocean resources) and joint use of the Mitsubishi, Mitsui, or Sumitomo name and trademarks are features of these groups.

Both the traditional and the banking *keiretsu* are clusters of major operating firms looking to a single bank as their "primary" capital source. Organizationally, such groups are cooperative business confederations, but they are also, in a sense, a part of the national administration of capital resources from (1) the Bank of Japan to (2) the "city banks" to (3) modern industry at large. These *keiretsu* all have the following characteristics:

1. The members are all "independent" major firms in their own oligopolistic industries.

2. The *keiretsu* is a confederation pursuing the "one-set" formula (*i.e.,* excluding competitors but aiming at representing all lines within the confederation).

3. Service firms (for example: banking, trading, insurance, and shipping companies) from within the *keiretsu* perform special functions for industrial member firms in varying degrees (not usually to the complete exclusion of outsiders).

4. Between the firms there are several cross-ties: *e.g.,* borrowing from the same banks, mutual shareholding, interlocking directors, use of the same trademark, same trading company, and liaison planning by presidents' clubs.

5. Much interfirm business, horizontal and vertical, is done within the group of firms.

6. Holding companies at the top (as in the prewar *zaibatsu*) have been eliminated so that the relationship between these groupings is now more cooperative than controlled.

It is essential to emphasize at the outset what the *keiretsu* is not; even the Mitsubishi, Mitsui, and Sumitomo groups are not the palest ghost of the prewar *zaibatsu,* loose journalism to the contrary not withstanding. They are not conglomerates either, because stockholding control is formally lacking; and it is not "monopoly capitalism," except as that term is pejoratively used in the abundant Marxist literature on the subject.[112]

Japan no longer has the prewar kind of combines that by 1945 had amassed 25 percent of Japan's entire capital in all fields in the "big four" (Mitsui, Mitsubishi, Sumitomo, and Yasuda—now traceable in part to the Fuji Bank). Concentration in the big four was even higher in finance (49.7 percent), heavy industry (32.4 percent), marine transport (60.8 percent), and foreign investment (80 percent).[113] Now, along different lines, a loose *keiretsu*-type of regrouping of the "big four" *zaibatsu* splinters has, however, occurred since 1952, for reasons mentioned above. But there can be no doubt about the considerable operational independence of member firms in the new *keiretsu,* compared to their *zaibatsu* status, which was then rather like that of controlled "divisions," even though they were legally separate from their top holding company, which was in turn dominated by powerful majority stockholding families (Mitsui, Iwasaki [Mitsubishi], Sumitomo, and Yasuda). SCAP reforms liquidated the holding companies and even split a few larger operating subsidiaries (*e.g.,* their trading firms, Mitsubishi Heavy Industry, Nippon Steel, and Oji Paper), but, significantly, the banks were not broken up.[114] These same reforms forced the sale of the great family shareholdings, proceeds of which (ten-year bonds) were 95 percent wiped out in time by postwar inflation.[115] It is said that Kichiemon Sumitomo is virtually the only member of former *zaibatsu* families who has retained important wealth.[116]

SCAP also purged roughly two thousand of the top executives in the former *zaibatsu* firms,[117] leaving control to a new professional group of their middle managers without appreciable equity interests. Today, at the highest ranks, they now work for salaries in the range of $50,000 to $75,000 compared to the $150,000 to $300,000 paid annually to their American counterparts. These figures are, however, somewhat misleading because so much of the Japanese executives' compensation comes in the form of facilities, services, expense accounts, and intangibles. Also in the postwar period the use of the former *zaibatsu* names or trademarks was discontinued, but after the Japanese Peace Treaty in 1952, former sister firms again began to merge and regroup under the old names, though several major firms (especially Fuji [Yasuda]) no longer use the *zaibatsu* name. See Appendix VII for a list of the other operating companies in the three traditionally based *keiretsu* represented in their respective Presidents' Clubs.

Though the "big three" *keiretsu,* as regrouped under the old flags, little resemble the prewar structures, these former *zaibatsu* lineages are still in a class by themselves[118] based on their prominence and size; in another sense they are the generic epitome of today's banking *keiretsu* (*kinyu keiretsu*) because their banks are at the center of their activities too. Their intertwining personal relations and clannish pride symbolized by the old trademarks have made them the prime examples of the new national financing groups under discussion here, each centered around a leading bank. There are, besides these "big three," several other such financial alignments, mostly around the larger "city banks" (see Appendix VII). Among the most important are the alignments around the Fuji Bank, the Sanwa Bank, and the Daiichi-Kangyo Bank, although each of the fourteen major banks have their string of major client companies. Because of their national importance, the top thirteen "city banks," are listed below, along with the Bank of Tokyo;[119]

Commercial Banks	Paid-up Capital ($1,000)	Deposits 1971 ($1,000)	Employees
Dai-Ichi Kangyo Bank	175,324	15,016,025	23,011
Fuji Bank	163,636	12,727,103	16,324
Sumitomo Bank	163,636	12,314,389	14,649
Mitsubishi Bank	163,636	12,008,373	15,907
Sanwa Bank	163,636	11,082,701	15,746
Tokai Bank	123,376	8,638,912	12,733
Mitsui Bank	90,909	8,353,162	11,037
Kyowa Bank	77,922	5,955,324	10,933
Daiwa Bank	77,922	5,406,097	8,807
Bank of Kobe	58,441	4,872,107	8,251
Bank of Tokyo	64,935	4,221,012	5,050
Saitama Bank	52,597	4,157,863	7,340
Taiyo Bank	51,948	3,702,123	6,852
Hokkaido Takushoku Bank	38,961	3,525,954	6,085

For a foreigner to fully appreciate the banking *keiretsu,* he must pay special attention to the key roles of the "city bank" and also pay attention to the trading company within each *keiretsu.* Banking in Tokyo, like most everything else Japanese, has some very unusual features. The bank's role cannot be appreciated without understanding its public function, for the city banks are highly regulated, quasi-public institutions, and thus their superior obligation is to the financial mechanisms implementing Japanese industrial policy, to be discussed later, and their operations and interest rates are well insulated from market forces.

Essentially, the bank draws in extraordinarily high Japanese personal savings (three times the American rate), plus increases in money supply drawn from the Bank of Japan, and rations them to those that are presumed to be the most deserving manufacturing firms among its *keiretsu* clientele. Such a critical function involves high public obligations that are enforced by law. In the first place, there are only fourteen so-called "city banks"[120] and some sixty-four provincial banks, plus several special-purpose banks including the Bank of Tokyo, which is a somewhat different foreign-exchange bank.[121] The above city banks have foreign-exchange privileges and drawing rights on the Bank of Japan. Actually, all banks are legally supposed to be able to borrow from the Bank of Japan, but, in fact, only city banks do so regularly. The some sixty-four "provincial banks" service smaller businesses in the outlying areas. Medium and small business depend on special banking institutions operating under separate enabling statutes and lending at higher rates of interest. City bank loans to individuals have only in 1972 climbed from 2 percent to a still meagre 4.5 percent of total lending.

In sum, then, the city banks serve the modern sector, but also they provide over 80 percent of the external funds even for financing of plant and equipment but on a commercial bank basis—relatively short terms but regularly renewed (*"tanki korogashi"*). Having been accorded such a privileged public function, it is understandable that city banks have, until recently, been limited by law as to interest rates and number of branches in their distribution of dividends to their shareholders,[122] and under the antimonopoly law they have been allowed to hold only 10 percent (changed from 5 percent in 1953) of the shares in any operating company.[123] Ranked themselves in Japanese banking, the banks are under constant pressure to maintain their own positions among the top ten. They too must maintain their "market share," just like the Japanese manufacturers. For this reason, the banks have become on occasion so committed to large industrial borrowers that they may be as dependent as they are depended upon. Industrial firms in turn borrow from their banks to increase plant capacity simply to "keep up with the Joneses." This "borrowed bigness," often insensitive to underlying market forces, causes overcapacity, excessive competition, dumping overseas, and "profitless prosperity." Ultimately it is a bootstrap gamble on its self-inducing market growth, which has so far turned out well enough. In the harsher climate of the 1970s, it might be imprudent to extrapolate from these successes to ever higher plateaus of growth at the same rates.

Though only a brief sketch, this summary of the money mechanisms underlying Japanese industrial expansion nevertheless properly focuses attention on the public regulatory and investment functions of the city bank at the center of the *keiretsu*. To complete the picture, it is necessary only to see, then, that the role of the Bank of Japan, which is 55 percent government owned, is to vary the credit supply by monetary (reserves, lending and discount rates) techniques in order to heat up or cool off the economy as desired. Loans to city banks are also varied by differential (penalty) interest rates and informal "window guidance" (*madoguchi kisei*), whereby the Bank of Japan tightens credit by simply telling the city banks to cut their loans across the board by a certain percentage, leaving it to them to do it through the "window" as applicants apply.[124] The OECD has well said that, because city banks are in a constant state of "over-loan" and their clients "over-borrowed" (85 percent debt and 15 percent equity), this puts the Bank of Japan in the peculiar position of being a bank of first recourse, rather than a central bank's usual position of final resort. Needless to say, this entire syndrome, amounting to over-loaning and over-borrowing, has caused much eyebrow raising in the western banking world[125] but has resulted in nothing but high performance in Japan to date. Serious questions do, however, underlie these differences of Japanese and western banking. Are the Japanese practices of mixing commercial banking with investment and central banking with ordinary capital lending viable in any other than the most expansive periods such as those of the postwar period to date? Is it viable only in the highly restricted international posture assumed by Japan to date? Given the high official role in funding and decision-making, can other nations afford to treat Japanese companies nurtured in this way as if they were operating in accordance with market forces? Other aspects of this so-called "borrowed bigness," "excessive competition," and "profitless prosperity" will be discussed in the next section on government and business. Enough has been said, however, to indicate the importance of the bank, both industrially and nationally as well as internationally, in the *keiretsu* structure. In Japan's global thinking the *keiretsu* trading company has an even larger role.

The largest trading companies in the world are not in the U.S. or in

Europe but in Japan. They are unique national institutions led by the "big four" (Mitsubishi Corporation, Mitsui Bussan, Marubeni, and C. Itoh); they have not only been prime movers in the nation's remarkable economic growth, but they have also had a potent global impact.[126] Their special importance to foreigners springs first from their functional role within the *keiretsu,* wherein they buy and market for sister companies to a degree.[127] Secondly, their international role is greatly enhanced by their extraordinary training and skills in solving both the Japanese and foreign businessmen's difficulties with Japanese language and culture. Conversely, these same difficulties have retarded direct marketing efforts by Japanese manufacturers in the international field.

The service aspect of the general trading company's role may be seen in their accounting records, which show that they have an extremely low margin (less than .2 percent of sales) on very high volume (e.g., Mitsubishi Corporation's $14 billion).[128] Incidentally, the *keiretsu* insurance companies and shipping companies seem to render similar services at bargain prices when required to enable their manufacturing siblings to deliver in a foreign market at a competitive price, though this behavior is probably most common in Mitsui, Mitsubishi, and Sumitomo.

The eleven major general trading companies and their major banking connections are as follows:[129]

Trading Company	*Keiretsu*	*Sales 1971 ($1,000)*
Mitsubishi Corporation	Mitsubishi	14,707,246
Mitsui & Co.	Mitsui	13,428,029
Marubeni Corporation	Fuji Bank	9,457,496
C. Itoh & Co.	Dai-Ichi-Kangyo	9,020,714
Sumitomo Shōji Kaisha	Sumitomo	6,451,746
Nissho-Iwai Co.	Sanwa and Dai-Ichi-Kangyo	6,251,909
Toyo Menka Kaisha	Mitsui	4,531,701
Toyota Motor Sales Co.	Tokai	3,722,964
Kanematsu-Gosho	Dai-Ichi-Kangyo	3,151,529
Ataka & Co.	Sumitomo	3,066,324
Nichimen Co.	Sanwa	2,980,220

In volume the big ten handle roughly 50 percent of Japanese exports and 60 percent of imports, and by volume they now handle about $75 billion annually; of this a major portion is domestic business, for they are as significant within Japan as they are externally. Typically, a top-ranking trading company has approximately ten thousand employees covering the world. They have personnel, both Japanese and foreign, stationed in most major cities, plus a roving staff that attends to existing markets in every country and searches for new customers or sources of raw material wherever they may be found at the best price.

However, the importance of the trading company is as much qualitative as quantitative. Besides their remarkable skill in cross-cultural, transnational transactions, the trading company routinely performs the following broader business functions:

1. Financing functions
2. Developmental functions
3. Organization and integration of business ventures
4. Distribution and marketing functions, both international and domestic

The investigative, financing, and entrepreneurial functions are important to the Japanese nation, as well as to the *keiretsu* industries specifically, especially in long-term developmental projects abroad to ensure reliable raw-material sources. To accomplish long-term reliability, the trading company often invests and participates in the operations of extractive industries abroad such as lumbering, coal, copper, and iron ore.

A prominent example is the steel industry. For its annual production of roughly 100 million tons of crude steel, Japan has to import 100 million tons of iron ore and roughly 50 million tons of coking coal. These enormous quantities cannot be handled by simple spot transactions in the international markets; rather, Japanese trading companies have joined in with local capital in places such as Australia (iron ore) and Canada (coal) to mine, transport, sell, export, and import as required to deliver regularly to the Japanese mills. Also, 25 percent of the same Japanese steel output is annually exported back to transoceanic markets; trading companies not only handle the sales and exports, but maintain yards overseas, provide the mills with market surveys, and finance the risk of credit extension to unknown foreign customers. Their services include advances of 80 percent of price to Japanese steel mills two months before the time of shipment abroad, then 20 percent when shipment is made, while the trading company's sales contract with the ultimate consumer may be net sixty or ninety days after delivery right into their overseas yard.[130]

The trading companies are also very important in Japan's technological revolution. They find new foreign machinery and processes, import sample units, and negotiate with the Japanese governmental officials controlling technological imports to acquaint them with the desirability of importing particular advanced plants and equipment. Trading companies even have real estate and general contracting facilities as well as building materials to assist in getting a plant in operation in Japan.

Looking outward, the trading companies also investigate, negotiate, and integrate many joint ventures for Japanese firms throughout the world. They also often invest themselves; for example, among the big ten trading companies, there are over four hundred controlled subsidiaries operating abroad. Of course, the trading company then participates in the export of equipment and the import of raw materials, often involving third-country to host-country transactions.[131]

Like everything else in Japan, the trading companies' function is shifting with continuous expansion. One negative trend is the tendency of the new heavy and chemical industries (70 percent of exports) to develop direct marketing channels, bypassing the trading firms, because of need for overseas assembly, repairs, and parts supply best handled by Japanese makers themselves.[132] Also, manufacturers of some consumer durables (*e.g.,* automobiles, electronics, and watches) are building their own international sales networks. Pharmaceuticals, toys, and personal accessories also seem to be less suitable for trading companies' transactions. In sum, roughly 30 percent of Japan's total exports and 20 percent of the nation's entire imports are now handled directly. But the continued vitality of these unique Japanese institutions is well shown by their five-fold increase in sales in the 1960s as compared to a three-fold growth in overall Japanese output.

In the future, then, trading companies are likely to strengthen in two other important areas: (1) the supply of fuel and raw materials from abroad, expected to increase at least 10 percent annually; (2) the rationalization of domestic retail business in which the multilayered, labor-intensive, inefficient wholesale system is expected to give way to large-scale retailing in supermarkets and the like.

Thus the trading company in any *keiretsu* has a key role, not only because it acts as the "foreign ministry" for its associates, but also because of its extraordinary sophistication and skill resulting from international specialization, global coverage, and a multifunctional approach. As one distinguished officer put it: "Trading companies are motivated by an awareness that their interest conforms to the national interest of Japan, and that they are also contributing to the well being of the people of the world through trade and development."[133]

However confidently the foregoing information about banking *keiretsu* may be offered for use of foreign enterprises contemplating Japanese ventures, it falls short of explaining the inner workings of this kind of financial *keiretsu* or its effect on overall competition. For one thing, the cast of firms in each *keiretsu* has changed some from year to year as a result of mergers and structural changes in the economy, but even more baffling is the variety of classifications to be found in any given year, even among Japanese writers, presumably because strong firms are only loosely related to any given *keiretsu*. In addition, there is no doubt that the Fuji, Sanwa, and Daiichi-Kangyo banking *keiretsu* have much less lateral liaison than Mitsubishi, Mitsui, or Sumitomo. So, too, the inner workings remain perplexing, not only because the sprawling *keiretsu* is extremely complex, but also because they are so subtle that our usual western analysis, based on a majoritarian mentality (and also its Japanese manifestations in the corporate law), confuses as much as it explains.

Eleanor Hadley's study[134] has been extremely useful in clarifying by careful scrutiny of data the very inadequacy of such analysis. In terms of western legal concepts (contract, ownership, and majoritarianism), the several crossties (cross-shareholding, interlocking directorates, lending, marketing, or liaison by corporate presidents), neither alone nor all together, amount to control as defined by corporate law or western majority decision-making. Cross-shareholding and interlocking directorates are dilute and unimportant by majoritarian analysis. The bank and the insurance company typically are the top shareholders but frequently neither holds even the mere maximum 10 percent allowed by law. Since each *keiretsu* typically has several financial companies (*i.e.,* the bank, the trust company, the life insurance company, the casualty insurance company), each of which often holds some sibling shares, their combined total is interesting, but it too seldom exceeds a minority interest, often a rather small minority. Even adding all sibling holdings, the total shareholding is, typically, still considerably less than 50 percent of firms nonetheless categorized as members of a certain bank's *keiretsu*.

Bank loans, by definition the key force in the banking *keiretsu,* are typically low by control standards, and the *keiretsu* bank is only the "primary bank." Looking at total loan contracts, key *keiretsu* siblings typically borrow from a half dozen banks, which by facile insiders-outsiders analysis is highly suspect. Similarly, the trading companies' percentage of total marketing is often little larger than that of outside, competitive traders. Likewise, the Presidents' Club obviously has no legal power to do anything but consult and plan. Western-style corporate or contractual *control* simply cannot be found, and this fact is satisfactorily demonstrated.

Still, the analysis does not tell the whole story or even the most important part. The next step, perhaps, in unraveling the inner workings is to start with Japanese thinking and business behavior.[135] Besides the government's preference for concerted action rather than free competition, two principles, which we have reviewed above, are particularly useful tools: (1) the familial insider-outsider psychology and the idea of hierarchical meritocracy; and (2) conciliar decision-making, especially its vertical dimensiion embodied in the *ringi-sei,* which acts as a solvent for the rigidity of the formal corporate hierarchy. These operate interstitially and explain more than the corporate law. Asserting their own superiority and unconsciously their own interests (seen no doubt as a kind of *noblesse oblige*), top management in each individual company, then at the next level in *keiretsu* management collectively (symbolized in the Presidents' Club), and finally in *zaikai* at the apex (Chapter II) —all bound together—constitute a special aristocratic insider interest (and also a trustee posture). Here is a group of people controlling at all levels of the decision-making process; these men alone essentially run the firms, *keiretsu,* and *zaikai* but in the Japanese tradition they run things interstitially from tea houses, by discussion, consensus, or compromise. In the end they manage resolutely and as effectively as a 51 percent vote, whether in the old-style holding company (*honsha*) or in the west. Indeed, the 51 percent vote is simulated, after all is decided, in a ritualistic ceremony once removed from real politics. This admittedly more diffuse managerial stratum is the legitimate successor of the old oligarchy or, by remote analogy, the old *samurai.*[136]

Important here is the fact that majoritarianism is not only un-Japanese but largely nonfunctional in publicly held corporations the world over, superficialities of the law to the contrary notwithstanding. The major Japanese corporations under discussion here are all publicly held; *ergo* their shareholder majorities (even director majorities in many Japanese corporations) have little policy function because management consistently commands the routine proxies needed to implement its goals. Especially in Japan, the shareholder meetings are perfunctory at best and theatrical at worst. Management is supported and opposed from the floor, depending on its fee-paying arrangements with "general-meeting pros" (*sōkaiya*), sometimes residing in the underworld.[137]

What is more important at the banking *keiretsu* level is the traditional Japanese conciliar technique required for successful operation of a confederation, which in business, at least, has been usually unsuccessful elsewhere. In conclusion, the *keiretsu,* which is in organizational principle little more than a confederation, is uniquely effective in Japan because of the familial insider-outsider psychology (very effective to integrate nationally for international competition) and the efficacy of conciliar decision-making techniques. In Japan, these can mold an operable unit from such an unlikely organizational pattern, but some of the resultant units pull together better than others, and it is clear that some of the journalistic treatment of *keiretsu* makes too much of the Sanwa, Daiichi-Kangyo, and Fuji (as well as other lesser groups).[138]

The intriguing question remaining is: why have shareholders and lending patterns developed as they have? Typically, major modern operating firms borrow from several banks and have shareholders among their top ten, which are from entirely different *keiretsu*. In other words, if each major bank (by some *keiretsu* analysis, presumably in the driver's seat) traded all of its shares in outside firms for shares of *keiretsu* firms, and did the same for loans, its *keiretsu* control would be vastly stronger by employing the very same resources. How and why did this confusing diffusion of interests occur to cloud our armchair *keiretsu* analysis? The answer seems to be in the way funds for lending became available over the past twenty years, coupled with the ups and downs of tight money for balance of payment reasons. Each primary bank simply was unable to supply all of the capital needed, when it was needed, for any of its core siblings. Also, there was doubtless some desire to spread the risk although legally there is no limit on bank loans to any individual company.

Enterprise keiretsu

As the name implies, the enterprise (*kigyō*) *keiretsu* is a much smaller-scaled organization than the banking *keiretsu*; it is a family of firms owned or dominated by a major manufacturing or trading enterprise. The key organizing principle is commercial dependence of the many lesser firms on the major. The dependent firms are of three types: (1) ordinary subsidiaries (51 percent); (2) affiliates (less than 50 percent); and (3) subcontractors.

Based on a single major firm, the enterprise *keiretsu* is overall a much more controlled, but much smaller-scaled, unit than the headless conglomerate of majors found in the banking *keiretsu,* but the enterprise *keiretsu* can still be quite extensive and complex. As a prime example, in 1971 Matshushita Electric had 536 subsidiaries and affiliates, in 195 of which Matsushita held over 50 percent. C. Itoh & Co. is another important example with 189 affiliates (61 majority owned) of which more than two-thirds are industrial. In 1971, Mitsui & Co. had even more affiliates (370; 177 were controlled), though their total capital (103 billion yen) was less, overall, than those of C. Itoh (193 billion yen). Taking all subsidiaries and affiliates in which the main enterprise held at least 10 percent, the FTC[139] discovered that Japan's top nonfinancial 100 firms held 7,612 affiliates, of which 37 percent were majority owned. These top 100 firms averaged 76 affiliates, and Matsushita, with 536, had the most.

When it is recalled that the Japanese law does not yet require consolidation of parent-subsidiary accounts, it becomes obvious that the enterprise *keiretsu* characteristic of Japanese majors makes the foreigner's evaluation of the same majors' performances difficult at the threshold of a venture. First, there is often much activity for which the parent is in fact obligated but which is difficult to see from the outside. Second, the parent can manipulate transactions within certain limits to produce accounting results desired in various parts of its empire. Also important is the risk that a Japanese major will regard its joint ventures with foreigners as but one more manipulable—possibly even expendable—subsidiary, whereas foreigners are likely to regard it as a more independent operation.[140]

Even more invisible, legally, are the numerous, wholly dependent subcontractors[141] encompassed within the enterprise *keiretsu* framework to perform specific services or manufacture components. We have already noted the profound effect this subcontracting practice has on the Japanese economy. We now need a glimpse of its business mechanisms.

Taking Isuzu Motors, a major motor vehicle manufacturer, Broadbridge[142] traced in detail the business relations and functions of four subcontractors in descending scale from 151 to 2 employees, all four of which firms were dependent on, and part of, the Isuzu enterprise *keiretsu* but not owned by Isuzu at all. The vivid detail set forth is worth summarizing here. Company A had 151 employees in 1964 and was dependent on Isuzu in the following typical way: (1) about 80 percent of its sales went to Isuzu; (2) Isuzu guaranteed one-third of Company A's loans (loans from Chūshō Kigyō Kinyū Kōko and the Jōnan Shinyō Kinko, since city banks are not interested in such small companies), amounting to 95,000,000 yen as against an equity capital of only 10,000,000 yen; (3) Company A's machinery was either bought secondhand from Isuzu or rented from Isuzu at 2 percent per month; (4) some retired workers from Isuzu were hired at about half their pre-retirement wage. Despite its dependence on Isuzu for funds, machinery, work force, and sales, Company A was not owned by Isuzu and was making business progress as a budding medium-sized firm.

Company B with eighteen employees was also independently owned and had been largely dependent upon Company A as a sub-subcontractor. It had a debt equity ratio of 94 to 6 percent and sold 70 percent of its output to one electrical firm, after breaking away from Company A in sales but not in other ways. Company B also had five tiny subcontractors of its own.

Company C had six employees and was making one small part for Company A on subcontract; Company A was in turn delivering it on subcontract. Company D had only two employees besides the owner; they were drilling holes in one auto part at the rate of 4,000 per month under a subcontract to Company A in turn subcontracted to Isuzu. Both C and D companies worked on an exacting piecework basis in dingy, even dangerous, facilities nine hours per day, six days a week, barely able in good times to eke out a profit after paying the price of high-interest debt capital.

Though Isuzu's enterprise *keiretsu* is not described in full,[143] this vivid glimpse does show how subcontracting works, in the machinery field especially, in some aspects like the nineteenth-century cottage-industry in Europe. During the 1961–65 period, the plight of all such small companies (like A, B, C, and D) was a classical example of "squeezing" (*shiwayose*), which occurs in tight money periods.[144] Typically the Bank of Japan, by raising the reserves, discount rates, or restricting funds, causes the city banks to call in funds, causing the majors to reduce orders to subcontractors and to reduce cash payment on delivery (usually 30 percent to say 10 percent with the rest due on long-term, six to nine months). Stronger subcontractors like Company A might survive by similar squeezing of their own subcontractors, but ultimately the domino effect sets in and multiple bankruptcies result at the end of the squeeze.

Our overview of the enterprise *keiretsu,* with its subsidiaries and dependent subcontractors, was intended to expose not only the concrete rigors of Japan's industrial dualism but also the dependence of large firms for their highly lauded performance on the miserable squeezing of many underprivileged Japanese, both entrepreneurs and workers. Without consolidated accounting requirements, the large firms have also been able to keep the subsidiaries' part in their productive technique from showing. Of course the very high "social cost" of subcontracting is quite beyond mere accounting. Fortunately improvements are being made in the lower tier by way of consolidations with more and more healthy medium-sized firms emerging as a result, and, again, critics of the dualistic harshness are less successful in suggesting plausible alternatives that at the same time will produce growth.

Trade Associations and Cartels

If, in Japan, the foreign enterpriser's ambience is restricted by both kinds of *keiretsu* described above, they are conditioned even more severely by the wondrous proliferation of trade associations and cartels since the Antimonopoly Law was amended (1953).[145] Despite their "un-American" character, such organizations are essential to the Japanese way.[146] We have already seen (Chapter II) how the ubiquitous industrial and trade associations have become federations (Keidanren, Dōyūkai, Nikkeiren, and Nihon Shōkō Kaigisho) at the top to influence politics and economic policy. We must eschew here details of cartelization since World War II, as well as the strands leading back to wartime experience. Essentially, though, the current structure of trade associations and cartels dates back to textile groupings in late Meiji period; and more directly it can be traced to beginnings in the 1920s. Today's types are a mild synthesis resulting from clashes between conservative forces (mostly in MITI) that are striving to reproduce some of the strictures of prewar, German-type control cartels (*Wirtschaftsgruppen*)[147] and progressive forces (initially in SCAP) attempting to suppress cartels completely as envisaged in the original version of the Antimonopoly Law (1947) and Trade Association Law (1948). A balance was struck in the 1953 amendments to the Antimonopoly Law by providing (Art. 8) for "rationalization" and "recession" cartels supervised by the FTC and abolishing the 1948 Trade Association Law, which had rigorously confined trade associations to innocuous purposes such as exchanges of scientific information, standardization, and the like. But informal guidance cartels are an important device in postwar regulations.

Actually, before MITI's pressures for better organization and control of horizontal industrial groups had run their course in the 1950s, the rationalization cartels and the recession cartels contemplated by the law had become relatively unimportant compared to a numerous array of special laws passed after 1953 to authorize cartels in specified industries. In a final phase, MITI utilized effectively "guidance cartels" on an entirely informal basis, without enabling legislation, to curtail output in certain industries suffering from overcapacity. These guidance cartels ordinarily operate through the trade associations and remain largely beyond public scrutiny, but in the famous *Idemitsu* case and the *Sumitomo* case,[148] the lack of MITI's legal authority to cut back on production (*sōtan*) in both instances came to the attention of the public when these major corporations resisted the "guidance." Ultimately, however, they were brought into line for a settlement by governmental pressure. Whether it was legally authorized by the Diet or not is still a question.[149]

Nothing reflects better than the guidance cartels the difficulties of rank and file Japanese officialdom in living with the antimonopoly idea in the modern sector. Because of the wartime experience, perhaps, both the government and the big-business bureaucracies felt an acute need for more horizontal industrial organization and control; the government has insisted especially upon business collusion in the modern and international sector to implement its investment, production, and export controls as auxiliaries to growth inducement, planning, and restructuring of heavy industries during the past twenty years. Business, too, has generally favored more lateral liaisons effected by trade associations, as noted by a member of the Japanese FTC: "Businessmen with a long tradition of cartels and trade associations can understand regulations arrived at after discussion among the competitors much more readily than they can the bizarre notion that concerted action constitutes an unreasonable restraint of trade."[150] This attitude is not easy to absorb for the foreigner who comes from the tradition articulated by Adam Smith: "People of the same trades seldom meet together even for merriment and diversion, but the conversation ends in a conspiracy against the public or in some contrivance to raise prices."[151] Without arbitrating between the two philosophies on their merits, it is clear enough that Japanese cartelization to avoid competition intramurally may work unfairness in dealing with outsiders subject to antitrust policies such as those of the U.S.

No doubt an understanding of the trade association's regulatory role, especially the prevalence of cartels in international trade and investment, is critical to successful integration and operation in Japan. Some 42 percent (by value) of all Japanese exports are cartelized. And this is not a situation about which "outsiders" can be "holier than thou"; for example, the American pleas for "voluntary quotas" have nurtured some of these export cartel tendencies because industries producing textiles, plywood, steel, footware, and flatware, and the like must organize into cartels to allocate among themselves the overall exports allowed by the "voluntary" quotas.[152] In fact, it has been questioned as to whether the U.S. government's role in these "quota talks" is consistent with the American laws.[153]

Also important to foreign manufacturing are the domestic Japanese investment quotas and credit facilities rigidly allocated by predetermined "market shares," which are in turn dependent upon past sales. This market allocation by production capacity leaves little room for newcomers and severely limits expansion by aggressive pricing and sales efforts used routinely by the Japanese abroad.

In a country where banking is "God" and production is "king," commerce has always, perhaps necessarily, taken a back seat to industry, and salesmen, if not underprivileged, certainly do not yet pace business as they sometimes do elsewhere. Foreigners are expected to accept the limitations of trade associations and cartels, or, as Japanese officials expect of them, "to do in Japan as the Japanese do," which is to conform to the prescribed "pecking order." In the 1970s, however, marketing and distribution innovations may well come into their own, as Japanese bureaucrats and businessmen continue to see the inefficiency in the traditional (but heretofore highly protected) distribution network. Indeed, since 1970, a marketing revolution seems to be getting under way.

As noted earlier (Chapter I), many foreigners have found the trade associations and cartels discriminatory against foreigners, especially during the period of strict foreign exchange and export-import licensing. Whether there has been domestic discrimination or not, there certainly has been an abundance of the usual charges of violation of the association rules, as well as international practices in trade. The uses and alleged abuses of cartels (*i.e.,* dumping and "neocolonialism") in the implementation of Japanese economic policy abroad and their effect on market structure and competition are discussed elsewhere; it is necessary here only to be aware that industry-wide trade associations and cartels are ubiquitous parts of the supracorporate business structure that is of great consequence to any Japan operation. With few exceptions, the integration of foreign operations into the trade associations has been incomplete and generally uncomfortable for both "outsiders" and "insiders." One may expect that they will prove to be extra-legal obstacles, if legal controls are finally lifted in the near future. A recent and not unusual example of association resistance to foreign competition is the objection raised by the Japan Auto Tire Manufacturers Association to Firestone's proposal to purchase Otsu Tire Company, and the "tissue paper" battle caused by the *chirigami* association when a joint venture decided to produce sheet tissue as well as rolls.[154]

Government Guidance of Free Enterprise

In economic policy, the Japanese government has steered its own mixed course between the poles of free enterprise and nationalized industry, drawing on its own wartime experience with tight German-type cartel controls and at the same time naturalizing, with ever greater confidence, some aspects of American antitrust policy introduced in the occupation days (1945–52).[155] At this point, we shall scrutinize the confluence of these two different regulatory approaches (German and American), relying on the background already sketched in this and prior chapters.

For perspective, four basic facts concerning Japan's century of industrialization (1870–1970) must be recalled. First, Japan's new heavy industrial complex has long been an instrument of national policy, initially in the Meiji period, endeavoring to become "rich and strong" (*fukoku kyōhei*) and now to become richer and stronger "surpassing the West." Second, heavy industry is in Japan a deliberate latter-day acquisition, not a natural evolution over the centuries. Third, with the aid of a vigorous group of entrepreneurs in this process, government officials have always been the instigating strategists making heavy industry not only a national mission but also a public pursuit. Fourth, the way in which modern industry was established in Japan was deliberately dualistic; modern industry was successfully brought to Japan "piggy back" and superimposed on small-scale traditional industries, which along with agriculture were expected to, and did, bear much of the burden. The result has been a national disposition to think of the two tiers as naturally separate—the western overlay built for national and public purposes, the old left untouched to supply the work force in building the new. Therefore, inequality of credit, wages, and opportunity between the two tiers was usually not seen as mistreatment of the lower tier; it was a natural result of the success of the separate national mission of which all were supposedly quite patriotically proud.

Given the late timing and its nature as a government-directed, forced march, it seems entirely clear that the success of Japan's modern industry could not have been left simply to the vagaries of the "invisible hand" in the market, which would likely have produced more tourist hotels, lipstick, beer, and teahouses than steel mills. It is also clear that immediate postwar antitrust policy, once SCAP shifted to rehabilitation of Japanese industries in the "cold war" context, paid insufficient attention to Japan's stage of development, institutional infrastructure, and past experiences—granting, as we do, that after adjustments and on balance its effect has been good. Reduced to its essence, early antitrust policy, after the "trust-busting" phase,[156] was intended to ensure future "economic democracy," which was thought to be a necessary concomitant of "political democracy" and was underwritten by the new Constitution (1947). Structurally, the kind of "democracy" SCAP envisaged meant popular sovereignty, which, legally, has always meant limited government power (*i.e.,* restricting official powers sufficiently to ensure personal freedoms requisite to meaningful popular choices at the ballot box). In western experience with governmental structure, effectively limited power has also meant divided power—functionally, geographically, or otherwise.

As a concomitant of political democracy, economic democracy implemented by the antitrust laws presumably proceeds on the same premises: it is necessary to limit economic power by division of the market among free competitors. Thus, concentration must be avoided by protecting the conditions for competition; and some would say that economic democracy requires the protection of numerous competitors, as well as competition itself—that is, no one is allowed to win.[157]

As we shall see, the foregoing American doctrine has had its difficulties in adjusting to Japanese guidance in the modern sector. In the first place, competitive conditions are necessarily quite different in Japan's two sectors of the persisting dualistic economy. In the lower tier, competition is endemic and, in fact, often excessive, causing heavy incidence of bankruptcy, lack of quality control, and instability in light manufacturing, such as parts, toys, and grass paper. Here the antitrust policy has become centered on "unfair trade practices."

In fact, however, the Antimonopoly Law (1947) was not imported into Japan with the problems of the small and medium sector primarily in mind, although it is here that it may have become most effective; it was primarily intended to create "economic democracy" from fragments of the "busted" *zaibatsu* empires. But it was here, too, that foreign antitrust ideology conflicted most sharply with Japanese national experience and international strategies. Such strategy was, indeed, required to achieve economies of scale in restructuring toward internationally competitive heavy industry. This often seemed to require avoidance of "excessive competition" at home, for there was vigorous competition for status in the oligopolistically structured modern sector. In a word, the real market competitors were seen as the "outsiders" (foreign business), and to "conquer" them Japanese officialdom deemed industry-wide domestic cooperative efforts as more appropriate tactics than the atomized internal competitive regime underwritten by the original antitrust laws. On balance, their judgment has been vindicated to date, but it poses problems for the future and especially for the foreign corporation dealing now with this latter-day united front from Japan.

Also, ironically, the antimonopoly laws originally passed in 1947 were in some respects more stringent than those in effect in their more congenial homeland (U.S.). For example, cartels were outlawed completely; monopoly power alone, not its exercise, was illegal; overlapping shareholding was prohibited; and mergers required prior approval. The history of the statutory revisions (*i.e.,* amendments of 1949 and 1953 and unsuccessful proposals in 1958, 1962, and again in 1966) is to be found elsewhere. Suffice it to say here that the law has been reshaped to accommodate governmental planning and controls that implement the official growth strategy; the law now permits Japanese industry to organize nationally "to surpass the west." Below we shall discuss the restrictive functions of the Antimonopoly Law, as revised and domesticated, in protecting competition; and then summarize, impressionistically, overall mechanisms (heretofore mentioned in specific contexts only) used by the government for positive restructuring and growth inducement.

Antitrust Law in Japan

Paradoxically, the Japanese beneficiaries of postwar antitrust legislation are now using it not against domestic concentration nor against collusive restraints in the home markets so much as in the field of small business "unfair business practices" and for incoming foreign licensing and joint ventures, in the latter as a substitute for foreign exchange and foreign investment controls now being dismantled in the international "liberalization" process.[158]

We have seen that the Japanese have never been able to place their industrial fate in the hands of the abstracted theories of market forces that are presumably universally sound and free of cultural bias and parochialisms. Indeed with modern institutionalized labor bargaining and with today's huge governmental spending, market forces alone do not have the ambience to work effectively in most western societies. Rather than trust the market, the Japanese have emphasized context and timing, in the German tradition, and consequently internal competition between their new heavy industrials has not often seemed the best way to induce growth, especially growth in the right direction.

Rather, a comprehensive hierarchical system supplemented by collusive horizontal cartels, all under the umbrage of the family-nation concept, has seemed better calculated to serve Japanese needs than conditions of equal opportunity and competitive performance.

There was another difficulty with the original Antimonopoly Law as passed in 1947. It was too restrictive in many respects, more so than anything to be found in the American law models existing at that time.

Such exuberance on the part of the SCAP reformers, though doubtless well-intentioned and in a sense understandable given the ambiguity resulting from an emergent cold war posture, was, nonetheless, inappropriate for Japanese rehabilitation. The inevitable amendments that occurred in 1949 and 1953 not only reflected Japanese needs but also brought the resultant Japanese law back closer to American doctrine.[159]

Some of the more avant-garde features, now abolished, are essential to an understanding of the law as it remains today. The original plan in the law was apparently to incorporate not only the essential features of the Sherman, the Clayton, and the Federal Trade Commission Acts but also to include refinements of antitrust doctrine developed by the American courts and administrative agencies as well. Art. 1 of the law shows a dual purpose: first, to prohibit "monopolization," "unreasonable restraint of trade," and "unfair business practices"; second, to promote enterprises and develop the national economy. This negative-positive dichotomy set the stage for a major debate that resulted in changes to harmonize efforts for the protection of competition with the necessity to rebuild the national economy. These two purposes, both important, have tended to fall within the jurisdiction of the FTC and MITI respectively.[160] At the same time, these two agencies have often opposed each other on policy issues stemming from their differences of perspective and function.

The latter positive regulatory measures to promote the national economy, within the Antimonopoly Law's conception, required a governmental agency to administer the law. In American fashion, the Fair Trade Commission (Kōsei Torihiki Iinkai) was established by the law,[161] providing for a chairman and, finally, four members appointed by the prime minister. Reporting directly to the prime minister's office, such an independent regulatory agency was an awkward novelty in Japan then and remains so today, with exceptional powers and legal practices (*i.e.,* the "substantial evidence rule" and "primary jurisdiction" problems, as well as special appeals to the Tokyo High Court). But by 1971 the FTC had become well established with 356 employees and 7 branch offices.[162] It had gone through two phases in the past twenty years: the first decade after the peace treaty (1952) was a period of adjustment, as the law was being constantly revised, cut back, and reinterpreted; but about 1960, especially in the area of "unfair business practices," the FTC and the Antimonopoly Law began to grow roots in Japanese soil, as its potentials began to be appreciated by consumers, academicians, and certain segments of business and government as well.

The act, which is in one hundrerd articles (ten major parts), has the omnibus purpose of developing, democratically, a sound national economy and protecting the general consumer.[163] MITI has dominated the developmental function with a different philosophy (controlled growth), but the FTC has pursued the developmental purpose in its own jurisdiction by two major techniques: first, prohibitions against monopolization, unreasonable trade restraints, and unfair business practices; and second, in the positive regulatory functions of promoting entrepreneurial initiative, employment, and increased national income for the benefit of three distinct divisions within the population—businessmen, employees, and general consumers. Such an economic magna carta inevitably has found many tensions built up within itself. With its maturation in Japan, the law has shifted, both by amendment and interpretation, toward a "rule of reason" and away from the strict per se violation philosophy originally embodied in the act. This means, as we have noted, that it is retrogressing toward an approximation of American standards.

The need that had always been felt by the Japanese bureaucracy (mainly MITI) for planning and controls found its toehold in the legal definition of "private monopolization," which forbade "substantial restraints of competition in any particular field of trade" if they were "contrary to the public interest." Soon after enactment two fundamental opinions arose as to what "public interest" meant in this context: the first view was that any economic order that restrains free competition contravenes the public interest per se, while the second view held that although free competition was the accepted rule, the public interest had a much broader national meaning often transcending the need of free competition. The per se argument was espoused originally by the FTC and certainly was underwritten by the original act, except that, as noted above, Art. 1 originally embodied, potentially, both interpretations, and it remains unchanged today to support the second view above. No doubt the test implied by "contrary to public interest"[164] is an additional test to the key phrase "a substantial restraint of competition," similar to the Clayton Act language,[165] which is intended to substantially lessen competition or tend to create a monopoly.

The original act (Arts. 4 and 5) used the per se test for price fixing, restrictive production, and allocation of markets and restraints on environment. Original Art. 8 required a stricter standard against monopoly than that found in the U.S. law: the Japanese law had a per se test, whereas the U.S. law struck down only monopolies subject to abuse.[166] The same was true for Arts. 10 and 11 that make any cross-shareholding, as well as interlocking directorates (Art. 13), in competing firms illegal. Merger law (Art. 15) was also more stringent than the American rules since the Japanese law required prior approval, and holding companies were outlawed completely (Art. 9).

By the 1953 amendment, Arts. 4 and 5 (per se test for cartel activity) were abolished, and Art. 8 was rewritten to incorporate parts of the Trade Association Act (1948), which was then abolished.[167] The new Art. 8 permits trade-association activities to be subject only to enumerated prohibitions (*e.g.,* they are not allowed to "substantially restrict competition in any particular field of trade"). Arts. 24-3 and 24-4 permit "depression cartels" and "rationalization cartels" respectively, and Art. 22 provides for special cartels and trade-association activities under special laws. Such special statuses did thereafter proliferate into a large number of important antitrust-law exemptions by special law.

Likewise, the provisions on cross-shareholding, interlocking directorates, and mergers (Arts. 10, 11, 13, and 15 respectively) were changed to permit these arrangements, unless it was found that they "substantially restrained competition in any particular field of trade." This really made such practices free, subject only to the standards of Art. 3. Thereafter, a series of cases[168] was appealed to the Tokyo High Court for interpretation of Art. 3, providing "No entrepreneur shall effect private monopolization or shall undertake any unreasonable restraint of trade."

As a result, monopolization has come to mean roughly what it means in the U.S.; namely, mere monopoly is not so much a problem as its abuse.

As far as "unreasonable restraint" is concerned, the Tokyo High Court has given that phrase a much narrower meaning than it would seem to imply (*i.e.,* Sherman Act, §1). After eliminating the per se restraints (Arts. 4 and 5 deleted in 1953), the courts further limited "unreasonable restraints" in the *Asahi Shimbunsha* case in 1953,[169] wherein an agreement among publishers of newspapers, allocating territories to distributors, found in unreasonable restraint by the Fair Trade Commission, was approved by reversal in the Tokyo High Court on the grounds that the restraint prohibited did not apply to vertical restraints. The only restraints forbidden would be those placed upon the publishers horizontally.

This Tokyo High Court decision is also the clue to the important emphasis on "unfair business practices," which thereafter became perhaps the most significant part of the Antimonopoly Law. Following the Tokyo High Court's suggestion there, the Fair Trade Commission has, by scheduled notifications, issued several general and specific designations of unfair trade practices in certain trades.

Except for Art. 9 outlawing holding companies, which was held firm, the other provisions against corporate controls (interlocking directorates, cross-shareholding, mergers, and the like) have become little more than auxiliary provisions, subject to the important condition that they may not cause "substantial restraint of competition in any particular field or trade." This standard includes the usual definitional refinements of "marketing area," "restraint," "competition," and levels of functional organization familiar to antitrust lawyers everywhere and subject to case-by-case expansion and contraction.

The foregoing outline of the development and current status of Japan's Antimonopoly Law serves to indicate its current vitality in several areas. Particularly, it shows the law's accommodation to the imperatives of governmental planning and control which is deemed best accomplished by extensive horizontal, industry-wide trade associations and cartels, especially in the international sector,[170] where it follows in a sense the Webb Pomerene Act.[171]

There remains, however, a provision of the Antimonopoly Law (Art. 6) specifically applicable to foreign controls. It is as follows:

Article 6. No entrepreneur shall enter into an international agreement or an international contract which contains therein such matters as coming under the purview of unreasonable restraint of trade, or unfair business practices.
2. In the event that an international agreement or an international contract is concluded, every entrepreneur shall file a report of the said effect, together with a copy of the said agreement or contract (in case of a verbal agreement or contract, a statement demonstrating the contents thereof), with the Fair Trade Commission within thirty (30) days as from the day of its conclusion pursuant to the provisions of its Regulation.
3. The provisions of the preceding paragraph shall not apply to an agreement or contract regarding a single transaction (excluding such transactions as the delivery period of the object thereof exceeding one [1] year), or to any agreement or contract merely granting power of attorney on matters in commerce and trade (excluding agreement or contract containing conditions that restrict the business activities of the other party or parties).

This peculiar provision is explained by its legislative history. The occupation forces, deploring the cartel growth in prewar Japan and Germany, specifically sought to control such arrangements through Art 6 and Art. 8 (prohibiting trade-association activities). The law has been changed now to require only filing of such contracts.

Generally, the only "entrepreneurs" who have been jurisdictionally subject to the law have been Japanese,[172] unless, of course, a foreign enterprise happens to have a place of business in Japan.

In 1971, in the case of *Novo Industri A/S* v. *Kōsei Torihiki Iinkai*,[173] the Tokyo High Court dismissed an appeal by a Danish company against an FTC order which found that Novo's licensee, Amano Pharmaceutical, was responsible for an "unfair business practice" in that the Novo-Amano contract contained a clause prohibiting Amano from producing or selling competing products for three years after termination and required Amano to eliminate the clause. The court decided the appeal against Novo on the grounds that Novo had no standing to appeal, because Novo was not a respondent in the FTC proceeding, and the order ran against Amano only. The order was only an administrative action (public law) against Amano and did not affect the underlying private-law obligations between Novo and Amano. So Novo was not affected by the order and not entitled to appeal against it. The High Court decision is now on appeal to the Japanese Supreme Court. This opinion thus indicated that, though nonresident foreign parties may not be subjected to FTC jurisdiction, they also may not attack FTC actions indirectly attacking provisions of their contracts.

During the stringent foreign-exchange and foreign-investment controls, this section was largely inoperative as far as foreigners were concerned because all contracts (licensing as well as investment) had to be cleared by the Foreign Investment Council (Gaishi Shingikai) on which the FTC was represented to prevent violations of the Antimonopoly Law. With the progress of liberalization, the provisions in Art. 6 will become more important, especially to foreigners whose place of business is in Japan. In fact, the Fair Trade Commission had issued guidelines on foreign licensing and investment in 1968, which will be discussed in Chapter VI, and more recently (1971) the FTC has issued another set of regulations on Art. 6 filing requirements.[174]

Like the new labor laws, Japan's Antimonopoly Law is another example showing the vagaries of the American law infusion in postwar Japan and pointing up the dangers of assuming that the mother law may serve as a reliable guide to understanding the meaning of its Japanese progeny.

The Government and Economic Planning

We have already seen that, unlike the west, Japanese business has little disposition to regard its government's prominent regulatory role as intermeddling with the natural forces of the marketplace. For, strictly speaking, there are no such "natural forces" in the domestic market for the modern sector. There is, however, "excessive competition" (*katō kyōsō*),[175] but, in part, this is a fierce "status-competition"[176] for governmentally sponsored privilege, funding, and position in the industrial hierarchy.[177]

In contrast with American images is the popular Japanese image of "big business." Historically, the large modern corporation and its individual elite entrepreneurs (*samurai*) have always been seen as doing great things *for* Japan rather than *to* the consumer. Literally, in postwar Japan, the bigger the firm the better, not only as one's employer, but as a symbol of national pride. With such attitudes, the Japanese government has not until recently[178] been cast in a role of protector of the consumer against predatory, self-seeking big business, as it has on occasion in the U.S. Emphasis on producers rather than consumers, the need for planning, the national industrial mission, the public pursuit thereof, and thus the identity of business and government interests— all have created in the modern industrial sector a close working partnership initially inhospitable to antitrust doctrine from another tradition. For one thing, in the Japanese context high production may be realized even in a near monopoly situation, because the monopolistic firm, made up of permanent members working with mostly borrowed capital, are motivated to produce more to enhance their own security and the position of the firm, without regard for maximizing shareholder profit by usual monopoly behavior and pricing.[179]

A "Naïve" Model

Our final concern here is to catch an overall glimpse of the entire mechanism of the Japanese economy, the major features of which have been set out piecemeal above. It is clear that, if there is any first-cause-of-all-causes in Japanese economic success, it is the popular capacity to work and save at a rate about double anywhere else in the "free world." Equally important is the fact that most of these remarkable individual savings have gone into time deposits controlled by the banks and the government. This may not be accidental either; there was little other investment opportunity for the Japanese saver, and the "city bank" as despository was a convenient, easily controlled, gathering mechanism facilitating governmental surveillance.

High corporate savings in the modern sector also deserve a word. They have been enhanced by three factors, particularly:

1. Higher increases of productivity than wages (partly illusory because of an unbalanced [young], growing labor force);

2. Interest costs of massive debt capital (85 percent) tax deductible, and other tax advantages;

3. Manipulatable (unconsolidated) accounting has permitted a controlled dividend policy at a fixed rate.

Next, two fundamental points in the Japanese capital market are relevant:

1. The long-term interest rate has been officially fixed and stable below its free-market level, causing dwarfed bond and long-term credit markets; city bank interest rates are also controlled and not competitive between banks.

2. The market for equity securities is also relatively undeveloped for institutional rather than economic reasons. Most new issues have gone to prior owners by "rights offerings" at par (usually well below market), and the major portion of equity securities has been held by financial institutions and other corporations. In fact, the ratio of personal (individual) to corporate shareholding has shifted from 60/40 percent to 39/61 percent from 1950 to 1970.

The individual's savings thus go into the banks' easily controlled time deposits of six months or one year. These huge funds, controlled by the city banks and increased proportionately by the fact that the individual's tax burden and the government's budget are both relatively small, have meant that governmental monetary policies and banking mechanisms have been quite effective regulators of the economy, and fiscal policies have been less efficacious and less used, until very recently.

But before tracing down the monetary pipeline, we need to restate the two most important national goals and their structural implementation in the economy:

1. The first national goal has been, of course, to establish an internationally competitive heavy industrial complex.

2. The second goal has been to capture the share of the world market necessary for its sustenance.

No doubt this dual purpose has been a continued national mission implemented by the dual economy. This dualism has been in a sense caused by an officially induced oligopolistic market structure in the top sector (heavy industries), which has been supply oriented because of the resultant single-minded emphasis on growth and export. Periodic overcapacity (excessive competition) caused by overinvestment (as high as 35 percent of the GNP) is relieved by underselling abroad in the cyclical troughs by use of the uniquely effective worldwide network of the Japanese general trading company (*sōgō shōsha*).

Now let us return to the uses of money in pursuit of a heavy industrial complex and a place for it "in the sun." First, direct government subsidies and the government banks' loans have been very significant, especially in the earlier years (*e.g.*, the Japan Development Bank's early postwar subsidy of iron, shipping, coal, and electricity). Postal savings have also been a major source of government influence on investment policy.

Focusing on the even more important private "commercial" banking, the dual economy's two tiers are separately financed, the lower layer at higher rates and by different cooperative and provincial bank sources; the heavy modern sector has been financed largely (80 percent) by "city banks" backed by the Bank of Japan at fixed lower rates on short term (renewable), probably dictated by the deposit sources and desire for more bank control. We recall that the central bank "of last resort" is really a bank of "first resort," lending to the "over-loaned" city banks, which in turn lend capital (not only commercial funds) to the "over-borrowed" industrials (80 percent of capital).

Furthermore, this over-borrowing is little short of compulsory, because, as noted in Chapter III, the oligopolistic industrial firms in each industry are a chosen few that are limited by government import licenses for technology and raw materials, without which none of these modern firms could turn a wheel. In turn, the planned oligopolistic structure of the heavy industries means that each participant has its ranking, its "market share," within the industry again perpetuated (actually positions do change some) by pro rata import licensing and borrowing quotas; with constant and rapid growth, each firm must, therefore, constantly and rapidly increase its capacity commensurate with its market share and resultant credit capacity, whether short-term market demand or profit prognosis justifies the expansion or not.

Finally, looking at the export picture, when overcapacity results from a corporation's investing to protect its "market share" instead of profit potential, the excess produce is sold abroad (even dumped) by the ubiquitous trading sibling as long as the variable costs are recovered, since high fixed costs for debt (interest) and wages (life employment) cannot be avoided anyway. This is "market penetration" by forcing other world producers to move over and make room for the new Japanese position "in the sun." Still, there is probably no other way, and surely this whole process is also welcomed by consumers abroad, though it is now drawing some new criticism of Japanese consumers paying the higher prices at home (see Chapter VII, n. 67).

We must repeat ourselves in recalling attention to the last step. Costs are further cut to enhance penetrative powers by the subcontracting relationship between the dual layers. The small and medium industries not only supply components on subcontract at bargain prices because of lower wages, longer hours, and inferior working conditions but also are useful in Darwinian finance through the squeezing process (*shiwayose*) as a cushion to absorb the shock of credit tightening when balance-of-payment strictures require it or, more recently, when world opinion discourages further penetration.

By this very rough sketch, it is clear that the Bank of Japan (and the Ministry of Finance)[180] has been in a pivotal position of great leverage applied by simple monetary techniques. To recapitulate, with a high saving rate and bond and equity markets atrophied, industrials must come to the city banks for the full measure of capital to protect their market shares. The city banks, also attempting to maintain their market share, must come to the Bank of Japan for discount. In reverse, when balance-of-payments or "orderly marketing" requires it, the Bank of Japan tightens up the money flow by raising the discount rate or by restricting the volume of loans by window guidance (*madoguchi shidō*). Major industrials in turn pass on the burdens to their subcontractors by lessening orders, diminishing the portion paid in cash, or by lengthening the term of notes issued for the rest. Bankruptcy is inevitable for any firm whose loans are not renewed in such a credit structure; but this is not done to major firms; such major semi-public institutions cannot be allowed to go bankrupt (*e.g.,* Yamaichi Shoken). For small firms, however, Darwinism is the principle, and the unsound and inefficient fail literally by the thousands annually in the periodic credit squeezes. This process is leaving only the stronger firms in the lower tier; in fact, it seems that sounder middle-sized firms are emerging from each application of tight money policy and pressure from the young labor shortage and steadily rising beginning wages.

It is little wonder then that the Bank of Japan's discount rate has become almost as much a part of the Japanese popular culture as the daily baseball scores, for it has been almost uniquely effective among world monetary controls. There is a certain grim irony in reflecting on tactics whereby the necessary foreign markets are captured by sacrificing the indefensible rear guard, the expendable firms in the small and medium sectors. But critics have not suggested a plausible better way with a prognosis for anywhere near as satisfactory an overall performance.

The foregoing model is "naïve" because it makes no pretense of quantitative precision or comprehensive analysis. All that can be said for it is that it brings together and correlates some very important factors in the workings of the Japanese business world and the economy.

But at the beginning of 1973 one senses a new regime for the future. From reading the recent white papers and financial news (1971–72), it seems that a rather different money market, fiscal policy, monetary regime, and business emphasis are shaping up in Japan, and many of the postwar features of Japanese business and economics, which in 1970 may have seemed fixed and permanent, are making important adjustments in response to a maturing appreciation of Japan's position in the world. For example, one such feature that is gone is the anxiety over balance-of-payment deficits; indeed the anxiety has shifted to fears of further revaluation of the yen as the reserves push toward $20 billion, a figure unimaginable but a year or two ago. Also, after two decades of short funds and borrowing voraciously at high interest rates, Japanese businesses in 1972 experienced for the first time easy money at interest rates as low as or lower than the U.S. or Europe. This was caused partly by a slackening of corporate borrowing for plant and equipment investment because of over-capacity, in turn caused by production cutbacks to avoid further protest from abroad against aggressive Japanese exporting thrusts. With interest rates down and plenty of money, corporations began to become more independent of city banks; indeed they even had funds to invest in the stock market to strengthen holdings in *keiretsu* siblings. This trend in stock market activity was enhanced by individual investors' entering the stock market with their savings, instead of putting them in time deposits at the city banks, because interest rates were hardly as high as the inflation rate. With the stock market prices thus raised by individuals' buying, as well as corporate buying, the corporate money managers were able to get huge amounts of capital by issuing shares at market prices, rather than issuing, as usual, to existing stockholders at par. An unprecedented amount of funding came from such issues at market prices in 1972. These money market features may well continue; as the Japanese assume a new international stature in the 1970s, Tokyo will become a financial center ranking with New York and London.

At the same time, fiscal policy is changing and huge governmental spending on environment, housing, resources development, and technological research is in the offing. Again these funds will go directly to industrial corporations, by-passing the banks, further leavening the financial structure by dividing the channels for funding growth. In the overall business structure (dualism), small firms are rationalizing quickly as the tertiary sector and distribution functions gain weight, and wage and productivity differentials of dualism continue to narrow in the face of labor shortages. The bias in favor of manufacturing may recede, just as banking seems to be losing some of its paralyzing grip on business. The action in the 1970s may well be in marketing directly to Japan's increasingly sophisticated and affluent consumers, since it seems that Japan's reserves are so high that her markets must be reciprocally opened to foreign goods and maybe even to foreign-styled sales programs. Only time can sketch in the details, but the imminence of change permeated the entire Tokyo atmosphere of 1972.

V

The Legal Environment for Foreign Enterprise

Concerned with the general legal environment for foreigners in Japan, we must at the outset consider a point that has caused widespread confusion in recent international discussion. We refer to the frequently cited penchant of Japanese businessmen to avoid law, to seek extralegal solutions, and to behave in accordance with emotive social norms rather than rationalized legal codes, to emphasize warm personal relationships rather than cold contractual commitments. In a sense all of these preferences are to a degree characteristic of Japanese dealings among themselves, and furthermore Japanese society functions well enough on such a basis. Indeed they are preferences by no means entirely lacking in business circles elsewhere.

Some otherwise astute observers have suggested that, given this Japanese disposition to avoid legalisms, the foreigner must "while in Japan do it the Japanese way."[1] After some years of experience, such a pat answer seems a bit facile, especially in the new era of internationalization, which Japan is now embracing—and with growing success. The trouble is that foreigners usually are not capable of behaving in all of the ethnocentric ways characteristic of Japanese business, admirable though those domestic ways may be. The reasons are already set out in the first few chapters of this study and cannot be briefly recapitulated, but the essential point is that not all indigenous Japanese patterns of business behavior and hierarchical organization are suited to free-world, international intercourse. Foreigners, in fact, are awkward and ineffective in such a context, but, more to the point, Japan itself has recognized that fact. Japan has law, codes, and courts, and, for international intercourse, foreigners are obligated to observe her law when applicable and are entitled to expect their Japanese business colleagues to do the same. Of course, there will continue to be some tension between traditional behavioral patterns and the legalities of international transactions as Japanese business continues to play an increasing and vital role in international finance and commerce. But, it is a fair prediction that this tension will be resolved, increasingly, by adherence to legal standards of the broader economic community. In fact, Japanese juristic developments at home are advancing rapidly in such a direction and in such ways that are readily perceptible over a decade if not day by day, and the developments are not simply in the nature of "catching up"; some of the trends are highly innovative, refined, and worthy of emulation.

We shall deal here with basic features of the Japanese legal system generally—*i.e.,* the derivation, organization, and role of law and lawyers as they affect foreign enterprises, both in making initial decisions to invest and in later management of investments once made. This limited focus leads us to emphasize practical questions such as: what minimal understanding must the foreign investor have concerning the Japanese legal system in order to frame his legal questions, address them to the proper Japanese expert, and then understand the answer once received? The assumption is that certain general features of the legal system—its derivation, structure, professional roles, decisional techniques, and formal materials—must first be understood to some minimal degree before a dialogue is possible between the foreigner and his advisers on Japanese law.

We have, therefore, undertaken to draw together some such information about the Japanese legal system. In such an overview, it may be useful to bear in mind several basic generalizations about English-language treatments of Japanese law. The first point is an obvious one: there is very little written in English on Japanese law, especially law related to business,[2] despite its international importance and its inscrutability in its original language. Secondly, all descriptions of Japanese law in English are comparative, of course, because one must start with English legal terms as tools of exposition. Yet English legal terms denote Anglo-American legal ideas, which may be all the way from wholly strange to rather similar to their nearest Japanese counterpart.[3] This means then that all translations, especially unannotated translations, being inevitably comprised of inadequate selections of English "equivalents,"[4] are at best an unsatisfactory approximation.

These observations lead to the third preliminary point. Some of the inadequacies of expression occasioned by an actual lack of conceptual equivalence, in both the languages and the laws, can best be overcome

by some perspective concerning the background—historical and social
—of both legal systems. In the first four chapters we have endeavored
to provide some useful background, but again more than the ordinary caution is in order, because unlike a comparison between two
western systems such as the French civil law and the American common
law, where the underlying cultural tradition is generally similar, a comparison of the American and Japanese legal systems involves differences
that go substantially deeper into diverse social structures and political
values.

A fourth threshold point to remember is that the Tokugawa (1603–
1868) traditional system has, of course, had a lingering influence in the
present-day society and hence on the overall performance of the legal
system. The influence of this extraordinary tradition on the modern law
goes to the structural, the fundamental, and the functional, and thus it
can easily be overlooked completely by craftsmen who are bent on
scrutiny of statutory formality and verbal detail.[5]

Fifthly, and very much related, is the tendency of traditional practices
to persist in behavior despite contrary formal law in some areas of
activity.[6] Above, we emphasized the fact that the traditional law had
become a part of the positive law system. Here we are focusing on an
important, different aspect; namely, the difference between book law
and "living law." When traditional ways conflict with the book law, the
latter is often ignored[7] in behavior and only observed in litigation, if
at all. Although the gap between law and practice is everywhere a problem, Japan has had this problem to a remarkable degree in the recent
past.

Sixth, one reason for the vast gap in Japan between the book law
and social practice is that in the Japanese conception even the role of
positive law itself has changed immensely with the adoption of the
German-style codes at the turn of the century. In the premodern era,
the Japanese (or such of them as had thought about it) had understood
law to be a sort of natural law—not made, or even found—that existed
in nature and had always been adhered to by the ancestors. Nevertheless, the Tokugawa had falteringly begun to use positive law in our own
sense (*i.e.,* state law made, verbalized, promulgated, and enforced—
more or less) to try to preserve the feudal status quo, whose principles
they understood to be in accordance with their Confucian natural law.
Against this background it is clear enough that the role of law, after
the codes, has been not only consciously positive and legislative, but it
sought to destroy past practices and shape future conduct of the populace into patterns as yet quite incomprehensible to them. This new role

for law has gained acceptance and efficacy gradually. But still, on its verbal face, the formal law often greatly overestimates its own power to shape society in its own image.[8]

A final caveat, before exploring the derivation of current Japanese law, is to note that despite its various western importations, Japanese law is today sui generis and the product of its own unique development. In the following story of the two main western law receptions in Japan, this important fact must not be forgotten.[9]

Derivation of Modern Japanese Law

There are three major phases of Japanese legal development that need to be sketched below in order to fathom the principal components of modern Japanese law: the Tokugawa phase (1603–1868), for the Japanese traditional institutions; the period before World War II (1868–1945), for the reception of civilian codes; and the postwar period (1945–73), for the Anglo-American influences.

Tokugawa

Many Tokugawa values have been adapted to modern uses and exercise to some degree a continuing influence in Japanese life today. Some of them have found their way into the law itself, others remain vigorous in spite of the law, and still others operate in the interstices, neither heeding nor hindering the formal rules. But, in general, the traditional elements are receding in importance year by year as Japan industrializes, urbanizes, standardizes, and democratizes the fabric of its society. The level of abstraction on which this chapter is cast does not permit us to notice any particular vestigial elements.[10] Rather, an understanding of the overall skeleton of the Tokugawa legal system, for our purposes here, is much more important, not only to indicate the starting point of modern legal development and consequently to show the vast distance traveled since 1868, but also to suggest some of the older ideas lingering at the very foundations of Japanese legal thinking.

In trying to achieve an overview of Tokugawa law, we find a new legal order emerging in Edo, which had developed the following relevant characteristics toward the end of the Tokugawa period:[11]

1. There was an emergent state centering around the Edo shogunate, and its control system, decrees, and precedents were the beginnings of a positive law system that was rationalized by an orthodox Confucian natural law. At the same time, private relations in large part continued to be governed by a residual customary law.

2. The administration of justice was highly decentralized in that each of literally hundreds of fiefholders had the right to govern and administer justice to the people within their fiefs. Even the shogunate, in a sense, was but one of these fiefs, occupying, however, about one-fourth of Japan and strategic posts throughout the other three-fourths.

3. But judicial and administrative functions were not yet organized separately either in the shogunate officers or in the fiefs.[12] The shogunate "judges" (*bugyō, daikan,* etc.) were primarily warrior-bureaucrats. Although some recording clerks (*tomeyaku*) in the commissions (*bugyō-sho*) became officials specialized in law suits, they were mere clerks and subject to the directives of their superiors.[13]

4. Criminal and civil procedures were not entirely distinct,[14] although generally the inquisitorial procedure (*gimmi-suji*)[15] was used in criminal trials and a petition procedure (*deiri-suji*)[16] was generally used in civil trials.

5. Torture was used legally in both criminal[17] and civil[18] proceedings.

6. The core of the centralized shogunate law, as is usual in early stages of positive legal growth, was a remarkably harsh criminal law, wherein conviction was based on confession extracted, if need be, by torture, and classified penalties were prescribed with revolting ingenuity.[19]

7. In theory all civil litigation was a matter of grace, not of right.[20]

8. The legal system had few professional jurists. The colorful tradition of licensed innkeepers accompanying out-of-town litigants to "court" has been told in sufficient detail[21] to show their shortcomings as lawyers. Yet there were no other lawyers in Tokugawa Japan.

9. Conciliation was the usual civil procedure, with veiled village coercion in the background to induce agreement.[22]

10. No appeals were allowed.[23]

11. The individual was legally only a member of a group; groups or their chiefs were the main objects of law and were vicariously liable for the conduct of members of their group (village, family, etc.).[24]

12. Hence, suits brought to shogunate courts without approval of the village authorities and overlords were illegal and the petitioner without approval would be punished severely.[25]

13. In no significant degree were schools and scholars factors in molding the positive law on a professional level,[26] except perhaps as teachers of the bureaucracy.[27]

14. Most personal and social relationships were governed by Confucianistic concepts of status, hierarchy, and authority, which left the individual wholly without legal recourse for abuse by his Confucianistic superior.[28]

These features of the Tokugawa legal tradition added up to make authority, status, hierarchy, and official discretion the outstanding legal characteristics of a society of 30 million people, which found itself after 1853 for the first time in the full current of world affairs. If any single feature of the legal system stands out more than others, besides its fixed, static, and durable qualities, it is probably the unfettered authority of the warrior[29] turned bureaucrat. His shadow has fallen noticeably over several decades of postrestoration legal development.

The present-day bureaucrat (See Chapter VI) is not, of course, identical with the warrior bureaucrat of the Tokugawa regime or even the new university-trained Imperial bureaucrat of prewar Japan. But they have all, until recently, been largely above the law in the sense of independent judicial review. It needs to be said, however, that, since the Meiji restoration, the civil branch of the bureaucracy has been generally motivated by a rather effective spirit of noblesse oblige, and judging from their overall performance in modernizing and, since World War II, rehabilitating Japan, they have shown a relatively high degree of competence and integrity.

Reception of Western Law

The forces behind the reception[30] of western law in Japan in the 1880s and 1890s sprang from both internal and external sources. Within the ruling clique, at least after the first inept attempts to revert to the Chinese-style Imperial institutions of eighth-century Japan,[31] there was no doubt a strong desire to centralize administrative power and to modernize Japanese legal institutions. By 1873 and onward, foreign legal advisers were employed to translate western legal materials and assist with the framing of new laws.

However, external pressures pushed the Japanese toward westernization of their law even more urgently. The chief reason was the unequal treaties that had established extraterritorial rights[32] for foreigners in Japan. We are told[33] that Townsend Harris had reluctantly included a provision for extraterritoriality in the U.S.-Japan Treaty of Amity and Commerce of 1858 in order to be sure that the U.S. Senate would consent to its ratification.[34] Even before this, Japan was forced to accept the consular courts of several European nations as well. Consequently, whatever the desire to reform for reform's sake may have been, the necessity to westernize Japanese law, before the treaties could be revised to abolish extraterritorial rights, was made clear enough.[35] Treaty revision thus became a part of the program of successive Japanese governments after 1875, and concurrently work amongst the ruling group for westernization of the law, as a precondition of foreign treaty concessions, quickened noticeably after 1875.[36] By 1900, a complete system of European-style codes had been adopted, and simultaneously extraterritoriality was expunged from all of the treaties, except that full tariff autonomy was not realized until a decade later.

We have spoken of the reason for the western codification, but how did it come about and what were the major influences that made up the final product? Two distinct stages were followed: the first was a period of preparation and education (1870–85); the second was a period of debate, revision, and final adoption (1886–99). The preparatory phase began in earnest with the employment of a French jurist, Boissonade,[37] in 1873. After Boissonade, several English, American, and German jurists also served in Japan as advisers and lecturers.

In addition, several Japanese jurists (*e.g.,* Kentarō Kaneko, Harvard, 1871–78; Nobushige Hozumi, English barrister; Kazuo Hatoyama; Okamura, and others) had studied in the U.S. or Europe. Until about 1890, it seems that the English jurists were personally the more influential, followed by the French-trained group. The German-trained lawyers became especially influential after Hirobumi Itō's European trip during 1882–83. In fact, during the 1880s, when Itō brought German ideas and advisers back to Japan, it was often necessary to have a foreigner translate from German into English, then into Japanese.

At about the same time, schools were established to teach foreign law, and we are told that they ordinarily taught in foreign languages because the Japanese language did not have the required vocabulary at the time to discuss western legal ideas. Later, such fundamental work as developing a new Japanese legal terminology for western legal concepts was a most important part of this preparatory work at the schools, and the new legal terms, in Chinese characters, were later exported to China after 1900.[38] "Taught law is tough law," and in applying the Japanese law,[39] "judicial officers and lawyers, in spite of their affecting to follow our own customs and written statutes, in most cases formed their views upon whatever foreign jurisprudence they had studied."[40]

By the end of the preparatory stage (1885), torture in legal proceedings had been banned (1879),[41] and a new criminal code (1880) and code of criminal procedure (1882), as drafted along French lines by Boissonade, had been enacted. A new constitution was under active consideration after the strenuous study of Hirobumi Itō and his group at home and abroad (1882–83). The drafting was in progress by his Japanese colleagues (mainly Kowashi Inoue and Kentarō Kaneko and Myoji Itō) using the ideas of his foreign advisers in Japan (mainly Hermann Roesler and Sir Francis T. Piggott) and abroad (mainly Professors Rudolph Gneist, Lorenz von Stein, and Albert Mosse, who later came to Japan as an adviser). A new civil code was being drafted along French lines by Boissonade, and a new commercial code was in progress under Roesler, incorporating German, French, and English ideas. Also, work on the Code of Civil Procedure had been started by Techow and, to a lesser extent, Mosse, incorporating strong German influences.

The reverse side of Japan's eager study of foreign law during this period was the noticeable neglect of the traditional customary law by the Meiji legal scholars,[42] especially after the compilations of customary law[43] were made in the early period. However as we shall see, certain traditional family institutions were adapted and woven into the Civil Code, Books IV and V, and it was this part of the Civil Code that underwent the most change after 1954.

The second stage of Japanese codifications after 1889 centered around one of the most significant episodes of modern Japanese legal history. The "postponement campaign," as Hozumi[44] called it, began as a dispute[45] between the English-trained Japanese jurists and the French-trained Japanese jurists to postpone the effectiveness of the new civil and commercial codes promulgated in 1890 and to become effective in 1893. It has been likened in some ways to the Savigny-Thibaut dispute,[46] but the issues were somewhat different in that the English school, though more traditional, did not recommend against codification. The arguments[47] advanced by both sides and reasons behind them are complex, but, generally speaking, the English-trained jurists headed by Nobushige Hozumi favored postponement primarily (1) to enable a more deliberate and scientific drafting process and selection of legal models, rather than what they felt to be an overemphasis on French law, and (2) to permit a better accommodation between the Civil Code and the Commercial Code and between native practice and the code law. Those in favor of immediate enforcement, headed by Kenjiro Ume,[48] were, like Boissonade, of a natural-law persuasion and held that the French-style codes embodied principles universally applicable to mankind. Therefore, the codes need not specifically incorporate Japanese elements, and should be enforced on schedule (1893). The later famous American jurist, John Henry Wigmore, in one of his lesser moments also supported immediate enforcement, though for slightly different reasons. The English-trained Japanese jurists (without Wigmore's support, of course) won a temporary victory when a bill[49] was passed to postpone effectiveness for four years, after acrimonious debate in the newly established Diet of 1892.[50] A drafting committee[51] of Hozumi, Ume, and Tomii substantially revised and improved the Civil Code, and another committee of Ume, Tabe, and Okano redrafted the Commercial Code.

Then the Civil Code became effective in 1898[52] and the Commercial Code followed in 1899.[53] Curiously enough, though French influences remained strong, the new German codes, then in draft form in Germany, were finally relied upon most heavily in the new Japanese codes. So, while the English and French lawyers were at battle, the Germans, relative latecomers in Japanese legal circles, made the greatest contribution to the new code, though actually much of the French doctrine remained.[54]

It would, of course, have been nearly impossible to adopt the American or the English law in their amorphous case-law form, faced with the political pressures for treaty revision growing annually. In fact, Wigmore early noted that the outcome might have been different had the English law been available at that time in some more convenient form, such as Sheldon Amos's later *Civil Code of England*. In any event, after 1900, the Japanese codes, even the provisions clearly drawn from the Code Napoleon, were taught and interpreted by civil-law standards learned from the works of German professors.[55] As Hozumi put it in 1912: "Within the past thirty years, Japanese law has passed from the Chinese family of law to the European family."[56] Although this is in a sense so, it is important to be aware, as Hozumi was, that the new Japanese codes were but an imported skeleton. Only when the Japanese university, bar, and bench could give it flesh and the observance of the people give it life would it become Japanese. This has happened to a remarkable degree since 1945.

In its constitutional and administrative aspects,[57] the new system was essentially authoritarian[58] and remained so with only one significant glimmering of nascent liberality in the 1920s. This glimmering was ultimately snuffed out in the field of constitutional development when the tides turned against Minobe in the Minobe-Uesugi (successor of Yatsuka Hozumi) debates in the 1930s.[59] Minobe contended that the Emperor was only an "organ" of state, not the source of state power. Minobe's position was one of noble aspiration, but it did not accord with the views of the founders,[60] nor was it easy to support by a literal interpretation of the text of the constitution either. It failed, and thus the prewar legal order achieved no more than what might be called a rule-by-law[61] (*Rechtsstaat*).

The Anglo-American Infusion

Disillusioned and industrially demolished, Japan signed its surrender to the Allied powers on 2 September 1945, and in accordance with the Potsdam Declaration,[62] the Supreme Command of the Allied Powers

(SCAP) set about democratizing Japan. The legal formulation of this novel project—an unprecedented democratic revolution initiated paradoxically by aliens from the top down—was of profound significance to the formal legal order and potentially for the society. The constitution was fundamentally rebuilt; all of the five major codes underwent revisions, presumably to render them consistent with the constitutional changes; and a number of special implementing[63] and regulatory laws (*e.g.,* antitrust, collective bargaining, securities exchange) previously unknown to Japan were enacted, with far-reaching implications[64] for both the legal system and the society.

Clearly the new constitution was the center from which most of the other reforms emanated.[65] In the sweeping amendments,[66] theocracy disappeared with the disestablishment of state Shintoism and the secularization of the Emperor's position in the state. National patriarchy was abolished by declaring the people, not the Emperor, sovereign[67] and by destroying the peerage, and, on the local scene, by abolishing the legal inequalities of individuals in the families and villages—the basic authoritarian units from which the structure of Japanese absolutism had been built over the centuries. Judicial supremacy and cabinet responsibility were two other key constitutional principles then novel to Japan, as noted above in Chapter II.

In the five basic codes, the most pervasive changes occurred in the Code of Criminal Procedure, which was completely revised effective in 1949 to provide for a Japanese "due process," right of counsel, and most of the other rights afforded by U.S. law,[68] except the right to trial by jury.[69] The Criminal Code required fewer changes, mostly in the areas in which the status of the victim had been the occasion for special crimes or penalties (*e.g.,* lese majeste, adultery as a crime for women but not for men, etc.[70]). In the Civil Code the changes were almost entirely confined to Books IV and V on family relations.[71] The political significance of these changes can, however, hardly be overestimated. Broadly speaking the changes meant first the abolition of the old house (*i.e.,* the extended family group, whose chief or head controlled the family property and marriage of the members) and secondly the abolition of the inequalities of the sexes.

Although perhaps less urgent from the constitutional standpoint, the changes in the Commercial Code and the Code of Civil Procedure are of more direct interest to foreign investors, affecting as they do the business patterns and the resolution of disputes arising therefrom. The Commercial Code was not changed until near the end of the occupation (effective 1 July 1951), and the most important changes were confined to Book II on company law, which were very substantial changes, however, covering 203 of the some 450 articles in Book II. Generally speaking, the major changes were related to shareholders' rights and management's responsibilities.[72]

The Code of Civil Procedure was left largely intact, but two changes were made in 1948[73] which tended to give Japanese civil trials a more Anglo-American, adversary character.[74] First, the power of the judge to take evidence ex officio was eliminated[75] except for certain special situations, and secondly, the burden of presenting and cross-examining witnesses was placed upon the litigants and their counsel.[76] These changes, supported by later Supreme Court Civil Procedure Regulations,[77] were interpreted to relieve the judges of first instance of their prewar duty of clarification,[78] and hence they have caused a shift somewhat away from the German-style, inquisitorial trial methods that lean heavily on the judge. This new tendency has increased the adversary character of Japanese civil trials, relying more on lawyers to present their cases.

In addition to the changes in the constitution and codes, profound changes were also effected in education by instituting nine years of compulsory education and a 6-3-3-4 graded progression up through the universities, the number of which was greatly increased; in the field of agriculture by the Land Reform[79] Law that created a host of new landowners; in the field of labor by setting up minimum standards of hours and wages and collective bargaining rights; in the field of business regulation by enacting antitrust laws and establishing a new Fair Trade Commission (*Kōsei torihiki iinkai*); in the field of securities by passing a Securities Exchange Act; and in maritime transportaton by passing a Marine Transportation Act—to mention some of the most important special postwar legislation.

In all of the latter acts, except the land reform, the legislative pattern followed models from the U.S. The most pronounced American influences found in the five codes themselves are in the Code of Criminal Procedure, the Commercial Code, and the Code of Civil Procedure. The postwar changes in the Criminal Code and the Civil Code might better be characterized more generally as a culmination of "western" rather than narrowly American trends, as they reflect the individualism of the western family and state which are inimical to the hierarchial Confucianistic family statuses.

Cumulatively, these changes after World War II amount to a considerable infusion of Anglo-American influence into the Japanese legal system. Furthermore, the cumulative effect of the experience has greatly influenced the Japanese juristic method by producing an increased interest on the part of Japanese jurists in case studies and in the study of the social effects of law in Japan. Interest in practical legal and social problems such as the efficacy of law and lawsuits and judicial administration has grown encouragingly, as testified by the annual increases of such literature readily noticeable in the bibliographies in these fields. Nevertheless, it is probably fair to say that the Japanese lawyer still feels closer to the civil law world than the common law—in respect to private law problems at least.

Be that as it may, the fact is that modern Japanese law is now reaching a stage of maturity at which it will henceforth live a more independent life of its own, consolidating and harmonizing its diverse borrowings from the west with the virility of its own tradition. Yet, in the future, Japan's law will also share the tendency of modern legal systems generally to grow more similar under the influences of massive travel, trade, and consequent standardization of modes of business and even ways of life.

The Structure of Japanese Law

General

However decentralized it may have been in the distant past, political power in Japan is geographically centralized now. The legal structure is unitary as in France or England, rather than federal as in the U.S. Just as in the prewar period, all law is still equally applicable throughout Japan, except for certain rule-making powers delegated to the prefectures or municipalities, not by specific provision defining local powers in the constitution but by statutes enacted by the Diet.[80] Thus, federalism as a constitutional problem is generally unknown and well-nigh unfathomable to all but the most sophisticated of Japanese lawyers and businessmen who might be concerned with it because of their interests in the U.S.

But, as we have seen, the internal organization of the national government in Japan has changed from the prewar idea of absolute monarchy, wherein the Japanese Emperor was formally, at least, divine, patriarchal, and omnipotent,[81] to the vastly different basic premise that power resides in the people who will rule through their elective representative in the Diet. Understandably, the implementation of this idea of popular sovereignty has encouraged many political[82] and legal problems in postwar Japan, as elsewhere, ranging from prosecutions for electoral corruption to policing against snake-dancing demonstrators and parliamentary fisticuffs. But what is more strictly relevant here, if less exciting, is the role of the courts[83] in enforcing a rule of law in the new constitutional scheme.[84]

Japanese governmental organization embodies a "double supremacy": legislative and judicial. The American type of separation of powers—legislative, executive, and judicial—is only partially observed in the new constitution since Japan now has a parliamentary type of government with a prime minister, not separately elected by the people, as in our presidential type, but elected by and responsible to the Diet,[85] roughly following the English pattern. This fusion of executive and legislative power resulting in the legislative supremacy of the Diet[86] is, however, accompanied by a sort of Japanese judicial supremacy much like that of the U.S., which is, of course, not found in parliamentary English practice. However, Japanese judicial supremacy is codified in the written constitution,[87] whereas ours was developed in the case law beginning with *Marbury* v. *Madison.*[88] This significant innovation in the formal Japanese law is still nurturing a traditionally weak consciousness of justiciable rights amongst the Japanese populace, although I would argue that socially the Japanese are quite conscious of their "due." Foreign lawyers dealing with Japanese legal affairs need to understand that Japan is on the threshold of this phase of her legal development. It is useful to remember that the U.S. did not have its second case[89] declaring a law unconstitutional until a half century after *Marbury* v. *Madison.*

Unique England aside,[90] judicial supremacy, organized in a variety of ways, has been made to carry a heavy burden in fostering a rule of law[91] and implementing and inducing popular government throughout the politically immature parts of the "free world," especially in two spheres. First, it has been useful to enforce the minimal individual rights of association, expression, and assembly that are deemed critical to a meaningful choice at the polls.[92] Secondly, on the routine administrative level it has been useful to enforce the concept of the "public servant," acting in accordance with the laws enacted by the popular representatives.[93] When we recall the Tokugawa and even the prewar Japanese official, often limited only by vague standards of Confucianistic or Imperial noblesse oblige, it is not difficult to comprehend the novelty of this key concept of law over power in postwar Japan. Against the background of Japanese tradition, judicial supremacy as a formalism to support nascent political interest in a rule of law and right consciousness is, therefore, a structural change of revolutionary importance; its basis in the constitution is clear enough, but its practical realization in the courts and in society has only begun.

In the new Japanese Constitution there were three major constitutional changes designed to implement the rule of law through judicial supremacy. First, the Supreme Court has been given the ultimate power to review all legislative, executive, and administrative acts for constitutionality.[94] Secondly, the prewar separate administrative court for suits against officials, which was really a token device, was abolished, and the regular courts were given jurisdiction[95] over all complaints alleging that officials had transgressed their authority or otherwise acted illegally. To date the volume of litigation against officials under this new arrangement has been very light, reflecting no doubt both the traditional Japanese awe of officialdom and the disinclination to sue even a private party. However, there is every sign that the courts are well aware of their new responsibilities and that they will strive to build soundly on their newly acquired powers. The biggest obstacle before them is probably budgetary;[96] if the courts are not given enough manpower to become more prompt and efficient, they may very well fail to keep pace with the current social interest in the new rule of law.

Thirdly, the regular court system was taken out from under the administrative supervision of the executive branch (Ministry of Justice), and now the Supreme Court not only administers the entire court system[97] but it also has rule-making power.[98] The extent of this power has been narrowly construed by U.S. standards, which might surprise the drafters of the constitution, but nevertheless many important rules of procedure have emanated from the court.[99]

Court Organization

The judicial organization as of 1968[100] is shown in the chart below:

Court	Number of Courts	Judges	Civil Jurisdiction
Supreme Court	1	15	Appeals from High Court
High Court	8	263	Largely, appeals from District Court
District Court	49	805	(1) Appeals from Summary Court (2) Original trial jurisdiction in cases involving over 300,000 yen (about $1000).
Family Courts	49	193	Domestic relations cases.
Summary Courts	570	734	Original trial jurisdiction in all cases involving less than 300,000 yen.

The Supreme Court sitting as a grand bench (*dai hōtei*; fifteen judges) has final power to determine the constitutionality[101] of all governmental acts, legislative and administrative. It sits in three petty benches of five members for nonconstitutional cases. Also to be noted is the fact that the courts shown above constitute the entire judiciary in Japan; there are no local or municipal courts established by the local subdivisions in Japan. Besides the judges listed on the above chart, there were in 1968 some 527 assistant judges (*hanjiho*), who ordinarily will become full judges after ten years of service. The 734 Summary Court judges need not be formally trained as judges and need not pass the rigorous judicial examination (*shihō shiken*).

Legal Professionals' Roles

Training of Japan's Legal Professions

To a remarkable degree the Japanese bachelor's degree in law (A.B. not LL.B.) is regarded as the most direct avenue leading to business and official power in Japan.[102] Consequently, most bright and ambitious young people in Japan clamber for entry into the best law departments as a first step to important careers. Some fifty universities with law departments throughout the country produce annually about eighteen thousand law graduates at the bachelor's level, but only about half of them take the national legal examination. About 3 percent (1968) of those who take the exam pass.

Significantly, upon passing the legal examination, judges, procurators, and lawyers now receive a common education[103] consisting of two years of professional training at the Legal Training and Research Institute (*Shihō kenshūjo*). However, after graduating from the institute these three branches of the legal profession go their separate ways. Those electing to become judges commence their work immediately as assistant judges and as a rule remain "career judges" for their entire active lives.[104] Procurators move directly to the procurator's office in the Ministry of Justice and continue to serve as government lawyers handling criminal or civil legal work for the government throughout their careers; and lawyers likewise go directly into the private practice of law, as a rule for life. There is some provision for appointment of procurators or lawyers to the bench, but the actual movement between these three branches of the profession has been relatively slight, though several practicing lawyers have been appointed to the Supreme Court. Thus, the practice of drawing from a common bar of practicing lawyers to fill legal positions on the bench and in the procuracy has not developed in Japan as it has in the Anglo-American countries. Under the slogan of "unification of the legal profession" (*hōsō ichigen-ka*)[105] some support has been given to this idea of unification, meaning selection of judges and procurators from the bar in the postwar period, but little progress in that direction has been made, largely because of the low compensation of judges and the consequent sacrifice that the more successful lawyers would be forced to make in moving to a judgeship. Thus, for practical as well as traditional reasons, the "career judge" is likely to remain in Japan for some time to come despite a recognition, in some circles at least, of the cogency of a program of drawing judges from the practicing bar.

The common training received at the institute has doubtless created a new and valuable common ground for cooperation amongst Japanese judges, procurators, and lawyers. Indeed, the inclusion of lawyer trainees in the postwar institute was properly regarded as a victory for the bar, for in the prewar days lawyers were not afforded educational opportunity and status equal to the other professions. However, the curriculum problems arising out of this three-way amalgamation at the institute are substantial obstacles to the training of lawyers for counseling roles, since the procurators and judges are concerned largely only with dispute settlement and court work, and the curriculum has inevitably reflected their predominance.[106]

Lawyers and Other Experts Useful to Foreigners

In any investment project in Japan, the foreign investor will need certain legal advice from the outset, and if he goes into a direct investment involving manufacturing and sales in Japan, he may need several other professional services. He, therefore, should know the way the various professionals are trained and organized, as well as the types of services that they are accustomed to render on the Japanese scene.[107]

In the early postwar years, foreigners tended to bring their own lawyers, accountants, and other experts to Japan with them or hire their own kind on the spot. Japanese language difficulties are only part of the explanation for this practice. Other reasons were an early lack of interest by the Japanese lawyers in foreign clients; low standards of competence for foreign work, real or imagined, of some professionals in some fields; and, to some extent, ignorance on the part of many foreigners of the availability of some types of services. We shall describe below several of the licensed professions that are required or could be useful to the foreign investor.

Liaison Lawyer

In the past, the foreign investor in Japan has usually found it necessary sooner or later to employ what has been informally called a liaison lawyer (*shōgai bengoshi*)—a lawyer who specializes in international transactions[108] involving Japan.[109] Liaison lawyers practicing in Tokyo have generally been American lawyers with Japanese partners and associates. There are, however, several such experts practicing in the U.S., and recently several Japanese lawyers[110] have entered the field in Tokyo without the assistance of foreign lawyers, except as correspondents abroad. Some Tokyo liaison lawyers maintain related offices in the U.S. and sometimes also in Europe. Others simply work more loosely with correspondents. In U.S.-Japanese ventures, the key person in these firms has been an American lawyer, preferably bilingual, who is admitted to practice in Japan[111] and is also a qualified lawyer in one or more of the states. Japanese language competence was not a requirement for foreign lawyers to join the Japanese Bar up until 1955, when foreign attorney admissions by easier rules than those applied to the Japanese were cut off. There are now no real possibilities for a foreigner to join. As mentioned below, the liaison lawyer often conveniently supplements the services of his Japanese lawyer colleagues, who are only recently commencing to regard the solution of tax problems, corporate documentation, and business counseling and negotiations in English as properly within their sphere of professional competence and activity.[112]

For several years there has been a shortage of competent liaison lawyers in Tokyo. The foreigners who are still registered for practice in Japan number thirty-eight, and about twenty of those are actually practicing in Tokyo, of which only a half dozen are able to read legal materials in Japanese with any facility. There are only two or three Europeans registered. Even adding the growing number of Japanese lawyers who are undertaking the substantial task[113] of qualifying for this bilegal, bilingual, and bilateral practice, still there is a pitifully small liaison bar to handle the vast volume of business flowing between Japan and the U.S. or Europe.

Monolingual Japanese Lawyers

Under postwar constitutionalism, Japanese lawyers are just now coming into their own.[114] Such professional antecedents as they had before 1868 were concurrently innkeepers with little status in or out of court.[115] Between 1886 and 1949,[116] the Japanese lawyer's role was largely courtwork like a barrister, although in the context of the Japanese tradition and the consequently congenial German-style, inquisitorial trial procedure adopted for prewar Japan, their role in the courts and in society as well was a mere shadow of that of their British brethren.[117]

Since the legal examination[118] is very restrictive,[119] a diminutive[120] but generally very competent bar of some 8,210 lawyers,[121] who are even now often essentially trial lawyers of a rather passive sort,[122] now serves a nation of over 100 million people. Most of the Japanese lawyers practice in the three or four large cities[123] and are still largely found in one-man offices. It stands to reason, then, that other types of experts must handle the vast volume of counseling, legal drafting, tax work, regulatory filings, and corporate documents and registration.

The Law-Trained Corporate Employee

Although the law-trained corporate employee is not a licensed or professionally trained lawyer, and as far as we are able to ascertain no careful empirical study has been done on his role in the legal affairs of Japanese corporations, it is logical in the Japanese scheme of things to mention at this point the A.B. law graduate who joins the Japanese corporation immediately after graduating from the four-year course of the law department of a university. Much of the law work handled in the U.S. by the corporate counsel or "office lawyer," or in England by a solicitor, is done in Japan by quasi-professionals of this sort. On the other hand, full-fledged and professionally licensed Japanese lawyers (two years of training after graduation from the law department and after passing the legal examination) almost never accept full-time employment with the government or a corporation as is common in the United States.[124]

As mentioned above, these law-trained employees are the peculiar product of the law departments of Japanese universities. Those graduates who decide to go into government or corporate offices directly without taking the legal examination or those who fail the examination are the ones who perform the bulk of legal work, aside from litigation,[125] in public offices and business. They lack the qualities of professionalism and the competence that come from intensive professional training, discipline, and organization, but in the specialized fields to which they are assigned, they often become skilled in technical legal matters. It is this type of quasi-professionals whom foreign investors will frequently encounter in joint-venture negotiations, contract drafting, tax filing, and corporate work. If a joint-venture corporation is established, several law-trained employees may be useful for the foreign staff. By the same token, the Japanese law graduate as such is a rather inadequate substitute for the lawyer as business counselor, as he is known in U.S. practice. For this purpose, besides the liaison lawyers, the American Chamber of Commerce lists a dozen or more "business" or "marketing" consultants who can supply a great deal of information on the business context in Japan, and in fact their functions often overlap with the liaison lawyer.

Patent Agents (benrishi)

Rather like the situation in the U.S., patent work in Japan is done by separate specialists. However, unlike our practice, these specialists are ordinarily not lawyers but members of a separate profession[126] called patent agents.[127]

By 1967, annual patent applications (85,364)[128] in Japan had increased four times over their prewar high (20,877) in 1940.[129] The professional work involved in filing, registering, and otherwise handling this large volume of patent work in Japan is ordinarily done by patent agents. Their association is regulated by the Ministry of International Trade and Industry,[130] and their qualifications, scope of work, organization, and other affairs are governed by a separate law and regulations.[131] However, any qualified Japanese lawyer (*bengoshi*) is also authorized to do patent work[132] although patent agents need not be lawyers. Of all the other legal specialists in Japan, only the patent agent is qualified to handle litigation[133] in his special area of competence.

The special status of the patent agent dates back to 1899,[134] but the present organization of the profession dates from the Patent Agents' Law of 1921. All qualified patent agents must register and become members of the Patent Agents' Association (*Benrishikai*), which was organized in 1922. It had 1,536 members[135] in 1967, almost two-thirds of whom (992) were in Tokyo. Japanese citizenship[136] is a requirement to become a patent agent, although foreigners may be authorized to handle specific matters on the basis of reciprocity.[137] Otherwise, to qualify to become a patent agent, one must pass two examinations,[138] the first of which is waived for graduates of Japanese universities. The final examination is given once a year in Tokyo and only roughly 4 percent are successful.[139] No special training institute is provided to train successful candidates such as the Legal Training and Research Institute for lawyers.

The Patent Agents' Association provides a list of suggested fees to be charged for application registration, defense against objections, litigation opinions, and the like. The basic structure of the fee system is a commencement fee (*tesūryō*) and a success fee (*shakin*)[140] at the end, although the latter is fixed and payable whether the work is successful or not. Also foreign-language work is handled by a separate and understandably higher schedule of fees. For example, a foreign-language application is $90, while a Japanese application is only 20,000 yen (about $55).[141]

Tax Agents (zeirishi)

As yet no sharp antagonism, such as we have had in the U.S., has developed in Japan between accountants and lawyers with respect to tax matters.[142] One reason is that tax administration has just recently reached a point where controversies over tax liability are emerging as legal problems, as opposed to negotiating and fact-finding problems. Another reason is the legal structure governing the various practitioners in Japan. Japanese law recognizes the tax agent as a specialist separate from the lawyers and accountants[143] in tax matters, but at the same time, both lawyers[144] and certified public accountants (*kōnin kaikeishi*),[145] including foreign C.P.A.s,[146] are authorized to handle tax matters as an incidence of their respective professions. However, despite their recent aspirations, the tax agents have not been given a right corresponding to that of the patent agents to handle tax cases in the courts; such work is reserved to lawyers.

An investigation in 1969 shows that the Tax Agents' Association's membership is a mixture of lawyers, C.P.A.s, and tax agents as such. Out of 19,622 members of the Tax Agents' Association,[147] 2,780 were also C.P.A.s, and only 485 were also lawyers, whereas the rest were simply tax agents as such and neither lawyers nor accountants.

The first national legislation to organize and control tax agents dates from 1942,[148] but it was not until Japan adopted the voluntary assessment system of tax returns of 1947 that the present basis for the tax agent's role was firmly laid.[149] Soon followed the new Tax Agent Law (*Zeirishihō*) of 1951, which provided that the government tax office must notify the tax agent who had been retained whenever certain investigations were to be undertaken regarding a return.[150]

The importance of the tax agent's work can be seen from the fact that as early as 1961, out of 976,020 individual proprietorships, 178,069 (18.2 percent) and, out of 578,241 corporate businesses, 398,072 (68.8 percent) filed their tax returns through tax agents.[151] For this business the average tax agent made fees of 2,555,000 yen ($7,000) per year, which for that time was very high and probably considerably in excess of the average Japanese lawyer's earnings.[152]

Control of the tax agents is under the Ministry of Finance, National Tax Agency. The agency director may fix the schedule of maximum (no minimum) fees,[153] although since the new law was passed in 1951, no such schedule has been issued. The Tax Agents' Association has, however, established a maximum fee schedule.[154]

To qualify, the tax agent must pass an examination supervised by a committee appointed by the minister of finance. In 1968 out of 35,516 candidates only 755 (2 percent) passed.[155] Those qualified must register with the government and also join the Tax Agents' Association[156] in the National Tax Bureau district where they are to practice. These local associations are then members of the national federation.[157]

Judicial Scriveners (shihō shoshi)

Judicial scriveners play an important role in drafting and registering legal documents for individuals and small enterprises, though they are less frequently used by larger corporations in Japan. Indeed, they may be characterized functionally as half lawyer and half legal secretary in our sense, as they perform many of the more menial of the legal services that our law offices or the English solicitor's offices provide.[158] Nothing that they do could not be done also by a Japanese lawyer, but the scrivener's fees are lower,[159] and they do a great deal of paper work of a legal nature which Japanese lawyers do not deign to do, notably documents for small incorporations.[160] Judicial scriveners also draft pleadings and other documents for use in litigation, but they cannot appear in court for a client. However, since in about 75 percent[161] of the cases in the Summary Courts of Japan one or both of the parties appear without lawyers, we can surmise that the scriveners may aid these litigants with their paper work but leave them on their own in court.[162]

The foreigner will have little occasion to use the judicial scrivener's services, except indirectly, because the scrivener generally works only in Japanese and would under the circumstances most often render his services to a foreigner through a responsible lawyer. Although their work dates back to the early Meiji period, judicial scriveners were not given a legal status until 1919, and their present status is defined in the new Judicial Scrivener Law of 1950. At present, there are 11,898[163] active judicial scriveners in Japan who are serving as second-rate "lawyers," often in rural areas for people who cannot afford the barrister-like *bengoshi* and who, therefore, have the scrivener prepare the pleading and then let the judge try to work out the facts in court.

Judicial scriveners must be selected from persons who have served for five or more years as court secretaries, court clerks, assistant court clerks, secretaries to the minister of justice, or the like.[164] These are, of course, all positions that are filled by special governmental examinations. The licensing of judicial scriveners is, however, done on a local level, and the judicial scriveners are supervised by the District Legal Affairs Bureau (*Chihō hōmukyoku*) of the Ministry of Justice. Thus, they do not have the independence from the executive branch that the bar enjoys. All judicial scriveners are required to maintain membership in the local Judicial Scriveners' Associations, which are federated at the national level.[165]

Administrative Scrivener (gyōsei shoshi)

The administrative scriveners in Japan originated in modern Japanese law as early as 1873,[166] but the modern system is based on the Administrative Scriveners Law of 1951[167] as amended through 1960.

To qualify as an administrative scrivener one must pass an examination given once a year by the governor of each prefecture in Japan.[168] Then, it is necessary to register with the local Administrative Scriveners' Association. However, all persons qualified as lawyers, patent agents, C.P.A.s, or tax agents are also qualified[169] as such to serve as administrative scriveners. Also, all employees of the local or national government who have handled administrative matters for eight years (or five years for those with a high school education) are qualified to become administrative scriveners.[170]

The law of 1951 defines the function of the administrative scrivener very broadly to include the drafting for compensation of all "documents to be presented to governmental or public offices or other documents concerning rights, obligations or certification of facts."[171] However, administrative scriveners may not do any drafting work that is restricted by other laws. This latter provision drastically narrows the work of the administrative scrivener because it is interpreted to mean that their work must not overlap with the work of the lawyer, legal scrivener, patent agent, tax agent, or C.P.A.[172] So their work is considerably more constricted than it might appear on the face of the law. Also, unlike the lawyer, who may appear in any court in Japan, the administrative scrivener is only licensed to work within his prefecture[173] and, of course, is not qualified to represent a client in any court.

The administrative scrivener must belong to the prefectural Administrative Scriveners' Association,[174] which in turn must be affiliated with the Japan Administrative Scriveners' Federation.[175] The prefectural association is regulated as to fees, discipline, and registration by the prefectural governor, and the national federation comes under the supervision of the Ministry of Domestic Affairs (Jichishō).

They have a schedule of fees fixed by the prefectural governor varying from 1,600 yen to 11,000 yen (mining) (about $30).[176] Because of their limited territorial license and their subordination to the various other nonlawyer specialists, the actual practice of the administrative scrivener tends to center around the problems of small operators. For example, they draft applications for restaurants and barber licenses and the like. Also, of the some 13,500 administrative scriveners registered as of June 1968,[177] about two-thirds of them are also qualified as legal scriveners or other professionals such as land and house investigators (*tochikaoku chōsashi*). Only about a third are exclusively engaged as administrative scriveners.

Certified Public Accountant (kōnin kaikeishi)

As we have seen, in the Japanese legal system, several professions are allowed to handle legal matters that in our terms belong in the lawyer's field—*e.g.,* patent agents, tax agents, judicial scriveners, and administrative scriveners, not to mention several others of less importance to foreign enterprise such as land and house investigators and marine assistants. However, these are all narrow specialties that perform altogether only part of the services that the Japanese lawyer is authorized to do, although, in fact, he does not usually compete with these specialties because he is too occupied in court and also because, probably with the exception of the tax agents, their fees are too low to interest him. However, there are two other related professions of quite independent status[178] which the lawyer may not enter without qualifying separately— that of the certified public accountants (*kōnin kaikeishi*) and the notaries.

Although their chief function is not to render legal services, the Japanese C.P.A.s are so important to foreign investments, especially direct investments, that a word about them is appropriate here. In the first place, it is significant that C.P.A.s did not appear as a profession in Japan until 1948,[179] and then it was a result of adopting the Securities Exchange Law under American influence. They have had a monumental task since 1948 of training, organizing, and setting their standards.[180] Before 1948, under the Registered Accountant Law of 1927 there were some 25,000 accountants (*keirishi*) registered, but since 1927 fewer than two hundred of them have entered the profession as accountants by examination for competence. Rather, since vocational college (*semmon-gakkō*) graduates were exempted from the examination, nearly all of the accountants entered their specialty through that route, and inevitably the competence of many of them beyond the elements of bookkeeping, as well as their sense of professionalism, was low. After 1942, these registered accountants were not able to handle tax work without qualifying as a tax agent, which many of them have now done. In March 1967 there were only about 2,586 registered accountants and 3,740 C.P.A.s,[181] all of whom are members of the C.P.A. Institute. Only 1,390 of the C.P.A.s have audit work under the SEC Law.

To become a C.P.A., all candidates must pass a three-stage examination and then join one of ten local chapters of the Japanese Institute of C.P.A.s (*Nippon kōnin kaikeishi kyōkai*). Foreign C.P.A.s with a certain knowledge of Japanese laws may be admitted to practice in Japan,[182] and since 1948, thirty-one[183] foreign C.P.A.s have qualified.

The mainstay of the new C.P.A. is the provision in the Securities and Exchange Law[184] that requires corporation accounting reports for corporations listed on the stock exchange to be certified by a C.P.A. As of December 1967, only 2,225 corporations were required to submit C.P.A. audits, and only 1,390 C.P.A.s had been retained by these corporations, showing a concentration of this work in about 37 percent of the C.P.A.s. Presumably the others work for those fortunate 1,390 C.P.A.s or do other work such as tax service.

The work of the C.P.A.s and tax agents overlaps to some extent in Japan and also some 2,586 accountants still do accounting work on a second level of competence, although they are tending to become tax agents. The C.P.A. and the corporate auditor (*kansayaku*)[185] have functions that overlap in some areas also. It is the need for strict accounting by internationally accepted principles, in order to administer certain royalty and profit formulae in joint-venture contracts, which makes the role of the C.P.A. critical in most direct investments in Japan, and it is fair to say that most foreigners have felt that accounting services of the competence and integrity required in English have been difficult to find outside of the half-dozen foreign firms that have established branch offices in Tokyo, though this may be changing in the 1970s.

Japanese Notary (kōshōnin)

It would be better if another term other than "notary" were available to refer to the Japanese *kōshōnin,* because his function is very different from that of the notary public in the U.S. However, the usage has become so established that to select another term might be even more confusing now.

The foreign investor will most often encounter the notary in the incorporation procedure, but the notary's more important functions are:[186] (1) making notarial deeds (*kōsei shōsho*); (2) attesting articles of incorporation; (3) and attesting all sorts of private documents. When he performs the above duties he authenticates the signatures or seals of the parties and keeps a copy of the document on file for a required period of thirty years. He is not paid a salary, but is paid by his clientele in accordance with a schedule of fees established by the Ministry of Justice. He is thus both a quasi-public official and in a sense a private practitioner.

Japanese notaries are assigned to a given district and supervised by the Ministry of Justice. They must not perform other duties. Frequently they are persons who have been appointed as notaries upon retiring from the bench or procuracy. There are 364[187] notaries in Japan, organized into associations in each district of the Judicial Affairs Bureau of the Ministry of Justice. As noted, the foreigner's most common encounter with them is in establishing corporations,[188] but foreigners should not overlook the efficacy of notarial deeds to express money obligations, because they can be executed on like a judgment in case of default.[189]

Authoritative Legal Sources and Japanese Decisional Techniques

Despite a century of borrowings from the west and despite the fact that it shares in the worldwide tendency of legal systems to draw closer together as industrialization, world trade, and travel increase, we have said that modern Japanese law is a product of its own peculiar development. It we were to search impressionistically for its most prominent feature, perhaps we should say it has been a law of bureaucrats, in the same sense that French law may be a law of professors; English law, a law of judges; and American law, a law of lawyers. Here we point not only to the traditional Japanese subordination of judicial officials to executive authority until 1947 but also to the preponderance of bureaucratic law-making and decision-making in the daily legal relations of the people even today. Focusing on the preponderance of bureaucratic law-making, we find it caused by the pronounced habit of drafting legislation at the ministries in overly broad generalities; the laws, on being perfunctorily passed by the Diet, then delegate authority back to the ministry to give the generalities concrete meaning by issuing regulations at their discretion. Thus ministerial rules abound, and most phases of Japanese life are highly regulated by the ministries, requiring licenses, reports, or registrations; yet there was almost total lack of judicial review[190] of official decisions in the prewar period, and still relatively slight use[191] of the new rights of judicial review of administrative acts made available in the regular courts by the new Constitution of 1947. However, for perspective, we might say that recent trends seem to indicate that recent judicial changes are working rather well with other democratic innovations; that judicial review, though it may be cautiously used, will continue to gain in acceptance; and that the independent judges and resourceful lawyers may very well play a larger role in the jural life of Japan henceforth.

However, the professors and bureaucrats in alliance have had a head start of over half a century before World War II. While the prewar judiciary was weak, the professor as text writer and as the teacher of officialdom has had a large voice in the development of Japanese law, both because of a rather Confucianistic respect for literati and because of a Confucianistic loyalty of bureaucratic disciples to the professors who trained them, often in the Law Department of Tokyo University. At the same time, these same prewar professors had little interest in limited government or a rule of law, except perhaps for Professor Minobe and his sympathizers.

On the other hand, as noted, the judge, until 1947, was limited to dispensing justice between private parties when he could not persuade them to compromise their differences in private. He was not a law-maker; nor was he an arbiter of the use or abuse of public power or authority. Now he is independent of the bureaucracy; he does have authority to judge official, as well as private, conduct for compliance with the law. In addition to these enormous increases in the judges' postwar stature in the whole complex of government, there has also been, especially in the 1960s, a noticeable tendency for both professors and judges to pay more attention to the practical effects of law in society, which significantly takes them both to the case reports for concrete analogies if not embodiments of law as such. Those currently discernible trends lead one to suspect that the bureaucrat's role may be tempered more by law, judicially determined, in the future than it has been in the past. Be that as it may, it behooves the foreign lawyer and businessman to acquaint himself with the techniques of decision in the Japanese legal system in the past, because he will find that, for practical purposes in his license and approval seeking particularly,[192] "bureaucratic justice" is virtually all that is available to him.

The Lawyers' Tools

The foreign lawyers concerned with legal problems related to Japan will be interested in the legal tools of the Japanese judges, officials, and lawyers, and in how they are used.[193] Much has been written about differences in decisional methods in the common-law–civil-law dichotomy, and the common antinomies, frequently mentioned, lend some insights, but they speak too broadly in generalities to fit the Japanese scene. Case law in Japan, for example, may be less authoritative than in the U.S., but it is, nevertheless, of considerable weight, despite the formalism of theory that says that only the statute is law.

Certainly the orthodox Japanese theory today does say that the sole source of law is statutory and that judicial precedents and juristic commentaries are only suggestive interpretations thereof.[194] Custom is effective to the extent that it is recognized by the legal system as effective.[195] Thus, the Japanese lawyer will generally peruse his library for a nice point of law in the following sequence. He will first read the relevant provisions of the code or special statutes and regulations or the annotated codes. If the answer is still uncertain, where for instance two interpretations are possible or the case is covered only by general principles ambiguously, then the next step in all likelihood would be to check the point in a text on the subject—very likely the text that he used in the law department at the university or a more detailed and practical commentary by a leading professor on the subject. The best of this type of book will give the professor's view, as well as the views of other text writers, and cite the leading cases, which may or may not be consistent with the professor's view. If the point is controversial amongst the jurists and not resolved satisfactorily by them, the Japanee lawyer will check the cases because the judges will usually follow the leading cases rather than academic theory (*gakusetsu*) in such a case. The lawyer will start with those cases cited in his text or by the use of case studies or case compendiums or digests. If the legal point is really difficult and important, he may check the periodical literature on the chance that a more detailed study on the point may have been done in the form of an article.

Note again that if the statutes and annotations are inconclusive, the lawyer goes to the text writers instinctively, but it is rather likely that, if the legal point is to be argued in court, nowadays the judges would follow the cases rather than the jurists' views to the contrary.[196] Seldom would a legal point be resolved differently by the cases and the leading writers.[197] However, it does happen.[198]

Regardless of whether the judges at present would follow the precedents in litigation, in the prewar period, company and governmental clerks handling routine administration not involving litigation paid much attention to the systematic theory of their professors. Hence, by the time these early clerical, out-of-court interpretations based on university lectures had later reached the courts, they had often already become too strong to change. So, although in the postwar period the judge's role has been enhanced, the professors have already consolidated their position and done much valuable systematizing of the law in accordance with their overall theories.

List of Japanese Standard Law Books for Practitioners

Unlike the scant legal materials published in some countries, Japanese legal literature is voluminous and more practical and sophisticated with each passing year. The books listed below are regarded as standard materials that would be generally adequate as a core library in a Tokyo law office dealing with the major areas of civil law—when supplemented by the monographs, periodicals, statutory collections, and textbooks required for any specialties that the lawyer might have, such as securities law, labor law, or shipping. It is worth noting that nearly all of the Japanese legal materials have been rewritten in the postwar period, and most of those listed below date after 1960, but occasionally older statutes, case reports, or texts are necessary to solve a legal problem. For a more complete list for older lawyers' tools, see *Hōgaku kenkyū no shiori* (A guide to the study of jurisprudence), 2 vols. (Tokyo: Yūhikaku, 1948).

Statutory Materials

1. *Roppō zensho* (complete collection of the six codes). This single-volume, up-dated annual includes the "six codes" (constitution, civil, civil procedure, criminal, criminal procedure, and commercial). In one version by Yūhikaku Publishing Company, about 600 other important statutes and regulations are also included. The *Roppō* is on the desk of almost every law student, lawyer, official, and business executive concerned with legal matters. It is republished annually to keep it up to date.
2. A complete compilation of the effective laws and regulations such as *Genkō hōki sōran* (General coverage of currently effective laws and

regulations). This is a multivolume, looseleaf, complete collection of effective laws that are classified and up to date. In other words, it may be used for locating more specialized laws and regulations not in the *Roppō* but still effective.

3. *Hōrei zensho* is a monthly collection of all laws, regulations, and treaties as they were when they were issued, arranged chronologically and by types of regulation (*i.e.,* statute, cabinet order, etc.). It is the standard work used in locating laws as they were at a past date, although if an old *Roppō zensho* can be found it may be more convenient in some instances since it integrates amendatory laws into the laws that have been amended.

Code Commentaries

Commentaries or annotated codes are designated by several terms (*chūkai, jōkai, shōkai, or commentāru*), and generally they are most useful to a practitioner. They usually give the leading view (*tsūsetsu*) rather than that of the author. Groups of leading professors from the better law departments have jointly compiled such commentaries in their respective fields. For example, those representative in the civil law area are:

1. *Constitution:* Hōgakukyōkai, *Chūkai Nippon koku kempō* (Tokyo: Yūhikaku, 1953), 3 vols.

2. *Civil Code:* Zennosuke Nakagawa and others, eds., *Chūshaku mimpō* (Civil code annotated) (Tokyo: Yūhikaku, 1965—), 27 vols. (projected).

3. *Code of Civil Procedure:* Hideo Saitō and others, eds., *Chūkai minji soshōhō* (Code of civil procedure annotated) (Tokyo: Daiichi hōki, 1968—) (several vols. projected).

4. *Commercial Code:* As yet there is no full-scale commentary for the complete Commercial Code, but the corporate law portion (Book IV) is covered. Tadao Omori and others, eds., *Chūshaku kaishahō* (Corporation law annotated) (Tokyo: Yūhikaku, 1967—), 10 vols. (projected).

Texts

In the civil law field most of the better law departments have their expert on the various codes, and each of them usually has a well-known text,[199] of which only the most detailed are convenient for practitioners.

For example, Tokyo University professors have published the following texts:

1. *Constitution:* Jiro Tanaka and others, eds., *Nihon-koku kempō taikei* (Systematic study of Japanese constitutional law) (Tokyo: Yūhikaku, 1961–70), 8 vols.

2. *Civil Code:* Wagatsuma Sakae, *Minpō kōgi* (Lectures on the civil code) (Tokyo: Iwanami shoten, 1955–68), 8 vols.

3. *Code of Civil Procedure:* Kaneko Hajime, *Minji soshōhō taikei* (System of civil procedure) (Tokyo: Sakai shoten, 1965).

4. *Commercial Code:* T. Ishii Teruhisa, *Shōhō* (Commercial Code) (Tokyo: Keisō shobō, 1967–70), 4 vols. Vol. 1, *Shōhō sōsoku* (General part); Vols. 2 and 3, *Kaishahō* (Corporation law); Vol. 4, *Tegata kogittehō* (Bills of exchange and checks).

Besides the texts on the main codes as a whole, most well-equipped law offices would have the compendium series, *Hōritsugaku zenshū* (Complete compilation of legal studies), projected in 60 volumes (54 published to date), some of which contain two or more subjects, each authored by an acknowledged authority on the subject. It is a convenient lawyer's tool for use in getting a start in an unfamiliar part of the law, such as bonds. See T. Ōtori, "Shasaihō" (Law on corporate bonds) 33 *Hōritsugaku zenshū* 1–241 (1958).

Case Reports

1. Actual reports of postwar cases are found in the following major official reports:

a. *Saikō saibansho hanreishū minji* (Compilation of Supreme Court decisions, civil).

b. *Saikō saibansho hanreishū keiji* (Compilation of Supreme Court decisions, criminal).

c. *Kōtō saibansho minji hanreishū* (Compilation of High Court civil decisions).

d. *Kōtō saibansho keiji hanreishū* (Compilation of High Court criminal decisions).

e. *Kakyū saibansho minji hanreishū* (Compilation of lower-court civil decisions).

f. *Kakyū saibansho keiji hanreishū* (Compilation of lower-court criminal decisions).

g. *Gyōsei jiken saiban reishū* (Compilation of court precedents in administrative cases).

All of these reports contain but a small part of the cases decided by their respective courts. They are selective, and often the Supreme Court report will append the High Court and District Court decisions in the instant case. Lower court decisions, not found in the official reports, are sometimes printed in *Hanrei taimuzu, Hanrei jihō,* or other periodicals.

2. A convenient lawyer's tool for finding precedents is the postwar *Hanrei taikei* (Compendium of decisions), 189 vols. (Tokyo: Daiichi Hōki Shuppan, K.K., Dec. 1970). It is organized by the articles of each of the major codes. Although it does not give complete reports of cases, it quotes relevant extracts on most of the important cases interpreting each section of the code. It is a looseleaf service, and therefore it is kept up to date and convenient for the lawyer to use.

PART THREE

Legal Problems of
Foreign Enterprises

VI

Administration of
Foreign Entry into Japan

Introduction

As noted in Chapter I, foreign enterprises have encountered more barriers at the threshold in Japan than in any other advanced nation, and
although Japan has had reasons for such a policy, we will reserve discussion of them until Chapter VII. Our task in this chapter is to examine
the legal basis for this restrictive behavior of the Japanese bureaucracy
responsible for management of capital entries into Japan. The story
must begin with the "economic ministries" (MITI and the finance
ministry) and the Foreign Investment Council and then turn to the
Foreign Exchange and Foreign Trade Control Law (hereafter FECL)[1]
and the Foreign Investment Law (hereafter FIL),[2] enacted in 1949 and
1950 respectively, because this comprehensive organization and highly
restrictive legal framework have persisted to serve shifting purposes
throughout the entire postwar period, and there is, as of 1972, no indication that it will be dismantled soon by legislative action in the Japanese Diet. Such gradual and piecemeal liberalization as there has been
(including the "100 percent liberalization" of 1 May 1973) has taken
place largely by administrative actions within the framework of these
major laws, as we shall see in Chapter VII.

One other preliminary point is important. Rather than a rule of law,
a rule of bureaucrats prevails in this field; in fact, in most countries
with threshold controls, there is little lawyer's law (or "justiciable" law)
involved in the regulation of foreign business entries. In Japan this is
doubly true,[3] because judicial review of administration, as a legal dimension of democracy, is essentially a postwar phenomenon and still in its
infancy.[4] Instead the "validation" (*ninka*) process for foreign invest-

ment is almost pure administration, where "guidance" and official discretion is all but unchallenged in the courts and has, in fact, remained unchallenged to date. Despite much dissatisfaction in foreign circles, not even an administrative complaint, as provided for in the FIL[5] itself, is known to have been filed in over twenty years. The reason for this appears to be the futility of asserting alleged legal "rights" in the bureaucratic realms of foreign-investment licensing, and this Japanese situation, allowing for differences in degree, is not much different in kind from foreign-investment licensing in most countries that have controls. In actual practice, however, the Japanese bureaucracy has been more restrictive than its counterpart in other major countries.[6] The reasons are as controversial as they are thought-provoking, but we will postpone discussion of them until the next chapter.

To say that this is not a field of justiciable law is not to say that foreign-investment management in Japan is entirely discretionary and unregulated by rules; rules there are, hundreds of pages of them supplementing the FECL and the FIL and found conveniently in annually updated handbooks for the use of officials and specialists.[7] Even the English-language versions, for example, run to nearly a thousand pages of translated regulations,[8] and these are only the more important regulations, under which still larger volumes of notification and "inside rules" (*naiki*) are issued to serve as guides for officials who are highly specialized in the application of them.

In other words, though this is not a field in which litigation is practical, neither is it a field for generalists, not even for general legal practitioners, who might, by their usual ad hoc preparation or on-the-spot briefing, try to raise their competence to the do-it-yourself level.[9] Generally, foreign applicants for validation consult specialists who work with the Japanese parties (for example, on application for licensing or approval of joint ventures), and both rely upon and usually accept the officials' interpretations and "guidance." We intend in this chapter, therefore, only to outline the bureaucratic milieu, the policy, the organization, and the validation processes. Only when this modicum of understanding is achieved can the conflicts over "liberalization" and national policies, and the recent international law disputes over treaty obligations, be summarized in the next chapter.

The Japanese Bureaucracy in General

Bureaucracies, as well as the individuals who comprise them, have their own professional characteristics from country to country, and the enormous political and economic role as well as the distinctive internal features of the Japanese bureaucracy are so important that some basic awareness of them is essential to students of Japanese foreign investment and also to foreign enterprisers and their advisers. The management of foreign investment by the Japanese government is accomplished by administrators entrusted with broad discretions, and in such a milieu there is a certain false emphasis in approaching the problems of foreign-capital entries initially by a close analysis of the laws and regulations without some minimal profile of the men who apply them, their organization, and their national outlook, for they make most of the policy and licensing decisions important to applicants.

The Bureaucracy as a Power Group

It is by now conventional wisdom that an elemental separation-of-power analysis that relegates administrators to a simple implementation of policy made by legislators is an oversimplification of policy-making in modern government; by now it is accepted dogma that if legislators make policy wholesale, administrators make their share retail.

Bureaucratic participation, directly, in policy-making requires double emphasis in the case of economic ministries in Japan, because they are an elite and powerful force, comprising one of the three major groups in what we have called (Chapter II) "the ruling triumvirate"—elective politicians, top business management, and the higher bureaucracy (see Chart I, p. 198).[10] The center of gravity of the Japanese polity is well within this elite tripartite core, a fact that conditions the functioning of Japanese democracy in a way not apparent from the formal institutions. In a sense, the tight interdependence of these three groups (likened to the paper-scissors-rock [jankempon] game, wherein no single element can dominate both of the others) amplifies the political power of each and all. For example, elective politicians, as appointive cabinet ministers, preside over the ministerial bureaucracies; yet retired bureaucrats are the single largest source of candidates for elective office; also, such a minister is quite dependent on his former colleagues in the bureaucracy because only he and his parliamentary vice-minister (seimu jikan) are appointive, so that the political probe into the realms of bureaucracy at the time of Cabinet changes is very shallow and frequent, making for near total dependence on the career men for actual implementation of policy. In turn, the politicians are dependent almost directly on election funds supplied by organized business; and the bureaucrats, who retire at the early age of fifty, depend greatly on a "second career" in politics or in major business firms with which they had earlier established congenial connections in their official capacities. This is all rather cozy,

Chart I

GOVERNMENT OF JAPAN

EMPEROR

DIET	CABINET	COURTS
House of Representatives	Board of Audit	Supreme Court
House of Councilors	Prime Minister's Office	High Courts (8)
Judge Impeachment Court	Ministry of Justice	District Courts (49)
Judge Indictment Committee	Ministry of Foreign Affairs	Family Courts (49)
National Diet Library	Ministry of Finance	Summary Courts (570)
	Ministry of Education	Nonindictment Review Committees (204)
	Ministry of Health and Welfare	
	Ministry of Agriculture and Forestry	
	Ministry of International Trade and Industry	
	Ministry of Transport	
	Ministry of Posts and Telecommunications	
	Ministry of Labor	
	Ministry of Construction	
	Ministry of Home Affairs	

effective, and power generative for all the participants. Hence, bureaucratic power in Japan, though not entirely self-sufficient, is not entirely derivative, instrumental, or indirect either; because of the relationships within the ruling triumvirate, the career bureaucracy is no ordinary force in its own right in Japanese policy-making.

Some mention of recent history is also necessary to clarify how present power arrangements came to be.[11] To a considerable extent, the power that the bureaucracy now holds has been carried over from prewar Imperial Japan. The top bureaucrats then were a homogeneous elitist group of "Imperial aides," underwritten by personnel policies that insulated them from popular Diet controls, because personnel affairs were handled directly by Imperial ordinances. Working closely with and for a "transcendental cabinet," responsible only to a sovereign emperor rather than to a popular Diet, the prewar Japanese bureaucracy was a well-trained, proud, and privileged elite of high performance and integrity, with few of the attributes of the "public servant" that are idealized in western democracies.[12]

After 1945, besides abolishing the special administrative court and providing for ministers from the elective Diet members of the majority party, SCAP attempted to convert the "Imperial aides" to public servants by several measures including the Civil Service Law (*Kokka komuin-hō*) and by establishing a National Personnel Authority (*Jinji-in*),[13] as well as by recommending a system of merit promotions by exams for specialties[14] and less emphasis on the generalists (law) and the Tokyo University bias (see below). But some of these measures were misguided in attempting to establish a public service consistent with the new ideals of Cabinet responsibility, legislative supremacy, and popular sovereignty without sufficient awareness of the context in which they were to be launched. A major fault lay in the carefully contrived independence of the National Personnel Authority, presumably to avoid a spoils system or, in effect to insulate the bureaucracy from the politics of the Cabinet and Diet, which possibly could have been a mechanism for guiding officialdom toward the public-servant role. Independence was, in other words, sought for the wrong reasons, since an American kind of spoils system had never been and still is not a major problem in Japan. Sectionalism (*e.g.,* the Todai law bias) and discriminatory hiring and promotion practices resulting from it are apparently problems and have remained embedded in the system. Thus SCAP may have perpetuated an old Japanese problem by attempting to solve an American problem imputed to Japan.[15]

Oversimplified as it is, the foregoing comment on postwar civil-service reforms gives an inkling of some reasons why much of the prewar elitism has carried over into the postwar Japanese bureaucracy and why it has been difficult to cultivate the "public-servant" concept implied by a rule of law. Some progress, however, has been made in that direction, and the postwar Japanese bureaucracy, whatever its own self-image and attitudes toward law and its clientele may be, has a positive public performance record in the postwar period.[16]

Certain aspects of Japanese juristic method become a third source (or effect?) of the enormous power wielded by the Japanese bureaucracy. These methods give the bureaucracy a dominant role in the technicalities of law-making, at least on the "retail" level where it counts with the citizenry. In a legal sense, this is a consequence of immaturity of the rule of law adopted in 1947 as applicable to administrators. (See Chapter V). There are two aspects to the bureaucratic law-making role worth emphasizing. First, the ministries draft and sponsor[17] most of the legislation (but, notably, only after considerable consultation through commissions, *shingikai,* and the like), which is even now often perfunctorily passed by the Diet; and this situation highlights the difficulty of the Diet in overcoming its prewar disabilities as little more than an advisory body in many areas. Also, in a society of "consensus" decisions, a majoritarian institution such as the Diet naturally has its tensions with the culture. Second, legislation originating in the ministries is characteristically drafted in very abstract terms that leave, at least in regulatory statutes, many important distributive decisions, as well as detailed application, to be worked out by the regulations, the making of which is again delegated to the self-same bureaucrats. Though the phenomenon of delegating to the administration important rule-making powers is not itself peculiarly Japanese, the net effect of the practice confers upon its bureaucrats law-making powers so enormous in degree[18] that it is almost different in kind from the results, striven for at least, in western countries more experienced with administration-under-law, buttressed by ideas of equal protection and procedural due process and implemented by a tradition of judicial review of administrative acts. These latter institutions are as yet little developed and of little practical relief to foreign business in Japan.

The so-called "administrative guidance" (*gyōsei shidō*) is an even broader extralegal source of independent bureaucratic power in Japan, quite apart from bureaucratic participation in executive and legislative powers. Or perhaps it is more accurate to say that the source of Japanese "guidance" power is derived again from traditional concepts of inherent power of the administration, largely a carry-over from Imperial theories, so that "administrative guidance" is more the mode of expressing these powers than their source. By way of analogy, in most modern-managed economies something akin to this same concept is appearing more and more useful even in the traditional democracies—witness American guidelines and the like.

Administrative guidance has remained such a pervasive condition of the business environment in postwar Japan that its characteristics are worth examining in some detail. Quite recently the Foreign Investment Council under the Japanese Finance Ministry has begun to suggest special guidelines for foreign enterprises as such in Japan. By its very nature, guidance is not legally defined, nor are there rules or court precedents on such a subject, though there is just recently some attention, worth noting here, to guidance in academia. As professorially defined in Japan, "guidance" means action by which administrative agencies influence parties through voluntary, nonauthoritative—as opposed to legally coercive—means to cooperate willingly with the agency's guidance toward what is academically called "integration of the social order" (*shakai chitsujo no keisei; Gestaltung*).[19] Even though "administrative guidance" may be defined broadly to include some official behavior supported, and some not supported, by statutory grants of power, that portion of administrative guidance for which specific statutory support cannot be readily identified is very large in Japan[20] and is, of course, the most difficult to accommodate under a rule of law, our main concern here. The weight of Japanese academic authority seems to justify such extralegal administrative activity under certain circumstances, because, it is said, the conveniences are great for both sides and the dangers from insufficient guidance in solving real problems still beyond the specific statutory coverage outweigh possible abuses.[21] Thus the main Japanese concern about extralegal, inherent administrative guidance is to prevent its abuses by confining its uses to interaction between official suggestions and voluntary compliance. The "administrative guidance" of concern has four essential elements: (1) the agency must not act beyond its specific field of administrative concern; (2) it must induce from the citizenry only voluntary action; (3) there need not be specific statutory authority; and (4) the agency uses only expressions of expectations or wishes, not legal orders, or sanctions for failure to comply. Needless to say, the crux of the matter is whether in any real sense one can say in each instance that compliance was in fact voluntary.

Actually, then, "administrative guidance" is not a formal legal idea or term found either in the official regulations or even in the scholarly literature until recently. It seems to have arisen as a usage in the governmental offices and the mass news media, where it was first widely dramatized in the famous *Sumitomo* case of 1965 to be described below.

Moving from *what* administrative guidance is to *how* it is practiced, we find that, instead of proceeding by legal orders, the bureaucracy practices administrative guidance by direction (*shiji*), requests (*yōbō*), warnings (*keikoku*), suggestions (*kankoku*), and encouragements (*kanshō*). Addressees of official "guidance" are presumably not forced to perform without consent, nor are they punished if they do not. With the growth of "jawboning" and wage and price guidance[22] of the Johnson era, as well as voluntary limitations of foreign-capital transfers in the pre-1968 era, recent experiences in the United States may make it easier for Americans to understand the modern use and limitations of this pervasive mode of controls long found throughout the Japanese economic and business structure. But German nonauthoritative economic guidance (*nicht-hoheitliche Wirtschaftslenkung*) may be regarded as closer to the theoretical model for administrative guidance in Japan.[23]

In prewar Japan, as in Germany, the predominance of national authority over the judiciary was such that, even in the formal legal exercise of authority, there was insufficient protection of the rights of individuals subjected to regulations. In such an environment, there would be even less questioning of informal bureaucratic pressures resembling administrative guidance today and little awareness of the problem that official action might be extralegal or illegal.[24] Much of postwar administrative guidance flowed rather directly from ongoing and accepted prewar practices, which are just now being raised to a level of consciousness under challenge from postwar constitutionalists. Yet, as noted, some Japanese authorities justify ongoing administrative guidance as an inherent power of responsible officialdom because, in broadest terms, the administration must step into the breach to "integrate society" (*Gestaltung*); in fact, where there is a legislative vacuum it is intolerable, they say, not to do the necessary in guiding the overall economy. However, an awareness that administration under law (*hōritsu ni yoru gyōsei*) requires a statutory base (*hōritsu no konkyo*) is growing and producing new scholarly theories that urge a more adequate legal proliferation into areas admittedly requiring positive governmental planning and coordination. Still, as late as 29 September 1964, when the Special Commission on Administration made its celebrated report after two years of study, it made no special note of the pervasiveness of administrative guidance and suggested no standards to measure its propriety or impropriety for the future.[25] Actually, much of the present Japanese guidance does have at least some abstract statutory basis for official suggestions concerning such things as structural reform in industry, fixed sales prices for depressed commodity markets, and levels of capital investment; but also much of it does not, and even where generalized substantive grants are found, the modes for exercising authority (substantive criteria, notice, and fair hearing) are little affected by legalities.

As we have seen, the type of guidance in which statutory criteria are totally lacking, or the sole basis for authority is in the broad legislation establishing the ministry itself, is the most troublesome type of administrative guidance for persons concerned with a rule of law. Such was the situation in the *Sumitomo* case in which action was taken by MITI in 1965, when market conditions in steel had declined to the point where drastic countermeasures were deemed necessary. MITI suggested that the some eighty-five producers curtail their output by self-imposed no-work days and other steps to adjust supply to demand, which they did. When the market conditions again deteriorated and MITI suggested further specific production limitations, one major company, Sumitomo Metal Mining Company (*Sumitomo kinzoku kōgyō*), considered its resultant quota unjustly low and refused to comply with the MITI "guidance," alleging that it was a wrongful interference in Sumitomo's managerial rights (*keieiken*). MITI authorities resorted to sanctions available in another area of its authority and cut off Sumitomo's coal imports that were necessary for continued production. Finally, by 11 January 1966, a settlement had been reached, but the publicity given to this famous *Sumitomo* case in the media firmly established the administrative guidance problem in the minds of the public.[26]

Some observers expressed the opinion that MITI abused its power by applying sanctions collateral to the issue, in this case a reduction (or threat) of coal imports.[27] The case was also particularly apt for future reference because soon thereafter MITI became much concerned with raising Japanese industry to the level of "international competitiveness" based on the "new industrial order theory" (*shinsangyō chitsujoron*), wherein MITI sought to restructure many of the units of Japanese production into larger, more competitive sizes by encouraging mergers, consolidations, increasing investments, and concentrations on fewer products. This was reminiscent, on a broader scale, of official encouragement of massive mergers in the shipping industry in the early 1960s, wherein mergers became a condition for cheaper financing officially proffered through the Japan Development Bank. The computer industry is now undergoing similar pressures to thin itself down to three producing units (Hitachi–Fuji Tsushinki; Toshiba–Nihon Denki; and Mitsubishi-Oki).[28]

In 1966, soon after the *Sumitomo* case was settled, Idemitsu Kosan, a leading Japanese oil company, was subjected to similar guidance and sanctions because it failed to comply, in this case, with curbs on crude petroleum set by the relevant industrial association (Oil Federation), which in turn demanded that MITI exercise administrative guidance.[29] Notice that the technique of extralegal "guidance cartels" is often in competition with specifically designed statutory cartels to be supervised by the FTC after designating an industry as a "depressed industry" needing concerted price or production controls. The FTC rule was legislatively designed to prevent such cartels from arising unsupervised in violation of the Antimonopoly Law.[30] Legal ambiguity still shrouds MITI's "guidance cartels," despite their widespread employment by MITI officials in various phases of Japanese industry. MITI's role in promoting several major mergers raises similar problems, as for example the shipping company mergers, the Yawata-Fuji steel consolidation (creating the Japan Steel Corporation from parts of the old prewar combine split up by SCAP), the Daiichi-Kangyo Bank merger (1971), and the proposed paper producers' merger, which alone was finally aborted by the FTC and other opposition.

So different is this approach to "guidance" from the antitrust philosophy against such collusive action in the United States[31] and increasingly in other parts of the world that some introduction to the Japanese professorial theorizing in justification of officially sponsored collusion coexisting with Japan's own Antimonopoly Law may be of some interest, in lieu of any more solid "law" on the subject.[32] The large questions are (1) how to square officially nurtured bigness (to match foreign competitors) with the domestic Antimonopoly Law and (2) how to square administrative guidance to this end with the principle of "administration-by-law," itself derived from principles of (1) "separation of powers," (2) respect for private rights and private competition, and (3) legislative supremacy, all pillars of postwar constitutionalism.

It is instructive (and symbolic) to note that a leading academic authority in this field, Professor Narita, chose to clarify these constitutional ideas by a parenthetical insertion of the term *"burgerlicher Rechtsstaat,"* showing the tendency to find meaning for the American-inspired constitution in German concepts.[33] Narita further suggests that it is helpful, in explaining administrative guidance under the new constitutionalism, to think of administration under law as having a positive and a negative aspect. He calls the positive aspect, again in German, *Vorbehalt des Gesetzes* or "reservation of law." The negative aspect is *Vorrang des Gesetzes* or "priority of law." He says the weight of Japanese authority accepts the proposition that administrative guidance is subject to the negative aspects (priority of law) of the principle of administration according to law, because, of course, administrative guidance may not violate specific legal requirements. But he argues further that, though subject to law, guidance would seldom in fact violate law if compliance is voluntary, as assumed by definition, leaving only the very large factual question of whether compliance is voluntary.

The more interesting theorizing occurs, then, in the area of the positive aspect (reservation of law), where again two main theories have been developed. First, the leading theory in both Germany and Japan is called reservation of injury (again characteristically specified in German—*Eingriffs Vorbehalt*), which holds that the only public administration (presumably excluding administrative guidance based on consent) subject to the reservation-of-law principle is official action injurious to the people's rights and liberties. Thus, nonauthoritative acts (guidance) or beneficial acts that confer benefits or exemptions proceed outside of the principle and thus need not find their basis in explicit statutory grant.

The second theory, called total reservation (*Totaler Vorbehalt*), subjects administrative acts to the reservation-of-law principle (that is, the positive aspect of the principle of administration according to law) on a much broader front, not limited, as in the first theory, to exercising a public authority that violates rights and liberties of the citizenry. These theorists regard the first and most influential theory in Japan and West Germany (reservation-of-injury theory) as a relic of nineteenth-century ideology, premised on constitutional monarchy and supremacy of the sovereign's administrative authority over the legislature, and on the idea of inherent authority (*originarer Gewalt*) of administrative power. The total-reservation theorists, therefore, find the reservation-of-injury theory too permissive toward officials and contrary to the new constitutionalism that subordinates administration to the Diet (Constitution, Art. 41) by placing all legislative authority in the Diet. Consequently, this more modern theory would require statutory authority for all administrative acts without distinguishing between injurious and beneficial acts.

Narita[34] confesses that he has some doubts about the newer total-reservation theory because (1) under the new constitutionalism the Cabinet administration presumably is responsive to the Diet, as distinguished from the prewar imperial bureaucracy; (2) it is also suggested (for reasons that are not entirely clear) that even under the new parliamentarianism, it is not necessary to have "complete constitutionalism" in the sense that every administrative act needs specific statutory authorization; (3) modern public administration is charged with dynamic "integration of society," in turn requiring a certain degree of free scope in synoptic supervision; and finally (4) even if strict authorizations are required in dynamic modern administration, the statutory grants would have to be so general and comprehensive that they would mean very little. Despite growing awareness of legal problems with guidance, Narita notes that the older reservation-of-injury theory is still dominant among academic circles. This position does require that administrative guidance be premised from the outset upon the parties' agreement. Even though the total-reservation theory requires statutory authority for all activities of administrative bodies regardless of their kind or character, it too could exempt administrative guidance from the requirement of statutory authority because again guidance depends on consent. So it seems that by Narita's interpretation both theories on legal controls for public administrators in Japan largely exclude administrative guidance.

The net effect of Japanese academic theorizing is, then, that positive legal authority by statute is not required for administrative guidance. Common types of controls imposed by the negative principles (priority of law) must, however, be followed: the administrative agent must not press his guidance to exceed the limits of its jurisdiction; in other words, an agency should not use administrative guidance for purposes outside its sphere of authority. Actually, MITI violations of this sort seem to be rather common in Japan; the aforementioned cutting of Sumitomo's coal import quotas in the steel-production curbing program has been suggested as such an example.[35] Another possible violation of the priority-of-law principle is the major jurisdictional conflict wherein MITI has favored many cartel arrangements to enhance competitiveness against foreigners, even though the cartels might infringe upon the "primary jurisdiction" of the FTC, charged with the maintenance of competition.

Foreign enterprisers operating in Japan, of course, are now, and in the future will be, expected to follow government guidelines on "check prices," reduction of production, investment quotas, and the like— whether filtered down through industrial associations or more directly enforced through "guidance cartels" and whether any basis in law can be found or not. Such guidance is a pervasive part of Japanese business and governmental relations to which foreigners must accommodate themselves. In fact, one of the major unstated official reasons for limiting foreign participation in Japanese industry has been precisely that the symbiosis of Japanese government and business is such that foreigners are awkward at best and disruptive at worst.[36]

Addressing itself to this problem, MITI is reported to be considering a set of guidelines specifically for foreign enterprise. The major points tentatively reported are:

1. The 50 percent principle, as established by Japanese policy in the past.

2. Where foreign enterprises entering Japan have powerful patents that threaten the domestic economy, such enterprises will be required to open such patents to the public by licensing at a fair royalty rate.

3. Foreign enterprises must refrain from unjust business transactions and unfair competition.

4. Foreigners should not excessively concentrate their activities on specific industrial divisions in their advance into Japan.

5. Foreigners should cooperate with Japanese industrial circles in the latter's voluntary efforts for maintaining good order.

6. Foreigners should respect established Japanese practices with relation to the employment and wage system.

7. Foreigners should not obstruct independent development of technologies by Japanese industries.

These will "be convenient for MITI for exercising its administrative guidance over foreign enterprises advancing into Japan after the fourth capital decontrol schedule."[37]

Even at the point of entry, foreign applicants for investments in the nonliberalized industries are soon introduced to still another specific kind of official guidance[38] in the form of intensive, case-by-case, official review of contract terms already negotiated and even signed between foreign and Japanese parties. Foreigners have often negotiated a licensing or joint-venture contract, with detailed terms representing their maximum concessions, assuming (we do not say with justification) that the contract would be approved or disapproved, as signed by the parties, under Japan's "free-enterprise" system. But the official practice was for years, and in the case-by-case screening of important cases still is, for the government to go over contract terms and suggest revisions in favor of the Japanese party. Of course, sophisticated foreigners with experience have long been aware of the "two-against-one" routine—as it was known among foreigners. But it often caught first-timers unawares, because there were for years no guidelines that specified the outer limits of key terms such as royalty rates or foreign management participation; nevertheless, the foreigners were frequently subjected to officially required reductions, sometimes beyond the point at which business was voluntarily possible and despite mutual interest between the parties on the agreed terms. Though administrative guidance of this sort was routinely practiced throughout the 1960s with virtually no useful promulgated legal guidelines, the new Fair Trade Commission (FTC) regulations, issued in 1966 to fill gaps left by eliminating screening in the "liberalization" process, have made the "law" more knowable in this respect for technological assistance contracts. (See Appendix VIII.)[39]

This kind of guidance—the foregoing "two-against-one" procedure in the negotiation of contracts—was and still is blandly described by officialdom as the case-by-case (*kobetsu shinsa*) validation and is still applicable to unliberalized areas, those most interesting to foreigners. Texas Instrument,[40] IBM, Avon, Norton Co., General Foods (curry), and Ampex are but a few of the more celebrated cases in which "guidance" of this sort bore heavily upon foreign leaders in technology.

In anticipation of our later discussion of "liberalization," we should mention that some specific criteria for validation appeared in 1967, but ironically enough, these appeared as conditions to be met in order to obtain the highly publicized "automatic" validations.

To summarize, the Japanese bureaucracy (and especially the "economic ministries" managing foreign enterprises) is a political force and wields major policy-making powers in its own right and in its own way (guidance). This is because of inheritance of the *samurai* image and because of effective leadership where and when the need is felt by itself and its partners (business and politicians) in the ruling triumvirate. One should not forget, however, that extensive consultation (see Chapter II) with advisory councils and private groups precede official actions at all levels and during all stages to avoid arbitrary actions. Query: Is this equivalent to, or better than, seeking legal authorizations?

The Japanese Bureaucracy as an Elite

Looking now at the internal aspects of the Japanese bureaucracy, its most striking quality is a deeply ingrained elitism derived from both its prewar heritage[41] and its postwar performance in Japanese society.[42] In addition to its élan, the Japanese bureaucracy has highly unusual organizational features[43] in nearly every aspect including training, recruitment, promotion, modes of operations, and retirement practices— all of which need to be understood not only because they are interesting for comparative purposes but also because they go a long way toward explaining how the Japanese bureaucracy operates and why it is so confident, prestigious, and effective, as well as officious. There is a tendency to think of the higher civil servant (section chief: *kachō* and above)[44] in Japan as the *samurai*'s (*shizoku*) successor, legitimized now by a merit system based on academic performance. Perhaps nothing in Japanese modernization exhibits more national genius than the smooth transition from hereditary status to the merit system so evident in modern Japanese society.[45]

The merit system has its peculiarities, however, the most important being the Tokyo University bias[46] and the fact that objective testing ends, by and large, with the first job; indeed, some would say its role is largely played out at the point at which the young Japanese passes the university entrance exam. But eligibility for that first job comes from passing civil service exams, even though the actual hiring by the ministers from the pool comprised of those who pass is done by a rather subjective interviewing procedure. The various Japanese school and government exams, like all exams, have their limitations, but the popular mythology in Japan still seems to support them, even though they are decisive forever at each stage from entrance to middle school to higher school to university to ministry (or major corporations). Massive eliminations at each stage produce a pyramid of disappointed people at the base and talented (as defined by the exam) people at the top. This makes for much social mobility up to graduation, because academic performance is more important than social origin, wealth, geographic factors, or political connections in obtaining a coveted position in the public service or with big business. (See Chapter IV.) For this reason, there is no more intense competition on entrance exams on each rung of the educational ladder anywhere in the world than in Japan. And at the time of hiring, the exam not only determines eligibility for preferred ministries but also one's entire career because of the lifetime employment system.

As noted, although there is much journalistic criticism, there is surprisingly little real challenge to the integrity of the Japanese examination system and the steeply graded hierarchy of universities which it has provided. Also, in the national universities, there is little evidence of admission because of money or political pressure and little evidence of bribery on exams.[47] Because of the critical interview[48] at the final stage of hiring into prestigious ministries, there is some room to doubt the complete objectivity of final selections for the ministries or the firms. Perhaps this is unavoidable; in any event, it is understandable that the graduate from a top university hired by a prestigious ministry feels a certain élan, just as it is understandable that society respects his ability. It is not surprising that members of this elite, all from the same exacting mold, respect and promote each other's interests and perform well, personally and collectively. However, the extraordinary extent to which Japan classifies everyone by exams, irrevocably and normally before he is eighteen, may in the long run create a troublesome class system because of the "strong inherited element in ability."[49]

The historical leadership role of the government service in developing the economy to "miracle" proportions, from the Meiji Restoration (1868) onward, has also enhanced its prestige—and privilege. Rather than an adversary business-government standoff as we had in American economic development, wherein a career in business or the professions was until recently favored over government service, in Japan government has been until recently[50] the favored career, because modern industry was early regarded as a western institution to be acquired and used offensively by a national effort in which the bureaucracy was in the vanguard. Thus, its *samurai* image and leadership role in early modernization and postwar reconstruction have made government careers highly coveted, which in turn assured the government of bright young officials from all strata of Japanese society (though not proportionately), whose talent was measured by a hierarchical education system of sufficient integrity to sustain itself at a high degree of efficiency. These are some of the reasons why the officials encountered in the economic ministries (among the most prestigious) are competent, purposive, and, though courteous, intensely nationalistic in thrust.

Given the aforementioned general qualities, it is also important to understand that in its training, recruitment, modes of operation, and retirement practices, the Japanese bureaucracy in almost every phase has peculiarities unparalleled, at least in degree, elsewhere in the world.[51] Eschewing details, we can only list some major features here.

In recruitment for the higher civil service, for example, it is standard practice to do virtually all of the hiring from a pool of "generalists," the group of bright young law graduates just out of the university; a disproportionate number come from one law faculty—Tokyo University. They stay with the ministries for their entire careers, leaving almost no room for mid-career hiring; in hiring, almost no attention is paid to specialties; the ministry buys raw material and trains its own because the long career justifies it.[52]

Probably no bureaucracy in the world emphasizes the generalist qualification (synonymous with legal training) to the extent that Japan does. To Americans, it comes as a surprise to find that the generalist role is performed largely by law graduates (B.A. not J.D. degrees; see Chapter V), whereas social science and humanities graduates are regarded as "specialists" and not favored in the hiring and promotion of officials. But since the young law-trained generalist normally stays with the service and with the same ministry throughout his entire career, he develops by in-service training a kind of specialty and deep competence over the years—in that ministry's work.

Promotions are made in an escalating fashion in accordance with age and seniority measured from the date of graduation rather than from birth; one major irregularity evident in the high levels of the civil service is the favoritism (even clearer than in the hiring) shown for Tokyo University (Todai) law graduates.[53] At least one study shows that they are promoted faster (seven years on the average) and higher than law graduates from other universities so that nearly 80 percent of the entire "higher civil service" (section chiefs up to vice-minister, hereafter HCS), are Todai graduates.[54] Comparative studies show that in the U.S. (1959) the only school with even 3 percent of the "higher civil service" was George Washington University,[55] and in England, even Oxford and Cambridge[56] together accounted for only 47 percent. Other departments (besides law) of Tokyo University seem to be discriminated against, with few hired, and those who are hired are promoted later than law graduates. All Japanese national universities (excluding Todai) had only 13 percent of the HCS, and private universities had only 3 percent. It must be remembered that Japanese private universities were only accorded equal status as universities in 1918. Only Kyoto University (law), Hitosubashi University (law), and Todai economics might be called important minorities with appreciable portions of the 13 percent mentioned above.[57]

To subject promotions to objective standards, SCAP attempted to initiate examinations for each important advancement in the service, but this seed fell on barren soil.[58] The factors in promotion are, first, a Todai law degree; among other university graduates, the university and specialty (meaning law) too were in the leading factors in promotion. Also, promotion occurs faster for members of some ministries than for others because of better opportunities (for example, in the "economic ministries") for "second careers" as described below. Though, in the HCS, Tokyo law graduates were promoted noticeably faster and higher than others, promotion within all such university groups proceeded almost automatically by age in lockstep from promotion to promotion with no exams and little attention given to ability, performance, personality, pull, or politics in status promotions. But certain differentiation is made as to positions, and thus the route of promotion is well known in advance, since certain sections in any ministry are more important than others. Individuals given a position in, for example, the General Affairs Section (*Sōmuka*) are marked for higher promotions. Automatic seniority promotions and the bias in favor of Todai are features not found to the same degree in most other countries.

Retirement practices are also unusual in Japan, especially "two-careerism" as explained before with regard to business. Retirement occurs early at an average age of about fifty for the HCS as a result of the automatic, lockstep promotion system. The aversion to status competition within a graduating group and in-service testing for specialties is so strong that, without any legal rules or regulations requiring it at all, the automatic promotion system (*nenkō joretsu*) forces the talented Todai type of official to proceed up and out by age fifty. This is because when a group of graduates, for example, from Todai reach the ultimate point at which they should be appointed to the next status up to administrative vice-minister (*jimu-jikan*)—a position, of course, requiring but one of them—the rest resign and make room for the next wave. Also, there is great pressure on the administrative vice-minister to hold the job only two or three years.

This early retirement at the height of productive capacity has meant that officials seek a second career in Japan. In fact, the system is greatly facilitated by availability of positions for these talented retired officials in business, politics, and public corporations or collateral agencies.[59] Typically, MITI officials find positions as high officers in the industries with which they work while in office. Finance retirees often go to public corporations. The law requires officials to obtain permission[60] before joining a firm related to their official duties, but permission is generally granted without difficulty. Others get LDP support to run for the Diet and if successful for several terms may even come back to the old ministry as the minister.

The Bureaucracy and Sectionalism

Without suggesting that Todai law graduates are not an extraordinarily talented group, it seems likely that part of the explanation for the remarkable Todai dominance of the HCS, after hiring, lies in the perpetuation of organizational advantages long held collectively by means of a peculiar sectionalism inherent in Japanese psychology, especially in the upper levels of society discussed here. This characteristic is of great importance to any understanding of the Japanese political, business, and bureaucratic milieu.[61]

In considering Japanese sectionalism,[62] one starts with the impression gained by daily observations that most Japanese upper-level social relationships are of a peculiarly tangible, intense, exclusive, and concrete kind, typical of the "frame," to use Professor Nakane's term. Though the same might be said of society everywhere, the peculiarity in Japan is that one can almost say that those people with whom one lives and works are all that matter. Relationships without daily contact (and outside the "frame") do not count; "neighbors are important; cousins are not." This unusually sharp and exclusive focus on tangible personal relations has both internal and external aspects, constituting two traditional principles that persist as a kind of fundamental social grammar actuating relationships of the elite, despite all of the remarkable changes during Japan's modern century. The internal principle is the primacy and exclusivity of vertical relationships between a superior and subordinate (*samurai*-retainer), emotionally bound by loyalty and mutual obligations, man to man; today it may be the prior and later graduates of the same school (*sempai-kohai*), or patron-client (*oyabun-kobun*) relationships in a myriad of contexts in Japanese everyday life. The strength of the vertical tie means, significantly, the weakness of horizontal ties, illustrated for example by the observation that Japanese professors are typically closer to their students than their professional colleagues, even though the faculty as a group is bound almost tribally together so that cooperation across faculty boundaries or with another university is weak.[63] For our purpose this is specifically significant in perceiving how the bureaucracy operates.

The external principle is the aforementioned primacy of the frame, the intimate (and often heterogeneous) group (*e.g.,* the work unit), over relations based on similarities or more universal attributes, such as occupation, academic degrees, professional qualifications, or similar work skills. To any Japanese, his group (his firm, village, school, or graduating class) is virtually his all. Relationships with outsiders are at best awkward or dull and often hostile. And, in contrast to American concern for "attributes"—work skills, academic or professional qualifications such as a Ph.D., or membership in the lawyers' bar or political science association—these are of minor concern in Japan. Illustrations are the aforementioned hostility often prevailing between faculties of the same subject matter but different groups (universities) and faculty inbreeding by hiring only their own, unless a lesser university is under wing (*i.e.,* staffed by disciples from a superior university).

Many a foreigner has mused over the near compulsion of the Japanese to offer a name-card (*meishi*) forthwith to any stranger (foreign or Japanese). This is not just a useful national habit; it is symbolic of the strength of these two basic principles at work. The card tells the stranger one's company (group) and his vertical position in it, and among Japanese it seems that both the donor and the donee of the card are quite uncomfortable—quite unable to behave properly—without it. In another way, group-over-attribute is well illustrated by the fact that a typist for a major Japanese firm undoubtedly outranks a skilled typist from a provincial firm; the company, not the skill, confers prestige.

This attention to basics is worth the space, because these are, in degree at least, distinguishing principles activating Japanese society, and their meaning is not always discernible to the outsider. The dual effect of these two principles also helps to explain the virulent sectionalism and informal factionalism found within larger Japanese organizations, whether it be company, political party, or ministry. The connection to the prior basics is, as one plausible explanation notes,[64] that sectionalism is a direct result of the exclusivity of the vertical principle described above, wherein a patron, A, has three subordinates, B, C, and D, with perhaps each in turn having his own subordinates as shown by the following model:

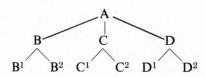

In this typical model of a Japanese clique organization patterned after the concrete and emotive ties of traditional Japan, the faction-producing potential lies in the fact, above noted, that there is little by way of horizontal ties, or even communication, between B, C, and D; nor does A have the kind of direct emotive ties that count with B^1 or B^2. These structural weaknesses allow, in fact almost inevitably cause, formal or informal factions to develop between B's group and C's group, especially if A disappears. With this simplified description in mind, it is easier to understand our suggestion that sectionalism, born of characteristic Japanese exclusive focus on groupings by vertical relations, may explain in part the persistent Todai dominance in the HCS of the major ministries, especially given their talent, historical priority, and numerical weight.

Of more practical significance is the effect within MITI of sectionalism on the execution of broader ministerial policies. An illustration in point here is the attempt to implement "liberalization." Starting with assumptions that liberalization policy originated from the top down (*i.e.,* with the Cabinet, in response to foreign pressures; see below), it seems clear that sectionalism on at least three levels has greatly impeded the execution of the policy over nearly a decade. The first type of sectionalism on the broadest level is economic nationalism itself[65] and one of its instruments, enterprise nationalism. Delicate as this subject is nowadays, there are rare but candid Japanese comments on the tendency of organized big business, as well as MITI, the protector of domestic business, to regard foreign competition with hostility. Whether abroad or on the domestic scene, the response becomes one of "we Japanese" banding together against foreign competition. More will be said on this point later. This kind of nationalism,[66] too, is not solely Japanese, of course, and we only note its intensity and historical roots here.[67]

The second type of factionalism in the liberalization struggle has taken the form of jousting among the three leading ministries concerned —MITI, the Ministry of Finance, and the Foreign Ministry. The latter, responsible for foreign relations and aware of the international requirements, has affirmatively favored a faster pace for Japanese "liberalization" whereas MITI has been the major drag,[68] with the Finance Ministry in the middle position.

The third type of sectionalism is even more interesting; it has grown out of the organizational pattern of MITI itself (see Chart II below), for MITI has several bureaus, one for each segment of industry. So a "horizontal" policy, ministry-wide, that is sponsored by one of the functional bureaus inevitably has rough going against the vertical commitment of each of the "industry" bureaus to its clients. Each bureau supports liberalization for other bureaus' industries and the maximum

Chart II

BUREAUS AND DEPARTMENTS UNDER THE
MINISTER OF INTERNATIONAL TRADE AND INDUSTRY
(*Tsūshō sangyō daijin*)

*Minister's Secretariat (*Daijin kambō*)
    Research and General Statistics Department (*Chōsa tōkei-bu*)
*International Trade Bureau (*Tsūshō kyoku*)
    International Economic Affairs Department (*Kokusai keizai-bu*)
*Trade and Development Bureau (*Bōeki shinkō kyoku*)
    Economic Cooperation Department (*Keizai kyōryoku-bu*)
*Industrial Policy Bureau (*Kigyō kyoku*)
*Environmental Protection and Safety Bureau (*Kōgai hoan kyoku*)
 Heavy Industry Bureau (*Jūkōgyō kyoku*)
 Chemical Industry Bureau (*Kagaku kōgyō kyoku*)
 Textile and General Merchandise Bureau (*Sen'i zakka kyoku*)
 Mining and Coal Mining Bureau (*Kōzan sekitan kyoku*)
    Coal Department (*Sekitan-bu*)
 Public Utility Industry Bureau (*Kōeki jigyō kyoku*)

*Functional Bureaus

of protection for its own (so-called *sōron sansei, kakuron hantai*).[69] So when the government approves a liberalization schedule at the Cabinet level, and the minister calls for suggestions (as to how much and when) by the usual procedure (*ringisei*), the result is suggestions for liberalization by each bureau, but for the other bureaus' industries. The identity of interest (with their industrial clientele) behind this behavior is enhanced by the practice of MITI bureaucrats of looking to these same industrial firms for their "second careers."

In ending a discussion of Japanese bureaucracy and foreign investment, one final comment may add some perspective. Because of the density of official attention lavished on the foreign enterprisers in Japan, it may be a surprise to some foreigners to learn that, in spite of official omnipotence and omnipresence in things economic, there is less bureaucracy in Japan in at least two respects than there is, for example, in the U.S.: first, there are fewer public employees per capita in Japan than in the U.S.;[70] and second, the bureaucracy disposes of less of the GNP through public spending than does, for example, the U.S. government, suggesting that, while "private enterprise" may not be quite as private in Japan, it has a larger role.[71]

The several suggestions and insights offered above regarding the Japanese bureaucracy will provide some clues as to its modes of operation in enforcing the Foreign Investment Law. In the foreign-investment licensing process, the attitudes and habits of officials occupying positions in the "economic ministries" are more important than any analysis of the law, or even of policy statements issued for international readers. Still, at least an understanding of the coverage and basic framework of the FIL is required as well and will be offered in the next section.

The Foreign Investment Law:
The Threshold Validation Process

The legal system described in Chapter V furnishes the general legal milieu in which foreigners must plan and operate their Japanese enterprises, but the more specific legal framework for the official licensing of foreign business at the threshold will be discussed here as a matter of purely domestic Japanese law and policy that restrict the entry of foreign business. International and policy issues are deferred until later, though at this point it is well to bear in mind that Japanese attitudes are shifting slowly toward a recognition that a more open economy at home is a condition of liberal treatment abroad and therefore in the national interest; the U.S. 10 percent surcharge, the *dōru shokku* (dollar shock), the December 1971 yen (308 to $1.00), and the early 1973 yen (260 to $1.00) were part of this process.

Two domestic statutes are directly involved in the licensing of foreign capital entry: the Foreign Investment Law[72] (FIL) of 1950 and the Foreign Exchange and Trade Control Law[73] (FECL) of 1949, with their many regulations. These are complex statutes with highly technical regulations,[74] but, simply put,[75] the FIL regulates investment by "foreign investors" as defined in the statute, whereas the FECL regulates (besides trade) currency transactions between "residents" and "nonresidents," as defined in the FECL. The two laws are interrelated in that they both deal with foreign money, and they both dovetail and overlap. Their systematic legal relationship is that the FECL is the "general law" (*ippanhō*), while the FIL is the "special law" (*tokubetsuhō*). By Japanese rules of construction, the FIL as a special law governs and prevails over the FECL in investment activities specifically placed within its jurisdiction, and the FECL governs all else; there is much cross-referencing to basic FECL definitions in the FIL.[76] Together, the FIL and FECL subject almost every imaginable transaction with a foreign contact to a licensing requirement; almost everything is prohibited, unless one first obtains approval. As is common to this species of controls, which run all human beings covered through a single wicket before they can accomplish their daily business, this legislation has spawned a maze of regulations full of abstruse and unintelligible cross-references in attempts to close "loopholes" and handle exceptions. Poignant as many landmarks (such as the yen-base company)[77] are to many of us, after nearly twenty years of working with the FIL, the past[78] does not warrant much attention here, for most of the past detail is now legally irrelevant or has been summarized already (Chapter I).

Purpose of Investment Controls

Still, after over ten years of "liberalization," the FIL is very much alive and operative in vital areas of interest to foreigners. Reflecting on the persistence of the FIL, it seems clear that two spirits lay within its bosom: one preferred by foreigners, who saw it largely as a mechanism that insures Japan's balance of international payments in an otherwise unrestricted enviroment, where faith in free market forces prevails, and provides, as a price for its restrictions, a guarantee for repatriation of "validated" investments; the other preferred by officialdom, which has always seen the FIL as primarily a tool for planners and a method for selective induction of technology—with no more foreign managerial participation in business than required to get the techniques. These polar readings of the law by Japanese and foreigners stems from the confusion in Arts 1 and 2, the texts of which are as follows:

[Purpose]
Article 1. The purpose of this law is to create a sound basis for foreign investment in Japan, by limiting the induction of foreign investment to that which will contribute to the self-support and sound development of the Japanese economy and to the improvement of the international balance of payment, by providing for remittances arising from foreign investment, and by providing for adequate protection for such investments.
[Principle concerning foreign investment]
Article 2. Foreign investment in Japan shall be permitted to be as free as possible, and the system of validation pursuant to the provisions of this law shall be relaxed and eliminated gradually as the necessity for such measures decreases.

It seems obvious in retrospect, FIL Art. 2 notwithstanding,[79] that Japanese officialdom has always used the FIL, at least since 1956 or 1957, to resist foreign direct investment as such, although the balance-of-payment rationale was so real until about 1965 that antiforeign motives did not clearly surface, as such, in the validation of direct investment until later. On the other hand, Japan has always favored the importation of foreign technology, though free importation, except in petty proportions, has not been the policy until July 1972; rather, importation has been allowed only selectively and on governmentally imposed conditions. The contract conditions have generally not been left to the parties nor imposed by law but provided by guidance. Also, many foreigners have felt that only when—by domestic competition, physical preemption of sites, or other discouraging circumstances—a particular business becomes impenetrable or unattractive to foreigners will the formal legal controls be "liberalized."[80] An exception to the foregoing conclusion, again borne out by experience, was that equity participation in new enterprises might be validated, sometimes after much renegotiation and delay, but only if a foreign enterpriser possessed legally secure technology that he would not offer to Japanese enterprisers on a straight licensing basis.

Coverage of FIL and FECL

Interrelated as they are, both as to subject matter and persons covered, the FIL and the FECL have important differences affecting their application in specific transactions. First, the FIL is formation (or transaction) oriented; it requires validation (*ninka*) of all investment "contracts" (*keiyaku*) and "acquisitions" (*shutoku*) within its purview,[81] whereas generally the FECL is performance oriented. It prohibits, among other things, all payments (*shiharai*) including deposits or credits between "exchange residents" (*kyojūsha*) and "nonresidents" (*hikyojūsha*), unless they have obtained "approval" (*kyoka*), and note that these approvals must be obtained not only for foreign currency payments but also for domestic (*yen*) payments, or even deposits or credits between residents and nonresidents.

As to persons concerned, the FIL requires validation for transactions with "foreign investors," which is defined by "nationality" criteria[82] to include individual foreign nationals and juridical persons incorporated abroad or with their main place of business abroad (even if Japanese), as well as foreign residents in Japan, including branches and subsidiaries controlled by foreign investors, even though located or incorporated in Japan. Also, the FIL includes in its definition of foreign investors specifically FECL "exchange nonresidents" (excluding juridical persons), as defined in FECL.[83]

The FECL applies to payments between "residents" and "nonresidents" and more generally to any person in Japan making payments abroad, whether the other party is nonresident or not.[84] "Exchange resident" means all natural persons who have their permanent place of abode or who customarily live in Japan; juridical persons (corporate bodies, enterprises) having their seat or place of administration in Japan; and Japanese branches of "exchange nonresidents," whether independent in law or not, even if the place of their administration or headquarters is located abroad. "Exchange nonresident" means all persons, natural or juridical, other than those who are exchange residents.[85]

Thus, the FIL definition of "foreign investors" includes all "foreign exchange nonresidents" under the FECL and, in addition, other investors, mainly those of foreign nationality or those that are foreign controlled, even though technically "exchange residents" under the FECL.

Another point of contact is important. Since the investment transactions validated under the FIL may confer remittance privileges for the foreign investor of all "fruits" (*kajitsu*) and "principal withdrawn" (*genbon kaishukin*) under certain conditions, these payments are "deemed"[86] to be approved under the FECL; this approval is conferred at the time of validation, provided special requests are made in the application forms and other procedures for handling remittances are followed.[87]

In terms of legal effects also, the FIL and FECL are different. The Japanese conceptualization, which produces the differences, flows from the public-law–private-law dichotomy that is central to civil law thinking. The latter sees regulatory (public) and contract (civil or private) law as separate so that it is quite possible to have a transaction that violates the regulations (public) and yet is enforceable as a valid contract between the parties. Especially in the area of foreign-exchange regulations the Japanese judges have not been enthusiastic about extending the legal effects of acts violative of the public regulations into the private law domain. This result is reached by the traditional Japanese analysis that classifies all economic control regulations into two basic categories: mandatory provision (*kyōkō hōki*) or directive provision (*torishimari hōki*). A contract violative of rules classified as *kyōkō hōki* not only subjects the parties to possible administrative sanctions and criminal penalties but is also invalid and unenforceable as a contract under the private law, whereas a contract violative of a mere *torishimari hōki* only subjects the parties to administrative or criminal sanctions and does not invalidate the contract.

The FIL has been labeled "mandatory" so that violative contracts are unenforceable. But the Japanese courts have consistently classified the FECL as "directive" and thus have been willing to enforce violative contracts in civil actions. Overall this Japanese approach seems a bit more flexible than the American approach to such illegal contracts. Although the FECL (Arts. 27–29) deals with performance (*i.e.,* payments), FECL Art. 30 requires prior approvals (*kyoka*) for the creation (*hassei*) of all obligations (*saiken*) between residents and nonresidents which are not excepted by ministerial ordinance. But because the FECL is merely directive, parties to a contract "created" without the essential prior approval may still sue for damages for breach, even though they are subject in public law to criminal penalties for not getting the prior approval. This point was decided for the first time by the Japanese Supreme Court in 1965 in the case of *Tomita* v. *Inoue*.[88] The defendant (resident of Japan) had borrowed $500 in Hawaii from the plaintiff's assignor, a Japanese resident in Hawaii. The plaintiff, as assignee of the lender, sued to collect the loan in the Saga District Court, where the suit was dismissed, which decision was affirmed at the Fukuoka High Court. The Supreme Court then reversed, holding that the FECL requirement of an approval (*kyoka*) for resident-nonresident loan payments did indeed only go to the payment. And an underlying loan contract without approval was valid and enforceable, though the plaintiff would have to get approval before he could collect on a judgment. In Japanese legal conception, the court held that the FECL requirements are merely "directive provision" (*torishimari hōki*), meaning in this case that the FECL only restricts performance (payment). It is not a mandatory provision (*kyōkō hōki*) invalidating the whole transaction, as the FIL would, for example, were it applicable.

This case may be regarded as settling, at least as to similar cases, a question that has been much debated. But note that Justice Jiro Matsuda wrote a cogent dissent suggesting that the majority opinion holding the contract effective was unnecessarily broad. Justice Matsuda proposed a concept of inconclusive invalidity (*fudōteki mukō*)—if approval for payment is later obtained, the transaction is retroactively valid.

A final interplay (respecting subject matter covered) between the FIL and the FECL should also be noted preliminarily: reporting of establishment of[89] branches by foreign enterprises and the transfer of capital[90] and technology to them in Japan has fallen under the FECL, rather than the FIL, largely for historical reasons (note that OECD treats branches as "direct investment," all other forms of which are handled under the FIL in Japan). Also, all technological assistance agreements are divided into Class A and Class B, and Class B (defined as those to be performed—or payment made thereon—within one year) are subject only to the payment approvals of the FECL, where Class A agreements lasting more than a year are treated as "foreign investment" and subject to FIL validation.[91]

Some emphasis should be placed at the outset on the fact that technological assistance agreements, including patents, know-how, and trademark transfers or licenses, are regarded as "foreign investments" under the FIL.[92] This is unusual conceptualization in international practice (*e.g.,* OECD or FCN treaties). It does, however, point to the paramount importance that Japanese policy has attached to the selective importation of technology on nationally favorable terms.[93]

We will next review the facilities, criteria, and procedures provided in the FIL and regulations for validation of foreign investments, since validation, whether "automatic" or case-by-case under it, is necessary for any legal investment in Japan, whether a loan, direct or indirect (portfolio) investment, or even a technological assistance agreement of more than a year's duration.

Bureaucratic Facilities for Validation

In the FIL, the authority to grant validations is conferred upon the "competent minister" (*shumu daijin*),[94] but, as we shall see, most of the real decision-making is delegated to other agencies so that the competent minister's final seal is usually rather perfunctory. For most acquisitions of stock, technological assistance agreements, and loans (formally, "claimable assets of loans" [*kashitsukekin saiken*]), the competent ministers are jointly the minister of finance and another minister concerned with the pertinent industry.[95] For example, if the investment were in shipping, the other minister would be the minister of transportation, but usually it is the MITI minister, because of his surveillance over the bulk of Japanese industry. Under the FECL, the competent minister is in most investment cases the finance minister, although MITI has FECL functions in import-export trade and in some investment matters involving industrial property.[96]

Generally, in investment matters, the finance minister must first request an opinion from the Foreign Investment Council[97] (*Gaishi shingikai*; hereafter FIC), which was established[98] as an organization attached to the Ministry of Finance and had up to fifteen councilors (all part-time). In 1967 the council was reconstituted, drawing its entire membership (Chart III, p. 223) exclusively from business and academic circles rather than government. They were asked to consider the question of liberalization put to them by the Ministry of Finance as follows: "Looking at recent conditions both internal and external, what sort of policy should we have concerning liberalization of direct investment in Japan?" At that time, the finance minister, who presides over the FIC and appoints the other members, also designated a distinguished business leader (Ataru Kobayashi) as his deputy to preside over the council's liberalization discussion.

The importance of the FIC may be perceived from the FIL description of its two functions: (1) rendering opinions (*iken*) on policy questions put to it by "administrative agencies" (*gyōsei kikan*) through the Finance Ministry,[99] and (2) rendering opinions to the competent ministers on validation applications,[100] except for matters of minor importance, which incidentally are increasing recently. The statute says that the finance minister "*shall request*" the opinion of the FIC; and then Art. 18-2(2) states specifically, "In case of granting the validation in accordance with the provisions of this law, the competent minister *shall respect* (*sonchō*) the opinion of the Foreign Investment Council. . . ."

In establishing the FIC,[101] the FIL provides for two-year terms of part-time service; reappointment is allowed. The council's decisions are by majority vote of the members present; it is authorized to have special commissioners up to five for the investigation of special projects; and

Chart III

MEMBERS OF THE FOREIGN INVESTMENT COUNCIL
(1973)

Ataru Kobayashi, Chairman
    Chairman, Arabiya Petroleum Company
Toshio Dokō, Acting Chairman
    President, Tokyo Shibaura Electric Appliances Company
Yoshishige Ashihara
    Chairman, Kansai Electric Power Company
Hiromi Arisawa
    Emeritus Professor, Tokyo University
    Member of the Atomic Energy Commission
Takashi Ihara
    President, Yokohama Bank
Hiroki Imazato
    President, Nihon Seikō (precision industry) K.K.
Kōhei Suzue
    Member of the New Technology Development Group
Michikazu Kōno
    Vice-president, Bank of Japan
Hideo Shinojima
    President, Mitsubishi Chemical Industry Company
Takeo Suzuki
    Emeritus Professor, Tokyo University
Gen Takagi
    Managing Director, Central Bank for Commercial and Industrial
    Associations
Shigeki Tashiro
    Honorary President, Toyo Rayon Company
Masahiro Tsukuda
    Executive Director, Nihon Keizai Shimbunsha
Seiichi Tōhata
    Emeritus Professor, Tokyo University
Sohei Nakayama
    Counselor, Japan Industrial Bank

up to seven experts may be appointed as necessary on temporary, part-time assignments. In 1973 they were as shown in Chart IV below:

Chart IV

FIC: Expert Commissioners (1973)
(*Semmon iin*)

Chairman: Takeo Suzuki, Professor of Law Emeritus, Tokyo University
Members: Yasuo Takeyama, Staff Editor, *Japan Economic Journal*
          Sōhei Mizuno, Director, Japan Consumers' Association
          Makoto Yazawa, Professor of Law, Tokyo University
          Toshihiro Tajima, Executive Director, Japan Industrial Bank

There is a staff (*kanji*) of up to fifteen persons of special knowledge and experience to serve only part-time. The housekeeping affairs of the council are handled for it by the Ministry of Finance, International Finance Bureau.

An important fact that does not show from such descriptions of the council is that it has concentrated its time on policy deliberations recently, and validation opinions have been largely delegated, in fact, if not in law, to the Foreign Investment Management Committee (*Kanjikai*) consisting (along with others) of administrative vice-ministers, one from each of the following governmental agencies: Ministry of Finance, MITI, Foreign Affairs, Transportation, Public Welfare, Agriculture and Forestry, Science and Technology Agency, Economic Planning Agency, Fair Trade Commission, and the Bank of Japan. Thus, it is important to understand that the "competent minister" who has formal authority to validate (usually the Finance Ministry and/or MITI) "must respect" the Foreign Investment Council's decision, which in turn is actually delegated to the high-ranking bureaucrats on the Foreign Investment Management Committee.

Applications must be signed by both parties[102] to technological assistance contracts and by the foreigner in case of stock acquisition. There are forms for various applications and they are submitted in Japanese. In this case-by-case screening still used for all important cases, applications are routed (see Chart V, p. 225) from the applicant to the Bank of Japan, to the competent minister, the Foreign Investment Management Committee (with possible adjustment directly made between the applicant or his agents), the Foreign Investment Council, back to the competent minister, Bank of Japan, and the applicant. The chart also shows that, as provided in the law, cases are divided into "major" and

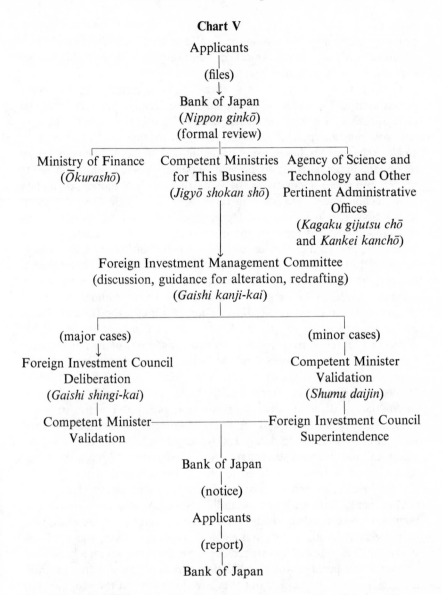

Chart V

Applicants

(files)

Bank of Japan
(*Nippon ginkō*)
(formal review)

Ministry of Finance   Competent Ministries   Agency of Science and
(*Ōkurashō*)   for This Business   Technology and Other
                 (*Jigyō shokan shō*)   Pertinent Administrative
                                        Offices
                                 (*Kagaku gijutsu chō*
                               and *Kankei kanchō*)

Foreign Investment Management Committee
(discussion, guidance for alteration, redrafting)
(*Gaishi kanji-kai*)

(major cases)   (minor cases)

Foreign Investment Council   Competent Minister
Deliberation   Validation
(*Gaishi shingi-kai*)   (*Shumu daijin*)

Competent Minister————————————Foreign Investment Council
Validation   Superintendence

Bank of Japan

(notice)

Applicants

(report)

Bank of Japan

"minor" cases, and minor cases, such as "automatic validations," are
not routed through the Foreign Investment Council. The foregoing outline shows the formalities by which applications for validation are
handled in the more complicated instances; that is, the individual screening process or the so-called "case-by-case" method (*kobetsu shinsa*)
that is used for unliberalized fields of investments, which is still where

most of the foreign interest lies. A recent appraisal emphasizes this point by reminding that during the first four years (1967–71) of "liberalization" only seventeen American ventures have been established by the "automatic" validation route.[103]

In certain areas, handling of applications is delegated[104] by the "competent minister" to the Bank of Japan.[105] Specifically, under the FIL and ordinances, the Bank of Japan has been delegated the authority to validate routinely all "portfolio" investments, except that in 1972 foreigners' stock-exchange purchases were being limited to hold down an inflow of dollars in an attempt to prevent Japan's high reserves from going higher. But more important is the Bank of Japan's authority to validate most technological assistance agreements[106] and applications for stock acquisitions within industrial categories qualifying for "automatic" validation—up to 50 percent of shares in most and 100 percent in a few industries, provided certain conditions are met. Furthermore, the "designation"[107] and "confirmation"[108] process dealing with derivative remittance rights from shares transferred between foreigners or acquired by stock dividends, splits, mergers, or inheritance are also ordinarily handled as a matter of routine by the Bank of Japan. Finally, the Bank of Japan is also authorized to act for the finance minister in handling the highly controlled "foreign investors' deposit accounts" (*gaikoku shihonka azukeire kanjō*) and deposits and withdrawals therefrom incidental to remittances (deemed approved with each validation) for repatriation of "fruits" and "principal withdrawn."[109] Thus, the Bank of Japan handles the myriad of details involved in controlling portfolio investment in the automatic category, as well as many remittances, confirmation, and designation problems. In doing this, we should add, much detail is delegated to major banks that have been designated "foreign exchange banks,"[110] authorized to deal in foreign currencies and to maintain the foreign investors' deposit accounts. There are some eighty "foreign exchange banks," divided into A and B types; A banks are allowed to maintain correspondent relationship abroad; among the A banks are over eighteen foreign banks and eighteen Japanese banks, and the Bank of Tokyo[111] is the only specialized Japanese foreign-exchange bank.

Many nice problems of classification and application of the proliferating rules have developed, but they are quite beyond the scope of any useful generalized description. Indeed, this whole field of administration has become so recondite that only the officials are able to speak with confidence from day to day. The reasons for rule proliferation seem purely for the benefit of administrators (*i.e.,* to insure complete control) rather than to precisely define the rights of those regulated, for again we emphasize there is no appreciable justiciable law in this field. In this regard, the modern Japanese bureaucrats have maintained an old principle of Tokugawa administration: *"Yorashimu-beshi; shirashimu-bekarazu"* (Keep them ignorant, thus dependent). Just how apt this adage is will become more apparent in the search for objective, predictable criteria and reliable procedures that are applied by the "competent minister" and his retainers.

The Screening Process: Standards and Procedures for Validation

The essence of the Foreign Investment Law is the legal authority of the competent ministers to screen all investment applications to determine their desirability, regardless of their nature or scope; it is this same screening procedure that has drawn foreign criticism[112] and has clouded Japan's image as an "advanced nation" (see Chapter VII).

In search for substantive criteria for validation in the FIL, as a domestic "law" or policy, we must approach it in the Japanese way. On an "us"-against-"them" national scale, the Japanese officials have regarded the FIL as an instrument for strengthening Japan's industrial competitiveness against the world, for protecting the weak substructure of industrial dualism at home, and for reorganizing the outward "cutting edge" of its modern industries by governmental guidance, thus contributing overall to a comprehensive industrial development plan with little room for foreigners.

On the positive side, such foreign capital and technology as is deemed useful to the governmental self-sufficiency plan would be validated. In all other respects, practice to date supports the conclusion that the FIL has been used negatively: to keep foreigners out. The criterion for handling applications is a matter of bureaucratic discretion, much as the procedures for shaping useful foreign inputs by renegotiating contracts are largely left to official "guidance." The applicant is seeking a privilege; screening is a simple administrative process, unencumbered by a foreign rule-of-law ideology, because there is no practicable way to judicially review the substance of restrictive decisions nor to challenge the procedures by which decisions are reached in the "due process" sense.

This is not to say, however, that the process is entirely discretionary or arbitrary. Screening procedures are different for several defined categories of investment, and some substantive standards for validation decisions (though not very specific, and often not published) do exist. Besides criteria deducible from the general purposes stated in Arts. 1 and 2 already discussed, the FIL, in Art. 8, lists both positive and negative standards for validation as follows:

Article 8. The competent Minister shall apply the following standards on validating contracts prescribed in this Law, and the priority shall be given to those which will most speedily and effectively contribute to an improvement of the international balance of payment.

(1) Directly or indirectly contributing to the improvement of the international balance of payments, or

(2) Directly or indirectly contributing to the development of essential industries or public enterprises, or

(3) Necessary for continuation of existing technological assistance contracts concerning essential industries or public enterprises or for the alteration of the articles of the contracts concerned, such as renewal.

2. The competent Minister shall not validate contracts prescribed in this Law which fall under any one of the following paragraphs:

(1) Contracts the provisions of which are not fair, or are in contravention of laws and regulations.

(2) Contracts which are deemed to be concluded or the alteration of articles of which such as renewal of the contracts is deemed to be made in a manner not free from fraud, duress or undue influence.

(3) When deemed to have an adverse effect on the rehabilitation of Japanese economy.

(4) Unless as provided for by cabinet order, in the event that the payment for the acquisition by a foreign investor of stock, proprietary interest, beneficiary certificate, debentures or claimable assets arising from loans is not made with any of the below-mentioned items. . . .

As early as 1963, just before Japan took the major step to join OECD (1964), much was made in the media of the decision to shift from emphasis on the strict positive standards to presumably less onerous negative standards; namely, unless the investment would have negative effect on the Japanese economy or business, it was to be validated. In practice, foreigners seem to have noticed little difference where anything but petty transactions have been involved.

Potential for a general standard may be found in Art. 7, which required MITI to make public a list of technologies desired from abroad, and such a list has been published.[113] But it is out of date and generally regarded by foreigners to be of little assistance as a standard, if the assumption might be that validations would flow smoothly forth to cover the listed items.[114] Since all of these standards mentioned in the FIL, with precious few exceptions, are subjective—varying with the "length of the chancellor's foot"—they underwrite broad official discretion. Foreign applicants must look elsewhere in predicting the permissibility of their proposals.

The four rounds of "liberalization" (1967–71) have produced some further guides and major categories of unliberalized and "liberalized" industries with rather detailed conditions that must be met before validations will issue "automatically." Similar percentages for portfolio investments (stock-exchange acquisitions) of 10 percent per individual (and up to 25 percent per company for all foreigners) continue the specific, if restrictive, guidelines in this area. In addition, the recent rules of the Fair Trade Commission (*Kōsei torihiki iinkai*) have furnished some criteria[115] for technological assistance agreements and AML Art. 6 filings of all contracts in order to avoid Antimonopoly Law violations (see Appendix VIII).

Hereafter we shall outline the specific methods for handling each type of investment included under the comprehensive coverage of the FIL and FECL, as follows:

1. technological assistance contracts (*gijutsu enjo keiyaku*)
2. corporate stocks and proprietary interests (*mochibun*)
3. claimable assets from loans (*kashitsukekin saiken*)
4. beneficiary certificates (*jueki shōken*)
5. corporate debentures (*shasai*)

As noted earlier, loans, corporate debentures, and technological assistance contracts of less than a year's duration are taken out of the Foreign Investment Law and handled as a payment matter under the FECL, as are Japanese bonds issued abroad (*gaisai*). Also, branch offices are handled under the FECL (see below).

Technological Assistance Agreements

This is the one type of "investment," requiring FIL validation, that the Japanese government has positively favored, on a selective basis, throughout the life of the FIL, and since 1 July 1972, most technology may enter Japan without difficulty. The reason is that foreign technology has been used to develop new and improved industries during the past two decades, though certainly Japan is entering a phase of growing self-sufficiency for the future. Still, a recent study states that roughly 30 percent of all Japanese industry operates on foreign technology.[116] Recently, however, major foreign owners of new technology, realizing the competitive effect of transnational licensing on multinational operations, seem less casual about entering into straight licensing as some of them have in the past when Japanese companies were less formidable as potential competitors.[117] For some time foreign business policy has favored a trade-off of high-grade technology for an equity in a Japanese joint venture. This typical direct investment "package" has required a validation for the stock acquisitions and technological assistance, as well as a possible loan (requiring a validation for "claimable assets from loan") and possibly import licenses from MITI for special foreign equipment or parts required to start manufacturing.

FIL Art. 3(1)(3) provides its own definition: " 'Technological assistance contracts' shall mean contracts concerning the transfer of patent [*tokkyo*] or utility model [*jitsuyō shinan*] rights for technologies, license agreements therefor, assistance covering technical and factory management, and other matters designated by the competent minister (hereafter referred to as 'technological assistance')."

Applications for validation are signed by both parties on forms provided.[118] Conclusion (also alterations or renewal) of the contract after validation must be reported to the competent minister (FIL Art. 24). The key to understanding the validation criteria for technological assistance agreements is the system of categories employed to classify such agreements. The first classification, established early,[119] divided all technological assistance into the two classes already mentioned: Class A and Class B.[120]

Class B agreements are usually of minor importance and are handled under the FECL; they include three types:

Type 1: contracts with a duration of a year or less covering a license or transfer of patent or utility model rights;

Type 2: contracts with a duration of a year or less covering only services, such as engineering or managerial assistance;

Type 3: all contracts, whether of more or less than a year's duration, between foreign parents and domestic branches.

FECL procedures vary for the three types of contracts as follows:

Type 1: Bank of Japan to MITI;[121]

Type 2: Bank of Japan to the Ministry of Finance;[122]

Type 3: Bank of Japan to either Finance or MITI, depending on whether transfers of industrial property are involved (MITI).

Notably Class B contracts calling for no compensation require no FECL approval, except branch-parent transfers.[123]

For Class A agreements, FIL validation is required,[124] though validation is "automatic" in most cases now. Because of their early importance to Japan (as evidenced, perhaps, by the fact that this type of "investment" is listed first throughout the laws and regulations), technological assistance applications have been carefully handled by the "case-by-case" method of screening, which as noted earlier has been characterized as a "two-against-one" contract process, whereby (after the parties sign) a second round of redrafting and renegotiation is imposed to accommodate MITI views, often in practice indirectly conveyed through the Japanese licensee. Most liaison lawyers in the field have examples of contracts previously signed by the parties but returned after preliminary talks with MITI, replete with interlineations of (1) reduced duration; (2) reduced royalties rates; (3) deletions of license-back and territorial clauses; and (4) reductions of items covered. This practice is dying out but is still likely to reappear whenever critical technology is involved.

Such redrafting is the kind of "administrative guidance" with which foreigners have become familiar. Legally it may be based on the FIL[125] permitting the competent minister to "stipulate necessary conditions" for validation, but such conditions, if legally imposed by formal administrative action, raise serious questions under the U.S.-Japanese FCN Treaty and IMF Art. VI.

In 1968 a major plan for liberalization of technological inflow was announced,[126] and with it technology was divided into three broad types.[127]

1. The seven types of technological assistance listed below were excluded from the liberalization with the effect that they remain subject to the screening requirements:

    1. technology related to aircraft;
    2. technology related to weapons;
    3. technology related to explosives;
    4. technology related to atomic power;
    5. technology related to space development;
    6. technology related to electronic computers;
    7. technology related to petrochemicals.

The foregoing technologies were, of course, most interesting to foreigners at the time; they are very broad, and at the fringes of each of the seven large categories were many problems of inclusion or exclusion to be resolved by officialdom. (See Appendix IX for a more detailed listing of the seven types.)

2. Technological assistance agreements calling for up to $50,000 in compensation, even when technology of the seven types listed in (1) above is involved. In these minor cases, validation has become virtually automatic, and processing has been delegated to the Bank of Japan.

3. A middle category of technological assistance falls between the case-by-case screening for excluded technology and the minor cases liberalized and handled routinely by the Bank of Japan ($50,000). This middle type is also validated automatically by the Bank of Japan, *unless* the competent minister issues a notice within one month (after receipt of his copy of the application) requiring the Bank of Japan to

withhold validation. Withholding power is to be exercised only when the contract will cause "grave harm" to Japanese industry if validated.

In addition, two specific exceptions[128] to the liberalization were retained for case-by-case handling, regardless of amount of royalty involved (*i.e.,* even if less than $50,000). The first concerns cross-licensing between foreign and domestic firms. The second excludes from automatic validation contracts between foreign investors and their Japanese subsidiaries. These exceptions to the automatic validation process are probably explained by difficulties of valuation: (1) in cross-licensing much technology may flow in both directions without any money changing hands; (2) in parent-subsidiary relationships the price paid for technology is often set for parental convenience unrelated to market forces.

After validation, the parties must report to the government [129] when the contracts are actually effected. Both parties must be applicants on the validation forms for technological assistance contracts, and remittance of royalties, when stipulated in the application, are deemed authorized[130] under FECL 27 and paid into Foreign Investors' Deposit Accounts.

At the end of June 1972, the Foreign Investment Council recommended liberalization of computer technology (both software and hardware) by 1 July 1974. Also, technology related to petrochemicals (exclusive of derivatives), aircraft, arms, explosives, atomic power, and space developments were to be freed by July 1972, and petrochemical derivatives by January 1973. The computer industry also framed up the usual counter-measures, such as use of subsidies to get out advanced models (a 3.5 generation computer) and contractual tie-ups with potential consumers.[131] But for now technology imports into Japan have become quite liberalized as shown by a total of 1,916 licensing contracts validated in the year 1972. But note that the FIL recognition is still required, though now easy to get in most instances.

Stock Acquisitions

Obtaining FIL validation is necessary before the foreigner may establish a Japanese operation by acquiring shares[132] in a new subsidiary (usually, in fact, a joint venture) or shares in an existing company. For opening a branch operation only a *report* under the FECL is required, but FECL *approval* is necessary for the transfer of funds to the branch.[133]

Of course, portfolio investments (up to 10 percent or 25 percent for all foreigners) in the shares of existing companies purchased through the stock exchange and without managerial participation constitute a separate category, and foreigners may obtain automatic validation for such investments routinely through their brokers and the Bank of Japan. Though 10 to less than 25 percent limits might occasionally interfere with foreign purchases, such limits on portfolio investments have not drawn the fire that Japanese barriers on direct investment have. In 1972, a new form of restriction on foreigners' portfolio purchases occurred when officials decided to limit purchases in order to hold Japanese dollar reserves down. On 1 May 1973, 100 percent became possible with the Japanese firm's management approval.

In practice, even if management participation might be envisaged by a foreigner's acquisition of 10 percent to less than 25 percent in an existing Japanese company (liberalized or unliberalized), these same automatic rules apply for lack of serious danger of foreign domination and lacking proof of managerial motives.[134] In the Japanese Commercial Code,[135] 25 percent is a critical point in that foreign shareholders with a joint 25 percent might demand cumulative voting, even though provisions to the contrary have been inserted into the Articles of Incorporation (*teikan*). Hence, provided it had a board of at least four directors, foreign owners of 25 percent could get on the board of, but hardly dominate, a Japanese company.

Under the 1968–71 liberalization program (see Chapter VII), which applied only to certain industries and only to new corporations therein, stock acquisitions in the "liberalized industries" are "automatically" validated[136] by the Bank of Japan without the usual screening, provided the holdings are limited to 50 percent in certain industries (Category I). But 100 percent is allowed in others (Category II), largely in inaccessible or unattractive fields. Thus, in newly established corporations, it is only where (1) foreigners apply for more than 50 percent in Category I, or (2) fail to comply with conditions, or (3) apply to acquire stock of a corporation in the nonliberalized industries that stock acquisitions for direct investment are still screened case by case. However, the nonliberalized industries are still the areas of major interest, which is why they are nonliberalized. Only twenty-eight foreign enterprises (seventeen American) have been established in the liberalized categories throughout the first four years (1967–71) of "liberalization."[137] In 1971 there were thirty-five and in 1972 there were seventy-five automatic validations.

Worth mentioning also is another special category of nineteen restricted industries listed[138] by Cabinet Order (see Appendix X) in which foreign shareholding is specially limited because of their highly public character. No special legal problem or foreign criticism is caused by this list because the industries on it fall into the category accepted internationally for restricting certain strategic industries.[139]

Exceptions in which FIL validation is not required are worth noting: (1) foreigners purchasing shares from other foreigners need not obtain validation; (2) nor do shares obtained as a result of amalgamation or inheritance require validation.[140] Under the FIL there are, however, provisions for "designation" of such shares so that any remittance rights "deemed" to have accrued to the former owner will accrue to the purchaser by following the procedures for designation.[141]

Loans

All loans between foreigners and Japanese involving foreign exchange are subject to controls. The FIL covers only those with a term of one year or more,[142] and the FECL approval system covers the rest.[143] FIL validation is routine through the Bank of Japan for all loans that comply with the following conditions:[144]

1. $300,000 or less;
2. three or more years' duration;
3. the purpose is not pleasure or luxury;
4. the interest rate is appropriate.

Japanese legal practice (the one-year rule for FIL recognition) is not in strict accord with international standards; for example, OECD defines only loans of five years or more as direct investment.[145] As with other types of investments, the Japanese guarantee for repatriation of principle and interest requires that the request be stipulated in the application, and there are provisions for reporting and confirmation in case of transfers of compensations. Additional validation is required for acceleration or alteration. Loans for repayment in currency other than "foreign-currency-conversion yen" need no validation under the FIL, but FECL permits are required.[146] Foreign enterprisers, especially smaller businesses, have some interest in foreign-loan validations, because credit is often part of the package arrangement in joint-venture transactions, or foreign loans may be advantageous later in operations because of interest differentials, though Japanese rates were low in 1972 for the first time in the postwar period.

However, the chief interest in loans was first stimulated not by foreign enterprises but by foreign banks and money managers because of the high Japanese interest rates for long-term loans, though the Japanese have succeeded now in bringing the rates down. By far the greatest amount of capital from foreign sources has flowed into postwar Japan through loans, largely because at the time when Japan needed foreign capital the Japanese officials preferred foreign debt to foreign equity. A very large part of the early foreign loans were from the International Bank for Reconstruction and Development (World Bank). Because so much Japanese corporate financing was by short-term loans from "commercial" (city) banks (perhaps 80 percent) at rather high interest rates in the past, the government has been concerned with making sure that outside capital at lower rates could not be made preferentially available to foreign favorites to the severe disadvantage of the domestic competitors who were borrowing huge sums at higher Japanese rates.

Corporate Debentures and Beneficiary Certificates

Acquisitions of corporate debentures[147] and beneficiary certificates[148] require FIL validation, but they are not a major concern of foreign enterprises, as they are instruments for money managers and passive investors essentially. The corporate bond market in Japan is still underdeveloped, and beneficiary certificates (securities investment trusts, which are like mutual funds, or loan trusts with compound interest for fixed terms) are not much known or used by foreigner entrepreneurs. Apparently they were included in the FIL coverage for balance-of-payment reasons.

Branch Operations

To the surprise of most foreigners, branch offices, shops, or factories are not covered by the FIL; furthermore, the FECL coverage was only extended to branch operations by special regulations at the time of abolishing the yen-based companies in 1963. Up to that time, there were few regulations treating branches as a form of investment.

Present FECL rules cover the branch office and impose detailed reporting duties at the time of establishment[149] and also at regular accounting intervals[150] on prescribed forms.[151] Most important, however, is the requirement that a branch operation of a foreign firm obtain approval for capital[152] or technology transfers (even if free and less than one year) from its parent abroad. The nonresident seeking to fund his branch must submit through the Bank of Japan to the Finance Ministry and MITI an application for approval to transfer the funds to the branch.

The approval system for funding branches has been quite restrictive, and manufacturing and processing by Japanese branches has therefore been inhibited by a lack of funding. Even at the end of 1971, one of the several complaints listed by a representative of the American government in Tokyo was that branches of American companies were not allowed to import ingredients and perform simple processing in their Japanese premises.[153] As noted earlier, transfers of technology from parent to foreign branch require validation regardless of the terms of the contract, even if it is royalty free. Repatriation of profits or capital also requires remittance approvals by the minister of finance.[154]

From the foregoing general survey of validation procedures and criteria in the several types of investments covered by the comprehensive FIL-FECL framework, it emerges that, after a decade of liberalization, the policy is to facilitate petty transactions, routinize validation somewhat in middle-size transactions, and reserve the areas of critical technology or attractive or established industries to a case-by-case screening method, which remained highly restrictive up to 1972. For direct investment all industries are covered by an elaborate hierarchy of categories, each with varying conditions for validation of share acquisitions under the "liberalization" restrictions, which are discussed in the next chapter.

In concluding this chapter, we call attention again to the fact that the foregoing validation requirements were affected in May 1973 by the government's change of policy from a 50 percent principle to approval in principle of 100 percent ownership in both new and established Japanese firms, but with an elaborate system of exceptions, which seem to cover, still, most of the possibilities attractive to foreigners, and ownership (beyond the prior 10 percent to 25 percent) in established firms is dependent on the firm's consent. The details of this latest "liberalization" may be seen in the Foreign Investment Council report appended to the Cabinet order putting it into effect. (See Appendix XII.)[155]

VII

Japanese Liberalization in International Law

Under U.S. and OECD pressures, Japan began in 1967 a programmed five-year liberalization of foreign investments. After four rounds, amidst a continuing bad foreign press,[1] the four-round schedule to liberalize direct investment came to an end by 1971 after an interim liberalization of technological assistance in 1968.[2] And further liberalization of technology followed in July 1972, and finally in May of 1973 the government announced a policy of allowing in principle 100 percent liberalization of direct investment subject to many exceptions. These exceptions still contain the main industries of interest to foreigners as explained above, and restrictions still prevail at all critical points. (See Appendix XII.) Nevertheless, there had been, by mid-1973, substantial liberalization of technology imports and business entries of minor importance. This chapter will review in detail the progress and limitations of the program to May 1973, since it has been the most significant Japanese effort since Perry to internationalize at home as well as abroad. Briefly, it has been a highly controlled liberalization, partial and incomplete, with many conditions attached; foreign equities were limited to 50 percent of new enterprises in most industries of interest, and foreigners are excluded from participating in all existing Japanese corporations (except up to 25 percent) without corporate approval. Partial liberalization of this sort falls short of international goals set by treaties under which Japan is a party (OECD and U.S.-Japanese FCN; see below), a point repeatedly made for years by foreign officials[3] as well as by the foreign business community.[4] Since Japan's capital liberalization has been largely a response to these international standards rather than an initiative flowing from felt needs at home, its performance understandably is measured accordingly against

237

the treaty standards;[5] and in the circumstances it is easy for foreigners to regard the problem as essentially a legal one (and on that level the recent case is strong), but they fail to look beneath the surface to consider Japanese reasons[6] for the slow pace and other limitations of her liberalization program. These Japanese reasons deserve careful attention; also, the remarkable growth of truly international outlooks in an expanding segment of Japanese opinion is even more important. We can only summarize these points here as a preface to our description of the liberalization program itself and then consider the legal issues raised by the "treaty problem" that continues into the future at least as part of the rhetoric of internationalism. The many shifts in Japanese opinion and the economic policy in 1973 would indicate that internationalization will have top priority with accelerating results in the future, especially Japanese activities abroad. Indeed, one senses that the lack of reciprocity in Japan is embarrassing Japanese abroad enough to force a reappraisal of domestic policy for 1973 onward. Our coverage below is focused on the situation to 1972 and the 1 May 1973 change.

The Japanese Philosophy of "Liberalization" (1967–1972)

Just as there is an international meaning for liberalization, it seems there is a local Japanese meaning[7] too, at the bureaucratic level, though it has been somewhat obscured by the fact that Japan has signed treaties embodying the international standards so that foreigners expect that such usage will govern Japanese bureaucratic behavior. From this foreign expectation, it would follow that either the treaty or the behavior should be changed. To anticipate a bit, our reading of the U.S.-Japan FCN Treaty requires liberalization in the international sense now; the OECD Treaty clearly commits Japan in spirit, but not in law, to liberalize direct investment and technological assistance fully in the future. What remains indefinite is timing, and therein lies the bone of contention with OECD (see below).

What then was the Japanese reasoning in support of semiliberalization (*i.e.,* to 50 percent and only in new enterprises)? There are diverse Japanese reasonings, both business and official, that shift with conditions and the passage of time. The nuances are not easy to discern because of the natural tendency of the official announcements, alluded to above, to emphasize the positive, Madison Avenue style,[8] so that the negative aspects, hidden in bureaucratic screening, and the reasons underlying them have not always been easy to follow in public.[9] However, the official position on semiliberalization is stated in much of its restrictive complexity in the first Foreign Investment Council (hereafter, FIC) report entitled *Concerning Liberalization of Inward Direct Investments* (1967) (hereafter, *FIC Report*) and supplements issued at rounds two, three, and four, as adopted by the Cabinet.[10] After a thorough review of all issues, the pros and cons of liberalization were framed by the FIC in lists of merits and demerits.[11] The following major demerits should be understood as much of the Japanese rationale for controlled liberalization and as background for our description of the program and the treaty problem to follow.

1. Up to 1972, there has been some official Japanese skepticism, particularly at the middle levels of bureaucracy, regarding the merits of the liberal economic philosophy underlying the international treaties, at least insofar as it might relate to Japan's domestic modern sector in the short run. The idea seemed to be that national advantage could be obtained by temporizing with continuing protectionism that responds only as much as necessary to keep the foreign heat below boiling.[12] Needless to say, this approach weighed the costs which might accrue rightly or wrongly to Japan's reputation abroad (*i.e.*, as a sharp dealer or a treaty violator, as parochial, antiforeign, or discriminatory) as worth it in terms of gains flowing from protecting their industrial clients. What seems more likely is that, at the lower levels of bureaucracy, these costs were not fully apprehended.[13]

The international theory, on the other hand (for example, OECD), means that liberalization of capital movements is but a removal of barriers to an ideal free world economy in which both domestic and foreign private firms may compete within, as well as across, national boundaries. This presumes ultimate advantage for all producers and consumers and also probably presumes relatively free domestic economies already moving toward a free world economy guided largely by market forces rather than officialdom; presumably these principles are important to a "free-world economy." In Japanese policy of the 1960s, free economics and consumers were not that important; national polity[14] has always been the center of gravity, despite current references to the "economic animal."[15] We have seen in Chapter IV that modern Japanese industry has been producer-oriented and guided by government precisely in order that the *nation* might succeed—so that the official and industrial coalition could enhance productivity and succeed against foreign competition.[16] There has been, therefore, a profound underlying protective nationalism and bureaucratic reluctance to dissolve this quasi-public (and self-serving) approach in favor of an open house economy that is free for both foreign and domestic firms. Of course, at this stage such a stance means a double standard: a free world economy but a controlled domestic economy—"insular internationalism" perhaps? Organized Japanese big business as a whole (*e.g., sanken* or *keidanren*) is more progressive, but even some segments there have preferred protection for themselves and liberalism for others. But, at least as a possibility, we must not overlook the evidence indicating that this nationalistic approach will be transitional only; timing is important and real internationalism is strengthening from within Japan.

2. We have noted that, besides a bureaucratic preference for a planned, quasi-public (as distinguished from a free private enterprise) economy, there has been a great deal of simple "enterprise nationalism" behind the reluctance to accept foreigners except on limited terms. This is inherent in very basic features of the society—loyalties within groups,[17] emphasizing "them against us," which is peculiar in degree to Japanese society.[18]

3. There is also, of course, the fact that Japanese capital formation and managerial performance is such that Japanese might well conclude that a foreign source for both will soon be superfluous.[19] This point is important to timing, especially when coupled with officialdom's doubts about excessive freedom in the economy ("market confusion"). In other words, if the free-economy theory were embraced, foreigners who were freely entering might be accepted as bonus, ballast, or a liability (depending on the evaluator), but if a free economy is of doubtful merit in the first place, one would not adopt it simply to make foreigners feel at home, especially if their contribution (except technology) seemed dubious in the long run.

4. Some Japanese doubtless feel that foreigners might actually have negative value, like a "foreign object."[20] Psychologically there is a highly emotive content and consequent high productivity in the familial principles of Japanese sociality underlying the "family company" and the "families of companies." Though seldom stated, conservative Japanese may very well feel that their traditional Japanese ways, ingeniously adapted to modern industrial demands, are more efficiently modern than even the methods of foreign merchants of modernity who still struggle at home with a hostile, antiquated industrial-relations regime[21] that is paralyzed by strikes and "cost-pushism." Japanese loyalties to company and nation extend vertically to the bureaucratic apex, and officialdom is fully aware that productivity stems from these popular attitudes and social talents and that exclusivity may well be essential to the formula. Admittance of foreigners is thus a delicate project.

5. At the level of official policy dissemination and implementation,

officialdom anticipates trouble from foreigners with "guidance," because they may be more right-conscious than imbued with the national program.[22]

6. Japan sees an independent research and development capacity as one of her most important goals for the near future. For the real competition henceforth is seen in technology and innovation, not simply in production, quality, and price as in the past. Some Japanese seem to fear that foreign branches and subsidiaries operating in Japan would tend to leave research and development to the foreign parent abroad[23] and not serve the national purpose.

7. The financial handicaps in Japan, especially high interest, long-term capital shortages, and thin capitalization (85-15 debt-equity ratio), have been such that restrictions are required to keep foreigners from taking over major companies at bargain prices or crushing them by financial superiority.

8. The inefficient substrata of small or medium-sized industries in Japan (employing half of the work force) must be sensitively shepherded through a transition period to modernization without excessive human costs in terms of bankruptcies and wrecked Japanese careers.[24] Consequently, foreigners must not be allowed, in the short run, to overwhelm these tiny companies by modern productive and distributive and financing advantages; an extended transition period is essential.

9. Accumulating worldwide experiences with multinational corporations is also creating deep concern, even skepticism, in some Japanese circles, just as it has elsewhere.[25] These giant corporations with flexible business policies attuned to profit, wherever they may be found even at the expense of national interest, are a challenge to the regulatory efficacy or even the sovereignty of some smaller governments; there is some reluctance in Japan to embrace an unrestricted direct investment policy, if it means weakening capacities to deal effectively in the national interest with such a challenge. Japan has been exploring (though not always practicing overseas) a policy favoring 50-50 joint ventures as an international direct investment standard,[26] and there already is considerable international support for some such policy, especially among lesser developed countries. In any event, to some influential Japanese, it was not obvious by 1972 that direct investment on the international scene is a purely economic or business matter to be left to a free world market populated by giant corporations. These are legitimate political and social interests that raise theoretical issues for the future over and above the confines of Japanese policy.[27]

10. While the foregoing points have considerable cogency, there is

also a more irrational kind of anxiety rooted in Japanese history: the "black ship" and "unequal treaties" syndrome. This is a reactionary view of foreign investment drawing upon Meiji experiences at a time when Japan was locked in a struggle to westernize without being colonized. The difference is that it is now Japan that is seeking a free international economy to insure markets (sometimes herself now accused of neocolonization of raw-material sources), which it is quite irrational to expect to secure for herself without full reciprocity. Consequently, many Japanese leaders have recently become fully aware of the need for reciprocal liberalization. Nevertheless, there is to some degree "black ship" fear and defensive antiforeignism underlying and limiting Japanese liberalization policy.[28]

From a review of these issues, as discussed in Japan, the gap appears enormous between the domestic attitudes in Tokyo and the "open economy" commitment that most foreign signators believe to flow from Japanese treaty law. N. Kobayashi's comment is interesting, not only in pointing to the legal problem, but in setting out the informal policy of the Ministry of Finance and its expectations from foreigners as informally announced (September 1967), quite without references to legalities:

> It would almost seem that the Ministry of Finance was ignorant of the law when it issued its "Ten Commandments for Foreign Investors," who are told that they should:
> 1. Invest in industries where a fifty percent equity is automatically approved rather than in industries where a hundred percent is possible;
> 2. Avoid industries in which goods are produced mainly by medium to small factories;
> 3. Avoid restrictive arrangements with overseas parent companies or affiliates;
> 4. Cooperate with Japanese producers in the same industry in order to avoid "excessive competition";
> 5. Contribute to the development of Japanese technology;
> 6. Help promote Japanese exports;
> 7. Ensure that in a joint venture the number of Japanese directors reflects the Japanese equity percentage;
> 8. Avoid layoffs and plant closures that might disrupt the Japanese labor market;
> 9. Cooperate in maintaining Japan's industrial harmony and help in the achievement of her economic goals; and
> 10. Avoid concentrating their investments in any particular industry or industries.[29]

The foregoing points are by no means all of the complex elements of the past Japanese debate over liberalization, nor can all of the listed points be attributed equally to all government policy-makers or to specific segments of public opinion. We mention these complexities, however, in order to emphasize especially that the Japanese process of consensus decision-making in the postwar democratic context is a very deliberate and generally rational process, wherein the sensitivity to domestic industrial input is often such that it is difficult to change policy at all, given these pressures. Possibly this is the major factor in the frustrating *timing* of Japanese liberalization and explains the lag between Cabinet announcements (*e.g., FIC Reports*) and what seems to outsiders to be niggardly implementation thereof for the past five years at the bureaucratic and industrial level. The *"doru shokku"* (dollar shock) ushering in the 308-yen dollar in late 1971[30] offered the occasion for the many leaders in Japan who favor liberalization and internationalization to make the necessary and difficult adjustments at home, not only to accommodate foreigners, but to achieve a better balance in the internal allocation of resources. Highly significant shifts have already resulted at home with encouraging implications for international business.

In sum, the foregoing points comprise the chief reasons that Japanese liberalization has been a "controlled liberalization" by stages so that each relaxation coincides with a counterbalancing competitiveness within each Japanese industry and the Japanese firms can live with foreign participants. The 50-50 (new companies only) rule means that only after foreigners have joined with an equal Japanese partner and learned the ways of guidance can they be allocated a separate "market share." As a response to foreign pressures for international reciprocity, this program still falls short, but it has had its own logic in the Japanese context and is necessary background in understanding the intricacies of "controlled liberalization" to be described below.

In such a milieu the Cabinet in 1967 made three basic decisions with respect to foreign direct investments, relying on the study[31] produced by the FIC and after much debate and anxiety in industry, government, and society at large. The first decision was to retain the comprehensive FIL control system without amendment and when necessary to liberalize direct investments by bureaucratic pronouncement within its framework. Second, substantive liberalization under the FIL was to be accomplished by an automatic approval system for all foreign-investment applications meeting specifications in two rigid categories: one up to 50 percent and the other up to 100 percent foreign ownership; all others would continue to get case-by-case screening. Third, the council recommended a number of countermeasures[32] to be effected in the domestic Japanese law to cope with threats of foreign domination, take-overs, and other harsh foreign practices, much feared (and in retrospect exaggerated) in the Japanese press of the time. These latter countermeasures have not all been implemented yet, but because they show better than Japanese public announcements the basic Japanese philosophy toward foreign business at the time, these measures are of great intrinsic interest and will be discussed at the end of this section.

"Liberalization" Program

To implement the 1967 liberalization decisions, the government program had two aspects related to direct investment. The first was a legal structure defining the categories of industries and their specifications; the second was envisaged as an elaborate classification of actual "industries" into the aforementioned categories, with reclassification to occur at intervals of about a year so that, with each ensuing "round" (of which there were four to 1972), the reclassification of more industries into the more liberal categories was to give the program a progressive thrust. Besides the categories and classifications, there were also two procedural aspects to the overall program: (1) rules by which the jurisdiction of the Bank of Japan was to be enlarged to routinely handle foreign applications that complied with stipulated conditions for automatic approval; and (2) even where the case-by-case screening was retained, the reform program sought some revamping of the procedures for internal processing and providing more precise criteria and less delay and paperwork. Both of these liberalizing procedures were recommended by the original *FIC Report* and adopted by the Cabinet (1967), but little has appeared at the bureaucratic level with regard to the latter measures for expediting procedures.

Two Categories of Nonliberalized Industries

The core of the system is the elaborate definitions of categories. Overall, there are four industrial categories. The first two categories were major segments of industry that were completely excluded by design from "liberalization" (*i.e.,* from eligibility for automatic approval) of direct investment (portfolio acquisitions up to 10%, 15%, or 25% allowed; see below). The first category excluded was a group of nineteen (actually now eighteen) restricted industries (*i.e.,* public and security-related industries commonly excluded in international investment relations).[33] The second category encompassed all investments in "existing corporations" in Japan, even in industries to be placed in one or the other of the automatic-approval categories. This, of course, subjects applications to case-by-case scrutiny for acquisitions by any foreigner of more than 10 percent (25 percent by all foreigners, or 15 percent in restricted industries) in all established Japanese corporations, whether listed on the exchanges or not. Also included in the second category were investments in all corporations (existing or new) in a residual group called "industries for case-by-case examination" (*kobetsu shinsa taishō gyōshū*),[34] a cosmetic renaming in 1971 for public relations effect of the prior category of "nonliberalized industries" (*hijiyūka gyōshū*), which presumably lack international competitiveness. After the four rounds (1967–72), there were still seven major areas (including some sixty "industries") left in the nonliberalized residual category, which foreign investors can enter only after a case-by-case screening under the FIL in either new or existing business. These seven industrial lines (though also called "industries") are quite broad and comprehensive, as can be understood from the list itself:

1. oil refining and sales
2. electronic computers and computer peripheral equipment[35]
3. data processing
4. leather products
5. retail chain of more than eleven stores
6. agriculture-forestry-fishery
7. real estate

Two Categories of "Liberalized" Industry: Conditions and Specifications

Both liberalized categories deal only with (1) direct investment in (2) newly established firms in (3) liberalized industries. In other words, direct investments in existing firms are not liberalized and are handled by different rules to be discussed later, as are indirect (portfolio) investments. Also, specific investments proposed by foreigners that do not fit the rigid mold imposed by the specifications of the categories are not "liberalized"; and many of the most important industries are categorized as nonliberalized.

In Category I, all foreign-investment applications for validation of acquisitions up to 50 percent of the total shares of a new company are entitled to automatic validation under the FIL, but only if they meet the following conditions:[36]

1. Not exceptionally harmful to Japan's interests (*Nihon no rieki*).

2. Property to be invested in kind (*genbutsu shusshi*) by the Japanese stockholders of the newly established company (meaning stockholders other than foreign investors; hereinafter the same) or property to be transferred from a former juridical person to a company to be established is immovable property (*fudōsan*) other than factories, shops, and warehouses.

3. The newly established company must not receive from a preexisting juridical person, right after its establishment, a transfer, lease, etc., of business or properties to be used continuously for its business (excluding properties other than factories, shops, and warehouses), and preexisting juridical persons must not merge (*gappei*) into a newly established company.

4. The total number of shares possessed by the new company's Japanese stockholders, which must be in the same business as the new company, must be half or more of the total shares issued; and, further, one Japanese stockholder, engaged in the same business, must possess one-third or more of the total.

5. Among the directors (*torishimariyaku*) and representative directors (*daihyō torishimariyaku*) of the newly established company, those elected by the Japanese stockholders must be in the same proportion as the Japanese shareholdings or higher.

6. The voting method of the newly established company must be based on the principles of the Commercial Code, and furthermore consent of a specific officer (*yakusha*) or the consent of all stockholders must not be required for conducting business.

In Category II, automatic validation for foreign shareholding up to 100 percent is granted, in Category II industries, if the application meets conditions 1 through 3 as established for Category I (above).

Finally, on authority of FIL Art. 14, automatic validations in both Category I and Category II will be made subject to two more conditions, but only when the foreign acquisitions contemplated are one-third or more of the total shares to be issued by a newly established company:

A. When a kind of business other than that originally specified in the charter (*teikan*) is planned, validation of the competent minister must be obtained in advance.

B. When it is intended to receive a transfer of a business, or to acquire assets (existing prior to establishment and to be used continuously in business, excluding immovables other than factories, shops, and warehouses, requiring a special shareholders' resolution), or when a merger is planned, validation of the competent minister shall be obtained in advance.

Validations for Share in Existing Corporations, Portfolio Investments, and the Residual Nonliberalized Category (10 percent to 20 percent)

For the nonliberalized category (and "restricted" industries), automatic validation is allowed even of applications for direct investments within the limits set for portfolio validations by the Bank of Japan (*i.e.,* 10 percent per individual and up to 25 percent for all foreigners, except the aggregate may be only 15 percent for "restricted industries").

Similarly, in "existing corporations" (regardless of category, *i.e.,* whether direct or portfolio, and whether within the liberalized or unliberalized category) validations will automatically issue through the Bank of Japan up to the 10 percent or 25 percent or 15 percent limits.

In portfolio investments, the fourth round of liberalization left automatic validation in the hands of the Bank of Japan as shown in Chart VI below.

Chart VI

LIMITS ON AUTOMATIC VALIDATION FOR EXISTING ENTERPRISES

Round	1 Foreign Investor	All Foreign Investors	
		Unrestricted Industries	Restricted Industries (19)
1st Round	5%	15% or less	10% or less
2nd Round	7%	20% or less	15% or less
3rd Round	7%	up to 25%	15% or less
4th Round	up to 10%	up to 25%	15% or less

Schematically, conditions for validations in all basic categories (existing and newly established; liberalized and nonliberalized; Category I, 50 percent, and Category II, 100 percent; direct and portfolio; restricted and nonrestricted) may be seen in Chart VII, p. 248.

Note should be taken of the fact that, even though a direct investment in shares up to 10 percent per foreigner or 25 percent aggregate is acquired and this in an existing company, still it will be treated as a "portfolio" investment and automatically validated up to those limits unless the fact of its direct investment character (*i.e.,* managerial interest) is made explicit in the validation processing.

Also, the liberalization regulations within the FIL framework have provided for all automatic validations to be handled routinely by the Bank of Japan on behalf of the competent minister. This is simply an executive expansion of authority of the Bank of Japan.[37]

Chart VII

CONDITIONS OF VALIDATION PROCESSES

Ratio of Foreign Ownership	Newly Established Companies (All Industries)			Existing Companies All Industries	
	Liberalized Industries		Nonliberalized Industries (7 Industries)	All Other Industries	Restricted Industries (19 Industries)
	Category II 228 Industries	Category I (All Other Industries)			
50–100%	automatic validation	case-by-case screening	case-by-case screening	case-by-case screening	case-by-case screening
25–50%	automatic validation	automatic validation	case-by-case screening	case-by-case screening	case-by-case screening
0–25% Subject to Limit of 10% on Each Investor	automatic validation	automatic validation	automatic validation	automatic validation	case-by-case screening
0–15%	automatic validation	automatic validation	automatic validation	automatic validation	automatic validation

All of the foregoing legal structuring (*i.e.,* definition of categories and Bank of Japan jurisdiction) has by and large remained stationary since the first promulgation of the liberalization program in 1967. The progressive thrust of liberalization has taken place by reclassifying Japanese industries so that more and more of them fall into the more liberal categories.

Classification of Japanese Industries

Bearing in mind that "restricted" and "nonliberalized" industrial categories (as well as all "existing" business regardless of category) are not covered, the round-by-round progress of the liberalization by reclassifications through 1972 shows in Chart VIII below.[38]

Chart VIII

CUMULATIVE NUMBERS OF INDUSTRIES
LIBERALIZED BY CATEGORIES

Rounds	I (50%)	II (100%)	Total
First (July 1967)	33	17	50
Second (May 1969)	160	44	204
Third (September 1970)	447	77	524
"Third and one-half" (Auto Industry, April 1971)	453	77	530
Fourth (August 1971)	562	228	790

In preparing round four (effective 4 August 1971) and in response to foreign criticism of the meaningless proliferation of unimportant "industries" (often actually only products) on a *poji risuto* (positive list), the Japanese government provided a negative list showing those "industries" (actually often several industries) that were not liberalized, even up to 50 percent. These were seven industrial fields (about sixty "industries") as listed above, among which were the most attractive investment opportunities for foreigners under Japanese business conditions existing in 1972. So, using the Japanese industrial classification system comprised of 850 "industries," 790 are now liberalized at least to 50 percent. Much has been made of those figures; frequently it was said that the liberalization rate had reached about 93 percent by 1972, of which 30 percent was in Category II (100 percent).[39] Actually the ratio of "automatic" to "screening" validations to 1971 was one to eight, suggesting by this more realistic standard that 12 percent liberalization had been reached. In 1971 (35 firms) and 1972 (75 firms) the automatic validations were still small, though growing.

Finally, with an eye to President Nixon's trade bill introduced to Congress in early 1973, the Japanese Cabinet ordered on 1 May 1973 a program of liberalization to allow "in principle" 100 percent ownership of both new and established Japanese firms, but five broad industrial areas were exempted and seventeen others delayed until as long as 1976. (See Appendix XII.) It really seems that "liberalization" occurs only over the "hot wire" between Washington and Tokyo.

Liberalizing Procedures in the Screening of Nonliberalized Industries

Even in the case-by-case screening (*kobetsu shinsa*) for investments (over 10 percent to 25 percent) in "existing companies," new companies in nonliberalized categories (*nega risuto*), and all investments in even "liberalized" industries in which the aforementioned conditions for "automatic" validation are not met, the Japanese government has attempted to meet foreign criticism by announcing and reannouncing a policy to simplify, expedite, and reduce delays and paperwork. The problem has been with implementation; not much progress had, in fact, been made by 1973 according to most foreign sources. As a beginning, in August 1966, the government issued a broad guideline to expedite individual screening of technological assistance agreements. A main feature of this guideline was the so-called "one-month rule," whereby applications were to be passed on to the Foreign Investment Committee (*kanjikai*) of the FIC within one month from the time they were received by the Bank of Japan. Apparently the "formal examination" conducted by the Bank of Japan or ministry was holding up applications.[40] Similar suggestions were repeated in the *FIC Report* on direct investment in June 1967 and adopted by the Cabinet; pertinent provisions were as follows:

A. The case-by-case examination will be conducted much more elastically than before in the light of the purpose of the current liberalization measures.

B. The government is to give free and courteous counsel when it is sought by a person planning to make an application, but any action which might be misconstrued as pre-application examination must be avoided.

C. Criteria for examination must be clarified and efforts must be made to simplify the forms and other details for application.

D. The rule that the application is referred to the Foreign Investment Committee (*kanjikai*) of the FIC in one month after it is submitted is adhered to.[41]

Also, it was provided that any application for acquisition of stocks in a liberalized industrial category, which might be shifted to case-by-case screening because of failure to meet conditions for the category of automatic approval, was to be screened only as to the particular unfulfilled condition.

As far as can be determined, there are still no published substantive guidelines other than those cited in Chapter VI, nor have even unpublished internal rules (*naiki*) to further expedite case-by-case screening come to our attention. Contrariwise, the experience of applicants indicates that nothing has liberalized to a noticeable degree. The fact that the problems of delay and excessive *paperasserie* still exist is clear also from candid comment and renewed suggestions in the FIC's statement[42] of 29 July 1971 on inaugurating the fourth round and from the fact that there was still need to do the things stated as new policy in 1967 so that more expeditious handling would be encouraged. The FIC again recommended that the government *actually* speed up and simplify the process. Such candid appraisals of nonliberalization of screening have been rare, since critical charges and liberal promises tend to emit from polar foreign and Japanese sources respectively with little in between.[43]

Though hardly 93 percent liberalization as the Japanese PR releases suggest, no doubt the "automatic" approval system is helpful for the few applicants (*e.g.,* 12 percent in 1970) who are able to meet the "unautomatic" conditions; but proving that the many conditions of each category have been met has itself been an onerous and time-consuming task. There are Japanese assertions that the overwhelming majority of all (automatic or otherwise) applications are being validated, amounting, as one journal has suggested, to a "de facto" liberalization.[44] However, the mere quantitative analysis using the government's figures of past validations tells little about the delays and conditions in the actual process of validation, with which businessmen and legal practitioners in the field have become all too familiar. Perhaps no figures tell the story so simply and clearly as the meager twenty-eight cases validated "automatically" in all 790 "industries" for all nations in over four years (1967–71) of liberalization.[45] It is true that the 1971 and 1972 figures are much higher, but still, through 1972, the bulk of investments were not "automatic."

Much negotiation and revision, imposed by the ministry before an automatic application can even be filed (or, more accurately, before it will be accepted) are still occurring; also, in case-by-case screening, as well as "automatic" cases in certain circumstances,[46] FIL Art. 14 authorizes a "conditional validation." This invites a kind of revision bargaining akin to administrative guidance, under which the competent minister (really the lower-level bureaucrats) imposes, in exchange for validation, conditions that might not be legal (or politic) in a more orthodox administrative milieu.[47] In the realities of Tokyo practice, however, there is little to prevent the guiding officials from exercising this discretionary power in unlegal ways within the limitless limits of the interests of the Japanese economy, as perceived by middle- or lower-level bureaucrats handling the applications.[48] In fact, the Japanese validation landscape is strewn with crippled ventures, validated with "necessary conditions" attached. Texas Instrument, Avon, and Ampex are but some of the better-known examples in which bureaucratic design has shaped or misshaped the venture rather than business negotiation.

Part of the problem has been the long-established practice of Japanese businesses to check out all foreign investments, informally and as a perliminary step, with MITI. Whether this is legally required or whether foreigners could or should also go along to assure that the official guidance is properly understood and transmitted is an academic, impractical question from the standpoint of the foreign individual applicant. The actual practice has usually been for the Japanese party to receive the official preliminary (and self-serving) view and transmit it to the foreigner. Usually foreigners have been told that they have been asked by the officials to change the terms in the Japanese favor. The ex parte aspect itself is questionable administrative practice under a rule of law, but equally important is the weakness of the system as a method of transmitting government views, because in most cases it is such an obvious self-serving use of public power by the Japanese party. This point (need for more self-reliant contracting) was also stressed by the FIC as early as its 1967 report, but the high-level business leaders on the FIC have not been able to induce the bureaucracy to follow their policy, even though it had been aided by the imprimatur of the Cabinet.

Liberalization of Technology

The Cabinet also ordered in 1968 that validations of technological assistance be liberalized in line with a separate *FIC Report* the same year.[49] This, too, is an important segment of the entire liberalization program. The 1968 Cabinet decision set forth a list of uniliberalized technology, and then provided that all inductions of technology involving less than $50,000 for the foreign licensor would be handled by automatic validation. In addition, all other inductions of technology would be automatically validated, unless the government stepped in (by notice) within one month. The details of this program may be found in Chapter VI above, but here the important point is that liberalization did not progress further until the spring of 1972, despite the fact that the technological assistance is not classified as a "capital movement" by OECD. It is liberalized under the OECD Code for Invisible Transactions, and no other advanced nation controls inward technology. Still, important foreign technological assistance is subjected to guidance and case-by-case handling to a considerable degree because of the Japanese drive for an independent capacity in advanced fields.

Saving the question as to whether Japanese handling of foreign technology recently has been "fair," the U.S. Commission on International Trade and Investment Policy (1971) recommended to President Nixon (p. 223): "Failing rapid progress in this regard, the U.S. Government should examine alternatives at its disposal to influence present Japanese investment restrictions. One question worthy of consideration is whether U.S. Government agencies such as the National Aeronautics and Space Administration and the Atomic Energy Commission should continue to grant licenses on U.S. Government technology to Japanese business firms on terms equally favorable to those accorded U.S. firms."

No part of the validation process has deserved and received more criticism than the procedures (or nonprocedures) discussed above, as Japan's own *FIC Reports* (1967 and 1971) themselves intimate. With MITI's preferences for unpublished criteria[50] and guidance (case-by-case screening), such scant information as there is about these troubles comes from individual businessmen (their lawyer's experiences are confidential and cannot be divulged), or from cases exasccrbated enough to surface in the media.[51] All of this is not entirely surprising because of the undeveloped state of Japanese administrative "law" (as opposed to administrative controls), which is largely lacking in the concepts of procedural due process and equal protection—ideas fashioned in another culture to rationalize and publicize administrative behavior.[52] But, howsoever unexplicit and disguised the Japanese government's policy to exclude foreign business may have remained by listings of liberalized "industries" (products) and employing the rhetoric of "liberalization" and "automatic" approvals, it has been clear enough that the policy was until 1972 restrictive rather than liberal in all areas of business and industry in which entry was, business-wise, viable (*i.e.,* in which Japanese firms, either privately by closing ranks within the industrial association or by government structuring [*taiseika*] and guidance, had not yet preempted the technology, sites, sources, manpower, or other factors of production). Such a conclusion seems justified from reading the evidence of the day-to-day validation process for several years. This is not to say that there are not cogent reasons for a temporizing exclusionary policy or that it has not been within certain arguable conceptions of the national interest.

Counter-Liberalization

From the foregoing, it is clear that, even in the two liberalized categories, "liberalization" has lacked both depth and breadth of coverage, and "automatic"' approvals are subject to many conditions. Coverage is limited in breadth to new companies that foreigners might establish; the existing corporate structure in Japan—and each company now participating in it—is excluded as a special Japanese preserve, except for case-by-case processing or for automatic validation of portfolio investments up to 10 percent per individual and 25 percent for all foreigners. The depth of the "liberalization" is limited also to 50 percent in practically all fields of interest to foreigners.

Given the Japanese anxiety over the foreign threat (real or imagined) reflected in the severe limitations built into the functioning aspects of the "liberalization" program of 1969–72, it is clear that internationalization of capital movements has not in fact been an immediate Japanese goal. It is understandable too, under the circumstances, that the Japanese government should consider countermeasures[53] to fend off foreigners and confine them to cooperative roles in "new enterprises," attempting to squeeze them into tight industrial structures already officially induced to close ranks against them. This meant a kind of restricted "market share" for foreigners by building barriers between new and existing companies, plugging loopholes in those barriers, and regulating competitive relations between the new and existing enterprises to prevent foreigners from becoming too effective and expanding beyond their assigned minor roles that are implicit in the "new enterprise" limitation.

There have been several interesting suggestions for legal reforms to fend off foreigners, which will be reviewed briefly here. In particular, the revision of the FIL regulations to prevent share acquisitions in yen (below) was clearly illiberal "liberalization" at the inception,[54] in much the same way that abolition of the yen-based corporation in 1964 was a step backwards.[55] The legal countermeasures may be divided roughly into negative and positive devices: the negative regulatory law was to prevent foreigners from entering the "existing" sector; the positive measures were official actions to strengthen concerted Japanese competitiveness against foreigners. Initially the psychology was not international, but the "black ship" philosophy was subsiding by 1972.[56]

Plugging the Yen Acquisition Loophole

At the beginning of "liberalization" (early 1967),[57] the rules permitted resident foreigners (or foreign corporations through their Japanese branches or subsidiaries) to purchase, with yen currency, stock in existing Japanese enterprises (without an FIL validation), even when the yen was not purchased with foreign currency. This was, of course, a loophole that might permit a foreign take-over of a Japanese enterprise through local stock-exchange transactions. The method is said to have been used in the widely publicized *Tokyo Simmons Bed* case.[58] This loophole was closed pursuant to the FIC recommendation at the beginning of the liberalization in June 1967, by requiring FIL validation even for yen acquisitions of Japanese stocks in existing companies, though an exception was made for acquiring stocks, even with yen, for the "operation of property" (*shisan no unyō*). "Operation of property" is a technical term that refers to corporate money management of surplus funds (investing surplus corporate funds for profit outside the regular productive operations of the company). This still qualifies as a legitimate purpose for foreign corporations to make yen stock acquisitions without FIL approval; but if the motive is direct investment (to acquire stock for control), then FIL approval now is required under the rules as amended in 1967.[59]

Illiberal though it was, the Special Committee of FIC opined in its report that the amendment to FIL regulations would not violate the spirit of FIL Art. 2 (requiring that foreign investment be as free as possible) since the general program was liberal. In order to effectuate the overall liberalization, this illiberal exception was required, given the expansion of resident foreigners to ensue, presumably, from the program. Also important is the ease by which stock-exchange purchases might enable foreigners to control even a major Japanese corporation because shares are widely held, and the shares issued are relatively few because of the high debt-equity ratio in corporate capital structures. But unlike the OECD policy, the Japanese premise of the amendment was that existing enterprises are exclusive preserves for Japanese, and access must be closed off before foreigners are allowed into even the "new enterprise." In this sense, the Special Committee's report in 1967 is understandable, coupled with popular agitation and official fears of the time. For example, in 1967 the Tokyo Chamber of Commerce sent a questionnaire to Japanese businessmen asking them, "How do you feel about take-overs?" The most frequent answer was: "We understand, logically, that a take-over is a natural phenomenon in the stock corporation system, but we cannot accept it emotionally."[60] Thus, the national psychology and high debt-equity ratio that lies just below the surface of liberalization discussions required this step backwards to deny previously permitted foreign acquisitions of existing shares with yen while embarking on "liberalization" at the same time. The Expert Committee's recommendations for use of the Antimonopoly Law (AML) are similarly interesting.

Antimonopoly Law as a Defensive Weapon

The committee, though it did not recommend immediate revision of the AML, did suggest that special interpretations and enforcement policies might be used under AML Art. 11 (limiting "financial institutions" to 10 percent shareholdings in industrial companies) and Art. 19 (unfair business practices)[61] (1) to prevent foreign take-overs and (2) to blunt the harsh effects of resident foreigners' competitive powers respectively. Ironically, the liberalization program has caused two inconsistent undercurrents in AML enforcement discussions. Industrial structuring and guidance to meet the foreign threat has caused the anti-concentration policies to be relaxed in favor of MITI-sponsored mergers, while in the area of "unfair business practices" (under discussion here), there are suggestions favoring more strict enforcement to prevent harsh foreign competitive practices.[62]

The Expert Committee suggested that the AML might be reinterpreted and enforcement policies redirected to assist in handling the anticipated advance of foreigners after the "liberalization." The first potentially useful provision was AML Art. 11 (proviso), which may be translated: "No company engaged in financial business [*kinyūgyō*] shall own or acquire stock, in the event that its ownership thereby exceeds 10% of the total issued of a domestic company; provided *that the foregoing shall not apply to such cases where the advance validation of the Fair Trade Commission [hereafter FTC] has been obtained in accordance with rules issued by the FTC. . . ."*

The idea here was that the proviso to Art. 11 could be interpreted to provide the FTC with authority to grant approvals for acquisitions of more than 10 percent of an existing corporation's shares by financial institutions in special cases for the purpose of turning back a threat of foreign take-over.

Such an interpretation has its problems, given the purpose of the law,[63] which was to prevent banks, insurance companies, and the like from becoming holding companies as in a prior era. In effect, the committee is urging administrative relaxation of the AML specifically for the purpose of shielding domestic enterprise against possible foreign managerial influence. The suggestion has more justification, in some cases, than might appear on the surface, again because of the typical Japanese debt-equity ratio and shareholding pattern mentioned above. Shares are widely held in a fractionated pattern, but usually the top six shareholders include several financial institutions that are fraternally linked with the industrial company's *keiretsu,* each with under 10 percent. Thus, the possibility of enlarging such shareholdings by relaxing the AML is attractive to the antiforeign segments of Japanese official-dom. Whether, legally, inauguration of such a policy change could take place by an FTC use of what should otherwise be an exceptional approval procedure, or only by a revision of the AML itself, is another question. Surely the draftsman of such a law would have his difficulties avoiding discriminatory implications. An amusing tactical move, pertinent to AML Art. 11, occurred in round three of the liberalization. To the surprise of the foreign-securities industry itself, the securities business was included in Category I (50 percent). Still, the domestic-securities dealers maintained their calm, even when international firms began surveying the Japanese market potential,[64] for the domestic confidence was buttressed by secure knowledge that the FIL regulations required 30 percent for a Japanese partner in each venture, (domestic-securities firms) to a 10 percent interest. That which was an impossibility under the AML Art. 11 that limits financial institutions given by the FIL was taken away by the AML; everyone remained unaffected as "liberalization" progressed. Actually, the securities market of Japan was opened up to foreign-securities dealers by a new law effective 1 September 1971. The law requires foreigners to operate through the relatively unattractive branch form. In March 1972, at least one U.S. firm was applying for branch approval.[65] A similar tactic occurred with banking. In the third round, banking was included in Category I (50 percent), but under the domestic administrative policy for banks (domestic and foreign), the establishment of new banks in Japan was not being approved.[66]

Illusory though the third-round liberalization of the banking and securities industry was, still it conveyed something of the flavor and tactics that lay always near the surface in the Japanese attempts (1967–72) to cope with foreigners by "liberalization," which was often fundamentally opposed by the authorities in the international sense, despite publicity to the contrary.

The Special Committee's second suggestion regarding the Antimonopoly Law was in the area of "unfair trade practice." In this case, rather than a relaxation in favor of domestic firms as in the first example, the committee found strict enforcement promising in order to prevent foreigners from using their superior technology, financial clout, or marketing innovations to disturb the Japanese market and possibly obtain more than the minor "market share" proffered.

The AML outlaws all unfair trade practices;[67] it then specifies six basic types[68] of unfair trade practices and empowers the FTC to designate unfair trade practices within these types. The FTC has designated unfair practices in the form of one regulation for general applicability and some seventeen regulations for specified industries. For foreigners, the FTC rules on requirements for technological assistance agreements are of interest (as noted above). Under the general regulations, provisions against unlawfully low retail prices and price discrimination were regarded by the FIC as especially pertinent to the foreign threat. Also pertinent is a special law[69] controlling sales promotions (through premiums and prizes) by authorizing self-regulation by industry-wide agreements banning suspect promotional and advertising activities, all of which are appropriate shields.

In sum, the committee suggests that the AML (Art. 11) should be leniently interpreted to promote "stable shareholdings" to exclude foreign influence and strictly enforced in the area of unfair trade practices (Art. 19) to prevent foreigners from becoming too competitive on the domestic scene. Critics say that the official promotion of international competitiveness, a prime objective of MITI, is but protection from competition for existing firms in the domestic modern sector at the expense of consumers,[70] smaller enterprises, and foreigners, because it creates an oligopolistic industrial structure. Little is heard about this matter in the mainstream of Japanese decision-making, but the opposition (*yatō*) frequently makes the point.[71] One president of a medium-sized Japanese enterprise has observed that he feared large domestic corporations more than foreign enterprises.[72] However, enlargement of domestic corporations and reduction of their numbers by merger is apparently national policy in order to create competitiveness with foreign enterprises, as the steel merger (Nippon Steel Co., from Yamata and Fuji) and the recent merger of Dai Ichi and the Kangyo Banks so well illustrate. Indeed, there has been a suggestion that all key industries, such as steel, automobiles, petrochemical, and synthetics be concentrated into two or three industrial groups. MITI has just proposed a plan for the six Japanese computer manufacturers to reorganize into three groups in order to better protect themselves when the investment restrictions are lifted. Six computer firms are apparently too many, creating "excessive" competition. In effect, MITI is proposing a state-sponsored (and subsidized) oligopolistic concentration in the computer industry for the sake of meeting international competition. Already joint-venture talks between Hitachi Ltd. and Fuji Tsushinki, as well as between Toshiba and Nihon Denki, have become well advanced.[73] This is but the latest of examples of state-sponsored, enterprise nationalism, infused with oligopolistic unity for attack purposes, which may continue to prove effective in world markets. But the question remains as to whether it deserves to be treated as "free private enterprise," when to do so may disadvantage more independent competitors not similarly backed by their government.

Patent Law

In its 15 November 1968 report[74] on liberalization of technological assistance contracts, as well as its earlier *FIC Report* on direct investment (1967), the Expert Committee concluded that Patent Law provisions[75] on compulsory, nonexclusive licensing could be used to prevent foreign use of patents to dominate an industry in Japan after liberalization. The gist of the law is the grant of authority to the MITI minister to compel nonexclusive licensing of a foreigner's Japanese patents if required by the "public interest" (*kōkyō no rieki*). There is no case history under the article, and its meaning remains vague. The committee suggested that it might be used where public health or public facilities were affected or possibly where mass unemployment or plant obsolescence would result from a foreign monopoly by patent.[76]

There are problems with this suggestion.[77] Compensation as required by the Japanese Constitution[78] could not be finally determined administratively (MITI). Also, whether compulsory licensing for these purposes might not be inconsistent with the Convention of the Union of Paris is a question, for the convention[79] provides only for "compulsory" licenses to prevent the abuses that might result from the exclusive rights conferred by the patent, for example, for failure to work. Are other "abuses" too indirect? The Japanese law also has another provision addressed to the problem of failure to work.[80] On the nonlegal level, foreign inventors might keep technology from Japan if this provision were used so as to undercut the major benefits of their patent rights. It is unlikely, however, that this patent-law provision will be much used, but it is interesting that MITI's tentative criteria for foreign firms also mention this possibility.[81]

Countermeasures in the Commercial Code

Plans for amending the Japanese Commercial Code (Book II, Ch. IV) on corporations have reached the draft stage. The amendment is aimed at resisting foreign encroachment on existing firms by abolishing compulsory cumulative voting.[82] A second suggestion, not yet so advanced, would relax rules against a corporation acquiring its own stock.

Regarding abolition of cumulative voting (*ruiseki tōhyō*), Japanese corporation law has a SCAP-inspired provision adopting cumulative voting in a compromise form as follows:

Article 256-3: Any shareholder may, in writing, demand of the company at least five days before the time set for convening a general meeting for the election of two or more directors that such election shall be held by the method of cumulative voting.

Article 256-4: The company may provide by the articles of incorporation that the election of directors shall not be made in accordance with the cumulative voting. Even in this case, any shareholder or shareholders who hold shares representing not less than one-fourth of the total number of the issued shares may make the demand mentioned in paragraph 1 of the preceding Article.

Proof of the lack of Japanese enthusiasm for cumulative voting is found in a recent survey, showing that 588 out of 589 companies answering a questionnaire have provisions against cumulative voting in their articles of incorporation.[83] Even in such corporations, however, cumulative voting may be required by demand of shareholders who have 25 percent of the votes. The foreign threat is slightly mitigated by the fact that, by current automatic validation provisions, foreigners (in the aggregate) may obtain up to 25 percent (not including 25 percent) of the shares by automatic approval (see above). To meet this danger, the tentative draft for Commercial Code revision provides as follows:[84] "Once a company establishes by its articles of incorporation that the election of directors shall not be made according to the cumulative voting, the shareholders may not demand that the election be made according to the cumulative voting."

This would, therefore, abolish even the power of a 25 percent shareholder to demand cumulative voting, in spite of provisions in the articles of incorporation prohibiting cumulative voting. The advisability, even from the Japanese standpoint, of such a new provision[85] is not entirely obvious. In other countries, outside directors have proven a useful source of perspective on corporate policies and operations. Quite apart from the outsider problem or possible foreign directorships, the cumulative voting device has been useful abroad to avoid abuse of power by incumbent management, which, surrounded only by directors of their own ilk, could perpetuate themselves and even insulate themselves from criticism, though it must be recognized that such checks on power do not have the role in Japanese corporate life that they do abroad. In Japan cumulative voting provisions are still regarded as a foreign device, useful mainly for foreigners, and the amendment is directed against them essentially. The policy discussions seem to be favoring this amendment, and it may soon be law.

Regarding acquisition by a corporation of its own shares, a Tokyo Chamber of Commerce survey[86] turned up 79 percent of those surveyed (761 corporations) favoring a relaxation of current laws prohibiting acquisition of own shares by issuing companies, while only 4.2 percent were content with the present law, which reads as follows:

Commercial Code, Article 210. A company cannot acquire its own shares or take them in pledge except in the following cases:
(1) Where the shares are to be retired;
(2) Where companies are amalgamated or the entire business of another company is acquired by transfer;
(3) Where in the course of the exercise of the rights of the company it is necessary to do so for achieving such object;
(4) Where the shares are to be purchased in accordance with the provisions of Article 245-2, Article 349 paragraph 1 or 408-3.

The code thus prohibits a corporation from acquiring its own shares except for limited purposes, then suspends voting rights[87] with respect to shares held by the corporation. Evasion is also discouraged by providing a criminal penalty for using a third person's name to acquire corporate shares.[88]

Apparently the government is looking into the system of "treasury shares" that is widely used in the U.S. as a possible model for reform, but as yet this reform has not reached the draft stage.[89] The usefulness of the device is reduced, because even its supporters (*e.g.,* MITI or *keidanren*)[90] would not apparently advocate the elimination of the no-vote rule for corporate holdings of its own shares, thus reducing its usefulness in countering foreign capital. Though the voting of owned shares is now impossible and is regarded by even the proponents as undesirable for the future, proponents of allowing own shares without voting rights point to the following possibilities: (1) an incipient take-over by foreigners might be countered by the company's entering the market and bidding the price up; (2) by corporate purchases of its own shares, the existing shareholders would be reduced, permitting an indirect consolidation and stabilization of the shareholding structure.[91]

As with banning of cumulative voting, however, there are other major disadvantages of the treasury share system. One major question is what funds to use for purchases of own shares. A second problem would be the scope and purpose for which the board of directors might be empowered to purchase shares, since an ulterior motive and managerial self-interest might become a real problem.[92] Would preventing foreigners from obtaining a directorship be an appropriate cause for spending scarce corporate funds and perpetuating at the same time the present board of directors? Presently, such dangers are apparently considered by some Japanese to be less dangerous than foreign participation in management.

Both of the above-mentioned reforms have a cogency in the Japanese environment which is unappreciated abroad. For example, there is less disposition of a minority to question authority (management) from the bottom up by the voting shareholder route (*sokaiya* aside)[93] in corporate life. Shareholders, providing typically only a small fraction of total corporate capital, are also financially less important (as are their dividends and risks).

Intracorporate Countermeasures

The Japanese FIC (through its Expert Committee)[94] has also discussed at some length, in the context of the foreign threat, measures that might be taken as intracorporate actions to prevent foreign domination. These include (1) restrictions on share transfers, (2) excluding foreign directorships in the articles of incorporation, and (3) stabilizing a controlling shareholders' group by employee shareholding plans. Also, capital increases for the same purposes have been mentioned in some other groups.

Concerning restricting share transfers, it seems that under present law a corporate charter could legally provide: "Approval of the board of directors is required for transfer of shares to foreigners." This is because the Commercial Code, as revised in 1966 to repeal prohibitions against share-transfer restrictions[95] (first written into the Commercial Code in 1950), has provided that board approval for transfers may be required. The 1966 amendments were apparently intended for the use of close corporations or family corporations, where share-transfer restrictions are often useful. The elaborate system to implement the powers to restrict transfers (Arts. 204–2 to 204–5) enables a shareholder to dispose of his shares and recapture his investment, but it also gives the corporation a right to screen purchasers, fix an appraisal price, and obtain alternative purchasers who are more congenial. Though the amendment was intended for other purposes, the board of directors could be used to screen out foreign investors by exercising its approval powers.

The Expert Committee (FIC) recommended this device for consideration by private corporations, but a major difficulty is a Tokyo Stock Exchange rule[96] that prevents listing a corporation with transfer restrictions in its charter. Consequently, as it now stands, the Stock Exchange rules prevent the proviso of Art. 204 from being useful in any but smaller, unlisted Japanese companies. The committee has suggested that the troublesome Tokyo Stock Exchange rules might be reconsidered,[97] but a change would create its own serious problems— for example, how to determine the foreign identity of stock-exchange buyers. The purchase might be invalidated, after determining the purchaser to be a foreigner, on the grounds that director approval was not obtained, and prevailing scholarly opinions seem to support this invalidation approach,[98] though in operation it would be troublesome for exchange transactions. Query: whether the Tokyo Stock Exchange, essentially a quasi-public body, could legally impose such discriminatory treatment on foreigners, especially U.S. citizens in view of the FCN Treaty provisions[99] (see below).

Basically, the Japanese interest in this device stems from the need to stabilize the fractionated stockholding pattern, as it exists even in most major firms. As noted before, typically, the debt-equity ratio is about 80 percent to 20 percent, meaning that much leverage can be obtained for relatively little money in such thin and widely held corporations; also the 10 percent rule for financial institutions under the AML Art. 11 (discussed above) means that in the family of companies (*keiretsu*), shareholding can be stabilized only to a point by sister company holdings, making even first-level companies vulnerable to take-overs by foreign investors. The take-over by tender offer is now less of a threat because of the SEC amendments of 1 July 1971.

No better example of the anxiety of MITI over unstable shareholding structures can be found than its worries about the joint ventures between Japanese automobile makers and the American "Big Three." For example, the Mitsubishi-Chrysler tie-up went smoothly (June 1971) only because of close-knit cross-shareholdings between Mitsubishi companies. As the *Japan Times* reported:[100] "MITI officials see no serious problem in the Mitsubishi-Chrysler partnership because the possibility is very small of Chrysler taking over Japan's No. 3 auto firm, whose ownership is firmly controlled by its giant parent corporation, Mitsubishi Heavy Industry." Also, President Yaichiro Makita of Mitsubishi Heavy Industry is quoted as saying:[101] "We view this relationship as one of Chrysler with the Mitsubishi group rather than as one between Chrysler and the Mitsubishi Motor Corporation."

Also, General Motors and the Isuzu Motor Company concluded a tie-up (July 1971) to be approved by MITI as soon as the condition of "stabilized shareholders" could be achieved.[102] But, the Ford–Toyo Kogyo negotiations were even more to the point, as MITI had reportedly required a "no take-over pledge" from Ford, presumably by "guidance." In March 1972, the Ford–Toyo Kogyo talks were abandoned for the time being, in part because Ford wanted representation on the board commensurate with the equity to be obtained in Toyo Kogyo. These negotiations were finally broken off.[103] Since the Japanese automobile firms involved are existing corporations, these tie-ups were in the nonliberalized area and subject to screening but note 1973 changes.

Share-transfer restrictions, colliding as they do with the listing rules of the Tokyo Stock Exchange, pose such serious legal problems that the direct approach of actually organizing a controlling group of domestic shareholdings has been proposed as a more realistic solution to the foreign take-over. Cited as a successful example is Toyota Motors, in which a group headed by the company itself controls 60 percent of all shares.[104] The entire Sumitomo group, well known as the closest of the major *keiretsu* with high interlocking shareholdings, is another example of closing of ranks within the group, and it renders its units impervious to foreign infiltration.[105] Heavy corporate buying of sister companies' shares is said to have been one reason why the Tokyo stock price index doubled in 1972, when corporations had excess funds to spend.

Turning to exclusion of foreign directors, this important legal device has already been litigated, ending in a judgment upholding the exclusion.[106] The case involved Toyota Motors, whose charter (Art. 17) provided the following: "Directors and auditors shall be limited to those possessing Japanese nationality." In a shareholder's suit, the charter provision was challenged by requesting nullification of a board resolution alleging that the charter provision violated the equality provisions of the constitution[107] as well as various Commercial Code provisions. The Nagoya District Court upheld the charter clause on the grounds that the constitution does not guarantee absolute equality between Japanese and foreigners in the internal affairs of private groups such as business corporations, which are essentially self-regulating, and where the court may not intrude unless the regulation is "unreasonable." The court then found it reasonable to limit by this method the extent of managerial participation in Toyota by foreign nationals. Most Japanese legal writers, commenting on the case, believe the Nagoya District Court's opinion will be upheld if appealed to higher courts.[108]

Of course, such a charter restriction could be overcome if foreigners obtained the necessary two-thirds to amend the charter. Still, the chances are marginal and the exclusion of foreign directors has appeal because of its deterrent effect on foreign investors planning take-overs, especially if it could be combined with transfer restrictions. The appeal of the device is further enhanced by the fact that an all-Japanese board would insure against disruptive foreign behavior at board meetings; Japanese directors presumably would be more constrained to maintain harmonious relations with colleagues and other enterprises and to follow cartel quotas and policies flowing from MITI guidance. Prevention of "dummy" Japanese directors acting for substantial foreign shareholders is a problem that is not yet seriously posed or satisfactorily solved.

The Expert Committee noted another legal problem with this device to exclude foreign directors. Although original charter provisions excluding foreign directors would clearly be valid, charter amendments in corporations already with foreign shareholders (*e.g.,* Hitachi, Toshiba, etc.) pose a more serious problem, though they too would probably be legal if foreign shareholders are still less than the 25 percent required to demand compulsory cumulative voting.[109] Some legal scholars have pointed to the policy of the Commercial Code that encourages the widest possible selection of directors as shown in Art. 254-2 (unlawful to confine directorships to shareholders only).[110] Most recent opinions seem to regard the right to a directorship as mere expectancy and say that present foreign shareholders might not even challenge the invalidity of an amendment excluding them as directors.[111]

Employee shareholding plans were another suggestion of the Expert Committee to stabilize the fragmented shareholding structure in Japanese corporations.[112] This plan gives employees preferential treatment in purchasing shares of their employer corporation, either by special credits extended by the corporation or by reduced prices. Of course, to police this system, some kind of share-transfer restrictions must be imposed to prevent employee-shareholder profiteering, though the Japanese lifetime employment system provides a sound institutional base, provided other problems can be solved. Some legal writers suggest that selectively restricting employees' share transfers poses legal problems,[113] and the difficulties of general restrictions colliding with the Tokyo Stock Exchange listing requirements have been discussed above. Shareholding trusts for employees have been considered too.[114]

Where the corporation finances its employees' purchases, the question is raised as to whether such a use of funds is within the corporate purposes: Is excluding foreign capital itself enough to justify this use of funds? Advocates are quick to point out that employee shareholding increases loyalty and promotes the employee's welfare enough to justify the plan in most companies.[115] In fact, employee shareholding plans are gaining popularity in Japan as an employee welfare program without focus on resisting foreign shareholders.

Employee shareholding plans based on favorable prices require a special two-thirds vote of shareholders present (quorum: more than one-half of total shares issued), as provided by the 1966 amendment to the Commercial Code.[116] Difficulties with this idea stem from the almost universal practice of issuing new shares to existing shareholders. Preemptive rights to buy new issues at par (usually below market) has been so strong as to almost wipe out the capital-raising potential of offering new issues to the general public even at market prices. During 1971–72, however, the practice of corporations issuing shares at market prices gained a remarkable acceptance and may indicate a new trend in Japanese corporate finance.

Other Measures Useful in Countering Foreign Business

Several other measures of more general applicability have been mentioned as collaterally useful in dealing with threats of foreign managerial participation or control of existing Japanese corporations.

Maintaining control by capital increases to nonforeigners is such a measure. Capital increases are subject to the aforementioned preemptive rights. However, the 1966 revisions of the Commercial Code authorize the board of directors to issue new shares to third parties if the issuing price is fair; and the shares may be issued at a favorable price, if approved by the shareholders.[117] Thus the capital issue has some promise in countering foreign domination, because it would first reduce the proportionate share of foreigners and secondly the new issue could be distributed to larger corporate brethren in the *keiretsu* or the financial institutions at its core, though if over 10 percent per financial institution, this latter requires FTC approval as mentioned.[118]

Revisions in the Securities Exchange Law were enacted 3 March 1971. They contain provisions[119] designed more generally to prevent takeover bids (*kōkai kaitsuke*), but since Japan had not yet had any experience with take-over bids (but note the Borg Warner tender offer, *Japan Economic Journal,* 7 March 1972), the revision was also aimed in part at preventing foreign firms, after liberalization, from using such devices to take over existing industrial firms.[120] These new provisions are intricate, but essentially they require disclosures ten days before the bid can be effective by filing, with the Ministry of Finance, information about all bids addressed to the public outside of the exchange market.[121] The law is not concerned with secret buying up of controlling shares on the exchange, or with private purchases from major shareholders without using the exchange. The filing must be by the person who will actually hold the shares sought, or, in the case of "nonresident" buyers,[122] filing is by the securities firm or bank acting for the foreigner.[123] Forms for disclosure filings are prescribed in the ministerial ordinance.[124]

Domestic regulatory laws for each industry are another source of restrictions on foreigners, though they apply equally to all enterprisers. The point is that the latecoming foreigner may be excluded completely or assigned a minor share that will be expected to remain minor so as not to cause confusion in the market or cause industrial disorder. We have already discussed the implications of the government-nurtured modern oligopolies and the resulting "market share" concept in general terms (Chapter IV), as well as the exclusionary effect of the laws regulating licensing of banking and securities firms, even after liberalization. Attention need only be drawn again to the fact that formal legal liberalization in Japan for foreign entries does not mean a liberal or free domestic environment once admitted; in many cases it will amount to government's protecting the domestic incumbents by quotas, licenses, and the like and restricting the new activities of foreigners. Indeed, these controls are so tight and pervasive that it would seem that Japan could abolish the FIL, thus avoiding international treaty problems and still adequately control the foreign operations in Japan. But even in the "100 percent liberalization" announced 1 May 1973, there is no mention of amending the FIL. Though the "countermeasures" would seem to be enough, the Japanese government still, in 1973, retains a double defense against foreign business entries—FIL and the countermeasures (SEC, AML, cartels, etc.).

Summary

My own feeling is that the foregoing limits and complexities of Japanese liberalization efforts, despite clear statements of liberal policy at the cabinet level, stem largely from the fact that Japan makes decisions by consensus, in this case extremely difficult because of the "vertical" industry principle in MITI organization and also because each industry tends to favor liberalization in principle but to except themselves specifically (*sōron sansei, kakuron hantai*). The limitations placed on the automatic approval system for certain percentages (50 percent Category I; 100 percent Category II) of *new* enterprises, as well as countermeasures to protect existing firms, should convey some of the interest politics and some of the real anxieties permeating Japanese society generally—but particularly business circles and officialdom—even after the last four years of "liberalization" (1967–72). Much as OECD and Americans have suggested that the foreign irritant will be to Japan as the pearl to the oyster because of the added efficiency and productivity implicit in competitive business, the Japanese middle-level officials have remained reluctant and unconvinced, except on their own cautious schedule and limited scale.

Liberalization has made some progress, but it is still behind international standards of "advanced countries." The 50 percent limits imposed on almost all industries in which practicable investments exist for foreigners is well below practices acceptable under OECD policy; and Japan does not practice the 50 percent rule abroad in her own investments in foreign industrial enterprises overseas. Still, the 50 percent limit is only accorded to foreigners in new enterprises; in unapproving, existing enterprises it is under 25 percent. The studied attempts by the countermeasures reviewed herein to deny rights to participate, even as a minority, in the management of an existing Japanese enterprise is a serious restriction, for one of the results of progressing industrialization the world over is the increasing difficulty of industrial entry for venture capital. Japan is no exception to this proposition. Arguably, new entry into Japanese heavy industry—steel, shipbuilding, automobiles, and the like—is more difficult in Japan because of government licensing, the domestic *keiretsu,* institutional solidarity, and other familial organization.[125] Thus, limiting of the 50 percent category to new enterprises makes the 1967–72 liberalization program quite shallow.

We have dwelt upon the counterliberalization in some detail because it poignantly conveys the deep misgivings of Japanese officialdom (and industry, too, to a lesser extent) regarding intrusions by foreigners into their highly integrated, hierarchical, and effective corporate and supracorporate institutions. Most of the countermeasures are surely illiberal in their thrust, and, by treaty and constitutional standards abroad (equal protection and due process), the kinds of discrimination implicit in some of them raise another set of legal questions that are little considered in Japan. We will consider the treaty problem next.

The Treaty Problem

In the discussion of Japanese liberalization, we dealt with recent developments in the Japanese internal law as related to inward capital movements to determine what it has actually accomplished by 1973. From the outside, there have been two kinds of "international standards" referred to in the foreign criticisms of the domestic program in the 1967–72 period.[126] First, "advanced-nation status" seems to imply in the U.S. and Europe certain capacities and resultant obligations (to LDCs) or reciprocity (to advanced nations) in maintaining a "free-world economy."[127] The content of this idea has never been entirely clear or uniform among nations involved; though a worthy ideal, it is long on economics and short on political cogency; it can thus operate best at the level of economic diplomacy, to be discussed later. The second standard is specifically legal, concerned with obligations flowing from Japanese treaty commitments in international law and premised largely on the economic theories promoted and documented by these treaties in the 1950s and early 1960s. It is this legal aspect that now deserves our attention as background for the economic diplomacy and adjustments unfolding in the 1970s. Though surely the incipient changes in the world economic regime will outweigh the importance of these dryly legal arguments of the past, they are part of the current background essential to ongoing Japanese internationalization, which is now much espoused by high Japanese officials in the process of reconnoitering for the future in the wake of the "dollar shock" and already two revaluations by 1973.

The Free-World Economy (1945–1971)

Under U.S. leadership, the legal structure of a "free-world economy" was established, piecemeal and imperfectly, after World War II in the form of several multilateral organizations (mainly IMF, OECD, and GATT), as well as a multitude of bilateral treaties. This the U.S. was in a position to do because her GNP and trade volume were predominant in the world, plus the fact that U.S. policy favored rehabilitation of other nations and a liberal international exchange;[128] the U.S. had not suffered the devastation of her allies and former opponents.

Japan entered into most major international multilateral commitments soon after gaining her autonomy by the San Francisco Peace Treaty in 1952.[129] The more important treaties with dates of Japanese accession are: the International Monetary Fund (IMF)[130] in 1952, first as an

"Article XIV nation" (for twelve years); also in 1952 Japan joined the International Bank for Reconstruction and Development (World Bank) and later the Asian Development Bank (1965).[131] Then she joined the General Agreement on Tariffs and Trade (GATT)[132] in 1955, accepting Art. XI[133] obligations in 1963, and was admitted to the United Nations on 18 December 1956, five years after the effective date of the San Francisco Peace Treaty on 28 April 1952 because of unresolved cold-war issues with the U.S.S.R.[134] Thereafter, she was elected to a nonpermanent membership on the Security Council for a two-year term commencing 1 July 1958, and she also participates in the major subsidiary UN organs.[135] In 1964 Japan joined the Organization of Economic Cooperation and Development (OECD)[136] and was widely acclaimed as a new member of the "advanced nations club," despite her numerous "reservations" to the Code of Liberalization of Capital Movements.[137] At the same time, she also accepted obligations to free all exchange restrictions in current transactions under IMF Art. VIII, thereby giving up the protective restrictions on foreign payments previously invoked under Art. XIV,[138] though she simultaneously increased restrictions on some of the underlying transactions.[139] In all of these international arrangements, the U.S. has been Japan's most forceful sponsor against the restrictive and reluctant attitudes of many of the European nations, which have invoked GATT Art. XXXV against Japan.[140]

In addition, Japan has signed a number of bilateral treaties regarding friendship, commerce, and navigation (FCN treaties) with some variations for different nations, but the most important in this context is that with the U.S., which was signed on 2 April 1953.[141] The "national treatment" provisions of the U.S.-Japanese treaty later (1962) inured to citizens of the United Kingdom by virtue of a "most favored nation" clause in the Anglo-Japanese treaty signed 22 April 1960.[142]

In addition to the general multilateral conventions and comprehensive bilateral FCN treaties that framed post-World War II economic relations, Japan also entered into a number of important multilateral and bilateral conventions more narrowly concerned with specialized subject matter of importance to international business. Japan became a signatory of the Convention of the Union of Paris (20 March 1883), as revised,[143] for the protection of industrial property and the Universal Copyright Convention[144] with its protocols. She also became a party to the United Nations Convention on the Recognition and Enforcement of Foreign Arbitral Awards (see Chapter IX), and among other private law conventions put into effect the International Convention for the

Unification of Certain Rules Relating to Bills of Lading through the enactment of her own International Carriage of Goods by Sea Act (COSGA) in 1962.[145] Also important to foreign enterprisers are the bilateral tax treaties of which the one between the U.S. and Japan is notable, with important revisions signed[146] on 8 March 1971 (ratified by Japan, 21 May 1971).

The foregoing treaties are the basic framework for Japanese participation in the international economic community, although the enumeration could be greatly extended to cover other agreements between Japan and her many trading partners the world over.[147] But the criticisms that have become a part of the liberalization issue are grounded largely in her commitments under the OECD agreement and the U.S.-Japanese FCN Treaty, with collateral references to IMF obligations.

Attention must be given first to terminology used in the FCN, OECD, and IMF agreements as they affect the "liberalization" issue—here limited to inward capital transfers, notably direct investment by foreigners wishing to invoke their right to do business not only with, but also in, Japan. "Liberalization" itself is not defined in the FCN, OECD, or IMF agreements, though it appears in the OECD codes (below); the word "capital"[148] is found in each of these agreements but not specifically defined in any of them. The FCN Treaty employs the term in the strategic Protocol Paragraph 6 (hereafter Protocol 6) with no explicit definition, but with cross-references that might take the analysis to the IMF agreement. The IMF agreement uses the terms "capital transfers"[149] and "capital movements"[150] as distinguished from "current transactions," and IMF, Art. XIX(i), defines current transactions circularly as follows: "Payments for current transactions means payments which are not for the purpose of transferring capital." The OECD terminology differentiates between "current invisibles" and "capital movements" in its two codes of liberalization, Code of Liberalization of Current Invisibles and Code of Liberalization of Capital Movements[151] (hereafter Invisibles Code and Capital Code), without explicitly defining the terms. Rather, the approach is to list in some detail transactions that fall into one category or the other, and one of the many transactions that is listed as a "capital movement" is direct investment.[152] We shall accept the OECD approach in delineating "capital movements" since IMF is only secondarily concerned with capital movements, and then only with transfers of money as opposed to underlying transactions.

While discussing terminology, we should again note the exceptional Japanese usage: the FIL includes technological assistance agreements, which the OECD does not regard as a "capital movement"; contrariwise, branches of foreign firms are not covered by the FIL though they are defined as direct investment by the OECD Capital Code; and finally, the FIL covers all loans of one year or longer in duration, whereas the Capital Code treats only loans of five years or more as direct investment.[153] The OECD Code applies only to private capital movements, and the term "capital movement" includes both the *transfers* and the underlying *transactions* involved, in a manner analogous (but with quite the opposite effect) to the FIL, as opposed to the FECL, which, though covering transactions (Art. 30), does not reach or invalidate them in civil law. (See Chapter VI, above). This calculated shallowness of the IMF and FECL (by court decisions) results from concern with international currency exchange and thus regulates primarily payments or transfers, leaving the validity of underlying contracts and transactions to private law. The restrictions on contracts and acquisitions, as found in the FIL, are contrary to the spirit of the OECD Capital Code.

The distinction between liberalization of payments and transactions has confused newcomers in international business, who presume that when foreign-exchange payments are liberalized their transactions are also to be freed. No better example may be found than the Japanese handling of the yen-based enterprises in 1964, whereby in the name of "liberalization" (foreign-exchange payments) the underlying transactions (acquiring stock for domestic yen) were prohibited, with the obvious effect that, from the investor's viewpoint, the important "transaction," which had previously been free, was thereafter restricted and the unimportant foreign-exchange payment (by definition unimportant since a "yen corporation" means that a foreigner had consciously chosen to forego repatriation) was "liberalized."[154] In the 1967 liberalization, this same phenomenon is found in new prohibitions against branches and subsidiaries of nonresident companies acquiring Japanese stock with yen without purchasing said yen with foreign currency—transactions previously free.

Liberalization and the U.S.–Japanese FCN Treaty

Our analysis will start with Japan's legal commitments under the FCN Treaty because here the argument[155] has recently been quite spirited and often framed in legal rhetoric, though in our view the U.S. treaty violation argument has little problem-solving potential (see below). The problems will more likely be solved by effective U.S. reactions to Japanese restrictions in ways that may produce opportunities to trade off restrictions. Still, the treaty argument has become a part of the background necessary to a future understanding, for, if anything other than constant power maneuverings are to govern international economic relations, it is, of course, imperative that compliance with appropriate treaties be taken seriously. It may well be that this treaty has outgrown its usefulness in its present form; if so, it should be revised or reinterpreted to cover the behavior preferred under new conditions. Such an approach would leave the U.S. free to pursue an overall national policy (hopefully forthcoming) toward the outside world and free to use denial of access to its major market as leverage in future dealings in which liberality is not reciprocated.

Allegations by U.S. officials that Japan has been violating the FCN Treaty commenced as far back as 1964[156] and have been renewed successively by American participants at the annual Joint U.S.-Japan Meetings on Trade and Economic Affairs.[157] Business interests in the United Kingdom[158] have also supported this view because of their most-favored-nation clause, which gives them the same "national treatment" rights as the U.S., and the Business and Industrial Advisory Committee (BIAC)[159] of OECD has also supported this view.

The allegations are based on the FCN Treaty, Art. VII, which should be read in its entirety:

Article VII

1. Nationals and companies of either Party shall be accorded national treatment with respect to engaging in all types of commercial, industrial, financial and other business activities within the territories of the other Party, whether directly or by agent or through the medium of any form of lawful juridical entity. Accordingly, such nationals and companies shall be permitted within such territories: (a) to establish and maintain branches, agencies, offices, factories and other establishments appropriate to the conduct of their business; (b) to organize companies under the general company laws of such other Party, and to acquire majority interests in companies of such other Party; and (c) to control and manage enterprises which they have established or acquired. Moreover, enterprises which they control, whether in the form of individual proprietorships, companies or otherwise, shall, in all that relates to the conduct of the activities thereof, be accorded treatment no less favorable than that accorded like enterprises controlled by nationals and companies of such other Party.

2. Each Party reserves the right to limit the extent to which aliens may within its territories establish, acquire interests in, or carry on public utilities enterprises or enterprises engaged in shipbuilding, air or water transport, banking involving depository or fiduciary functions, or the exploitation of land or other natural resources. However, new limitations imposed by either Party upon the extent to which aliens are accorded national treatment, with respect to carrying on such activities within its territories, shall not be

applied as against enterprises which are engaged in such activities therein at the time such new limitations are adopted and which are owned or controlled by nationals and companies of the other Party. Moreover, neither Party shall deny to transportation, communications and banking companies of the other Party the right to maintain branches and agencies to perform functions necessary for essentially international operations in which they are permitted to engage.

3. The provisions of paragraph 1 of the present Article shall not prevent either Party from prescribing special formalities in connection with the establishment of alien-controlled enterprises within its territories, but such formalities may not impair the substance of the rights set forth in said paragraph.

4. Nationals and companies of either Party, as well as enterprises controlled by such nationals and companies, shall in any event be accorded most-favored-nation treatment with reference to the matters treated in the present Article.

These straightforward provisions established the rights of U.S. citizens to "national treatment" in the establishment and operation of businesses in Japan and vice versa, and the apparent purpose is to accord the "foreign enterprise" the same rights, duties, and privileges, legally, as those enjoyed by domestic business.

Persons experienced in Japan will immediately sense that the real problem here, from the Japanese point of view, has been that foreign enterprises could not be fitted into the Japanese milieu comfortably, unless their rights to do business in Japan are read as conditioned by the many peculiar duties and limitations of the Japanese business world. In other words, freedom to do business in Japan is not freedom to do business there as foreigners would do business at home, and since doing business as the Japanese do is difficult for foreigners, the Japanese officials seem to feel it is necessary to grant entry with great care and deliberation. Actually, I have not found such Japanese reasoning directly offered by the Japanese government as a basis for official behavior under FCN Treaty Art. VII, but I suspect my statement underlies the Japanese position.

To the grant in favor of foreign enterprises, the treaty sets out four major exceptions, two of them in Art. VII. Art. VII-2 excepts from national treatment sensitive industries such as public utilities, water transport, banking, land and resource exploitation. Art. VII-3 permits the host country to require "special formalities" in connection with the establishment of alien-controlled enterprise within its territories, provided such formalities do not impair the substance of the rights provided in Art. VII-1.

A third exception[160] for national security interests (munitions, atomic energy, and the like) is found in Art. XXI-1. Such provisions are common in international agreements and are intended to satisfy the interests of host countries in excluding foreigners from defense and other sensitive industries.

Finally, a more important explicit limitation, upon which Japan's defense of her foreign-investment restriction in ordinary industries is usually based, is found in Protocol 6, which reads as follows:

Either party may impose restrictions on the introduction of foreign capital as may be necessary to protect its monetary reserves as provided by Article XII, paragraph 2.
Article XII(2) provides:
Neither party shall impose exchange restrictions as defined in paragraph 5 of the present Article except to the extent necessary to prevent its monetary reserves from falling to a very low level or to effect a moderate increase in very low monetary reserves. It is understood that the provisions of the present Article do not alter the obligations either Party may have to the International Monetary Fund or preclude imposition of particular restrictions whenever the Fund specifically authorizes or requests a Party to impose such particular restrictions.

To paraphrase, the effect of Protocol 6, plus Art. XII-2, is to permit "exchange restrictions" on inward capital transfers to prevent reserves from falling to a *very low level* or to effect a moderate increase in *very low monetary reserves*, provided restrictions are consistent with IMF obligations.

Noteworthy also is Art. XXIV, which provides for consultation between the two governments concerning operation of the treaty and provides for submission of such disputes as cannot be settled by diplomacy to the International Court of Justice.[161] Also, the treaty may be terminated by giving one year's written notice (Art. XXV).

Within the treaty framework summarized above, has Japan violated "national treatment" obligations by excluding U.S. business for existing industries (except 25 percent) or by subjecting investors, even in new enterprises, to conditions not imposed upon domestic business? Since rights to national treatment are clear (Art. VII [1]) and severe restrictions still exist which exclude U.S. direct investment, Japan's justification for continuing restrictions on entry (as opposed to regulation once admitted in) of direct investment, in particular in ordinary industries, must be found in the above-mentioned exceptions. And, assuming no "sensitive industries" (Art. VII [2] or Art. XXI) are involved, Japan is presumed to argue necessity to protect its monetary reserves under Protocol 6. Note that the exact standard allows restrictions necessary to protect monetary reserves *from falling to a very low level* or to effect a *moderate increase in very low* monetary reserves, provided they are consistent with the IMF obligations. Application of Protocol 6 is not clear in all circumstances: first, within a certain range it is always arguable in good faith that the reserves are "very low" by one party and not "very low" by the other party; second, it is not always clear whether restrictions are "necessary" or for the purpose of protecting reserves; third, it is not always clear whether the means (restrictions) for protecting reserves are sufficiently cogent to those ends.

But preliminarily, Art. XII (2) raises the question as to how IMF provisions might affect the application of Protocol 6. The last sentence (XII [2]) provides: "It is understood that the provisions of the present Article do not alter the obligations either Party may have to the International Monetary Fund or preclude imposition of particular restrictions whenever the Fund specifically authorizes or requests a Party to impose such particular restrictions."

Looking to the IMF agreement,[162] its general purposes and particularly Art. VI and official interpretations thereof, it is clear that such IMF rules as may be incorporated by reference into Protocol 6 are concerned primarily with current payments; generally, the IMF is not concerned with capital transfers. This can be seen from IMF, Art. VI, which is concerned with exceptional uses of the fund for capital transfers:

Article VI. Capital Transfers
Section 1. Use of the Fund's Resources for Capital Transfers.—

(a) A member may not make net use of the Fund's resources to meet a large or sustained outflow of capital, and the Fund may request a member to exercise controls to prevent such use of the resources of the Fund. If, after receiving such a request, a member fails to exercise appropriate controls, the Fund may declare the member ineligible to use the resources of the Fund.

(b) Nothing in this Section shall be deemed

(i) to prevent the use of the resources of the Fund for capital transactions of reasonable amount required for expansion of exports or in the ordinary course of trade, banking or other business, or

(ii) to affect capital movements which are met out of a member's own resources of gold and foreign exchange, but members undertake that such capital movements will be in accordance with the purposes of the Fund.

Section 2. Special Provisions for Capital Transfers.—

If the Fund's holdings of the currency of a member have remained below seventy-five percent of its quota for an immediately preceding period of not less than six months, such member, if it has not been declared ineligible to use the resources of the Fund under Section 1 of this Article, Article IV, Section 6, Article V, Section 5, or Article XV, Section 2(a), shall be entitled, notwithstanding the provisions of Section 1(a) of this Article, to buy the currency of another member from the Fund with its own currency for any purpose, including capital transfers. Purchases for capital transfers under this Section shall not, however, be permitted if they have the effect of raising the Fund's holdings of the currency of the member desiring to purchase above seventy-five percent of its quota, or of reducing the Fund's holdings of the currency desired below seventy-five percent of the quota of the member whose currency is desired.

Section 3. Controls of Capital Transfers.—

Members may exercise such controls as are necessary to regulate international capital movements, but no member may exercise these controls in a manner which will restrict payments for current transactions or which will unduly delay transfers of funds in settlement of commitments, except as provided in Article VII, Section 3(b), and in Article XIV, Section 2.

Thus the IMF is only peripherally involved (Art. VI) with capital movements as a facility to members, as Art. VI (1 and 2) provides a limited use of IMF resources for capital outflows (not inward). Art. VI (3) then authorizes members to control "capital movements" (both inward and outward) provided they do not "restrict payment for current transactions," which is the major concern of IMF.[163] It is these obligations (not to control capital in a manner restricting current payments) that are the IMF obligations that are not to be altered by FCN Art. XII (2) as incorporated in Protocol 6.

At this point in marshaling all cross-referenced provisions for a consistent reading of FCN Protocol 6, a critical term used in FCN Art. XII (2) (as defined in XII [5] and relating to IMF Article VI) is "exchange restrictions." Art. XII (5) provides: "5. The term 'exchange restrictions' as used in the present Article includes all restrictions, regulations, charges, taxes, or other requirements imposed by either Party which burden or interfere with payments, remittances, or transfers of funds or of financial instruments between the territories of the two Parties."

The FCN Art. XII (2) states (though as an exception) that "exchange restrictions" consistent with IMF duties may be imposed for "very low" reserves; and Protocol 6 extends the right to impose "restrictions" for "introduction of foreign capital" to protect "monetary reserves," again consistent with IMF (presumably to maintain free payments of current transactions). From this interplay the most plausible purpose emerging from Protocol 6, in relation to FCN Art. VII, is that it too authorizes only "exchange restrictions" on inward capital transfers (not contracts or transactions) out of concern for maintaining reserves necessary to assure IMF payments on current accounts. Furthermore, since, in the actualities of international finances, it is primarily the comings and goings of short-term deposits or loans and port-folio investments that are the capital movements with the most potential for disrupting settlements of *current accounts,*[164] it can be seen that the restrictions of Protocol 6 were intended to apply only to them, rather than to inward direct investment. This is because, in all but exceptional cases, inward direct investments increase reserves immediately and are not usually withdrawn soon to create reserve problems; hence it would seldom be "necessary" to restrict direct investment inward.

Though not entirely clear, because Protocol 6 uses only "restrictions" (not "exchange restrictions"), still this interpretation, which limits Japan's rights to control capital entries only to "exchange restrictions" on payments inward aimed at short-term loans, capital deposits, and portfolio purchases, is nonetheless the most plausible reading for this critical provision,[165] given its cross-referencing to Art. XII and the IMF obligations that, as far as inward movements are concerned, deal only with exchange restrictions as they relate to payments not underlying transactions. Such an interpretation of Protocol 6, of course, removes it, for all practical purposes, as a justification for restrictions (FIL validations) on share *acquisitions* or technological assistance *contracts,* as opposed to foreign exchange *payments* thereunder, even where re-strictions are "necessary" because the reserves are "very low." We repeat, it seems doubtful that even the "exchange restrictions" on pay-ments as a device authorized by Protocol 6 to protect reserves would apply to inward *direct investors,* because they immediately add to these reserves and do not ordinarily contemplate, or, in fact, soon make, a withdrawal except dividends after taxes. If withdrawals later do become a threat to reserves, then is the time to restrict.

But supposing *arguendo* that Protocol 6 does apply to restrictions of both transactions and payments on inward direct investments made by U.S. citizens, then it only applies to prevent reserves from falling to a "very low level" and when the restrictions are "necessary" to protect the reserves.

Long-Term Considerations and Low-Level Reserves

The influence of timing on the concept of preventing "very low re-serves" becomes a major issue in the interpretation of Protocol 6, if we grant *arguendo* that Protocol 6 contemplates restrictions on inward direct capital transfers and/or transactions. The only time, according to one view, when restrictions may be placed on inward foreign capital is when monetary reserves are (or are about to become) in fact low or when it is desired to "effect a moderate increase." Such restrictions are thus preventive or corrective in a present or imminent balance-of-payments crisis. This seems to be the proper context for use of Protocol 6 timewise, but applied to inward direct investment capital it makes little sense.

The second view, allegedly espoused by the Japanese government,[166] sees the restrictions as long-term planning tools, if not a desirable way of life. This view brings "long-term considerations" into the interpretative problem. Presumably it would be framed like this: to maintain her reserves, Japan must compete effectively abroad, and to compete effectively, appropriate industrial specialties must be planned, organized, and placed in competition with the outside world. Government can do this better than individual enterprisers guided by the invisible hand of market forces. A comprehensive permanent plan implemented by restrictions (FIL) is necessary to insure that foreign participation in the plan is fully complementary, thus productive for Japan in exports or import substitutes, preventing monetary reserves from falling to a very low level. "Liberalization" is a relative program within these restrictions, which is allowed whenever Japanese international competitiveness grows to the point at which foreigners are not likely to find entry profitable. Thus, the official industrial plan, the nationalistic focus, and quasi-state trading characteristic of the Japanese economy (implemented largely by restrictions on trade, foreign exchange, and inward capital entry) are all rationalized as necessary auxiliaries to a foreign reserve maintenance strategy, and these "long-term considerations" (planning, subsidizing, industrial structuring, and administrative guidance) are necessarily buttressed by restrictions on foreign capital under Protocol 6. Also implicit in the argument is the assumption that free inward direct investments, in the long run, take more out of the economy than they produce by way of increased productivity, export potential, or technological and managerial innovations.

What Is a "Very Low Reserve?"

No matter which of the two views outlined above is appropriate to the interpretation of Protocol 6, it is clear that restrictions on inward capital (whether simple exchange restrictions or controls on transactions) may not be imposed at all under the treaty in ordinary industries except in relation to a "very low reserve." In the first view, the reserve has to be already or imminently low, whereas in the second view, presumably, advanced restrictions may be imposed as part of a planned economy to prevent a very low level of reserves. But in either case it becomes necessary to determine what a very low reserve is.

As of the end of 1972, Japanese reserves stood at $18 billion, and it is doubtful that the Japanese government could have responsibly argued that the reserves were then at a "very low level," especially if both outward and inward flows of capital are considered. Under the second view ("long-time considerations"), protagonists might argue that the FIL restrictions are proper preventive measures against some future low reserves, even though the present reserves in hand are high. Overall, this position makes Art. VII all but meaningless, but since this point is so important to the Japanese position, we should note four interesting issues inherent in the argument. First, a comprehensive and permanent control of capital entries to complete the symmetry of a planned and controlled economy is a great deal to pack into an appended clause such as Protocol 6, appearing rather as an afterthought in the treaty; also, such an interpretation places Japan on a double standard in that, internally, the long-term consideration view of Protocol 6 becomes the pivotal point for a controlled economy, whereas externally the philosophy of the FCN Treaty, OECD, IMF, GATT, and all of the rest of the free-world economic structure upon which Japan depends for trade is to maximize free international competition and free economic interplay. Third, there is the problem of the cogency of the means employed to obtain the ends (adequate reserves), since inward capital immediately increases reserves at entry, whereas restriction of such inward transfers obviously keeps reserves lower. This had led proponents of Japanese restrictions to say that only the "long-term considerations" can rescue Protocol 6 from the anomaly of seeming to authorize, in aid of reserves, restrictions that keep reserves low. They seem to be saying that the long-term cost of direct investments (repatriated principal, plus appreciation and dividends) is so high that actually to prevent them from being added to the reserves now will protect reserves later.

Is this really true? There is, of course, another prominent theory of cost-factor analysis that holds, without nationalistic bias, that the costs of capital and managerial talent have their own price, which would tend to be reduced (though not necessarily) in a larger, more competitive market across national boundaries. This analysis, as a premise of the "free-world economy," also holds that the price of entrepreneurial capital paid off the top presumably first produces its worth in terms of higher productivity, cheaper consumer goods and services, export potentials, import substitutes, technological know-how, and managerial innovations—amounting to more than their price costs in monetary reserves even if such capital is repatriated rather than reinvested, which in fact is often the case for some time. The price of capital and managerial talent, as well as its yield, may depend, in fact, on how free both internally and externally the competition is. If this view is correct, then the FIL restrictions on inward direct investment will not only keep reserves lower by prohibiting the initial transfer but will continue to keep them low by preventing contributions to both the economy and reserves by later yield of foreign capital within Japan. Needless to say, this means-end inquiry just raised relates fundamentally to the basic commitments to internationalism and connects with prior questions as to whether Japan has not had a dual standard at home and abroad.[167] But it is clear enough that the FCN Treaty has legally committed Japan to internationalism on a bilateral basis concerning entry of direct investments; once entered, foreign direct investment may, of course, be regulated consistent with the "national treatment" concept of the treaty.

The fourth question goes to the internal manipulability of reserves and the relationship of restrictive maneuvers to the interpretation of Protocol 6. For example, because of concern with avoiding yen revaluation, Japan had engaged in several programs throughout the 1970–72 period, frequently discussed in the Japanese media, which were intended to reduce reserves (for example, freeing outward capital movements, encouraging yen usage in commercial transactions, acceleration of foreign loan payments).[168] Is it then permissible for a country that is committed to free capital entries (Art. VII) except when reserves are low (Protocol 6) to require foreign investors to stand in line—waiting to add to the reserves by their capital transfers—until each Japanese wishing to withdraw capital from the same reserves for an investment abroad has been satisfied so that for governmental arguments the reserves will be low? The urgency of this question, as it relates to FCN Treaty interpretation under discussion here, has increased with mounting Japanese outward investments, which had by 1972 brought her total direct foreign investments to a higher figure than those admitted into Japan in the postwar period—usually at higher equity rates than she allows. The "low reserve concept" can scarcely be so open at one end and so closed at the other, convenient as such a device might be for nationalistic planners.

A final important question arises from the problem of manipulable "very low reserves." Assuming that Japan is not now suffering from "very low" reserves with an $18 billion balance and that "restrictions" are not now "necessary to prevent its monetary reserves from falling to a very low level or to effect a moderate increase in very low monetary reserves," what is the minimal reserve? Or when in the past did Japan's reserves exceed the "very low level," placing upon her the obligation to dismantle entry restrictions vis-à-vis U.S. investors (FCN, Art. VII [1])? This is a legal question important to foreigners who have thus far been deprived of investment opportunities.

The question is, of course, not susceptible to an exact answer, but surely $2 billion was the bottom of the range in, say, 1960, and $6 billion[169] is near the top now, with much evidence favoring placing the "low level" needed to justify any capital restrictions at $2 or $3 billion *if, as a matter of treaty law, limits on inward direct investments are contemplated by Protocol 6 at all* (see above).

If for discussion we fix $2 billion as the lower limit (before the 1971 revaluation), Chart IX below shows that Japan has been above that limit since 1962.

Chart IX

JAPANESE FOREIGN CURRENCY RESERVES
(1 = $1,000,000)

	(A) Reserves	(B) Imports	(A)(B)%
1959	1,447	3,599	40.2
1960	1,949	4,491	43.4
1961	1,666	5,811	28.7
1962	2,022	5,637	35.9
1963	2,058	6,737	30.5
1964	1,999	7,938	25.2
1965	2,107	8,170	25.8
1966	2,074	9,523	21.8
1967	2,030	11,663	17.4
1968	2,906	12,989	22.3
1969	4,263	16,003	26.2
1970	6,324	19,374	32.4

Again the reserve levels are a rather meaningless manipulable standard, unless set by free international payments and transactions *both ways;* presumably if Japan were to liberalize in the international sense (both trade and investment), a somewhat larger reserve could be justified as a cushion against otherwise uncontrolled short-term or cyclical outflows. But surely inward restrictions alone would not square with low reserve standards of FCN Art. VII, even when reserves are at a minimal $2 or $3 billion, without some balancing controls on outflow. In this context, when reserves are over $5 billion, the present FIL restrictions seem clearly unjustifiable under the U.S.-Japanese FCN Treaty. But not all rights have their remedies, a problem to be discussed later.

Japan's Commitments for Capital Liberalization under the OECD

In OECD,[170] such obligations as Japan may have had since 1964 to liberalize inward foreign investment are defined in the Code of Liberalization of Capital Movements.[171] The Capital Code was approved in 1959 as an OECD Council "decision" binding on members under Art. V(a) of the OECD Convention. The code's purpose is stated in Art. 1(a): "Members shall progressively abolish between one another . . . restrictions on movements of capital to the extent necessary for effective economic cooperation. Measures designed to eliminate such restrictions are hereinafter called 'measures of liberalization.' "

Liberalization under the code takes place by abolishing restrictions concerning capital transactions appearing on Lists A and B in Annex A covering capital "items." These capital "items" on Lists A and B are drawn from a "General List" (Annex D, which serves simply as a catalog for OECD reference). Members are obligated then to "grant any authorization required for the conclusion or execution of transactions and for transfers specified" (Art. 2 [a]). Obligations to liberalize under the OECD Code Art. 2(a) (see also Annex D, Introduction) reach both (1) transactions and (2) payments, as distinguished from IMF, which reaches only payments. Based on the General List of International Capital Movements (Annex D), the two OECD Liberalization Lists are set out in Annex A as List A and List B, and reservations may be lodged and listed in Annex B to the code. For List B, generally, reservation rights are broader and may be asserted at any time, whereas reservation against List A items can be asserted only at specific times. In this framework, direct inward investment is on List A as Item 1 and the comment provides:

Investment for the purpose of establishing lasting economic relations with an undertaking such as, in particular, investments which give a possibility of exercising an effective influence on the management thereof:
A. In the country concerned by non-residents by means of:
1. Creation or extension of a wholly-owned enterprise, subsidiary or branch, acquisition of full ownership of an existing enterprise;
2. Participation in a new existing enterprise;
3. A long-term loan (5 years and longer).

There is a "Remark ii" for List A, Item I(A) (inward direct investment) that provides: "Transactions and transfers under A and B shall be free unless: (ii) In view of the amount involved or of other factors a specific transaction or transfer would have an exceptionally detrimental effect on the interests of the member concerned." Notice under Art. 11(b) must be given to OECD, with reasons, whenever restrictions are imposed (based on this Remark ii).

Significantly, under the code,[172] reservations may be lodged by any member with respect to any item on either of the lists, subject only to time limitations of Art. 2(b) i-iii. Reservations act as exemptions, but it is the intention that they should be removed as soon as possible, and a member must periodically notify OECD of its reasons if it intends to retain existing exemptions.[173] In addition, the code provides[174] for an examination by OECD itself of all reservations maintained by a member at intervals of not more than eighteen months. The examinations are made by OECD's Committee for Invisible Transactions (CIT), provided in Art. 19(a) of the code. The committee reports to the OECD Council, but no sanctions (other than the periodic examinations and pressures engendered by them) are imposed against retention of reservations, thus leaving enforcement of the whole Capital Code to economic diplomacy and political pressures.

Japan signed the Memorandum of Understanding Between the Organizations of Economic Cooperation and Development and the Government of Japan Concerning the Assumption by the Government of Japan of the Obligations of Membership of the Organization in July 1963. Beside accepting the obligations of OECD membership, Japan made the following statement of intentions in Annex B (Reservations) to the memorandum: "It is the intention of the Government of Japan that upon its accession to the Convention of the Organization for Economic Cooperation and Development, Japan would adhere to the Code of Liberalization of Current Invisible Operations and to the Code of Liberalization of Capital Movements. The Government of Japan endorses the objectives of these Codes, and has given careful consideration to their provisions and is prepared to accept any obligations and commitments arising therefrom." Annex B also then includes Japan's eighteen reservations. One of the reservations covers direct investment, although a full Japanese reservation was not made until the "remark" was amended by OECD in 1964 to require a higher degree of liberalization, after Japan's accession.

Among the six major nations (total membership twenty-three), Japan's reservations are the most numerous, though some smaller nations (*e.g.*, Portugal and Spain) have more reservations. Among the six major nations, only Japan has lodged a reservation against inward direct investment. After examination by CIT, Japan added a "remark" to its reservations on direct investment and portfolio share transactions to include the gist of the "liberalization" programs in 1967–71. The fact that the first measures failed to satisfy OECD is clear from the extended report of 1968, which, though largely descriptive of Japanese regulations, nevertheless remarked as follows:[175]

It is recalled, however, that when she joined the OECD her Government informed the Organization that they would "in future deal with all applications for inward and outward direct investments in the spirit of the item in question and [would] disapprove applications only in exceptional cases where serious detrimental effects to the economy are to be feared." It might thus have been assumed that no obstacles would be placed in the way of the greater part of bona fide direct investments, but in the experience of certain foreign investors and of some of the official representatives of other Member States this expectation has not so far been fulfilled to their satisfaction. The obstacles encountered are partly of a policy nature, partly procedural. These sources feel that rejection of the original application—unless there were substantial modifications of the proposed terms—can rarely be ascribed to "exceptional cases" which might have "serious detrimental effects" for Japan. So far the impression is that refusals of what has been asked for, or failure to approve, are general rather than exceptional.

Legal Remedies under OECD against Persisting Restrictions

There is no case against Japan for violating legally enforceable obligations to liberalize under the OECD Capital Code.[176] This is because she is entitled to lodge reservations and has no legal obligations to withdraw any of them; her only duty is to allow examinations by CIT at intervals up to eighteen months and to notify OECD regularly whether she desires to retain reservations and for what reasons.

Law aside, Japan has clearly committed herself to liberalize under Art. 1 of the Capital Code: "Members shall progressively abolish between one another restrictions on movements of capital to the extent necessary to effect economic cooperation." Besides undertaking the commitments of the code (subject to reservations), Japan made other positive statements of intention to liberalize, and her performance since has been largely considered as a violation of the spirit, though not the letter, of these commitments. The methods to enforce such commitments are not legal but diplomatic and political, and OECD (and its member nations, of course) has not been reluctant to point out that they regard Japan in violation of the spirit of the commitment, especially since she has done little to reduce her long list of reservations.[177] On the other hand, the inch-by-inch liberalization movement starting in 1967 has made some progress, as has been noted in detail above.

Remedies against Japanese Restrictions

Since in both the FCN and OECD provisions the commitment to free direct investment inures to the benefit of thousands of would-be private investors, their indignation and frustrations with Japanese restrictions (quite aside from their dialogue at the governmental level) have become a major source of criticism, tension, and demands for remedial action.

Aside from such coaxing as OECD is entitled to do under its periodic examinations and reporting, no legal remedy for private parties is available there, for Japan is surely entitled in international law to maintain her OECD reservations. Joint political or economic sanctions and diplomacy are the major implements in OECD circles for inducing Japanese reciprocity.

Under the FCN Treaty, the legal rights and duties are different; the time has come when reserves are not "at a very low level," nor are they likely to be soon. It had not been "necessary" to have restrictions on inward capital for those purposes for several years, however convenient they might be for other bureaucratic purposes. In the unlikely event of litigation of the substantive issue, FIL restrictions could hardly be justified with a reserve over, say, $5 billion, regardless of the position on the other issues (*i.e.,* whether Protocol 6 applies to inward direct investment or "transactions" as opposed to merely transfer of payments).

Practicable remedies are, however, another matter again, for two important reasons. Aggrieved though many have felt, no U.S. businessman has wanted to squander his time, money, and good will in a long legal contest in the Japanese courts to establish the fact that FIL restrictions were inconsistent with his FCN Treaty rights. Indeed, there are many procedural obstacles, including the "exhaustion-of-local-remedies rule" in public international law, which would require initial litigation in the Japanese courts by a plaintiff whose investment application had been denied, delayed, or otherwise handled in violation of the treaty. Given the way the administration operates (without promulgated criteria, without written reasoned actions during "guidance"), an investor would have to be bent on litigation rather than business in order to build a record to support his complaint.

Certainly there can be no doubt about the competence and integrity of Japanese courts, though international politics have influenced some critical constitutional decisions on the lower level.[178] Under present circumstances, however, a plaintiff might ultimately get a Japanese court judgment in his favor. But the Japanese legal apparatus to implement such a lawsuit is on the whole discouraging.[179] For example, the Japanese courts are only beginning to develop a case law around their post-World War II jurisdiction to review administrative actions and thereby subject official behavior to justiciable law.[180] They generally have been reluctant to substitute court judgment for that of an entrenched officialdom, perhaps subconsciously because of the political countermeasures that excessive boldness could evoke. Also, as a procedural matter, apparently the plaintiff contesting administrative action would have the burden of showing that official discretion was unreasonably exercised. These are sobering burdens in the Japanese milieu and are correctly recognized by businessmen to be poor business. There is the further question of the legal effect of the treaty. Is it self-executing, so that the court may measure official behavior (or the FIL itself) against its standards? The answer is probably affirmative in both cases.[181]

If the Japanese courts were to hold against the investor contesting FIL restrictions, then in public international law, where normally the "contracting states" become the litigating parties, the U.S. would be positioned to take the case up, first by negotiations and consultations with the Japanese government and, failing solution, would possibly submit it to the International Court of Justice under Art. XXV(1) of the FCN Treaty. However, it is not entirely clear whether at that stage Art. XXV(1) requires a specific submission of each particular case by both nations, or whether by merely signing the treaty they have submitted all cases that they are unable to solve by diplomacy, so that a filing by the dissatisfied party alone is all that is required. It is probably the latter case.

In litigation, a rejected U.S. investor might have a strong substantive case, but even legally he has a problematical remedy, and, of course, the entire topic makes no business sense at all to an individual investor. Such has been the case for two decades of operations under the Foreign Investment Law, and this explains the lack of foreign plaintiffs to date. Even more basic, however, is the fact that the fabric of U.S.-Japanese political relations is so important and the economic interests, since the treaty was signed, so changed and changing that the issue is much better viewed today as a problem for negotiation and economic diplomacy rather than one for litigation.

Economic Diplomacy: Pressurized Internationalization of Japan

In the global context, U.S.-Japanese economic relations reached by the early 1970s an era of readjustment that must proceed in a rhetoric differing from FCN rights and obligations. Rather, the flexible approach of OECD negotiations is more suitable for the transitions of the 1970s. In the aftermath of polarizing journalistic excitement (*e.g.*, the "American challenge" and the "Japanese superstate") and now the multinational corporate threat, a broader perspective should remind us that the task of rehabilitating Japan's industries for international competition has required some leeway in timing, just as time is also needed for a new confidence and a less nationalistic attitude on the part of Japanese decision-makers (both in government and business circles) appropriate to Japan's new stature and her new goals of internationalization. Liberalization will continue in most areas of trade and technology. But direct investment may remain limited to new companies simply because Japan, like most nations, including the developing world in general, is not yet ready to concede the merits of foreign controls of certain major domestic industries.

After following the arguments for the past decade, free-traders may feel some sympathy with the view that Japanese protectiveness has persisted longer than justified in either law or economics. But timing is seldom perfect in relation to power shifts of the magnitude Japan's own success has recently helped to engender. Since all major actors on the global scene are experiencing a reshaping of roles, not only in the free world itself, but in global power relations generally, the broader view again cautions one to emphasize the progress, to encourage the liberal trends in the future, and to minimize the abrasions of the past. Japan has also recently absorbed some persuasive counterabrasions produced by the short-lived U.S. surcharge of 1971, continuing import quotas, intensified anti-dumping actions, and revaluations. Sometimes these foreign countermeasures have seemed narrowly protective (textiles) and illegal (surcharge). But these reciprocally invoked tactical tools should not be allowed to cloud strategic objectives of freer, if not absolutely free, trade and investment. There is much evidence that Japan will take more care in the future to prevent a triggering of U.S. protectionism, not only because Japan stands to be injured most by such tactics, but also because U.S. protectionism shows signs of becoming strategic instead of merely tactical, because of the structural and institutional weaknesses in the cost-push, labor-management regime, following, it seems, the prior English example without learning much from it.

In preparing for flexibility and transition in the 1970s, we need hard thinking about current international investment practices themselves, as they exist at the "end of the postwar period." We need clearer statements also of Japan's present and future inward investment policies, which in the past have been so inaccurately stated in her public relations in trying to square the circle (*i.e.,* make them appear consistent with the FCN Treaty or the OECD arrangements). In fact, some critics may find more fault with this lack of straightforwardness than with the restrictive policies themselves, which can be defended, to a point, on "infant industry" grounds. Nonetheless, the latest announcement of "100 percent liberalization" (1 May 1973) was full of the same kind of overstatements in the media, while in fact accomplishing relatively modest liberalization in areas of interest to foreigners.

Also for the 1970s, we may well ask: What is the proper global role of foreign enterprise and of direct investment? In the era of multinational businesses, mostly American, direct investment has recently been depicted as not just a business or economic problem but possibly a challenge to national regulatory competence that could not be understood exclusively in old-fashioned economic terms. There are political and social undertones that, at least in the case of Japan, are paramount, because by virtue of her insular development she has become a unique polity. The managerial strata (in Japanese official and business circles) intend to continue to man and operate that polity and its carefully nurtured, modern industrial sector with little foreign participation; other nations may, on recognizing this exclusivity, choose to exclude Japanese reciprocally. There is also a highly emotive content to the forces supporting Japanese corporate exclusivity which is based on the "vertical" organization of society and the them-versus-us frame of mind. This phenomenon generates its own kind of intensive competition between groups (including the nation) and has proven to be a productive internal formula for Japan; it is likewise nationalistic and a serious barrier to true internationalization (*i.e.,* internationalism at home as well as expansion abroad). The social-psychological wellsprings of individual loyalties to group and nation, and particularly enterprise nationalism, also extend to the apex of the politico-bureaucratic pyramid wherein officialdom is fully aware that Japanese productivity may be in part directly traced to these attitudes and organizational principles. Policy-makers may continue to feel that exclusivity is important to Japan's national competitive efforts and also indispensable to enhance the entire elite strata as managers of the national polity. Confronted with such nationally sponsored industrial forces, of course, other nations will have to fashion policies more appropriate than those of the past simplistically premised on idealized free private competition on the global scene.

Rather, the Japanese imagery and rhetoric has relied on the dreaded "black ships" of Perry and the "unequal treaties"[182] of the Meiji period to spur the citizenry to greater competitive output. This is not to say that there is a sinister xenophobia behind each stage of planning; but it is useful to see clearly that nationalism and exclusivity are significant operative forces, even if Japanese pronouncements for the foreigners do not make them explicit. It is however not a virtue for Japan's international associates to ignore these forces countering internationalization, for there are elements within Japan which will be trying to ameliorate, maturate, and accept more international responsibility commensurate with a new stature in the world community. For foreigners to use powers available to evoke reciprocity will assist these domestic Japanese forces favoring a freer international policy. This calls for awareness of the past limitations of the respective images held by Japanese and outsiders of each other.

VIII

Contracts between Japanese and Foreign Enterprises

Japanese "contracts" (*keiyaku*) are conceptually different from American contracts, and also Japanese businessmen rely on the legalities of "contracts" among themselves less than, for example, Americans do.[1] Still, from Tokugawa times at least, there has been a tradition of very full and careful documentation of agreements including extensive uses of third-party witnesses and registries to assure understanding, compliance, and proof, especially in the lender-borrower, master-servant, and landowner-tenant relationships.[2] In contemporary Japan, sophisticated businesses[3] (*e.g.,* trading companies, banks, and large industrials) are aware of the functional importance of the English-language contracting process in achieving real understanding in the more complex foreign transactions. We may say, then, that whatever the practices may have been in the past, or may be today in certain purely parochial relationships, in transnational transactions, and especially in arranging licensing and joint-venture corporations,[4] foreign-language written "agreements" are essential and invariably used.[5] Furthermore, when made in contemplation of a major new enterprise involving large labor forces and long terms, such contracting is a highly creative activity worthy of the deliberate and careful attention of the best professionals available.

Four points are of critical importance at the outset: first, of course, nothing can substitute in a joint business relationship for a properly selected, internationally sophisticated Japanese associate; second, however much Japanese businesses may do without formal contracts in dealing among themselves in their own cultural setting—and in big business today this lack of a "contract sense" perhaps has been exaggerated[6] —foreigners (outsiders) are quite disqualified to participate in such ethnocentricities and are entitled, if they deal at all, to rely on Japan's own codes.[7]

Third, in licensing and joint-venture negotiations, another crucial fact has not been stressed enough: the option not to do business in Japan is quite often the most valuable alternative, and to perceive that fact is critical. Japanese may have earned the reputation, in some circles, of weak commitment to contracts because they "agree" sometimes to provisions that foreigners have improvidently insisted upon, when the Japanese deep down know they cannot live with them. A negotiator more culturally attuned would have sensed this in advance and backed out, realizing that necessary mutuality did not exist. In the past the most prominent example has been the case where the Japanese wants licensing (technology) and the foreigners want an equity position to exploit the technology themselves in Japan. The result has often been a contract signed the way the foreigners wanted it and performed the way the Japanese wanted it—that is, the so-called "conduit company," whereby the Japanese early siphons off to the Japanese parent the coveted know-how and leaves the joint corporation to wither away. Then, too, there are many times when Japanese instinctively depart from the signed contract in the performance phase, feeling from their own psychological and social make-up that adjustments are appropriate, man-to-man, when circumstances pose new problems.

Fourth, lawyers especially need to appreciate the relative business inefficacy of legal enforcement of joint-venture or licensing contracts. Whether trans-Pacific agreements ultimately have much legal bite as "contracts" cannot be answered prospectively without an elaborate "systems analysis" of enforcement possibilities, calculated to discount appropriately a potential claimant's legal rights by all of the contingencies and expenses of trans-Pacific litigation with enormous lingual, jurisdictional, and choice-of-law hazards potentially involved, over and above the costs, frustrations, and delays usual even in simple domestic litigation.[8] Actually, however, careful contracting between foreigners and Japanese is not justified in legal enforcement of obligations so much as in the need for accurate communication and the give-and-take involved in writing it down in a detailed document in terms defined by business experience and litigated precedent so that the plans of both parties are identical and understood as guides to a program of united actions.

With only minority positions in new Japanese firms allowed as a rule by the Japanese government in industries where opportunities actually exist, it is not surprising that foreign investors have long attempted to mitigate the weaknesses of their corporate position by special corporate control provisions inserted in preincorporation joint-venture contracts[9] with the Japanese partner. In this chapter our main focus will be on this complex range of problems raised in the interstices of Japanese contract, corporate, and administrative law. The discussion below will be limited to actual problems as they appear to the drafting businessman or lawyer in the initial contracting phase,[10] although, of course, in drafting the lawyers look prospectively to performance and enforceability for reference, meaning, deterrence, and, only in the most marginal situations, to litigation.

Emphatically, again, the facile desk lawyer's transition from the clever clause to the courtroom victory must be avoided. Litigated results can be only a minor guide in this peculiarly complex drafting and creative type of private law-making. Rather, the legal doctrine and enforcement apparatus of the law function more as aids to understanding and clarity of communication, as voluntary guides to performance or possibly as moral deterrents to breach. This is because the efficacy of law in the international private contracting process of joint ventures, as noted above, is premised on good faith and mutual purpose—things that cannot be legally compelled. Thus, litigation invariably means little more than salvage, not specific performance or even adequate compensation, even though the Japanese legal system on the level of doctrine is reasonably adequate in this area.[11] U.S. domestic experience with affirmative enforcement of domestic partnerships or close corporate relations also generally bears this proposition out,[12] but aforementioned factors peculiar to Japanese transactions amplify this basic premise.

To reiterate, foremost among these peculiarities is the Japanese businessman's attitude toward contracts. In his domestic business affairs he uses detailed formal contracts relatively little[13] and litigation[14] even less, depending more on traditional organizational patterns, social hierarchy, and authority, which we have seen in Chapter IV always have been the dominant features of what is perhaps the world's most *socially* (not legally) organized society. More will be said on contract flexibility in contracting later.[15] A second point worth repeating is the ambiguity of transnational law and the inefficacy of transnational litigation generally. This is not just the usual problem of judicial administration—expense, time, and inept procedures and remedies; transnational lawsuits generally, and U.S.-Japanese actions specifically, reach an exquisite degree of disutility by the combination of ambiguous conflicts rules, possibly unenforceable prorogation and choice-of-law clauses[16] (meaning multiple law potentially applicable), translation and foreign-law proof problems, and a paucity of truly adequate, bilingual legal experts.[17]

Saving for another time (in Chapter IX below) the difficulties of as-
suring that any single law will actually turn out to govern bilateral
arbitration or litigation, it will be assumed for the purpose of discussion
that Japanese law governs because often it is stipulated (and the parties
think it governs, which for reasons mentioned above is important),
because the operation is in Japan, and because invariably the joint-venture corporation and often the Japanese partner are not suable elsewhere.[18]

The Scheme of Japanese Law Applicable
to Joint-Venture Contracts

The first elemental question for the foreign lawyer with a Japanese
contract is: where in the Japanese codes is the law of contracts[19] relevant to joint ventures to be found? Because this law is interwoven into
both the Civil Code and the Commercial Code along with several
special laws, it is useful to approach contract law in the German fashion,
as the Japanese lawyer would. He sees the codes as deductively systematic: the Civil Code is the source of general principle, perhaps
analogous in this sense to the historical position of the common law in
our system, but much more accessible. On contracts, Civil Code Book I
(especially Arts. 3–20, 90–137) covers juristic acts (*hōritsu kōi*) and
capacity (*nōryoku*), which, as far as it applies to contracts, corresponds
roughly to our various problems of mutual assent, especially when
considered with Book III (Arts. 399–696) on obligations (*saiken*),
particularly Arts. 399–548 on the formation and effect of contracts
generally and Arts. 549–696 covering thirteen specific types of contracts. Then a special and separate Commercial Code (Book III) elabo-
rates the law governing any commercial transaction (*shōkōi*), including
all transactions of business enterprises (*kigyō*),[20] which are the main
objects to which the Commercial Code is applicable. To determine the
applicability of the Commercial Code, the first question is whether the
joint-venture contract is such a commercial transaction[21] or between
such enterprises. It clearly is, because any Japanese corporation is a
trader (*shōnin*), and all transactions of a trader which are related to
his business are commercial transactions under the Commercial Code
whether the other party is a trader or not.[22] Commercial Code, Art. 1,
then provides for the priority of the Commercial Code over commercial
transactions: the code shall govern, but if it contains no applicable
provisions, the customary law shall apply, and if there is no applicable
customary law, the Civil Code shall apply.

The formation of a contract is generally determined by the Civil Code provisions[23] and the basic requirement to form a contract is mutual consent (*i.e.,* offer and acceptance). Such questions as capacity, fraud, mistake, duress, or illegality are considered to bear only upon the effect of the contract after mutual assent.[24] There are no general requirements of consideration[25] or writing.[26] Since U.S.-Japanese joint-venture contracts are always written embodiments of mutual bilateral promises duly signed, generally there would be no formation problems even under our law.[27]

The general approach of the rest of the Civil Code (*i.e.,* Book III) is to elaborate general rules for obligations and particular rules for thirteen kinds of typical contracts (*tenkei keiyaku*),[28] none of which includes a joint-venture contract as such, but the typical partnership contract (*kumiai keiyaku*) would undoubtedly apply to these joint ventures before incorporation and also, when appropriate, after incorporation, as shall be seen later. Of course, the general provisions in Civil Code (Book I) and other general provisions, such as those on obligations and contracts, Book III (Arts. 399–548), are applicable to all contracts,[29] including joint ventures. In a proper case some of the specific provisions on other typical contracts may be applied by analogous application (*ruisui tekiyō*) or mutatis mutandis (*junyō*), which are techniques found in Japanese theories of statutory construction.[30] Also, there are a number of special laws supplementary to the codes, affecting certain contracts[31] or certain aspects of contracts generally.

The exact legal equivalent of the "joint-venture" concept does not seem to exist in Japanese contract law.[32] But, much as in the U.S. system,[33] the joint-venture contract would be treated as a Japanese type of partnership subject to the rules of a typical partnership contract[34] since it contemplates all the elements of a Japanese partnership: (1) an agreement; (2) group organization (*dantai*); and (3) joint assets.[35] The important thing to be remembered, however, is that, in Japanese legal concepts, the "joint venturers" stand in several relationships to each other when moving from the simple contract to promotion of the new corporation and finally to an operative corporation in which they are shareholders and officers. First, the U.S. and Japanese firms are legally Japanese partners by virtue of the joint-venture contract. When they set about organizing the corporation, they must assemble incorporators[36] (*hokkinin*), and Japanese jurisprudence subjects these seven to the typical partnership contract rules with regard to their activities in establishing a new corporation.[37] Thus, at this stage, if both joint venturers become "promoters" (incorporators) formally, they are legally members of two separate partnership arrangements, one under the joint-venture contract and one as "promoters." In addition, they can represent the embryo company (*seiritsuchū no kaisha*) and can commit it to certain obligations as long as these commitments are limited to matters of incorporation rather than commencement of business.[38] Also, under the corporation law, all seven of the incorporators will have fixed and distinct duties, powers, and liabilities to the corporation and third parties.[39] After the new corporation is formed, the partnership relationship under the original joint-venture contract may subsist, if such is intended, in parallel with the corporate relationships among the same joint venturers as shareholders. Joint-venture or preincorporation agreements coexist in a similar way in close corporations in some U.S. jurisdictions.[40] However, the parallel spheres of contract and corporate law are much more distinct in Japanese law than in most American law, as will be demonstrated. In summary, then, the applicable law for the interrelations of joint venturers and promoters is the partnership contract law. The promoters, later the corporate shareholders, are, in addition and at the same time, subject to the corporate law in relation to the corporation and certain third parties.[41]

Problems of Form

As mentioned, Japanese contracts with few exceptions need not be in writing; nor must there be consideration.[42] Since joint-venture contracts are invariably in writing with mutual bilateral promises, these points would hardly be problems anyway.

Who is the proper officer to sign a contract for a Japanese corporation? While it is easy, given the time and requisite know-how, to determine from the public corporate registry (*shōgyō tōkibo*) who is the person registered as the representative director (*daihyō torishimariyaku*) or manager of any Japanese corporation at a given office,[43] still it frequently happens that hastily concluded contracts are signed by other officers or agents of a Japanese company. This does not necessarily mean that the corporation is not bound because others may have authority by power-of-attorney from the representative director or even by "apparent authority (*hyōken daihyō*)."[44] To avoid difficulty, it is preferable to make sure that the representative director signs a document as important as a joint-venture agreement. Also, in some cases, the usual license agreements, sales contracts, and other arrangements for the new corporation should be signed by the majority joint venturer as representative of the promoters in order to bind the new corporation and the majority joint venturer.

Most Japanese individuals have registered seals that they affix to documents instead of signing them by hand,[45] although the custom of using the handwritten signature by Japanese is becoming common in international transactions. The very cautious person might find it advisable to check both the registry certificate of the corporation to ascertain the corporate existence and the registered representative's correct name and the seal certificate (*inkan shōmei*) of the representative at the commercial registry[46] if he uses his seal. Thus, the impression can then be compared with that used on the contract.

Another formal matter of importance should be mentioned—the normal practice of providing in the contract that conflicts in interpretation arising out of differences in the Japanese and English language versions will be resolved by reference to the English. One of the major language problems of these contracts relates to corporate control devices in the pro forma articles of incorporation that are annexed to the contract. These are required by law to be in Japanese.[47] One wonders whether, in a dispute on the contract in such a situation, the Japanese language would not in fact govern, at least concerning the rights of the joint-venture corporation and third parties.

Share Restrictions and Corporate Control Devices

Introduction

The problem here involves the interplay between the corporation law and the preincorporation contract that the parties intend shall control their future action (as shareholders, directors, or officers) and, through them, certain actions of the future joint corporation. Under the circumstances assumed, this immense field is essentially a Japanese corporation and contract law problem, but any lawyer with situational sense will be equally concerned with evidence, burdens of proof, procedural efficacy, and remedies. In this situation, inquiry will be made as to whether in Japanese law pertinent kinds of preincorporation obligations can subsist and be enforced after incorporation and, if so, what the efficacy of enforcement actions might be. The latter inquiry extends to the effect on (1) the contracting joint venturers as shareholders, (2) the joint corporation, and (3) third parties where relevant. The availability of these remedies is particularly important in case of violations of the agreements in three critical areas: (a) restrictions on share transfers; (b) corporate control mechanisms that vary from the normal meeting and voting procedures of the corporation law; and (c) transactions contemplated in the contract to be accepted and carried out by the future joint corporation, such as trademark, patent and know-how licenses, sales agencies, supply contracts, capital equipment imports, employment contracts for key engineers, and a host of other items that may be critical in the overall bargain to one or the other of the parties.

It is a major problem of draftsmanship, after the creative planning, negotiating, and adjusting have produced a bargain, to sort out the parts of the overall complex and to document them in optimum form— a master contract, pro forma articles of incorporation, and various side agreements or annexes. One problem is that official practice requires[48] that the joint-venture contract must annex draft articles of incorporation and legally the parties may find it advisable to include some of the above-mentioned policies in the articles. Others may simply subsist in the master contract or in side agreements, depending on whether they need approval and how long they are intended to be effective. It shall be seen that it can make a difference under Japanese law, as it does in some American jurisdictions, whether the restrictions are in a side agreement or the articles. Japanese corporation practice does not have any exact counterpart to our bylaws, but something similar is often instituted by the directors or shareholders to govern details of directors' meetings and share transfer procedure.[49] As disinguished from American[50] practice, however, such "bylaws" do not seem to have been used for the redistribution of corporate control powers in close corporations.[51] Obviously, the joint-venture corporation under discussion resembles the close corporation,[52] which in our domestic parlance has been largely an operational rather than a technical term because they have traditionally received little special legislative support in the states until very recently. However, Japanese corporation law since 1938 has provided for a juristic person called a limited company (yūgengaisha),[53] which was legislatively intended as a vehicle for this kind of close-corporate enterprise. Like the English private company[54] and the German company with limited liability (Gesellschaft mit beschränkter Haftung),[55] the yūgengaisha law limits the number of members (shain) and permits informal meetings; it restricts membership transfers and provides simpler incorporation procedures, corporate structures, records and notices; but it still provides the desired juristic separateness and limited liability.[56] Thousands of small, closely-held enterprises avail themselves of this juristic form in Japan, but the word yūgengaisha must appear in the company's name.[57] Thus, unfortunately, in Japanese business and financial circles it has a diminutive connotation[58] and therefore joint ventures have seldom, if ever, availed themselves of it. Instead, joint ventures have generally chosen the stock corporation (*kabushiki kaisha*) that is designed for wide public shareholding, and thus they have invited upon themselves many of the same problems of our clumsy close corporation. Yet, the availability of the *yūgengaisha* means that legal guidelines for close *kabushiki kaisha* have been relatively unnecessary and, therefore, undeveloped in Japan for fitting the requirements of a close corporation into the formalistic framework and procedure of the stock corporation. In contrast, our U.S. law (despite a multitude of close corporations) has never provided an adequate separate juristic entity designed for them.[59] Only recently are these special problems beginning to get partial recognition in our statutes and judicial precedents, and even these changes are taking place largely within the ponderous corporation law framework designed for publicly held corporations.[60] Ironically, then, our long and awkward experience with the close corporation has produced precedents, literature, and even a treatise,[61] all of which are useful as comparative guides for coping with partnership-type enterprises that choose to avoid, for reasons of prestige, the legally most appropriate vehicle in Japan and instead set up a *kabushiki kaisha*.

Restrictions on the Transfer of Shares

Having usually invested considerable time and effort in carefully selecting each other for the enterprise at hand, U.S.-Japanese joint venturers understandably want to restrict the sale of shares to insure that the joint Japanese corporation will continue to be jointly owned by them alone. To this end they usually agree on some restriction such as first-refusal rights for the other party in case one shareholder wants to sell. The first question raised by such a contract clause is its relationship to the intricate mechanisms found in the recently revised Commercial Code provisions[62] (Arts. 204 to 204–5), which, since 1966, have changed the law from outright prohibition of share transfer restrictions to allow restrictions on the transfer of shares of *kabushiki kaisha*,[63] but only in elaborately limited ways. The incorporators may insert in the articles of incorporation (*teikan*) a provision that board approval is required for a share transfer. Elaborate new provisions are then spelled out (Commercial Code, Arts. 204 to 204–5) for the board to arrange for an alternative purchaser for shares offered, if the board does not approve the seller's proposed sale to a stated buyer. Of course, for the close corporation, these new provisions are an improvement over the prior outright prohibition of transfer restrictions, and certainly in many, perhaps most, cases the joint venturers may wish to follow them as is. But, on pricing, timing, and third-party decisions (*e.g.*, court evaluation), the new law poses its own problems and ambiguities.

All of the manifold variations in close corporate relations that the parties may devise to accomplish their own purposes can scarcely be foreseen in the abstract, but certainly there will be occasions upon which the contracting parties will wish to depart from the strict procedures of the code (Arts. 204 to 204–5) to provide for transfer prices or arbitration. Corporations established without requiring board approval in their articles must rely on contracts, or amend their articles to comply with the new procedures.[64]

The question then remains as to whether different transfer restrictions contained in the joint-venture contract are enforceable as contract obligations of the parties quite apart from the fact that they do not bind the corporation. Contractual limitations, apparently violative of these new cumbersome Commercial Code provisions against share transfer restrictions except as stipulated, are still considered valid and enforceable. The key to understanding the limited legal effect given to Art. 204(1) (*i.e.,* so that the code's transfer restrictions are not exclusive) is in the systematic code structure of Japanese law which separates contract and corporate law principles and gives them parallel validity in their own spheres: the contract binds the parties and the code governs the corporation in case of conflict with a contract. Thus, Art. 204(1) would prevent all share transfer restrictions, except the requirement of board approval, in the intracorporate structure (*i.e.,* articles of incorporation, rules [bylaws], and resolutions). So, on this theoretical level, restrictive contracts (1) between the corporation and a shareholder or (2) between shareholders are legally outside the operative sphere of corporation law, and despite Art. 204(1), which limits restrictions to requiring board approval, they will be enforced by the usual remedies for breach of contract. Only one relevant case since 1950 has been found,[65] and the treatise authority is divided on the enforceability of the corporation-shareholder (as opposed to shareholder-shareholder) agreements.[66] On upholding shareholder-shareholder contracts that restrict transfers, however, the authorities are almost unanimous.[67] Judge Matsuda is a notable exception.[68] Inadequacy of remedies, in fact, is the problem.

Given the general validity of shareholder agreements restricting transfers as described above, the remaining question is: How useful are the legal remedies of the nontransferring shareholder against the transferor, the transferee, or the corporation? Can he get damages, injunctive relief, or recover from the transferee and correct the registration of the shares on the corporation shareholder list?

Consistent with the contract-corporate law dichotomy, most scholars[69] seem to agree that contractual restrictions on transfer of shares not conforming with Art. 204 can only bind the parties and do not affect the right of the transferee, whether he takes notice of the restrictions or not.[70] The nontransferring shareholder has a damage claim against the transferor, but the proof of damages for a violative transfer of shares without a ready market would be difficult, especially since most of the damage would result from the risk to the enterprise introduced by a strange new shareholder,[71] a practically immeasurable factor. Thus, the most effective remedy would be an injunction to prevent any transfers in breach of the agreement, but again the chances of getting enough information and court action on the threshold of an illegal transfer are highly unlikely. If the situation permits, however, the law is encouraging. The courts can grant an injunction[72] and order that a notice thereof be inserted in the registry of the company or, alternatively, the court may order that the shares be delivered to the bailiff for safe-keeping.[73] Note, however, that injunctions are limited to the parties to the action or the persons named therein. A case regarding a disputed telephone right held that, if a violative transfer occurs, the company that was not mentioned in the injunction must register the right at the request of the transferee[74] (even after an injunction against the transfer, and even though the transfer occurred with notice). Being nonnegotiable, the telephone right is hardly comparable to a corporate share, which is necessarily negotiable, and so a transferee of a corporate share in violation of an injunction would unquestionably obtain good title.[75]

In summary then, despite the clear language of Commercial Code, Art. 204(1), limiting restrictions on transfer to requiring board approval, the legal effect is limited to the intracorporate law sphere. The authorities support the parallel validity and enforceability of contractual restrictions for damages or a preventive injunction in the case of a shareholder-shareholder contract, howsoever impractical the latter might be in the usual case. Some authority, notably Ishii, would support reasonable corporation-shareholder contracts as well. No remedy either against the corporation to cancel the registry or against the transferee to regain title is generally supported by the authorities except in a case in which the transfer proceeded in violation of an active injunction. Matsuda[76] would strike down such restrictive contractual clauses under Art. 204(1) and deny them enforcement of any sort, but no decision has been found following his interpretation.

It should be noted again that, despite the validity of and legalistic remedies for breach of share transfer restrictions, the fact is that usually a timely injunction to prevent a sale is impossible, and if a violative sale occurs, the amount or even the fact of actual damages is often prohibitively difficult to prove. The parties are, therefore, well advised to include a reasonable liquidated damage clause in the joint-venture agreement providing that, if a wrongful sale is made, the seller will pay the other party a sum fixed in advance. The Japanese Civil Code provides for such clauses and forbids the courts to vary the amount.[77] This provision thus seems to prevent a court from refusing to enforce a liquidated damage clause because it is too high or a "penalty,"[78] in our terms. Extreme amounts have been struck down, however, as violating public policy,[79] but generally Japanese law has no overriding concept of penalty. Rather, such clauses are upheld without superimposing the court's judgment as to the adequacy of the amount or even the existence of any damages, unless they are *contra bonos mores*. Since both parties may be equally interested in such a provision at the time of contracting, it may be feasible, in spite of the disenchantment usually occasioned by introducing such ideas into the final stages of negotiations.

Corporate Control Devices for Protection of Minority Interests

In the U.S. a variety of devices including preincorporation agreements between prospective shareholders are used to effect custom-made controls over close corporations—voting trusts, pooling agreements, irrevocable proxies, specific employment and management contracts, as well as diverse charter and bylaw arrangements to insure veto power for the minority by requiring extraordinary quorums and votes of both the shareholders and the board or by shifting decision-making power between them to achieve a veto effect over specific critical corporate actions. The utility of one or combinations of these measures in the U.S. depends on the promoters' bargain, the nature of the business, the statutes of the state[80] chosen for incorporation, and other factors.[81]

In U.S.-Japanese joint ventures, the shareholders similarly desire to act as partners among themselves, but as shareholders with limited liability toward the outside world. They want to be able to act informally by agreement, and in order to insure a position for itself in corporate policy-making, the minority, in particular, must rely on such agreements to avoid coercive majority votes. It has been demonstrated that, as their corporate vehicle, they ordinarily choose the *kabushiki kaisha,* which is as ponderously over-equipped for close corporation purposes as our general corporation. Specific attention, therefore, must be given to control problems in each venture and each problem requires its own specific solution. The purpose here is only to indicate from the richer U.S. experiences which devices may be most useful in drafting joint-venture contracts for Japan operations.

Corporate Controls: Effect of FIL Approvals on the Contract

It should again be noted that in Japan the character of this kind of corporate control problem is significantly conditioned by the shape of the venture imposed by the postwar Japanese governmental policy of excluding foreign majority equities in Japanese enterprises. Ordinarily the parties also stipulate that FIL approval is a condition precedent to the effectiveness of the master joint-venture contract. One of the strong reasons for the Japanese policy against foreign majorities is to prevent foreign management control. Even in the 1967 "liberalization," the "automatic" approval for 50-50 joint ventures was conditioned on observing corporate control provisions of the Commercial Code, but arguably this condition includes the right to vary code control techniques to the extent that the code itself permits variations; hence the situation seems little changed. So whatever the motivation or wisdom of the policy, the American investors' problems are limited to protecting minority interests by veto provisions and the like. It also means that adroitly patterned, multi-class share structures that aim at giving the foreign minority a control over major policies, at least where documents are to be submitted for approval, would ordinarily not be any more acceptable to the Japanese foreign investment authorities than more forthright requests for approval of majority ownership. Since the official validation is still a condition precedent even in "automatic" cases of a foreigner's right to acquire shares in a Japanese corporation[82]—however much this may conflict with the spirit of the U.S.-Japanese Friendship, Commerce and Navigation Treaty (1953) now that reserves are above the $5 billion level—it becomes important to decide just what parts of the total bargain need FIL approval. This can influence the choice between the two general methods of formalizing veto devices agreed upon by the joint venturers: (1) shareholder agreements; and (2) provision in pro forma articles of incorporation. Also, for the parties' ease of future reference, certain kinds of obligations fit best in separate contracts; that is, those agreements that are intended to have subsisting effect between the parties even after incorporation.

There are three parts to this drafting and distribution question: first, what parts of the total arrangements does the FIL say must be submitted and approved, and second, in doubtful instances involving risks, what are the administrative law consequences of mistake and violation? The third and related question inquires into the contract law effects of a shareholder's agreement that should have been, but has not been, validated. The answer to the first two questions would depend on specifics, but in general the FIL[83] requires in these situations validation of share acquisitions (thus requiring submission of the proposed articles of incorporation) and inductions of certain restricted technology only, leaving open the possibility that other side arrangements between the joint venturers as prospective shareholders need not be submitted or might be submitted later. The law does not specifically forbid foreign control, and there may be some side agreements giving a veto with legal efficacy only as a contract between the parties, which, depending upon the situation, would not need validation. If it is deemed necessary to make the veto binding in the corporate law, then it must be put into the articles and receive FIL approval. If approval is required and not obtained, penalties, even including imprisonment, may be incurred.[84]

When approval is required by the administrative law, the third question relating to the effect between the parties of an unapproved contract has been of interest to foreigners throughout the period of tight Japanese foreign-exchange controls, but contract validity under the Foreign Exchange Control Law (FECL) was only recently litigated and no cases have been decided under the FIL. The FECL cases[85] examined have all held that such unapproved contracts are valid, but what sort of enforcement they might be entitled to in court is not as clear. The result of the cases upholding contractual validity is consistent with earlier scholarly theory[86] and by analogy consistent also with some precedents[87] of Japanese law which also in a general way compartmentalize the operative spheres of administrative (public) and contract (private) law, much as they do contract and corporate laws, as noted in the transfer restriction discussion above.

But under new FIL requirements (as opposed to FECL) enacted in April 1964 to the effect that certain contractual obligations themselves (not just payments) between Japanese and foreign investors must be approved, the policy is basic and restrictive enough to justify finding the unapproved contract void, or at least unenforceable, to this writer's way of thinking.[88]

Corporate Controls: Shareholder Control Agreements

In this connection there is another interstitial problem of Japanese contracts and corporation law similar to the one noted in the discussion of share transfer restrictions.[89] In Japan, as elsewhere, the enforce-

ability of shareholder agreements affecting corporate structure, procedures, and control is greatly influenced by the basic theory underlying corporations in the legal system. For example, in English law the
limited liability corporation evolved from partnership, which was in
turn based on contract, and this approach still influences English statutes
and decisions to allow the incorporators to fix the corporate procedures
and control features (*i.e.,* voting and quorums) freely by contract. The
English corporate law rules in this area are thus largely optional and
for convenience if the parties do not wish to supersede them by special
arrangement.[90]

On the other hand, in both Japan and the U.S., the concept of corporation law is different in that the rules are, to a degree at least, mandatory and not subject to overriding contractual arrangements of the
incorporators. In the U.S., this theory stems from the early practice of
granting corporate charters by special acts of the legislature, which gave
rise to the so-called concession theory of incorporation. In the later
general incorporation laws, it came to mean that the "corporate norms"
embodied in the law were conceived as mandatory and designed mostly
for publicly held corporations and to protect the public and shareholders.

Japan, without such a history of special charter grants, nevertheless
treats the corporate rules as mandatory, unless the law otherwise provides. In addition, however, the systematic character of the code tends
to support the theory that the corporate law requirements are only
mandatory in the intracorporate structure and as to corporate action as
such,[91] leaving open the question of the validity of actions agreed upon
by contract.

In consequence then, though U.S. and Japanese law both tend to
treat the corporate law control requirements as more generally imperative than the English contract theory, the Japanese law has little difficulty at the same time in holding that contrary contracts in their separate
spheres are both valid and enforceable *between the parties,* for damages
at least.

The U.S. cases show their usual variety of holdings, exacerbated
especially in this instance by early failures to recognize in the legislation
the obviously different needs of close and publicly held corporations.
Some U.S. cases hold that the shareholders cannot vary the control
mechanisms fixed by the corporate law, and if they try to do so, the
bylaw[92] or contract[93] will not be enforced. Others will enforce shareholder contracts, as such, even though they may be invalid as bylaws.[94]
Overall, however, the needs of the close corporation in the U.S. seem
to be leading to more enforcement of contracts that are contrary to
the corporate law provisions. Similar separate and distinct treatment of

corporate and contract law has been forthrightly recognized in Japanese law from the beginning, and thus contrary contractual provisions are normally valid. The only question is whether there are any useful remedies, given the fact that the corporate law is adverse and no action is possible against the corporation in case of breach.[95]

Corporate Controls: Provisions in the Articles

Because of the inherent inadequacy of affirmative injunctions to enforce contracts entirely dependent upon cooperation in a close corporation, the desired veto devices for a foreign minority in Japan are probably best achieved in the articles of incorporation by adjusting quorum and voting ratios required for decision within the scope allowed by the code, coupled with cumulative voting in electing directors. At the outset, however, it should be noted that this technique will not insure a veto for a minority of one-third or less because a two-thirds vote will amend the articles, and, though scholarly opinion is divided, the majority view is that this vote is not legally subject to variations in the articles.[96] Also, it is necessary to provide for preemptive rights to new shares in the articles in order to enable the minority to maintain its shareholding ratio. Otherwise the code authorizes the board to decide upon a share issue, although, if preemptive rights are allocated to outsiders, a two-thirds vote under Commercial Code, Art. 343, is required (Art. 280-2[2]). If preemptive rights are provided and the minority can block an amendment, then the articles can insure a veto power by extraordinary vote on most matters.

The reason for this approach where the minority has more than one-third is that the irrevocable proxy, the voting trust, and share classes are ordinarily not practicable in Japan. The scholars are unanimous in the view that voting trusts and irrevocable proxies[97] are not legal in Japanese corporate law.[98] This conclusion flows from the requirement that shareholder proxies be limited in effect to a single meeting,[99] which rules out irrevocable proxies and has been interpreted to bar voting trusts also. Presumably they are, however, effective as contracts, subject to the weaknesses of affirmative remedies discussed above.

On the other hand, different classes of shares are possible in Japanese corporation law,[100] including preferred shares (up to 25 percent of the total shares) that may be nonvoting as long as preferred dividends are not suspended.[101] In practice, however, preferred shares, in general, are exceedingly rare in Japan (or any type except par value, nonbearer common), and preferred shares seem to carry implications of fiscal weakness. Besides, they are cumbersome for attaining no more than veto power in an otherwise simple close corporate arrangement, and if they do more, they could complicate the official validation process.

In placing minority veto power in the articles of incorporation, draftsmen must pay careful attention to the code provisions. They specify certain items that must be in the articles (*zettaiteki kisai jikō*); others are made optional in various provisions of the code, but they must be placed in the articles if they are to be effective (*sōtaiteki kisai jikō*), even though they are not treated in the codes as long as they do not violate the law or contradict the basic corporate concepts or public policy.[102]

The details of corporation law and incorporation procedure are a separate subject, so only the code provisions defining the boundaries for draftsmanship will be indicated here. The most basic provision is, of course, the amending power in Commercial Code, Art. 343, which requires a two-thirds vote, and, as mentioned, this vote is, by the majority view, not subject to modification in the articles. Thus, if courts follow this view, minorities with less than a third cannot be given a veto power in the articles which is secure against amendments. Given the requisite one-third of the voting shares, the code provisions relevant to a veto power over corporate policy are those that specify quorums, votes required for resolutions of the board or shareholders, those regarding election of directors and representative directors, those specifying the powers of the board or shareholder meetings, and those specifying the points that may be freely decided in the articles. Arts. 239 and 260-2 require a simple majority of a quorum of half of the issued shareholdings or directors for shareholders' and directors' resolutions respectively, but significantly, both articles authorize provisions for larger majorities and quorums in the articles of incorporation. Art. 230-2 then allows the articles of incorporation to fix matters to be decided by the shareholders in addition to those specified in the code. There are doubtless some policy limits to these options, though it is difficult to define the degree of flexibility permitted. For example, some scholars say that shareholders may not be authorized to elect the representative director (ordinarily elected by the board),[103] and one decision has held that the articles may not give the president the power to determine the retirement allowance (*taishōkukin*) of directors because this is a power reserved to the shareholders by Commercial Code, Art. 269, unless retirement matters are fixed in the articles. Thus, delegation to the president in the articles was deemed inappropriate.[104]

Election of directors is by the shareholders and cumulative voting may be provided or prohibited (Art. 256-4) in the articles of incorporation, but even if it is prohibited in the articles, 25 percent or more of the shareholders may require it by simply filing a request before any given meeting. If cumulative voting is not prohibited in the articles, any shareholder may demand it before an election (Art. 256-3). Of course, in U.S.-Japanese joint ventures, both preemptive rights to new shares and cumulative voting should be provided in the articles, though, as a matter of practice, this is seldom done by purely Japanese corporations. Arithmetic will show what number of directors must be correlated with the ratio of shareholdings to get the most out of a minority by cumulative voting.[105] In general, the smaller the minority shareholding, the larger the board must be to reflect true voting strength. If more than the minimal three are desired, a larger number of directors can be fixed by the articles that cannot be amended except by a two-thirds shareholder vote.

*Agreements between the Joint Venturers Committing the Joint
Corporation to Future Specific Policies and Transactions*

Most U.S.-Japanese joint-venture contracts envisage future transactions between the new joint company and one or both of its parents.[106] These transactions may be critical to the overall bargain, as, for example, transfers of property such as capital equipment, plant sites, patent licensing, supplies, agreements, or other arrangements, such as sales agencies and employment of specific personnel. Drafting responsibility requires a lawyer to first decide whether such arrangements can, and if so should, be made binding on the embryo joint corporation or its promoters, or whether they should be provided only in an initial side agreement unvalidated by the FIL authorities and binding only betwen the joint venturers as future shareholders. To anticipate, ordinarily it seems that the shareholders' agreement is preferable, although legally the new corporation and promoters can be bound by following prescribed procedures at the proper stage. The most important exception to such a formula is a case in which the FIL requires approval. For example, all licensing agreements once required approval, and, by past official standards, a share acquisition ordinarily would not gain validation without a licensing agreement inducting technology otherwise unavailable to Japan. So the licensing transaction would have to accompany the application for validation of the share acquisition, leaving only the question of whether the licenses (or transfers) of technology may be treated for FIL purposes as separate transfers to be entered into by the new corporation after validation and after corporate establishment by the Commercial

Code, Art. 246, adoption (see below). Or, must the licensing be treated as a concurrent transaction, such as a contribution in kind (*gembutsu shusshi*) under Art. 168(1)v, or property to be taken over later under Art. 168(1)vi, both to be entered in the articles.[107] Note that timing is also critical in these problems: (1) first, a joint-venture contract (perhaps with several side agreements, separate, annexed, or incorporated by reference) is signed; (2) then seven persons (probably including one or both joint venturers) become "promoters" (*hokkinin*, incorporators) by signing the articles; (3) the constituent shareholders' and directors' meetings are held at which elections occur and evaluations of contributions are reviewed; (4) after that, registration is effected, at which time the new corporation comes into existence and can act on its own.

Generally, there are two ways to proceed in order to transform the contemplated obligations arising from these transactions from mere plans of the joint venturers to commitments of the new corporation. The commitment to transfer property can either (1) be made by entering (a) the name of the transferor (subscriber, "promoter," or third person), (b) the property (anything that can be entered on the balance sheet), and (c) its value in the articles[108] before the constituent meeting;[109] or (2) the transactions can be adopted by the new corporation after it is registered. However, if this latter course is followed, the contract must be recognized as a new one between the new corporation and the parent involved, meaning either can actually refuse to enter into the arrangement. In addition, the new corporation can only enter into such a transaction[110] by a two-thirds vote of the shareholders,[111] and an attempt to adopt the old obligation, without contracting anew, will fail because the old contract is void for lack of entry in the articles.[112] It is also useful to remember at this point that "promoters" are not competent to act for or to bind the embryo corporation in any matters looking to the commencement of business (*kaigyō jumbi kōi*) as opposed to acts necessary to incorporation.[113]

Of course, the thrust of these rules is to prevent evasion of the requirement of similar entries in the articles when a contribution of property (instead of cash) is to be made for the initial shares of the corporation,[114] which contribution in kind must be delivered before the corporation can be registered and come into legal existence. When either of these types of transfers is planned, the Commercial Code requires that they be listed in the articles and that a court appoint an inspector to investigate and report on the propriety of the evaluation and other aspects of the transaction. If improprieties are found, changes may be ordered by the constituent meeting[115] or the court,[116] depending on which of the two available incorporation procedures is being followed.[117] All of these are, of course, to protect the subscribers and the public from depletion of assets by inside deals. The provision allowing postincorporation transfers, as long as they were listed in the articles and inspected by the court, was enacted as late as 1938 after a decision that unlisted transfers were void.[118]

A review of these rules is especially pertinent to a joint venture because the parties often want to transfer intangible industrial property or capital equipment to the new corporation, and difficulties, real or imagined, of proving its value and delivery have motivated the parties to avoid the court inspections during incorporation where legally possible, even though they submit technology transfers for FIL approval. So, for corporate law purposes, instead of a direct single transaction whereby a contribution in kind of patents, know-how, etc., is transferred for shares, they arrange to pay cash for the shares (without mention of the property transfer contemplated later), and after incorporation the shareholder receives his money back in exchange for his patents. This kind of prearrangement is entirely void against the joint corporation. Also, whether the technology is to be a contribution in kind or transferred after incorporation, it has usually required FIL approval and can involve some of the most difficult tax problems as well. But now much technology may enter Japan more freely (see Chapter VI).

Leaving these latter problems aside, such a result may not be so disadvantageous to suggest listing the transaction in the articles, because if the joint venturers are bound contractually to cause the new company to act in accordance with the plan, there should be little difficulty in obtaining the new corporation's acceptance of a new contract to transfer the property by the two-thirds vote required. Should the majority shareholder fail to carry through, surely the venture will fail anyway, and for salvage operations a claim against the other joint venturer for damages, especially if liquidated damages are specified, is as good as any remedy against the ineffectual new corporation. However, for maximum security the other party must be made to specifically undertake to cause the new corporation to do as stipulated or compensate the other party for the loss. In summary, then, it seems that because of the formalisms of the *kabushiki kaisha* law, it is preferable in most of these matters (except licenses of technology that need FIL approval) to rely on side agreements between prospective shareholders for legal commitments of a specific nature, such as transfers of property to the new corporation. Of course, for guarantees of corporate positions or employment contracts, there is no alternative because they cannot be put into the articles legally.

Joint-Venture Corporation's Third-Party Beneficiary Rights

From the joint company's point of view, it could be important to know what right the new corporation has in Japanese law to accept and enforce the benefits conferred upon it by the side contract of the parents. Again, consistent with general Japanese theory, one might suppose that the contract should be enforceable despite the corporate law stricture, since the Civil Code recognizes the right of a third-party beneficiary,[119] even though the third party may be a corporation not yet in existence at the time of contracting.[120] But the right is only perfected when the beneficiary notifies the obligor of his acceptance of the benefit and obligation.[121]

It has been demonstrated, however, that in one case[122] the court held that the contract for transfer of land, concluded between a "promoter" and the seller for benefit of an embryo corporation but not listed in the articles, was void and the third-party new corporation could not, after incorporation, accept the benefits and enforce the contract against the seller, even by compliance with Commercial Code, Art. 246 (two-thirds vote). Doubtless, the holding in this case is understandable as an example in which, as in U.S. law, a contract is not enforceable when the state specifically forbids that the corporation be bound as a party by such contract itself without conforming to the prescribed procedures, which is apparently the effect of Art. 168(1)vi.[123]

There are, however, other types of obligations such as employment and advisory services that the joint venturers undertake for the new corporation as third-party beneficiary which cannot and need not be entered into the articles because they involve no property transfer. With respect to these arrangements, the joint corporation as a third-party beneficiary would have a right to accept the benefit and duty if any, and it could enforce the contract directly against the obligor parent.

Frustration and Modification

We have emphasized throughout that, whatever the legalities of the situation may be, a court cannot affirmatively enforce the continued confidence and cooperation required for the success of a close corporate operation any more than it could in a marriage. These relationships depend for continuance of effective operations almost entirely on confidence born of mutual interest and understanding. In a situation where the parties are dependent upon private law enforcement as well as private law-making, legal obligations, if clearly understood by the parties to be such, may have preventive and deterrent functions; or in case of failure of the enterprise, they may be legally useful in litigation to salvage some pieces. But the law will rarely put together what the parties have put asunder, and the wise lawyer, like the wise bamboo, will bend with the wind and use his skills to induce initial mutuality and clarity of legal commitment—only theoretically enforceable—for whatever value of the sort mentioned above it may turn out to have.

But even though the original bargain seems clear enough, both between the parties and in law, there is the additional problem, particularly relevant to a minority position, of subsequent coerced modifications[124] —a danger that a majority may be peculiarly able to exploit in a joint venture in which the bullied minority knows full well that success is dependent on continued cooperation and that legal remedies to that end are ineffectual. An analogous situation in our law is the position of a contractor in the middle who is confronted with demands for a higher price by a subcontractor.[125]

There are three Japanese factors—one, a matter of Japanese business practice, and the other two legal points bearing on the potential problem of coerced modification of U.S.-Japanese joint-venture agreements, points that a draftsman needs to bear in mind. First, we have noted that Japanese businessmen, unlike Americans, do not habitually use formal detailed contracts drafted with a view to strict performance and enforcement if necessary by litigation in their domestic business relations;[126] they traditionally have preferred flexibility in their hierarchical relationships to meet problems as they unfold and social power and conciliation to resolve disputes. In their domestic society, uniquely organized both in degree and kind, that approach seems to work well enough. But an awkward foreigner can hardly "while in Japan do as the Japanese ethnocentrically and particularistically do,"[127] and a foreign minority position is thus untenable, unless the basic bargain is faithfully observed in accordance with the universalistic codes and unless the terms of the bargain are observed without unwarranted requests for changes or subsequent renegotiation.

Novation (*kōkai*) is, of course, provided for in the Japanese Civil Code, and it presents no special legal problems here, requiring as it does the agreement of both parties.[128] It is significant, in this discussion of security for contractual commitments to a minority interest, to note, however, that in Japanese law a later promise by one party to do more than the signed contract calls for, based for example on threats of nonperformance by the other and without any change in the other's obligations, is binding,[129] even though the subsequent promise is oral and, in our common-law conception, without consideration.[130]

In avoiding erosion of the initial bargain, it is, therefore, important to know when a request for modification has some *legal* support; for example, what sort of changed circumstances will excuse nonperformance. Impossibility is, of course, recognized as an excuse for nonperformance and, as a general rule, the risk of loss is on the obligor,[131] with the exception of sales of identified specific goods where the risk is shifted to the purchaser even before payment and delivery.[132]

The doctrine on change of circumstance (*jijō henkō no genosku*) is more closely related to our inquiry here.[133] As exemplified in the Japanese precedents, it is a far different thing from a flexible contract to allow adjustments for inconvenient contingencies. In a leading case, *Iguchi* v. *Ikegami,* the Supreme Court, while refusing to recognize a defense of changed circumstances, laid down four criteria that seem to be generally accepted law:[134]

1. Substantial change of circumstances must have occurred since the contract was formed.

2. The change must have been unforeseeable.

3. The change must have been caused by forces for which neither party was responsible.

4. And thus, to enforce the contract would violate the principle of faith and trust (*shingi seijitsu no gensoku*).

The code basis for this doctrine is Civil Code, Art. 1(2),[135] requiring that rights be exercised faithfully and in accordance with the principles of trust. The weight of scholarly opinion says that an objective, unforeseeable change for which the parties were not responsible must be found first; then the situation is examined to see whether the parties' own positions and actions warrant excuse of performance under Art. 1(2).[136] The cases have been very strict in the postwar period,[137] and it is safe to assume that argument for a change in contractual terms on this basis will have to be supported by real hardship without fault and caused by extreme and unforeseeable changes of circumstance after the contract was made.

In summary, Japanese substantive law as administered by the courts furnishes ample security against legal claims for modifications merely convenient for one side. Also, for a Japanese operation, the draftsman does not need an elaborately tailored *force majeure* clause, at least from the minority point of view. Nonetheless, Japanese parties occasionally wish to insert a clause to the effect that, in case of changed conditions or disagreement, the parties will discuss the matter and reach an amicable agreement. In this innocuous-sounding suggestion is often planted the seed of traditional flexibility that may come to be understood as a *right* to change. In the interest of security of the commitments, it is advisable to discuss these matters thoroughly and to leave such clauses out, especially since legally the parties can always agree to a partially or wholly new arrangement. In this area of contract nonperformance and modification, Sawada has explored the Japanese business practices and attitudes and compared these practices with the law. His conclusion is that in practice the legal rights and obligations of the code are largely ignored.[138]

Conclusion

Experienced international practitioners will know that the role of law and the efficacy of courts vary from place to place and that, consequently, businessmen choose to give formal contracts a role that varies with the country. Compared to us, the Japanese rely less on formal contracts domestically, and they rely even less on litigation. This point of behavior regarding the uses of contract law (and the role of law generally) needs to be understood, even though increased international business contracts are focusing more attention on Japanese positive law.

Additionally, it is common sense that the legal meaning of a transnational contract in the Holmesian sense (the law is what the court says it is) cannot be understood prospectively unless we know from which law it derives its meaning. And we cannot, in fact, determine with certainty which law would govern *in litigation* until we know where a suit will be brought, which in turn is indeterminable as long as the parties can sue in more than one country—and they can—considering both of them separately as potential plaintiffs. When the American federalistic complex is involved in any bilateral problem with some states showing little or no respect for foreign judgments, prorogation, and choice-of-law clauses, the single-law standard for understanding the legal meaning of a contract as an enforceable instrument, prospectively, is largely illusory at the only point at which the law can add anything more to the security of the transaction than the parties' good faith— namely, in a lawsuit.

In U.S.-Japanese joint ventures, nearly all American firms have a minority position because of Japanese official policy against foreign majority equities in Japanese enterprises though, since 1970, controlled Japanese subsidiaries are becoming more numerous. This fact molds the constitutive contracts in a fairly fixed pattern, and by all odds the most important problem is to protect the foreign minority interest within the limits possible under the Japanese contract, administrative, and corporation laws. Now, since 1966, it is possible to restrict the transfer of shares under the Commercial Code, Art. 204. Also, this can be done by a contract valid between the parties, but then enforcement is not possible against the corporation or third parties; specific performance is available in the law, but it is unlikely to be useful against the other party. Damage claims are similarly ineffectual unless liquidated damages are included in the contract; if they are, they will be upheld unless they are so excessive as to be *contra bonos mores,* which is a standard apparently much more permissive than the U.S. concept of "penalty."

A minority veto power over certain critical transactions is given in the Commercial Code itself to the shareholder with more than one-third of the votes, and the veto can be extended legally in the articles, but despite some differences of opinion among scholars, small minorities cannot be confidently protected, because the articles can be amended by a two-thirds vote and this required vote cannot be with confidence increased to 75 or 80 percent by the parties in the articles. To protect a veto power, it is necessary to provide for preemptive rights for the existent shareholder in the articles. The veto power can be extended to the board by properly calculating the number of directors and providing for cumulative voting, in addition to adequate extraordinary board votes, in the articles; even more than two-thirds could apparently be required.

Prospective commitments for later property transfers between the parents and the new joint corporation can be made effective against the new corporation only by including them in the articles and by getting a court inspector's approval at the time of incorporation. Often it would be reasonably safe and much simpler to bind the other joint venturer, on the risk of otherwise paying liquidated damages, to cause the new corporation to enter a new contract and to approve the transfer by a two-thirds shareholder vote required for certain transfers within two years after incorporation. Where transactions other than property transfers are contemplated for the future company, they can only be fixed as legal obligation between the joint venturers, but the Japanese law provides benefits for the third-party new corporation.

The conclusion that comes through more clearly is that, without good faith and cooperation, no affirmative legal remedy is adequate to make a joint venture work. Nevertheless, a well-planned legal structure that is set up and operating will make the bargain understandable, operable, and then, given the modicum of initial good faith, sustainable. Careful legal planning will also help salvage something from a stalemate. Liquidated damage clauses are as useful in a breakdown as they are difficult to negotiate.

IX

Dispute Settlement:
The Uses of Arbitration

Most of the foreign dissatisfaction with business in Japan has been directed toward Japanese official restrictions, but still there have been private differences between Japanese and foreign enterprisers noted in the Japanese literature;[1] for example, Nichiro-Heinz, Nihon Dixie (American Can, Daiwa Can, Daishowa Paper, Toppan Printing), and Safeway-Sumitomo. Many, many others have been kept quiet and settled among the parties, in the usual routine of business. Probably the best-known joint-venture dispute that has gone to litigation is the Hilton-Tōkyū dispute (Tokyo Courts) over the Tokyo Hilton Hotel management.

As noted above (Chapter VIII), inadequacies of "trans-Pacific litigation" are such that arbitration, despite its shortcomings, has come to play a dominant role in Japanese business relations with foreigners, both in contract drafting and in subsequent dispute resolution. This is true especially because joint-venture contracts normally provide for sales and export arrangements; and in the resultant commercial disputes especially, arbitration has often proved to be most useful. Furthermore, arbitration has become even more effective since the 1970 amendments to the Federal Arbitration Act (FAA) to implement the U.S. accession (29 December 1970) to the United Nations Convention on the Recognition and Enforcement of Foreign Arbitral Awards (hereafter the UN Convention). This is particularly true because the UN Convention makes arbitral agreements enforceable, too, even though only awards are mentioned in the convention title.

Still, arbitration is not always appropriate for certain issues,[2] and each enterpriser must weigh the merits and demerits and make his own choice of forum. Hereafter discussed are some of the advantages and disadvantages with their historical backgrounds, followed by a review of legal facilities available to support arbitration in Japan. Specifically, the U.S.-Japanese comparative legal framework will be used in an illustrative way in this chapter because the realities of trans-Pacific dispute resolution can only be adequately seen in full by scrutiny in a bilateral context, not only because the laws of at least two countries must be understood to make a proper choice of law and forum in contracting, but also because the parties, whether consistent with their contract or not, may choose either country when a dispute arises and the time comes to sue.

Arbitration Experience and Facilities[3]

Use of Arbitration in the U.S.

The operational advantages and the legal efficacy of arbitration are so interrelated[4] that businessmen and lawyers need a grasp of both subjects in order to draft a workable arbitration clause for transnational dealings. Yet, according to recent Japanese and U.S. surveys, most American lawyers as well as businessmen are rather uninformed about arbitration.[5] This is probably because arbitration is largely excluded from "taught law"[6]—and apparently "taught business" also—even though it has now emerged in the American dispute-settlement process as a major technique,[7] especially in the commercial, labor, accident, and investment fields.

American arbitration enthusiasts have argued that, comparatively, arbitration is more informal, flexible, confidential, and expert, as well as quicker and cheaper, than litigation. Generally, these things are true, but the result may be less reliable and contain a large element of compromise. Also, the implications that may underlie these assertions (*i.e.,* lawsuits and lawyers are highly dysfunctional) have not been taken passively by the lawyers, though one lawyer has agreed from a sampling of personal observations that attorneys are not very useful in arbitration proceedings.[8] Other lawyers have pointed out that arbitration has its problems, too, from the legal standpoint: little respect for precedent or consistency of results; fewer safeguards during the hearing, *e.g.,* generally no transcript[9] or evidence rules;[10] uneven competence of lay arbitrators;[11] unreasoned awards;[12] failures to comply with law,[13] thus unpredictable results; and no opportunity for appeal except on the narrow grounds of fraud, misconduct, or lack of notice.[14]

These dialectics in the American literature have done much to clarify the issues in the admittedly delicate relationship between arbitral and legal remedies; at the same time, occasional lingering examples of the old rhetoric may have had the unfortunate effect of partially obscuring the growing complementary role of arbitration in the modern dispute-settlement process in the U.S. as reflected in the recent statutes and cases. Rather than "ousting" the courts, arbitration is a useful auxiliary, such as compromise, mediation, conciliation, and other private settlements.

But certainly arbitration is more useful in some circumstances than in others. One area in which the usefulness of arbitration is recognized almost universally is international business.[15] On reflection, the reasons are not altogether happy ones; most of the benefits as seen by the proponents of arbitration seem to flow from the inadequacies of litigation, which are especially pronounced in the transnational context, as alluded to in Chapter VIII above. The effect of impracticalities in transnational suits has been to cause the structuring of transactions with Japan in such a way as to avoid disputes and to use methods other than lawsuits to settle those which do occur. For example, the Japanese government has in the past used its tight foreign-exchange controls and import-export licensing powers to standardize delivery and payment terms so that documents of title and payment are exchanged for most Japanese export goods on C.I.F. or F.O.B. Japan terms.[16] Buyers in both countries have reduced breach of warranty claims by preshipment inspection, insuring that the goods conform to the contract specifications. We shall pursue in the next section the question of whether arbitration facilities have been useful in making up the deficiencies of international lawsuits with Japanese parties.

Use of Arbitration in Japan

At the outset it is critical for foreigners to understand that Japanese arbitration (*chūsai*) is quite different in concept and psychology from arbitration in the U.S. or Europe. This fact foreigners must bear firmly in mind when considering whether to use an arbitration clause in dealings with Japanese, especially a clause under which arbitration might take place in Japan. Basically Japanese arbitration has a flavor of compromise;[17] the word "*chūsai*" itself literally means "to decide in the middle" or compromise. Likewise, the very first article on arbitration in the Code of Civil Procedure (CCP) lays the foundation for the compromising approach in Japanese "arbitration": "CCP Article 786:

An agreement for submission of a controversy to one or more arbitrators shall be valid insofar as the parties are entitled to effect a compromise regarding the subject matter in dispute."

Nor is the compromising nature of Japanese arbitration simply a legal and lingual matter, for conciliation and compromise have deep roots in Japanese psychology and traditional methods of dispute resolution so that, when German-styled arbitration was early inducted into Japan as a part of the new Code of Civil Procedure (1891), it was natural for the Japanese to adjust this alien institution, in its actual operations, to the local psychology of compromise.[18]

In comparing, for the first time, Japanese and foreign arbitral institutions, it is, therefore, important to note the vastly different role that law plays in such a process. Japanese law does not require arbitrators to apply substantive law in deciding the dispute before them unless the parties so require; nor do Japanese disputants expect it; rather, they expect arbitrators to compromise, if necessary, to reach a "fair" result. In this respect CCP Art. 801(5), requiring that arbitrators give reasons in their awards, may mislead some western lawyers who might suppose that this means to support the award with reasoned application of the pertinent rules of law. But Japanese lawyers interpret Art. 801(5) to mean only that some reasons are supplied; they need not be legally correct reasons.[19]

All draftsmen must consider what this contrasting psychology underlying Japanese arbitration means to their arbitral clauses in contracts with Japanese. It is clear enough that, to the extent that a foreigner might wish to see his legal rights enforced by arbitration, he should avoid arbitration in Japan under Japanese law or he should clearly stipulate that the arbitrators must apply a specifically stipulated governing law. By stipulating a foreign arbitrator or Japanese arbitrators experienced in foreign practices and a different applicable law, arbitration in Japan might be had there, which would conform to international practice. If a subjective conciliatory result based only on the Japanese arbitrators' feelings of fairness, without attention to legalities, is deemed adequate, Japanese arbitration will cause no problem.

Even though Japanese arbitrators need not apply the substantive law, Japanese procedural law adequately supports arbitration so that Japanese arbitration has not been saddled with adverse judicial attitudes against enforcing arbitral agreements such as is found in the American common law. In 1891, a modern system for enforcing arbitration, rather similar to that found in our modern statutes beginning with the New York Arbitration Act of 1920, was first enforced in Japan by enactment of the Code of Civil Procedure, of which the arbitral system was the final part.[20] This enactment of arbitration provisions as a part of the Code of Civil Procedure predated enforceable arbitral contracts covering future disputes in the U.S. by three decades. It was, however, not a response to demands from the business community but a part of a larger, superimposed codification process wherein largely German procedural law was inducted into Japan in response to foreign demands that the legal system be modernized. At that time, the chief methods of indigenous dispute settlement were conciliatory and based upon mutual agreements and concessions of the parties themselves. In contrast, both litigation and arbitration, which are based upon third-party decisions, were largely alien to the culture.[21] Consequently, arbitration was little used for decades,[22] especially because the usual trade associations and other institutional frameworks that have been prominent in the development of commercial law and arbitration facilities in the Western world were not developed yet in Japan. Likewise, Japanese business is only recently developing standard contract forms with arbitration clauses for use in their trade associations.[23] One authority has stated that in the first half century of Japanese arbitration (up to 1938), only 209 cases of arbitration had been filed,[24] and it is estimated that not more than another 200 cases of arbitration were handled between 1938 and 1950. Even these cases were presumably handled in accordance with Japanese concepts of mediation and compromise, as opposed to the legalistic, third-party arbitral process common in the West.

It was not until after World War II that the use of arbitration facilities began to increase rapidly, gaining momentum from the encouragement of the Allied occupation authorities.[25] The Japan Commercial Arbitration Association (hereinafter JCAA) was established by 1950, and in the past fifteen years it has concluded agreements with its counterparts in the U.S. (1952), India (1955), Russia (1956), Poland (1957), Rumania (1957), Pakistan (1958), the Inter-American Commercial Arbitration Commission (1958), West Germany (1959), Western Canada (1961), Bulgaria (1961), Hungary (1961), Sweden (1962), and The Netherlands (1962).[26] The Japanese government has also concluded bilateral treaties providing for commercial arbitration with ten countries.[27]

Even this expansion, however, has not changed the emphasis on arbitration and compromise. For, besides administering arbitration and conciliation services, the JCAA conducts an extensive preliminary "consultation" and "adjustment" service. The scope of these entire dispute-settlement activities may be understood from the following statistics on

disputes (domestic and foreign) filed with the JCAA for the year
1970:[28]

	1970
Consultation	2,445
Adjustments on complaints (import or export)	814
Conciliation	13
Arbitration pending	9
Arbitration awards	0
	3,281

In its consultation and adjustment services, the JCAA acts informally
as mediator and tries to induce a settlement between the parties. From
the huge gap between the figures for consultation and those for the
disputes actually submitted to conciliation or arbitration, it is clear that
less than 1 percent of the disputes that are brought to the JCAA actually
go to arbitration or formal conciliation. Even there, compromise is the
dominant element, unless foreign arbitrators are appointed.

International disputes that have been actually decided by an arbitration award in Japan have been even scarcer. Between 1957 and 1967,
only nineteen international arbitrations were formally concluded by
the JCAA, three of which were settled by withdrawals (*torisage*) and
sixteen by awards. The average time required to complete the arbitration was 28.6 months. Americans were involved in eight of these
cases, five as plaintiffs and three as defendants. All but one case involved over $10,000, and ten of the cases involved over $100,000 each.

Quite apart from the question of the legal content of the awards or
what role substantive law may play as a criterion for the arbitrators'
decision, arbitration, by definition a consensual process, is most useful
when it operates voluntarily throughout—from contract to payment of
the award—without recourse to courts and law for its enforcement.
Only when voluntary participation breaks down does the law have a
role, and then the chief legal enforcement problems are: (1) whether
arbitration clauses will be supported by the courts, either by requiring
participation from a party who has agreed in advance to arbitrate but
refuses once a dispute is at hand, or by enjoining, staying, or dismissing
a lawsuit in favor of the agreed arbitration; and (2) whether the courts
will recognize and enforce an arbitration award against a party who
does not voluntarily comply with it, especially when the opponent has
willfully refused to even participate in the proceeding as agreed. In the

usual case, the parties have never foreseen the host of legal difficulties that then appear. Rather, they had usually thought that they had avoided such problems by reliance upon arbitration. For example, the losing party may question the validity of the main contract or the arbitration agreement itself, the arbitrability of the issues in dispute either under the applicable law or under the agreement, the propriety of the arbitration procedures; or he might attempt to challenge the award, for example, because of misconduct of the arbitrator. Unfortunately, arbitration is not as free of legal problems as businessmen often think or wish unless both parties voluntarily accept what it yields, and when legal enforcement is required, arbitration loses much of its advantages in speed and economy. This insight leads one to the conclusion that, if arbitration is to fulfill its role, courts should limit their review at all points, except at the threshold to insure that the parties did in law and in fact agree to arbitrate the dispute in question. In American law terms, this much would seem to be required for "due process" under the U.S. Constitution.[29]

Also, where the parties to an international contract fail to specify precisely the law applicable to the main contract and to the arbitration, a complex of conflict-of-laws questions may arise which are rarely foreseen at the contracting stage but which can be highly practical to the arbitrator during the proceeding or later at the point of enforcement. For example, which law is applicable to the main contract or to the arbitration clause itself (for they may in some cases be different laws)? Which law applies to the arbitration proceeding[30] (since arbitration is not "in court," it does not necessarily, at least in Japanese theory, apply the local court rules or even the local arbitration procedures[31])? Which law does an enforcing court apply to determine whether the award has the legal validity required for local recognition? Does the procedure for executing domestic awards apply in granting execution on a foreign award once it is recognized as a valid foreign award? Below we shall refer to these problems only in passing, but we shall discuss in detail the legal structure to enforce arbitration contracts and awards in Japan and the U.S.

Law and Facilities for U.S.-Japanese Arbitration

There are several sources of law and arbitral procedure in U.S.-Japanese trade relations. First, there is the Treaty of Friendship, Commerce, and Navigation between the U.S. and Japan (1953) (hereinafter FCN Treaty),[32] which, insofar as it has not been superseded by the UN Convention (see below), applies to arbitration in both countries.[33] Second, there are the abitration provisions of the Japanese Code of Civil Procedure[34] and the arbitration statutes in the U.S., state[35] and federal,[36] including the new federal legislation of 1970 implementing the UN Convention. For sales, the Uniform Commercial Code (hereinafter UCC), Section 1-105,[37] is important. Third, the United Nations Convention on the Recognition and Enforcement of Foreign Arbitral Awards (hereinafter the 1958 UN Convention)[38] is most important because the U.S. just joined[39] in 1970, and Japan is also a member.[40] Finally, there is the Japan-American Trade Arbitration Agreement,[41] entered into by the American Arbitration Association (AAA), and the Japanese Commercial Arbitration Association (JCAA). Though this agreement is a private arrangement between the respective associations and does not have the force of law, it provides rules of procedure for arbitration in either country, if the parties include in their contracts the standard clause that incorporates the association rules.

Private Arbitration Rules

An examination of arbitration agreements actually used in U.S.-Japanese transactions reveals that they ordinarily are brief, boiler-plate clauses that are usually too general and follow a certain pattern that fails to deal with most of the common U.S.-Japanese legal problems. Often arbitration clauses are used without much understanding of their legal consequences. Double emphasis is thus required in warning businessmen that boiler-plate to cover dispute-resolution problems (governing law, forum, language, arbitration, etc.) needs more care than it usually gets in the U.S.-Japanese contract process. Most licensing and sales executives and their lawyers have had most of their early international experience in Europe, and European boiler-plate may fit there, but it does not fit in Japan. For example, in a recent survey 312 contracts between Japanese and Americans were examined,[42] and 82 contracts had arbitration clauses. Thirty-four of them designated the International Chamber of Commerce rules (Hdqrs. Paris), whereas only eighteen invoked the rules provided under the U.S.-Japanese Arbitration Association Agreement (1952), which is a great deal more appropriate in many ways for settling U.S.-Japanese disputes. Here, then, is an instance in which we can tell, by a careful count, what the behavior has been; it has been to act, when in Japan, as though we were still in Europe.[43]

The clause recommended by the Japan-American Trade Arbitration Agreement (1952) is as follows:[44] "All disputes, controversies, or differences which may arise between the parties, out of or in relation to or in connection with this contract, or for the breach thereof, shall be finally settled by arbitration pursuant to the Japan-American Trade Arbitration Agreement of September 16, 1952, by which each party hereto is bound."

Although other international facilities may be used (*e.g.,* postwar marine charter parties in Japan often provided for London arbitration; also the International Chamber of Commerce[45] has facilities), the AAA-JCAA facilities are, overall, probably the best suited for U.S.-Japanese trade; but, as discussed hereafter, the standard clause was never intended to displace the parties' preferences, and it should usually be supplemented to fit the particular needs of the parties to negotiated contracts. The following discussion will, therefore, center around the legal problems of arbitration as structured by the Japan-American Trade Arbitration Agreement, with only occasional reference to less structured arrangements.

The AAA and the JCAA agreed in 1952 that the foregoing clause incorporates the terms of the Japan-American Trade Arbitration Agreement into any contract containing the clause. The agreement thus incorporated into the contract in turn provides that arbitration in Japan will be conducted under the 1971 rules of the JCAA[46] and that arbitration conducted in the U.S. will be conducted under the rules of the AAA.[47] Once invoked by a party, these rules then provide most of the necessary organizational and procedural machinery required for the arbitration to get under way and proceed to an award. Without incorporating by references such supplemental rules—to determine where the arbitration will take place, the qualifications of arbitrators, how they are selected, and by what procedural rules the hearing will be held and the award reported and enforced—the usual brief arbitral agreement would be troublesome in practice. Nor is it ordinarily practicable to provide this technical detail by ad hoc provisions in each contract, particularly since most trade contracts are negotiated under pressure by businessmen, not lawyers. And most lawyers and businessmen know little about arbitration—though international specialists probably are the group best informed about arbitration within their respective professions.[48]

It is important for lawyers and businessmen to understand exactly what the foregoing U.S.-Japanese arrangement means on three points in particular: (1) the place of arbitration, (2) selection of arbitrators, and (3) choice-of-law. This understanding is important because the contracting parties may want to provide a different arrangement from that which would automatically ensue if they simply used the standard clause.

Where the place is not designated by the contracting parties, the Japan-American Trade Arbitration Agreement will fix the place for arbitration in any given case through a joint arbitration committee in the following manner:

2. If the place where the arbitration is to be held is not designated in the contract, or the parties fail to agree in writing on such place, the party demanding arbitration shall give notice to the Arbitration Association of the country in which the party resides. That Association shall notify the parties that they have a period of about 14 days to submit their arguments and reasons for preference regarding the place to a Joint Arbitration Committee of three members, two appointed by the respective Associations, and the third, to act as Chairman, to be chosen by the other two. The third member shall not be a member of either Association. The seats of the two Committees shall be in Tokyo and in New York. The determination of the place of arbitration by the Joint Arbitration Committee shall be final and binding upon both parties to the controversy.

In lieu of a place stipulated by the parties, this provision is designed to pick the most convenient place for arbitration of a dispute after the dispute has actually arisen. But, of course, if the parties want all arbitration to be held in a specific place, they will have to so provide in their contract. Although Tokyo and Osaka[49] are the logical places for most international arbitration in Japan, business is not so centralized in the U.S., and parties from various parts of the U.S. will want to designate a certain convenient city.[50] Note below that by usage the designation of a place for arbitration often implies the applicable law as well, although, by applicable conflicts principles, such a result does not necessarily follow from the choice of a location without implying such an *intent*.

Nothing could make the contract more meaningless as a standard for predicting the legal rights and duties of the parties, given the wide differences in U.S. and Japanese contract law,[51] than these rules for choosing the arbitral place (and therefore the law applicable). Until the complaint is filed and the site selected, it cannot be known which law (U.S. or Japanese) applies. Japanese law and foreign law differ enough so that this eleventh-hour decision will often mean the difference between liability or not for parties who cannot possibly know in advance what their enforceable legal obligations will turn out to be. Deplorable as this ambiguity of place may be for legalists, it is quite often the best that the parties can do in negotiating for arbitral clauses in binational contracts. This is because each party strongly prefers arbitration at home, and to break the stalemate posed by each wanting an arbitration in his own country, the place is not infrequently left for later determination.[52]

In cases of the parties having made no provisions in the contract for the selection of arbitrators, the Japan-American Trade Arbitration Agreement leaves the choice to the specific rules of either the AAA or the JCAA, depending on where the arbitration is held. Both the AAA and JCAA rules (1971) provide for a single arbitrator, unless the parties agree to a larger number.[53] The selection in both countries is made from an international panel of arbitrators, which the Japan-American Trade Arbitration Agreement (paragraph 3) requires each association to maintain. The AAA, for example, appoints from its international panel as follows:

Section 12. *Appointment from Panel*—if the parties have not appointed an Arbitrator and have not provided any other method of appointment, the Arbitrator shall be appointed in the following manner: Immediately after the filing of the Demand or Submission, the AAA shall submit simultaneously to each party to the dispute an identical list of names of persons chosen from the Panel. Each party to the dispute shall have seven days from the mailing date in which to cross off any names to which he objects, number the remaining names indicating the order of his preference, and return the list to the AAA. If a party does not return the list within the time specified, all persons named therein shall be deemed acceptable. From among the persons who have been approved on both lists, and in accordance with the designated order of mutual preference, the AAA shall invite the acceptance of an Arbitrator to serve. If the parties fail to agree upon any of the persons named, or if acceptable Arbitrators are unable to act, or if for any other reason the appointment cannot be made from the submitted lists, the AAA shall have the power to make the appointment from other members of the Panel without the submission of any additional lists.

The JCAA rule is substantially the same except that the new rules (No. 15[2]) disqualify all persons not resident in Japan at the time of appointment. If the parties want more than one arbitrator in either the U.S. or Japan and want the arbitrators selected by other means in either country, they must so provide in their agreement. A very common practice in arbitration, although not necessarily a good one, is to have two arbitrators selected, one by each of the parties, and a third "umpire" selected by the first two.[54] When this is done, it is important to stipulate that once the moving party appoints an arbitrator, the opposing party must appoint an arbitrator within a fixed period of time. Section 13 of the AAA and Section 19(2) of the new JCAA rules are well devised to take care of this situation. For example, AAA, Section 13: "If the agreement specifies a period of time within which an Arbitrator shall be appointed, and any party fails to make such appointment within that period, the AAA shall make the appointment. If no period of time is specified in the agreement, the AAA shall notify the parties to make the appointment and if within seven days after such Arbitrator has not been so appointed, the AAA shall make the appointment."

This, of course, avoids the inconvenience of requesting a court appointment as in the U.S. federal statute[55] and in the Japanese procedure.[56] Also, the rules anticipate the problem when the first two arbitrators are unable to agree on a neutral third arbitrator. The AAA simply appoints one when the stipulated period expires or after seven days if there is no stipulated period. Also AAA, Section 16 (and JCAA, Section 20), solves a sensitive nationalistic problem by affording either party to a U.S.-Japanese dispute arbitrated in the U.S. an opportunity to require that the sole arbitrator, or the neutral arbitrator, be appointed from among the nationals of a country other than the U.S. or Japan. Lawyers will, of course, note that such a foreigner will rarely have a deep familiarity with the law of either the U.S. or Japan; but for a foreign party who is interested in a result consistent with his legal rights, a third party may be better than a Japanese arbitrator (unless experienced in international transactions), given the psychological compromising attitudes toward arbitration found in Japan and underwritten in its law.[57]

If incorporated into their contract by the parties, the foregoing JCAA and AAA rules will handle most of the problems that a draftsman might overlook or squander considerable time solving in an ad hoc fashion. On the other hand, if a fixed place, a different number of arbitrators, or a specific method of selection is desired, they must be written into the contract because the rules provide otherwise, as indicated. If the parties hope to seek a result consistent with law, one useful device would be to agree that arbitrators be picked from among lawyers familiar with the law of the transaction. Needless to say, however, the dilemma of nationalistic bias versus legal competence is well-nigh insoluble because, especially for application of Japanese law, only Japanese nationals are likely to be competent, with precious few exceptions.

It is also imperative to explicitly set forth the parties' choice of governing law on all phases of the contract and arbitration, for it is quite possible that the simplicities of assuming that the law of the place of arbitration will turn out to be the governing law will become, instead, a costly complication in the enforcement phases, especially since the place of arbitration remains indeterminable under the standard clause. The clause recommended by the AAA and JCAA does not adequately deal with this problem, nor does the FCN Treaty provision (Art. IV[2]).

Enforcement of the Arbitration Agreement

Court Assistance in Requiring Arbitration under the UN Convention

In describing the specific legal supports[58] for U.S.-Japanese arbitration, let us suppose that the AAA-JCAA clause has been included in a contract between a U.S. company and a Nippon K.K. and that a dispute has arisen. One of the commonest problems is that the defendant refuses to appear or to appoint an arbitrator.

To begin with the U.S. side, treaty law is of critical importance in the enforcement of U.S.-Japanese arbitral agreements, and arbitration was greatly strengthened in 1970 by the U.S. accession to the UN Convention and by attendant amendments to the Federal Arbitration Act (FAA).[59] Unfortunately, the 1970 amendments did no more than was necessary to implement the UN Convention, leaving the complexities, ambiguities, and inadequacies that had developed in the decisional law under the original FAA still with us to vex practitioners in all U.S.-Japanese arbitration that might still fall outside the ambit of the UN Convention. However, the UN Convention will cover most, but not all, U.S.-Japanese arbitration; it covers only "commercial" arbitrations located in "contracting countries." It thus excludes noncommercial arbitrations (*e.g.,* patent infringements?), and since several countries important to international arbitration, such as England and Canada, are not yet "contracting parties" of the UN Convention, there could be U.S.-Japanese parties arbitrating in such countries outside the ambit of the convention. Such U.S.-Japanese arbitrations would still be governed by the FCN treaty and the old FAA. The brief new act retains all provisions of the FCN treaty and the old FAA that were not inconsistent with the convention; and these old provisions and their case law gloss will still operate, even for arbitration covered by the 1970 law, where not inconsistent. There are therefore three levels of authorities in the U.S. for U.S.-Japanese arbitration, starting with the original FAA (1925); the FCN Treaty (1954), which makes the old act applicable in some international arbitrations; and finally the UN Convention and the 1970 FAA amendments, which cover all commercial international arbitrations within the territories of contracting parties but still rely on parts of the old FAA for implementation. In view of past problems with federal arbitration law, experienced practitioners might have hoped for a bolder legislative stroke than we find in the 1970 amendments. Nevertheless, the 1970 amendments are a great improvement, covering many problems and greatly facilitating most future U.S.-Japanese arbitration and award enforcement. Hereafter, both U.S. and Japanese businessmen will be spared many of the contingencies, risks, and frustrations of the American state-law morass in the enforcement of both arbitral agreements and awards. This is no small step forward, as will become clear in the following summary of the convention and amendments. Because of the continued reliance on the old FAA, even in convention cases, and also because of the gaps left by the convention, where the prior law and the FCN treaty remain the only law applicable, we will discuss also U.S.-Japanese arbitration under the FCN Treaty and federal and state law as still operative in the interstices.

The 1970 act is too new to have any decisional gloss or much scholarly commentary helpful to practitioners, but we can review its text and interrelationships with prior law to determine in a general way what it does and does not do in implementing the UN Convention. First, it has two limiting features, as noted; the U.S. availed itself of the opportunity provided in the UN Convention (Art. I[3]) to lodge two reservations at the time of accession: (1) only arbitral agreements and awards taking place in "contracting parties" come under the convention as applied in the U.S., meaning, for example, that awards involving U.S.-Japanese disputes from such important nonconvention countries as the United Kingdom or Canada may only be enforced under the old law; (2) the U.S. also reserved the right to apply the UN Convention only to "commercial" arbitral agreements and awards. This latter reservation raises questions as to whether, for example, patent licensing problems would be sufficiently "commercial" to come under the convention as applied in U.S. courts.[60] Certain arbitrations between citizens of the U.S. may also fall under the convention, provided these relationships involve property located in Japan or another foreign country, envisage performance abroad, or have some other reasonable relationship with Japan or another foreign state (§ 202). The 1970 act covers a very large segment of the potential for arbitration in U.S.-Japanese transactions, and, as we shall see, the act will undoubtedly vastly facilitate the enforcement of arbitral agreements and awards between the two countries at the federal level.

In brief, the 1970 act forms a new Chapter 2 in the FAA (Section 201 through Section 208). After stating that the UN Convention on the Recognition and Enforcement of Foreign Arbitral Awards of 10 June 1958 will be enforced in the U.S. courts, and setting forth the arbitral agreements falling under the convention, the 1970 act solves in the next three sections (203, 204, and 205), subject to the foregoing limitations on its coverage, some of the very serious jurisdictional, venue, and removal problems previously hampering the usefulness of the FAA.

First the act states that contracts falling under the convention are deemed to arise under the laws and treaties of the U.S., and then the federal district courts are given original jurisdiction over arbitral problems arising therefrom, regardless of the amounts in controversy.[61] This overcomes the serious shortcoming of the prior federal law that, through court interpretation, has held that even arbitration procedures and agreements "in commerce" are not a separate source of federal jurisdiction and that "commerce" simply limits, legislatively, the scope of the statute's coverage, thus creating serious procedural-substantive (or "outcome determinative") classificatory problems for application of the act to diverse cases before the federal courts and in state courts in general. Happily, this problem is greatly reduced in future U.S.-Japanese transactions that fall under the convention.

Next, the act broadens the venue of the district courts to handle arbitration enforcement proceedings by providing that actions may be brought in any court which would have jurisdiction, save for the arbitration agreement, or in the district or division designated as a place of arbitration in the U.S.[62]

Thirdly, the act provides a more effective method for avoiding the morass of state legal disabilities for arbitration by allowing the removal of convention enforcement actions from any state court to the federal district court embracing the place where the action is pending, and also the act provides that grounds for removal need not show on the face of the complaint.[63] For purposes of the old Federal Arbitration Act, to the extent that its provisions are still applicable, the action is deemed to have been brought in the district court to which it was removed. This enables a U.S.-Japanese party wishing to enforce arbitration to avoid problems found in nearly half of the states of the U.S. which do not effectively enforce arbitrations, as we shall see.

The enforcement powers are much improved in the new federal law (1970)[64] because it specifically authorizes the federal courts to order arbitration, even abroad; whereas under the old FAA, Art. 4, the court could compel only local arbitration. This restricted result was worked out in the case law based on differences in the language of Art. 4 and Art. 3; that is, a stay of suit could be had under Art. 3 to prevent a local suit contrary to an arbitration contract, but a positive order to arbitrate abroad was unavailable under Art. 4.

As to enforcement of awards, the act allows an action to confirm the award and enforce it within three years in any court having jurisdiction.[65] Finally, the 1970 act provides that the old law (Chapter I) still applies to all enforcement proceedings, even under the convention, to the extent that they are not in conflict with the new provision of the convention.

This patchwork legislative technique, instead of a more ambitious attempt to codify and unify all of the federal arbitration law in a harmonious way, leaves first some important problems of interpretation regarding the coverage of the act and, secondly, some vexing unsettled problems for that portion of arbitration in U.S.-Japanese transactions which may turn out to be excluded by the new act. This, and other problems of the local law in both the U.S. and Japan, will be explored in the next section.

Court Assistance under the U.S.-Japanese FCN Treaty and Auxiliary Statutes

The FCN Treaty (1954) is helpful generally, but its protection is not positive.[66] It provides[67] only that arbitral contracts shall not be unenforceable merely on grounds that the arbitrators or place of arbitration is foreign. It is left to the Japanese law, or the federal or state law in the U.S., to determine first which law governs the arbitration agreement and, secondly, whether it is enforceable by an order to arbitrate, dismissal of a local lawsuit, a stay of such litigation,[68] or enjoining a suit in another court.[69] Thus, in the U.S., before the 1970 amendments to the federal act to accord with the UN Convention, the FCN Treaty was all we had, and it does little to make arbitration contracts more enforceable than they would be under existing federal or state law in the U.S.[70] Because of jurisdictional and venue problems, the cases in which arbitration abroad had been ordered by the U.S. federal courts were indeed rare.[71] Now the 1970 act specifically empowers the federal courts to order arbitration abroad where it is appropriate. Such arbitration clauses are, however, more secure legally in some of the U.S. than are prorogation clauses specifying a foreign court for litigation.[72]

In looking to the local "American"[73] law, aside from treaties, on enforcement of arbitration agreements, the U.S. has inherited the long, adverse, common-law history[74] that is now giving way to a strong trend toward general enforceability under modern statutes. During the transition, however, there is much diversity; and here we can only refer to the extensive "American" law literature[75] and set forth the basic principles of interest in U.S.-Japanese trade arbitration.

Because of developing uniform legislative patterns, "American" law fortunately is not as multiheaded as it might be in the arbitration field, especially since the 1970 act permits removal of international cases to the federal courts on broader terms than before 1970. Fifty jurisdictions have split rather evenly into two groups: one (currently twenty-two states[76]) with weak arbitration facilities following common-law doctrine to the effect that general arbitral agreements covering future disputes are revocable by the parties and unenforceable in court;[77] the other (twenty-eight states[78] and the federal jurisdiction[79]), by modern statutes,[80] has made arbitral clauses enforceable, including stays of law suits for foreign arbitration.[81] Until the 1970 act, however, federal courts generally have held that they could not order arbitration abroad in an FAA, Section 4, proceeding.[82] Furthermore, the latter group of statutes, where arbitral clauses are enforceable, is growing and already includes all of the states with substantial commercial relations with Japan, as well as the federal courts in which most U.S.-Japanese commercial suits may be filed, or removed to and handled under the federal act, because they would usually come within the UN Convention and thus arise under "treaties of the U.S."[83] (*i.e.,* "commercial" as defined therein).[84] Significant to uniformity is the holding of the U.S. Supreme Court that such questions as the validity and interpretation of an arbitral clause affecting "commerce" are questions of federal substantive law, not local state law,[85] and the question is whether this federal "substantive" law must be applied even by the state, as well as federal, courts.[86] However, under the Erie doctrine in a federal diversity case, state substantive law would govern the question of the validity and enforceability of arbitral clauses not related to "maritime transactions" or in "commerce,"[87] but such a case would be rare in U.S.-Japanese trade relations. As noted, patent licensing and infringement cases may be the most important area of ambiguity in U.S.-Japanese relations. If only FCN treaty provisions and the old federal statute (§4) apply, it is problematical whether the federal courts would order foreign arbitration; they almost never have.[88]

"American" law will thus serve reasonably well the American and Japanese businessmen who stipulate for arbitration, except in the infrequent cases in which enforcement can only be sought in the state courts of one of the twenty-odd jurisdictions still operating under influences of the common law. The statutory trend strengthening arbitration in some of the state systems includes Maryland (1965), Illinois (1961), and Texas (1965),[89] which were about the last of the major trading states with no modern arbitration statute. Nevada, Colorado, and Minnesota enforced, by case law,[90] arbitral clauses covering future disputes without the support of a modern statute; Minnesota and Nevada have since enacted (1957 and 1969 respectively) the Uniform Arbitration Act. California and New York have had modern statutes since 1920 and 1927 respectively, but both have recently further modernized their statutes.[91] The overall effect of the trend in the past two or three decades has been to change not only the laws but also the courts' attitudes at most of the major commercial centers in the U.S. from a rather negative attitude to an approach generally favoring arbitration.[92] And, by the UN Convention (Art. XI[1][c]), the U.S. federal government is obligated to recommend compliance with the convention to the states, for whatever effect this might have.

Under the Japanese law,[93] there is adequate legal support to enforce contracts obligating the parties to arbitrate either in Japan[94] or in the U.S.[95] There are several postwar Japanese lower court cases enforcing arbitration contracts,[96] though Supreme Court cases are lacking on this point. In the *Kobayashi*[97] case, the seller failed to ship goods from Australia; therefore, the Japanese buyer cancelled the contract and sought damages through a clause in the contract calling for arbitration in Japan. The defendant refused to appoint an arbitrator or otherwise participate. The plaintiff went to court, and the court granted an order appointing an arbitrator on defendant's behalf and rejected defendant's *force majeur* defense for nonperformance, holding that it went to the merits and was to be presented only to the arbitrator later.

A little different kind of support was lent to an arbitration clause in *Rose Int'l. Corp.* v. *Japan Commercial Arbitration Ass'n.*[98] Appellant Rose, an American motion picture company, chartered a ship from the complainant. Under the charter, disputes over the charter hire were to be settled by arbitration in Japan. Rose refused to pay the charter hire, so the shipowner commenced the arbitration proceeding. Rose, refusing to participate, sought a court injunction against the arbitration association to prevent it from administering the arbitration proceeding. Finding Rose's court action without merit, the court refused the injunction, and presumably the association appointed an arbitrator and proceeded with the arbitration, ending in an award or settlement.

Perhaps even more specifically useful, however, is the enforcement procedure built into the AAA and JCAA rules incorporated into the Arbitration Agreement. These rules provide that when a party fails to perform his duty to appoint an arbitrator and to arbitrate, the competent association in either country will automatically, after due notice and lapse of a proper period of time, appoint an arbitrator for him. This is a convenient and generally effective method of insuring that, when a dispute arises, the arbitration will progress efficiently to an award, despite the bad faith of an opponent. Once such an award is rendered, the scope of challenge is quite restricted. For example, in *G. M. Casaregi Compagnia di Navigazione e Commèrcio, S.P.A.* v. *Nishi Shōji K.K.*,[99] plaintiff Casaregi, an Italian shipowner, contracted to sell a ship to Nishi, a Japanese buyer, for $162,000 (U.S.), and Nishi agreed to use its best efforts to obtain an approval from the Japanese government; such approval was required before Nishi could make foreign-exchange payment in dollars. The approval was not obtained, and Casaregi sought London arbitration under English law, as provided in the contract, to recover for the loss occasioned by failure of the sale. Nishi refused to appoint an arbitrator; thus, under the English Arbitration Act of 1950, Casaregi's arbitrator became legally the sole arbitrator. Defendant failed to appear on the appointed date though he had been given adequate notice; therefore, under the English law, the arbitrator was empowered to proceed to an award without Nishi's presence. Casaregi was awarded damages (20,966 pounds), based on a finding by the arbitrator that Nishi breached its duty to use its best efforts to obtain government approval. When the award was presented to the Tokyo District Court for enforcement, the court enforced it, despite the fact that Nishi had not been represented at the London arbitration proceedings.

These holdings will, of course, go a long way toward establishing the point that in Japan failure to participate in an agreed arbitration for various make-weight reasons can be done only at one's own peril.[100]

Dismissal of Litigation

The second problem in enforcing arbitral clauses is presented when either a U.S. company or Nippon K.K. files a suit in the U.S. or Japan instead of resorting to arbitration as agreed. Will the courts in the U.S. or Japan dismiss the suit or stay the litigation? Or enjoin a suit in another court pending arbitration?

In the U.S., despite its negative common-law history, the federal courts can be expected to stay a suit that has been brought in violation of an agreement to arbitrate in Japan.[101] Similar support is becoming the rule in U.S. state courts as well.[102] Dismissal of Japanese suits in violation of an agreement to arbitrate in London,[103] New York,[104] and elsewhere may also be expected.

In an early postwar case,[105] a Panama shipowner, Compania, agreed to carry 8,280 tons of wheat from the Columbia River to Japan for defendant, Mataichi, which failed to deliver the cargo. Plaintiff sued in Tokyo for lost freight and Mataichi defended with a clause calling for New York arbitration. Despite plaintiff's plea that a foreign arbitration clause could not prevent a suit against a Japanese in Japan, because a foreign award would not be enforceable, the court dismissed. Note that the Japanese courts do not "stay" litigation contrary to arbitral clauses. The Japanese lower courts have been true to this holding ever since, although there has been no postwar Supreme Court holding on the point.

In *Hinode Kagaku Kōgyō K.K.* v. *Sankō Kisen K.K.*,[106] plaintiff Hinode, an importer of phosphorus for fertilizer, contracted for defendant to transport 8,000 tons of raw phosphorus material from Egypt to Japan. Leakage caused loss to the cargo in transit, and plaintiff sued in Osaka despite a clause for London arbitration. The court dismissed in favor of arbitration, rejecting plaintiff's argument that a clause for arbitration in a place foreign to both parties and all phases of the contract as well were void and that an award resulting from such an arbitration would be unenforceable in Japan. Note that the law of the forum (Japan), not the law of the contract (New York), has been held to govern the method of relief to be granted where an arbitration clause was asserted as a defense to a Japanese suit requesting dismissal.[107]

Reference to local law to provide the remedy is the general rule in the U.S. too, and it means that some state courts, applying their own law in this regard, will still refuse to stay or dismiss a suit brought by a party violating his agreement to arbitrate,[108] even though the agreement is valid by the proper law of the contract and though it "may not be deemed unenforceable" merely because of the place of arbitration or nationality of arbitrators under the FCN Treaty, Art. IV(2).[109] Still the party requesting arbitration may be able to prevail, after the *Prima Paint* case (*supra*), in such a state court if he can persuade the court to extend the *Prima* doctrine and find that the issue of enforceability is "substantive" and federal law applies to matters of federal "commerce" even in the state court.[110]

Threshold Legal Questions for the Courts

Even where arbitration is enforceable under modern treaties and legislation, the enforcing courts must first decide whether there is an arbitral contract between the parties and, if so, what its scope is. In

Japan, the authorities[111] are clear that the question of the existence of a contract (*keiyaku*) is a legal question for the court, provided it is raised before the arbitration gets under way. If the arbitration gets started, then the Code of Civil Procedure, Art. 797, requires that all challenges be postponed to the time of award enforcement. More important, perhaps, is the fact that questions of fraud and the like, which affect "validity" in American terms, are not often raised in considering whether a contract exists. In a very recent case, the Tokyo District Court[112] routinely, in the course of ordering enforcement of an award, reviewed a foreign-trade transaction to confirm that an arbitral "contract" in this limited sense did in fact exist to support the arbitration proceeding, in response to the loser's challenge on the point.

In the U.S., the established rule has generally been the same,[113] though its breadth has been traditionally much wider, embracing challenges to validity such as allegations of fraud. But, in 1967, the U.S. Supreme Court, following federal courts in New York,[114] decided the *Prima Paint Corp.* v. *Flood and Conklin Mfg. Co.*,[115] which narrows the range of questions for the court and enlarges substantially arbitrators' powers over the threshold question of fraud by, in effect, shifting to the person attacking the clause the burden of proving that the fraud went specifically to the arbitral clause itself. To do this, the *Prima Paint* case upheld the "separability" doctrine created by Judge Medina[116] in *Robert Lawrence Co.* v. *Devonshire Fabrics, Inc.*[117] Where an issue of fraud in the inducement of a "container" contract containing an arbitration clause is raised in an action to enforce the arbitration clause, the arbitration clause may be severed from the main contract; the arbitral clause will be enforced "separately" unless the plaintiff alleges and proves fraud in inducing the arbitral clause itself. If the court finds no fraud in the clause, then arbitration is enforced, and the arbitrators decide the fraud issue in the principal contract, if that issue is within the agreed scope of the arbitral clause; presumably this is a court question. The doctrine has drawn scholarly fire,[118] and in dissent Justice Black (joined by Justices Douglas and Stewart) have exposed the legal, constitutional, and theoretical weaknesses of the doctrine.[119] Also, in an earlier case, faced with a similar threshold legal question (condition precedent to a contract with an arbitral clause), the second circuit court did not find the clause separable and enforced arbitration. It decided the threshold issue itself[120]—a holding that is difficult to square with the fraud cases except on a narrow factual basis. In practice, the separability doctrine places a burden on the plaintiff asserting fraud in the container contract to plead and prove fraud[121] as to the arbitration clause specifically, when it seems in fact, or in commercial practice, that the parties seldom intend any agreement on arbitration at all separate from the underlying contract. Under such circumstances, the usual lack of evidence on a point neither party consciously considers makes the burden so heavy that plaintiffs will seldom be able to sustain it—again because the transactions are seldom put together in two separate steps the way the majority of the Supreme Court in *Prima* chose to presume they are negotiated.

Lawyers opposing arbitration in a fraudulent contract will, therefore, want to observe two important points in presenting this issue in the federal courts. First, because in most states (*e.g.,* New York) fraud in the inducement only makes the contract voidable, the plaintiff must seek rescission of the contract rather than sue for damages on it;[122] second, even this will not avoid arbitration being foisted upon the parties by way of the separability doctrine unless the plaintiff alleges fraud in inducing the arbitration clause itself.[123]

The New York state courts have not unambiguously embraced the separability doctrine,[124] but in two recent cases they have rendered decisions that have allowed arbitrators to decide threshold questions (condition precedent[125] and lack of mutuality[126]), which, it is submitted, should have been decided by the court as threshold questions addressed to insuring the consensual nature of arbitration.[127] This shifting of the balance between the powers of courts and commercial arbitrators in New York by allowing arbitrators, in a sense, to determine their own authority may have been improperly influenced by the Supreme Court's recent expansive approach to arbitration in the labor field.[128] Or perhaps the judges see arbitration as a solution to New York court congestion.[129] Precedents in labor cases and the ulterior goal of reducing court congestion seem to be producing an unsound relaxation of judicial control over business arbitration in the federal courts—and at precisely the point at which even friends of arbitration should see the need for close court scrutiny in order to insure the consensual nature of arbitration. Otherwise, there is a forceful denial of access to the nation's courts and due process.

The New York trend is important in U.S.-Japanese arbitration because of the volume of U.S.-Japanese business through New York—and two-thirds of all AAA arbitrations. Indeed, two Japanese firms already have been involved in cases involving these points. In a federal case involving the Japanese firm Kinoshita & Co.,[130] Judge Medina followed the separability doctrine, his own creation, but he then found the separable arbitral clause too narrow to cover the issue of fraudulent inducement; so the court itself found no fraud in favor of Kinoshita. In a state case,[131] the New York Court of Appeals reversed the appellate division that had found there was no valid arbitral agreement, because the agreed condition precedent to the entire contract had failed. Thus the reversal left the question to the arbitrators, who found, agreeing with both lower courts, that the condition precedent had not been fulfilled; the petitioner was relieved from performing.

Compared with Japanese law, this federal and New York trend to relax threshold review of arbitration agreements is moving in the Japanese direction, though Japan may have even more laxities of judicial control of arbitration than the U.S. once the arbitration has commenced.[132] Neither the U.S. nor Japan attempts to see that arbitrators use law as a criterion in their awards to the extent that the English do, for example. Both the Japanese and the U.S. arbitral systems, as developed in recent decades, rather generally operate outside the substantive law, presumably justified by their consensual character. If this is the rationale, it is appropriate for the courts to maintain a stricter review of the precise question of whether, in fact, there was consent to arbitrate, especially since, in the "battle of form" characterizing much of the commercial contracting process, the negotiated and bargained-for arbitral clauses are greatly outnumbered by their "adherent" cousins.[133]

Arbitration Awards: Enforcement (Recognition and Execution) in Japan or the United States

Introduction

Though an arbitral agreement is revocable and not entitled to specific enforcement in American common law, domestic awards are enforced under the same common law without a court review on the merits, once arbitration is voluntarily concluded by an award; errors of law or fact are usually not fatal to enforcement.[134] Common-law awards are, in theory at least, subject to less court review than either inferior court judgments or decisions of administrative tribunals.[135] Note that common-law arbitrations still coexist with statutory arbitration in some states.[136] Unlike federal law, the modern American statutes in the states have further facilitated award enforcement (including foreign awards) by routine procedures leading to a confirming judgment,[137] not only supporting local compulsory execution, but also entitling it to federal "full faith and credit" in sister states. In Japan, after the arbitration provisions became law in 1891 as a part of the Code of Civil Procedure, domestic awards have been routinely enforced as provided in the code.[138] We need only review here the special problems of enforcing the foreign award[139]—enforcing an American award in Japan, or vice versa.

Since domestic awards in both the U.S. and Japan can be confirmed routinely (note old FAA §9 restrictions) by a domestic court judgment, the winner of a local award in either country has an option: (1) he can enforce the local award in the other country as a foreign award there, or (2) he can reduce it to a judgment locally and then try to enforce it as a foreign judgment in the other country. In the U.S.-Japanese context under the UN Convention, there is now much reason to conclude that direct enforcement of the award may be easier than enforcing it indirectly by first reducing it to a local judgment. On the other hand, in areas in which the UN Convention might not apply, it is easier to reduce the award to a judgment and let all periods for appeal run, in order to prove finality under the FCN Treaty, thus foreclosing most legal challenges. Use of a judgment is also wise because FAA award enforcement procedures (9 USCA §9) are not readily adaptable to foreign awards, and federal handling is uncertain and state court treatment variable. Incidentally, since Japan and New York do not follow the "merger" doctrine, the award will survive infirmities that might eventuate in the judgment.[140] We are concerned below, however, only with direct enforcement of Japanese awards in the U.S. or vice versa.

Foreign awards, like domestic awards, cannot be enforced directly in either Japan or the U.S.; the foreign award must first be reduced to a judgment in the enforcing country. Under the 1970 amendments to the U.S. federal law (§207), there are, for the first time in U.S. federal law, legal provisions specifically authorizing a confirmation judgment for foreign awards as there are, for example, in Germany[141] and Sweden.[142] In Japan, however, such procedures as there are for judgment on awards are in their terms concerned only with domestic awards. But still by analogy much procedure, precedent, and practice for domestic awards will generally be applied by Japanese courts in enforcing foreign awards (see below).

Foreign Awards: Recognition of Validity

The UN Convention and the 1970 Federal Arbitration Act / Two steps are involved in enforcing foreign awards under the UN Convention or the FCN Treaty: (1) recognition by a local confirmation judgment; and (2) execution thereof. Under the UN Convention, an award is covered as "American" or "Japanese" only if it was rendered in the U.S. or Japan, whereas under the FCN Treaty an award is covered no matter where it was rendered as long as it was pursuant to a contract made by Japanese or American nationals. In order to recognize a foreign award, the 1970 FAA §207 provides:

§ 207. Award of arbitrators; confirmation; jurisdiction; proceeding:
Within three years after an arbitral award falling under the Convention is made, any party to the arbitration may apply to any court having jurisdiction under this chapter for an order confirming the award as against any other party to the arbitration. The court shall confirm the award unless it finds one of the grounds for refusal or deferral of recognition or enforcement of the award specified in the said convention.

This formula refers directly back to the UN Convention itself for the details of proving the agreement and award by the winner in Art. IV as follows:

Article IV.
1. To obtain the recognition and enforcement mentioned in the preceding article, the party applying for recognition and enforcement shall, at the time of the application, supply:
(a) the duly authenticated original award or a duly certified copy thereof;
(b) the original agreement referred to in article II or a duly certified copy thereof.

This arrangement makes the burden of recognition of the foreign award in the U.S. court relatively simple for the enforcing party; all he needs are certified or authentic copies of the agreement and award. Then the burden shifts to the party resisting the award to prove his defenses, which, however, are quite broad, indeed somewhat more so than those in the old FAA for domestic awards.

The act (§207) provides that the only challenges that may be raised against an award in the federal district courts are those listed in the UN Convention (Art. V), which are as follows:

Article V.
1. Recognition and enforcement of the award may be refused, at the request of the party against whom it is invoked, only if that party furnishes to the competent authority where the recognition and enforcement is sought, proof that:
(a) the parties to the agreement referred to in article II were, under the law applicable to them, under some incapacity, or the said agreement is not valid under the law to which the parties have subjected it or, failing any indication thereof, under the law of the country where the award was made; or
(b) the party against whom the award is invoked was not given proper notice of the appointment of the arbitrator or of the arbitration proceedings or was otherwise unable to present his case; or

(c) the award deals with a difference not contemplated by or not falling within the terms of the submission to arbitration, or it contains decisions on matters beyond the scope of the submission to arbitration, provided that, if the decisions on matters submitted to arbitration can be separated from those not so submitted, that part of the award which contains decisions on matters submitted to arbitration may be recognized and enforced; or

(d) the composition of the arbitral authority or the arbitral procedure was not in accordance with the agreement of the parties, or, failing such agreement, was not in accordance with the law of the country where arbitration took place; or

(e) the award has not yet become binding on the parties, or has been set aside or suspended by a competent authority of the country in which, or under the law of which, that award was made.

2. Recognition and enforcement of an arbitral award may also be refused if the competent authority in the country where recognition and enforcement is sought finds that:

(a) the subject matter of the difference is not capable of settlement by arbitration under the law of that country; or

(b) the recognition or enforcement of the award would be contrary to the public policy of that country.

FCN Recognition of Awards / The FCN provisions also require two steps in determining the enforceability of foreign awards in the U.S. or Japan: (1) is the award entitled to *recognition* (*i.e.,* is it valid?); (2) what procedural *remedies* are foreign awards, once recognized as valid, entitled to in enforcement proceedings?

Concerning recognition of Japanese awards in the U.S., the FCN analysis starts then with the treaty provision:[143] "Awards duly rendered pursuant to any such contract, which are final and enforceable under the laws of the place where rendered, shall be deemed conclusive in enforcement proceedings brought before the courts of competent jurisdiction of either Party, except where found contrary to public policy." An award rendered in Japan against a U.S. firm will be valid in the state and federal courts, provided it is (1) "duly rendered pursuant to" the recommended U.S.-Japan clause under discussion here; (2) final and enforceable in Japan; and (3) not against public policy in the particular U.S. jurisdiction where enforcement is sought.

The problem with U.S.-Japanese awards in the federal courts is that the old FAA §9 provides only for recognition of domestic awards, and in the U.S. there have been no cases indicating specifically how the three treaty criteria would be applied to a Japanese award,[144] but for the state courts the treaty criteria are not much different from the standards for interstate[145] or foreign[146] awards in the U.S. in cases where no special provisions are applicable, such as the treaty provides in the U.S.-Japanese situations.

A preliminary question must be answered by the United States court in enforcing a Japanese award: Which law governs the review under each criteria? For the second criterion (final and enforceable) the treaty provides that the law of the place of arbitration governs (Japan), which is the general American rule anyway. For the third criterion (not contrary to public policy), of course, U.S. law would apply. The only troublesome treaty test is the first: "duly rendered pursuant to" an arbitration contract. Note that the question is similar to the one raised under the UN Convention, Art. V(a) (see page 340 above). The American court would presumably apply its own law to determine the scope of review authorized by this phrase under both treaties.

As a second step, the court would apply the governing law of the contract to issues contesting the validity or scope of the arbital contract, but only if such points are found to be covered by the review defined in the first step. Detailed analysis of these conflicts problems must be passed over here,[147] but note the capriciousness of the answers produced in simply trying to fix the law governing the contract. Unless the parties have stipulated the governing law, the various issues found by interpretation to be subsumed under this first phrase would be governed by the law of the arbitration contract as indicated by the conflicts rules. In the first place, under some circumstances the U.S. court and the arbitrator might quite properly apply different conflicts rules to determine the law governing the contract, but assuming U.S. conflicts rules (state or federal rules in "commerce" contract?[148]) are applied, an anomaly will often arise from the fact that in applying, for example, the place-of-contracting rule to a U.S.-Japanese contract, the U.S. and Japanese answers would always be different on the same facts where the contract is concluded by mail.[149] So the contingencies of how and where the dispute is eventually arbitrated will determine which law governs and then who wins in certain cases, all of which is, of course, no more rational than flipping a coin.

Governing-law niceties aside, an American court's review under this first treaty criterion (duly rendered pursuant to a contract) would vary greatly with the jurisdiction, its statutes, and the court precedents.[150] Generally, however, American review of awards is limited to validity and compliance with the arbitral agreement and does not go to the merits;[151] errors of law[152] or fact in reaching an award are not grounds to vacate. To repeat, courts only consider questions of procedural compliance or fairness and the validity[153] or scope of the contract. Some states' statutes do, however, allow appeals from awards on questions of law related to the merits, much like the review of inferior court judgments.[154] But there is a trend to restrict the review of awards, and the AAA practice of discouraging reasoned opinions in awards makes it more difficult to ascertain legal or factual errors therein.[155] This would suggest that parties might prefer to agree[156] to omit reasons in their Japanese awards to lessen the chance of review in the U.S. Note that the Japanese popular understanding, as well as the legal conception of arbitration, does not even require or expect arbitrators to apply strict legal standards in deciding their cases, and, therefore, the reasons required in CCP 801(5) need not be "correct" reasons.

In recognizing an award, ordinarily the U.S. court might be expected to review challenges to the validity and scope of the arbitration contract (*i.e.,* duly rendered pursuant to a contract), but only if these contract questions had not been at issue in the Japanese courts already and if they had not been waived by participation or lost by laches. Cases in which such issues would still be timely would be rare, but conceivably challenges to the "contract" could be made in a proceeding to enforce, for example, an ex parte Japanese award, where the U.S. defendant had not appeared because he denied the contract. Except in such unusual cases with legitimate threshold issues still unresolved, the review under this first treaty criterion would be limited to procedural challenges asserting that the arbitration had not been conducted by agreed procedures for appointing arbitrators and the like (*i.e.,* duly rendered pursuant to a contract). To read any more meaning into this first phrase would cause overlapping with the next treaty criterion.

When a U.S. court is asked to enforce a Japanese award under the second treaty criterion ("final and enforceable . . . where rendered"), the court must look to the Japanese Code of Civil Procedure to determine when the award is final. Under the code a domestic award has the effect of a final judgment, and it can be enforced immediately by an execution judgment,[157] subject only, at the time of the application for execution, to specified objections:[158]

Motion for cancellation of an award shall be made in the following cases:

(1) In case an arbitration procedure should not be allowed [*i.e.,* the issue is not legally arbitrable];

(2) In case an award condemns a party to perform an act the performance of which is prohibited by law;

(3) In case the parties were not represented in accordance with the provisions of law;

(4) In case the parties were not examined in the arbitration procedure;

(5) In case the award is not accompanied by reasons;

(6) In the case of Article 420 items (4) and (8) inclusive, there exist

conditions allowing a suit for retrial [Art. 420 deals with grounds for retrial (*saishin*) such as false evidence, etc.].

Cancellation of an award shall not be made for reasons mentioned in items (4) and (5) of this Article in case parties have otherwise agreed.

Notably, a Japanese award is "final and enforceable" even though a revision action (*saishin*) may be brought (Art. 803) for certain very special reasons (Art. 801[6]) for as long as five years after the execution of judgment (Art. 804).

Regarding the third treaty standard (public policy), there are no American cases involving Japanese awards, but the cases in which domestic awards have been set aside as against public policy will give an idea of the standard that American courts would use in applying the public policy criterion in the treaty.[159] Generally "public policy" in the U.S. courts has meant a modicum of review of points of law, despite generalizations disclaiming any power to do so. Courts have, therefore, been criticized[160] for its use, but actually few awards have been set aside on public policy grounds; most of them have been in labor cases.[161]

Concerning recognition of a U.S. award in Japan under the FCN treaty provisions, of course, in Japanese courts, the three treaty standards similarly control the *recognition* of American awards. There are three cases that shed some light on the Japanese courts' application of the treaty, although only one of them dealt specifically with an American award under the treaty.

Concerning the first treaty criterion, a recent case[162] in the Tokyo District Court is interesting. The challenged award was a domestic award rendered ex parte in Tokyo, and the court enforced it against allegations that there had been no arbitration contract between the parties and that the defendant had not been served with proper notice. The court, as a matter of course, passed on the issue challenging the existence of an arbitral contract, and there is no reason to believe it would not do so where the point is properly raised in enforcing an American award. But there is an opinion among Japanese, it seems, supporting the rule that arbitral clauses are to be treated as separably valid and that questions going to the validity of the container contract should be committed to the arbitrator as long as the validity of the clause itself is not challenged in court.

Under the second treaty criterion, a Japanese court must look to the American law to determine finality and enforceability when asked to enforce an American award. "American" law has its usual multiplicities, but taking the U.S. Federal Arbitration Act[163] as an example, Section 9 provides that a party may within one year obtain a confirmation judgment unless the award is vacated, modified, or corrected as prescribed in Sections 10 and 11. On the question of finality, Section 12 provides that all motions to vacate, modify, or correct an award must be served upon the adverse party within three months after the award is filed or delivered to the parties. The grounds for vacation are set out in Section 10,[164] and grounds for modification or correction are found in Section 11.[165]

The case of *American President Lines* v. *C. Subra K.K.*[166] is the only precedent where the Japanese court has enforced an American award under the FCN Treaty (1954). The award was obtained in New York under the U.S. Arbitration Act on a claim for demurrage on a ship chartered by APL to a Japanese corporation, C. Subra K.K. (correctly romanized from Japanese "Subura" and actually spelled by the defendant "Soubra"[167]). The award was confirmed by the New York federal District Court in a judgment that added interest at 6 percent from the date of the award until payment. APL then sought enforcement of the judgment in the Tokyo District Court, which recognized the award and granted an execution judgment in an opinion that sheds little light on the application of the treaty.

The case is interesting on three collateral points; first, since it enforced the award rather than the judgment (defective because of interest added illegally), the court indicated that the doctrine of merger is not accepted in Japanese law; hence, even though the confirming judgment may be defective, the underlying award can be enforced. Second, from the standpoint of tactics, the facts of the case show the advantage of having first obtained a U.S. judgment confirming the award, even though such judgment may be unenforceable in Japan. This advantage is that the U.S. court hearings and the running of formal appeal periods, necessarily entailed in obtaining the U.S. judgment, will foreclose for practical purposes most legal challenges against the underlying award in Japanese enforcement proceedings. Third, the opinion shows the difficulty in proving the foreign law and its effect on award (and judgment) enforcement abroad.[168]

Regarding the third treaty criterion (public policy), the recent Japanese case[169] (*Casaregi*) involving Japanese court enforcement of an English award indicates that Japanese courts will probably make very limited use of public policy arguments to defeat foreign awards. In that case, the Japanese defendant, who was the buyer under a contract to purchase a ship from an Italian seller, lost an arbitration conducted in London under "third country" law (English) as specified in the contract. In fact, he refused to appoint an arbitrator and refused, though properly notified, to attend or be represented at the hearing. Notwithstanding, he was found by a sole arbitrator, acting properly under the English Arbitration Act,[170] to have breached his duty to obtain the required Japanese government approval for his purchase, thus causing the sale to fail and causing the plaintiff damages (20,966 pounds). Against defendant's argument that such an award was against Japanese public policy on a number of grounds, including the defendant's absence from the hearing, the court enforced the award and held that it did not violate Japanese public policy because the defendant was absent by choice. Also, the court held that the criteria for enforceability were not to be sought in Japanese Code of Civil Procedure, Art. 801, but in the treaty (here the 1958 UN Convention). One would expect Japanese courts to treat public policy challenges to American awards similarly under the FCN Treaty.

The FCN Treaty does not solve a practical lawyer's problem of proof by specifying the methods of proving[171] validity for purposes of recognition abroad, nor does it distribute the burden of proof[172] to favor the winner of an award, as is done in the UN Convention. With the convention now applicable to U.S.-Japanese trade, these proof problems at the stage of recognition will be more easily handled where it is applicable than where the FCN alone applies.

Foreign Awards: Procedures for Execution Thereof

Execution of Awards under the 1970 FAA and the UN Convention /
Once a foreign award covered by the UN Convention is recognized under FAA §207, then presumably the usual procedures for execution of federal judgments are available. The major advantage of the 1970 act is that, at the federal level, it supplies the need in the U.S. for procedures to *recognize* certain foreign awards, thus overcoming the parochialism of the old statutory law (9 USCA §9), which provided for recognition of only domestic awards.

When the UN Convention does not apply, the limitations of §9 to domestic awards leave a gap in the federal statutory law and raise awkward questions for federal courts when requested to recognize and enforce a foreign award entitled to recognition under the FCN Treaty. To honor the treaty commitments, must the federal courts, when properly petitioned, fashion federal common-law rules for recognition of foreign (FCN) awards? Do the federal courts have jurisdiction? If so, is it limited to diversity cases? And, if so, do they then apply state rules for enforcement? These are all questions unanswered after half a century under the federal statute and two decades under the FCN Treaty. The lack of federal experience can be attributed to the lack of positive federal provisions, a situation that forces parties to seek other remedies. Either the winners in a foreign arbitration have confirmed their awards abroad and then sought federal execution on the resultant judgment, or they have sought enforcement of the foreign award in the state courts. We will consider experience concerning execution of foreign awards in the U.S. (mostly the state courts) and in Japan.

FCN Treaty / On the question of execution, the FCN Treaty provides that "such awards [*i.e.,* those which are recognized as valid] shall be entitled to the privileges and measures of enforcement appertaining to awards rendered locally." In the U.S., "locally" has its usual federalistic complications, and we have alluded to the inadequacies of the old FAA (§9) to enforce foreign awards. But the treaty provides also that Japanese awards are entitled in state courts "to the same measure of recognition as awards rendered in other states," meaning sister states of the U.S. We have noted that, unlike some foreign countries,[173] neither Japan[174] nor the U.S.[175] will enforce even a domestic award directly; nor does either country have rules applicable to foreign awards as such (except the U.S. provisions in the new 1970 act). But actions for an execution judgment on a foreign award are generally brought under the procedures for domestic awards in the competent domestic court, unless, as in the case of the federal law, the provisions are difficult to apply to foreign awards. The states will apparently grant a judgment on an award, although the scope of judicial review practiced in various states at this stage is actually quite varied, despite common generalizations to the effect that awards are not reviewable on the merits, either on issues of fact or law.[176]

The FCN Treaty does not mean that a prior confirmation action under Japanese procedure would strengthen the award by entitling it to "full faith and credit" in an enforcement proceeding in those state courts in which such an award would otherwise be more strictly reviewed. It is a local question whether such a Japanese judgment would receive more favorable treatment than an award.[177] But where an American defendant's property located in a progressive state is insufficient to satisfy a Japanese award, perhaps the award could be reduced to judgment there, and then that sister state's judgment would be entitled to full faith and credit in a state that otherwise practices strict legal review of all awards.

In Japan, a very recent decision[178] of the Tokyo District Court upheld and granted under Code of Civil Procedure, Art. 802, an execution judgment on a domestic award against the defendant, a foreign party. After the adverse award, the defendant in the arbitration brought two court actions seeking to nullify the award by voiding the arbitration contract. In one action he sued as an individual and in the other as a firm. His defense was that he acted only as an agent for a foreign company. Then the winner in the arbitration brought a court action under Code of Civil Procedure, Art. 802, for an execution judgment on the award. The court consolidated these three actions, dismissed the attack against the arbitral contract, and granted an execution judgment on the award.

In Japan, the Code of Civil Procedure provides only for domestic awards in Art. 800: "As between the parties the award has the effect of a final and conclusive judgment of a court of justice."

Then Art. 801 provides the grounds for annulling an award, and Art. 802 provides for an execution judgment: "Execution to be undertaken by virtue of an award shall be made only when an execution judgment has been rendered for the admissibility thereof. 2. The foregoing judgment shall not be rendered in case there exists a reason under which cancellation of award may be moved."

In a recent case,[179] involving an English award, the court held that, lacking separate procedures in Japan for the enforcement of foreign awards, the usual procedure for enforcing domestic awards would be applied to avoid rendering the applicable Geneva Convention nugatory. This same domestic procedure should be applied by analogy to executions on American FCN awards in Japan, except that the grounds for nullification in Art. 801 are not applicable, for, as noted above, the FCN (or UN Convention) sets different standards for recognition of the validity of an award.

Conclusion and Sample Clause

In U.S.-Japanese business there is an increasing use of arbitration. Its popularity is based on its own merits and also on the fact that there is a better enforcement framework for trans-Pacific arbitration than there is for U.S.-Japanese litigation. For example, when the arbitration takes place in Japan the proceeding can[180] and probably should be in English because the transactions are handled in English, and English is usually understood by both parties. This is not legally possible in the courts in which the proceeding and evidence must be in Japanese—a much more onerous requirement for the foreigner than most monolingual "outsiders" (*gaijin*) might imagine; whereas the inconvenience to Japanese parties from arbitrating in English, though sometimes considerable, will be reduced by the fact that their international dealings are almost invariably documented in English and the transactions conducted in English.

As has been seen, the UN Convention and 1970 FAA have limited the risks of restrictive state law by clarifying federal jurisdiction, venue, removal, and power of enforcement of arbitration abroad; also the FCN Treaty solution to the trans-Pacific legal vacuum has been to neutralize the stigma of foreignness and to rely on domestic remedies in both countries to enforce arbitral contracts and awards. The domestic provisions are quite adequate in Japan, and the same is true in all major U.S. jurisdictions. Indeed, recent case law trends may ultimately even extend the coverage of the U.S. federal act to disputes in U.S.-Japanese "commerce" handled by those state courts that cannot now enforce arbitration under their own law. But this will depend on future U.S. Supreme Court decisions to resolve questions left open in the *Prima Paint* case (*supra*) regarding the full implication of the constitutional "commerce" rationale of the federal act. Where the UN Convention does not apply, interesting questions arise: Can the U.S. Federal Arbitration Act, Section 2, be an independent basis (without diversity) for federal subject matter jurisdiction over disputes in "commerce"? Must Section 2 then be applied in enforcement of arbitral agreements involving commerce in state courts?

Whatever the U.S. Supreme Court may eventually decide, it is clear that the basic formulae for integrating arbitration into the legal systems of the U.S. and Japan are sufficiently different to require specific attention in drafting arbitral clauses. The same may be said for differences (*e.g.*, the Japanese preference for compromise) in the approach to the arbitral proceeding itself. The most important differences are (1) the federalistic pattern (and gaps) in "American" arbitration law, (2) the degree of reliance on written reasons in Japanese arbitration results, as opposed to the tendency to avoid explicit reason in American awards, and (3) the U.S. separability doctrine that dilutes court control over arbitration at the threshold. In American practice, judicial control only goes to review of threshold questions (validity and scope) to insure that the parties have agreed to arbitrate, now in law, if not in theory, weakened by the separability doctrine. In AAA commercial arbitrations, such an agreement means, in enforcement proceedings, that the parties have bargained away their substantive law rights to the extent that they are not observed voluntarily by the arbitrators.

No doubt American arbitrators, though often not legally trained, intend in most cases to render an award consistent with the legal rights of the parties. No doubt some American parties expect a result consistent with their legal rights. To the extent that this is true, there is much to be said for a choice-of-law clause and appointment of lawyers as arbitrators so that the arbitrator knows some law and which law to apply. There is also much to be said for stipulating the law that the arbitrator may know best. For example, one problem with appointing third-country arbitrators (*i.e.,* ICC rules)[181] is that they are therefore unlikely to be expert with either of the laws most relevant to a bilateral transaction. After such precautions to assure that the arbitrators can apply relevant law, there is then much to be said for restricting court review to threshold consent, because further control would tend to cancel out the benefits of arbitration by adding litigation on top of arbitration. This theory underlies American arbitration, and it is also authorized in Japanese law, but its effectiveness in Japan is enhanced by the parties' agreement not to have reasons stated in the award.

Given these different methods of integrating arbitral and judicial remedies in the American and Japanese legal systems, arbitration clauses must be tailored to fit the U.S.-Japanese context. There are four points that might better be handled specially in the arbitral clause rather than waiting for the eventuation of prospectively unpredictable results imbedded in the procedures of the general clause recommended by the AAA-JCAA agreement. First, the place of arbitration should be specified, if at all possible; but often, unfortunately, the parties cannot agree on this delicate point and prefer to leave it ambiguous. Second, the law governing the container contract, the arbitration clause, and all phases of the arbitration proceeding and award should be specified, and in most cases should be the same law and the law of the arbitrator, if possible. Third, arbitrators should then be freed specifically from the Japanese law requirement of reasoning in their awards. Reasoned results are important in most methods of settling disputes; but the point here is that the enforcement of reasoned results tends to suffocate arbitration with legal action, causing its alleged advantages to disappear. If the parties really want a reasoned result, they might better litigate from the beginning. Fourth, rather than a general catch-all clause, parties should draft a provision expressive of their own needs. For example, if the place of arbitration is New York, they may want to consider a specific clause reserving threshold questions for the court and specifying that the arbitral clause is not intended to be "separable." We suspect that a behavioral study, which the court did not have in the *Prima Paint* case, would show that very few enterprisers ever dreamed of "separability" so that arbitrators could determine questions of mistake, lack of mutuality, or fraud in the container contract.

No boiler-plate clause will fit all purposes, nor will it fit any individual contract relationship perfectly. Complex long-term relationships, particularly, will benefit from specially drafted arbitral clauses. Nevertheless, all or part of the following provisions, which we have built around the AAA-JCAA clause, may prove helpful in solving the four problems mentioned above:

Settlement of Disputes

1. This clause is an integral part of this entire contract and is not separable and has no independent validity.

2. Questions of validity of this contract and the scope of this arbitral clause are reserved for the court, but if such questions are raised and decided in court, the loser shall pay all costs including a reasonable fee for the winner's attorney.

3. All other disputes, controversies, or differences which may arise between the parties, out of or in relation to or in connection with this contract, or for breach thereof, shall be finally settled by arbitration pursuant to the Japan-American Trade Arbitration Agreement, of 16 September 1952, by which each party hereto is bound except as modified by these provisions.

4. All arbitrations will be held in English in _____ (city), and this sales contract (including this arbitral clause), and all arbitral proceedings and awards hereunder, will be governed by the internal law of _____ (usually the place of arbitration).

5. The parties hereto also agree that they will instruct, and, by this provision in this contract, they do hereby instruct, the arbitrator in any proceeding hereunder to make his decision in accordance with the governing law but not to specify his reasoning in his award.

Such a clause would integrate litigation and arbitration only on the critical issue of consent. Parties wishing the efficiencies of arbitration can, therefore, have them by conscious choice; however, at the same time, they must give up certain judicial protections that are inconsistent with arbitral efficacy. Finally, the courts must continue to scrutinize the legality and factual basis for consent whenever a party raises the issue, for the policy of both Japanese and U.S. law is to allow the parties to choose arbitration as a substitute for a lawsuit—not as a substitute for the legal system itself.[182]

Appendixes
Notes
Glossary
Bibliography
Index

Appendix I

Table 1. *Distribution of Foreign-Related Firms by Industry*

I. *Manufacturing Industries*	*Number of Foreign-Related Companies (1968)*	*Number in 1971*
Food products	17	24
Textiles	10	10
Paper and pulp	5	5
Chemicals	73	115
Pharmaceuticals	14	24
Petroleum	7	10
Rubber goods	7	5
Porcelain, glass, and cement	10	15
Nonferrous metals	11	12
Metal goods	12	17
General machinery	65	112
Electrical machinery	26	50
Transportation machinery	2	18
Precision machinery	11	19
Others	16	33
SUBTOTAL (*manufacturing*)	286	469
II. *Commercial Enterprises* (*Sales and service*)	111	223 (Sales) 65 (Service)
III. *Other Productive Industries* (*Sangyo*)[a]	57	19
TOTAL	454	776

SOURCE: From *Gaishi-kei kigyō* (1968), p. 5, and MITI, *Gaishi-kei kigyō no dōkō* (1971), p. 5.

a. The category "Other Productive Industries" includes construction, poultry raising, mining, advertising, and the like—mostly, in fact, foreign businesses of minor scope.

Table 2. Kind of Foreign Interest

Category	Number (*1968*)	Number (*1971*)
Purely foreign companies (mostly minor "commercial")	118	220
Joint-venture companies (mostly Japanese controlled)	285	502
Companies with foreign capital introduced (all Japanese controlled)	51	54
TOTAL	454	776

SOURCE: From *Gaishi-kei kigyō* (1968), p. 6, and *Gaishi-kei kigyō no dōkō* (1971), p. 3.

Table 3. Foreigner's Share Ratio

Foreign Holdings	Number (*1968*)	Number (*1971*)
Under 30%	42	31 (over 20%)
30% to 50%	156	236
50%	103	232
Over 50% to under 95%	31	57
95% and over	122	220
TOTAL	454	776

SOURCE: From *Gaishi-kei kigyō* (1968), p. 6, and *Gaishi-kei kigyō no dōkō* (1971), p. 3.

Table 4. Size of Capital of Foreign-Related Firms

In yen (*360 yen to $1.00*)	Number in 1968	Number in 1971
Under 10,000,000 ($27,778)	85	175
Over 10,000,000 and under 50,000,000 ($139,000)	128	228
Over 50,000,000 but under 100,000,000 ($278,000)	49	96
Over 100,000,000 but under 1 billion ($2,778,000)	133	209
Over 1 billion but under 10 billion ($27,778,000)	52	63
Over 10 billion	7	5
TOTAL	454	776

SOURCE: From *Gaishi-kei kigyō* (1968), p. 6, and *Gaishi-kei kigyō no dōkō* (1971), p. 3.

Table 5. *Number of Employees*

9 employees or under	100
10 to 49 employees	132
50 to 299 employees	132
300 to 999 employees	52
1,000 employees or over	38
TOTAL	454

SOURCE: From *Gaishi-kei kigyō* (1968), p. 6.

Table 6. *Number of Direct Investments Validated per Year*[a]

1950	30
1951	38
1952	31
1953	22
1954	16
1955	9
1956	23
1957	22
1958	18
1959	21
1960	34
1961	41
1962	43
1963	92
1964	125
1965	106
1966	142
1967	200
1968	248
1969	391
1970	455
1971	445

SOURCE: Marunouchi Research Center, *Nihon ni okeru gaikoku shihon no jittai* (1972),
a. These figures do not show numbers of companies; rather, they show numbers of stock acquisitions validated annually, including capital increases.

Table 7. Foreign-Related Firms by Industry, Type, and Share Ratio (1968)

Type / Industry	Wholly Owned	Joint Venture						Firms with Foreign Capital Introduced						Total					
Foreign Share	100	Less than 30%	30–50%	50%	51–95%	96–99%	Total	Less than 30%	30–50%	50%	51–95%	96–99%	Total	Less than 30%	30–50%	50%	51–95%	96–99%	Total
Food	8	0	1	5	3	1	10	0	0	0	0	0	0	0	1	5	3	9	18
Textiles	0	1	2	5	1	0	9	0	1	0	0	0	1	1	3	5	1	0	10
Paper and pulp	1	0	2	2	0	0	4	0	0	0	0	0	0	0	2	2	0	1	5
Chemicals	6	5	30	30	3	0	68	2	1	0	1	1	5	7	31	30	4	7	79
Pharmaceuticals	5	0	1	8	2	0	11	0	0	0	0	0	0	0	1	8	2	5	16
Oil	0	0	0	2	0	0	2	0	1	4	0	0	5	0	1	6	0	0	7
Rubber goods	0	0	4	0	0	0	4	2	1	0	0	0	3	2	5	0	0	0	7
Ceramics and earthern ware	0	2	4	3	0	0	9	0	1	0	0	0	1	2	5	3	0	0	10
Nonferrous metal	0	1	9	0	0	0	10	0	0	2	0	0	2	1	9	2	0	0	12
Metal products	0	2	9	2	0	0	13	1	1	0	0	0	2	3	10	2	0	0	15
General machinery	6	3	35	12	4	0	54	4	4	0	4	0	12	7	39	12	8	6	72
Electrical machinery	2	4	18	3	1	0	26	0	0	1	0	0	1	4	18	4	1	2	29
Transportation machinery	0	1	1	0	0	0	2	1	0	0	0	0	1	2	1	0	0	0	3
Precision machinery	0	0	4	3	1	0	8	1	0	0	1	0	4	1	6	3	2	0	12
Other manufactures	3	2	6	2	0	0	10	2	2	0	0	1	4	4	8	2	0	3	17
Sales	79	1	14	16	12	1	44	1	3	1	5	1	11	2	17	17	17	81	134
Other (services)	43	3	11	7	4	0	25	3	3	0	0	0	6	6	14	7	4	42	73
TOTAL	153	25	151	100	31	2	309	17	20	8	11	2	58	42	171	108	42	156	519

SOURCE: From *Gaishi-kei kigyō* (1968), p. 265.

Table 8. Foreign Firms by Industry, Type, and Capital (1968)

Type	Wholly Owned							Joint Venture							Firms with Foreign Capital Introduced							Total						
Foreign Share / Industry	I	II	III	IV	V	VI	Total	I	II	III	IV	V	VI	Total	I	II	III	IV	V	VI	Total	I	II	III	IV	V	VI	Total
Food	2	2	0	2	2	0	8	0	5	2	2	1	0	10	0	0	0	0	0	0	0	2	7	2	4	3	0	18
Textiles	0	0	0	0	0	0	0	0	2	3	2	2	0	9	0	0	0	1	0	0	1	0	2	3	3	2	0	10
Paper and pulp	1	0	0	0	0	0	1	0	0	0	2	2	0	4	0	0	0	0	0	0	0	1	0	0	2	2	0	5
Chemicals	0	1	2	3	0	0	6	6	10	3	38	11	0	68	0	1	0	2	2	0	5	6	12	5	43	13	0	79
Pharmaceuticals	1	2	1	1	0	0	5	0	2	3	2	4	0	11	0	0	0	0	0	0	0	1	4	4	3	4	0	16
Oil	0	0	0	0	0	0	0	0	0	0	0	2	0	2	0	0	0	0	2	3	5	0	0	0	0	4	3	7
Rubber goods	0	0	0	0	0	0	0	0	1	0	2	1	0	4	0	0	0	1	2	0	3	0	1	0	3	3	0	7
Ceramics and earthen ware	0	0	0	0	0	0	0	0	2	2	3	2	0	9	0	0	0	0	1	0	1	0	2	2	3	3	0	10
Nonferrous metal	0	0	0	0	0	0	0	0	1	0	6	3	0	10	0	0	0	0	1	1	2	0	1	0	6	4	1	12
Metal products	0	0	0	0	0	0	0	1	3	3	6	0	0	13	0	1	0	1	0	0	2	1	4	3	7	0	0	15
General machinery	2	2	1	1	0	0	6	10	21	4	17	1	1	54	2	2	0	5	3	0	12	14	25	5	23	4	1	72
Electrical machinery	0	0	0	1	0	1	2	0	4	4	16	2	0	26	0	0	0	0	1	0	1	0	4	4	17	3	1	29
Transportation machinery	0	0	0	0	0	0	0	0	0	0	2	0	0	2	0	0	0	0	0	1	1	0	0	0	2	0	1	3
Precision machinery	0	0	0	0	0	0	0	0	3	1	4	0	0	8	0	2	1	0	1	0	4	0	5	2	4	1	0	12
Other manufactures	1	1	0	1	0	0	3	2	5	1	2	0	0	10	0	0	0	4	0	0	4	3	6	1	7	0	0	17
Sales	35	21	10	9	4	0	79	9	20	6	9	0	0	44	6	3	1	1	0	0	11	50	44	17	19	4	0	134
Other (services)	22	14	2	2	2	0	42	9	11	3	1	0	1	25	0	5	0	0	1	0	6	31	30	5	3	3	1	73
TOTAL	64	43	16	20	8	1	152	37	90	35	114	31	2	309	8	14	2	15	15	4	58	109	147	53	149	54	7	519

SOURCE: From *Gaishi-kei kigyō* (1968), p. 266.

NOTE: I—Under 10 million yen ($27,800)
II—More than 10 less than 50 million yen ($139,000)
III—More than 50 less than 100 million yen ($278,000)
IV—More than 100 million less than 1 billion yen ($2,778,000)
V—More than 1 billion less than 10 billion yen ($27,778,000)
VI—Over 10 billion yen ($27,778,000)

Appendix II

*Foreign Firms with Majority Holdings (100 Million Yen +)
in Japanese Joint Ventures*

		Paid in Capital (*1 million yen*)	Percentage Held by Foreign Company
1965–67	Esso Standard Eastern, Inc.	7,000.	100
1951–65	National Cash Register Co.	4,000.	64.7
1951–63	Shell Petroleum Co., Ltd.	2,430.	100
1960–67	L'Air Liquide Société Anonyme l'Etude et l'Exploitation des Procédés Georges Claude Société d'Osygene et d'Actylene d'Extrême Orient	2,222.6	82.33
1966	Nestlé Alimentana, S.A. Participations Industriellis afib, S.A. Itag, S.A.	1,680.	100
1963–67	Unilever N.V.	1,500.	70
1967	Japan Light Metals (Nihon Keikinzoku K.K.)	1,012.	59.5
1961–68	Bell & Howell Co.	864.	75
1965–67	H. J. Heinz Co.	725.	80
1966	General Foods Corp.	622.6	100
1965–66	Olivetti International, S.A.	540.	100
1966	Duco Aktiengesellschaft Schering Asia GmbH	495.	100
1951–65	Carrier Corp.	450.	75
1954–66	Radio Corporation of America	444.	100
1965–67	Siber Hegner & Co., Ltd.	400.	100
1970	Bulova Watch Co.	360.	51
1964–67	British United Shoe Machinery Co., Ltd.	300.	100
1965	Kellogg Co.	300.	100

		Paid in Capital (1 million yen)	Percentage Held by Foreign Company
1951–52	Otis Elevator Co.	300.	80
1965	F. W. Woolworth Co.	270.	79
1966	Sandoz, Ltd.	250.	100
1966–67	S. C. Johnson & Son, Ltd.	237.5	97
1951	J. & P. Coats, Ltd.	210.	60
1966	Bristol Laboratories International, S.A.	200.	100
1970	Donald B. Poynter	200.	81
1970	Sybron Corp.	192.	100
1972	Dmark Caribbean, Inc.	175.	100
1960	Ciba, Ltd.	170.	100
1970	Kaiser Trading Co.	160.	100
1956	Farbenfabriken Bayer A.G.	150.	82
1960	Gulf and Western Industries, Inc.	150.	100
1970	Th Muhlethaler, S.A. Givaudan Far East, Ltd.	150. Givaudan—35; Muhlethaler— 40; Atlantic Industries—25	100
1970	Agriculture and Fishery Development Corp.	142.9	100
1971	Olivier, International, S.A.	125.	100
1966–67	Pepsi-Cola Co.	120.	100
1969	Esso Hotels & Restaurants Far East, Inc.	100.	100
1966	Farbwerke Hoechst Aktiengesellschaft Vormals Maister Lusius & Bruning	100.	100
1951	Linen Thread Co., Ltd.	100.	60
1964	Productos Natuales y Senteticos, S.A.	100.	60
1967	Rhone-Poulene, S.A.	100.	75

SOURCE: Selected from *Gaishi donyū nenkan* (1968–69), pp. 190–223; MRC, *Nihon ni okeru gaikoku shihon no jittai*, Appendix, p. 62 (1972); MITI, *Gaishi-kei kigyō no dōkō* (1971), pp. 154–77.

Appendix III

Foreign Firms with Fifty-Fifty Holdings (100 Million Yen or More) in Foreign-Related Joint Ventures

		Paid in Capital (1 billion yen)
1963–66	Caterpillar Overseas, S.A.	16.800
1961	Aluminum, Ltd.	10.976
1951–59	California Texas Oil Corp.	8.000
1960	E. I. DuPont de Nemours & Co.	6.480
1950–67	California Texas Oil Corp.	4.800
1951–63	Anglo-Saxon Petroleum Co., Ltd.	4.500
1952–66	Dow Chemical International A.G.	4.000
1960–63	Union Carbide Corp.	3.600
1960	E. I. DuPont de Nemours & Co.	3.510
1951–62	Dunlop Rubber Co., Ltd.	3.000
1963	Monsanto Chemical Co.	3.000
1964–67	Kimberly Clark Corp.	2.304
1953–66	Pfizer Corp.	2.130
1959–68	Minneapolis-Honeywell Regulator Co.	2.100
1970	Union Carbide Corp.	1.800
1963–64	Scott Paper Co.	1.620
1963	E. I. DuPont de Nemours & Co.	1.440
1967	International Harvester Co.	1.110
1969	Ford Motor Co.	1.080
1970	The Goodyear Tire & Rubber Co.	1.080
1971	General Electric	1.000
1967	Mobil Petroleum Co., Inc.	1.000
1964	Phillips Petroleum Co.	.900
1963	Universal Oil Products Co.	.830
1969	Farbenfabriken Bayer A.G.	.800
1968	Frueharif International, Ltd. and Nihon Keikinzoku	.800
1963–64	Rank Xerox, Ltd.	.800
1968	Columbia Broadcasting System, Inc.	.720
1963	E. I. DuPont de Nemours & Co.	.720
1967	Esso Eastern Chemical, Inc.	.720
1964	Continental Oil Co.	.600

		Paid in Capital (*1 billion yen*)
1969	Kearney & Trecher Corp.	.600
1953	American Cyanamid Co.	.560
1946–71	Superscope, Inc.	.560
1971	Burlington Industries, Inc.	.540
1971	Crown Zellerbach International, Inc.	.500
1970	Honeywell, Inc.	.500
1972	Kawachi Berylco, Inc.	.422
1970	Crown Zellerbach International, Inc.	.400
1965	Eli Lilly & Co.	.400
1970	Kraftco Corporation	.400
1970	Anery Products Corp.	.360
1971	Control Data Corp.	.360
1964	Cyprus Mines Corp.	.360
1961	Mineo Corp., Ltd.	.360
1968	Norton Co.	.360
1966	Owens-Illinois, Inc.	.360
1970	Uniroyal, Inc.	.360
1964	Utah Construction & Mining Corp.	.360
1964	Chemetron Corp.	.355
1967	Hercules, Inc.	.350
1966	General Electric Co.	.342
1970	Norton Co.	.340
1965	American Can Co.	.300
1967	Farbwerke Hoechst Aktiengesellschaft Vormals Maister Lusius und Bruning	.300
1967	Sola Basic Industries, Inc.	.252
1969	Encyclopaedia Britannica, Inc.	.250
1968	Phillips Petroleum Co.	.250
1966–67	Deutsche Gold-und Sillbel-Scheideanstalt Vormals Roessler	.240
1967	Huck Manufacturing Co.	.220
1969	Bureau Engraving, Inc.	.200
1969	Lips N.V.	.200
1972	Carl Zeiss Co., Ltd.	.200
1971	Société des Electrodes et Réfractaires	.200
1965	Stauffer Chemical Co.	.200
1970	Union Carbide Corp.	.200
1968	United Shoes Machinery Corp. (George Tucker Eyelet Co., Ltd.)	.200
1970	U.S.M. Corp.	.200
1971	Bailey Meter Co.	.180
1970	Economics Laboratory International, Inc.	.180

		Paid in Capital (*1 billion yen*)
1966–67	Englehard Hanova, Inc.	.180
1967	Vender, Ltd.	.180
1965	Singer Co.	.160
1964	Borg Warner Corp.	.150
1966	British Paints (Holding), Ltd.	.150
1971	H. B. Fuller Co.	.150
1965	General Mills, Inc.	.150
1966	United Shore Machinery Corp.	.150
1963–64	Beckman Instrument, Inc.	.144
1966	Dow Corning International, Ltd.	.144
1970	Chemische Werk Huls, A.G.	.140
1970	Bryant Grinder Corp.	.125
1971	N. V. Philips-Duphor	.125
1971	British Oxygen Co.	.120
1966	General Mills, Inc.	.120
1970	Borden, Inc.	.108
1966	Elastomer A.G.	.108
1968	Samuel Moore & Co.	.108
1963	Armour & Co.	.100
1971	Artosinter Machinery Corp., S.A.	.100
1966	AMF Overseas Corp., S.A.	.100
1970	Ballast Nedom Groep, N.V.	.100
1970	Bopparder Machinenbaugesellschaft	.100
1971	P. Beiersdorf and Co., A.G.	.100
1965	Donaldson Co.	.100
1970	Eckhart Werke Standard Brenzepulver-werk	.100
1969	Eko Products, Inc.	.100
1971	Emery Air Freight Corp.	.100
1972	Essilor International	.100
1965	W. R. Grace & Co.	.100
1972	Loreal Société Anonyme	.100
1969	Mine Safety Appliances Co.	.100
1969	Pacemaker Corporation	.100
1965	Panalfab Pacific, Inc.	.100
1971	Schenck Maschinen, A.G.	.100
1971	Signode Corp.	.100
1970	Siemens Asia Investment, A.G.	.100
1965	Tektronix, Inc.	.100
1966	United Carr, Inc.	.100

SOURCE: Selected from *Gaishi donyū nenkan* (1968–69), pp. 190–223; MRC, *Nihon ni okeru gaikoku shihon no jittai*, Appendix, p. 62 (1972); MITI, *Gaishi-kei kigyō no dōkō* (1971), pp. 154–77.

Appendix IV

World Enterprises in Japan

(Top Ten World Enterprises in Twelve Major Industries, Showing Those with Japanese Operations)

Foods	Japanese Operation	Textiles	Japanese Operation
Unilever (Eur.)	yes	Burlington Ind.	yes
Swift		Courtaulds (Eur.)	
Armour	yes	Stevens (J.P.)	yes
N.D.P.		A.K.U. [AKZO] (Eur.)	
Nestlé (Eur.)	yes	United Merchants & Mfg.	
Gen'l Goods	yes	J. & P. Coats	yes
Borden	yes	West Point-Pepperell	
Corn Prod.	yes	Philadelphia Reading	
Wilson		Snia Viscosa (Eur.)	
Coca-Cola	yes	Kaysen-Roth	

Paper and Pulp		Chemical	
International Paper	yes	DuPont	yes
Weyerhaeuser	yes	I.C.I. (Eur.)	yes
Crown Zellerbach	yes	Proctor & Gamble	yes
St. Regis Paper		Union Carbide C.	yes
Reed Paper Group (Eur.)		Montecatini-Edison (Eur.)	
Mead	yes	Eastman Kodak	yes
Kimberly-Clark	yes	Monsanto	yes
Bowater Paper (Eur.)		Hoechst	yes
Scott Paper	yes	Bayer	yes
MacMillan Bloedel (Can.)		Dow	yes

Drugs		Oil	
American Home Product	yes	Standard Oil (N.J.)	yes
Pfizer	yes	Shell (Eur.)	yes
Roche	yes	Mobil Oil	yes
Rexall Drug & Chemical		Texaco	yes
Warner Lambert	yes	Gulf Oil	yes
Merck	yes	Shell Oil	yes
Sterling Drug	yes	Standard Oil (Ind.)	
Lilly	yes	Standard Oil (Cal.)	yes

365

Drugs	Japanese Operation	Oil	Japanese Operation
Abbott Laboratories	yes	British Pet. (Eur.)	
Upjohn	yes	Continental Oil	yes

Rubber Goods		Ceramics, etc.	
Goodyear	yes	Pittsburgh Plate Glass	yes
Firestone	yes	Owens-Illinois	yes
Uniroyal	yes	Saint-Gobain (Eur.)	
B. F. Goodrich	yes	Johns-Manville	yes
General Tire & Rubber		Corning-Glassworks	yes
Dunlop (Eur.)	yes	Owens-Corning Fiberglass	yes
Pirelli (Eur.)		Associated Portland	
Michelin (Eur.)		Cement (Eur.)	
Continental Gunmi-		U.S. Gypsum	
Werke (Eur.)		Libbey-Owens-Ford Glass	yes
Armstrong		National Gypsum	

Electrical Machinery		Transportation Equipment	
G.E.	yes	G.M.	yes
I.B.M.	yes	Ford	
Western Elect.		Chrysler	yes
Westinghouse	yes	V.W. (Eur.)	
R.C.A.	yes	Boeing	yes
Gen'l Tel. E.	yes	Lockheed	yes
Philips (Eur.)	yes	North-American	
I.T.T.	yes	General Dynamics	
Siemens (Eur.)	yes	Fiat (Eur.)	
Sperry-Rand	yes	United Aircraft	

Nonferrous Metals		General Machinery	
Alcoa	yes	Int. Harvester	yes
Anaconda	yes	Caterpillar	yes
Alcan (Can.)	yes	Gutehoffnung (Eur.)	
Metallgesellschaft (W. Ger.)	yes	Deere	
Reynolds Metals	yes	Singer	yes
Pechiney		F.M.C.	yes
Kaiser	yes	N.C.R.	yes
National Lead		Massey-Ferguson (Can.)	
Kennecott		Allis Chalmers	
Inter. Nickel (Eur.)	yes	S.K.F. (Swed.)	

SOURCE: From *Gaishi-kei kigyō* (1969), p. 21, plus supplementation from MITI, *Gaishi-kei kigyō no dōkō*, p. 62.

Appendix V

Profitability of 100 Leading Foreign-Related Firms in Japan
(*1971 Tax Filings*)

Company	Income Tax Returns (*$1,000*)	Foreign Capital Ratio (*percent*)
IBM Japan	127,685	100
Coca-Cola Japan	58,853	100
Nestlé Japan	34,662	100
Toa Nenryo Kogyo	27,285	50
Nippon Petroleum Refining	23,811	50
Fuji Xerox	23,133	50
National Cash Register (Japan)	22,944	70
Matsushita Electronics	22,415	35
Nippon Brunswick	19,448	50
AMF-C. Itoh Bowling	13,801	50
Japan Upjohn	11,918	55
Showa Oil	11,620	50
Pfizer Taito	11,282	80
Nippon Univac	10,646	40
Max Factor	10,464	100
Mitsubishi Oil	10,305	50
Asahi-Dow	9,993	50
Yokohama Rubber	7,951	33.6
Toyo Ink Mfg.	7,688	21
Esso Standard Sekiyu	7,353	100
Shell Sekiyu	7,318	100
Lederle Japan	7,055	50
Shinko-Pfaudler	6,944	33.3
Sumitomo 3M	6,899	50
Revlon	6,636	100
Caterpillar Mitsubishi	6,480	50

Company	Income Tax Returns ($1,000)	Foreign Capital Ratio (percent)
AMP (Japan)	6,444	100
Nippon Merck-Banyu	5,824	50
Yamatake-Honeywell	5,805	50
Mobil Sekiyu	5,568	100
Nippon Oil Seal Industry	4,857	25
Nippon Light Metal	4,694	50
Sumitomo Rubber Industries	4,386	43.7
Nihon Schering	4,142	99
Teijin Hercules Chemical Industry	4,103	49
Sega Enterprises	3,935	100
Polyplastics	3,915	45
Mitsui Polychemicals	3,532	50
Karonite Chemical	3,431	45
Nippon Polaroid	3,415	100
Oki Univac	3,133	49
Japan Elanco	3,107	50
Parke-Davis	3,003	100
Texas Instruments Japan	2,822	50
Mitsubishi Monsanto Chemical	2,821	50
Kao-Atlas	2,779	49
Teikoku Sanso	2,740	82.3
Nihon Tokushu Noyaku Seizo	2,720	50
Parke-Davis & Sankyo	2,659	50
Japan Vilene	2,629	28.2
Nippon-Lubrizol Industries	2,594	45
Tokyo Organic Chemical Industries	2,490	47.5
AMF Japan	2,483	100
Toshiba Musical Industries	2,448	50
Nippon Unicar	2,373	50
Koa Oil	2,227	50
Japan Tupperware	2,214	100
Pepsi-Cola (Japan)	2,211	100
Gadelius	2,159	100
CBS-Sony Records	2,064	50
Toyo Stauffer Chemical	2,019	50
Yokogawa-Hewlett-Packard	2,019	49
Sony-Tektronix	1,873	50
Mitsui Fluorochemicals	1,857	50
Toppan Moore Business Forms	1,824	45
Sanyo Scott	1,823	50
Bristol Laboratories (Japan)	1,737	100
Ebara-Infilco	1,720	50

Company	Income Tax Returns ($1,000)	Foreign Capital Ratio (percent)
Vendo (Japan)	1,701	75
Toyo Otis Elevator	1,691	80
Hoechst Japan	1,672	100
Kondo Sewing Machine	1,603	35
General Foods	1,587	100
Showa Neoprene	1,532	50
American Drug	1,506	100
Nippon Sealol	1,505	24
Aishin-Warner	1,451	50
Tokyo Nickel	1,438	40
Tokyo Keiki	1,418	31.47
Interpublic-Hakuhodo	1,392	51
Toyo Aluminium	1,383	50
Yuka Badische	1,363	50
Miles-Sankyo	1,344	45
Keisokki Kogyo	1,298	50
Sintobrator	1,282	40
Nisso Master Builders	1,275	50
Security Control	1,162	46.6
Max	1,087	25
American International Under- writers Japan	1,084	100
The Hilton of Japan	1,081	100
Niigata Worthington	1,064	49
Sandoz Pharmaceuticals	1,055	100
Lubrizol Japan	1,042	100
Mitsubishi Acetate	1,019	30
Japan Acrylic Chemical	1,016	47.5
Nippon Goodyear	993	100
Nippon Abbott	967	50
Sanyo Vending Machine	961	40
Glaxo-Fuji Pharmaceuticals Laboratories	912	40
Toshiba Ampex	857	49

SOURCE: *The President Directory, 1973*, (Tokyo: Diamond-Time Pub. Co., 1972).

Appendix VI

*The 100 Largest Japanese Mining-Manufacturing Corporations,
Ranked by Sales*

Rank 1971	Company	Sales ($1,000)	Paid-up Capital ($1,000)	Employees
1	Nippon Steel	3,975,357	746,753	87,755
2	Toyota Motor	3,331,412	137,142	41,024
3	Nissan Motor	3,187,701	139,282	48,413
4	Hitachi	2,541,672	397,214	97,353
5	Matsushita Electric Industrial	2,431,522	148,538	45,930
6	Mitsubishi Heavy Industries	2,268,818	326,327	78,316
7	Nippon Kokan	2,025,899	330,668	43,473
8	Tokyo Shibaura Electric	1,997,217	300,496	72,927
9	Nippon Oil	1,694,801	73,051	3,041
10	Sumitomo Metal Industries	1,416,253	269,402	32,521
11	Mitsubishi Electric	1,348,522	176,870	57,001
12	Kawasaki Steel	1,339,496	289,772	39,963
13	Ishikawajima-Harima Heavy Industries	1,308,607	126,152	36,654
14	Kirin Brewery	1,216,720	93,506	7,704
15	Kobe Steel	1,208,636	247,253	33,451
16	Honda Motor	1,080,944	59,025	18,164
17	Toray Industries	968,925	139,746	25,908
18	Kawasaki Heavy Industries	944,398	136,363	32,932
19	Asahi Chemical Industry	886,506	88,535	20,264
20	Maruzen Oil	878,902	53,327	5,224
21	Toyo Kogyo	878,357	83,454	26,984
22	Sanyo Electric	804,487	81,685	17,245
23	Kanebo	793,467	42,727	22,618
24	Sumitomo Chemical	785,379	145,454	14,767

370

Rank 1971	Company	Sales ($1,000)	Paid-up Capital ($1,000)	Employees
25	Nippon Electric	777,701	129,870	36,530
26	Mitsubishi Chemical Industries	777,048	122,954	9,015
27	Nippon Mining	765,314	79,870	9,477
28	Taiyo Fishery	749,587	48,701	10,349
29	Mitsubishi Oil	741,409	48,701	2,840
30	Komatsu	694,876	77,977	19,000
31	Unitika	694,282	72,483	19,214
32	Teijin	693,551	92,350	13,482
33	Hitachi Shipbuilding & Engineering	674,707	68,051	25,463
34	Toyobo	673,613	91,126	26,994
35	Kubota	657,581	107,967	14,812
36	Isuzu Motor	641,360	123,376	11,369
37	Snow Brand Milk Products	562,516	24,350	10,582
38	Takeda Chemical Industries	556,038	79,269	12,893
39	Showa Denko	540,574	137,012	10,872
40	Fujitsu	532,970	92,324	29,253
41	Daikyo Oil	522,496	19,480	1,748
42	Toa Nenryo Kogyo	516,181	47,772	2,342
43	Bridgestone Tire	510,821	32,467	17,757
44	Sony	502,961	16,386	11,407
45	Sumitomo Electric Industries	496,581	58,441	11,334
46	Ube Industries	493,240	99,350	11,560
47	Furukawa Electric	483,237	48,707	9,479
48	Matsushita Electric Works	481,347	38,961	10,761
49	Suzuki Motor	481,275	38,961	9,815
50	Mitsubihsi Rayon	481,250	49,025	9,145
51	Mitsui Shipbuilding & Engineering	474,600	65,584	14,844
52	Asahi Glass	474,237	93,506	11,609
53	Nissan Shatai	457,577	15,584	6,759
54	Nisshin Steel	453,720	105,194	10,734
55	Showa Oil	449,324	14,610	2,133
56	Sapporo Breweries	445,467	32,727	4,280
57	Ajinomoto	437,574	26,967	6,217
58	Mitsui Toatsu Chemicals	435,675	71,272	9,903
59	Sharp	435,305	37,506	13,834
60	Mitsubishi Metal Mining	419,779	73,051	10,777
61	Meiji Milk Products	412,191	22,727	6,208
62	Fuji Electric	410,383	67,532	22,035
63	Morinaga Milk Industry	404,717	19,480	5,284

Rank 1971	Company	Sales ($1,000)	Paid-up Capital ($1,000)	Employees
64	Hino Motors	392,366	40,519	6,700
65	Dai Nippon Printing	385,688	32,467	10,867
66	Kuraray	378,840	32,467	11,555
67	Fuji Photo Film	376,087	35,834	10,465
68	Mitsui Mining & Smelting	371,740	52,597	9,022
69	Jujo Paper Manufacturing	370,512	24,350	7,765
70	Nippon Denso	368,279	16,655	12,917
71	Shiseido	366,061	11,688	2,737
72	Fuji Heavy Industries	357,980	32,467	13,482
73	Sumitomo Shipbuilding & Machinery	354,948	34,876	11,431
74	Nippon Suisan	354,928	32,467	7,720
75	Toppan Printing	351,116	25,974	8,080
76	Dainippon Ink & Chemicals	337,152	32,467	5,731
77	Nisshin Flour Milling	333,396	19,480	2,915
78	Daihatsu Kogyo	333,243	59,415	8,561
79	Asahi Breweries	332,012	32,727	3,721
80	Sumitomo Metal Mining	331,282	40,944	5,007
81	Mitsubishi Petrochemical	329,610	50,730	5,327
82	Oji Paper	324,707	26,103	4,983
83	Victor Co. of Japan	321,766	17,532	10,809
84	Nippon Gakki	302,727	14,555	13,980
85	Koa Oil	300,873	15,584	1,287
86	Nippon Reizo	297,198	29,220	3,828
87	Hitachi Metals	296,334	24,883	6,606
88	Chiyoda Chemical Engineering & Construction	287,678	8,766	2,874
89	Honshu Paper	283,110	13,639	5,686
90	Sanyo-Kokusaku Pulp	282,512	39,935	5,700
91	Oki Electric Industry	277,211	36,922	15,521
92	Yamaha Motor	268,324	6,250	5,573
93	Sekisui Chemical	267,103	18,418	5,031
94	Hitachi Cable	265,821	32,467	5,150
95	Daido Steel	262,935	40,584	9,398
96	Daishowa Paper Manufacturing	258,616	27,597	5,423
97	Onada Cement	255,847	64,935	3,749
98	Eidai	254,396	15,688	3,971
99	Arabian Oil	252,704	81,168	1,558
100	Japan Steel Works	252,376	40,584	8,606

SOURCE: *The President Directory 1973* (Tokyo: Diamond-Time Pub. Co., 1972), p. 24.

Appendix VII

A. Mitsubishi Keiretsu (1971)

(*Kin'yokai—26 Members*)

Corporation	Total Capital (*1 billion Yen*)	President
Finance		
The Mitsubishi Bank, Ltd. (K.K. Mitsubishi Ginkō)	50.4	Toshio Nakamura
The Mitsubishi Trust & Banking Corporation (Mitsubishi Shintaku Ginkō K.K.)	16.0	Hidetomi Sendo
Meiji Life Insurance (Meiji Seimei Hoken Sōgō Kaisha)	(5th assets rank in Japan)	Yoshimi Seki
Tokyo Marine and Fire Insurance Co., Ltd. (Tokyo Kaijō-Kasai Hoken K.K.)	13.5	Genzaemon Yamamoto
Mining and Industry		
Mitsubishi Mining Co., Ltd. (Mitsubishi Kōgyō K.K.)	7.5	Bumpei Ōtsuki
Mitsubishi Metal Mining Co., Ltd. (Mitsubishi Kinzoku Kōgyō K.K.)	22.5	Mitsuo Aikyō
Mitsubishi Heavy Industries, Ltd. (Mitsubishi Jūkōgyō K.K.)	100.4	Shigeichi Koga
Mitsubishi Electric Corporation (Mitsubishi Denki K.K.)	54.5	Sadakazu Shindō

373

Corporation	Total Capital (1 billion Yen)	President
Mining and Industry		
Mitsubishi Steel Mfg. Co., Ltd. (Mitsubishi Seikō K.K.)	7.2	Masaki Nakajima
Mitsubishi Chemical Machinery, Ltd. (Mitsubishi Kakōki K.K.)	2.0	Itsuo Matsushita
Mitsubishi Chemical Industries, Ltd. (Mitsubishi Kasei Kōgyō K.K.)	37.9	Hideo Shinojima
Mitsubishi Plastic Industries, Ltd. (Mitsubishi Jushi K.K.)	3.2	Tokuzō Sugiyama
Asahi Glass Company, Ltd. (Asahi Garasu K.K.)	28.8	Motoharu Kurata
Nippon Kogaku K.K. (Nippon Kōgaku K.K.)	3.9	Yutaka Sugi
Mitsubishi Rayon Company Limited (Mitsubishi Reiyon K.K.)	15.1	Kisaburō Shimizu
Mitsubishi Monsanto Chemical Co., Ltd. (Mitsubishi Monsanto Kagaku K.K.)	4.0	Tatsuaki Nishikawa
Mitsubishi Gas Chemical Co. (Mitsubishi Gasu Kagaku K.K.)	11.0	Yoshio Shigi
Mitsubishi Oil Co., Ltd. (Mitsubishi Sekiyu K.K.)	15.6	Shingo Fujioka
Mitsubishi Petrochemical Co., Ltd. (Mitsubishi Yuka K.K.)	15.0	Hisashi Kurokawa
Mitsubishi Paper Mills, Ltd. (Mitsubishi Seishi K.K.)	5.6	Shūichi Kozeki
Mitsubishi Cement Co., Ltd. (Mitsubishi Semento K.K.)	5.3	Masao Yamanaka
Kirin Brewery Co., Ltd. (Kirin Bīru K.K.)	23.0	Chōjirō Takahashi

	Total Capital	
Corporation	*(1 billion Yen)*	*President*

Commerce and "Other"

Mitsubishi Corporation (Mitsubishi Shōji K.K.)	30.0	Chūjirō Fujino
Mitsubishi Warehouse & Trans- portation Co., Ltd. (Mitsubishi Sōko K.K.)	3.0	Masanao Matsumura
The Japan Mail Steamship Co., Ltd. (Nihon Yūsen K.K.)	30.0	Yoshiya Ariyoshi
Mitsubishi Estate Co., Ltd. (Mitsubishi Jisho K.K.)	33.0	Otsuichi Nakata

Some other Mitsubishi (or affiliated) companies:

Caterpillar-Mitsubishi K.K.	Mitsubishi Development Company
Mitsubishi-York, Ltd.	Mitsubishi Motor Sales Co., Ltd.
Dai-Nihon Toryo K.K.	Mitsubishi Kensetsu K.K.
Mitsubishi Atomic Power Industries, Inc.	Diamond Credit Co., Ltd.
Nippon Carbide K.K.	Mitsubishi Acetate
Shimazu Seisakusho K.K.	Mitsubishi Precision
Chiyoda Kako Kensetsu K.K.	

B. Mitsui Keiretsu (1972)

(Getsuyokai—31 Members; and Nimokukai—22 Members)

	Total Capital	
Corporation	*(1 billion yen)*	*President*

Finance

*Mitsui Bank, Ltd. (K.K. Mitsui Ginkō)	28.0	Gorō Koyama
*Mitsui Trust & Banking Co., Ltd. (Mitsui Shintaku Ginkō K.K.)	16.0	Senkichi Ikuno
*Taisho Marine and Fire Insurance Co., Ltd. (Taishō Kaijō-Kasai Hoken K.K.)	9.6	Takahisa Hanai
*Mitsui Mutual Life Insurance (Mitsui Seimei Hoken Sōgō Kaisha)	(6th assets rank in Japan)	Y. Yoneyama

Corporation	Total Capital (*1 billion Yen*)	President
Mining and Industry		
*Mitsui Mining Co., Ltd. (Mitsui Kōzan K.K.)	3.0	Okito Kurata
*Mitsui Mining & Smelting Co., Ltd. (Mitsui Kinzoku Kōgyō K.K.)	16.2	Shinpei Omoto
*Hokkaido Colliery and Steamship Co., Ltd. (Hokkaidō Tankō-Kisen K.K.)	7.0	Yoshitarō Hagihara
*Japan Steel Works, Ltd. (K.K. Nihon Seikōsho)	12.5	Sasaburō Kobayashi
*Mitsui Shipbuilding & Engineering Co., Ltd. (Mitsui Zōsen K.K.)	20.2	Isamu Yamashita
Mitsui Precision Machinery (Mitsui Seiki Kōgyō K.K.)	3.3	Shinohara Kinjiro
Showa Aircraft Industry Co., Ltd. (Shōwa Hikōki Kōgyō K.K.)	5.0	Shūsuke Noda
Mitsui Sugar Co., Ltd. (Mitsui Seitō K.K.)	3.3	Kinjirō Shinohara
*Mitsui Toatsu Chemicals, Inc. (Mitsui Tōatsu Kagaku K.K.)	21.9	Toshio Sueyoshi
Mitsui Miike Machinery Co., Ltd. (Mitsui Miike Seisakusho K.K.)	1.0	Choyo Inoue
*Mitsui Petrochemical Industries, Ltd. (Mitsui Sekiyu Kagaku Kōgyō K.K.)	10.0	Hoji Torii
*Toray Industries, Inc. (Tōre K.K.)	43.0	Seiichro Hirota
*Japan Flour Mills Co., Ltd. (Nihon Seifun K.K.)	3.4	Motohiko Ban
*Tokyo Shibaura Electric Co., Ltd. (since 1973) (Tokyo Shibaura Denki K.K.)	92.0	Keizo Tamaki

	Total Capital	
Corporation	*(1 billion Yen)*	*President*

Mining and Industry

*Oji Paper Co., Ltd. (since 1973)
(Oji Seishi K.K.)   7.8   Fumiō Tanaka

Commerce and "*Other*"

*Mitsui & Co., Ltd.
(Mitsui Bussan K.K.)   22.6   Sueyuki Wakasugi

General Petroleum   1.7   Takasu Kurō

*Mitsukoshi Department Store
(since 1973)
(Mitsukoshi K.K.)   11.5   I. Matsuda

Toshoku Ltd.
(K.K. Tōshoku)   2.8   Matajirō Hasegawa

Toyo Menka Kaisha, Ltd.
(K.K. Tōmen)   7.4   Kazuo Yasumoto

*Mitsui Warehouse Co., Ltd.
(Mitsui Sōko K.K.)   5.0   Jieki Takeuchi

Mitsui Wharf Co., Ltd.
(Mitsui Futō K.K.)   0.36   Sōji Nakamura

*Mitsui Real Estate Development Co.,
Ltd.
(Mitsui Fudōsan K.K.)   7.2   Hideo Edo

*Mitsui O.S.K. Lines, Ltd.
(Osaka Shōsen-Mitsui Senpaku K.K.)   30.0   Hisao Fukuda

Mitsui Agriculture and Forestry
Co., Ltd.
(Mitsui Nōrin K.K.)

*Sanki Engineering Co., Ltd.
(Sanki Kōgyō K.K.)   4.0   Setsu Kakumu

*Mitsui Construction Co., Ltd.
(Mitsui Kensetsu K.K.)   5.0   Noboru Inagaki

Other major companies with some Mitsui affiliations (past or present):

Toyota Motors Co., Ltd.

Ishikawajima-Harima Heavy Industries Co., Ltd.

Onodo Cement Co., Ltd.

Denki Kogaku Kōgyō Co., Ltd.

Fuji Photo Film Co., Ltd.

Asahi Breweries

Tōyō Bearing Co., Ltd.

SOURCES: Mainichi Daily News, *Mitsui Group* (Tokyo: Mainichi Shimbunsha, 1971), p. 16; "Mitsui Group," *Oriental Economist* 40 (Oct. 1972): 23–28; Akira Kubota, *Mitsui* (Tokyo: Chūō Kōronsha, 1966).
a. The twenty-two Nimokukai members have an asterisk.

C. Sumitomo Keiretsu (1972)

(Hakusuikai—16 Members)

Corporation	Total Capital (1 billion Yen)	President
Finance		
Sumitomo Bank, Ltd. (K.K. Sumitomo Ginkō)	50.4	Shōzō Hotta
Sumitomo Trust & Banking Co., Ltd. (Sumitomo Shintaku Ginkō K.K.)	16.0	Hiroshi Yamamoto
Sumitomo Marine & Fire Insurance Co., Ltd. (Sumitomo Kaijō-Kasai Hoken K.K.)	6.0	Yoshio Morokatsu
Sumitomo Mutual Life Insurance (Sumitomo Seimei Hoken Sōgō Kaisha)	(3rd assets rank in Japan)	Masaaki Akai
Mining and Industry		
Sumitomo Coal Mining Co., Ltd. (Sumitomo Sekitan Kōgyō K.K.)	3.3	Kanji Kawafuku
Sumitomo Metal Mining Co., Ltd. (Sumitomo Kinzoku Kōzan K.K.)	12.6	Kenjirō Kawakami
Sumitomo Metal Industries, Ltd. (Sumitomo Kinzoku Kōgyō K.K.)	83.0	Hōsai Hyūga

Corporation	Total Capital (*1 billion Yen*)	President
Mining and Industry		
Sumitomo Electric Industries, Ltd. (Sumitomo Denki Kōgyō K.K.)	18.0	Isamu Sakamoto
Nippon Sheet Glass Co., Ltd. (Nihon Itagarasu K.K.)	12.0	Jirō Kawase
Nippon Electric Co., Ltd. (Nippon Denki K.K.)	40.0	Kōji Kobayashi
Sumitomo Shipbuilding & Engineering Co., Ltd. (Sumitomo Jūkikai Kōgyō K.K.)	10.7	Nobuhiko Iwasaki
Sumitomo Chemical Co., Ltd. (Sumitomo Kagaku Kōgyō K.K.)	44.8	Shūjū Hasegawa
Sumitomo Cement Co., Ltd. (Sumitomo Semento K.K.)	10.0	Susumu Koga
Commerce and "Other"		
Sumitomo Shoji Kaisha, Ltd. (Sumitomo Shōji K.K.)	10.8	Yukio Shibayama
Sumitomo Warehouse Co., Ltd. (K.K. Sumitomo Sōko)	2.7	Nagahiro Senseki
Sumitomo Real Estate Co., Ltd. (Sumitomo Fudōsan K.K.)	2.5	Seigorō Seyama

Other major companies with some Sumitomo affiliations:[a]

Matsushita Electric

Tōyō Kōgyō (Motors)

Asahi Chemical Products (Kasei)

Takeda Pharmaceutical Products (Yakuhin)

Kubota Iron Works (also contacts with Fuyōkai of Fuji Bank)

Bridgestone Tires

Sanyō Electric

Komatsu Industries

Kuraray Textile Co.

Matsushita Electric Chemicals (Denkō)

Dai-Shōwa Paper Mfg.

Nihon Victor

Tōyō Sheet Steel (Kōban)

Uraga Heavy Industries

Kōyō Precision

Idemitsu Kosan (also working with the Mitsubishi Group)

SOURCES: Kenichi Suzuki, *Sumitomo* (Tokyo: Chuō Kōronsha, 1971); "Keieisha-mondai tokushūgō" (Special Symposium on problems of managers), in *Daiyamondo keizai jōhō: Bessatsu*, 10 April 1971.
a. See *Oriental Economist*, Nov. 1972, p. 15–21. Also listed as "Affiliated": (1) Meidensha; (2) Asahi Breweries; (3) C. Itoh & Co. (tendency toward Daiichi Kangyo Bank); (4) Ataka and Co.; (5) Kajima Construction. It did not list (1) Kuraray; (2) Matsushita Denkō; (3) Nihon Victor; (4) Tōyō Sheet Steel (Kōban); (5) Uraga Heavy Industries; or (6) Kōyō Precision.

D. Daiichi Kangyo Bank (DKB) Group

(Merged 1971)

(I) Former Daiichi Ginko Group:[a]
     (a) Furukawa "Sansuikai"—29 members;
         organized 1954:

Corporation	Total Capital (1 billion Yen)	President
Daiichi Kangyo Bank	54.0	Kaoru Inoue
Asahi Mutual Life Ins. (Asahi Seimei Hoken Sogo K.K.)	(4th assets rank in Japan)	K. Kazuno
Furukawa Mining (Furukawa Kōgyō)	5.5	Heiji Shimizu
Furukawa Electric (Furukawa Denki Kōgyō)	15.0	Jiro Sizuki
Asahi Electro-Chemicals (Asahi Denka Kōgyō)	2.2	Yoichi Kawai
Yokohama Rubber (Yokohama Gomu)	5.3	Toshio Shimazaki
Fuji Electric Mfg. (Fuji Denki Seizo)	20.8	Hichinosuke Maeda

Corporation	Total Capital (1 billion Yen)	President
Fujitsu	28.4	Yoshimitsu Kora
Nippon Light Metal (Nippon Kei-kinzoku)	15.0	Ichiro Nakayama
Nippon Zeon	6.0	Shuji Koga
Toa Paint	1.0	Tokusuke Okazoe
Nippon Agricultural Pesticide (Nippon Noyaku)	5.0	Yutaka Yoshida
Fuji Electro-Chemical (Fuji Denki Kagaku)	1.6	Tadanori Sugita
Nikkei Aluminum (Nikkei Arumi)	3.0	Shiro Sugimoto
Shibusawa Warehouse (Shibusawa Sōko)	1.5	Shingi Yasoshima
Nippon Seihaku	5.0	Hideo Iizuka
Taisei Fire & Marine Ins. (Taisei Kasai-Kaijo Hoken)		
Furukawa Battery (Furukawa Denchi)	1.2	Tsutomu Yamamoto
Furukawa Magnesium		
Furukawa Sangyō		
Nikkei Trading Co. (Nikkei Shōji)		
Tokai Metals (Tokai Kinzoku)		
Furukawa Casting (Furukawa Chuzo)		
Fuji Diesel		
Furukawa Special Metal (Furukawa Tokushu Kinzoku Kōgyō)		

Corporation	Total Capital (*1 billion Yen*)	President
Fujitsu FACOM		
Daiichi Developer (Daiichi Kaihatsu)		
Sea'ai Chemical (Sea'ai Kasei)		
Kanamachi Rubber (Kanamachi Gomu)		

(b) Kawasaki "Sansha"

Corporation	Total Capital (*1 billion Yen*)	President
Kawasaki Heavy Industries (Kawasaki Jūkōgyō)	42.0	Kiyoshi Shimoto
Kawasaki Steel (Kawasaki Seitetsu)	89.2	Ichiro Fujimoto
Kawasaki Line (Kawasaki Kisen)	20.2	Mamoru Adachi

(II) Former Kangyo Bank "Group of Fifteen Companies" (Jugosha-kai; organized 1970):[b]

Corporation	Total Capital (*1 billion Yen*)	President
Kanematsu Gosho	5.6	Gota Machida
Korakuen Stadium	4.0	Haruo Niwa
Sankyo (Drugs)	5.3	Manbei Suzuki
Shiseido	3.6	Hideo Okauchi
Denki Kagaku Industries (Denki Kagaku Kōgyō)	10.4	Yaroku Hanaoka
Niigata Steel (Niigata Tekkosho)	9.5	Tomio Nojima
Nissan Fire & Marine Ins. (Nissan Kasai-Kaijo Hoken)	2.4	Yoshio Ohishi
Nippon Columbia	3.6	Kiyoshi Nishi
Nippon Express (Nippon Tsūun)	43.5	Takayoshi Sawamura

Corporation	Total Capital (1 billion Yen)	President
Fukoku Mutual Life Ins. (Fukoku Seimei Hoken)	(10th assets rank in Japan)	T. Mori
Honshu Papers (Honshu Seishi)	4.2	Toshiro Kawaguchi
Yasukawa Electric (Yasukawa Denki)	7.0	Minoru Yasukawa
Dentsu		
Seibu Department Store (Seibu Hyakkaten)		
Nippon Kangyo Kakumaru Securities (Nippon Kangyo Kakumaru Shoken)		

(III) DKB Affiliated Trading Companies

C. Itoh and Co. (Increasing relations) (Itō-Chu Shōji)	20.5	Eikichi Itoh (Chairman)
Nissho-Iwai Co. (Declining relations)	11.1	Yoshio Tsuji
Kanematsu Gosho	5.6	Gota Machida

(IV) Other companies more or less affiliated with DKB:[c]

Seibu Railway (Seibu Tetsudo)	Shinko Electric (Shinko Denki)
General Corporation	Shimura Kako
Nagasakiya	Hokuetsu Paper Mills (Hokuetsu Seishi)
Ishikawajima-Harima Heavy Industries (Origins: Mitsui) (Ishikawajima-Harima Jukōgyō)	Shimizu Construction (Shimizu Kensetsu)
Isuzu Motors	Hasama Gumi
Showa Oil	Sato Kogyo

Ebara Manufacturing
(Ebara Seisakusho)

Kobe Steel
(Kobe Seikosho)

Yokogawa Bridge
(Yokogawa Kyoryo)

Asahi Kōgaku

Iseki Agricultural Machinery
(Iseki Noki)

Nippon Oil
(Nippon Sekiyu)

Ando Construction
(Ando Kensetsu)

Yamaha Motors

K. Hattori & Co.

Nippon Gakki

Prima Meat Packers

Morinaga Milk Industries

Nissan Agricultural Industries
(Nissan Nōrin Kōgyō)

a. *Sankei Shinbun* (24 Feb. 1972), p. 4.
b. *Sankei Shinbun* (24 Feb. 1972), p. 4.
c. *Oriental Economist* (Aug. 1972), "Industrial Groups under Reorganization," pp. 14–20.

E. Fuji Banking Keiretsu (1972)

(*Fuyōkai*[a]—29 Members)

Corporation	Total Capital (1 billion Yen)	President
Finance		
Fuji Bank, Ltd.	50.4	Kunihiko Sasaki
Yasuda Fire & Marine Insurance Co., Ltd. (Yasuda Kasai Kijō Hoken K.K.)	12.0	Takeo Miyoshi
Yasuda Trust & Banking Co., Ltd. (Yasuda Shintaku Ginkō K.K.)	10.0	Yoshio Tozawa
Yasuda Mutual Life Insurance Co., Ltd. (Yasuda Seimei Hoken Sōgō Kaisha)	(8th assets rank in Japan)	M. Mizuno
Industrials		
Tōa Nenryō Kōgyō K.K.	14.7	Masaji Nambu

Corporation	Total Capital (*1 billion Yen*)	President
Industrials		
Japan Steel Tube Co., Ltd. (Nippon Kokan K.K.)	101.8	Hisao Makita
Shōwa Denkō K.K. (Same)	42.2	Haruo Suzuki
Hitachi, Ltd. (K.K. Hitachi Seisakusho)	122.4	Hirokichi Yoshiyama
Nissan Motor Co., Ltd. (Nissan Jidōsha K.K.)	44.0	Katsuji Kawamata
Nihon Cement Co., Ltd. (Nihon Semento K.K.)	10.5	Chiharu Takeyasu
Nippon Seiko Co., Ltd. (Nippon Seiko K.K.)	7.3	Kōki Imazato
Canon Inc. (Canon K.K.)	7.2	Takeshi Mitarashi
Kureha Chemical Industry Co., Ltd. (Kureha Kagaku Kōgyō K.K.)	8.0	Saburō Araki
Kubota, Ltd. (Kubota Tekkō K.K.)	34.7	Keitarō Hiro
Nippon Reizo Co., Ltd. (Nippon Reizō K.K.)	9.0	Iwao Asanaga
Yokogawa Electric Works, Ltd. (K.K. Yokogawa Denki Seisakusho)	3.8	Iwao Yamazaki
Oki Electric Industry Co., Ltd. (Oki Denki Kōgyō K.K.)	11.3	Akira Mori
Toho Rayon Co., Ltd. (Tōhō Rayon K.K.)	2.5	Seizō Manabe
Nisshin Spinning Co., Ltd. (Nisshin Bōseki K.K.)	5.0	Tatsu Tsuyuguchi
Sanyo-Kokusaku Pulp (Recent merger of Sanyō Pulp & Kokusaku Pulp)	12.3	

Corporation	Total Capital (*1 billion Yen*)	President

Industrials

Sapporo Breweries, Ltd. (Sapporo Bīru K.K.)	10.0	Kurato Uchida
Nisshin Flour Milling Co., Ltd. (Nisshin Seifun K.K.)	6.0	Eisaburō Shōda
Nippon Oil and Fats Co., Ltd. (Nippon Yushi K.K.)	4.3	Tsutomu Murata

Commerce and "Other"

Marubeni Corporation (Marubeni K.K.)	27.5	Hiro Hiyama
Showa Shipping Co., Ltd. (Shōwa Kaiun K.K.)	6.7	Toshiharu Suenaga
Keihin Electric Express Railway Co., Ltd. (Keihin Kyūkō Dentetsu K.K.)	13.6	Kōichi Nakagawa
Tobu Railway Co., Ltd. (Tōbu Tetsudō K.K.)	13.6	Kaichirō Nezu
Taisei Construction Co., Ltd. (Taisei Kensetsu K.K.)	25.0	Yukiharu Minami
Tokyo Tatemono Co., Ltd. (Tokyo Tatemono K.K.)	3.0	Takeshi Yataomi

Other companies jointly owned by Fuyokai members:
Fuyo Sōgō Kaihatsu K.K.
Fuyo General Lease
Fuyo Information Center
Fuyo Ocean Development
Penta Ocean Construction

Other corporations said to have some affiliation with the Fuji Bank:[b]

Okura Shōji	Nihon Suisan
Katakura Kōgyō	Nihon Diners' Club
Goyo Kensetsu	Palace Hotel
Suminoe Orimono	Hitachi Kaden Hambai

Tōa Kowan Kōgyō

Hikojima Kensetsu

Nishimatsu Kensetsu

Nihon Orefin Kagaku

Nichido Kasai Kaijō
 Hoken K.K.

Nihon Gakki Seizo

Hitachi Kasei Kōgyō

Yamaichi Shōken

Yuraku Tochi

Yodogawa Seikojo

Fuji Ad System

Maeda Kensetsu Kōgyō

SOURCES: *The Oriental Economist* (Sep. 1972), pp. 15–21; *Sankei shimbun* (24 Feb. 1972), p. 4; *Shukan Tōyō keizai* (24 Nov. 1970), p. 43; Kata keizai kenkyūjo, ed., *Kaisha keiretsu o saguru* (Search for corporate lineages) (Tokyo: Kata keizai kenkyūjo, 1972), p. 705.
 a. The Fuyōkai was established in 1966.
 b. This list is from *Sankei Shimbun* (24 Feb. 1972), p. 4.

F. Sanwa Banking Keiretsu (1972)

(Sansuikai—36 Members)[a]

Corporation	Total Capital (1 billion Yen)	President
Finance		
Sanwa Bank, Ltd. (K.K. Sanwa Ginkō)	50.4	Tadao Watanabe
Nippon Life Insurance (Nippon Seimei Hoken K.K.)	(1st assets rank in Japan)	G. Hirose
Toyo Trust Banking Co., Ltd. (Tōyō Shintaku Ginkō K.K.)	10.0	Shigeo Arimitsu
Industrials		
Maruzen Oil Co., Ltd. (Maruzen Sekiyu K.K.)	16.4	Kazuo Miyamori
Kobe Steel Works, Ltd. (K.K. Kōbe Seikōsho)	76.1	Kenkichi Sotozima
Nakayama Steel Works, Ltd. (K.K. Nakayama Seikōsho)	1.0	Ikuo Nakayama
Hitachi Shipbuilding & Engineering Co., Ltd. (Hitachi Zōsen K.K.)	28.0	Takao Nagata

Corporation	Total Capital (*1 billion Yen*)	President

Industrials

Daihatsu Kogyo Co., Ltd.[b] (Daihatsu Kōgyō K.K.)	18.3	Yoshikichi Ise
Osaka Cement Co., Ltd. (Osaka Semento K.K.)	6.7	Kiyoshige Matsushima
Ube Industries, Ltd. (Ube Kōsan K.K.)	30.6	Kan'ichi Nakayasu
Tokuyama Soda Co., Ltd. (Tokuyama Sōda K.K.)	3.2	Nyoshin Kageyama
Kansai Paint Co., Ltd. (Kansai Peinto K.K.)	4.4	Noritaka Kotani
Toyo Rubber Industry	5.0	Wataru Mejiro
Teijin Limited (Teijin K.K.)	28.4	Shinzō Ōya
Hitachi Ltd.[c] (K.K. Hitachi Seisakusho)	121.9	Ken'ichirō Komai
Unitika, Ltd. (Yunichika K.K.)	22.3	Kazuo Tomii

Commerce and "Others"

Nissho-Iwai Co., Ltd. (Nisshō-Iwai K.K.)	11.1	Yoshio Tsuji
Nippon Express Co., Ltd. (Nippon Tsūun K.K.)	43.5	Takayoshi Sawamura
Ohbayashi-gumi, Ltd. (K.K. Ohbayashi-gumi)	15.0	Yoshio Obayashi
Takashimaya Co., Ltd. (K.K. Takashimaya)	7.5	Shin'ichi Iida
Keihanshin Express Railway Co., Ltd. (Keihanshin Kyūkō Dentetsu K.K.)	16.5	Kaoru Mori

	Tatal Capital	
Corporation	*(1 billion Yen)*	*President*

Commerce and "Others"

Corporation	Capital	President
Yamashita-Shinnihon Steamship Co., Ltd. (Yamashita-Shinnihon Kisen K.K.)	7.9	Saburō Yamashita
Nichimen Co., Ltd. (Nichimen Gitsugyō K.K.)	7.5	Seikyo Kambayashi
Iwasaki Tsushinki Co., Ltd. (Iwasaki Tsushinki K.K.)	3.2	Kan'ichi Ōhashi
Iwatani Sangyo K.K.	7.2	Naoji Iwatani
Shin-Meiwa Kōgyō K.K.	3.2	Toshiō Itō
Sekisui Kagaku Kōgyō K.K.	5.67	Kenzō Obata
Tōyō Bearing Seizo K.K.	8.1	Kōtarō Ōtsū
Tōyō Kensetsu K.K.	4.7	Hachirō Fujii
Hitachi Kasei Kōgyō K.K.	3.3	Sanshirō Fujikubo
Hitachi Kinzoku K.K.	7.6	Ryūichi Nakamura
Hitachi Densen K.K.	10.0	Takayoshi Matsuura
Sharp K.K.	11.5	Tokuji Hayakawa
Tanabe Seiyaku K.K.	8.0	Gōbei Tanabe
Orient Lease	0.8	
Fujisawa Yakuhin Kōgyō K.K.	4.0	Yukichi Fujisawa

NOTE: The following are new firms in the Sansuikai admitted in 1972: Iwatani Sangyo; Hitachi Densen; Hitachi Kinzoku; Hitachi Kasei Kōgyō; Tōyō Kensetsu K.K.; Sharp K.K.; Tanabe Seiyaku K.K.; Fujisawa Yakuhin Kōgyō K.K. Also the following have tended to become neutralized by the merger of the Daiichi-Kangyo Bank: Kobe Steel; Nissho-Iwai; and Hitachi, Ltd. Other major companies in the Sansuikai are quite independent; for example: Nippon Life Insurance; Nippon Express; Kei-Han-Shin Express Railway; and Hitachi, Ltd. (including Hitachi Densen, Hitachi Kasei Kōgyō, and Hitachi Kinzoku).

Other major companies with some Sanwa affiliations (i.e., membership in the Clover-kai, Midori-kai*, or both**):

> Daido Mutual Life Insurance**
> Koa Fire and Marine Insurance*
> Nomura Securities*
> Fukusuke**
> Tōyō Umpanki**
> Mitsubashi Betting**
> Morishita Juntan*
> Zendaka-Gumi*
> Nissan Construction*
> Osaka Soda*
> Konishiraku Photo Ind.*

SOURCES: *Oriental Economist* (Nov. 1972), pp. 22–27; *Shukan Tōyō Keizai* (24 Nov. 1970), p. 48.

a. Formed only in 1967, and it has an affiliate (Clover-kai), with members drawn from the level of executive and managing directors of Sansuikai companies.

b. Daihatsu Kōgyō has shifted to a closer relationship with Mitsui and Toyota. *Oriental Economist* (Nov. 1972), p. 22.

c. Also a member of the Fuyōkai of Fuji Bank.

Appendix VIII

Antimonopoly Act Guidelines for International Licensing Agreements

May 24, 1968
Fair Trade Commission

I. Among the restrictions which are liable to constitute unfair business practices in international licensing agreements on patent rights or utility model rights (hereinafter referred to as patent rights, etc.) the following are outstanding:

1. To restrict the area to which the licensee may export the goods covered by patent rights, etc. (hereinafter referred to as patented goods).

a. In case the licensor has patent rights, etc. which have been registered in the area to which the licensee's export is restricted (hereinafter referred to as the restricted area);

b. In case the licensor is selling patented goods in the restricted area in his normal business;

c. In case the licensor has granted to a third party an exclusive license to sell in the restricted area.

2. To restrict the licensee's export prices or quantities of patented goods, or to make it obligatory for the licensee to export patented goods through the licensor or a person designated by the licensor.

However, such cases are excluded where the licensor grants license to export to the area coming under either of the preceding a, b, or c and the said restrictions or obligations imposed are of reasonable scope.

3. To restrict the licensee from manufacturing, using or selling goods, or employing technology which are in competition with the licensed subject.

However, such cases are excluded where the licensor grants an exclusive license and imposes no restriction on goods already being manufactured, used or sold, or technology already being utilized by the licensee.

4. To make it obligatory for the licensee to purchase raw materials, parts, etc. from the licensor or a person designated by the licensor.

5. To make it obligatory for the licensee to sell patented goods through the licensor or a person designated by the licensor.

6. To restrict the resale prices of patented goods in Japan.

7. To make it obligatory for the licensee to inform the licensor of knowledge or experience newly obtained regarding the licensed technology, or to assign the right with respect to an improved or applied invention by the licensee to the licensor or to grant the licensor a license thereon.

However, such cases are excluded where the licensor bears similar obligations and the obligations of both parties are equally balanced in substance.

8. To charge royalties on goods which do not utilize licensed technology.

9. To restrict the quality of raw materials, parts, etc. or of patented goods.

However, such cases are excluded where such restrictions are necessary to maintain the creditability of a registered trademark or to insure the effectiveness of the licensed technology.

II. The aforementioned guidelines shall apply to international know-how licensing agreements.

III. In international licensing agreements on patent rights, etc., the following acts shall be regarded as the exercise of rights under the Patent Act or the Utility Model Act:

1. To grant a license to manufacture, use, sell, etc. separately;

2. To grant a license for a limited period within the life of patent rights, etc. or for a limited area within the whole area covered by patent rights, etc.;

3. To restrict the manufacture of patented goods to a limited field of technology or to restrict the sale thereof to a limited field of sales;

4. To restrict the use of patented processes to a limited field of technology;

5. To restrict the amount of output or the amount of sales of patented goods or to restrict the frequency of the use of patented processes.

Appendix IX

List of Nonliberalized Technology (1968–1972)*

AIRCRAFT:

1. Technology concerning the manufacture of aircrafts.

2. Technology concerning the manufacture of parts or attached equipment of aircrafts.

WEAPONS:

3. Technology concerning the manufacture of weapons.

4. Technology concerning the manufacture of parts or attachments of weapons.

5. Technology concerning the manufacture of electronics equipment for military use.

EXPLOSIVES:

6. Technology concerning the manufacture of explosives.

NUCLEAR ENERGY:

7. Technology concerning the manufacture or use of nuclear reactors (including nuclear fusion reactors, and the same definition will be applied hereafter), their parts, attached equipment of component materials, or turbines for nuclear power or generators for nuclear power.

8. Technology concerning the manufacture, use or reprocessing of nuclear fuels, or the manufacture of devices used for such purposes.

9. Technology concerning the manufacture or utilization or processing of radio-active materials, or the manufacture of devices used for such purposes.

10. Technology concerning the utilization of nuclear reaction without the use of a nuclear reactor.

SPACE DEVELOPMENT:

11. Technology concerning the manufacture or use of space vehicles (except meteorological sounding rockets, and the same definition will be

* Only computer technology is subject to case-by-case screening (until July 1974); see p. 232 above.

applied hereafter) or the devices especially designed for launching, guidance and control, tracking or utilization of the space vehicles.

12. Technology concerning the manufacture or use of testing devices especially designed for the development of the space vehicles.

13. Technology concerning the manufacture or use of propulsion for space vehicles, or of the parts, attached equipment or materials especially designed for (11) or (12) mentioned above.

ELECTRONIC COMPUTERS:

14. Technology concerning the manufacture of electronic computers (including attached equipment).

15. Technology concerning the manufacture of devices for applied use of electronic computers.

16. Technology concerning the utilization of (14) and (15) above.

PETROCHEMICALS:

17. Technology concerning the cracking of naphtha or inflammable natural gas.

18. Technology concerning the manufacture of derivatives.

19. Technology concerning engineering for petrochemical plants.

Appendix X

Nineteen Restricted Industries

1. Waterworks and supply works of city water under Article 3 paragraph 2 and paragraph 4 of the Water Supply Law (Law No. 177 of 1957).

2. Local railway business to which Local Railway Law (Law No. 52 of 1919) applies (excluding such railway or cable railway which is constructed for an exclusive use of a private person).

3. Light railway business under Article 1 paragraph 1 of Light Railway Law (Law No. 76 of 1921).

4. Trust business to which Article 65 of Trust Law (Law No. 65 of 1919) applies.

5. Banking business to which Article 2 of Bank Law (Law No. 21 of 1927) applies.

6. Marine transportation business to which Article 2 paragraph 1 of Marine Transportation Law (Law No. 187 of 1949) applies (excluding, however, business under paragraph 7 to 12 of the same Article).

7. Express business under Article 2 paragraph 2 of Express Business Law (Law No. 241 of 1949) (these under items 3 and 5 of paragraph 1 of the same Article only).

8. Fishing business under Article 2 paragraph 1 of Fishing Law (Law No. 267 of 1949).

9. Deleted.

10. Broadcasting business under Article 2 paragraph 1 of Broadcasting Law (Law No. 132 of 1950).

11. Mining under Article 4 of Mining Law (Law No. 289 of 1950).

12. Harbour transport business under Article 2 paragraph 2 of Harbour Transport Law (Law No. 161 of 1951).

13. Road transport business under Article 2 paragraph 2 of Road Transport Law (Law No. 183 of 1951) (excluding business under paragraph 4 to 5 of the same Article and Article 3 paragraph 2 item 3 of the same Law).

14. Mutual banking business to which Mutual Banking Law (Law No. 199 of 1951) applies.

15. Business of Long Term Credit Bank under Article 2 of Long Term Credit Bank Law (Law No. 187 of 1952).

16. Air transport business under Article 2 item 17 of Air Transport Law (Law No. 231 of 1952).

17. Electric business under Article 2 item 5 of Electric Business Law (Law No. 179 of 1964).

18. Gas business under Article 2 paragraph 5 of Gas Business Law (Law No. 51 of 1954).

19. Foreign exchange banking business under Article 2 item 1 of Foreign Exchange Banking Law (Law No. 67 of 1954).

Appendix XI

Agreement between the Japan Commercial Arbitration Association and the American Arbitration Association to Facilitate the Use of Commercial Arbitration in Trade between Japan and the United States of America

Being convinced that a wider use of commercial arbitration would lend confidence and stability to commercial transactions between firms in Japan and in the United States of America, the Japan Commercial Arbitration Association and the American Arbitration Association are agreed henceforth to recommend that firms engaged in such trade should insert in their contracts the following clause:

"All disputes, controversies, or differences which may arise between the parties, out of or in relation to, or in connection with, this contract, or for the breach thereof, shall be finally settled by arbitration pursuant to the Japan-American Trade Arbitration Agreement of September 16, 1952, by which each party hereto is bound."

The terms of the agreement referred to in this clause are as follows:

(1) Arbitration to be held in Japan shall be conducted under the rules of the Japan Commercial Arbitration Association; arbitration to be held in the United States of America shall be conducted in accordance with the rules of the American Arbitration Association.

(2) If the place where the arbitration is to be held is not designated in the contract, or the parties fail to agree in writing on such place, the party demanding arbitration shall give notice to the Arbitration Association of the country in which the party resides. That Association shall notify the parties that they have a period of about 14 days to submit their arguments and reasons for preference regarding the place to a Joint Arbitration Committee of three members, two appointed by the respective Associations, and the third, to act as Chairman, to be chosen by the other two. The third member shall not be a member of either Association. The seats of the two Committees shall be in Tokyo and in New York. The determination of the

place of arbitration by the Joint Arbitration Committee shall be final and binding upon both parties to the controversy.

(3) The Associations each agree to establish such International Panels of Arbitrators as may be necessary to carry out the provisions of this agreement and to advise each other of the personnel of these panels.

(4) Both Associations will cooperate in advancing international commercial arbitration, through increased use of the facilities of their organization, and will advise each other concerning mutual policies and progress in the interests of Japanese-American trade.

The foregoing shall be known as the Japan-American Trade Arbitration Agreement, and shall be deemed to be incorporated in any contract containing the following clause:

"All disputes, controversies, or differences which may arise between the parties, out of or in relation to or in connection with this contract, or for the breach thereof, shall be finally settled by arbitration pursuant to the Japan-American Trade Arbitration Agreement of September 16, 1952, by which each party hereto is bound."

Dated: September 16, 1952

The Japanese Commercial Arbitration Association
    By: Aiichiro Fujiyama

The American Arbitration Association
    By: A. C. Croft

Appendix XII

Concerning Liberalization of Inward Direct Investment

April 27, 1973
Cabinet Decision (*Kakugi kettei*)

Concerning the captioned matter, the Government received on April 25 the response to a query previously referred to the Foreign Investment Council (FIC).

The Government respects the gist of that response in its entirety and decides as follows concerning the basic thinking related to liberalization of inward direct investment and the content of liberalization measures:

Furthermore, these liberalization measures will be enforced from May 1, 1973.

1. BASIC VIEW

It is already nine years since Japan undertook the obligations embodied in "The Code of Liberalization of Capital Movements" of the Organization for Economic Cooperation and Development (hereinafter referred to as the OECD Code), the principal objective of which is the complete liberalization of international capital movements, and, although the four consecutive rounds of liberalization measures have been introduced in the intervening period in connection with inward direct investment, many reservations to liberalizations in this area are still in force.

On the other hand, in line with the marked improvement of Japan's economic position in recent years, the role the Japanese economy plays in the international economy has grown and the business activities abroad of Japanese enterprises have been increasing.

In view of this situation, it is deemed necessary for Japan to demonstrate

399

to the world its determination and posture aiming at promoting in a most positive manner the internationalization of its economy, on the belief that this type of action will help avoid possible surges of protectionism in the world economy, and thus prove instrumental to the maintenance of world peace and prosperity, which depends on the spirit of international cooperation.

In pursuance of this purpose it is an urgent necessity that the Government should now resolutely liberalize inward direct investment to the maximum extent Japan's present economic situation permits, and adopt the 100 percent liberalization principle stipulated in the OECD Code, departing from the existing framework based primarily upon the so-called 50 percent principle. Also by virtue of this action, the further development of the Japanese economy is to be expected through freer international exchanges of capital and technology.

As to those remaining restrictive measures which are deemed appropriate to be maintained in the context of the present liberalization, it is necessary to subject them to continuous reappraisal with a view to exploring the possibility of liberalization taking into account progress to be made in creating an improved structure and system, including legislative measures, and to promote a further liberalization in this area. Flexibility in operating these remaining restrictive measures is, in the meantime, warranted.

Even after implementing the liberalization measures contained herein, it is of course possible for the Government to take necessary measures, should serious damages be incurred by related industries, inter alia, by medium and small scale enterprises or agriculture, due to the establishment of new companies or participation in the management of existing companies by foreign capital. It also goes without saying that unfair business practices on the part of foreign capital in Japan are not to be permitted.

However, all Japanese enterprises should reaffirm their determination to achieve sound development by their own efforts under free and fair international competition.

2. CONTENT OF LIBERALIZATION MEASURES

Liberalization measures connected with inward direct investment and inward portfolio investment to be implemented are as follows:

(1) Approval of share acquisitions by foreign investors provided in Article 11 of the Law Concerning Foreign Investment will be given automatically by the competent Minister in accordance with the OECD Code, except in cases where

(i) it is not clear whether there is consent by an existing enterprise as to the acquisition of its shares by foreign investors—such cases to be dealt with as hitherto, or

(ii) the acquisition of shares of an enterprise, either newly established or existing, which belongs to any of the industries listed in Annex I, would continue to be treated as hitherto, and the acquisition of shares of an enterprise, either newly established or existing, which belongs to any of the industries listed in Annex II, would continue to be dealt with as hitherto up to the date mentioned in the Annex.

(2) The confirmation procedures for the automatic approval mentioned

in (1) above and screening procedures currently in use will be progressively simplified.

ANNEX I

Five* Restricted Industries Subject to Case-by-Case Screening

1. Primary industry related to agriculture, forestry and fisheries
2. Mining (50 percent liberalized as at percent)
3. Oil industry
4. Leather and leather products manufacturing industry
5. Retail trade operations (50 percent liberalization for those with less than 11 stores)

ANNEX II

Seventeen Industries to be Decontrolled on Set Dates in the Future

(NOTE: Present restrictions, in parentheses, and the order of the industries have been changed to show times and degrees of liberalization.)

Industries to be completely liberalized on December 1, 1974:

1. Integrated circuit (IC) manufacturing (50 percent liberalized)

Industries to be completely liberalized on May 1, 1975:

2. Meat packing—limited to production of ham, sausage, bacon and processing of meats and poultry (50 percent liberalized)
3. Tomato products manufacturing (50 percent liberalized)
4. Formula feed manufacturing (50 percent liberalized)
5. Manufacturing of prepared food products for food service businesses (50 percent liberalized)
6. Apparel manufacturing and wholesale—limited to woven or knitted clothing for men, women and children (50 percent liberalized)
7. Drug, medicine and agricultural chemicals manufacturing—including quasi-pharmaceuticals and animal drugs (50 percent liberalized)
8. Ferro-alloy manufacturing (50 percent liberalized)
9. Hydraulic machinery manufacturing (50 percent liberalized)
10. Packaging machinery manufacturing (50 percent liberalized)
11. Electronic precision machine manufacturing—limited to those for medical or electric measuring use (50 percent liberalized)
12. Phonograph record manufacturing (50 percent liberalized)
13. Real estate business (case-by-case screening)

* Actually there are 46 "industries" in No. 1 (primary industries) and 67 "industries" in No. 2 (mining) above, according to the Japanese method of classification generally adhered to in bureaucratic circles. See Gyōsei kanrichō, *Nihon hyōjun sangyō bunrui* (Japanese standard classification of industries) (Tokyo: Gyōsei kanrichō, 1972), p. 468.

Industries to be liberalized up to 50 percent on August 4, 1974, and to be completely liberalized on December 1, 1975:

14. Manufacturing, sale or leasing of electronic computers—including peripheral equipment, terminal units, parts and accessories—and computer aided systems (case-by-case screening)

Industries to be liberalized up to 50 percent on December 1, 1974, and to be completely liberalized on April 1, 1976:

15. Data processing industry, including computer software industry (case-by-case screening)

Industries to be completely liberalized on May 1, 1976:

16. Fruit juice and fruit drinks manufacturing (50 percent liberalized)
17. Sensitized photographic materials manufacturing (50 percent liberalized)

NOTE:

1. Acquisitions of shares of a company, newly established and engaged in manufacturing, sale or leasing of electronic computers (including peripheral equipment, terminal units, parts and accessories) or computer aided systems, will be subject to the same procedure as heretofore applied to Class-1, newly established companies (the so-called 50 percent liberalized industries) from 4th August, 1974 until 30th November, 1975.

2. Acquisitions of shares of a company, newly established and engaged in information processing (including software), will be subject to the same procedure mentioned in 1 above from 1st December, 1974 until 31st March, 1976.

3. The processed cheese manufacturing industry is liberalized on condition that domestic natural cheese accounts for more than one third of the raw materials used in the manufacturing of the product.

Notes

CHAPTER I

1. See U.S. Department of Commerce, *The Multinational Corporation* (Washington D.C.: GPO, 1972). For background information and citations to the literature, see Sydney E. Rolfe, *The International Corporation* (Paris: International Chamber of Commerce, 1969), p. 202; for Japanese discussion of the requirements for internationalization of Japanese business, see Keizai shingikai kokusai shihon idō kenkyū iinkai, ed., *Shihon jiyūka to kaigai kigyō shinshutsu* (Capital liberalization and the advance of enterprise abroad) (Tokyo: Ōkurashō insatsukyoku, 1969), p. 129.

2. See Leon Hollerman, *Japan's Dependence on the World Economy* (Princeton U. Press, 1967), pp. 4–19, for a discussion of Japan's advanced status by numerous criteria. Throughout my first four chapters, I have drawn widely from my own experience and impressions over twenty years concerning various aspects of Japanese business and legal practice, and the footnotes for this sketchy summary are only intended to indicate reliable sources that I have found useful.

3. A "professional futurologist" says, "Japanese are among the most forward-looking and future-oriented people in the world—if not the most so. . . . [Japan] soon would possess the most productive economy in the world. . . . It would not be surprising if the twenty-first century were the Japanese century. . . ." Herman Kahn, *The Emerging Japanese Superstate: Challenge and Response* (Englewood Cliffs, N.J.: Prentice-Hall, 1970), pp. 1–2.

4. See Kagaku gijutsu-chō, *Gijutsu yosoku hōkokusho* (Report on technological forecasts) (Tokyo: Kagaku gijutsuchō, 1971); *Nihon no mirai gijutsu* (Japan's future technology), in *Shūkan daiyamondo bessatsu* (Nov. 1971); Sōrifu tōkeikyoku (Bureau of Statistics, Office of the Prime Minister), *Kagaku gijutsu kenkyū chōsa hōkoku* (Report on the survey of research and development in Japan) (Tokyo: Sōrifu tōkeikyoku, 1972); and *Wall Street Journal*, 9 Feb. 1972, p. 1. Also see Arthur H. Livermore, ed., *Science in Japan* (Washington: American Association for the Advancement of Science, 1965), pp. 1–24; Hideomi Tuge, *Historical Development of Science and Technology in Japan*, rev. ed. (Tokyo: Kokusai bunka shinkōkai, 1968), p. 84; and Tsūshō-sangyōshō, Kōgyō gijutsu-in (Ministry of International Trade and Industry [MITI], Agency of Industrial Science and Technology), *Gijutsu kakushin to Nihon no kōgyō* (The technological revolution and Japanese industry) (Tokyo: Nippon kōgyō shimbunsha, 1964), p. 13, for the modern background.

5. *Gaishi ni kansuru hōritsu* (The foreign investment law), Art. 3 (Law No. 163, 1950); English, 5 *EHS Law Bulletin Service* (hereafter EHS) No. 5410.

6. *E.g.*, K.K. Marunouchi resāchi sentā, *Nihon ni okeru gaikoku shihon no jittai* (Actual condition of foreign capital in Japan), ed. Gorō Saitō (Tokyo: K.K. Marunouchi resāchi sentā, 1972) (hereafter *MRC*). Gaishi dōnyū nenkan henshū iinkai, ed., *Gaishi dōnyū nenkan* (Annual of foreign capital induction) (Tokyo: Shōkō kaikan,

1969), p. 22 [hereafter *Gaishi dōnyū nenkan*]; and MITI (Tsūshō sangyō-shō, kigyō-kyoku), ed., *Gaishi-kei kigyō—sono jittai to eikyō* (Foreign related enterprises—their actual condition and influence) (Tokyo: Ōkurashō insatsu-kyoku, 1969), p. 9 (hereafter *Gaishi-kei kigyō*); and the earlier survey, Tsūshō sangyō-shō, Kigyō-kyoku, ed., *Waga-kuni no gōben gaisha no jittai* (Actual condition of joint ventures in our country) (Tokyo: Fuji kōhōsha, 1964).

7. C. R. Boxer, *The Great Ship from Amacon: Annals of Macao and the Old Japan Trade, 1555–1640*, 2d ed. (Lisbon: Centro de Estudos Historicos Ultramarinos, 1963); C. R. Boxer, *The Christian Century in Japan* (U. of Cal. Press, 1951), p. 18. Note that earlier Marco Polo reported, however, that he had heard of a place called "Zipangu," referring to Japan.

8. George Sansom, *The Western World and Japan* (New York: Alfred A. Knopf, 1950), p. 105, notes that the warm welcome to the first Westerners and the keen interest in their weapons and wares set the Japanese off at the very beginning from the Chinese, who regarded the Portuguese as simply barbarians.

9. See generally Ludwig Riess, "History of the English Factory at Hirado (1613–1622)," *Transactions of the Asiatic Society of Japan* (1898; reprint, 1964), 26: 1–114, 163–218; and R. Cocks, *Diary of Richard Cocks, Cape-merchant in the English Factory in Japan, 1615–1622*, ed. N. Murakami (Tokyo: Sankōsha, 1899).

10. Boxer, *The Christian Century*, p. 78; Yosaburō Takekoshi, *The Economic Aspects of the History of the Civilization of Japan* (1930; reprint ed., London: Dawson of Pall Mall, 1967), 2: 67–68, gives a vivid account of the execution by Ieyasu of two Christian daimyo after their defeat at the battle of Sekigahara (1600).

11. S. Noma, *Arts of Japan*, trans. Glen Webb (Palo Alto: Kōdansha Int'l., 1967), 2: 179.

12. N. Mody, *A Collection of Nagasaki Color Prints and Paintings* (1939; reprint ed., Tokyo: Tuttle, 1969), plate 25 ff.

13. E. Kaempfer, *The History of Japan* (Glasgow: James Maclehose & Sons, 1906 [written 1690–92]), 2: 89–92.

14. *Kinreikō zenshū* (Consideration of Tokugawa regulations, first compilation) (Tokyo: Sōbunsha, 1959), 6: 375.

15. Osamu Ōba, *Edo jidai ni okeru karabune mochiwatarisho no kenkyū* (Study of books brought over by T'ang [Chinese] ships in the Edo period) (Osaka: Kansai University, 1967), p. 32.

16. Quoted in Sansom, *The Western World*, p. 201.

17. Dan Fenno Henderson, "Promulgation of Tokugawa Statutes," *Journal of Asian and African Statutes* 1 (1967): 9.

18. There is a vast modern literature accumulating on the problems encountered by businessmen arising out of these Japanese differences. Limiting ourselves to hard-cover works, the following are some of the more recent books: Robert J. Ballon and Eugene H. Lee, eds., *Foreign Investment in Japan* (Tokyo: Sophia University, 1972); Robert J. Ballon, ed., *Japan's Market and Foreign Business* (Tokyo: Sophia University, 1971); James C. Abegglen, ed., *Business Strategies for Japan* (Tokyo: Sophia University, 1970); T. M. F. Adams and Noritake Kobayashi, *The World of Japanese Business* (Tokyo: Kōdansha International Ltd., 1969); F. Herbert Glazer, *The International Businessman in Japan* (Tokyo: Sophia University, 1968).

Also see, Ichirō Kawasaki, *Japan Unmasked* (Rutland, Vt.: Charles E. Tuttle Co., 1969), by a former Japanese Ambassador to Argentina; Boyce De Mente, *How Business is Done in Japan—A Personal View* (Tokyo: Sampson-Doyle Co., 1963); Boyce De Mente, *Japanese Manners and Ethics in Business* (Tokyo: East Asia Pub. Co., 1960). On aspects of Japanese business the two books by M. Yoshino are of the highest authority (see bibliography).

19. See Tsuneo Tamba, *Yokohama ukiyoe* (Tokyo: Asahi shimbunsha, 1962), plate 15.

20. Also concerned with the difference in nose sizes was Luis Frois, S.J. (1532–1597) quoted in Cooper, *They Came to Japan*, p. 239: "We pick our noses with our thumb or index fingers; the Japanese use their little finger because their nostrils are small."

21. G. C. Allen and Audrey Donnithorne, *Western Enterprise in Far Eastern Development: China and Japan* (London: George Allen & Unwin, Ltd., 1954), p. 199; and *Japan Gazette*, March 12, 1881.

22. John R. Black, *Young Japan: Yokohama and Yedo, 1858–79* (1883; reprint ed., London: Oxford U. Press, 1968), 1: 32.

23. See generally, F. C. Jones, *Extraterritoriality in Japan* (Yale U. Press, 1930), p. 47.

24. Thomas C. Smith, *Political Change and Industrial Development in Japan: Government Enterprise, 1868–1880* (Stanford U. Press, 1955), p. 11.

25. W. W. Lockwood, *The Economic Development of Japan: Growth and Structural Change, 1868–1938* (Princeton U. Press, 1954), p. 322.

26. Allen and Donnithorne, *Western Enterprise*, p. 196.

27. John E. Orchard, *Japan's Economic Position* (New York: McGraw-Hill, 1930), p. 107, for special foreign processing of tea; and see also, Y. Hattori, "The Foreign Commerce of Japan Since the Restoration, 1869–1900," *Studies in Historical and Political Science: Social and Industrial History* 22 (Johns Hopkins U. Press, 1904): 485.

28. Allen and Donnithorne, *Western Enterprise*, p. 270, show that foreign experts hired by the Meiji government dwindled down to 237 in 1880, from 507 in 1873; Tokutarō Shigehisa, "Foreigners in Early Meiji," *Japan Advertiser*, Oct. 1939, p. 28, says 5% of the entire budget (early Meiji) went for foreign experts' salaries. Grace Fox says in her introduction to Black, *Young Japan*, p. iii, that there were 528 British subjects in Yokohama in 1879.

29. Hazel Jones, "The Formulation of Meiji Policy toward the Employment of Foreigners," *Monumenta Nipponica* 23 (1968): 9–30, and Hazel Jones, *The Meiji Government and Foreign Employees, 1868–1900* (Ph.D. diss., U. of Mich., 1967), p. 472.

30. Lockwood, *The Economic Development of Japan*, pp. 151, 320; Sanzō Hidemura, "Meiji shonen Zōheiryō ni okeru o-yatoi gaikokujin no kaiyō mondai" (The problem of terminating employment of hired foreigners in the early Meiji Mint), in *Osaka no kenkyū* (Studies of Osaka), ed. Mataji Miyamoto (Osaka: Seibundō shuppan, 1968), 2: 377–401.

31. M. Matsukata, *Report on the Adoption of the Gold Standard in Japan* (Tokyo: Japanese Government Press, 1899), p. 173.

32. Lockwood, *The Economic Development of Japan*, p. 329.

33. Allen and Donnithorne, *Western Enterprise*, pp. 208, 226.

34. Keiji Ohara, ed., *Nichibei bunka kōshō-shi: tsūshō sangyō-hen* (History of Japanese-American cultural exchange: part on commerce and industry) (Tokyo: Yōyōsha, 1954), 2: 27.

35. Allen and Donnithorne, *Western Enterprise*, p. 231; and see E. B. Schumpeter, ed., *The Industrialization of Japan and Manchukuo, 1930–1940* (New York: Macmillan Company, 1940), pp. 804–5.

36. Ohara, *Nichibei bunka kōshō-shi*, p. 412. Unless otherwise indicated, my prewar information comes from Ohara, Lockwood, or Allen and Donnithorne (*supra*).

37. *Gaishi-kei kigyō*, p. 267.

38. Allen and Donnithorne, *Western Enterprise*, p. 235.

39. See Lockwood, *The Economic Development of Japan*, p. 260. Cf. H. G. Moulton, *Japan, An Economic and Financial Appraisal* (Washington, D.C.: Brookings Inst., 1931), p. 524. Also see Y. Horie, "Foreign Capital and the Japanese Capitalism after World War I," *Kyoto U. Econ. Rev.* 20 (1950): 38–59.

40. Hōmushō (Ministry of Justice), *Gaikokujin tōroku kokuseki-betsu jin'in chōsa geppō* (Monthly report of investigation into the registration of aliens, classified by nationality) (Tokyo: Hōmushō, 1970), p. 1.

41. The Ministry of Justice (*hōmushō*), Civil Affairs section, kindly supplied these statistics upon my special application, and I wish to express my gratitude again for the very helpful attitude that I have always found upon properly explaining my academic interests to Japanese governmental agencies whose statistics are not only well kept and frequently published but generously made available even before publication when requested.

42. U.S. Dept. of Commerce, *Statistical Abstract of the U.S.* (Washington, D.C.: GPO, 1971), p. 76.

43. *MRC*, 1972, p. 2. This massive report of 1,400 pages (plus 116 pages of materials) is based on an investigation completed July 1972, covering questionnaires sent to 899 (out of a total of 1,002 foreign firms in Japan), of which 772 responded. Also see Bank of Japan, *Manual of Foreign Investment in Japan*, Nov. 1971, pp. 40–41.

44. U.S. Dept. of Commerce, *Survey of Current Business*, Oct. 1971, p. 32.

45. See *MRC*, p. 21, and Keizai Hatten Kyōkai, *Wagukuni no kaigai tōshi* (Overseas investments of our country) (Tokyo: Kenzai hatten kyōkai, 1972), p. 28; also Japan Economic Research Center (hereafter JERC), *Quarterly Forecast: Japan's Economy (1971 Apr.–June—1973 Apr.–June)*, Dec. 1971, p. 45; also World Economic Information Services, ed., *Economic Information File: Japan*, Supplement No. 2 (1972), p. 7; and Supplement No. 3 (1972), p. 3.

46. Cabinet Order No. 228, 29 June 1963, effective 1 July 1963, which amended the Cabinet Order Concerning Exceptions, etc., to Standards of Validation Based on the Law Concerning Foreign Investment (*Gaishi ni kansuru hōritsu no kitei ni motozuku ninka no kijun no tokurei-tō ni kansuru seirei*) (Cabinet Order No. 221, 1 July 1952), in 5 EHS No. 5470. Thus, the FIL was left in its original form until 1 April 1964, and it seems that between 1 July 1963 and 1 April 1964 (when the FIL was amended), there was no legal basis for preventing yen-base investments, since the unamended FIL Art. 10 only prohibited acquisitions requiring foreign-exchange payments.

47. *Gaishi-kei kigyō*, p. 267.

48. Tsūsho sangyōshō, kigyō kyoku (MITI), ed., *Gaishi-kei kigyō no dōkō* (Trends of foreign-related enterprises) (Tokyo: Ōkurashō insatsu-kyoku, 1971), p. 1 (hereafter *Gaishi-kei kigyō dōkō*).

49. See *MRC*, p. 35. *Gaishi-kei kigyō*, pp. 4–35. This survey of both validated and "yen-base" enterprises covered 519 foreign-related firms in Japan, 85% of those to which questionnaires were addressed. Some of the major firms were also interviewed and substantially all major firms as of June 1967 were contacted one way or another. Indeed, the major problem with using the report is the mass of classifications and categories that are set up and quantified by percentages of "firms" as units when many times the sheer number of minority interests and minor operations obscures the whereabouts and the weight in the resultant statistics of the really foreign firms and especially those with some scale. A selected group of seventy-six manufacturing firms with at least 100 million yen ($278,000) in capital was tabulated (p. 7), overcoming this difficulty to some extent. There were only sixteen controlled firms (51%–100%) of this scale.

50. *Gaishi-kei kigyō*, p. 265.

51. Up to 1952, when the Allied occupation ended, there were roughly twenty foreign sales enterprises validated, of which twelve were majorities. All were small scale, but they included a few major names (*e.g.*, B. F. Goodrich Co. and Goodyear Tire). From 1952 to 1963 virtually all requests for approval of sales firms were denied or delayed by Japanese officialdom; so some of them entered on a yen basis. After new yen companies were prohibited in 1963, the Japanese government began validating more sales enterprises (*e.g.*, 16 in 1964; 14 in 1965; 37 in 1966; and 65 in 1967). *Gaishi dōnyū nenkan*, p. 188. Still only 24 of 134 surveyed in 1968 were capitalized at over 100 million yen ($278,000), and only 30 of 223 in 1971. And of those surveyed in 1968 only Rank Xerox, Sperry Rand, and Olivetti had capital over $1,000,000, besides of course the oils— Shell, Mobil, and Esso.

52. *MRC*, p. 25, and *Gaishi-kei kigyō dōkō*, p. 18. *MRC*, p. 62 (*shiyro-hen*) has a list of new direct investments 1970 through July 1972.

53. *Gaishi-kei kigyō*, p. 64.

54. *MRC*, p. 27.

55. Ibid., p. 29.

56. *E.g.*, see "Gaishi tokushū" (Special symposium on foreign capital), *Tōyō keizai* 3 (31 July 1969), for Japanese anxieties and some more balanced suggestions for the future; or "Keiei mondai" (Management problems), in *Chūō kōron; bessatsu* 51 (Fall 1967).

57. *MRC* (1972), p. 42.

58. *Gaishi-kei kigyō dōkō* (1971), p. 11, for 1969–70 statistics quoted hereafter.

59. Ibid., p. 38.

60. *MRC*, p. 35.

61. Confirming this point, *Gaishi-kei kigyō dōkō*, p. 29, showed that manufacturing FRF spent 0.7% of sales on R & D, whereas domestic Japanese enterprises spent more than double that much (1.5%).

62. Ibid., p. 16.

63. *See* generally M. Y. Yoshino, *Japan's Managerial System: Traditions and Innovation* (MIT Press, 1968), p. 225.

64. *Gaishi-kei kigyō*, p. 70. Rate: 360 yen to $1.00.

65. See, *e.g.*, Nobuyoshi Araki, "Shihon yushutsu no hitsuyō takamaru kongo no Nihon keizai" (The Japanese economy hereafter as the need to export capital increases) *Tōyō keizai*, 13 July 1969, p. 35, and Gaishi shingikai, *Shihon jiyūka to kaigai kigyō shinshutsu* (Tokyo: Ōkurashō insatsukyoku, 1969), p. 31; and Jūkagaku kōgyō tsūshinsha, ed., *Kaigai tōshi, gijutsu yushutsu yōran* (Tokyo: Jūkagaku kōgyō tsūshinsha, 1970), p. 421.

66. See the military terms previously used to report the "attacks" and "landing" of foreign capital in *Tōyō keizai*, No. 3528 (11 Apr. 1970), p. 16. But see also the recent tendencies, *Japan Economic Journal*, 26 Dec. 1972, p. 1, for a story that the Foreign Investment Council was considering 100 percent liberalization of new enterprises.

67. *Gaishi-kei kigyō dōkō*, p. 18.

68. Several Tokyo-based executives of controlled foreign firms quite candidly made these points, even in answering an official questionnaire.

69. Ryūtarō Komiya, "Shihon jiyūka no keizaigaku" (The economics of capital liberalization), *Ekonomisuto*, 25 July 1967, p. 4, and Tsuneo Iida, "Kokueki-ron ni hisomu Nihonjin no higaisha ishiki" (Japanese injured feelings concealed in the national-interest theory), *Tōyō keizai*, No. 3486, 31 July 1969, p. 14.

70. See U.S. Dept. of Commerce, *The Multinational Corporation*, 1: 12. From 1946 to 1967 U.S. enterprises increased their foreign investments four-fold from $12 to $55 billion, twice the rate of domestic capital increases. R. Vernon, "The Role of U.S. Enterprise Abroad," *Daedalus* (Winter 1969), p. 113.

71. Statement of Takeo Fukuda, *The President Directory* (Tokyo: Diamond-Time Co., 1971), p. 4. But note the comment of one of Japan's most objective observers of the economic ministries (Kobayashi, "Management Differences," in *World of Japanese Business*, Adams and Kobayashi, p. 254): "He [the foreign investor] may enjoy meeting the *uppermost echelon of the bureaucracy*, he may find people at that level more sympathetic because they have had more experience with international business, but he must remember that he will also have to deal with officials on other levels who may think and act quite differently from the top-level bureaucrats. If he approaches the latter in a manner that juniors may consider highhanded or untimely, he may well find that he has created a bureaucratic antagonism in the Ministry that will be both irksome and obstructive" (italics added).

72. See editorial, *Fortune*, Oct. 1967.

73. D. Vagts, "The Multinational Enterprise," 83 *Harv. L. Rev.* 739 (1970), for a marshalling of business information as well as business, legal, and policy issues posed by the growing multinational corporations.

CHAPTER II

1. See report of a panel of the American Chamber of Commerce in Japan as reported in T. F. M. Adams and N. Kobayashi, *The World of Japanese Business* (Toyko: Kōdansha International, Ltd., 1969), p. 145; also Howard Van Zandt, "The Japanese Culture and the Business Boom," *Foreign Affairs* 48 (1970): 355.

2. See Dan Fenno Henderson, *Conciliation and Japanese Law: Tokugawa and Mod-*

ern (U. of Tokyo and U. of Wash. Press, 1965), Vol. 1. For a provocative discussion, also see Hisao Ōtsuka, "Modernization Reconsidered," *The Developing Economies* 3 (1965): 387–403; and *cf.* John W. Hall, "Changing Conceptions of the Modernization of Japan," in *Changing Japanese Attitudes Toward Modernization*, ed. Marius B. Jensen (Princeton U. Press, 1967), p. 7.

3. Dan Fenno Henderson, "Law and Political Modernization in Japan," in *Political Development in Modern Japan*, ed. Robert E. Ward (Princeton U. Press, 1968), p. 387.

4. See Yasumasu Kuroda, "The Protest Movements in Japan: A New Politics," *Asian Survey* 12 (Nov. 1972): 947, and Chie Nakane, *Japanese Society* (U. of Cal. Press, 1970), p. 85. For a Japanese view of the limitations of such a circumstance, see Hisao Ōtsuka, "The Formation of Modern Man: The Popular Base for Democratization," *The Japan Interpreter* 6 (1970): 1.

5. Dan Fenno Henderson, "Perspectives on the Japanese Constitution after Twenty Years," in *The Constitution of Japan: Its First Twenty Years, 1947–67*, ed. Dan Fenno Henderson (U. of Wash. Press, 1968), p. xi.

6. Henderson, "Japanese Judicial Review of Legislation," in ibid., p. 115.

7. *Sakagami* v. *Japan*, 7 Saikō saibansho minji hanreishū (hereafter Minshū) 1562 (Sup. Ct. G.B., 8 Oct. 1953).

8. *Nakamura* v. *Japan*, 16 Saikō saibansho keiji hanreishū (hereafter Keishū) 1953 (Sup. Ct. G.B., 28 Nov. 1962).

9. 5 U.S. (1 Cranch) 137 (1803).

10. *Tomabechi* v. *Japan*, 14 Minshū 1206 (Sup. Ct., G.B., 8 June, 1960). For full discussion see D. C. S. Sissons, "Dissolution of the Japanese Lower House," in *Papers on Modern Japan*, ed. D. C. S. Sissons (Canberra: Australian National U. Press, 1968), p. 116.

11. *Suzuki* v. *Japan*, 6 Minshū 783 (Sup. Ct., G.B., 8 Oct. 1952); English translation in Maki, *Court and Constitution in Japan* (U. of Wash. Press, 1964), p. 364.

12. *Japan* v. *Sakata* (the Sunakawa case), 13 Keishū 3225 (Sup. Ct., G.B., 16 Dec. 1959). English translation in Maki, *Court and Constitution*, p. 305.

13. Though the LDP scored a resounding victory in 1969, capturing three hundred seats (counting twelve independents), the party accomplished this feat while losing 1.2% of the LDP popular vote received in the prior election.

14. "Neutralist" may be a euphemism for anti-Americanism in some elements of the party; see Etō Shinichi, "Japan and the Chinas," in Princeton University Conference, *The New Japan: Prospects and Promise* (Princeton U. Press, 1963), pp. 55–65.

15. Haruhiro Fukui, "Liberal Democratic Party and Constitutional Revision," in *Papers on Modern Japan*, edited by D. C. S. Sissons (Camberra: Australian National U. Press, 1968), pp. 26–45.

16. Masao Maruyama, *Thought and Behavior in Modern Japanese Politics*, ed. Ivan Morris (New York: Oxford U. Press, 1963), pp. 15, 17, 230.

17. Peter Duus, *Party Rivalry and Political Change in Taishō Japan* (Harvard U. Press, 1968), p. 107. Also see Tetsuo Najita, *Hara Kei in the Politics of Compromise (1905–1915)* (Harvard U. Press, 1967), p. 185.

18. See, generally, Robert A. Scalapino, *Democracy and the Party Movement in Prewar Japan: The Failure of the First Attempt* (U. of Cal. Press, 1953), p. 200.

19. Const., Art. 41: The Diet shall be the highest organ of state power and shall be the sole lawmaking organ of the state.

20. See Allen B. Cole, George O. Totten, and Cecil H. Uyehara, *Socialist Parties in Postwar Japan* (Yale U. Press, 1966), p. 452.

21. At last we have two helpful studies on the LDP: Nathaniel B. Thayer, *How the Conservatives Rule Japan* (Princeton U. Press, 1969), and Haruhiro Fukui, *Party in Power: The Japanese Liberal Democrats and Policy-making* (Canberra: Australian National U. Press, 1970).

22. See Dan Fenno Henderson and T. Matsuo, "Japan's Trade Experience with the People's Republic of China," mimeo., 1972; William D. Hartley, "Eating Humble Pie:

In Trading with China, Japan Sometimes Gets More Abuse Than Goods," *Wall Street Journal*, 11 Nov. 1970. See also Chae-Jin Lee, "The Politics of Sino-Japanese Trade Relations, 1963–68," *Pacific Affairs* 42 (1969): 129–44; and George P. Jan, "Japan's Trade with Communist China," *Asian Survey* 9 (1969): 900–918.

23. Haruhiro Fukui, "Twenty Years of Revisionism," in *The Constitution of Japan*, ed. Henderson, p. 41; Robert E. Ward, "The Commission on the Constitution and Prospects from Constitutional Changes in Japan," *J. Asian Studies* 24 (1965): 401–29.

24. See, generally, Cole, Totten, and Uyehara, *Socialist Parties in Postwar Japan*, p. 98.

25. See Chae-Jin Lee, "Factional Politics in the Japan Socialist Party: The Chinese Cultural Revolution Case," *Asian Survey* 10 (1970): 230; see also J. A. A. Stockwin, *The Japanese Socialist Party and Neutralism* (U. of Melbourne Press, 1969), p. 112.

26. Allen B. Cole, "Political Tendencies of Japanese in Small Enterprise," mimeo. (New York: Inst. of Pac. Relations, 1959), p. 19.

27. See, generally, James A. Dator, *Sōka Gakkai: Builders of the Third Civilization* (U. of Wash. Press, 1969), p. 106. James W. White, *The Sōkagakkai and Mass Society* (Stanford U. Press, 1970), p. 28.

28. Jooinn Lee, "Kōmeitō Sōkagakkai-ism in Japanese Politics," *Asian Survey* 10 (1970): 510.

29. See John K. Emmerson, "The Japanese Communist Party after Fifty Years," *Asian Survey* 12 (1972): 564; and Hoover Institute, *Yearbook of International Communist Affairs* (Stanford U. Press, 1972), p. 241. For prewar background see George M. Beckmann and Genji Ōkubo, *The Japanese Communist Party, 1922–1945* (Stanford U. Press, 1969), p. 453; and Robert A. Scalapino, *The Japanese Communist Movement, 1922–1966* (U. of Cal. Press, 1967), p. 292.

30. Robert A. Scalapino and Junnosuke Masumi, *Parties and Politics in Contemporary Japan* (U. of Cal. Press, 1962), p. 125.

31. Nathan B. Thayer, "The Election of a Japanese Prime Minister," *Asian Survey* 9 (1969): 477.

32. Thayer, *How the Conservatives Rule Japan*, p. 148.

33. Fukui, *Party in Power*, pp. 57–80, discusses the numbers, education, and occupations of LDP members and emphasizes the definitional problem in trying to calculate the LDP membership. But certainly the active dues-paying group is relatively small.

34. Even the *kōmeitō* has its factions. See Jooinn Lee, "Kōmeitō," *Asian Survey*, p. 514, note 21.

35. Fukui, *Party in Power*, p. 107; Michael Leiserson, "Factions and Coalitions in One-Party Japan," *Am. Pol. Sci. Rev.* 62 (1968): 770.

36. *Asahi Shimbun*, 15 May 1972, p. 10.

37. See Gerald. L. Curtis, *Election Campaigning Japanese Style* (Columbia U. Press, 1971), p. 126; and Gerald L. Curtis, "The Kōenkai and the Liberal Democratic Party," *Japan Interpreter* 6 (1970): 216, for conflict between party and *kōenkai* organization at the local level.

38. Thayer, "The Election," *Asian Survey*, p. 34.

39. Compare Fukui, *Party in Power*, pp. 102–6, for pessimistic comments on LDP modernization efforts.

40. For background generally, see U.S. Dept. of Commerce, *Japan: The Government-Business Relationship* (Washington, D.C.: GPO, 1972); and Chitoshi Yanaga, *Big Business in Japanese Politics* (Yale U. Press, 1968), p. 371; Thayer, *How the Conservatives Rule Japan*, p. 58; Fukui, *Party in Power*, p. 144; Takeshi Ishida, "The Development of Interest Groups and the Pattern of Political Modernization in Japan," in *Political Development in Modern Japan*, ed. Robert E. Ward (Princeton U. Press, 1968), p. 293.

41. *Japan Times Weekly*, 20 Jan. 1973, p. 1, budget for social security up 29%, etc.

42. Yanaga, *Big Business*, p. 34.

43. See Hidetoshi Katō, "Sanken: A Power above Government," *The Japan Interpreter* 7 (1971): 36. The original members: Masao Anzai, president, Shōwa Denkō

(Electric Industry); Toshio Dokō, president, Tōshiba Electric; Chūjirō Fujino, president, Mitsubishi Shōji (Trading); Hasegawa Norishige, president, Sumitomo Chemical; Hiroki Imasato, president, Nippon Seikō Bearings; Yoshihiro Inayama, president, Yawata Steel (now president of Japan Steel); Yoshizane Iwasa, president, Fuji Bank; Katsuji Kawamata, president, Nissan Motors; Kazutaka Kikawada, president, Tokyo Electric Power; Shigeo Kitano, board chairman, Shōkō Chūkin (Central Commercial and Industrial Trust); Kōji Kobayashi, president, Nippon Electric; Fumihiko Kōno, board chairman, Mitsubishi Heavy Industries; Tatsuzō Mizukami, board chairman, Mitsui Bussan (Trading); Moriatsu Minato, president, Nikkō Securities; Shigeo Nagano, president, Fuji Steel (now board chairman of Japan Steel); Sōhei Nakayama, board chairman, Nippon Kōgyō Bank; Minoru Segawa, board chairman, Nomura Securities; Wataru Tajitsu, president, Mitsubishi Bank; Toyosaburō Taniguchi, board chairman, Tōyōbō (Spinning); Shigeki Tashiro, board chairman, Tōyō Rayon.

44. World Economic Information Services, *Economic Information File: Japan*, Supplement No. 2 (1972), pp. 3–4.

45. James R. Soukup, "Comparative Studies in Political Finance: Japan," *J. of Politics* 25 (1963): 727–56; but see Frank Langdon, "Big Business Lobbying in Japan: The Case of Central Bank Reform," *Am. Pol. Sci. Rev.* 55 (1961): 538, for limitation on the ability of business to influence; also Frank Langdon, "Organized Interests in Japan and Their Influence on Political Parties," *Pacific Affairs* 34 (Fall 1961): 271–78.

46. For data on faction finances, see Fukui, *Party in Power*, p. 154; and Frank Langdon, "The Political Contributions of Big Business in Japan," *Asian Survey* 3 (Oct. 1963): 465–73.

47. James R. Soukup, "Business Political Participation in Japan: Continuity and Change," *Studies on Asia* (1965): 163–78.

48. Yanaga, *Big Business*, p. 79.

49. *Arita v. Kajima et al.* (Yawata Steel Case), 14 Kakyū minshū 657 (Tokyo D. Ct., 5 Apr. 1963).

50. *Arita v. Kajima et al.*, 24 Minshū 625 (Supreme Ct., 24 June 1970); see also *Shōji hōmu kenkyū* (No. 529), p. 43.

51. See generally, the Keizai dōyūkai, *Keizai dōyūkai jūgonen-shi* (Fifteen-year history of the Committee on Economic Development) (Tokyo: Keizai dōyūkai, 1963), p. 319.

52. Langdon, "The Political Contributions," *Asian Survey*, p. 466.

53. *Cf.* 18 USCA § 611 (1951).

54. Note the chronology and contacts set out in Hirotatsu Fujiwara, *I Denounce Soka Gakkai* (Tokyo: Nisshin hōdō Co., 1970), pp. 277–87. Also see Yomiuri Shimbunsha, *Sōri daijin* (Prime Minister) (Tokyo: Yomiuri shimbunsha, 1971), p. 34.

55. See Yomiuri Shimbunsha, *Sori daijin*, pp. 34, 35, 142, 151, 184, 185; and Thayer, *How the Conservatives Rule Japan*, p. 65.

56. Fukui, *Party in Power*, p. 58.

57. Yanaga, *Big Business*, p. 26.

CHAPTER III

1. See Raymond Vernon, "Future of the Multinational Enterprise," in *The International Corporation*, ed. Charles P. Kindleberger (MIT Press, 1970), p. 374; and Jack N. Behrman, "Some Pattern in the Rise of the Multinational Enterprise," University of North Carolina School of Business Administration Research Paper, No. 18, 1969, p. 3.

2. Economic Planning Agency, *Survey of Japan* (1964–65) (Tokyo: Japanese Times, 1966), p. 99.

3. Shin'ichirō Michida, "Capital Liberalization as a Treaty Question and Offensive and Defensive Strategies Concerning Foreign Capital," 2 *Law in Japan: An Annual* 1 (1968); *cf.* Yasuhiro Fujita, "Does Japan's Restriction on Foreign Capital Entries

Violate Her Treaties—In Response to Michida Article," 3 *Law in Japan: An Annual* 162 (1969).

4. Editor, "Natural Resource Problems," *Oriental Economist* 40 (June 1972): 40, says per-ton freight on ores is down from $5.50 in 1960 to $3.65 in 1970. Jūkagaku kōgyō tsūshinsha, *Nihon no kaigai shigen kaihatsu* (Japan's natural resource development abroad) (Tokyo: Jukagaku kōgyō tsūshinsha, 1972), p. 23, gives a list of some 256 projects overseas in fourteen different industries. Also see, generally, Edward A. Ackerman, *Japan's Natural Resources and Their Relation to Japan's Economic Future* (U. of Chicago Press, 1953), p. 559, for a minute analysis of Japan's post-World War II raw-material problems.

5. Naomichi Nakanishi, "Changes in Living Patterns Brought about by Television," *Developing Economies* 7 (1969): 572.

6. Ezra Vogel, *Japan's New Middle Class* (U. of Cal. Press, 1963), p. 54; Ken'ichi Tominaga, "Trend Analysis of Social Stratification and Social Mobility in Contemporary Japan," *Developing Economies* 7 (1969): 471, shows that inter-generational social mobility through education and occupational achievment has been as high in modern Japan as in Europe and that it has significantly increased even in the past ten years (1955–65).

7. *Japan Economic Journal* (11 April, 1972), p. 20. For discussions of the rise in educational levels and the ratio of white collar–blue collar see Shigeru Susato, "The White Collar Strata in Postwar Japan," *Developing Economies* 7 (1969): 451; Miyohei Shinohara, *Structural Changes in Japan's Economic Development*, Economic Research Series No. 11 (Tokyo: Hitotsubashi U., 1970), p. 30; Yoshi Hara and Masakazu Yano, "Changes in Education in Postwar Japan: A Graphic Explanation," *Developing Economies* 7 (1969): 640.

8. See Michio Nagai, *Kindaika to kyōiku* (Modernization and education) (Tokyo: Tokyo daigaku shuppankai, 1969); and Michio Nagai, "University Problems in Japan," *Bulletin* (Int'l. House of Japan) 23 (1969): 1–25; and Hara and Yano, "Changes in Education," *Developing Economies*, p. 648.

9. *Japan Times Weekly* (16 Dec. 1972), p. 12; Hara and Yano, "Changes in Education," *Developing Economies*, p. 648.

10. Countless observers, one might say all thoughtful students of Japan, have tried their hand at articulating this Japanese penchant for sociality—familism, groupism, nationalism. See Michio Nagai, "Social Change in Postwar Japan," *Developing Economies* 7 (1969): 404, for its effectiveness on the national level beginning with the Meiji policy of *fukoku kyōhei*.

11. U.S. Dept. of Commerce, *The United States in the Changing World Economy* (Washington, D.C.: GPO, 1971), 2: 60. Minoru Tachi and Yōichi Okazaki, "Japan's Postwar Population and Labor Force," *Developing Economies* 7 (1969): 170; and Robert Evans, Jr., *The Labor Economies of Japan and the United States* (New York: Praeger, 1971), p. 97.

12. Ibid., p. 177.

13. See "Wages in Major Enterprises," *Oriental Economist* 40 (Dec. 1972): 16, where it reports that even in 1972 wages were up 16.2% despite the recessions, and now 85% of middle school graduates go to high school.

14. Robert E. Cole, *Japanese Blue Collar: The Changing Tradition* (U. of Cal. Press, 1971), p. 122; Ken'ichi Kobayashi, "The Employment and Wage Systems in Postwar Japan," *Developing Economies* 7 (1969): 187; Solomon B. Levine, "Labor Markets and Collective Bargaining in Japan," in *The State and Economic Enterprise in Japan*, ed. William W. Lockwood (Princeton U. Press, 1965), p. 633; and Solomon B. Levine, "Postwar Trade Unionism, Collective Bargaining, and Japanese Social Structure," in *Aspects of Social Change in Modern Japan*, ed. Ronald P. Dore (Princeton U. Press, 1967), p. 277.

15. Hiromitsu Kaneda, "Long Term Changes in Food Consumption Patterns in Japan," in *Agriculture and Economic Growth: Japan's Experience*, ed. Kazushi Ohkawa,

Bruce F. Johnston, and Hiromitsu Kaneda (Princeton U. Press and U. of Tokyo Press, 1970), p. 398; John W. Bennett, "Japanese Economic Growth: Background for Social Change," in *Aspects of Social Change in Modern Japan*, ed. Dore, p. 435.

16. Tachi and Okazaki, "Japan's Postwar Population," *Developing Economies*, p. 177, show forty-seven years in 1935 and sixty-eight years in 1965 for males.

17. Kaneda, "Long Term Changes," in *Agriculture and Economic Growth*, ed., Ohkawa, Johnston, and Kaneda, p. 417, note 22, shows $700 to $800 million in 1960; $1.5 million in 1963.

18. This is a 1968 summary and 1975 estimates by Kazu Nukazawa, *Japan's Foreign Economic Policy: Options for the Seventies* (Washington, D.C.: U.S.–Japan Trade Council Inc., 1970), p. 4. See also Tsūshō sangyō-shō, *Shigen mondai no tembō* (Prospects concerning the resources problem) (Tokyo: Tsūshō sangyō chōsakai, 1971), p. 10.

19. JERC, *18 Month Forecast of Japan's Economy* (1970): 30, shows the ratio at 45% in 1968 and 43.9% in 1970.

20. See, *e.g.*, *Japan Economic Journal* (4 Apr. 1972), p. 10, where Keidanren suggests that the government set several billion dollars of this reserve aside for creation of a natural resource corporation; and JEJ, 26 Dec. 1972, p. 10, for MOF and MITI suggestions that overseas investment corporations be formed with government participation.

21. Kōzō Yamamura, *Economic Policy in Postwar Japan* (U. of Cal. Press, 1967), pp. 61–63. "Dumping" may have different technical meanings for lawyers and economists, and much difficulty has been experienced to date in establishing the fact of dumping as legally required in the administrative fact-finding process. *E.g.*, the *N.Y. J. of Commerce*, 16 Feb. 1966, reports that from 1934 to 1965 there were 487 complaints and only 17 penalties assessed. See Robert A. Anthony, "The American Response to Dumping from Capitalist and Socialist Economies—Substantive Premises and Restructured Procedures after the 1967 GATT Code," 54 *Cornell L. Rev.* 159 (1969); and Thomas Shannon and William Marx, "The International Anti-Dumping Code and United States Anti-Dumping Law—An Appraisal," 7 *Columbia J. of Transnational Law* 171–202 (1968). Note that Japanese officials were warned in December 1972, because Japanese prices for exports had not gone down after revaluation of the yen. They feared that this might be treated as evidence of dumping. *Japan Economic Journal*, 11 Apr. 1972, p. 12, and 5 Dec. 1972, p. 1.

22. For an American view see Philip H. Trezise, "The Realities of Japan–U.S. Economic Relations," *Pacific Community* 1 (1970): 358; also in the popular media, evidence of growing irritation against Japanese trade practices is plentiful: *e.g.*, "U.S. Hits Japan TV Sets," *New York Times*, 29 Aug. 1970, reporting allegations of dumping (*i.e.*, selling in the U.S. under Japanese home prices and injuring U.S. producers of TV sets, an export that has captured about 20% of the U.S. market—by unfair means, if the allegations are proved; "U.S. Companies Aren't Excited by Easing of Japanese Investment Rules, Poll Finds," *Wall Street J.*, 22 Sept. 1970; Jacob K. Javits, "A Senator Looks at U.S.–Japan Relations," *Am.-Japan Soc'y. Bull.* 18 (November, 1969–January, 1970): 8: "It is clear that in any impartial court of world opinion, Japan's continuing appeal for free market access to other markets of the world must be judged as seriously flawed since Japan does not accord the same free market access to its trading partners"; *Asahi Shinbun*, 22 Aug. 1970 (*Gyōshu dake de wa fujūbun*); and "The Sharp Side of the Rising Sun," *Business Week*, 6 Sept. 1969, p. 124.

23. See, *e.g.*, JERC, *The Outlook for a Trillion Dollar Economy: Japan's Economy in 1985* (Tokyo: JERC, 1971), but note that the shift to social welfare and antipollution emphases had changed the more recent predictions, *Japan Economic Journal* (14 Mar. 1972), p. 1. Also see Tsūshō sangyōshō, *Tsūshō hakusho* (Commerce white paper) (Tokyo: Tsūshō sangyō chōsakai, 1972), 1:217.

24. Martin Broufenbrenner's remark, "The figures prosper, the people suffer," was at least true as to the figures. See Eleanor Hadley, *Antitrust in Japan* (Princeton U. Press, 1970), p. 396.

25. Throughout, statistics are drawn from the convenient summary, Japan, *Statistical*

Survey of Japan's Economy (1971) (Economic Affairs Bur., Ministry of Foreign Affairs, Japan, 1972) (hereafter, *Statistical Survey*); and Japan, Bur. of Statistics, Office of Prime Minister, *Nihon tōkei nenkan* (Annual of Japanese statistics) 1971 (hereafter *Annual Statistics*); Statistics Dept., the Bank of Japan, *Keizai tōkei nenpō* (Economic statistics annual) (Tokyo: Bank of Japan, Mar. 1970). For forecasts, I have used: Japan Economic Research Center (JERC), *Outlook for the Trillion Dollar Economy*, (Tokyo: JERC, 1972); JERC, *Japan's Economy in 1975* (Tokyo: Mar. 1970); and Keizai kikaku-chō (Economic planning agency), ed., *Shin-keizai shakai hatten keikaku* (New plan for economic and social development) (Tokyo: Ministry of Finance Printing Office, 1970).

26. See Shinohara, *Structural Changes*, p. 149 (Chapter 5, "Japan's Industrial Level in International Perspective").

27. JERC, *Japan's Economy in 1975*, p. 3.

28. *E.g.*, see Hugh Patrick, "The Phoenix from the Ashes: Postwar Japan," in *Modern East Asia: Essays in Interpretation*, ed. James B. Crowley (New York: Harcourt Brace Jovanovich, Inc., 1970), p. 333.

29. Kazushi Ohkawa and Henry Rosovsky, "A Century of Japanese Economic Growth," in *The State and Economic Enterprise in Japan*, ed. Lockwood, p. 47.

30. See Kazushi Ohkawa, "Phases of Agricultural Development and Economic Growth," *Agriculture and Economic Growth*, ed. Ohkawa, Johnston, and Kaneda, p. 3. *Cf.* James K. Nakamura, "Growth of Japanese Agriculture, 1875–1920," in *State and Economic Enterprise in Japan*, ed. Lockwood, p. 249, where the early growth is put at about 1%.

31. See *e.g.*, "Japan's Remarkable Industrial Machine," *Business Week*, 7 Mar. 1970, p. 59; "How the Japanese Mount the Export Blitz," *Fortune*, Sept. 1970, p. 126.

32. *Japan Times Weekly* (6 Jan. 1973), p. 9. Fiscal 1971 (ending 31 Mar. 1972) has a GNP of $242 billion (using 334 yen to $1.00 as an average exchange rate for that troubled year). Also see JERC, *Japan's Economy in 1975*, p. 19.

33. Nakanishi, "Changes in Living Patterns Brought about by Television," *Developing Economies*, p. 572.

34. Ezra Vogel, "Beyond Salary: Mamachi Revisited," *Japan Interpreter* 6 (1970): 105.

35. JERC, *Japan's Economy in 1975*, p. 4.

36. Ibid., p. 13.

37. Shinohara, *Structural Changes*, p. 21.

38. Hadley, *Antitrust in Japan*, p. 403.

39. Figures from Yamamura, *Economic Policy*, p. 163, note 13.

40. See Shinohara, *Structural Changes*, p. 303. Another incipient structural change may eventuate in the next few years in that "easy money" may change the relationship between banking and manufacturing, and increased sales activity aimed at the consumer market may upgrade the sales of service and sales entities.

41. Kazushi Ohkawa, "Agriculture and Turning Points," *Developing Economies* 3 (1965): 486.

42. Trezise, "The Realities of Japan–U.S. Economic Relations," p. 363.

43. Theories of Japanese dualism, its causes and effects, are diverse and controversial. See Shinohara, *Structural Changes*, p. 303, for a discussion of recent debates. Also see Yamanaka Tokutarō, *Small Business in Japan's Economic Progress* (Tokyo: Asahi Evening News, 1971); and Seymour Broadbridge, *Industrial Dualism in Japan* (Chicago: Aldine Pub. Co., 1966), p. 8; review of the Broadbridge book by Masaharu Toike, *Developing Economies* 7 (1969): 253; and MITI, Chūsho kigyō-chō, *Chūsho kigyō hakusho* (Medium and small enterprise white paper) (Tokyo: Okurashō insatsu-kyoku, 1972).

44. See Henry Rosovsky and Kazushi Ohkawa, "The Indigenous Components in the Modern Japanese Economy," *Econ. Dev. and Cultural Change* 9 (Apr. 1961): 488; also Ohkawa, "Agriculture and Turning Points," p. 481.

45. Shinohara, *Structural Changes*, p. 305.

46. Ibid., p. 307.

47. Broadbridge, *Industrial Dualism in Japan*, p. 50.

48. Ibid., p. 51.

49. MITI, 1970 *Chūshō kigyō hakusho* (White paper on medium and small enterprises) (Tokyo: Ōkurashō insatsu-kyoku, 1971), p. 10 (Fuzoku tōkei-hyo) (Attached list of statistics).

50. See Shinohara, *Structural Changes*, p. 308.

51. Yamamura, *Economic Policy*, p. 166.

52. Rōdōshō, ed., *Rōdō hakusho* (Labor white paper) (Tokyo: Ōkurashō insatsu-kyoku, 1971), p. 4.

53. MITI, Medium and Small Enterprise Agency, *Medium and Small Industry*, *White Paper* (1969), pp. 45–62.

54. Medium and Small Enterprise Agency, *Supplement* (1971), p. 29, chart 28(2).

55. Both Marxist and non-Marxist views are summarized in Shunjūsha, ed., *Nihon keizai no kiso kōzō* (The basic structure of Japan's economy), 9th ed. (Tokyo: Shunjūsha, 1971); also see discussions in Yamamura, *Economic Policy*, pp. 163–72.

56. See Yamamura, *Economic Policy*, pp. 173–86, for thoughtful evaluative comments (p. 180) and summaries of several positions (pp. 173–80) that are somewhat dated now by narrowing differentials and annual wage raises higher than annual increases in productivity, in some sectors at least, since 1967.

57. There is a growing literature, popular and otherwise, on Japanese economic growth. A useful survey: Ohkawa and Rosovsky, "A Century of Japanese Economic Growth," in *State and Economic Enterprise in Japan*, ed. Lockwood, pp. 47–92. Two recent books synthesize much of the prior research product: Shinohara, *Structural Changes;* and Ohkawa, Johnston, and Kaneda, *Agriculture and Economic Growth*. Also four recent issues of the journal *Developing Economies* (Vol. III, No. 4, Dec. 1965; Vol. V, No. 2, June 1967; Vol. VII, No. 2, June 1969; Vol. VII, No. 4, Dec. 1969) have relevant up-to-date studies. An earlier collection edited by Ryūtarō Komiya, *Postwar Economic Growth in Japan* (U. of Cal. Press, 1966), is also useful. For special monographs in English, see the Shinohara volume, *Structural Changes*. The following show refreshing outsiders' insights by experts in their respective fields who do not claim to be Japan specialists: E. Wight Bakke, *Revolutionary Democracy: Challenge and Testing in Japan* (Hamden, Conn.: Archon Books, 1968), p. 152; Marshall E. Dimock, *The Japanese Technocracy* (Tokyo: Walker-Weatherhill, 1968), p. 22; Herman Kahn, *The Emerging Japanese Superstate: Challenge and Response* (Englewood Cliffs, N.J.: Prentice-Hall, 1970), p. 75; also Norman McCrea, "The Risen Sun," *The Economist*, 27 May 1967.

58. Shinohara, *Structural Changes*, p. 21.

59. See U.S. Dept. of Commerce, *Japan: The Government-Business Relationship* (Washington, D.C.: GPO, 1972), p. 11.

60. M. Yoshino, *Japan's Managerial System* (MIT Press, 1968), p. 254; Kiyoaki Tsuji, "Decision Making in the Japanese Government: A Study of *Ringisei*," in *Political Development in Modern Japan*, ed. Robert E. Ward (Princeton U. Press, 1968), p. 457.

61. Byron K. Marshall, *Capitalism and Nationalism in Prewar Japan: the Ideology of the Business Elite* (Stanford U. Press, 1967), p. 30.

62. See, *e.g.*, Vogel, *Japan's New Mdidle Class*, p. 3; Kazuko Tsurumi, *Social Change and the Individual: Japan Before and After Defeat in World War II* (Princeton U. Press, 1970), p. 183; Chie Nakane, *Kinship and Economic Organization in Rural Japan* (New York: Humanities Press, Inc., 1967), p. 130; Tadashi Fukutake, *Man and Society in Japan* (Tokyo: U. of Tokyo Press, 1962), p. 105; Arthur M. Whitehill, Jr. and Shin'ichi Takezawa, *The Other Worker: A Comparative Study of Industrial Relations in the U.S. and Japan* (Honolulu: East-West Center Press, 1968), p. 95; James C. Abegglen, *The Japanese Factory: Aspects of Its Social Organization* (Glencoe, Ill.: Free Press, 1958), p. 11; Ronald P. Dore, *City Life in Japan* (U. of Cal. Press, 1960), p. 15.

63. See Shinohara, *Structural Changes*, p. 107; for background, Henry Rosovsky, *Capital Formation in Japan, 1868–1940* (Glencoe, Ill.: Free Press, 1961), p. 358.

64. Angus Maddison, *Economic Growth in Japan and the USSR* (London: George Allen and Unwin, Ltd., 1969), p. 51.

65. Tuvia Blumenthal, *Savings in Postwar Japan* (Harvard U. Press, 1970), p. 12.

66. See, generally, Toshiyuki Mizoguchi, *Personal Savings and Consumption in Postwar Japan* (Tokyo: Kinokuniya Bookstore, 1970), p. 301; and Ryūtarō Komiya, "The Supply of Personal Savings," in *Postwar Economic Growth in Japan*, ed. Ryūtarō Komiya and trans. Robert S. Ozaki (U. of Cal. Press, 1966).

67. Blumenthal, *Savings in Postwar Japan*, p. 94.

68. See *Far Eastern Economics Review* (9 Dec. 1972), p. 31, where it says that real estate prices are rising 20% per year in Japan.

69. Hadley, *Antitrust in Japan*, p. 414. Compare Yamamura, *Economic Policy*, pp. 20, 33.

70. For example, Trezise, "The Realities of Japan–U.S. Economic Relations," p. 363.

71. From James Morley, "Growth for What? The Issues of the Seventies," in *Japanese-American Relations in the 1970's*, ed. Gerald L. Curtis (Washington, D.C.: Columbia Books, 1970), p. 83.

72. Shinohara, *Structural Changes*, p. 8.

73. Hadley, *Antitrust in Japan*, p. 393; *Japan Economic Journal* (15 Feb. 1972), p. 10.

74. *Japan Times Weekly* (2 Jan., 1973), p. 1.

75. Hadley, *Antitrust in Japan*, p. 393.

76. Leon Hollerman, "Recent Difficulties in Japan's Economic Development," *Banca Nazionale del Lavoro Quarterly Review* 88 (March 1969): 3.

77. JERC, *Japan's Economy in 1975*, p. 15, and U.S. Dept. of Commerce, *The United States in the Changing World Economy*, 2: 9.

78. Japan Industrial Promotion Association, *The Key to the Japanese Market: Its Possibilities and Prospects* (Tokyo: Japan Industrial Promotion Association, 1968), 1: 171, 176; Alan Gleason, "Economic Growth and Consumption in Japan," in *State and Economic Enterprise in Japan*, ed. Lockwood, p. 391; Boyce De Mente and Fred Perry, *The Japanese as Consumers* (Tokyo: Walker Weatherhill, 1968), p. 21.

79. *M. C. K.K.* v. *Schulyro [Shiro?] Trading Co., Ltd.* (Osaka Dist. Ct., 27 Feb. 1970. English translation: 16 *Japanese Annual of International Law* 113 (1972). See *Japan Economic Journal* (22 Feb. 1972), p. 2.

80. Kyung-Mo Huh, *Japan's Trade in Asia* (New York: Praeger, 1966), pp. 85, 121. Also see, Alfred K. Ho, *The Far East in World Trade* (New York: Praeger, 1967), pp. 152, 342.

81. Leon Hollerman, *Japan's Dependence on the World Economy* (Princeton U. Press, 1967), p. 43.

82. Yamamura, *Economic Policy*, pp. 61, 63, notes 26, 66, and 184. See also exchange between Ted Kennedy and Prime Minister Tanaka re this point in *Japan Economic Journal* (22 Feb. 1972), p. 12.

83. *Japan Stock Journal* (14 Sept. 1970), p. 9.

84. See Kiyoshi Kojima, *Non-Tariff Barriers to Japan's Trade* (Tokyo: JERC, 1971), p. 37, for a candid collection of export incentives and subsidies of many sorts.

85. In March 1971 Japan's overseas direct investments stood at $3.6 billion and have been increasing annually at a rate of 33% from 1966 to 1971. *Japan Economic Journal* (14 Nov. 1972), p. 2. The *JEJ*, 4 July 1972, reported that Japan controlled 40 U.S. firms, while England had 70 and West Germany, 120. Keizai shingikai, Kokusai shihon idō kenkyū iinkai, ed., *Shihon jiyūka to kaigai kigyō shinshutsu* (1969), p. 129.

86. See U.S. Dept. of Commerce, *The United States in the Changing World Economy*, 2: 46; and Sidney E. Rolfe, *The Multinational Corporation* (New York: Foreign Policy Association, 1970), p. 20.

87. See the annual reports on imported technology; *e.g.*, Gaishi dōnyū nenkan henshū iinkai, ed., *Gaishi dōnyū nenkan* (Annual on foreign capital induction), Part 3 (Tokyo: Shōkō kaikan, 1969), p. 22; and for background, Hideomi Tuge, *Historical Development of Science and Technology in Japan*, rev. ed. (Tokyo: Kokusai bunka shinkōkai, 1968). Compare JIPA, *The Key to the Japanese Market* (Tokyo: Japan Industrial

Promotion Association, 1968), 1: 98, where it puts the sales based on foreign technique at 10% of total sales, which is highly misleading, if the impression to be left with the reader is that 90% of Japanese industry is functioning today free of postwar imported technology.

88. Jūkagaku kōgyō tsūshinsha, ed., *Kaigai tōshi gijutsu yushutsu yōran* (Survey of overseas investment and exports of technology) (Tokyo: Jūkagaku kōgyō tsūshinsha, 1970), p. 348.

89. JERC, *Japan's Economy in 1975*, p. 17. Keizai shingikai, Kokusai shihon idō kenkyū iinkai, ed., *Shihon jiyūka to kaigai kigyō shinshutsu* (Capital liberalization and the advance of enterprise abroad) (Tokyo: Ōkurashō insatsukyoku, 1970), pp. 1–31.

90. See Kagaku gijutsu-chō, ed., *Kagaku gijutsu hakusho* (Science and technology white paper) (Tokyo: Ōkurashō Insatsukyoku, 1972), p. 348.

91. *E.g.*, see Jūkagaku kōgyō tsūshinsha, ed., *Kaigai tōshi*, pp. 382–415, for detailed list of Japanese licensors and foreign licensees, etc. The statistics below are taken from this report. See pp. 339 ff.

92. *Japan Economic Journal* (14 Nov. 1972), p. 2, and Editor, "Japan's Overseas Investments," *Oriental Economist* 40 (July 1972): 16.

93. JERC, *Japan's Economy in 1975*, p. 48.

94. Keizai shingikai, *Shihon jiyūka to kaigai kigyō shinshutsu*, p. 130. Note that the figures show amounts approved by the Japanese government for investment abroad. Repatriations, amounts never actually invested, or accumulated capital after the initial investment do not show, but since all Japanese holding virtually started anew in 1951, the figures are adequate to grasp the general magnitude.

95. *Far Eastern Economic Review* (9 Dec., 1972), p. 33, says only $511 million was government aid; the rest was tied loans at higher than standard aid interest. Saburō Sakita, "Japanese Economic Cooperation in Asia in the 1970's," in *Japanese-American Relations in the 1970's*, ed. Curtis, p. 94. Also see Masao Sakurai, *Wagakuni no keizai kyōryoku* (Our economic cooperation) (Tokyo: Ajia keizai kenkyūjo, 1972).

96. See Kahn, *The Emerging Japanese Superstate*, p. 160.

CHAPTER IV

1. In bringing together and attempting to present the essentials of the Japanese business environment, I have drawn heavily upon both Japanese and English secondary literature, besides the official publications and my own experiences with trans-Pacific enterprises. Particularly useful in Japanese are the following: Noritake Kobayashi, *Nihon no gōben gaisha* (Japanese joint venture companies) (Tokyo: Tōyō keizai shimpōsha, 1967); Chie Nakane, *Tate-shakai no ningen kankei* (Human relationships in a vertically [organized] society) (Tokyo: Kōdansha, 1967); Takeyoshi Kawashima, *Ideorogī to shite no kazoku seido* (The family system as an ideology) (Tokyo: Iwanami shoten, 1964); Giichi Miyazaki, *Gendai Nihon no dokusen shihon, Vol. V, Shikin chōtatsu* (Monopolistic capital in contemporary Japan: capital formation) (Tokyo: Shiseidō, 1966); Noriyoshi Imai, *Gendai Nihon no dokusen shihon, Vol. I, Dokusen keitai* (Monopolistic capital in contemporary Japan: monopolistic forms) (Tokyo: Shiseidō, 1964); Hiroshi Mannari, *Za bijinesu erīto: Nihon ni okeru keieisha no jōken* (The business elite: the background of business leaders in Japan) (Tokyo: Kōdansha, 1965); Hitoshi Misono, *Nihon no dokusen* (Monopoly in Japan) (Tokyo: Shiseidō, 1965); Giichi Miyazaki, *Sengo Nihon no keizai kikō* (Economic structure in postwar Japan) (Tokyo: Shin hyōronsha, 1966); Shūichirō Nakamura, Sekio Sugioka, Ichiō Takenaka, and Kimishirō Masamura, *Nihon sangyō to kasen taisei* (Japanese industry and oligopolistic structure) (Tokyo: Shin hyōron, 1966); Kazutarō Sugano, *Nihon kaisha kigyōshi no kenkyū* (Studies in the development of joint stock companies in Japan) (Tokyo: Tōyō keizai shimpōsha, 1966); Yasuo Takeyama, *Nihon no keiei: sono fūdo to tembō* (Japanese

management: its climate and perspective) (Tokyo: Kashima kenkyūjo shuppankai, 1965); Takao Tsuchiya, *Nihon no keieisha seishin* (Managerial mentality in Japan) (Tokyo: Keizai ōraisha, 1963).

The following recent works have also multiplied substantially what can be learned, in English, about various aspects of Japanese business: M. Y. Yoshino, *Japan's Managerial System: Tradition and Innovation* (MIT Press, 1968), and my review, 11 *Harvard J. of Int'l. Law* 287–93 (1970); M. Y. Yoshino, *The Japanese Marketing System* (MIT Press, 1971); T. F. M. Adams and Iwao Hoshii *A Financial History of the New Japan* (Tokyo and Palo Alto: Kōdansha International, Ltd., 1972); Kōzō Yamamura, *Economic Policy in Postwar Japan* (U. of Cal. Press, 1967); Eleanor M. Hadley, *Antitrust in Japan* (Princeton U. Press, 1970); Robert Evans, Jr., *The Labor Economies of Japan and the United States* (New York: Praeger, 1971); Solomon B. Levine, *Industrial Relations in Postwar Japan* (U. of Ill. Press, 1958); Kōji Taira, *Economic Development and the Labor Market in Japan* (Columbia U. Press, 1970).

The following works, oriented to foreigners' problems, contain extremely useful information and insights because of the practical experience that their respective authors possess after long tenure in Japan: Shunzo Arai, *The Intersection of East and West: Japanese Business Management* (Tokyo: Rikugei Publishing House, 1971); Robert J. Ballon and Eugene H. Lee, eds., *Foreign Investment in Japan* (Tokyo: Sophia University, 1972); James C. Abegglen, ed., *Business Strategies for Japan* (Tokyo: Sophia University, 1970); T. F. M. Adams and Noritake Kobayashi, *The World of Japanese Business* (Tokyo: Kōdansha International Ltd., 1969); Robert J. Ballon, *Doing Business in Japan* (Tokyo: Sophia U. and Tuttle, 1968); Robert J. Ballon, *The Japanese Employee* (Tokyo: Sophia U. and Tuttle, 1969); Herbert F. Glazer, *The International Businessman in Japan: The Japanese Image* (Tokyo: Sophia U. and Tuttle, 1968); Iwao Hoshii, *The Dynamics of Japan's Business Evolution* (Tokyo and Philadelphia: Orient-West, 1966); Japan Industrial Promotion Association, *The Key to the Japanese Market* (Tokyo: Japan Industrial Promotion Association, 1968–69); also the monthly *Journal of the American Chamber of Commerce in Japan* frequently contains useful summaries of up-to-date information.

Much other valuable specialized literature is cited where appropriate below.

2. Interesting here, for example, is the "sociology-over-economics controversy" centered on the Japanese life employment system (*shūshin koyō*). Compare Robert E. Cole, *Japanese Blue Collar: The Changing Tradition* (U. of Cal. Press, 1971), p. 7, with James C. Abegglen, *The Japanese Factory* (Glencoe: Free Press, 1958), p. 11, and Abegglen, *Business Strategies for Japan*, p. 37; see also Taira, *Economic Development and the Labor Market in Japan*, p. 97; Kōya Azumi, *Higher Education and Business Recruitment in Japan* (Columbia U., Teachers College Press, 1969), p. 31; and Ken'ichi Kobayashi, "The Employment and Wage System in Postwar Japan," *The Developing Economies* 7 (1969): 202, 210. For a blend see Solomon B. Levine, "Labor Markets and Collective Bargaining in Japan" in *The State and Economic Enterprise in Japan*, ed. William W. Lockwood (Princeton U. Press, 1965), p. 640.

3. Asahi Shimbun Staff, *Pacific Rivals: A Japanese View of Japanese-American Relations* (Tokyo: Weatherhill-Asahi, 1972), p. 2 (foreword by Edwin O. Reischauer).

4. Arthur M. Whitehall, Jr., and Shin'ichi Takezawa, *The Other Worker: A Comparative Study of Industrial Relations in the U.S. and Japan* (Honolulu: East-West Center Press, 1968), p. 352, have well demonstrated, in almost ponderous detail, what experienced observers can intuitively sense: a marked difference in attitudes of younger workers on a wide range of industrial relations questions carefully canvassed.

5. For a discussion of the logic of industrialization, see Clark Kerr, John T. Dunlop, Frederick H. Harbison, and Charles A. Myers, *Industrialism and Industrial Man: The Problems of Labor and Management in Economic Growth* (Harvard U. Press, 1960), p. 14. See also Solomon B. Levine, "Postwar Trade Unionism, Collective Bargaining, and Japanese Social Structure," in *Aspects of Social Change in Modern Japan*, ed. Ronald P. Dore (Princeton U. Press, 1967), p. 246.

6. Besides Levine, Ballon, and Taira (cited in note 1 of this chapter), I have benefited most from the following books on labor generally:

Kazuo Ōkōchi, Shōjirō Ujihara, and Wakao Fujita, ed., *Rōdō kumiai no kōzō to kinō* (The structure and function of labor unions) (Tokyo: Tokyo daigaku shuppankai, 1959); Shin'ichi Takezawa, *Ningen no kanri* (Management of men) (Tokyo: Kōdansha, 1960); Shizuo Matsushima, *Rōmukanri no Nihon-teki tokushitsu to hensen* (Japanese characteristics and fluctuations in labor managment) (Tokyo: Daiyamondosha, 1962); Gorō Mori, *Sengo Nihon no rōmukanri* (Labor management in postwar Japan) (Tokyo: Daiyamondosha, 1961).

Cole, *Japanese Blue Collar;* Iwao F. Ayusawa, *A History of Labor in Modern Japan* (Honolulu: East-West Center Press, 1966), pp. 232–388; Whitehall and Takezawa, *The Other Worker;* Alice H. Cook, *An Introduction to Japanese Trade Unionism* (Cornell U. Press, 1966).

7. See Nakane, *Tate-shakai no ningen kankei*, p. 4. Kobayashi says, quoting a 1964 *Keizai Dōyūkai* survey report: "In fact, the great majority of top managers in Japan who attempt to evaluate thoughtfully the results of managerial decisions are of the opinion that their corporate activities should contribute first to the satisfaction of their employees and second to the social and economic betterment of the greater company of Japan." (Adams and Kobayashi, *World of Japanese Business*, p. 279.)

We can find rather early American statements about the private corporation's public duties to the community they serve, but little suggestion that their major responsibilities are to their employees. See, for example, E. Merrick Dodd, "For Whom Are Corporate Managers Trustees?" 45 *Harvard L. Rev.* 1145 (1932).

8. See Takeyoshi Kawashima, *Nihon shakai no kazokuteki kōsei* (The familial structure of Japanese society) (Tokyo: Nihon hyōronsha, 1950).

9. Indeed, a major obstacle to understanding the Japanese has been the parochial disposition of certain monolingual foreigners, happily in decreasing numbers, to persist in thinking that the problem is a mere language difficulty that can be solved clerically (*i.e.*, by hiring a translator), or, as it were, "Everyone understands English, if we shout." See, for the inseparability of language, thought, and behavior, Hajime Nakamura, "Consciousness of the Individual and the Universal among the Japanese," in *The Status of the Individual in East and West*, ed. Charles A. Moore (Honolulu: East-West Center Press, 1968), p. 441; and for a succinct special example that makes the pivotal point about language efficiently, see L. Takeo Doi, "*Amae:* A Key Concept for Understanding Japanese Personality Structure," in *Japanese Culture: Its Development and Characteristics*, ed. Robert J. Smith and Richard K. Beardsley (Chicago: Aldine Publ. Co., 1962), p. 132.

10. For a perceptive summary see "The Ladder of Success" in Herbert Passin, *Society and Education in Japan* (Columbia U., Teachers College Press, 1965), p. 132; and Ezra Vogel, *Japan's New Middle Class* (U. of Cal. Press, 1963), pp. 40–70.

11. Another tough issue, concerning the capacity of "insiders" to explain, was raised in the East-West Philosophers' Conference. See Charles A. Moore, ed., *The Japanese Mind* (Honolulu: East-West Center Press, 1968), Preface.

The difficulty I referred to in the text above is not that of the Japanese scholars to see themselves objectively, but that of the journalist and ordinary Japanese businessmen met in daily transactions in Tokyo.

Certainly the following recent books, for example, demonstrate amply the capacity of a growing group of Japanese scholars "to get outside of themselves" and explain Japanese psychology and behavior, even in English: Hajime Nakamura, *Ways of Thinking of Eastern Peoples: India, China, Tibet and Japan* (Honolulu: East-West Center Press, 1964), p. 449; Kazuko Tsurumi, *Social Change and the Individual: Japan Before and After Defeat in World War II* (Princeton U. Press, 1970); Moore, *The Japanese Mind*, with useful articles by fourteen distinguished Japanese; Tadashi Fukutake, *Man and Society in Japan* (U. of Tokyo Press, 1962); Chie Nakane, *Japanese Society* (U. of Cal. Press, 1970).

12. Let it be said emphatically that, while referring to the "minuet" or "diplomatic" personal relations, I do not deprecate at all the merits or the yield of these methods of cross-cultural cultivation; they certainly compare favorably with foreigners' treatment of Japanese. I am simply emphasizing the things that they do not explain to the foreigner. Glazer, *The International Businessman in Japan*, p. 9, makes this point well.

13. As noted (Chapter II), many have wrestled on a general philosophical level with the Japanese personality and psychology. For early examples see Inazō Nitobe, *Japanese Traits and Foreign Influence* (London: Kegan & Co., 1927), p. 20; F. S. C. Northrop, *The Meeting of East and West* (New York: Macmillan Co., 1946), p. 436.

For recent short statements see chapters by Hajime Nakamura, Tesshi Furukawa, Masaaki Kōsaka, and Takeyoshi Kawashima, in *The Status of the Individual in East and West*, ed. Charles A. Moore (Honolulu: East-West Center Press, 1968), pp. 141, 301, 361, and 429 respectively; and chapters by Shōson Miyamoto, Hideki Yukawa, Ichirō Hori, and Moore ("Editor's Supplement: The Enigmatic Japanese Mind"), in Moore, *The Japanese Mind*, pp. 4, 52, 201, and 288 respectively; also stimulating summaries, Maurice Bairy, "Motivational Forces in Japanese Life" in *The Japanese Employee*, ed. Ballon, p. 41, and Bairy, "Japanese Ways," in *Doing Business in Japan*, ed. Ballon, p. 3.

14. Ryōkichi Hirono, "Personnel Management in Foreign Corporations," in *The Japanese Employee*, ed. Ballon, p. 267, says that on balance the Japanese group in fact requires and often gets more service than it provides in self-fulfillment, quite apart from the ideal.

15. See Moore, *The Japanese Mind*, p. 288; and Bairy, "Japanese Ways," in *Doing Business in Japan*, ed. Ballon, p. 8.

16. Azumi, *Higher Education and Business Recruitment in Japan*, p. 6, has an interesting synthesis rather like my own, though he treats age ("gerontocracy") more as a separate category.

17. Doi, *"Amae"* in *Japanese Culture*, ed. Smith and Beardsley, pp. 132–39.

18. Azumi, *Higher Education and Business Recruitment in Japan*, p. 68.

19. Whitehall and Takezawa, *The Other Worker*, p. 352, confirm, from their extensive questionnaires answered by employees of large firms, that major work motivation for Japanese laborers was related to the social harness they constantly find themselves in.

20. The classics on this subject are E. H. Norman, *Japan's Emergence as a Modern State* (New York: Institute of Pacific Relations, 1938); William W. Lockwood, *The Economic Development of Japan: Growth and Structural Change, 1868–1938* (Princeton U. Press, 1954); and Thomas C. Smith, *Political Change and Industrial Development in Japan: Government Enterprises, 1868–1880* (Stanford U. Press, 1955). For a vivid synopsis see Robert J. Ballon, "The Japanese Dimension of Industrial Enterprises" in *The Japanese Employee*, ed. Ballon, pp. 3–40.

21. Byron K. Marshall, *Capitalism and Nationalism in Prewar Japan: The Ideology of the Business Elite, 1868–1941* (Stanford U. Press, 1967), p. 30.

22. Note the rather recent finding that with a growing scarcity of temporary workers some life-employees have recently resigned their firms to obtain higher immediate pay as temporary employees. Ken'ichi Kobayashi, "The Employment and Wage Systems in Postwar Japan," *The Developing Economies*, p. 187.

23. See, generally, Ken'ichi Kobayashi, *Gendai Nihon no koyō kōzō* (Employment structure in present-day Japan) (Tokyo: Iwanami-shoten, 1966), pp. 25–44, 194–257; and Yoshino, *Japan's Managerial System*, pp. 225–53.

24. In English, Yamamura, *Economic Policy in Postwar Japan*, p. 168, and Seymour Broadbridge, *Industrial Dualism in Japan* (Chicago: Aldine Pub. Co., 1966), pp. 72–86, make this point clear.

25. For details see Azumi, *Higher Education and Business Recruitment in Japan*, p. 50.

26. See Editor, "Wages in Major Enterprises," *Oriental Economist* 40 (Dec. 1972): 18; and Robert J. Ballon, "Lifelong Remuneration System," in *The Japanese Employee*, ed. Ballon, p. 123.

27. This term *kimatsu teate* is preferred by organized labor to strengthen the argument that it is simply deferred wages, not a reward for profits earned.

28. Iwao Tomita, "Labor Cost Accounting," in *The Japanese Employee*, ed. Ballon, p. 176.

29. Whitehill and Takezawa, *The Other Worker*, p. 158, have confirmed these sharp differences in concrete terms.

30. Ballon, *The Japanese Employee*, ed. Ballon, p. 65, quoting Tadao Umesao.

31. But note that in periods of recession or stagnation, Kobayashi, "The Employment and Wage Systems in Postwar Japan," *Developing Economies*, points out that anti-rationalization disputes have been common, if it involves cutting the "permanent" worker force, as has happened, and can happen again unless we are to assume, euphorically, that the Japanese economy will expand at a uniformly high rate forever.

32. Chūshō kigyō-chō, *Chūshō kigyo hakusho* (Medium and small enterprise white paper) (Tokyo: Ōkura-shō insatsu-kyoku, 1972), p. 42.

33. Ibid., p. 210, points out that during the 1962–64 slump many were rationalized out of their "life employment" in shaky firms.

34. Azumi, *Higher Education and Business Recruitment in Japan*, p. 38.

35. See generally on organization: Hiroshi Gōhara, *Nihon no keiei soshiki* (Organization of Japanese management) (Tokyo: Tōyō keizai shimpōsha, 1968); Nakane, *Tateshakai no ningen kankei*, p. 114; Noritake Kobayashi, "Management Differences" in *World of Japanese Business*, Adams and Kobayashi, p. 278; Yoshino, *Japan's Managerial Systems*, pp. 196–224; Abegglen, *The Japanese Factory;* Herbert F. Glazer, "The Japanese Executive" in *The Japanese Employee*, ed. Ballon, pp. 77–93.

36. Susumu Takamiya, "Business Organization," in *Doing Business in Japan*, ed. Ballon, p. 170.

37. Adams wryly notes: "*Ex oriente lux, ex occidente lex*," in *World of Japanese Business*, Adams and Kobayashi, p. 132.

38. See Chapter V (*infra*); also, Dan Fenno Henderson, *Conciliation and Japanese Law* (U. of Wash. Press, 1965) 2: 183.

39. For astute comparative insights, see Hirono, "Personnel Management in Foreign Corporations," in *The Japanese Employee*, ed. Ballon, pp. 251–71.

40. Yoshino, *Japan's Managerial System*, p. 208.

41. Toshio Sawada, *Subsequent Conduct and Supervening Events* (U. of Tokyo Press, 1967), p. 167, notes that disputes with buyers are seldom reported to others in the firm by sales sections.

42. See generally, in English, Misao Tatsuta and Dan Fenno Henderson, eds., *Cases and Materials on Japanese Business Corporation Law*, University of Washington School of Law, mimeo. (1967), 3 vols.; Makoto Yazawa, "The Legal Structure for Corporate Enterprise: Shareholder-Management Relations under Japanese Law," in *Law in Japan: The Legal Order in a Changing Society*, ed. Arthur T. von Mehren (Harvard U. Press, 1963), p. 547; and *cf.* Lester N. Salwin, "The New Commercial Code of Japan: Symbol of Gradual Progress Toward Democratic Goals," 50 *Georgetown L. J.* 478 (1962).

43. See, *e.g.*, Commercial Code, Arts. 263, 267, and 272. For an English translation see Eibun Hōreisha, *The Commercial Code of Japan* (No. 2200) (1967). All code translations pose nearly as many problems as they solve, but the EHS version is "under authorization of the Ministry of Justice and the Codes Translation Committee."

44. Com. Code, Art. 260.

45. Ibid., Art. 261.

46. See Ibid., Arts. 273 to 280. Though now standard usage in translation, "auditor" as an English equivalent for *kansayaku* can easily confuse foreigners with the CPA (*kōnin kaikeishi*); hence I have put it in quotation marks.

47. Akira Tanabe, "Shōhō o ichibu kaisei suru hōritsu-an yōkō ni tsuite" (Concerning the summary of a bill to amend a part of the Commercial Code), *Shōji hōmu kenkyū* (No. 517) 2 (1970); see Gerhard G. Mueller and Hiroshi Yoshida, *Accounting Practices*

in Japan (Seattle: Graduate School of Bus. Adm., U. of Wash., 1968), for general information on Japanese accounting.

48. T. W. M. Teraoka, "Accounting Practice," in *Doing Business in Japan*, ed. Ballon, p. 150. Also note his candid comment on the San'yō Steel case, which he compares with the McKesson-Robbins case in the U.S.

49. Commercial Code, Art. 262 provides: "A company shall be liable to a bona fide third person for any act done by a director invested with any title such as president, vice-president, chief [*semmu*] director or managing director from which it may be assumed that he has authority to represent the company even in cases where such person has no power of representation."

50. See Kobayashi's comment, in Adams and Kobayashi, *World of Japanese Business*, p. 280.

51. A recent cartoon showed the expert as his own division-head, sitting on top of a highchair with no one under him, captioned "*Ekisupāto wa ippiki ōkami*," translated, "The expert is emperor of a one-animal kingdom." Glazer, "The Japanese Executive," in *The Japanese Employee*, ed. Ballon, p. 88.

52. See, generally, Kigyō Kenkyūkai, *Ringi-teki keiei to ringi seido* (*Ringi*-style management and the *ringi* system) (Tokyo: Tōyō keizai shimpōsha, 1966); Toyoaki Ono, *Nihon-teki keiei to ringi seido* (The system of *ringi* and Japanese-style management) (Tokyo: Daiyamondosha, 1960); and Akira Yamashiro, *Keiei* (Management) (Tokyo: Nihon keizai shimbunsha, 1958). The same *ringi* system is used in the government; see Nikō Kawanaka, *Gendai no kanryōsei* (The contemporary bureaucratic system) (Tokyo: Chūō daigaku shuppanbu, 1962).

In English, Yoshino, *Japan's Managerial System*, pp. 254–72; Ichiro Hattori, "Management Practices," in *Doing Business in Japan*, ed. Ballon, pp. 159–68; Takamiya, "Business Organization," in ibid., p. 170; and concerning government uses, see Kiyoaki Tsuji, "Decision-making in the Japanese Government: A Study of *Ringi-sei*," in *Political Development in Modern Japan*, ed. Robert E. Ward (Princeton U. Press, 1968), pp. 457–75.

53. Yoshino, *Japan's Management System*, p. 262.

54. Ono, *Nihon-teki keiei to ringi seido*, pp. 4–5.

55. Takamiya, "Business Organization," in *Doing Business in Japan*, ed. Ballon, p. 169.

56. Kazuo Noda, *Nihon no jūyaku* (Japan's top executives) (Tokyo: Daiyamondosha, 1960), p. 109.

57. See generally, on Japan unionism, Kazuo Ōkōchi, Shōjiro Ujihara, and Wakao Fujita, eds., *Rōdō kumiai no kōzō to kinō* (The structure and function of labor unions) (Tokyo: Tokyo daigaku shuppankai, 1959); Robert Evans, Jr., *The Labor Economics of Japan and the United States* (New York: Praeger, 1971); Cole, *Japanese Blue Collar*, p. 225; Levine, *Industrial Relations in Postwar Japan;* Cook, *Japanese Trade Unionism;* Yamamura, *Economic Policy in Postwar Japan*, pp. 152–72; Levine, "Postwar Trade Unionism, Collective Bargaining, and Japanese Social Structure," in *Aspects of Social Change in Modern Japan*, ed. Dore, p. 245; Levine, "Labor Markets and Collective Bargaining in Japan" in *The State and Economic Enterprise in Japan*, ed. Lockwood, p. 633; Robert A. Scalapino, "Labor and Politics in Postwar Japan" in ibid., p. 669; and chapters by Paul T. Chang, Makoto Sakurabayashi, and Tadashi Hanami, in *The Japanese Employee*, ed. Ballon, pp. 201, 227, and 241 respectively; Kang Chao, "Labor Institutions in Japan and Her Economic Growth," *J. of Asian Studies* 28 (1968): 5–17.

58. These figures come from the *Rōdō kumiai kihon chōsa* (Basic survey of labor unions) (Tokyo: Ministry of Labor, 1966), p. 80.

59. Levine, "Postwar Trade Unionism, Collective Bargaining, and Japanese Social Structure," in *Aspects of Social Change in Modern Japan*, ed. Dore, p. 251.

60. Makoto Sakurabayashi, "Enterprise Unionism and Wage Increases," in *The Japanese Employee*, ed. Ballon, p. 238.

61. See Cook, *Japanese Trade Unionism*, p. 30.

62. Yamamura, *Economic Policy in Postwar Japan*, p. 155, shows the productivity index rising from 100 to 216 (1953 to 1963), but the labor share rising only from 47.7 to 53.9, compared with U.S., 71.1, and W. Germany, 63.5 (in 1962). Of course both nominal and real wages in Japan were rising very rapidly, regardless of the only slight improvement in labor's share.

63. See the book review by Makoto Sakurabayashi of Cook, *Japanese Trade Unionism*, in *Monumenta Nipponica* 23 (1968): 220.

64. On the rights to unionize and bargain, Japanese public employees submitted a complaint (and the Japanese government gave the necessary consent) to the Fact Finding and Conciliation Commission on Freedom of Association of the International Labor Organization in Geneva in 1964, which reported at length. See *Report of the Fact Finding and Conciliation Commission on Freedom of Association Concerning Persons Employed in the Public Sector in Japan* (Geneva: International Labor Office, 1965). During the hearing (on 14 June 1965) the Japanese government ratified the *Freedom of Association and Protection of the Right to Organize Convention*, thus clearing the air somewhat. The report found certain grounds for labor's dissatisfaction, as well as much wrong with labor attitudes, especially antigovernment politics extending even to obstructionism in routine labor management affairs.

65. The full development is summarized in Levine, *Industrial Relations in Postwar Japan*, pp. 21, 59, and Levine, "Postwar Trade Unionism, Collective Bargaining, and Japanese Social Structure," in *Aspects of Social Change in Modern Japan*, ed. Dore, p. 245. See also Scalapino, "Labor and Politics in Postwar Japan," in *The State and Economic Enterprise in Japan*, ed. Lockwood, p. 669.

66. Richard J. Smethurst, "The Origin and the Politics of the Japan Teachers' Union 1945–56," in Center of Japanese Studies, U. of Mich., *Occasional Papers*, No. 10 (U. of Mich. Press, 1967), pp. 117–60. Cole, *Japanese Blue Collar*, p. 267, offers an interesting insight, saying that Marxist ideology serves as a symbol of willingness to confront management for worker interests, but the worker, though appreciating this symbol, does not express commitment to the ideology itself by voting for a Marxist. To some extent, I share this view.

67. Kichiemon Ishikawa, "The Regulation of the Employer-Employee Relationship: Japanese Labor-Relations Law," in *Law in Japan: The Legal Order in a Changing Society*, ed. von Mehren, p. 441.

68. See, for example, Wakao Fujita, *Rōdō kumiai to rōdō kyōyaku* (Labor unions and collective labor agreements) (Tokyo: Hakutō shobō, 1963).

69. The better view in Japan is that Const., Art. 12, qualifies all of the rights conferred in the Japanese Constitution (Chapter III). Art. 12 reads: "The freedoms and rights guaranteed to the people by this Constitution shall be maintained by the constant endeavor of the people, who shall refrain from any abuse of these freedoms and rights and shall always be responsible for utilizing them for the public welfare." See Lawrence W. Beer, "The Public Welfare Standard and Freedom of Expression in Japan," in *The Constitution of Japan: Its First Twenty Years, 1947–67*, ed. Dan Fenno Henderson (U. of Wash. Press, 1968), p. 205.

70. See Kichiemon Ishikawa, "Rōsohō to kempō 28 jō to no kankei" (The relationship between LUL and Const. Art. 28), 87 *Hōgaku kyōkai zasshi* 1–14 (1970).

71. It was replaced by *Rōdō kumiai-hō* (Labor Union Law) (Law No. 174, 1949), in 8 EHS No. 8000; see Levine, *Industrial Relations in Postwar Japan*, p. 24.

72. National Labor Relations Act of 1935, 49 Stat. 449 (1935) 29 U.S.C.S. 101 (1956).

73. LUL, Art. 7.

74. *Rōdō kankei chōsei-hō* (Labor relations adjustment law) (Law No. 25, 1946), in 8 EHS No. 8010.

75. *E.g.*, *Kōkyō kigyō-tai to rōdō kankei-hō* (Public Enterprise, etc., labor relations law) (Law No. 257, 1948), in 8 EHS No. 8020; *Chihō kōei kigyō rōdō kankei-hō* (Local public enterprise labor relations law) (Law No. 289, 1952), in 8 EHS No. 8030; and *Denki jigyō oyobi sekitan kōgyō ni okeru sōgi kōi no hōhō no kisei ni kansuru hōritsu*

(Law covering the regulations of the methods of acts of dispute in the electricity business and the coal industry) (Law No. 171, 1953).

76. *Rōdō kijun-hō* (Labor standards law) (Law No. 49, 1947); 8 EHS No. 8040.

77. Koyō sokushin jigyōdan-hō (Law for enterprises to facilitate employment) (Law No. 116, 1936).

78. U.S. Dept. of Commerce, *The United States in the Changing World Economy* (Wash., D.C.: GPO, 1971), p. 61; Nobuo Narutomi, "From the Rule of Force to the Rule of Law in Labor-Management Relations," 15 *Bus. Lawyer* 607–32 (1960); Nobuo Narutomi, "Collective Action in Industrial Disputes," 58 *Law Society's Gazette* 15–20 (1961).

79. See Kichiemon Ishikawa, "Futō rōdō-kōi no shinsa sokushin ni tsuite" (Proposals for expediting examinations of unfair labor practices), in Akira Mikazuki, ed., *Saiban to hō* (Law and Trials) (Tokyo: Yūhikaku, 1967), pp. 111–27; in English, 4 *Law in Japan* 17 (1971).

80. *Odaka* v. *Japan*, 4 *Keishū* 2257 (Sct. G.B. Nov. 15, 1950). Union leaders were charged with misappropriation of the employer's funds, where the union took over a steel plant, expelled management, and operated the business.

81. See Mitsutoshi Azuma, ed., *Chūkai rōdō kumiai-hō* (Commentary on the Labor Union Law), 3rd ed. (Tokyo: Seirin shoin, 1960), p. 83, which defines picketing as follows: "(1) to watch the conduct of union members, high officials of the employer, and nonmember workers; (2) to persuade those workers who have seceded or who are going to secede from the union to come back or remain; (3) to prevent the employer from using means to break up the union; (4) to prevent nonmember workers or 'scabs' from entering into or working in the establishments; (5) to prevent the employer from delivering raw materials or finished or semifinished products into or from the premises; and (6) to discourage the employer from using strikebreakers."

82. *Tokiyasu* v. *Japan*, 12 Keishū 1694, 1696–97 (Sup. Ct. G.B., 28 May 1958).

83. *Japan* v. *Hirata*, 10 Keishū 1605, 1608–9 (Sup. Ct., 11 Dec. 1956).

84. See recent cases that might be so interpreted: *Yonago Sagyō K.K.* v. *Katō*, 19 Rōminshū (No. 21, 577) (Tottori D. Ct., 25 Apr. 1968); *Gakkō Hōjin Juntendō Daigaku* v. *Mitsui*, Rōhansoku (No. 656) (Tokyo H. Ct., 30 Oct. 1968); *Taki* v. *K.K. Fukui Shimbunsha*, Rōhansoku (No. 660.1) (Fukui D. Ct., 15 May 1968).

85. LRAL, Art. 7: (Act of Dispute) "In this Law, act of dispute shall mean strike, soldiering [*sic;* slowdown], lockout and other acts and counter-acts, hampering the normal course of work of an enterprise, performed by the parties concerned with labor relations with the object of attaining their respective claims" (EHS).

86. Apparently soon after the LUL was passed in 1945, again lacking experience with the statute and still without judicial precedents, the union practice of storming the plant to get in was justified by scholarly commentators. See Tokyo daigaku rōdō-hō kenkyūkai, ed., *Chushaku rōdō kumiai-hō* (Commentary on the labor union law) 32 (Tokyo: Yūhikaku, 1949), p. 32. See Ishikawa, *Law in Japan*, p. 456, note 43.

87. *Cf. Daikō denki* case, *Rōkeisoku* (No. 644) (Utsunomiya D. Ct., 29 Feb. 1968).

88. *Akita* v. *Dai Nippon Kōgyō K.K. Hatsumori Kōgyōjo Rōdō Kumiai*, 11 Rōminshū 1081, 1101 (Akita D. Ct., 29 Sept. 1960).

89. See, for example, *K.K. Meguro Seisakusho* v. *Sōhyō*, 12 Rōminshū 161 (Tokyo D. Ct., 28 March 1961), where the court held it was unnecessary for management to organize a superior force to exercise its right to close a plant occupied by the union. Typical, however, of the Marxist interpretation was the union's position in this dispute. After the union had split during a lengthy strike, the union leaders with their loyal members occupied the plant to prevent resumption of work by the others. The occupier refused to leave when the employer announced closure for an indefinite period. The employer then got an order to vacate from the Tokyo District Court. But on the union's refusal to grant entry to the plant even to the court's marshal, the police finally went into the plant and arrested the union leaders, who one must say exercised their so-called "rights" to the full throughout the dispute.

90. See a recent case, *San'yō denki* case, *Rōjun* (No. 682) (Yamaguchi D. Ct., 29 Mar.

1968); and the *Daikō denki case, Rōkeisoku* (No. 644) (Utsunomiya D. Ct., 29 Feb. 1968).

91. Indeed the term often translated "industrial relations" (*rōshi kankei*) really means "labor utilization relations" or "management of labor" rather than labor/management relations. See Ballon, "Participative Employment," in *The Japanese Employee,* ed. Ballon, p. 69.

92. An example of an actual Japanese "collective labor agreement" (*rōdō kyōyaku*) translated into English may be seen in Trade Bulletin Corporation, *Social and Economic Laws of Japan,* mimeo. (Tokyo: Trade Bull. Corp., 1969), pp. A1–A36. This example was adopted by a manufacturer with about 500 employees, but it is much larger than the typical contract in use in Japan.

93. LSL, Art. 89.

94. LSL, Art. 90.

95. A set of employment rules (*shūgyō kisoku*) are translated, Trade Bull. Corp., *Social and Economic Laws of Japan,* pp. B1–B49. Also under LSL, Art. 89 (2), a set of separate Wage Rules may be filed by the employer. See pp. C1–C12 for a sample.

96. LUL, Art. 20, and LRAL, Art. 29, both provide for arbitration, though it is little used, as noted in the text.

97. The court's jurisdiction is not spelled out anywhere explicitly but the theories say that it comes from the Const. 28 and so in discharge cases involving allegations of unfair labor practices the action violates Civil Code, Art. 90, making acts against public policy or good morals void, or amounts to abuse of right under Civil Code, Art. 1 (3).

98. Ishikawa, "Futō rōdō-kōi no shinsa sokushin ni tsuite," in Mikazuki, ed., *Saiban to hō,* pp. 111–27.

99. For example see Hadley, *Antitrust in Japan,* p. 421, for a summary showing gain during 1953–62 of 175% in wages but 222% in productivity.

100. *Japan Economic Journal* (Apr. 1972), p. 3. In 1971, productivity was up only 6.7%, but wages increased 13.7%.

101. On all aspects of postwar business organization above the corporate level see: Kōsei torihiki iinkai (FTC), ed., *Dokusen kinshi seisaku nijūnen-shi* (A twenty-year history of antimonopoly policies) (Tokyo: Ōkurashō insatsukyoku, 1968). Also see, generally, Miyazaki Yoshikazu, *Sengo Nihon no keizai kikō* (Mechanics of the postwar Japanese economy) (Tokyo: Shinkyōron, 1966); Jimpū Yoshida, *Nihon no karuteru* (Japanese cartels) (Tokyo: Tōyō keizai shimpōsha, 1964); Keizai chōsa kyōkai, ed., *Nempō, keiretsu no kenkyū* (Annual report, studies of *keiretsu*) (Tokyo: Keizai chōsa kyōkai, 1962); "Zen jōjō gaisha no keiretsu saimoku chōsa" (A detailed investigation of the *keiretsu* of all listed companies), *Tōyō keizai* (Special issue, 15 Nov. 1967). In English: Yamamura, *Economic Policy in Postwar Japan,* pp. 87–129; Hadley, *Antitrust in Japan,* p. 205 ff.

102. Ōkurashō, *Hōjin kigyō tōkei nenpō* (Annual report of statistics on incorporated enterprises) (Tokyo: Ōkurashō, 1970), p. 120.

103. See Kōsei torihiki iinkai (FTC), Jimū-kyoku, *Nihon no kigyō shūchū* (Concentration in Japanese enterprise) (Tokyo: Ōkurashō insatsukyoku, 1971), p. 11.

104. MITI, *Chūsho kigyō hakusho* (1972), p. 42; *Jurisuto nenkan* 1969 (No. 425), p. 466.

105. See Yoshihiro Tajima, *How Goods Are Distributed in Japan* (Tokyo: Walton-Ridgeway and Co., 1971); M. Y. Yoshino, *The Japanese Marketing System* (MIT Press, 1971), p. 10; Robert J. Ballon, *Japan's Market and Foreign Business* (Tokyo: Sophia University, 1971), p. 159. Adams and Kobayashi, *The World of Japanese Business,* p. 190, say there are in Japan 13.8 retailers per 1,000 people (U.S.: 6.7).

106. *Fortune,* Aug. 1970, p. 142.

107. Ibid., May 1970, p. 82.

108. *The President Directory, 1971* (Tokyo: Diamond-Time, 1971), p. 66.

109. See Kōsei torihiki iinkai (FTC), *Nihon no kigyō shūchū* (1971), pp. 33 and 127.

110. Miyazaki, *Sengo Nihon no keizai kikō,* p. 48.

111. FTC, *Dokusen kinshi seisaku nijū nen-shi* (1968), p. 207.
112. For example, see Dokusen shihon kenkyūkai, ed., *Gendai Nihon no dokusen shihon* (Monopoly capital in contemporary Japan) (Tokyo: Nihon hyōron shinsha, 1958), and S. Giga, *Gendai Nihon no dokusen kigyō* (Contemporary Japanese monopoly enterprise) (Kyoto: Mineruba shobō, 1962).
113. Hiroshi Iyori, *Antimonopoly Legislation in Japan* (New York: Fed. Legal Publications, 1969), p. 6.
114. This whole process supervised by SCAP is chronicled in detail in Hadley, *Antitrust in Japan*, pp. 3–201, and T. A. Bisson, *Zaibatsu Dissolution in Japan* (U. of Cal. Press, 1954), pp. 1–200.
115. Yamamura, *Economic Policy in Postwar Japan*, p. 11; *cf.* Hadley, *Antitrust in Japan*, p. 23.
116. Hadley, *Antitrust in Japan*, p. 252.
117. Iyori, *Antimonopoly Legislation in Japan*, p. 11, says 2,200 *zaibatsu* firms were purged by SCAP Directive No. 550 of 1946; *cf.* Hans Baerwald, *The Purge of Japanese Leaders under the Occupation* (U. of Cal. Press, 1959), p. 91.
118. See Eleanor Hadley's impressive work on the prewar *zaibatsu* and post-World War II forms. Hadley, *Antitrust in Japan*, pp. 3, 9 ff.
119. *The President Directory, 1971*, p. 90. See note 121 for Bank of Tokyo.
120. See for background T. F. M. Adams and Iwao Hoshii, *A Financial History of the New Japan* (Tokyo and Palo Alto: Kōdansha International, Ltd., 1972), p. 91; Nihon ginkō chōsa-kyoku, *Wagakumi no kinyū seido* (The money system of our country) (Tokyo: Nihon ginkō, 1971); Shirō Hara, *Nihon no ginkō* (Japanese banks) (Tokyo: Tōeidō, 1972); Fuji Bank, *Banking in Modern Japan* (Tokyo: Fuji Bank, 1967); Miyazaki, *Sengo Nihon no keizai kikō*, p. 43, deals with this as part of his economic analysis. On aspects of Japanese banking generally, see Bank of Japan, *The Bank of Japan: Its Function and Organization* (Tokyo: Bank of Japan, 1962); Hugh T. Patrick, *Monetary Policy and Central Banking in Contemporary Japan* (Bombay: U. of Bombay, 1962); Hubert F. Schiffer, *The Modern Japanese Banking System* (New York: University Publishing, Inc., 1962); Phra Sarasas, *Money and Banking in Japan* (London: Heath Cranston, Ltd., 1940); and Abe Motoo, *A Monetary Model of the Japanese Economy* (Ann Arbor: University Microfilms, 1969).
121. Adams and Hoshii, *Financial History of the New Japan*, p. 105, notes that the Bank of Tokyo is the "de facto" successor of the Yokohama Specie Bank, important in foreign exchange business during the prewar period.
122. See *Rinji kinri chōsei-hō* (Temporary money-rate adjustment law) (Law No. 181, 13 Dec. 1947).
123. Antimonopoly Law, Art. 11.
124. The devices used and other technical explanations may be found in Patrick, *Monetary Policy and Central Banking*, p. 63; also see Hugh Patrick, "Japan's Interest Rates and the Gray Financial Market," *Pacific Affairs* 38 (1965–66): 326–44, for problems arising from the artificialities of the fixed long-term interest rates.
125. See Frank Langdon, "Big Business Lobbying in Japan: The Case of Central Bank Reform," *Am. Pol. Sci. Rev.* 55 (1961): 527–38, for an account of the pressures involved in considering the issue of relative independence appropriate to the Bank of Japan's role in monetary matters; also see Morgan Guaranty Trust Co., *The Financing of Business in Japan* (Tokyo: Morgan Guaranty Trust Co., 1965), p. 20.
126. See M. Yoshino, *The Japanese Marketing System*, pp. 171, 210; Editors, "Contemporary Monster: Sōgō shōsha," *Oriental Economist* 40 (June 1972): 22. I have also gained several insights from a speech of Eikichi Itoh, chairman of C. Itoh and Co., Ltd., given at the 2nd International Conference on U.S.-Japanese Business, 21–23 Sept. 1969, in Los Angeles, California, sponsored by the Japan American Society of Southern California.
127. But the share of total sales of each *keiretsu* industrial firm, which is handled by the *keiretsu* trading firm, is not as large as might be assumed. See Hadley, *Antitrust in Japan*,

426   Notes

p. 148 (on prewar role), and compare p. 246 for present role. Note that the Antimonopoly Law, Art. 5, that forbids exclusive dealings was deleted in the 1953 amendments, which point Hadley seems to have overlooked (p. 247).

128. *President Directory, 1973*, p. 45.

129. Ibid.

130. Eikichi Itoh, speech at Conference on U.S.-Japanese Business.

131. Kōsei torihiki iinkai, *Nihon no kigyō shūchū* (1971), p. 142.

132. A leading example is the auto export business, where Toyota has its own sales corporation that now ranks high among exporters, though it handles mostly Toyota products.

133. Eikichi Itoh, speech at Conference on U.S.-Japanese Business.

134. Hadley, *Antitrust in Japan*, pp. 205–90.

135. Here I think prewar motivations of the top men (*jūyaku*) are, with accommodations for the times, still relevant. See for this mentality Marshall, *Capitalism and Nationalism in Prewar Japan*, p. 30; and Johannes Hirschmeier, *The Origins of Entrepreneurship in Meiji Japan* (Harvard U. Press, 1964), p. 162; Yoshino, *Japan's Managerial Class*, p. 48.

136. Collectively there is within the top nonfinancial one hundred companies a most remarkable cross-holding of shares, as well as a remarkable concentration of banks and insurance firms as major shareholders. See Kōsei torihiki iinkai, *Nihon no kigyō shūchū* (1971), pp. 44–45. This tendency to strive for "stable shareholders" is increasing through corporate buying of shares in sister companies during the easy-money conditions in 1972. In fact this corporate buying phenomenon is said to have been a major cause sparking a doubling of the Japanese Dow averages in 1972.

137. Symposium, "Sōkaiya no genjō to taisaku" (Present condition and policy concerning "general meeting manipulators"), *Jurisuto* 340 (1966): 22–64.

138. See generally Rowland Gould, *The Matsushita Phenomenon* (Tokyo: Daiyamondosha, 1970), and "Japan's Industrial Konzerns—Hitachi Group," *Oriental Economist* (Nov. 1970): 9.

139. FTC, *Dokusen kinshi seisaku nijū nen-shi* (Tokyo: Ōkurashō insatsu-kyoku, 1968), p. 304. The term FTC used was "shihon keiretsu."

140. My own experiences have included examples of corporate operating difficulties hidden in manipulatable subsidiaries, as well as what seem to have been threshold intentions (only later becoming apparent) to limit severely the scope of joint venture operations and profitability. In fact such problems are rather typical of the difference between the standardized American and Japanese views of what a joint venture is all about.

141. The Japanese technical term sometimes used (see FTC below p. 304) is "*kankei gaisha*," which includes subsidiaries, affiliates, and subcontractors. The current picture can be well seen from Chūshō kigyō-chō [MITI], *Chūshō kigyō hakusho* (White paper on medium and small enterprises) (Tokyo: Ōkurashō insatsu-kyoku, 1970), pp. 100–19; also for the legal developments for subcontractors' protection see FTC, *Dokusen kinshi seisaku nijū nen-shi*, p. 283.

142. Broadbridge, *Industrial Dualism in Japan*, p. 72; Cole, *Japanese Blue Collar*, pp. 57, 61, describe other similar situations.

143. Chūshō kigyō-chō, *Chūshō kigyō hakusho*, pp. 101–2, shows a synopsis of the whole subcontracting process in the auto industry. Attached to the thirteen makers of finished vehicles are 350 parts-makers with an estimated 8,000 subcontractors at the primary, secondary, and tertiary levels noted by Broadbridge.

144. Yamamura, *Economic Policy in Postwar Japan*, p. 163.

145. Iyori, *Antimonopoly Legislation in Japan*, p. 138, says there were 19,105 trade associations registered under the Antimonopoly Law, Art. 8, by 31 March 1968; see also Akira Shōda, *Karuteru to hōritsu* (Cartels and law) (Tokyo: Nihon hyōronsha, 1968).

146. FTC, *Dokusen kinshi seisaku nijū nen-shi*, pp. 89, 207, 327.

147. Yoshio Kanazawa, "The Regulation of Corporate Enterprise," in *Law in Japan*, ed. von Mehren, p. 484. See especially Chūshō kigyō dantai no soshiki ni kansuru hōritsu (Law concerning the organization of medium and small enterprise associations)

(Law No. 185, 1957), Art. 55, providing compulsory membership for the first time in the postwar period. This raises some doubts about its legality under Const., Art. 21, on freedom of association.

148. In this case Sumitomo Kinzoku Kōgyō refused to comply with a MITI order to reduce production of ordinary steel ingots (*futsū koatsu-nobeyo kōkai*) applicable to all (85) producers, alleging MITI interference with managerial prerogative (*keieiken*). MITI went for the jugular (*i.e.*, cut Sumitomo's coal import quota). For further details see *Daiyamondo* (No. 56) 88 (1965) and *Jurisuto* (No. 338) 56–57 (1966). In English, U.S. Dept. of Commerce, *Japan: The Government-Business Relationship*, p. 137.

149. Yoriaki Narita, "Gyōsei shidō" (Administrative guidance), in *Gendai-hō* (Tokyo: Iwanami shoten, 1966), 4: 131–68; translated 2 *Law in Japan: An Annual* 45 (1968).

150. M. Ariga and L. Rieke, "The Antimonopoly Law of Japan and Its Enforcement," 39 *Wash. L. Rev.* 459 (1964).

151. Quoted by Hadley, *Antitrust in Japan*, p. 372.

152. For a detailed study, see John Lynch, *Toward an Orderly Market: An Intensive Study of Japan's Voluntary Quota in Cotton Textile Exports* (Tokyo: Sophia U. and Charles E. Tuttle Co., 1968); also Editorial, *Wall Street Journal*, 9 Mar. 1971, p. 14, and 12 Mar. 1971, p. 5.

153. Comment, "Executive Authority and Antitrust Considerations in Voluntary Limits on Steel Imports," 118 *U. of Penn. L. Rev.* 105 (1969).

154. *Japan Economic Journal* (4 Apr. 1972), p. 5; *Japan Times*, 15 Jan. 1967, p. 2.

155. In Japanese a very full description may be found in FTC, *Dokusen kinshi seisaku nijū nen-shi*.

156. See Eleanor Hadley, "Trust Busting in Japan," 26 *Harvard Bus. Rev.* 425–40 (July 1948).

157. Ariga and Rieke, "Antimonopoly Law," *Wash. L. Rev.*, p. 448.

158. See Yuichi Nakamura, ed., *Gijutsu dōnyū keiyaku nintei kijun no kaisetsu* (Explanation of validation standards for contracts inducting technology) (Tokyo: Shōji hōmu kenkyūkai, 1968), p. 25; and Tōru Ōnuma *et al.*, "Current Developments in Antitrust and Trade Practice Laws and Policy in Japan and the Relation thereto of Industrial Property Rights," 7 *Patent, TM, and Copyright Journal of Research and Education* [Georgetown] 25–44 (1963); Ariga and Rieke, 39 *Wash. L. Rev.* 437 (1964).

159. A complete historical summary in Japanese is found FTC, *Dokusen kinshi seisaku nijūnen-shi.* A well-indexed, voluminous commentary is: Akira Shōda, *Dokusen kinshihō* (The Antimonopoly Law) (Tokyo: Nihon hyōronsha, 1966); also Tsūshō sangyō-shō daijin kansho chōsaka, ed., *Nihon sangyō to dokusen kinshi-hō* (Japanese industry and the Antimonopoly Law) (Tokyo: Tsūshō sangyō kenkyūsha, 1968).

See useful English-language summaries: Kanazawa, "The Regulation of Corporate Enterprise" in *Law in Japan*, ed. von Mehren, p. 480; Iyori, *Antimonopoly Legislation in Japan.*

160. Besides opposing positions on recent initial merger proposals (for example, Ōji-Jūjō–Honshū Paper, Yawata-Fuji Steel), see their positions on the Special Industries Law proposed in the early 1960s (which was never passed, partly because industry joined academicians for the first time to support the FTC). See MITI, *Nihon sangyō to dokusen kinshi-hō*, p. 10.

161. Antimonopoly Law, Art. 29 ff.

162. Kōsei torihiki iinkai, *1971 Dokusen hakusho* (1971 Monopoly white paper) (Tokyo: Kōsei torihiki iinkai, 1971), p. 265.

163. *Cf.* Shigekazu Imamura, "Dokusen kinshi-hō" (The Antimonopoly Law) 52 *Hōritsugaku zenshū* (Tokyo: Yūhikaku, 1962), p. 110, note 1.

164. Art. 2 (5) and (6).

165. Clayton §3 and §7.

166. See Learned Hand in *U.S.* v. *Aluminum Co. of America*, 148 F. 2d 416, 429–30 (2d Cir. 1945).

167. Yamamura, *Economic Policy in Postwar Japan*, pp. 196–216, has a useful English

translation of both the original and the amended texts of the Antimonopoly Law lined up for comparison.

168. *Asahi Shimbunsha* case, 8 Kōsai minshū (No. 2), p. 177 (1953).

169. Ibid.

170. See Iyori, *Antimonopoly Legislation in Japan*, p. 108.

171. Webb-Pomerene Export Trading Act, Ch. 50, 40 Stat. 516 (1918), 15 U.S.C. §§61–65 (1958).

172. See Michiko Ariga, "The Antimonopoly Law," in *Joint Ventures and Japan*, ed. Robert J. Ballon, (Tokyo: Sophia U. and Charles E. Tuttle Co., 1967), p. 59.

173. *Hanrei Taimuzu* (No. 264) 215–17 (1971).

174. *Kokusai-teki kyōtei mata wa kokusai-teki keiyaku no todokeide ni kansuru kisoku* (Regulations concerning reporting of international agreements or international contracts), FTC Regulation No. 1, 1971.

175. For an illuminating clue to the difficulties later experienced by the Japanese with fair competition as a constitutive principle of business, see Eiichi Kiyo'oka, trans., *The Autobiography of Fukuzawa Yukichi* (Tokyo: Hokuseidō, 1960), p. 190. Fukuzawa stated that he coined the new word "*kyōsō*" (race fight) for the English term "competition," which incidentally he found in "Chamber's Book on Economics." See Ballon, ed., *The Japanese Employee*, p. 26.

176. Masao Maruyama, *Thought and Behavior in Modern Japanese Politics* (London: Oxford U. Press, 1963), pp. 15, 17, calls this phenomenon "sectionalism," and it is the result of this "sectionalism" (or status competition, *i.e.*, over-capacity) that the Japanese usually refer to when they say "excessive competition" (*katō kyōsō*).

177. See Imamura, "Dokusen kinshi-hō," *Hōritsugaku zenshū*, p. 53, for a discussion of appropriate competition.

178. See *Futō keihinrui oyobi futō hyōji bōshi-hō* (Law to prevent unfair prizes and false marking) (Law No. 134, 15 May 1962).

179. There were at least thirty-eight formal antidumping cases against the Japanese before the U.S. Tariff Commission (1964–71). See, *e.g.*, *TV Dumping* case, *Federal Register* 36 (No. 46) 9 (Mar. 1971): 4576; also *Glass* case, *Federal Register* 36 (17 April 1971): 7330.

180. The degree of independence that should properly be accorded to the Bank of Japan has been a major public issue in postwar Japan. Certainly since its policy board of outsiders was established as its control device in the postwar period, the bank now has more independence, but MOF influence is still strong.

CHAPTER V

1. For example, see Noritake Kobayashi's comment, T. F. M. Adams and Noritake Kobayashi, *The World of Japanese Business* (Tokyo: Kōdansha, 1969), p. 248: "It is useless for the foreign investor to decry the system or to point out that that is not the way things are done in his country. It *is* the way things are done in Japan—and the only sensible solution for the foreigner who wants to do business in Japan is to accept that fact and to cope with the difficulties arising from it as best he can. He really has no choice."

2. A useful and quite complete bibliography of English material, to 1961, on Japanese law has been compiled by Rex Coleman, *An Index to Japanese Law (1867–1961)*, mimeo. preliminary draft (1961). Since 1961, the major additions on business law have been published in the annual symposium of the *Washington Law Review*, Vols. 38–43 (1963–68) and in the journal *Law in Japan: An Annual*, Vols. 1–4 (1967–71). Also see Albert E. Ehrensweig, Sueo Ikehara, and Norman Jensen, *American-Japanese Private International Law*, Bilateral Studies in Private International Law, No. 12, Parker School (New York: Oceana, 1964); and Arthur von Mehren, ed., *Law in Japan* (Harvard U. Press, 1963).

3. Germans would have less trouble with language equivalence than Americans be-

cause the Japanese legal terminology has developed largely as equivalents of German legal terms after 1890. But at the very beginning (say 1868–82), when the Japanese language did not have a vocabulary to cover Western legal concepts, the English and French jurists were dominant in Japan and contrived equivalents. It was not uncommon for the Meiji lawmakers, once their interest turned to German law in the 1880s, to translate German drafts into English and then translate the English into Japanese. See Kingo Kobayakawa, *Meiji hōeishiron* (Treatise on the legal history of the Meiji era) (Tokyo: Ganshōdō, 1940), 2: 1101.

4. See Fritz Moses, "International Legal Practice," 4 *Fordham L. Rev.* 244, 248–51 (1935); Nobushige Hozumi, *The New Japanese Civil Code as Material for the Study of Comparative Jurisprudence* (Tokyo: Maruzen, 1912), p. 57; *cf.* Francisco Capistrano, "Mistakes and Inaccuracies in Fisher's Translation of the Spanish Civil Code," 9 *Philippine L. J.* 89 (1929).

5. *E.g.*, it has been traditional in Japan for a man to divorce his wife without court formalities, and still today over 90% of the divorces in Japan are by "agreement" simply registered at the ward.

6. *E.g.*, the traditional landlord and tenant relationships remained in effect long after the Civil Code made the lease a matter of free bargaining. See Noboru Koyama, *Minji chōteihō gaisetsu* (General survey of the civil conciliation law) (Tokyo: Yūhikaku, 1954), pp. 5–6; and Ryōsuke Ishii, *Nihon hōseishi gaisetsu* (Tokyo: Sōbunsha, 1960), pp. 512–23, for the traditional relationships.

7. Another example is the elaborate arbitration (*chūsai*) system, which has been in the Code of Civil Procedure, Arts. 786–805, since 1891, perhaps intended as a substitute for Meiji encouraging settlement (*kankai*) or Tokugawa conciliation (*naisai*). But the code arbitration is little used domestically, and the traditional forms of dispute settlement continue to operate extensively. See generally, Dan Fenno Henderson, *Conciliation and Japanese Law: Tokugawa and Modern* (U. of Wash. and U. of Tokyo Presses, 1965).

8. *E.g.*, provisions for bearer shares, preferred shares, and convertible bonds are found in the Commercial Code, Arts. 227–29, Art. 222, and Arts. 341–2 through 341–6, respectively, but they hardly exist in practice.

9. See Dan Fenno Henderson, "Review: Von Mehren, *Law in Japan*," 16 *Stanford L. Rev.* 1132 (1964).

10. Many employment and "contractual" relationships—the pawn broker, the mutual banks, the family register, and the personal seal—are but a few of the institutions that, though of course not unchanged, still have more or less direct lineage back past 1868.

11. For an earlier summary of Tokugawa legal principles, see Dan Fenno Henderson, "Some Aspects of Tokugawa Law," 27 *Wash. L. Rev.* 85–109 (1952); for a more detailed analysis in English see Henderson, *Conciliation and Japanese Law*, Vol. 1, Chapters II, III, and IV; and Edwin Reischauer and John Fairbank, *A History of East Asian Civilization—East Asia: The Great Tradition* (Boston: Houghton Mifflin, 1960), pp. 579–688, for a recent, rather detailed summation of the various strands of Tokugawa history.

12. For organization of the shogunate "courts," see Yoshirō Hiramatsu, *Kinsei keiji soshōhō no kenkyū* (Study of the law of criminal procedure in recent era) (Tokyo: Sōbunsha, 1960), p. 415; Henderson, *Conciliation and Japanese Law*, Vol. 1, Ch. IV.

13. Kaoru Nakada, "Tokugawa jidai no minji saiban jitsuroku" (Actual records of civil trial in the Tokugawa period), 3 *Hōseishi ronshū* 756–85 (1943); Hiramatsu, *Kinsei keiji soshōhō no kenkyū*, pp. 421, 755.

14. Ishii, *Nihon hōseishi gaisetsu*, p. 471.

15. Hiramatsu, *Kinsei keiji soshōhō no kenkyū*, pp. 404, 762.

16. Tokugawa civil trials have been explored by the following: Nakada, "Tokugawa jidai no minji saiban jitsuroku," *Hōseishi ronshū*, pp. 756–904; Heiichirō Kaneda, "Tokugawa jidai no tokubetsu minji soshōhō—kanekuji no kenkyū" (Special civil procedural law of the Tokugawa period—study of money suits), 42 *Kokka gakkai zasshi* 1934–84, 1136–64, 1423–45 (1929); Kingo Kobayakawa, *Kinsei minji soshō seido no kenkyū* (Study of the civil litigation system in the recent era) (Tokyo: Yūhikaku, 1957),

p. 696; Kingo Kobayakawa, *Nihon kinsei minji saiban tetsuzukihō kenkyū* (A study of civil trial procedure in the Japanese recent era), 18 *Nihon hōri sōsho* (Series on Japanese legal theory) (Tokyo: Nihon hōri kenkyūkai, 1942).

17. Hiramatsu, *Kinsei keiji soshōhō no kenkyū*, p. 774.

18. Henderson, *Conciliation and Japanese Law*, Vol. 1, Ch. VI.

19. See John C. Hall, "The Tokugawa Legislation (Part IV)," 51 *Transactions of the Asiatic Society of Japan (TASJ)* (Part V) 683 following 804 for illustrations of torture techniques.

20. Hozumi, *The New Japanese Civil Code*, pp. 57–58, notes this point in suggesting that a word for "right" (*kenri*) had to be concocted in Japanese because of the exclusive emphasis on duty in Tokugawa law.

21. Nakada, "Tokugawa jidai no minji saiban jitsuroku," *Hōseishi ronshū*, pp. 753–904; Masaijirō Takigawa, *Kujiyado no kenkyū—Nihon bengoshi zenshi—Kujiyado kenjutsu "Hikae" no shōkai* (A study of the suit inns—a pre-history of the Japanese lawyer—an introduction to the "Hikae" compiled by a suit inn) (Tokyo: Waseda daigaku hikakuhō kenkyujo, 1962), pp. 2–76.

22. Kenji Maki, "Kinsei bukehō no wakai oyobi chōtei" (Conciliation and compromise in the law of the military houses of the recent era), *Saitō hakushi kanreki kinen, hō to saiban* 201 (1942); Heiichirō Kaneda, "Tokugawa jidai ni okeru soshōjō no wakai" (Reconciliation in litigation in the Tokugawa period), 1 *Shien* (No. 2) 64–88; (No. 3) 44–53 (1928); Shinzō Takayanagi, "Wakaishugi ni tatsu saiban" (Trials based on the principle of compromise), 56 *Chūō kōron* (No. 4) 139 (1941); Henderson, *Conciliation and Japanese Law*, 1: 128.

23. Kingo Kobayakawa, "Kinsei no saiban soshiki to shinkyū oyobi kankatsu ni kansuru jakkan no kōsatsu" (Some considerations of the organization, appeals, and jurisdiction of the courts of the recent era), 31 *Hōgaku ronsō* 994–1020 (1934); 32 ibid. 100–21, 801–44 (1935).

24. Ishii, *Nihon hōseishi gaisetsu*, p. 486.

25. Kingo Kobayakawa, "Kinsei minji saiban no gainen to tokushitsu" (General concepts and special characteristics of civil litigation of the recent era), 5 *Hōgaku ronsō* 372–402 (1921); in English see Viscount Hayashi, *For His People* (London: Harper & Brothers, 1903).

26. An exception might be Hayashi Razan and the Buddhist Suden, in the work on the early Tokugawa legislation. See Hikoroku Okuno, *Kinsei Nihon koyūhō ronkō* (Inquiry into Japanese traditional law of the recent era) (Tokyo: Kasahara shoten, 1943), p. 39. Also Ogyū Sorai and other Confusianists had a role in the compilation of the "Osadamegaki." See Yoshio Koide, "Osadamegaki hyakkajō hensan no jijō ni tsuite" (Concerning the conditions of compilation of the Osadamegaki Hyakkajō), *Shichō* (No. 3) 112–37 (1934); and Dan Fenno Henderson, "Chinese Legal Studies in Early 18th-Century Japan: Scholars and Sources," *J. of Asian Studies* 30 (1970): 21.

27. John W. Hall, "The Confucian Teacher in Tokugawa Japan," in *Confucianism in Action*, ed. David S. Nivison and Arthur F. Wright (Stanford U. Press, 1959), pp. 268–301.

28. Kobayakawa, *Kinsei minji soshō seido no kenkyū*, pp. 616–96.

29. Note *kirisute gomen* (cut down and throw aside without further ado), the oft-cited privilege recognized in the "Osadamegaki," Second Book, Art. 71, Para. 44 (1742) in *Shihō Shiryō Bessatsu* (No. 17), *Nihon kindai keiji hōreishū* (*jō*) (Tokyo: Shihōshō, 1942), p. 45: "Even though he be a mere footsoldier, a warrior who has no recourse but to cut down a petty townsman or farmer who addresses him with insolence will not be interfered with; provided, an investigation leaves no doubt as to the facts."

Although this point has perhaps been overemphasized in some earlier works, because the privilege was probably little used in the later Tokugawa period, it nevertheless symbolizes the undoubted superiority of officialdom—what has been often called the rule-of-man in the Japanese tradition. Still, the warrior's bark was probably worse than his bite, but that is another complex issue.

30. For the most complete work in English, see Ryōsuke Ishii, *Japanese Legislation in the Meiji Era*, tr. William Chambliss (Tokyo: Pan-Pacific Press, 1958); also see short summaries: Kenzō Takayanagi, "A Century of Innovation: The Development of Japanese Law, 1868–1961," in *Law in Japan*, ed. von Mehren, pp. 5–40; Kenzō Takayanagi, *Reception and Influence of Occidental Legal Ideas in Japan*, Western Influences in Modern Japan, No. 4 (Tokyo: Institute of Pacific Relations, 1929); and Hozumi, *The New Japanese Civil Code*.

31. See *e.g.*, Yutaka Tezuka, *Meiji shoki keihō-shi no kenkyū* (Study of history of early Meiji criminal law) (Tokyo: Keiō gijuku daigaku hōgaku kenkyūkai, 1956), pp. 3–76; Ishii, *Japanese Legislation in the Meiji Era*, p. 23.

32. See F. C. Jones, *Extraterritoriality in Japan* (Yale U. Press, 1931), p. 28; G. H. Scidmore, *United States Courts in Japan* (Tokyo: Igirisu hōritsu gakkō, 1887), p. 43; Luke T. Lee, *Consular Law and Practice* (New York: Praeger, 1961), p. 205.

33. Chitoshi Yanaga, *Japan Since Perry* (New York: McGraw-Hill, 1949), p. 26.

34. See a copy of the treaty in Mario Emilio Cosenza, ed., *The Complete Journal of Townsend Harris*, Rev. ed. (Tokyo: Tuttle, 1959), p. 578. The extraterritoriality provision is Art. VI at 581.

35. M. Sugii, "Paakusu hinan ronsō" (The dispute over Parkes's criticism), 38 *Shirin* (No. 4); Kikuo Nakamura, *Kindai Nihon no hōteki keisei* (The legal formation of modern Japan) (Tokyo: Yūshindō, 1956; reprint 1963), p. 52.

36. Voluminous material on the westernization of the public law is found in Kobayakawa, *Meiji hōseishiron*.

37. Ken Mukai and Nobuyoshi Toshitani (Dan Fenno Henderson, trans.), "The Progress and Problems of Compiling the Civil Code in the Early Meiji Era," in 1 *Law in Japan: An Annual* 25–59 (1967); also, Robert Epp, "The Challenge from Tradition: Attempts to Compile a Civil Code in Japan, 1866–78," *Monumenta Nipponica* 22 (1967): 15–48.

38. See Dan Fenno Henderson, "Japanese Influences on Communist Chinese Legal Language," in *Contemporary Chinese Law: Research Problems and Perspectives*, ed. Jerome A. Cohen (Harvard U. Press, 1970), pp. 158–87.

39. It has been suggested that in the early days before codification these diverse foreign laws entered the Japanese law as an expression of reason (*jōri*), a source of law in the 1875 *Rules for the Conduct of Judicial Affairs*, Art. 3: "Judgments in civil cases shall be governed by custom in the absence of written law; and in the absence of written law and in the absence of custom, judgment should be based on reason (*jōri*)." Ishii, *Japanese Legislation in the Meiji Era*, pp. 37–56. See also Takayanagi citing Hozumi, *The New Japanese Civil Code*, pp. 38–40.

40. K. Hatoyama, "Japanese Personal Legislation," in *Fifty Years of New Japan*, ed. Shigenobu Ōkuma (London: Smith & Elder Co., 1909), p. 276.

41. Tezuka, *Meiji shoki keihō-shi no kenkyū*, pp. 109–148. Also see George Sansom, *The Western World and Japan* (New York: Alfred A. Knopf, 1950), p. 445, note 1: "A curious story is told of Boissonade's experiences while working in the Ministry of Justice, which shows how old evils existed alongside of new ideals in the confusion of early Meiji. Boissonade, seated at his desk before a draft dealing with civil rights, heard a commotion downstairs. He investigated and found in a cellar an unfortunate suspect being tortured by officers of the law. He threatened to resign, and after some delay torture was made illegal in 1876." Actually torture was abolished in stages, but it was not finally banned until 1879. See Ishii, *Japanese Legislation in the Meiji Era*, pp. 328–29.

42. John Henry Wigmore, while he was in Tokyo, 1889–92, was struck by the fact that the Japanese lawyers' disdain for the traditional practices had gone to the point where, as he said, the opportunity of recording practices of the unique Tokugawa system was being lost forever by the destruction of documents and the passing of a generation of men who had served in the shogunate offices. See J. H. Wigmore, "The Legal System of Old Japan," 4 *Green Bag* 403–11, 478–84 (1892).

43. These Meiji compilations of customary laws have been printed. See Seiichi Taki-

moto, ed., "Zenkoku minji kanrei ruishū" (Country-wide classified collection of civil customary practices), 50 *Nihon keizai taiten* (Tokyo: Hakutōsha, 1932; reprint Tokyo: Meiji bunken, 1971), p. 390, originally compiled in 1877; Seiichi Takimoto, ed., "Shōji kanrei ruishū" (Classified collection of commercial customary practices), 49 and 50 *Nihon keizai taiten* (Tokyo: Hakutōsha, 1932; reprint Meiji bunken, 1972), p. 1130, originally compiled 1883–84; *Zenkoku minji kanrei ruishū* (Country-wide classified collection of civil customary practices), originally compiled by the Shihōshō in 1880 and printed in 50 *Nihon keizai taiten* (Tokyo: Shishi shuppansha, 1930), pp. 3–390. Perhaps the most useful of the printed versions of these compilations is Yasoji Kazahaya, ed., *Zenkoku minji kanrei ruishū* (Tokyo: Nihon hyōronsha, 1944), because it combines the better features of both the 1877 and 1880 compilations. John H. Wigmore spent several years after 1936 translating these and other Tokugawa legal materials, but World War II prevented their publication although an earlier part of the translation may be found in 20 *TASJ* (Pt. 2) (1893). See Henderson, "Japanese Legal History of the Tokugawa Period: Scholars and Sources," in *U. of Mich. Center of Japanese Studies Occasional Papers* (No. 7), ed. Robert Ward, 100–21 (1957), for a description of Wigmore's project. At last the entire set in ten volumes is being printed by Tokyo daigaku shuppankai.

44. Hozumi, *The New Japanese Civil Code*, p. 15.

45. A considerable literature has been accumulated particularly in the last two decades on this problem. *E.g.*, see Tōru Hoshino, *Meiji mimpō hensanshi kenkyū* (Study of the history of the Meiji compilation of the civil code) (Tokyo: Daiyamondosha, 1943); Tōru Hoshino, *Mimpōten ronsōshi* (History of the civil code dispute) (Tokyo: Kawade shobō, 1949), pp. 124–26, for bibliography; and see Nakamura, *Kindai Nihon no hōteki keisei*, pp. 297–301, for a list of books and articles. Particularly note the debate in the journals among Nakamura, Hoshino, and others over certain aspects of the civil code: Kikuo Nakamura, "Mimpōten ronsō no keika to mondaiten," 29 *Hōgaku kenkyū* 473–97, 753–71, 853–75 (1956).

46. Hozumi, *The New Japanese Civil Code*, p. 16.

47. Hoshino, *Meiji mimpō hensanshi kenkyū*, pp. 349–545, collects many arguments advanced by the two groups during the controversy; *e.g.*, see Yatsuka Hozumi, "Mimpō idete, chūkō horobu" (The civil code emerges: loyalty and piety collapse), p. 415 (1943). Also Shigeki Tōyama, "Mimpōten ronsō no seijishiteki kōsatsu" (Historical political considerations of the civil code dispute), 40 *Hōgaku shirin* 56–87 (1951).

48. Jōji Matsumoto *et al.*, "Ume Kenjirō hakushi no omoide" (Memories of Dr. Kenjirō Ume), 49 *Hōgaku shirin* 88–104 (1951); also both Wigmore and Boissonade were against postponement: J. H. Wigmore, "New Codes and Old Customs," *Japan Weekly Mail* (15 Oct. 1892), Boissonade, *Les Anciennes Coutumes du Japon et Le Nouveau Code Civil* (Tokyo: Hakubunsha, 1894), p. 40.

49. Law No. 8, 1892.

50. Hoshino, *Mimpōten ronsōshi*, pp. 80–83, gives the persons who voted for and against the measure proposing postponement.

51. See Tōru Hoshino, "San hakushi to mimpō seitei" (The three doctors and the enactment of the civil code), 49 *Hōgaku shirin* 33–35 (1951).

52. Civil Code, Law No. 89 (1896).

53. Commercial Code, Law No. 48 (1899).

54. For comparisons of the Civil Code ("old") and the new "Meiji" Civil Code, see Kiyoshi Miyagawa, *Kyū-mimpō to Meiji mimpō* (The old civil code and the Meiji civil code) (Tokyo: Aoki shoten, 1965).

55. Zentarō Kitagawa, *Nihon hōgaku no rekishi to riron* (Theory and history of Japanese jurisprudence) (Tokyo: Nihon hyōronsha, 1968).

56. Hozumi, *The New Japanese Civil Code*, p. 154.

57. See Hirobumi Itō, *Commentaries on the Constitution of the Empire of Japan*, 2d ed. (Tokyo: Chūō Daigaku, 1906), p. 72; Hirobumi Itō, "Some Reminiscences of the Grant of the New Constitution," in *Fifty Years of New Japan*, ed. Shigenobu Ōkuma (London: Smith & Elder Co., 1909), 1: 122; and George Beckmann, *The Making of the*

Meiji Constitution (U. of Kansas Press, 1957), p. 70, where he tells of Itō's nine months abroad during 1882–83 studying foreign constitutional models. Though he went briefly to England, he spent nearly all of his time studying under Gneist, Stein, and Mosse; see also Yasuzō Suzuki, *Kempō seitei to Roesureru* (Establishment of the constitution and Roesler) (Tokyo: Tōyō keizai shimpōsha, 1942), pp. 3–55.

58. See Shin'ichi Fujii, *The Essentials of Japanese Constitutional Law* (Tokyo: Yūhikaku, 1940), and Niichirō Matsunami, *The Constitution of Japan* (Tokyo: Maruzen & Co., 1930). Both of these English-language treatises seem bizarre by democratic standards. Fujii's work, though written in 1940, has a foreword by K. Kaneko, who traveled in 1889–90 to Europe at Itō's request for the specific purpose of eliciting comment from constitutional authorities. Kentarō Kaneko, *Kempō seitei to ōbeijin no hyōron* (Establishment of the constitution and European and American comments) (Tokyo: Nihon seinenkan, 1937), p. 3, and Shin'ichi Fujii, *Teikoku kempō to Kaneko-haku* (The imperial constitution and Count Kaneko) (Tokyo: Dai-nihon yūbenkai kōdansha, 1942), p. 416. Such men as Dicey, Holmes, and Gneist are said to have approved in general the Meiji constitution for the time and place. In English, see Takayanagi, "A Century of Innovation," in *Law in Japan*, ed. von Mehren, pp. 7–8.

59. See an excellent study by Frank O. Miller, *Minobe Tatsukichi* (U. of Cal. Press, 1965); also Toshiyoshi Miyazawa, "Minobe sensei no gyōseki" (Accomplishments of teacher Minobe), 62 *Kokka gakkai zasshi* 327–36 (1948); Nobushige Ukai, "Minobe hakase no shisō to gakusetsu—sono rekishiteki igi" (Theory and thought of Dr. Minobe —its historical significance), 20 *Hōritsu jihō* 381–85 (1948). See Richard H. Minear, *Japanese Tradition and Western Law* (Harvard U. Press, 1970), on Yatsuka Hozumi.

60. Hirobumi Itō's oft-quoted letter on this point is revealing: "By studying under two famous German teachers, Gneist and Stein, I have been able to get a general understanding of the structure of the state. Later I shall discuss with you how we can achieve the great objective of establishing Imperial authority. Indeed, the tendency in our country today is to erroneously believe in the works of British, French, and American liberals and radicals as if they were Golden Rules, and thereby lead virtually to the overthrow of the State. In having found principles and means of combating this trend, I believe I have rendered an important service to my country, and I feel inwardly that I can die a happy man."

Takeshi Osatake, *Nihon kenseishi taikō* (Outline of the history of Japanese constitutional government) (Tokyo: Nihon hyōronsha, 1939), 2: 676, translated Nobutaka Ike, *The Beginnings of Political Democracy in Japan* (Johns Hopkins Press, 1950), pp. 175–76; but also note some rather cogent reasoning by Itō on the Japanese conditions relevant to self-government: Itō, "Some Reminiscences of the Grant of the New Constitution," in *Fifty Years of New Japan*, ed. Ōkuma, p. 128; and see Johannes Siemes, *Herman Roesler and the Making of the Meiji State* (Tokyo: Sophia U. and Tuttle, 1968), p. 252.

61. George Akita, *Foundations of Constitutional Government in Modern Japan, 1868–1900* (Harvard U. Press, 1967), p. 292. Itō, "Some Reminiscences of the Grant of the New Constitution," *Fifty Years of New Japan*, ed. Ōkuma, p. 127; Nobushige Ukai, "The Individual and the Rule of Law under the New Constitution," 51 *Nw. U. L. Rev.* 733–37 (1956–57).

62. Potsdam Declaration, Proclamation by the Heads of Governments, United States, United Kingdom, and China, July 26, 1945, Article 10: "We do not intend that the Japanese shall be enslaved as a race or destroyed as a nation, but stern justice shall be meted out to all war criminals, including those who have visited cruelties upon our prisoners. The Japanese Government shall remove all obstacles to the revival and strengthening of democratic tendencies among the Japanese people. Freedom of speech, of religion, and of thought, as well as respect for the fundamental human rights, shall be established."

63. For an official collection of relevant documents and English translations of some of the implementing laws, see 2 SCAP, Government Section, *Political Reorientation of Japan (1945–1948)*, (Washington, D.C.: GPO, 1947).

64. Perhaps the most complete survey of the occupation legal reforms is: "Sengo hōsei no hensen" (Changes in the postwar legal system), *Jurisuto* (No. 100) 2–189 (1956) (hereafter cited *Jurisuto* [100]); and Hiroshi Suekawa, ed., *Shiryō sengo nijūnen-shi* (Materials twenty-year postwar history) (Tokyo: Nihon hyōronsha, 1966), p. 673.

65. The SCAP official story emphasizes their point of view: SCAP, Government Section, *Political Reorientation of Japan (1945–48)*, 1: xxiii–xxxv; Theodore H. McNelly, "Domestic and International Influences on Constitutional Revision in Japan, 1945–1946" (Ph.D. diss., Columbia University, 1952), p. 444.

66. The formal method of the revision was by amendment to the Meiji Constitution by its amendment procedure in Art. 73. See Toshiyoshi Miyazawa, *Nihon koku kempō taikei* (Commentary on the Japanese national constitution) (Tokyo: Yūhikaku, 1955), p. 16.

67. Const., Art. 1: "The Emperor shall be the symbol of the State and of the unity of the people, deriving his position from the will of the people, with whom resides sovereign power." Shigemitsu Dandō, *Japanese Criminal Procedure*, tr. B. J. George, Jr. (South Hackensack, N.J.: Fred B. Rothman & Co., 1965), p. 663.

68. *Jurisuto* (100) 91 (1956); A. Nagashima, "The Accused and Society: The Administration of Criminal Justice in Japan," in *Law in Japan*, ed. von Mehren, p. 297; Richard B. Appleton, "Reforms in Japanese Criminal Procedure under the Allied Occupation," 24 *Wash. L. Rev.* 401 (1949).

69. Japan has never had a jury for civil trials, but in 1923 a jury was authorized for criminal trials, Law No. 50 (1923). But the jury decided by majority; certain appeals were precluded by jury trial; and the judge was free to disregard the verdict, plus the fact that psychologically defendants did not favor a jury. So, it was suspended (Law No. 88 [1943]) and it has not been revived since.

70. *Jurisuto* (100) 88 (1956); Ryūichi Hirano, "Some Aspects of Criminal Law," in *Law in Japan*, ed. von Mehren, p. 274; Howard Meyers, "Revisions of the Criminal Code of Japan During the Occupation," 25 *Wash. L. Rev.* 104 (1950).

71. *Jurisuto* (100) 63 (1956); also see, among a growing literature, Kurt Steiner, "Postwar Changes in the Japanese Civil Code," 25 *Wash. L. Rev.* 286 (1950); Sakae Wagatsuma, "Democratization of the Family Relations in Japan," 23 *Wash. L. Rev.* 405 (1950); Kurt Steiner, "The Revision of the Civil Code of Japan: Provisions Affecting the Family," 9 *Far. E. Q.* 169 (1950); Yōzō Watanabe, "The Family and Law: The Individualistic Premise and Modern Japanese Family Law," in *Law in Japan*, ed. von Mehren, p. 364.

72. *Jurisuto* (100) 73 (1956); Lester N. Salwin, "The New Commercial Code of Japan: Symbol of Gradual Progress toward Democratic Goals," 50 *Georgetown L. J.* 478–512 (1962); Thomas Blakemore and Makoto Yazawa, "Japanese Commercial Code Revisions," 2 *Am. J. Comp. L.* 12–24 (1953).

73. Law No. 149, 12 July 1948.

74. For a summary of these changes see Kōji Tanabe, "The Process of Litigation: An Experiment with the Adversary System," in *Law in Japan*, ed. von Mehren, p. 73.

75. Code of Civil Procedure, Art. 261; deleted by Law No. 149, 12 July 1948.

76. See new Code of Civil Procedure, Art. 294.

77. Civil Procedure Regulations, Sup. Ct. Reg. No. 2 (1956).

78. Tanabe, "Process of Litigation," in *Law in Japan*, ed. von Mehren, p. 85.

79. Ronald P. Dore, *Land Reforms in Japan* (London: Oxford U. Press, 1959).

80. Local Autonomy Law (*Chihō jichihō*), Law No. 67, 1947. The local powers granted in the law have been gravitating back to the central government for lack of funds to wield them on the local scene. See Kurt Steiner, *Local Government in Japan* (Stanford U. Press, 1965), p. 564. Ardath Burke, *The Government of Japan* (New York: Crowell, 1961), pp. 196–222, has an interesting chapter on local government.

81. Meiji Const., Art. 3: "The Emperor is sacred and inviolable," and Art. 4: "The Emperor is the head of the Empire, combining in Himself the rights of sovereignty and exercises them, according to the provisions of the present constitution."

82. Robert A. Scalapino and Junnosuke Masumi, *Parties and Politics in Contemporary Japan* (U. of Cal. Press, 1962), pp. 125–53.

83. A standard introduction to the Japanese courts is: Hajime Kaneko, *Saibanhō* (Law of trials), 34 *Hōritsugaku zenshū* (Tokyo: Yūhikaku, 1959). In English see, generally, John M. Maki, *Court and Constitution in Japan: Selected Supreme Court Decisions (1948–1960)* (U. of Wash. Press, 1963), pp. i–xlvi; Alfred Oppler, "Japan's Courts and Law in Transition," 21 *Contemporary Japan* (Nos. 1–3) 1–37 (1952); Alfred Oppler, "The Reform of Japan's Legal and Judicial System under Allied Occupation," 24 *Wash. L. Rev.* 290–324 (1949); Supreme Court of Japan, *Outline of Japanese Judicial System* (Tokyo: Supreme Court, 1961).

84. *E.g.*, a standard simple Japanese text is Toshiyoshi Miyazawa, *Kempō* (Constitution) (Tokyo: Yūhikaku, 1949). In English see Dan Fenno Henderson, *The Constitution of Japan: Its First Twenty Years, 1947–1967* (U. of Wash. Press, 1968), p. 115; McNelly, "Domestic and International Influences on Constitutional Revisions in Japan, 1945–1946"; and Govt. Section, SCAP, *Political Reorientation of Japan*, 2 vols. (undated).

85. Const., Art. 66 (3): "The cabinet, in the exercise of executive power, shall be collectively responsible to the Diet." Both the new and old constitutions may be found in Leonard Quigley and John E. Turner, *The New Japan* (U. of Minn. Press, 1956), p. 407.

86. Const., Art. 41: The Diet shall be the highest organ of state power, and shall be the sole lawmaking organ of the state.

87. Const., Art. 81: The Supreme Court is the court of last resort with power to determine the constitutionality of any law, order, regulation, or official act.

88. 1 Cr. 137 (1803).

89. *Dred Scot* v. *Sanford*, 19 How. 404 (1857). Japan's first two Supreme Court cases declaring legislation unconstitutional were: *Sakagami* v. *Japan*, 7 Minshū 1562 (Sup. Ct., G.B., 8 Oct. 1953); *Nakamura* v. *Japan*, 16 Keishū 1593 (Sup. Ct., G.B., 28 Nov. 1962).

90. Sir William Ivor Jennings, *The Law and the Constitution*, 5th ed. (London: Univ. of London Press, 1959), pp. 305–17, states the enviable and perhaps unique fact of English political life; namely, that the free election alone can insure a rule of law. Jennings is critical of Dicey's earlier and more formal definition of the rule of law emphasizing court enforcement. A. V. Dicey, *Law of the Constitution*, 10th ed. (London: Macmillan, 1959).

91. Rule of law, limited government, and constitutionalism are often used in a synonymous way. Of course none of them are strictly legal terms; they all convey the idea that law is superior to power, even the power of a majority. They therefore have a highly political content concerned with popular sovereignty and the freedoms necessary to make a ballot meaningful. *Cf. International Commission of Jurists, the Rule of Law in a Free Society* 194 (1959).

92. Masami Itō, "The Rule of Law: Constitutional Development," in *Law in Japan*, ed. von Mehren, pp. 221–38, gives postwar case development in certain critical civil-rights areas. Also Nathaniel L. Nathanson, "Constitutional Adjudication in Japan," 7 *Am. J. of Comp. L.* 195 (1958).

93. *Cf.* Kiminobu Hashimoto, "The Rule of Law: Some Aspects of Judicial Review of Administrative Action," in *Law in Japan*, ed. von Mehren, p. 239.

94. Const., Art. 81.

95. Const., Art. 76. We are not asserting here that a separate court, as in France, would be less conducive to a rule of law; we are noting that the Japanese separate court was ineffectual to that end.

96. This judicial and bureaucratic balance in the Japanese government is such that, unless popular legislative support is forthcoming, judicial financing will likely remain inadequate. In a very real sense then it may be a melancholy truth that the people get no better courts than they deserve.

This is an old and ubiquitous problem, of course. See the uninhibited remarks in F. Shroeder, *Notes on the Civil Code of Japan* 77 (1898). "The few articles of the code [on torts] therefore will not be of much use to judges or parties; only the former will be pretty certain to be blamed for the shortcomings of the code, which ninety-nine times out of a hundred will throw them entirely upon their own resources, which the ill-advised and, we may say, blind and ruinous, economy of the Government in judicial salaries cannot fail to reduce to a very narrow limit."

97. Const., Art. 77.

98. Ibid.

99. *E.g.*, Civil Procedure Regulations, Sup. Ct. Reg. No. 2 of 1956.

100. Saikō saibansho jimusōkyoku, *Saibansho Binran* 1, 40–41, 44–45 (1968); Sup. Ct. of Japan, *Outline of Japanese Judicial System* 8–13 (1961).

101. To date, it seems that the court has only reversed two lower-court decisions on the basis of the unconstitutionality of the otherwise applicable laws. See citations in note 89 above. For discussion see Dan Fenno Henderson, "Japanese Judicial Review of Legislation," in *The Constitution of Japan: Its First Twenty Years, 1947–1967*, ed. Dan Fenno Henderson (U. of Wash. Press, 1968), p. 115.

102. Hakaru Abe, "Education of the Legal Profession in Japan," in *Law in Japan*, ed. von Mehren, p. 174.

103. See generally articles by two successive presidents of the Legal Training and Research Institute: Jirō Matsuda, "The Japanese Legal Training and Research Institute," 7 *Am. J. Comp. L.* 366 (1958); Abe, "Education of the Legal Profession in Japan," in *Law in Japan*, ed. von Mehren, p. 153; and Hiroshi Abe, "Hōritsuka no yōsei" (Training of jurists), 14 *Hōsō Jihō* 1–35 (1962).

104. See generally Hideo Saitō, "Wagakuni no saibankan no tokushoku" (Special characteristics of judges in our country), *Jurisuto* (No. 239) (1961), (Nos. 245 and 246) (1962); Hideo Saitō, *Saibankanron* (Treatise on judges) (Tokyo: Ichiryūsha, 1963).

105. The bar is a strong advocate of the system. For recent views see Saizō Suzuki *et al.*, "Hōsō ichigen no airo" (Bottleneck in unification of the legal profession), 13 *Jiyū to seigi* (No. 11) 1–17 (1962); Kikuji Ōyama, "Hōsō ichigen seido" (The system of unification of the legal profession) 14 *Jiyū to seigi* (No. 2) 1–21 (1963); Umon Takagi, *Bengoshi kara mita saibankan* (Judges as viewed by lawyers) (Tokyo: Yūhikaku, 1963), pp. 95–100.

106. Abe, "Education of the Legal Profession in Japan," in *Law in Japan*, ed. von Mehren, p. 171.

107. See generally Dan Fenno Henderson, "The Roles of Lawyers in U.S.-Japanese Business Transactions," 38 *Wash. L. Rev.* 1–21 (1963).

108. See for general, rather than transactional or bilateral, analysis, Milton Katz, "The International Role of Law and Lawyers," in *Proceedings of the International Association of Law Libraries for 1961*, p. 33; Mark S. Massel, "The Lawyer's Role in International Trade," in *Legal Problems in International Trade and Investment* (World Community Ass'n., Yale Law School, 1962); Walter Surrey, "American Investments Abroad —Foreign Legal Aspects for American Lawyers," 7 *Prac. Law* (No. 8), Pt. I, 13 (1961) and Pt. II, 8 (1962); also similar material in ABA-ALI, Joint Committee on Continuing Legal Education, *Law Governing International Transactions*, 1 (1962); George W. Ball, "The Role of the Lawyer in International Investment Fields," 11 *Virginia Law Weekly— Dicta 1* (1959–60); John Fayerweather, "Lawyers, Foreign Governments and Business Abroad," 44 *Va. L. Rev.* 185 (1958); Corwin Edwards, "The Internationality of Economic Interests," 111 *U. Pa. L. Rev.* 183 (1962); Fritz Moses, "International Law Practice," 4 *Fordham L. Rev.* 244 (1935); and *cf.*, for various subject-matter approaches, Arthur Dean, "The Role of International Law in a Metropolitan Practice," 103 *U. Pa. L. Rev.* 886 (1955); V. Alexander Scher, "What Foreign Patent Attorneys Think of American Patent Practice," 44 *J. Pat. Off. Soc'y.* 544 (1962); Kingman Brewster, "Legal Aspects of the Foreignness of Foreign Investment," 17 *Ohio St. L. J.* 267 (1956); Walter W. Brudno, "Basic Questions in Foreign Trade and Investment—A Lawyer's Check-List," 3 *Inst. of Private Investment Abroad* 5 (1961); Robert C. Kelso, "Check List of Legal Problems in Considering Foreign Investment," *U. Ill. L. J.* 416 (1959).

109. Henderson, "The Roles of Lawyers in U.S.-Japanese Transactions," *Wash. L. Rev.*, pp. 1–21.
110. Takeo Suzuki, "Shōgaihō no kenkyū o suishin shitai" (We want to promote studies of liaison law), *Shōji hōmu kenkyū* (No. 192) 2 (1960); Junkichi Koshikawa, "Nihon shōgai minji soshōhō no juritsu" (Establishment of a Japanese liaison civil-procedure law), *Hōkei ronshū* (No. 28) 205 (1959); (No. 30) 65 (1960).
111. Foreigners were admitted by a special article (*Bengoshihō*, Art. 7), which was deleted in 1955 (Law No. 155, 10 August 1955). Atsushi Nojima, "Gaikokujin no bengonin wa Nihon no hōtei ni tateruka" (Can foreign lawyers appear in Japanese courts?), 10 *Hōritsu no hiroba* (No. 9) 16 (1957). See also Akira Senō, "Zainichi beijin bengoshi no gyōmu seigen mondai" (The problem of limiting the practice of American lawyers resident in Japan), 5 *Jiyū to seigi* (No. 1) 12 (1954).
112. Chū Matsushita, "Bengoshi no chii kōjō to shokuiki kakujū" (Advancement of the lawyers' social status and expansion of their scope of services), *Nihon hōritsu shimbun* (No. 81) 3 (1963).
113. Of the difficulties of the common law for Japanese, see Kenzō Takayanagi, "Common and Civil Law in Japan," 4 *Am. J. Comp. L.* 63 (1955): "To the common run of Japanese jurists, the Anglo-American law became more and more strange and incomprehensible."
114. Takaaki Hattori, "The Legal Profession in Japan: Its Historical Development and Present State," in *Law in Japan*, ed. von Mehren, pp. 111–52, is an excellent article that pulls together most of the issues confronting the bar, as well as the issues posed for society generally because of the present posture of the legal profession.
115. Takigawa, *Kujiyado no kenkyū* 2–76 (1962); and Masajirō Takigawa, *Nijō Jin'ya no kenkyū* (Study of Nijō Jin'ya) (Tokyo: Waseda daigaku hikakuhō kenkyūjo, 1962), pp. 1–102.
116. There are a number of histories of the Japanese bar in Japanese; the most recent is Nihon bengoshi rengōkai, *Nihon bengoshi enkakushi* (History of the development of the Japanese lawyer) (Tokyo: Nihon bengoshi rengōkai, 1959), pp. 5–280; in English, for the period after 1868, see Richard Rabinowitz, "The Historical Development of the Japanese Bar," 70 *Harv. L. Rev.* 61–81 (1956). See also Judson F. Woodruff, "The Japanese Lawyer," 35 *Neb. L. Rev.* 429–457 (1956).
117. Kumao Terada, "Bengoshi gyōmu no hatten hōsaku" (A plan for the development of the lawyer's business), 10 *Jiyū to seigi* (No. 3) 21 (1959).
118. Kaname Ōhira and George Stevens, "Admission to the Bar, Disbarment and Disqualification of Lawyers in Japan and the United States—A Comparative Study," 38 *Wash. L. Rev.* 22–57 (1963); Hajime Kaneko, "Saibanhō" (Law of trials), 34 *Hōritsugaku zenshū* 246–56 (1959); Michitaka Kainō, "Nihon no bengoshi" (Japan's lawyers), 32 *Hōritsu jihō* 432 (1960).
119. See the early query as to whether the administration of the Japanese legal examination is not too restrictive in Woodruff, "The Japanese Lawyer," *Neb. L. Rev.*, p. 455.
120. Takeichi Amano, "Hōsō jinkō" (Lawyer population), *Jurisuto* (No. 249) 40–63 (1962); Eizō Sawa, "Soshō chien to hōsō jinkō (Delay of lawsuits and lawyer population), *Shōji hōmu kenkyū* (No. 94) 2 (1958).
121. Rounded figures for lawyers per capita show:

	Population	Lawyers	Persons per lawyer
Japan	103,700,000	8,900	11,650
Germany	55,000,000	18,700	2,900
United States	203,200,000	276,000	736

Retired and government lawyers (62,964) in the U.S. have been excluded because in Japan and Germany bar members as such seldom work as government employees. It is also questionable as to whether another 40,486 U.S. salaried lawyers should not be excluded. For German figures see 12 *Anwaltsblatt* 115 (May 1962); for the Japanese figures, see *Nihon bengoshi rengōkai, Kaiin meibo* (Japanese Bar Ass'n., Membership Register) (1968); for U.S. see American Bar Foundation, *The 1971 Lawyer Statistical Report 6*, 11 (1972).

122. Toshimasa Kozeki, "Saibankan yori bengoshi e no chūmon" (A request from a judge to lawyers), 12 *Jiyū to seigi* (No. 8) 2–6 (1961); Reisaku Takiuchi *et al.*, "Hōtei gijutsu to hōtei tōsō" (Conflict and technique in court), 33 *Hōritsu jikō* (No. 12) 4–7 (1961).

123. "Bengoshi no daitoshi shūchū tō ni kansuru sankō shiryō" (Reference materials regarding the concentration of lawyers in large cities, etc.) 13 *Jiyū to seigi* (No. 3) 45–47 (1962).

124. Arthur C. O'Meara, "Organizational Structure, Operation, and Administration for Large Corporate Law Department" (25 or more lawyers), 17 *Bus. Law* 584 (1962); *Continuing Education of the Bar* [Calif.], *Functions of Corporate Legal Departments* 1 and *Bibliography* 229 (1961). Note that in 1971 there were 33,593 salaried house counsel in the United States—10% of the lawyer population. American Bar Foundation, *The 1971 Lawyer Statistical Report* 11. To hold a job such as director of a corporation, a Japanese lawyer would have to obtain special permission from the bar. Lawyer's Law, Art. 30 (3), as amended.

125. See "Kigyōnai hōritsu gyōmu ni kansuru jittai chōsa" (Survey of legal work within the enterprise), *Shōji hōmu kenkyū* (No. 360) 7, 173 (1963).

126. Patent Agents' Law (*benrishihō*), Law No. 100, 30 Apr. 1922. See generally Benrishikai, ed. (Patent Agents' Association), *Benrishikaishi* (History of the patent agent association) (Tokyo: Benrishikai, 1959).

127. Our use of the English equivalent "patent agent" for the Japanese term *benrishi* varies from the official translation (*i.e.*, patent attorney). Since the *benrishi* is not a lawyer, the use of "patent attorney" would be unnecessarily confusing to Americans.

128. Tokkyochō, *Tokkyochō kōhō* 79 (1971).

129. Benrishikai, *Benrishikaishi* 211–12 (1959).

130. Patent Agents' Law, Art. 13.

131. Order for enforcement of the Patent Agents' Law (*Benrishihō shikōrei*) (Imperial Ordinance No. 466, 16 Dec. 1921).

132. Lawyers' Law, Art. 3: "A lawyer may, as a matter of course, perform the business of a patent agent and a tax agent." The Patent Agents' Law, Art. 3, provides that a lawyer is eligible to register as a patent agent without taking a special examination. Hence, there is a discrepancy in the two laws, since by the Lawyers' Law registration is not necessary for the lawyer to do patent work. However, because of the convenience of obtaining information and sharing the advice of other patent specialists the lawyer ordinarily does register as a patent agent, if he is at all active in patent work.

133. Patent Agents' Law, Art. 9 (2).

134. For a useful summary of the history see Benrishikai, *Benrishikaishi* 1–98 (1959).

135. Benrishikai, *Benrishi meibo* (A list of members) 286 (1970); also note Tokkyochō (Patent Office), *Tokkyochō nempō* (Annual report of the Patent Office), Nos. 12 (1959), 13 (1960), 14 (1961), that the number of patent agents has dropped to half what it was before World War II.

136. Patent Agents' Law, Art. 2 (1) (i); compare the Lawyers' Law that had such a provision in the prewar period (Lawyers' Law, Law No. 53, Art. 2, 1933), but no such provision was included in the new law after World War II. However, it has been said that admission to the required two-year course at the Legal Training and Research Institute has been limited to citizens (*i.e.*, a Taiwanese who passed the examination was excluded). See Nojima, "Gaikokujin no bengonin wa Nihon no hōtei ni tateruka," *Hōritsu no hiroba*, p. 14.

See also Isao Kumekawa, "Benrishi no shokumu han'i ni tsuite" (Concerning the scope of the patent agents' services), 11 *Patento* (No. 12) 7–8 (1958); Kunihiko Matsuo, "Benrishi no gyōmu han'i o kakudai" (The expansion of the patent agents' business), *Toki no hōrei* (No. 352) 10–15 (1960); and Keikichi Okuyama, "Benrishi no chii kōjō" (Improvement of the patent agents' status), 14 *Patento* (No. 10) 3 (1961).

137. Patent Agents' Law, Art. 2 (1) (i); MITI Ministerial Order, Art. 2 (1) (i) (No. 93, 24 Dec. 1952).

138. MITI Ministerial Order for the Patent Agents' Examination (Order No. 207, 4 June 1938), in Benrishikai, *Benrishikai reiki* (Patent agents' ass'n. rules and orders) 101 (1962).

139. The examinations are given annually and are very restrictive as can be seen from the following postwar statistics obtained from inquiry to Tokkyochō, 10 Feb. 1971.

Results of Annual Patent Agents' Examination

	Applicants	Successful Applicants
1962	655	68
1963	729	63
1964	985	48
1965	1073	51
1966	1329	49
1967	1417	47
1968	1844	49
1969	2138	48
1970	2365	49

140. See Benrishikai, "Tokkyo jimu hyōjungakuhyō," Ass'n. Order (*kairei*) No. 8.

141. Benrishikai, *Benrishikai reiki* 58–61 (1967). And see, generally, Shin'ichi Ishida, "Benrishi hōshū o meguru shomondai" (Various problems concerning the compensation of patent agents), 14 *Patento* (No. 11) 39–44 (1961).

142. See Sadao Hattori, "Kōnin kaikeishi to bengoshi to no kengyō tō ni tsuite" (Concerning the overlap of CPA and lawyer business, etc.) 10 *Jiyū to seigi* (No. 3) 16 (1959); *cf.* Joseph V. Anderson, "The Tax Practice Controversy in Historical Perspective," 1 *Wm. & Mary L. Rev.* 18 (1956).

143. Tax Agents' Law (*Zeirishihō*), Art. 2 (Law No. 237, 15 June 1951):

Article 2. A tax agent shall, on other persons' commission in regard to the income tax, corporation tax, estate tax, municipal inhabitant's tax, gift tax, enterprise tax, fixed assets tax and other taxes prescribed by Cabinet Order (hereafter referred to as "the taxes") conduct professionally the following business:

(1) To act as an agent in regard to reports, applications, protests, or requests for refunds of overpaid taxes, and other matters (excluding litigation);

(2) To prepare returns, applications, requests and other documents to be filed with tax offices (excluding custom offices; hereinafter the same);

(3) To give counsel on the matters under item (1).

This statute and various other laws, orders, and regulations affecting tax agents may be found in Nihon zeirishikai rengōkai, *Zeirishi kankei hōrei ruishū* (Classified collection of laws and regulations related to *zeirishi*) (Tokyo: Nihon zeirishikai rengōkai, 1970).

144. Lawyers' Law, Art. 3 (2) (Law No. 205, 10 June 1949). There is a conflict between the Lawyers' Law and the Tax Agents' Law, much like that regarding patent agents; namely, the Tax Agents' Law, Art. 3 (1) requires the lawyer to register under Art. 18 (3) or report to the director of the bureau under Art. 51 (1), but it is not necessary according to the Lawyers' Law.

145. Tax Agents' Law, Art. 3 (1) and Art. 51 (2). See Nihon zeirishikai rengōkai, "Zeirishihō chikujō kaisetsu" (Article-by-article commentary on the tax agents' law) 2–8 (1958).

146. Tax Agents' Law, Art. 3, and CPA Law, Art. 16 (2).

147. The reason all "tax experts" are not members of the Tax Agents' Association is, of course, that some lawyers and CPA's who handle tax matters do not join the association, while others do.

148. "Zeirishi no oitachi" (The growth of tax agents), in the newspaper *Zeirishikai*

(Tax agents' world) (No. 250), 18 Dec. 1962, p. 7. This is a newspaper for tax agents, and the 18 Dec. 1962 issue marks the twentieth anniversary of the Tax Agents' Association.

149. Before 1947, bookkeeping and accounting methods were such that Japanese tax assessment was necessarily done by a method sometimes called "assess and collect" (*fuka chōshū shugi*) whereby the tax office assessed the tax based on its best judgment of the liability and without consideration for the taxpayer's representations to the contrary. The tax agent's role was rather limited in such a practice.

150. Tax Agents' Law, Art. 34, as amended 1956.

151. "Zeirishi no jittai chōsa" (Empirical investigation of tax agents), in *Chōsashitsu shiryō* (44–2) July 1969. Investigation by the National Tax Agency (*Kokuzei chō*) made every five years through 1962 were reported in *Zeirishikai* (No. 267), 11 June 1963, pp. 4–5, Table 1. But in 1967 the authorities consented to the *zeirishi*'s own self-investigation as reported above.

152. No authoritative figures are available on lawyers' income, but one sampling (1960) showed that the income of those few who reported averaged only $275 a month (*i.e.*, $3,000 per year). Yasuhiro Matsui *et al.*, "Bengoshi no seikatsu to ishiki" (Life and thought of lawyers) 32 *Hōritsu jihō* 458 (1960). See 23-ki shūshūsei yūshi, "Shinjin bengoshi no keizaiteki jittai" (Economic status of newly born lawyers) 43 *Hōritsu jihō* 83 (1971).

153. Tax Agents' Law, Art. 39 (1951).

154. Japanese Tax Agents' Association, "Regulation on compensation for tax agents" (*Zeirishi hōshū kitei*), in Nihon zeirishikai rengōkai, *Zeirishi kaigyō no tebiki* (Guide to opening a tax agent's business) 12–16 (1962).

155. *Zeirishikai* (extra) 25 May 1963, p. 1; about the small percentage of the successful candidates, it must be noted that the candidates must pass five subjects, and usually they take one subject per year so that it takes five or more years to pass the whole examination. There were 23,497 registered tax agents, 31 Dec. 1970, but only 21,105 actively practicing members.

156. Tax Agents' Law, Art. 52, as amended 1956. This is a new requirement since 1956.

157. Ibid., Art. 49–14.

158. Takunaga Yumoto, "Shihō shoshi no shokuiki kakuritsu ni tsuite" (Concerning the marking out of a field of competence for the judicial scrivener), *Nihon shihō shoshikai rengōkai kaihō* (Report of the Japanese federation of judicial scriveners' association) (No. 1) 6–7 (1959).

159. Editor, "Shihō shoshi hōshū kitei kijun" (Standard fees for judicial scriveners), *Nihon shihō shoshikai rengōkai kaihō* (No. 67), p. 48 (1970). Fees were revised as of 1 Jan. 1970 in Tokyo. Each local association has a schedule of fees fixed by the Legal Affairs Office, Tokyo Shihō Shoshikai. See also "Hōshū kitei kijun'an" (Draft standards for computing compensation [for the Tokyo judicial scriveners' association]), ibid., p. 58; and Setsuo Tateishi, "Hōshū kitei no chūkai" (Comments on the compensation regulations), in ibid. (No. 4) 11 Nov. 1962, p. 13.

160. Judicial Scriveners' Law, Art. 1 (1950), amended 18 July 1967: "(1) A judicial scrivener's business shall be to draft an official document or official documents to be presented by that person to a Court, a Public Procurator's Office, a Legal Affairs Bureau or a District Legal Affairs Bureau, and also take the procedures regarding registration or deposition on behalf of any other person, in compliance with such person's request. (2) A judicial scrivener shall not be permitted to, even if it is a business mentioned in the preceding paragraph, do this, in cases restricted by other laws."

161. *Shihō tōkei nempō* (Annual report of judicial statistics, civil and administrative) 530 (1967).

162. See criticism by Toshio Muramatsu, "Shihō shoshi to shitei dairinin" (Judicial scriveners and appointed attorneys), 29 *Hōritsu jihō* (No. 9) 50–51 (1957); and reply by Rikimatsu Yamanaka, "Shihō shoshi to soshō kōi—Muramatsu hanji no shoron ni kotau" (Judicial scriveners and acting in litigation—in response to Judge Muramatsu's argument), 20 *Hōritsu jihō* (No. 11) 87 (1957).

163. Ichirō Kurimoto, "Saikin no shomondai" (Recent problems), *Nihon shihō shoshikai rengōkaihō* (No. 4) 1 Nov. 1962, pp. 1–4. Japan Judicial Scriveners' Association, "Dai-21-kai teiji sōkai shiryō" 181 (June 1968).

164. Judicial Scriveners' Law, Art. 2 (1950).

165. Ibid., Art. 14 and Art. 17.

166. Letter, 24 Apr. 1963, from Masaharu Hashimoto, chairman of the Administrative Scriveners' Association, wherein it was stated that Sanetomi Sanjō established such a system in 1873.

167. Administrative Scriveners' Law (*Gyōsei shoshihō*) (Law No. 4, 22 Feb. 1951).

168. Ibid., Art. 2 (1) and 4.

169. Ibid., Art. 2 (2).

170. Ibid., Art. 2 (2) (5) and Art. 3.

171. Ibid., Art. 1:

    1. An administrative scrivener's business is to draft, upon request by any other persons, for obtaining compensation, documents to be presented to governmental or public offices or other documents concerning the rights, obligations or certification of facts.

    2. An administrative scrivener shall not practice his business in connection with even those documents in the preceding paragraph, if the business is restricted by other laws.

172. This provision against overlap prevents the administrative scrivener in most cases from drafting documents for presentation to the Patent Office, Courts, Legal Affairs Offices, or Tax Offices. The association petitioned in 1963 to rescind Art. 1 (2) and Art. 19 (1) proviso. See Masaharu Hashimoto *et al.*, "Gyōsei shoshihō kaisei ni tsuite no seigansho" (A petition concerning the amendment of the administrative scriveners' law) in *Kaihō* (Ass'n. Report) (No. 3). There were 13,000 members in 1970.

173. Administrative Scriveners' Law, Art. 6 (3).

174. Ibid., Art. 15.

175. Ibid., Art. 18.

176. See, *e.g.*, *Gyōsei shoshihō shikō saisoku* (Rules for enforcement of the administrative scriveners' law) (Tokyo City Reg. No. 61, 7 Apr. 1951, amended to 1 June 1968); also amended 1 Aug. 1970.

177. The Association Members' List, 3 June 1968.

178. Sadao Hattori, "Kōnin kaikeishi to bengoshi to no kengyō tō ni tsuite," *Jiyū to seigi*, pp. 16–18.

179. Certified Public Accountants' Law (Law No. 103, 6 July 1948).

180. "Japanese Institute of CPA's," *CPA's in Japan* (Tokyo: Japanese Institute of CPA's, 1962), pp. 7–15; for standards of accounting suggested by the Ministry of Finance, see Ministry of Finance, "Kigyō kaikei gensoku" (General principles for enterprise accounting), in *Kigyō kaikei kisokushū* (Collection of regulations in enterprise accounting), ed. Makoto Yazawa (Tokyo: Yūhikaku, 1961), pp. 11–24; for auditing procedures recommended by the Ministry of Finance, see Kigyō kaikei shingikai, *Kansa jisshi kisoku* (Regulations for performing audits), in ibid., p. 125 (1961); Report, "Ōkurashō—Rikō Tokei ni chōsei todokeide shohōkokusho no teishutsu o meirei" (Ministry of finance order against Rikō Watch [company] to submit revised submissions and reports), *Shōji hōmu kenkyū* (No. 283) 25 (1963).

181. The Law on Registered Accountants (*keirishihō*) was abolished as of 31 March 1968. But those accountants who had been qualified by that time are allowed to continue their work as before; CPA Members' List, 1 Jan. 1970, shows 3,992 members; also see "Japanese Institute of CPA's," *CPA's in Japan*, p. 74.

182. CPA Law, Art. 16 (2).

183. CPA Members' List, 1 Jan. 1970.

184. Securities and Exchange Law, Art. 193 (2) (Law No. 25, 13 Apr. 1948).

185. See *e.g.*, Kō Yoshida, "Kansayaku kōnin kaikeishi no kensa" (Audit by auditors and audits by CPA's), 28 *Hōritsu jihō* (No. 6) 22–31 (1956).

186. Notary Law (*Kōshōninhō*), Art. 1 (Law No. 53, 14 Apr. 1908): "The notary

public shall, upon entrustment of the parties concerned or other interested persons, have the power to make notarial deeds in respect of a juristic act and other facts concerned with private right, or to attest a private deed and to attest articles of incorporation in accordance with the provisions of Article 167 of the Commercial Code and the *mutatis mutandis* application thereof."

187. Japan Notaries' Ass'n. Members' List (1 Sept. 1970) shows 380 members.

188. Commercial Code, Art. 167.

189. Code of Civil Procedure, Art. 559 (3). See Katsuyoshi Takanashi, "Kōsei shō-sho" (Notarial deeds), *Jurisuto* (207) 59–66 (1960).

190. Gyōsei saibansho, *Gyōsei saibansho gojūnenshi* (History of fifty years of the administrative court) (Tokyo: Gyōsei Saibansho, 1941), pp. 509–12, and charts show statistics on the work of the prewar court.

191. *Shihō tōkei nempō* (Annual reports of judicial statistics), p. 27, shows only 1,232 newly filed cases at first instance including tax cases in 1967. There were 1,562 cases filed in 1968. Ibid. (1968), p. 262.

192. In this area of foreign exchange and investment, administration is especially characterized by virtually unchallengeable discretion in many other countries too.

193. Shihō kenshūjo (Legal training and research institute), *Hōrei hanrei gakusetsu no chōsa ni tsuite* (Concerning investigation of laws, judicial precedents, and academic theories) (1962), is a very useful beginner's guide to Japanese legal research materials and techniques. It was compiled by Asst. Judge Tanno (laws), Judge Kawakami (judicial precedents), and Judge Tanabe (academic theories).

194. Ibid., pp. 87–90.

195. Law Concerning the Application of Laws in General (*Hōrei*), Art. 2 (Law No. 10, 21 June 1898).

196. *Cf.* Shihō kenshūjo, *Hōrei hanrei gakusetsu no chōsa ni tsuite*, p. 52.

197. Ibid., pp. 31–32, 51–53. Judge Kawakami points out that search of the precedents and the academic theories is a rather indivisible operation. This is because the text writers are so often the case compilers and annotators and also because the text writers influence the cases and vice versa.

198. *E.g.*, the cases generally say that it is not necessary to give notice of the next hearing to the parties; the text writers (Kaneko, Wada, Mikazuki) say it is necessary. See ibid., p. 53, note 3.

199. Beginners will find the selective bibliography in *Hōgaku annai* (Guide to legal studies), *Jurisuto* (extra issue), July 1967, useful.

CHAPTER VI

1. *Gaikoku kawase oyobi gaikoku bōeki kanrihō* (Foreign exchange and foreign trade control law) (Law No. 228, 1 Dec. 1949); English: EHS No. 5010.

2. *Gaishi ni kansuru hōritsu* (Foreign investment law) (Law No. 163, 10 May 1950); English: EHS No. 5410.

3. See OECD, *Liberalisation of International Capital Movements: Japan* (Paris: OECD Pub., 1968), p. 157, ¶321 (hereafter OECD, *Liberalisation*).

4. For a comparative summary of administrative law development by a Supreme Court Justice (formerly Tokyo University professor) see Jirō Tanaka, *Gyōseihō kōgi, jō* (Lectures in administrative law, Vol. One) (Tokyo: Ryosho fukyūkai, 1965), pp. 1–19; also see Ichirō Ogawa, "Gendai ni okeru gyōsei to hō" (Law and contemporary administration), in 4 *Gendaihō* (Contemporary law) (Tokyo: Iwanami shoten, 1966), p. 3; Masumi Ogata, *Gyōsei soshō seido no rekishi-teki kenkyū* (Historical study of the system of administrative litigation) (Kyoto: K. K. Mineruba shobō, 1963), p. 31.

In English see Ichirō Ogawa, "Judicial Review of Administrative Action in Japan," in *The Constitution of Japan: Its First Twenty Years, 1947–67*, ed. Dan Fenno Henderson (U. of Wash. Press, 1969), p. 185.

5. FIL, Art. 20 (1950).

6. See OECD, Business and Industry Advisory Committee (BIAC), "The Control of

the Inflow of Investment into Japan," Annex to Circular C-438 of 17 March 1967. Also see OECD, *Liberalisation*, pp. 57, 61 ¶116, 99.

7. See, for example, Ōkurashō, kokusai kinyū-kyoku (Ministry of Finance), *Gaikoku kawase bōeki sho-roppō* (Small compilation of laws on foreign exchange and trade) (Tokyo: Gaikoku kawase kenkyūkai, 1971).

8. Foreign Exchange Study Association, *Japan Laws, Ordinances and Other Regulations Concerning Foreign Exchange and Foreign Trade* (Tokyo: Foreign Exchange Study Ass'n., 1971) (hereafter *Japan Regulations*).

9. A Japanese trial judge, well known as an expert in handling judicial review of administrative actions, writes: "Administrative law and regulations lately have become more and more complex and have become specialized and technical things, and there are not a few instances where, if he is not a specialist, not only the layman plaintiff, but even the lawyer and the judge cannot easily understand." Judge Kenzō Shiraishi, "Gyōsei jiken soshō no arikata" (A model for administrative case litigation), *Hanrei jihō* (No. 428) 4 (1966).

10. For general reference, see Kiyoaki Tsuji, *Nihon kanryōsei no kenkyū* (Study of the Japanese bureaucracy) (Tokyo: Tokyo daigaku shuppankai, 1969), pp. 155, 324. Also an interesting journalistic treatment: Yukio Suzuki, *Keizai kanryō; shin-sangyō kokka no purodyūsā* (The economic bureaucracy, producers of the new industrial state) (Tokyo: Nihon keizai shimbunsha, 1969).

11. See Robert M. Spaulding, Jr., *Imperial Japan's Higher Civil Service Examinations* (Princeton U. Press, 1967); and Mikio Higa, "The Role of Bureaucracy in Contemporary Japanese Politics" (Ph.D. diss., University of California, University Microfilms #69-3612, 1968), p. 148; also Tadao Okada, "The Unchanging Bureaucracy," *Japan Quarterly* 12 (No. 2) (1965): 168.

12. Kiyoaki Tsuji, *Nihon kanryōsei no kenkyū* (Study of the Japanese bureaucracy) (Tokyo: Tokyo daigaku shuppankai, 1969), p. 89.

13. Ibid., p. 3.

14. See Higa, "The Role of Bureaucracy," p. 334, for description of a SCAP-inspired exam for promotion held on 15 Jan. 1950. Out of 2,488 positions to be filled, all but 18 were filled by those already in the service, and 78% of the positions went, by exam, to prior incumbents.

15. See ibid., p. 372.

16. Suzuki, *Keizai kanryō*, p. 10, has an interesting summary of the controversy over the extent to which the Japanese bureaucracy should be credited with the economic "miracle," and he makes it clear that the high evaluation placed on bureaucratic guidance by some (such as fellow-journalist Norman MacCrae of the London *Economist*) is by no means universally accepted. A major segment of Japanese opinion would say the credit should go to business management and labor diligence with the bureaucrats helping at best, or obstructing at worst.

17. See Higa, "The Role of Bureaucracy," p. 362, citing Shūgiin Sangiin, ed., *Gikai seido shichijūnen-shi: Kokkai gian kemmeiroku* (Seventy-year history of the legislative system: National Diet registry of bills) (Tokyo: Ōkurashō insatsu-kyoku, 1961), p. 959, for statutes: 4,389 bills considered, 3,333 adopted (1st Diet, May 1947, to 35th Diet, July 1960); the cabinet sponsored 71% and succeeded in getting 87% of its bills passed.

18. OECD, *Liberalisation*, p. 140, notes the enormous powers of the "economic bureaucracy" in the field of foreign investment derived directly from this technique of drafting the "governing law" so that it is a mere shell—thus liberalization occurs by bureaucratic decision to relax the blanket prohibitions in the "law": "1. The Law [FECL] is duly prohibitive or restrictive against all transactions likely to adversely influence this country's balance of payments or add to its international indebtedness, and restrictions are to be eased or removed through revisions of the orders and ordinances issued under the Law. Legally speaking, as will be noted later, foreign exchange and trade controls are liberalized by means not of revising the Law itself but of easing or removing restrictions through revisions of the Cabinet Orders and the Ministerial Ordinances."

19. Yoriaki Narita, "Gyōsei shidō" (Administrative guidance) 4 *Gendaihō* 131 (Tokyo: Iwanami shoten, 1966), translated by James L. Anderson, 2 *Law in Japan* 45 (1968).

20. Ichirō Ogawa, Yoshio Kanazawa, Yoriaki Narita, Kinzō Matsuo, Makoto Yazawa, and Kazuo Yamauchi (Symposium), "Gyōsei shidō no kihon mondai" (Basic problems of administrative guidance), *Jurisuto* (No. 342) 23–24 (1966).

21. *Jurisuto* (No. 342) 21.

22. Guidelines have some similarity to "guidance" as used in Japan. See George P. Shultz and Robert Z. Aliber, eds., *Guidelines: Informal Contracts and the Market Place* (U. of Chicago Press, 1966), p. 209.

23. Narita, "Gyōsei shidō," *Gendaihō*, p. 132.

24. Tsuji, *Nihon kanryōsei no kenkyū*, p. iii.

25. See Rinji gyōsei chōsakai, *Gyōsei no kaikaku* (Reforms in administration) (Tokyo: Jiji tsūshinsha, 1967).

26. Hirotarō Kawasaki, "Gyōsei shidō no jittai—saikin no mittsu no kēsu ni miru" (Actualities of administrative guidance—as seen in three recent cases), *Jurisuto* (No. 342) 51 (1966).

27. Ogawa *et al.*, "Gyōsei shidō no kihon mondai," *Jurisuto* (No. 342) 38 (1966).

28. See *Japan Economic Journal*, 27 July 1971, p. 1.

29. Kawasaki, *Jurisuto* (No. 342) 53 (1966).

30. See *Japan Economic Journal*, 9 Nov. 1971, p. 1. By mutual three-cornered agreement among the steel industry, MITI, and the FTC, it was agreed that a "depression cartel" would be set up under the AML, Art. 24–4, though MITI had first recommended collusion (a so-called "guidance cartel") to cut production without complying with the AML, until the FTC intervened. Also see *Japan Economic Journal*, 16 Nov. 1971, p. 1, where it is reported that ten more industries were under study by MITI for "depression cartel" privileges to be approved presumably by the FTC but reflecting MITI guidance. The industries mentioned were: steel, electrolytic copper, aluminum, machine tools, desktop calculators, heavy electrical equipment, paper pulp, synthetic fiber, cement, and petrochemicals. See Hiroshi Iyori, "Dokusen kinshi-hō to gyōsei shidō" (Administrative guidance and the AML), *Jurisuto* (No. 342) 59; also Ogawa *et al.*, *Jurisuto* (No. 342) 35 (1966).

31. For the status of such Japanese cartels in the U.S., see *U.S.* v. *Lerner Co.*, 215 F. Supp. 603 (1963).

32. See, however, *Domex International Co.* v. *Yokohama Tsūshō K.K. et al.*, *Hanrei Jihō* (No. 430) 17 (1966) (Tokyo D. Ct., 6th Dept., 28 Oct. 1965) for a case where "check prices" (*i.e.*, minimum prices imposed by MITI on Japanese export sellers) were held to have no legal effect as a defense by a Japanese seller (Yokohama) in a suit by the American buyer for damages for failure to perform a contract to sell below check price. The court noted that the "check price" was fixed without promulgation or legal authority and was not binding, therefore no excuse for nonperformance.

33. Narita, "Administrative Guidance," *Law in Japan*, p. 60.

34. Ibid., p. 62.

35. This point is discussed in Ogawa *et al.*, *Jurisuto* (No. 342) 38.

36. OECD, *Liberalisation*, p. 67, notes: "The [Japanese] Government is more closely and more deeply involved in economic activities than in other Member States. . . . In addition to overall orientation of economic and especially industrial development, the State feels it has specific responsibilities for newly developing sectors which in some instances it discharges through 'official guidance'. . . . Questions arise in the minds of the authorities: would foreign-controlled concerns respond to official direction in the same way? Would foreign capital dominate limited domestic resources to the detriment of orderly industrial development as government plans it? Would foreign investors defer to the rules and be responsive to the practices and needs of the dual economy? Would they respect the traditional role and position of the small enterprises? Would they appreciate that Japan is 'different'?"

37. "MITI Studies Criteria on Conduct of Foreign Companies," *Japan Economic*

Journal, 27 July 1971, p. 2. Compare Panel on Foreign Investment in Developing Countries, U.N. Econ. and Social Council, *Agreed Statement on Private Foreign Investment in the Developing Process* (Panel Doc. #17, 20 Feb. 1969). At a meeting in Amsterdam of developing nations' officials, businessmen from industrial countries, and officials of international organizations, those in attendance noted the need for businesses to accommodate their activities to the host countries abroad, because they best know their needs.

38. FIL, Art. 14, might be construed as authority for this practice: "Art. 14. The competent Minister or the Minister of Finance may, on making validation, designation or confirmation pursuant to the provisions of this Law, stipulate necessary conditions upon which validation is based."

39. *Kokusai-teki gijutsu dōnyū keiyaku ni kansuru nintei kijun* (Validation criteria concerning international contracts introducing technology) (FTC, 24 May 1968), in Yuichi Makaura, ed., *Gijutsu dōnyū keiyaku nintei kijun no kaisetsu* (Explanation of validation criteria concerning international contracts introducing technology) (Tokyo: Shōji hōmu kenkyūkai, 1968), p. 125; English version, p. 127.

40. *JEJ*, 6 Sept. 1966; note the following conditions for a validation of Texas Instruments' application filed Jan. 1964, granted 1968:

    1. 50/50 equities;

    2. The joint venture to refrain from disturbing domestic companies' production (*i.e.*, curtailed production for several years);

    3. Texas Instrument patents to be made public by licensing (*i.e.*, Sony, Mitsubishi Electric, Hitachi, Toshiba, and Nippon Electric Co. were all to be licensed).

Also see *JEJ*, 11 April 1967, and *JEJ*, 22 Nov. 1966.

41. Bernard S. Silberman, "The Bureaucracy and Economic Development in Japan," 5 *Asian Survey* 529–37 (1965).

42. As noted, at least two schools of thought discount considerably the government's causal connection with the postwar economic "miracle": (1) some writers emphasize the quality of the Japanese work force and the role of *zaikai* (business leadership); (2) some, mainly the opposition (*yatō*) Marxists, emphasize the self-interest of the bureaucrats and conversely the fact that today's prosperity has come out of the hide of those in the substructure of dualism, who are kept captive and running to keep body and soul together, while delivering parts and services at cut-rate prices to the modern sector. See, for discussion of several views, Suzuki, *Keizai kanryō*, p. 13.

43. The most useful, concise study in English is Akira Kubota, *Higher Civil Servants in Postwar Japan* (Princeton U. Press, 1969).

44. Hereafter the following English terms are used in the text as equivalent for Japanese organizational units:

        Secretariat—*kambō*

        Bureau—*kyoku*

        Division—*bu*

        Section—*ka*

        Parliamentary vice-minister—*seimu jikan*

        Administrative vice-minister—*jimu jikan*

        National Personnel Authority—*jinjiin*

45. But see an interesting caveat registered by Ronald Dore, "The Future of Japan's Meritocracy," *Bulletin of the Int'l House of Japan* (No. 26) 30 (1970).

46. See Hideo Shimizu, *Tokyo daigaku hōgaku-bu* (The law department of Tokyo University) (Tokyo: Kōdansha, 1965).

47. For prewar cases, see Spaulding, *Imperial Japan's Higher Civil Service Examinations*, p. 293.

48. Kōya Azumi, *Higher Education and Business Recruitment in Japan* (New York: Columbia U., Teachers College Press, 1969), p. 82, describes the procedures for business hiring, where the interview is probably even more important.

49. Dore, "The Future of Japan's Meritocracy," *Bulletin*, p. 48.

50. M. Y. Yoshino, *Japan's Managerial System* (MIT Press, 1968), p. 71, indicates that big business is now favored over government as an initial career by the young elite.

51. Kubota, *Higher Civil Servants in Postwar Japan*, p. 160.

52. Ibid., p. 92.

53. Shimizu, *Tokyo daigaku hōgaku-bu*, p. 196, for reference to "*hōka bannō*" (Omnipotence of law study); also Kubota, *Higher Civil Servants in Postwar Japan*, p. 84.

54. Kubota, *Higher Civil Servants in Postwar Japan*, p. 127. Much of the specific information hereafter on the HCS is drawn from this book, unless otherwise attributed.

55. Reinhard W. Lloyd Warner, Paul P. Van Piper, Norman H. Martin, and Orvis F. Collins, *The American Federal Executive: A Study of Social and Personal Characteristics of the Civilian and Military Leaders of the U.S. Federal Government* (Yale U. Press, 1963), p. 373.

56. R. K. Kelsall, *Higher Civil Service in Britain from 1870 to the Present Day* (London: Routledge & Kegan Paul, 1955), p. 136.

57. Kubota, *Higher Civil Servants in Postwar Japan*, p. 67 ff.

58. Higa, "The Role of Bureaucracy," p. 334.

59. In 1959 about 29% of the HCS went into business, 30% into public corporations, 8% foreign service (ambassadors), and 5% Diet members. (Kubota, *Higher Civil Servants in Postwar Japan*, p. 155). But 60% of MITI retirees went into business firms (ibid., p. 157).

60. *Kokka kōmuin-hō* (National public servants' law), Art. 103(2), prohibits a government official from taking a position in business within two years of leaving office, and Art. 103(3) authorizes the National Personnel Authority to grant approvals.

61. Nowhere is there a better simple statement of the special organizational principles of Japanese society than in Chie Nakane, *Japanese Society* (U. of Cal. Press, 1970), p. 23. *Cf.* Takeshi Ishida, *Japanese Society* (New York: Random House, 1971), p. 37.

62. Nakane, *Japanese Society*, p. 53, defines sectionalism as "creation of groups within a group" (*tōchū tō o tsukuru*).

63. Ibid., p. 38.

64. Ibid., p. 42.

65. The spate of "Black Ship" journalism concerning foreign capital is one manifestation of this phenomenon, though it is mixed with genuine anxiety, too. See, *e.g.*, "Gaishi no shinsenryaku o tenken suru" (Reivewing the new battle strategies of foreign capital), *Tōyō keizai* (No. 3585) 44 (13 Mar. 1971).

66. See what has been called "structural" nationalism, Kenneth B. Pyle, "Some Recent Approaches to Japanese Nationalism," *J. of Asian Studies* 31 (1971): 8.

67. See, *e.g.*, Misao Kanno, *Shihon jiyūka to kokusai hyōsōryoku* (Capital liberalization and international competitiveness) (Tokyo: K. K. Shiseidō, 1956), p. 71.

68. See, *e.g.*, report of disagreement (MOF for 100% liberation; MITI for retaining 50% limit on foreign ownership) in *Japan Times Weekly*, 20 Jan. 1973, p. 8. See also "Foreign Ministry Sets Policy for U.S.," *Japan Economic Journal*, 9 Nov. 1971, pp. 1, 12. Tsuneo Iida, "Kokueki-ron ni hisomu Nihonjin no higaisha ishiki" (Japanese injured feelings concealed in the national-interest theory), *Tōyō keizai* (No. 3486) 14 (31 July 1969).

69. Hiroshi Tomizawa, "Dai yon-ji shihon jiyūka ni tsuite" (Concerning the 4th round of capital liberalization), *Toki no hōrei* (No. 761) 36 (1971).

70. Per capita, the U.S. bureaucrats (including military and teachers) are nearly double those in Japan.
Japan:

	1970
Local	2,463,296
National	1,992,793
Total Japan	4,456,089

From Bureau of Statistics, Office of the Prime Minister, *Nihon tōkei nenkan* (Japan statistical yearbook) (Tokyo: Ōkurashō insatsukyoku, 1970), pp. 594–95.

U.S.:

Federal (civilian)	2,716,000
(military)	3,066,000
State and Local	10,147,000
Total U.S.	15,929,000

U.S. Dept. of Commerce, *Statistical Abstract of the U.S.* (Washington, D.C.: GPO, 1971), pp. 252, 421.

71. U.S. federal, state, and local roughly 30%, U.S. Dept. of Comm., *Statistical Abstract of the U.S.*, pp. 305, 373, 407. Japan roughly 15%, Bureau of Statistics, *Nihon tōkei nenkan*, p. 449.

72. *Gaishi ni kansuru hōritsu* (Foreign investment law) (Law No. 163, 10 May 1950); EHS No. 5410.

73. *Gaikoku kawase oyobi gaikoku bōeki kanrihō* (Foreign exchange and foreign trade control law) (No. 228, 1 Dec. 1949); EHS No. 5010.

74. Because it is well indexed, detailed, and kept up to date by expert officials, I have found the following loose-leaf work one of the most useful for up-to-date interpretations of the ever-changing regulations under the FECL and FIL: Zaisei kinyū hōki kenkyu iinkai, ed., *Zaisei kinyū hōki kaisetsu zenshū: Boeki kawase-hen* (Complete compilation of explanations of financial and banking regulations: Volume on trade and exchange) (Tokyo: Taisei shuppansha, 1969 plus supplements to date) (hereafter cited simply *Boeki kawase-hen*). A more detailed legal reference is: Yoshio Kanazawa, ed., *Bōeki kankeihō* (Laws related to trade), in Hōritsugaku taikei, Vol. 25 (Tokyo: Nihon hyōron-shinsha, 1956), pp. 615–734. Unfortunately it is outdated in many respects. For practitioners, see Michio Matsueda, *Gōben kaisha no hōritsu jitsumu* (Legal business for a joint-venture company) (Tokyo: Daiyamondosha, 1969), p. 369; Tokyo ginkō chōsabu, ed., *Gaikoku kawase* (Foreign exchange), in 8 *Shin-ginkō jitsumu kōza* (New essays on bank practice) (Tokyo: Yūhikaku, 1967), p. 3.

75. For a quick, initial overview, newcomers will find current official guidebooks useful, since they are regularly up-dated. For example, see Ministry of Finance (Int'l. Finance Bur.) and Bank of Japan (For. Dept.), *Manual of Foreign Investment in Japan* (Tokyo: Ōkurashō insatsukyoku, Nov. 1971). Also Robert S. Ozaki, *The Control of Imports and Foreign Capital in Japan* (New York: Praeger, 1972), p. 75. Somewhat more detailed and up-to-date information may be found in looseleaf English work: Inst. of Foreign Exchange and Trade Research, *Japan: Foreign Exchange and Trade Control Handbook* (Tokyo: Inst. of For. Exchange and Trade Research, 1971). More detailed and critical analysis in English may be found in OECD, *Liberalisation*.

76. FIL, Art. 3.

77. OECD, *Liberalisation*, p. 60, shows the status of yen-base investments.

78. Ibid., p. 171, has a "Calendar of Japanese Exchange Control Dates." The change in Japanese exchange restrictions from year to year, and also a brief current summary of those restrictions, can be found in the IMF *Annual Reports* on exchange restrictions. *E.g.*, IMF, *22nd Annual Report: Exchange Restrictions* (Washington, D.C.: IMF, 1971), covering calendar year 1970.

79. Note that the same legalistic ambivalence is found in the FECL (Articles 1 and 2) as follows:

(Purpose)

Article 1. The purpose of this Law is to provide for the control of foreign exchange, foreign trade and other foreign transactions, necessary for the proper development of foreign trade and for the safeguarding of the balance of international payments and the stability of the currency, as well as the most economic and beneficial use of foreign currency funds, for the sake of the rehabilitation and the expansion of the national economy.

(Review)

Article 2. The provisions of this Law and orders issued thereunder to implement this Law shall be reviewed with the objective of gradually relaxing and eliminating the restrictions established by this Law or the orders issued thereunder, as the need for them subsides.

80. In the Japanese-language literature, too, there has been much consciousness of "liberalization" without liberalization. *E.g.*, see Iida, "Kokueki-ron ni hosomu," *Tōyō keizai*, p. 15. The official objective is—if we may reciprocate and play with language—to "liberalize" only when officialdom is certain that no substantial Japanese business will be "liberated."

81. FIL, Arts. 10, 11, 12, 13.

82. FIL, Art. 3(1).

83. FECL, Arts. 6(5) and 6(6).

84. FECL, Art. 27. Also note that Articles 28 and 29 prohibit exchange residents abroad from making payments for property, etc., abroad and from receiving pay abroad for account of a resident for property abroad.

85. FECL, Art. 6(5) and (6).

86. FIL, Art. 15 and 15–2.

87. *Gaishi ni kansuru hōritsu no kitei ni yoru sōkin no tetsuzuki ni kansuru shōrei* (Ministerial ordinance concerning procedures of remittance in accordance with the FIL), Article 1 *et seq.* (MOF and MITI Ord. No. 2, 16 Nov. 1950 as amended) (hereafter Jt. Remittance Ordinance).

88. *Tomita* v. *Inoue*, 19 Minshū 2306 (1965). For comments on the case in English see: Teruo Doi, "The Validity of Contracts Made in Violation of Forum's Exchange Controls," 2 *Law in Japan* 180–193 (1968); and Tomohei Taniguchi, "Comment on *Tomita* v. *Inoue*," 2 *Law in Japan* 194–97 (1968). An unusual lower court case where the court found the FECL to be "mandatory" was *International Union Lines, Ltd.* v. *Banno Brothers*, 12 Kakyū minshū 1552 (Osaka D. Ct., 30 June 1961). The district court held the charter party invalid as violative of the FECL (mandatory) but granted damages on the basis of unjust enrichment in the amount of the charter hire, which would have been due had the contract been valid.

On appeal to the Osaka High Court, *Hanrei jihō* (No. 416) 78 (Osaka H. Ct., 13 May 1965), the judgment was affirmed, but the court disapproved, by way of dictum, the classification of the FECL as a "mandatory" provision. All other recent cases, we have found, held the FECL to be a directive provision. For example, see: *K.K. Greenhill-Katō Shōkai* v. *Shirō Trading Corp.*, 13 Kōsai minshū 696 (Tokyo H. Ct., 29 Oct. 1960); *Lewin* v. *Greenberg*, 11 Kakyū minshū 2034 (Tokyo D. Ct., 30 Sept. 1960); *Ryūkyū Bank* v. *Tōkai Denki-Kōji K.K.*, *Hanrei jihō* (No. 602) 90 (Nagoya D. Ct., 31 Jan. 1970); *Ralph A. Fields* v. *K.K. Taiheiyō TV*, *Hanrei jihō* (No. 586) 73 (Tokyo D. Ct., 6 Sept. 1969); *Domex International Co.* v. *Yokohama Tsūshō K.K. et al.*, *Hanrei jihō* (No. 430) 17 (1966) (Tokyo D. Ct., 6th Dept., 28 Oct. 1965); *Marubeni-Iida K.K.* v. *Ajinomoto K.K.*, 10 Kakyū minshū 594 (Tokyo D. Ct., 26 Mar. 1959). For general theoretical discussion of these points, see Charles Szladits, "Illegality of Prohibited Contracts: Comparative Aspects" in *XXth Century Comparative and Conflicts Law: Legal Essays in Honor of Hessel E. Yntema* (Leyden: A. W. Sythoff, 1961), p. 221, for discussion of English, French, and German approaches to these problems.

89. *Hikyojūsha no honpō-nai no shiten, kōjō sono ta no eigyōsho no hōkoku ni kansuru shōrei* (Ministerial ordinance concerning report of branch, factory, or other place of business in Japan of an exchange nonresident) (MOF and MITI Joint Ministerial Ordinance No. 1, 1 July 1963) (hereafter Branch Reporting Ordinance).

90. *Gaikoku kawase kanrirei* (Cabinet order for control of foreign exchange) (Cabinet Order No. 203, 27 June 1950, as amended); *Japan Regulations*, p. C-9. Also, *Hyōjun kessai hōhō ni yori hikyojū-sha kara shiharai no jun'yō o suru koto ga dekinai baai no shitei* (Designating cases where receipt of payment from exchange nonresidents under the standard methods of settlement is not allowed) (MOF Notification, No. 191, 1 July 1963); *Japan Regulations*, p. C-395.

91. FIL, Art. 10.

92. FIL, Art. 3(3): " 'Technological assistance contracts' shall mean contracts concerning the transfer of patent [*tokkyo*] or utility model [*jitsuyō shin'an*] rights for technologies, license agreements therefor, assistance covering technical and factory management, and other matters designated by the competent minister (hereafter referred to as 'technological assistance')."

93. FIL, Arts. 7 and 10.

94. *E.g.*, FIL, Art. 10.

95. *Gaishi ni kansuru hōritsu no kitei ni motozuku ninka no kijun no tokurei nado in kansuru seirei* (Cabinet order concerning exceptions to standards of validation, etc., based on the FIL), Art. 7 (Cab. Order No. 221, 1 July 1952) (hereafter Exceptions Order); English: *Japan Regulations*, p. D-115; or EHS No. 5470.

96. *Gaikoku kawase kanrirei* (Cab. order on control of foreign exchange), Art. 21 (Cab. Order 203, 27 June 1950, as amended); *Japan Regulations*, p. C-1 at C-18 (hereafter Cab. Foreign Exchange Order). *Bōeki kankei bōeki-gai torihiki no kanri ni kansuru shōrei* (Min. ordinance concerning control of invisible transactions relating to foreign trade), Attached List No. 9; Form 12-2 (MITI Ord. No. 49, 1 Apr. 1963, as amended); EHS No. 5222 (hereafter MITI Invisibles Ordinance).

97. FIL, Art. 18 and 18-2.

98. FIL, Art. 19-2 and 19-3.

99. FIL, Art. 18.

100. FIL, Art. 18-2.

101. Details for the FIC are found in: *Gaishi shingikai-rei* (Foreign investment council order) (Cab. Order No. 3091, 31 July 1952, as amended); English: EHS No. 5475.

102. *Gaishi ni kansuru hōritsu shikō kisoku* (Regulations for enforcement of the FIL) (FIC Regulation No. 2, 28 June 1950, as amended); EHS No. 5430; *Japan Regulations*, p. D-51 (hereafter FIL Enforcement Regs.).

103. John F. Shaw, "What Prompted President Nixon's Economic Program?" *The Journal of the American Chamber of Commerce in Japan* 8 (No. 10) (5 Oct. 1971): 10.

104. FIL, Art. 25-2.

105. *Gaishi ni kansuru hōritsu no kitei ni yori Nihon Ginkō ni toriatsukawaseru jimu no han'i o kimeru seirei* (Cabinet order fixing scope of business to have the Bank of Japan handle under provisions of the FIL) (Cab. Order No. 412, 11 Sept. 1952, as amended); EHS No. 5488; *Japan Regulations*, p. D-128 (hereafter BOJ Cab. Order); and Ministerial Ordinance fixing business scope to be handled by BOJ under the provisions of the FIL (Jt. Min. Ordinance No. 2, 30 June 1967) (hereafter BOJ Min. Ord.); *Japan Regulations*, p. D-131; EHS No. 5480A.

106. BOJ Min. Ord. No. 2, 30 June 1967, Art. 1(1)(a).

107. FIL, Art. 13-2; BOJ Cab. Order, Art. 7; *Japan Regulations*, p. D-129.

108. FIL, Art. 13-3; BOJ Cab. Order, Art. 10.

109. *Gaikoku tōshika yokin kanjō ni kansuru seirei* (Cabinet order concerning foreign investors' deposit accounts) (Cab. Order 427, 20 Sept. 1952); EHS No. 5460; *Japan Regulations*, p. D-194; also MOF Ordinance No. 120, 30 Sept. 1952; EHS No. 5461; *Japan Regulations*, p. D-196.

110. Jt. Remittance Ordinance, Art. 2 (Jt. MOF-MITI Min. Ordinance, No. 2, 16 Nov. 1950, as amended); *Japan Regulations*, p. D-93.

111. *Gaikoku kawase ginkō-hō* (Foreign exchange bank law) (Law No. 67, 30 Apr. 1954); EHS No. 5045.

112. Specific criticisms are catalogued in OECD, *Liberalisation*, pp. 42–44, 57, 156–58. Also see BIAC, *The Control of the Inflow of Investments in Japan* (Annexed to Circular C-438 of 17 Mar. 1967).

113. FIC Notification No. 5, 28 July 1950; *Japan Regulations*, p. D-90.

114. The OECD Committee for Invisible Transactions expressed its surprise that "a country with high growth targets and great technical skill should find it necessary to have any restrictions at all." OECD, *Liberalisation*, p. 57.

115. See Yūichi Nakamura, ed., *Gijutsu dōnyū keiyaku nintei kijun no kaisetsu* (Ex-

planation of validation criteria concerning international contracts introducing technology) (Tokyo: Shōji hōmu kenkyūkai, 1968), p. 126.

116. OECD, *Liberalisation*, p. 32; a Japanese official said in 1960 it was 9.2% of ex-factory deliveries.

117. See, *e.g.*, Zenith's refusal to license Japanese TV makers to use its superior patented technology called the "black matrix formula."

118. FIL Enforcement Regs. (FIC No. 2, 28 June 1950), Art. 3, and attached Form No. 1; *Japan Regulations*, p. D-59.

119. For a convenient summary of contract problems, see Tsūshō sangyōshō, kigyō-kyoku, gaishika (MITI), *Gaikoku gijutsu dōnyū keiyaku* (Contracts introducing foreign technology) (Tokyo: Tsūshō sangyō chōsakai, 1970), pp. 1–8; Arekisan Nagai and Yoshimitsu Noguchi, *Kaitei gijutsu enjo keiyaku no jissai* (Revised: Practice technological assistance contracts) (Tokyo: Nihon kōgyō shimbunsha shuppan-bu, 1967), p. 41.

120. FIL, Art. 10.

121. *Gaikoku kawase kanrirei* (Foreign exchange control order), Art. 17 (Cab. Order No. 203, 27 June 1950); *Japan Regulations*, p. C-1 at C-14; (hereafter Cab. Foreign Exchange Order); and MITI Invisibles Ord., Art. 3.

122. Cab. Foreign Exchange Order, Art. 17; and *Bōeki-gai torihiki no kanri ni kansuru shōrei* (Ministerial ordinance concerning control of invisible transactions), Attached list No. 4, and Form 3-d (MOF Ord. No. 58, 2 Nov. 1963, as amended to 1971); EHS No. 5221; (hereafter MOF Investment Ord.).

123. MITI, *Gaikoku gijutsu dōnyū keiyaku*, p. 103, but parent-branch or parent-subsidiary contracts are subject to license even if compensation is not called for.

124. FIL, Art. 10.

125. FIL, Art. 14 reads:

The competent Minister or the Minister of Finance may, on making validation, designation or confirmation pursuant to the provisions of this Law, stipulate necessary conditions upon which validation is based.

2. In the event that a foreign investor who was granted the validation, designation or confirmation as prescribed in this Law has filed an application with the competent Minister or the Minister of Finance in accordance with the Ordinance of the competent Minister or the Ministry of Finance Ordinance for alteration of conditions as stipulated pursuant to the preceding paragraph, the Competent Minister or the Ministry of Finance may alter them only in case where the competent Minister or the Ministry of Finance finds inevitable reasons concerning the application concerned.

126. *Gijutsu dōnyū no jiyūka ni tsuite* (Concerning liberalization of induction of technology) (FIC decision, 10 May 1968); BOJ Min. Ord., Art 1(1)(a) (Jt. Min. Ord. No. 2, 30 June 1967, as amended); *Japan Regulations*, p. D-28.

127. BOJ Min. Ord., Art. 1(1)(b) and Attached List (Jt. Min. Ord. No. 2, 30 June 1967, as amended).

128. BOJ Min. Ord., Art. 1(1)(a) and 1(2)(d). (Jt. Min. Ord. No. 2, 30 June 1967, as amended).

129. FIL, Art. 24.

130. FIL, Art. 15.

131. *Japan Economic Journal* (27 June 1972), p. 1.

132. FIL, Arts. 11 and 18–2 (FIC approval).

133. MOF Invisibles Ord., Art. 11(1).

134. BOJ Min. Ord., Art. 2(1), but under Art. 1(c) the automatic approval for 10/25% does not apply, if the buyer intended to influⁿce management.

135. Com. Code, Art. 256–4.

136. *Tainai chokusetsu tōshi tō no jiyūka ni tsuite* (Concerning liberalization of inward direct investment, etc.) (Cab. decision, 6 June 1967, as amended); English: *Japan Regulations*, p. D-138.

137. Tomizawa, "Dai yon-ji shihon jiyūka ni tsuite," *Toki no hōrei* (No. 761), p. 31.

138. Exceptions Order, Art. 4(2) (Cab. Ord. No. 221, 1 July 1950, as amended).
139. U.S.-Japan FCN Treaty, Art. 7(2), and OECD, *Liberalisation*, Art. 3.
140. FIL, Art. 11(2).
141. FIL, Art. 13–2.
142. FIL, Art. 13(1).
143. FECL, Art. 30.
144. Yoshida, *Shihon jiyūka to gaishihō*, p. 115.
145. Note OECD, *Liberalisation*, Annex A, List A(I)A3.
146. Exceptions Order, Art. 4–2.
147. FIL, Art. 13.
148. FIL, Art. 12.
149. Branch Reporting Ordinance, Art. 1 (MOF-MITI Jt. Min. Ord. No. 1, 1 July 1963); *Japan Regulations*, p. A-98.
150. Branch Reporting Ordinance, Art. 2.
151. *Japan Regulations*, pp. A-99 and A-101.
152. Cab. Foreign Exchange Order, Art. 11(2) (8 exclusions) (Cab. Order No. 203, 27 June 1950, as amended); *Japan Regulations*, p. C-9; and MOF Invisibles Ordinance, Art. 11(1), Attached List 18(1)A (MOF Min. Ord. No. 58, 2 Nov. 1963, as amended); *Japan Regulations*, p. C-233 (1971).
153. Shaw, "What Prompted President Nixon's Economic Program?" *Journal ACCJ*, p. 13.
154. MOF Invisibles Ord. Attached List No. 18(II) and Form 1-A (MOF Min. Ord. No. 58, 2 Nov. 1963, as amended); *Japan Regulations*, p. C-279 (1971).
155. *Tainai chokusetsu tōshi tō no jiyūka ni tsuite* (Concerning liberalization of inward direct investment), Kakugi kettei (Cabinet order), 27 April 1973, effective 1 May 1973.

CHAPTER VII

1. See, for example, the perceptive headline in a leading Japanese paper: "Amae tōranu jitsuryoku" (Actual power warrants no more indulgence), *Asahi Shimbun*, 24 April 1969. This was about an OECD report on the Japanese liberalization shortcomings after five years of membership. Also see Special Symposium, "Fukuro dataki no Nippon" (Japan in a bag), *Gekkan ekonomisuto* 16–61 (Oct. 1971), especially the part entitled, "Zainichi gaijin wa chūkoku suru" (Advice from foreigners living in Japan), pp. 44–50 (Hedburg, Adachi, VanZandt); and Committee for Economic Development, *Japan in the Free World Economy* (New York: CED, 1963), p. 51; BIAC, *The Control of the Inflow of Investment in Japan* (Annex to Circular C-438 of 17 Mar. 1967, BIAC), reproduced in Fujio Yoshida, *Shihon jiyūka to gaishihō* (Capital liberalization and the FIL) (Tokyo: K.K. Zaisei kōhō-sha, 1967). And note Japanese concern about their image, in a speech by Kōgorō Uemura (Pres. of Keidanren), *Challenge for Responsible Partnership* (Washington, D.C.: U.S.-Japanese Trade Council, 15 June 1971); and Kōgorō Uemura, "New Challenge for Japan's Foreign Economic Policy," *Journal ACCJ* 8 (Nov. 1971): 38.

2. *Gijutsu dōnyū no jiyūka ni tsuite* (Concerning liberalization of induction of technology) (Cab. Decision, 10 May 1968); untranslated. Also see Makoto Yazawa, "Gijutsu dōnyū no jiyūka ni kansuru hōteki taisaku" (Legal countermeasures concerning liberalization of induction of technology), *Shōji hōmu kenkyū* (No. 450) 2–12 (1968).

3. *E.g.*, see John T. Connor (Sec. of Commerce), "Expanding the Fabric of U.S.-Japanese Economic Relations," *The Department of State Bulletin* 50 (8 Aug. 1966): 219; Lester E. Edmunds (Minister, U.S. Embassy Tokyo), "Japan's Present Foreign Capital Liberalization: Woefully Short of International Standards," *Journal ACCJ* 7 (Dec. 1970): 39; and Stanley Nehmer (Deputy Ass't. Secretary of Commerce), "Japan's Trade and Investment Policies," *Journal ACCJ* 8 (No. 6) (5 June 1971): 49; and John F. Shaw, "Valedictory Remarks of a Commercial Counselor," *Am. Jap. Soc'y. Tokyo* 20 (No. 2)

(Aug.–Oct. 1971): 6. Also "1/4 jiyūka ni suginu" (Not more than 1/4 liberalization), *Asahi Shimbun*, 30 July 1971.

4. Editorial, "Liberalization," *Journal ACCJ* 7 (Oct. 1970): 5, 9–11.

5. Shaw, "Valedictory Remarks," *Am. Jap. Soc'y Tokyo*, p. 7, note 3; BIAC, *Control of Inflow*, p. 305, note 1.

6. Among articulate bureaucratic spokesmen, see views of Shintarō Hayashi (MITI), "Shihon jiyūka to keiki chōsei-saku" (Capital liberalization and counter-cyclical measures), *Bōeki to kanzei* 10–11 (1967); and Naohiro Amaya (MITI), "Shihon jiyūka to nashonaru intaresuto" (Capital liberalization and national interest), *Tōyō keizai* 4 (31 July 1969). Also see Masao Kanno (Japan BIAC), *Shihon jiyūka to kokusai kyōsōryoku* (Capital liberalization and international competitiveness) (Tokyo: K.K. Shiseidō, 1968), p. 151; T. F. M. Adams and Noritake Kobayashi, eds., *The World of Japanese Business* (Tokyo: Kōdansha International, 1969), Kobayashi's remarks, p. 248. Also see, for further discussion in English, Robert S. Ozaki, "Japanese Views on Foreign Capital," *Asian Survey* 11 (Nov. 1971): 1071–83; Leon Hollerman, "Liberalization and Japanese Trade in the 1970s," *Asian Survey* 10 (May 1970): 27–37; and Alan R. Pearl, "Liberalization of Capital in Japan," 13 *Harvard International Law Journal* (1972), pp. 59, 245.

7. Several comments refer to the Japanese usage: "liberalization" meaning more liberal than before, not "free to enter." See, *e.g.*, Editorial, "Liberalization," *Journal ACCJ*, p. 9; Iwao Hoshii, "Japan and European Economic Community," *Orient-West* 7 (No. 11) (1962): 13: "The bureaucrats, however, do not know the real meaning of 'free' trade, which has not existed in Japan for thirty years. Whatever they consider a relaxation of restrictions they call 'liberalization,' no matter how much red tape and direct or indirect control remains. . . ."

8. See in the liberalization publicity reference to continual expansive use of the term "industries" when "product" would be more accurate (*e.g.*, the oatmeal "industry" is liberalized). But note that "agriculture-forestry-fisheries" becomes but one industry on the nonliberalized "screening list." Or see the palliatives involved in announcing "Negative List Is Revised to Screening," *Japan Economic Journal*, 27 July 1971, p. 1. Similarly unhelpful is the use of large numbers of "industries" ("liberalized") to imply large quantities of liberalization, which is all but meaningless in terms of real investment opportunity. Editorial, "Liberalization," *Journal ACCJ*, p. 13.

9. Note Kōgorō Uemura's speech, p. 4, note 1, which states this problem accurately. When persons of his stature perceive the problem, the odds are that corrective measures will be taken. "The government is seen as imposing an all-encompassing web of administrative guidance. Japanese announcements of liberalization are viewed as inadequate at best, and a mockery at worst. . . ."

10. "Tainai chokusetsu tōshi tō no jiyūka ni tsuite" (Concerning liberalization of inward direct investments, etc.) in Yoshida, *Shihon jiyūka to gaishihō*, p. 183 (English) and p. 145 (Japanese); also Foreign Exchange Study Association, *Japan Law, Ordinances and Other Regulations Concerning Foreign Exchange and Foreign Trade* (Tokyo: Foreign Exchange Study Ass'n, 1971), p. 138 (hereafter *Japan Regulations*), and the recent FIC Report 4th Round is in *Zaisei keizai kōhō* (No. 1422) 3 (16 Aug. 1971).

11. See Yoshida, *Shihon jiyūka to gaishihō*, p. 33, note 10.

12. The view of N. Amaya, "Shihon jiyūka to nashonaru intaresuto," *Tōyō keizai*, p. 4, is interesting in this regard. The Japanese press (Asahi and Mainichi, 30 April 1973) mentioned this reasoning in relation to the 1 May 1973 liberalization.

13. See the candid comment of one of Japan's more astute observers, N. Kobayashi, in *The World of Japanese Business*, Adams and Kobayashi, p. 232, to the same effect: ". . . [Historical] isolationism has resulted in a state of profound ignorance among most Japanese about conditions prevailing in the rest of the world. . . . It is that same ignorance which now, as the century approaches its three-quarter mark, tends to promote fear of the foreigners who come to do business in Japan and suspicions as to their motives."

14. See Robert Bellah, *Tokugawa Religion* (Glencoe: Free Press, 1957), p. 6; James C.

Abegglen, *The Japanese Factory: Aspects of Its Social Organization*, Chapter 2, made the important point that Japanese labor is socially too strongly bound to its work place to respond fully to strict economic analyses. See a typical expression by a distinguished business leader, Kazutaka Kikawada, *Ningen-shugi no keizai shakai* (Humanistic economic society) (Tokyo: Yomiuri shimbunsha, 1971), p. 21.

15. Frank Gibney, "The View from Japan," *Foreign Affairs* 50 (Oct. 1971): 102.

16. Kobayashi, in *The World of Japanese Business*, Adams and Kobayashi, p. 232: "That there is a basis for the belief that both Japanese government and business share both the 'foreign capital phobia' and a kind of 'enterprise nationalism' cannot be questioned."

17. Bellah, *Tokugawa Religion*, p. 6.

18. Chie Nakane, *Japanese Society* (U. of Cal. Press, 1970), pp. 9–10.

19. Arguments that Japan should have used foreign capital to increase its growth rate in the 1956–70 period are not persuasive when fast growth was already creating problems. Hollerman, "Liberalization and Japanese Trade in the 1970s," *Asian Survey*, p. 427.

20. The point, too, is well put by Uemura, *Challenge for Responsible Partnership*, p. 13: "Transnational investments are indeed transfers of the totality of managerial resources and are bound to have influence on local business practices, employment patterns, working rules, community relations and the sense of participation among workers. This is a profound social and political hurdle in such a homogeneous nation as ours. This cultural and psychological factor also explains the Japanese insistence on equal ownership."

21. Note a different kind of American advertisement, Warner and Swasey Co., unusually perceptive on this precise point. *U.S. News and World Report*, 6 Dec. 1971, p. 1: "In prosperous Japan, government, unions and business are partners—not antagonistic."

22. In *FIC Report* there is a section entitled, "What We Expect of Foreign Investors," which quite understandably requires that foreigners "refrain from actions which might hamper our efforts or harm the economic interests of our people." The report is reproduced in Yoshida, *Shihon jiyūka to gaishihō*, p. 191.

23. See *FIC Report*, where concerns for technological creativity are stressed on nearly every page, ibid., p. 183. Also Hayashi, "Shihon jiyūka to keiki chōsei-saku," *Bōeki to kanzei*, pp. 10–11, states: "Technology is the engine of economic development. The long range prospect of economic development of a country largely depends upon how much of technology is mobile across national boundaries; hence, short-term growth is possible with borrowed technology. However, the chronic and excessive dependence upon borrowed technology destroys the internal capacity to develop new technology and dims the hope for the nation's playing a leading role in global development. The world enterprise typically lets its parent corporation in the home country concentrate on the R and D efforts. If we allow world enterprise with that sort of behavioral pattern to come and operate in Japan as they please, we will likely suffer a critical slow down of technological progress in our own factory" (as translated by Ozaki, "Japanese Views on Foreign Capital," *Asian Review*, p. 1081).

24. Amaya, "Shihon jiyūka to nashonaru intaresuto," *Tōyō keizai*, p. 4, note 12, stresses this point.

25. Uemura, *Challenge for Responsible Partnership*, p. 13: ". . . I urge restraint on the part of international corporations. As first-class citizens of the business world and roving ambassadors for free trade, they should be constantly seeking to harmonize with the communities in which they operate."

See, generally, Seymour Rubin, "The International Firm and the National Jurisdiction," in *The International Corporation*, ed. Charles P. Kindleberger, Jr. (MIT Press, 1970), p. 179.

26. Besides MITI's study of the 50–50 principle, *FIC Report* (*Ikensho*) *Zaisei keizai kōhō* (1422) 4 (16 Aug. 1971), see Uemura, "New Challenge for Japan's Foreign Eco-

nomic Policy," *Journal ACCJ*, p. 40. See "Perspective: Concept toward Decontrol of Capital is Changing," *Japan Economic Journal*, 9 Mar. 1971, p. 3: "It has been the basic concept of government leaders, including MITI Minister Kiichi Miyazawa, that equal ratio of investment by foreign and Japanese enterprises is the most desirable form of joint ventures in Japan *and that Japan should make other countires recognize this formula as an international criterion. This concept is making an about-face*" [emphasis added].

27. See Detlev Vagts, "The Multinational Enterprise," 83 *Harv. L. Rev.* 739 (1970).

28. See Jun Etō, "Japan and the U.S.: A Personal Reflection," *Bulletin Int'l House of Japan*, No. 28 (Oct. 1971): 2, for a vivid description of Japanese reactions.

29. Kobayashi, in *The World of Japanese Business*, Adams and Kobayashi, pp. 239–40.

30. See "Yen Revaluation Comes as a Relief in Japan after Uncertainty," *Wall St. J.*, 22 Dec. 1971.

31. "Report Concerning the Liberalization of Inward Investment by the FIC," reprinted in Yoshida, *Shihon jiyūka to gaishihō*, pp. 183–204.

32. See ibid., p. 369. An English translation of a summary of the countermeasures recommended by the FIC Committee of Experts headed by Takeo Suzuki (professor emeritus, Tokyo University Law Faculty) may be found as "Domestic Rules Recommended for Investment Liberalization," in *Journal ACCJ* 4 (No. 7) (Special Supplement, 5 July 1967): 20–23.

33. *E.g.*, U.S.-Japanese FCN Treaty Arts. VII(2) and XXI, 4 *UST* 2063, TIAS 2863, 206 *UNTS* 143.

34. This nomenclature was selected for public relations purposes in the last phases of preparing round four in the summer of 1971. It was thought to be better than calling the nonliberalized list a "negative list" (*nega risuto*), which had been requested by foreigners weary of liberal statistics and little liberality. See "Negative List Is Revised to Screening," *Japan Economic Journal*, 27 July 1971, p. 1.

35. Even before the fourth round, the government announced, under foreign pressure, that it would liberalize new computer businesses up to 50% foreign ownership over the next three years (1974), during which time MITI has determined to promote joint ventures or mergers of the six leading Japanese companies. See "Decontrol of Computers Will Be 3 Years Hence," *Japan Economic Journal*, 27 July 1971, p. 1. Fuji Tsūshinki and Hitachi; Tōshiba and Nihon Denki; Mitsubishi Denki and Oki are to be combined by government subsidy into three teams. *Asahi Shimbun*, 22 Oct. 1971.

36. FIC Report, in Yoshida, *Shihon jiyūka to gaishihō*, p. 157; *Japan Regulations*, p. D-138.

37. FIL, Art. 25–2.

38. Toshihiro Kiribuchi, "Daiyonji shihon jiyūka no mondaiten" (The problems of the 4th round capital liberalization), *Zaisei keizai kōhō* (No. 1423) 1–3 (23 Aug. 1971); also *Japan Economic Review*, 15 Sept. 1971, p. 19.

39. See Kiribuchi, "Daiyonji shihon jiyūka," *Zaisei keizai kōhō*, p. 4, for refreshing suggestions that the tactical subterfuges were wearing pretty thin in OECD circles, such as using the long "positive lists" (*poji risuto*) of "industries" (actually, many of them only petty products) instead of a readily understood negative list (not liberalized), or calling validations subject to many conditions "automatic validation," or indeed calling "liberalization" (up to 50%) liberalization, or, as to procedure, calling a process subject to prior consultations with resultant imposed conditions (plus voluminous documentation and delays) "automatic validation." He suggests that it will be important in the future to *actually* liberalize, but he is careful to point out that such ideas are personal, presumably not to be confused with the thinking of MITI, his employer. As foreigners, and Japanese too, frequently point out, the "automatic" validation has only been given in 28 cases in more than four years (17 American). There were 2 in 1968, 2 in 1969, 19 in 1970, and 5 to August 1971, of which about half were in Category I and half in Category II; 8 in distribution, 4 in foods, and 4 in chemicals.

40. *Gaishi dōnyū ni kansuru shinsa tetsuzuki kanso-ka sochi* (Provisions concerning

expedition of screening procedures covering capital induction). Reprinted in Yoshida, *Shihon jiyūka to gaishihō*, p. 367.

41. *FIC Report*, ibid., p. 200.

42. See text of "Opinion (*ikensho*) of the chairman (Ataru Kobayashi) of the FIC to Minister of Finance Mikio Mizuta," 29 July 1971, *Zaisei keizai kōhō* (No. 1442) 4 (16 Aug. 1971), saying: "We think there is an urgent need, concerning cases handled by individual screening, to dispose of them in a flexible, and moreover in a straightforward, manner, so as to produce actual liberalization in fact."

43. See OECD, *Liberalisation of International Capital Movements: Japan* (Paris: OECD Pub., 1968), pp. 61 ff., for both criticisms and government rejoinders (hereafter OECD, *Liberalisation*).

44. Editors, "Towareru seifu no shihon jiyūka seisaku" (Government capital liberalization policy questioned) 48 *Ekonomisuto* (No. 30) 7–8 (21 July 1970).

45. Hiroshi Tomizawa, "Daiyonji shihon jiyūka ni tsuite" (Concerning the 4th round of capital liberalization), *Toki no hōrei* (No. 761) 30 (1971).

46. *FIC Report*, in Yoshida, *Shihon jiyūka to gaishihō*, p. 196.

47. Kiribuchi, "Daiyonji shihon jiyūka," *Zaisei keizai kōhō*, p. 4, makes the point that in the process of checking as to whether conditions are met for "automatic" approval much delay and guidance are problems; and Tomizawa, "Daiyonji shihon jiyūka," *Toki no hōrei*, p. 37, notes that the strict conditions attached to the "automatic" validations probably accounts for the very few (28) cases approved. See the comment of one of Japan's most perceptive comparativists, N. Kobayashi, in *The World of Japanese Business*, Adams and Kobayashi, p. 239: "In fact, the way that Japan implements her obligations is determined not by the express provisions of the law but rather by the unexpressed practices of officials of the Ministries of Finance and the International Trade and Industry who screen applications for foreign-exchange validation."

48. Note in the *FIC Report*, 29 July 1971, in *Zaisei keizai kōhō* (No. 1422) 4 (16 Aug. 1971), there is a clear implication that, despite cabinet and FIC policies to make the procedures conform more with published criteria and legal requirements, as well as a spirit of liberality, little had happened in that direction in four years. I read this to confirm my conclusion that at the middle level, the control-minded, as well as protectionist-minded, nationalistic bureaucrats were lagging behind and not complying with policy established above, in the direction of internationalizing. This difference between levels of government remained important only for two or three years (say 1969–71). By 1972 the leaders among the younger men were also talking of the advantages—to Japan and Japanese business—of opening up the economy. See also Kobayashi, in *The World of Japanese Business*, Adams and Kobayashi, p. 247, to this same general effect: "Many officials working on this [middle] level come to feel that they are now defenders of the national interest. Being members of the elite, they are incapable of taking advice from more experienced people, and as defenders of Japan, they are prone to a xenophobia that may actually be harmful to the best interests of the country. For example, it is well known that a group of officials on this level are determined to defend to the death the Japanese electronics industry, which they claim to be still in an embryonic stage and which they say must be permitted to develop by itself, free from all foreign intervention. People of this sort will regard anyone with a more flexible attitude as in disagreement with them and will refuse to listen to anything he may have to say. It is generally believed that the so-called Ten Commandments . . . were prepared by people on this level of the hierarchy in the Ministries of Finance and International Trade and Industry."

49. *Gijutsu dōnyū no jiyūka ni tsuite* (Concerning liberalization of induction of technology) (Cab. Decision, 10 May 1968).

50. On the need for postwar Japanese administrative law to develop a procedural dimension of "fair hearing" and "notice," plus rights to know standards being applied, see the critique of a well-known judge on the subject, discussing a case in which taxi licensing criteria were not even known by the examiner, much less the applicants. Kenzō Shiraishi, "Gyōsei jiken soshō no arikata" (A model for administrative case litigation),

Hanrei jihō (No. 428) 4 (1966). The case has since been reviewed by the Japanese Supreme Court. *Tokyo Rikuunkyoku* v. *Kawakami, Hanrei jihō* (No. 647) 22 (11 Dec. 1971). For problems of judicial review of administrative actions, see Ichirō Ogawa, "Judicial Review of Administrative Action in Japan," in *The Constitution of Japan: Its First Twenty Years, 1947–67,* ed. Dan Fenno Henderson (U. of Wash. Press, 1969), p. 185.

51. See John F. Shaw, "What Prompted President Nixon's Economic Program?" *Journal ACCJ* 8 (No. 10) (5 Oct. 1971): 18, for a list of problems, some related to this discussion.

52. See Nathaniel L. Nathanson and Yasuhiro Fujita, "The Right to Fair Hearing in Japanese Administrative Law," 45 *Wash. Law Rev.* 273 (1970). Also see N. Kobayashi, in *The World of Japanese Business,* Adams and Kobayashi, p. 254: "These remarks may seem almost incomprehensible to British and American readers, for in their countries the actions of administrative officials are always regulated by laws that define as precisely as possible the scope of executive action. In Japan, on the other hand, the purpose of law is to express minimum protection of national interest. Whenever the force of law diminishes, administrative action must increase. The Westerner may find this system unsatisfactory (just as the Japanese might find the Western way unsuitable), but the fact remains that if the Westerner wants to do business in Japan, he must do it the Japanese way. Only after he accepts that fact will he be able to find practical means of meeting the situation."

53. For text of the official report on countermeasures, see "Gaishi shingi-kai senmon iinkai hōkoku" (Report of the expert committee of the FIC), in *Shōji hōmu kenkyū* (No. 415) 4 (5 June 1967). The report was issued 17 May 1967 by the seven-man committee headed by Takeo Suzuki, professor emeritus, Tokyo University Law Faculty. See comments, Takeo Suzuki, "Shihon jiyūka no seido-teki taisaku" (Systematic countermeasures for capital liberalization), *Shōji hōmu kenkyū* (No. 415) 8 (5 June 1967). English summary: 4 *Journal ACCJ* (No. 7) 20 (July 5, 1967).

54. Suzuki, "Shihon jiyūka," *Shōji hōmu kenkyū,* p. 3.

55. Masayasu Sakuragi, "Shihon no jiyūka to hōritsu mondai" (Capital liberalization and legal problems), 24 *Hōritsu no hiroba* (No. 12) 18 (Dec. 1971), notes candidly the obvious fact that the abolition of the yen-base company was a tightening of controls rather than a loosening.

56. See Tomizawa, "Daiyonji shihon jiyūka" *Toki no hōrei* (No. 761) 36 (Sept. 1971), where he refers to the "so-called foreign pressure problem"; or Kiribuchi, "Daiyonji shihon jiyūka," *Zaisei keizai kōhō* (No. 1423) 1 (23 Aug. 1971), "black ships" (*kurobune*). For background on this reference, see Arthur Walworth, *Black Ships Off Japan,* (1946; reprint ed., Hamden, Conn.: Archon Books, 1966).

57. *Gaishi ni kansuru hōritsu no kitei ni motozuku ninka no kijun no tokurei-tō ni kansuru seirei* (Cabinet order concerning exception to standards of validations, etc., based on the FIL) (Cab. Order 203, 27 June 1950, as amended to 1967); English: *Japan Regulations,* p. D-115; or EHS 5470.

58. See Yoshida, *Shihon jiyūka to gaishihō,* p. 84.

59. Ministerial Ordinance fixing cases where foreign investors perform operations of property in addition to acquisition of stock or beneficiary interest (Jt. Ord. No. 1, 30 June 1967).

60. "Tokyo shōkō kaigisho ruiseki tōhyō seido, jiko kabushiki shutoku seigen ni kansuru iken chōsa kekka o happyo" (Publication of Tokyo Chamber of Commerce results of opinion poll concerning cumulative voting and restrictions on acquiring own shares), *Shōji hōmu kenkyū* (No. 552) 18 (15 Mar. 1971).

61. AML, Art. 2(7).

62. Suzuki, "Shihon jiyūka," *Shōji hōmu kenkyū,* p. 3, stresses that as far as his committee was concerned this strict enforcement would not be discriminatory against foreigners. Foreigners are subject to the same enforcement policy as the Japanese. So unless the idea is to focus special attention on them, we wonder why it should be made a topic in a major national policy report concerning foreigners.

63. Sakuragi, "Shihon no jiyūka," *Hōritsu no hiroba*, p. 24, says it's like killing an ox while trying to straighten its horns *(tsuno o tamete, ushi o korosu)*. Also see K. Kakinuma (FTC), "Shihon jiyūka to dokusen kinshihō," *Shōji hōmu kenkyū* (No. 552) 19 (15 Mar. 1971).

64. *Japan Economic Journal*, 30 Mar. 1971, p. 15, reports that N. M. Rothschild & Sons, Lehman Brothers, Goldman, Sachs and Co., and Bache & Co. were investigating the Japanese possibilities.

65. *Gaikoku shōken gyōsha ni kansuru hōritsu* (Law concerning foreign-securities dealers) (Law No. 5, 1 Sept. 1971). See *Kaisei shōken torihikihō no kaisetsu* (Commentary on the revised securities-transactions law) (Tokyo: Shōji hōmu kenkyūkai, 1971), p. 137; also *Gaikoku shōken gyōsha ni kansuru hōritsu-an* (Draft of law concerning foreign-securities dealers), *Zaisei keizai kōhō* (No. 1396) 9 (15 Feb. 1971). See *Japan Times* (10 March 1972), p. 10, for a report of the Merrill, Lynch, Pierce, Fenner, and Smith application for government approval.

66. Sakuragi, "Shihon no jiyūka," *Hōritsu no hiroba*, p. 24, says this is like "crying mutton, but selling hare" *(yōtō kuniku)*.

67. AML, Art. 9.

68. AML, Art. 2(7).

69. *Futō keihinrui oyobi futō hyōji bōshi-hō* (Law to prevent unfair prizes and false marking) (Law No. 134, 15 May 1962).

70. See "Nipponese Naderism," *Wall St. J.*, 29 Jan. 1971, p. 1, for information on Japanese consumer protests because Japanese TVs could be bought in the U.S. almost as cheaply as in Japan. Government policy has always been "producer" oriented, but these are signs that consumers will demand more consideration.

71. See Hirozumi Iwao, *Biggu bijinesu to kaihō taisei* (Liberalization and big business) (Tokyo: Nihon hyōronsha, 1970), p. 64, and Kin'ya Kimoto, *Gendai shihonshugi to keizaihō* (Contemporary capitalism and economic law) (Tokyo: Shin hyōron, 1970), p. 51.

72. Editors, "Towareru seifu no shihon jiyūka seisaku" *Ekonomisuto*, p. 9.

73. *Japan Times*, 14 July 1971, p. 5.

74. Published in *Shōji hōmu kenkyū* (No. 444) 20 (25 Mar. 1968).

75. *Tokkyohō* (Patent law) Art. 93 (Law No. 121, 13 Apr. 1959); English: EHS 6850A. Art. 93:

> When the working of a patented invention is specially necessary for public interest, a person who desires to work such patented invention may, with the permission of the Minister of International Trade and Industry, demand of the patentee or the exclusive licensee a consultation as to the granting of an ordinary license.
>
> 2. When the consultation mentioned in the preceding paragraph has not successfully been concluded or it is impossible to hold such consultation, the person who desires to work the patented invention concerned may demand the arbitration of the Minister of International Trade and Industry.
>
> 3. The provisions of Article 84, Article 85 para. 1 and Article 86 to Article 91–2 inclusive shall apply with the necessary modifications to the arbitration mentioned in the preceding paragraph.

76. Suzuki, "Shihon jiyūka," *Shōji hōmu kenkyū*, p. 4.

77. See Makoto Yazawa, "Gijutsu dōnyū no jiyūka ni kansuru hōteki taisaku" (Legal countermeasures concerning liberalization of induction of technology), *Shōji hōmu kenkyū* (No. 450) 2 (25 Mar. 1968); and N. Mon'ya, "Gijutsu dōnyū no jiyūka to tokkyohō" (Liberalization of induction of technology and the patent law), *Keizaihō* (No. 11) 16 (1968).

78. Const., Art. 29(3): "Private property may be taken for public use upon just compensation therefor."

79. Convention of the Union of Paris for the Protection of Industrial Property, 20 Mar. 1883, as amended, 78 Stat. 1748. Art. 5 reads:

(1) The importation by the patentee into the country where the patent has been granted of articles manufactured in any of the countries of the Union shall not entail forfeiture of the patent.

(2) Each country of the Union shall have the right to take legislative measures providing for the grant of compulsory licenses to prevent the abuses which might result from the exclusive rights conferred by the patent, for example, failure to work. . . .

80. *Tokkyohō* Art. 83 reads:

When the working of a patented invention has not been appropriately carried out in the State of Japan continuously for three years or more, a person who desires to work such patented invention may, with the permission of the Director of the Patent Office, demand of the patentee or the exclusive licensee a consultation as to the granting of an ordinary license. Provided, however, that this shall not apply when four years have not elapsed from the day on which the patent application relating to such patented invention was filed.

2. When the consultation mentioned in the preceding paragraph has not successfully been concluded or it is impossible to hold such consultation, the person who desires to work the patented invention concerned may demand the arbitration of the Director of the Patent Office.

81. See "MITI Studies Criteria on Conduct of Foreign Companies," *Japan Economic Journal*, 27 July 1971, p. 3.

82. Sakuragi, "Shihon no jiyūka," *Hōritsu no hiroba*, p. 23.

83. Akira Tanabe, "Shōhō no ichibu kaisei hōritsuan yōkōan tsuika kōmoku no kaisetsu" (Commentary on supplemental items to the draft of a partial revision of the Commercial Code), *Shōji hōmu kenkyū* (No. 540) 32 (15 Nov. 1970).

84. Ibid.

85. Ichiro Sakai, "Ruiseki tōhyō seido no kaiseian ni tsuite" (Concerning the draft revision of the cumulative voting system), *Shōji hōmu kenkyū* (No. 549) 2 (15 Nov. 1970).

86. *Shōji hōmu kenkyū* (No. 552) 18 (15 Mar. 1971).

87. Com. Code, Art. 241(2).

88. Com. Code, Art. 489(2).

89. Sakuragi, "Shihon no jiyūka," *Hōritsu no hiroba*, p. 23.

90. Ichirō Kawamoto, "Jiko kabushiki no shutoku kinshi kanwa ron no haikei to sono kankyō," (Background and basis of argument for relaxing acquisition of own shares), *Shōji hōmu kenkyū* (No. 535) 3 (15 Sept. 1970).

91. Ibid.

92. See Hiroshi Imai, "Shihaiken kakuho no tame no jiko kabushiki shutoku" (Acquisition of own shares in order to preserve the power to control), *Shōji hōmu kenkyū* (No. 547) 2 (25 Jan. 1971).

93. *Sōkaiya* are professional shareholders who sometimes exploit their nuisance value at Japanese general shareholder meetings.

94. See the 1967 report: *Shōji hōmu kenkyū* (No. 415) 8 (5 June 1967).

95. Com. Code, Art. 204, 204-2 to 204-5 (as amended 1966). See Tadeo Ōmori and Makoto Yazawa, eds., 3 *Chūshaku kaishahō: kabushiki* (Annotated commentary on company law: part on stock) (Tokyo: Yūhikaku, 1967), pp. 57–120.

96. *E.g.*, Tokyo Stock Exchange, *Jōjō shinsa kijun* (Listing screening standards), Art. 4(1)(10). In English, see Tokyo Stock Exchange, *Listing of Securities Regulations of the Tokyo Stock Exchange* (Tokyo: Tokyo Stock Exchange, 1970), p. 15. See also English: OECD, *Liberalisation*, p. 168.

97. See Ichirō Kawamoto, "Jōto seigen-tsuki kimei kabushiki to jōjō seido" (Listing system and transfer-restricted shares), *Shōji hōmu kenkyū* (No. 423) 144 (25 Aug. 1967); *Shōji hōmu kenkyū* (No. 415) 9 (5 June 1967).

98. Ōmori and Yazawa, *Chūshaku kaishahō*, p. 76.

99. U.S.-Japan FCN Treaty, Art. 9(2) (1953).

100. *Japan Times*, 13 May 1971, p. 1.

101. Ibid.
102. *Japan Economic Journal*, 27 Apr. 1971, p. 5.
103. Ibid., 9 Mar. 1971, p. 1; *Asahi Evening News*, 10 March 1972, p. 10.
104. T. Asayama, "Shihon jiyūka to kabushiki kaishime no hōteki kōsa," (A legal analysis of capital liberalization and buying-up shares), *Jiyū to seigi* 39 (Jan. 1968).
105. Attempts to stabilize shareholdings to avoid outsiders' influences may account in part for the significant shift of individuals' shareholdings on the Tokyo Stock Exchange. Conversely, of course, corporate shareholding has increased to 60%. See Zenkoku shōken torihikijo, *Kakushiki bumpu jōkyō chōsa* (Investigation of the share distribution system) (Tokyo: Zenkoku shōken torihikijo, 1971), p. 9.
106. *Oba v. Toyota* (Nagoya D. Ct., 30 Apr. 1971), reported in *Shōji hōmu kenkyū* (No. 560) 16 (25 May 1967).
107. Const., Art. 14, reads:
All of the people are equal under the law and there shall be no discrimination in political, economic or social relations because of race, creed, sex, social status or family origin.
2. Peers and peerage shall not be recognized.
3. No privilege shall accompany any award of honor, decoration or any distinction, nor shall any such award be valid beyond the lifetime of the individual who now holds or hereafter may receive it.
108. See Eiichi Hattori, "Teikan ni yoru gaikokujin yakuin no senshutsu seigen ni tsuite" (Concerning restrictions on election of foreign directors by articles of incorporation), *Shōji hōmu kenkyū* (No. 421) 2 (25 July 1967); cf. K. Ōsumi, *Kaishahō-ron* (Theory of company law) 85–86 (1962).
109. *Shōji hōmu kenkyū* (No. 415) 10 (5 June 1967).
110. Ken'ichiro Ōsumi, *Kaishahō-ron* (Theory of company law) (Tokyo: Yūhikaku, 1962), pp. 85–86.
111. Hattori, "Teikan ni yoru," *Shōji hōmu kenkyū*, p. 3.
112. For the report see *Shōji hōmu kenkyū* (No. 415) 10 (5 June 1967); also see "Jūgyōin mochikabu seido no saiyō ni tsuite" (Concerning adoption of an employee shareholding system [Kawasaki Seitetsu's]), *Shōji hōmu kenkyū* (No. 536) 5 (25 Sept. 1970); and entire issue on this subject: *Shōji hōmu kenkyū* (No. 448) (30 April 1968).
113. Suzuki, "Shihon jiyūka," *Shōji hōmu kenkyū*, p. 6.
114. Ibid., pp. 6–7.
115. O. Ajimura, "Jūgyōin mochikabu seido" (Employee shareholding system), *Shōji hōmu kenkyū* (No. 430) 3 (15 Nov. 1967).
116. Com. Code, Art. 280–2(2).
117. Ibid. A fair price may be as low as 10–15% below market. Ōmori and Yazawa, *Chūshaku kaishahō*, p. 52.
118. See "Zōshi hakusho" (White paper on capital increases), *Shōji hōmu kenkyū* (No. 577) 12–13 (20 Apr. 1971).
119. "Shōken torihikihō no ichibu o kaisei suru hōritsu o koko ni kōfu suru" (Herein promulgating the law revising a part of the securities exchange law), *Hōrei zensho* 1 (March 1971); *Shōken torihikihō* (Securities exchange law), Arts. 27 to 27–8 (Law No. 25, 1948, as amended effective 1 July 1971); see also *Yūka shōken no kōkai kaitsuke ni kansuru shōrei* (Min. Ord. concerning take-over bids for securities.)
120. This aspect is discussed in Zadankai, "Shōken torihikihō kaisei no mondaiten" (Problem points in the revision of the securities exchange law), *Jurisuto* (No. 484) and (No. 485) 83 (1 Aug. 1971); details of filing forms and disclosure requirements for tender offers as well as other aspects of the law may be found in "Shōken torihikihō kaisei ni tomonau jūyō jikō no kaisetsu" (Commentary on the chief items relating to the revision of the securities exchange law), 23 *Kigyō kaikei* (Enterprise accounting) (No. 11) 2–69 (Sept. 1971).
121. Securities Exchange Law, Art. 27–2(1).
122. FECL, Art. 6(1)(6).

123. *Yūka shōken no kōkai kaitsuke ni kansuru shōrei*, Art. 7 (1971).
124. *Yūka shōken kōkai kaitsuke no todokeide ni kansuru shōrei* (Min. Ord. concerning filings for public take-over bids for securities), Form 1 (1971). See generally Kōzō Maekawa (MOF), "Kōkai kaitsuke no todokeide seido ni tsuite," (Concerning the filing system for public take-over bids), 23 *Kigyō kaikei* (No. 11) 99 (Sept. 1971).
125. See Maekawa, "Kōkai kaitsuke," *Kigyō kaikei*, p. 97.
126. See " 'Amae' no kokusai kankaku" ("Indulgence" in the international sense), *Gekkan ekonomisuto* 44 (Oct. 1971).
127. Commission on International Trade and Investment (CITI), *United States International Economic Policy in an Interdependent World* (Washington, D.C.: GPO, 1971), pp. 35, 214 (hereafter *CITI Report 1971*); also OECD, *Liberalisation*, pp. 61, 101, 136, 154. Here the criticisms proceed largely in the vein mentioned in the text.
128. *CITI Report 1971*, pp. 1–42, gives a summary of the free-world structure and policy problems facing the U.S. because of economic growth, power shifts, and other changes.
129. Treaty of Peace with Japan, San Francisco, 8 Sept. 1951, *TIAS* 2490, 3 *UST* 3169.
130. Treaty No. 13, 26 Aug. 1952, 141 *UNTS* 355, *TIAS* 1501, 60 Stat. 1705.
131. World Bank: Treaty No. 14, 26 Aug. 1952, 141 *UNTS* 356, *TIAS* 1502, 60 Stat. 1440. Asian Development Bank (4 Dec. 1965): [1966] 2 *UST* 1418, *TIAS* No. 6103, 571 *UNTS* 123 (effective 2 Aug. 1966).
132. For the GATT agreement, with annexes and schedules, and protocol of provisional application, Geneva, 30 Oct. 1947, see *TIAS* 1700, 61 Stat. (5), (6). For protocol of terms for Japanese accession, Geneva, 7 June 1955, *TIAS* 3438, 6 *UST* 5833.
133. GATT Arts. XI and XII:
ARTICLE XI: General Elimination of Quantitative Restrictions
1. No prohibitions or restrictions other than duties, taxes or other charges, whether made effective through quotas, import or export license or other measures, shall be instituted or maintained by any contracting party on the importation of any product of the territory of any other contracting party or on the exportation or sale for export of any product destined for the territory of any other contracting party.
2. The provisions of paragraph 1 of this Article shall not extend to the following:
(a) Export prohibitions or restrictions temporarily applied to prevent or relieve critical shortages of foodstuffs or other products essential to the exporting contracting party;
(b) Import and export prohibitions or restrictions necessary to the application of standards or regulations for the classification, grading or marketing of commodities in international trade;
(c) Import restrictions on any agricultural or fisheries product, imported in any form, necessary to the enforcement of governmental measures which operate:
(i) to restrict the quantities of the like domestic product permitted to be marketed or produced, or, if there is no substantial domestic production of the like product, of a domestic product for which the imported product can be directly substituted; or. . . .
ARTICLE XII: Restrictions to safeguard the Balance of Payments
1. Notwithstanding the provisions of paragraph 1 of Article XI, any contracting party, in order to safeguard its external financial position and balance of payments, may restrict the quantity or value of merchandise permitted to be imported, subject to the provisions of the following paragraphs of this Article. . . .
134. See Yasushi Akashi, "Japan in the United Nations," *Japanese Annual of International Law* (JAIL) 15 (1971): 23; and see generally, for the early developments, Y. Takano, "Japan and the International Organizations," 1 *Japanese Annual of International Law* (JAIL) 38–42 (1957).

135. Japan had been admitted to the leading UN-affiliated organizations before her admission to the UN, such as United Nations Educational, Scientific and Cultural Organization (UNESCO), International Labour Organization (ILO), Food and Agricultural Organization of the United Nations (FAO), World Health Organization (WHO), Universal Postal Union (UPU), International Telecommunication Union (ITU), International Civil Aviation Organization (ICAO), and World Meteorological Organization (WMO). See ibid., p. 40. On Japan's political activities during the eventful years following her admission to the UN, see K. Nakamura, "Japan's Role in the United Nations," 3 *JAIL* 92–102 (1959).

Japan at the present time belongs to United Nations Specialized Agencies, including also the Intergovernmental Maritime Consultative Organization (IMCO), the UN Children's Fund (UNICEF) and the International Atomic Energy Agency (IAEA). See Yūichi Takano and Wakamizu Tsutsui, *Kokusai keizai soshiki-hō* (The law of international economic organizations), 147–239 (1961); T. Minagawa, "ILO kenshō no shuyō mondai" (Major problems regarding the ILO charter), in Nihon kokusai mondai kenkyūsho, *Kokusai keizaihō no shomondai* (Problems of international economic law) (No. 4) 1–35 (1962); Zengo Ōhira, "Kokusai tōshihō no josetsu," (An introduction to international investment law), in *Kokusai keizaihō no shomondai*, 214–230.

136. *Memorandum of Understanding between the Organization for Economic Cooperation and Development and the Government of Japan Concerning the Assumption by the Government of Japan of the Obligations of Membership of the Organization* (Paris: OECD, 1963). A convenient text of the OECD Convention is provided in OECD, *The OECD* (Paris: OECD, 1969), p. 43. Also the codes are included (Invisibles, p. 163; Capital Movements, p. 121).

137. See *Code of Liberalisation of Capital Movements* (Paris: OECD, 1969) (hereafter *Capital Code*). This is updated to show changes in reservations and amendments.

138. IMF Arts. VIII(2) and XIV read as follows:

ARTICLE VIII(2):

2. *Avoidance of restrictions on current payments.*

(a) Subject to the provisions of Article VII, Section 3(b), and Article XIV, Section 2, no member shall, without the approval of the Fund, impose restrictions on the making of payments and transfers for current international transactions. . . .

ARTICLE XIV:

2. *Exchange restrictions.* In the post-war transitional period members may, notwithstanding the provisions of any other articles of this Agreement, maintain and adapt to changing circumstances (and, in the case of members whose territories have been occupied by the enemy, introduce where necessary) restrictions on payments and transfers for current international transactions. Members shall, however, have continuous regard in their foreign exchange policies to the purposes of the Fund; and, as soon as conditions permit, they shall take all possible measures to develop such commercial and financial arrangements with other members as will facilitate international payments and the maintenance of exchange stability. In particular, members shall withdraw restrictions maintained or imposed under this section as soon as they are satisfied that they will be able, in the absence of such restrictions, to settle their balance of payments in a manner which will not unduly encumber their access to the resources of the Fund. . . .

139. Sakuragi, "Shihon no jiyūka," *Hōritsu no hiroba*, p. 18.

140. GATT, Basic Instruments, Article XXXV:

ARTICLE XXXV: Non-Application of the Agreement between Particular Contracting Parties.

1. This Agreement, or alternatively Article II of this Agreement, shall not apply as between any contracting party and any other contracting party if:

(a) the two contracting parties have not entered into tariff negotiations with each other, and

(b) either of the contracting parties, at the time either becomes a contract party, does not consent to such application.

2. The CONTRACTING PARTIES may review the operation of this Article in particular cases at the request of any contracting party and make appropriate recommendations.

Generally, by negotiating accommodations, the number of European nations discriminating against Japan has been reduced. The accommodations have contained provisions allowing remedial action against Japanese exports deemed to threaten serious injury to domestic industry. For example, see the 1962 Treaty of Commerce, Establishment, and Navigation between the United Kingdom of Great Britain and Northern Ireland and Japan, First Protocol Concerning Trade Relations, 478 *UNTS* 6934, p. 132. For a Japanese exposition of the most-favored-nation clause, see T. Kuwabara, "Saikeikoku jōkō no seigen ni kansuru shomondai" (Various problems relating to limitations on the most-favored-nation clause), in Nihon kokusai mondai kenkyūsho, *Kokusai keizai-hō no shomondai* (Problems of international economic law) (No. 3) 1–51 (1961), especially "Kanzei dōmei to saikeikoku jōkō" (Customs unions and the most-favored-nation clause), p. 23. For a discussion of the reasons for the invocations of Art. XXXV against Japan, see M. Yokoi, *Gatto no kitei to sono un'yō* (The provisions of GATT and their application), 32 *Hōritsu jihō* 635–36 (1960). See *CITI Report 1971*, p. 219, for recommendation that the U.S. government seek a more open market for Japanese exports in Europe, in order to take the pressure of Japanese exports off the U.S. import market. The U.S. absorbs 30% of Japanese exports, European Common Market, 6.7%.

141. 4 *UST* 2063, 2082, *TIAS* 2863, 206 *UNTS* 143.

142. 478 *UNTS* 6934. Signed London, 14 Nov. 1962.

143. 53 Stat. 1748.

144. *TIAS* 4110, 9 *UST* 1247.

145. *Kokusai kaijō buppin unsōhō* (International carriage of goods by sea act) (Law No. 172, 13 June 1962).

146. *TIAS* (Tax), 8 Mar. 1971.

147. An annual list of bilateral and multilateral treaties concluded by Japan may be found in volumes of the *Japanese Annual of International Law*. E.g., see Vol. 15, p. 215 (1970 treaties) and Vol. 16, p. 178 (1971 treaties).

148. *E.g.*, FCN, Protocol Paragraph 6; IMF Art. VI; OECD Convention, Art. 2; and the *Capital Code* generally.

149. 2 CCH *Tax Treaties* (Income Tax), Japan, p. 4399, ¶4393.

150. IMF, Art. VI(3).

151. Convenient copies of both codes are found in OECD, *The OECD*, but memberships and their respective "reservations" change somewhat from year to year. *E.g.*, Australia became a new member in 1971.

152. *Capital Code*, Annex D (I).

153. *Capital Code*, Annex D (I); FIL, Articles 10 and 13.

154. Sakuragi, "Shihon no jiyūka," *Hōritsu no hiroba*, p. 18, notes the "reverse course" mentioned in the text.

155. The FCN Treaty problem has been the occasion for an exchange of academic views, interestingly enough, by Japanese scholars on opposite sides of the "violation" issue: Shin'ichirō Michida, "Jōyaku mondai to shite no shihon jiyūka to gaishikōbō no senryaku" (Capital liberalization as a treaty question and offensive and defensive strategies concerning foreign capital), *Jurisuto* (No. 364) 48 (1967); in English: 2 *Law in Japan: An Annual* 1 (1968); Yasuhiro Fujita, "Gaishi kisei wa jōyaku ni ihan suru ka" (Do Japan's controls of foreign capital violate treaties?), *Jurisuto* (No. 426) 124 (1969); in English: 3 *Law in Japan* 162 (1969). Also see Yoshio Ohara (FTC), "Shihon jiyūka no kokusai jōyaku-jō no mondaiten" (Problem points of capital liberalization from the standpoint of international treaties), *Keizaihō* (No. 11) 2 (1968). Note Professor Michida's significant statement (p. 2) implying that really Japan would not liberalize direct investment at all, were it not for the treaty requirements and pressures from the U.S. and OECD: ". . . As a matter of strategy, all questions of liberalization,

whether in regard to the so-called strategic industries or medium and small enterprises, probably will have their roots in treaty questions because, in terms of the genesis of the capital liberalization question as it has developed until now, the core of the problem is that there would be no liberalization if there were no treaty. Surprisingly, here in Japan we seem to overlook the fact that 'foreign pressures' for so-called capital liberalization exist only because there are treaties."

This is probably an accurate assessment of the real situation up to 1972, though the Japanese government avoids such straightforward enunciations of the actual position. Japan needed aid, free access to markets, and raw materials abroad; this required her to sign treaties supporting a free international economy (including capital movement into Japan), because the other side wanted it; she has since performed her commitments only when "pressured" into it, which was very little until recently.

156. Michida, "Jōyaku mondai," *Jurisuto*, pp. 10–14, sets out this background. See a recent subdued comment by an experienced commercial counselor in Tokyo, John F. Shaw, "What Prompted President Nixon's Economic Program?" *Journal ACCJ*, p. 12: "6. *FCN Treaty*. The United States and Japan should take a fresh look at the treaty of friendship, commerce and navigation between our two countries and particularly Article VII of the treaty which relates to the activities of our businessmen engaging in commercial, industrial, financial and other business activities within our respective countries. This document provides a reasonable basis on which to conduct our commercial relations. The U.S. Government believes it is extending to Japanese nationals and companies all of the rights set forth in that instrument and in turn it urges that U.S. nationals and companies be permitted to enjoy the same treatment in Japan. Possibly the U.S. would be better understood if there was greater acceptance on the part of Japan's economic ministries, that this treaty sets forth the commercial code by which commercial relations with the U.S. should be guided."

157. See Agreement for the Establishment of a Joint U.S.-Japan Committee of Trade and Economic Affairs, 22 June 1961, 12 *UST* 731, *TIAS* 4776.

158. See Confederation of British Industries, *Japanese Restrictions on Free Capital Movements* (London: CBI, July 1966), also reference to it in *Asahi Shimbun*, 7 Dec. 1966, p. 2.

159. Yoshida, *Shihon jiyūka to gaishihō*, p. 295 (English) and p. 286 (Japanese); also see mention of a third criticism of BIAC in *Asahi Shimbun*, 15 Dec. 1970.

160. FCN, Art. XXI(1), text:

1. The present Treaty shall not preclude the application of measures:

(a) regulating the importation or exportation of gold or silver;

(b) relating to fissionable materials, to radioactive by-products of the utilization or processing thereof, or to materials that are the source of fissionable materials;

(c) regulating the production of or traffic in arms, ammunition and implements of war, or traffic in other materials carried on directly or indirectly for the purpose of supplying a military establishment;

(d) necessary to fulfill the obligations of a Party for the maintenance or restoration of international peace and security, or necessary to protect its essential security interests; and

(e) denying to any company in the ownership or direction of which nationals of any third country or countries have directly or indirectly the controlling interest, the advantages of the present Treaty, except with respect to recognition of juridical status and with respect to access to courts of justice and to administrative tribunals and agencies.

161. FCN, Art. XXIV, reads:

1. Each Party shall accord sympathetic consideration to, and shall afford adequate opportunity for consultation regarding, such representations as the other Party may make with respect to any matter affecting the operation of the present Treaty.

2. Any dispute between the Parties as to the interpretation or application of

the present Treaty, not satisfactorily adjusted by diplomacy, shall be submitted to the International Court of Justice, unless the Parties agree to settlement by some other pacific means.

162. *TIAS* 1501 (1946); for reference see Fritz Machlup, *Remaking the International Monetary System* (Johns Hopkins U. Press, 1968); IMF, *International Monetary Fund* (Washington, D.C.: IMF, 1969), Vol. 3 (Documents); Joseph Gold, *Stand-by Arrangements* (Washington, D.C.: IMF, 1970); Hans Aufricht, *International Monetary Fund: Legal Bases, Structure, Functions* (Washington, D.C.: IMF, 1964); Hans Aufricht, "Exchange Restrictions under the Fund Agreement," 2 *J. of World Trade Law* 297–323 (1968).

163. See Decisions of the Executive Directors, Nos. 71–72 (26 Sept. 1946); 1238–(71/43), 28 July 1961; 541–(56/39), 25 July 1956 in IMF, *International Monetary Fund,* 3: 245–46.

164. This has proven to be a major concern to both Japan and the U.S. since the treaty was signed (1954). See *CITI Report 1971*, p. 36, recommending that "techniques to deal with large and destabilizing movements of short-term funds also require immediate attention."

165. Aufricht, "Exchange Restrictions," *J. of World Trade Law*, p. 297.

166. *Nichibei keizai kankei no shomondai* (Problems of Japanese-American economic relations), 203 (Tokyo: Keizai dantai rengokai [Keidanren], 1967). Formal documentation of the Japanese position on this whole treaty question is difficult to find. The chief sources are reactions voiced in response to the U.S. allegations at the Joint Committee meetings, *e.g.*, as reported in 10 *Journal ACCJ* (1971); also see Sakuragi, "Shihon no jiyūka," *Hōritsu no hiroba*, p. 18, which notes the clear conflct between the FIL and the treaty, but he does not discuss the point, nor speak, for the MOF.

167. Philip H. Trezise, "The Realities of Japan-U.S. Economic Relations," 1 *Pacific Community* 358 (1970).

168. The Japanese publications and press generally have many accounts of Japanese government moves to reduce the embarrassingly high black balances. *E.g.*, see 39 *The Oriental Economist* 14 (June 1971).

169. Fujita, "Gaishi kisei," *Jurisuto*, p. 173 n. 31: "The issue of discretion will center around the adjective wordings: When are monetary reserves *very low?* What is the permissible range of *long*-term considerations? The writer personally *feels* that 5 billion dollars and 5 years should be reasonable standards, respectively, in view of the situations of France, West Germany and Italy."

170. For general reference, see OECD, *The OECD;* Henry G. Aubrey, *Atlantic Economic Cooperation: The Case of the OECD* (New York: Praeger, 1967).

171. *Capital Code*, with updated reservations and amendments.

172. Ibid., Art. 2(b).

173. Ibid., Art. 12(a) and (b).

174. Ibid., Art. 12(c).

175. OECD, *Liberalisation*, pp. 61–62.

176. Ibid., p. 61.

177. Four reservations have been removed, leaving 14 of the original 18 reservations in 1972.

178. See, *e.g.*, *Japan v. Sakata*, 13 Keishū 3225 (Sup. Ct., G.B., 16 Dec. 1959), where the lower court (holding the U.S.-Japan Security Treaty was unconstitutional under Const., Art. 9) was reversed, the Supreme Court holding that the matter posed a "political question" to be left to political arms of government, Cabinet, or Diet.

179. See Fujita, "Gaishi kisei," *Jurisuto*, p. 172, for a discussion of these problems.

180. "Tokushū: gyōsei jiken soshōhō goshūnen" (Special symposium: five years under the administrative case litigation law), *Jurisuto* (No. 383) 22–75 (1967); Ogawa, "Judicial Review of Administrative Action in Japan," *The Constitution of Japan*, ed. Henderson, p. 185; Nathanson and Fujita, "Right to Fair Hearing in Japanese Administrative Law," *Wash. L. Rev.*, p. 273.

181. Isao Satō, "Treaties and the Constitution," in *The Constitution of Japan*, ed. Henderson, p. 167.

182. See Louis Jerold Adams, "Theory, Law and Policy of Contemporary Japanese Treaties" (Ph.D. diss., University of Washington), p. 264.

CHAPTER VIII

1. See Eiichi Hoshino, "Gendai ni okeru keiyaku" (Contemporary contract), 8 *Gendaihō* 206–70 (1966), translated as "The Contemporary Contract," 5 *Law in Japan: An Annual* 45 (1971); Takeyoshi Kawashima, *Nihonjin no hō ishiki* (Japanese legal consciousness) (Tokyo: Iwanami shoten, 1967), pp. 87–123. Toshio Sawada, *Subsequent Conduct and Supervening Events* (Tokyo: U. of Tokyo Press, 1967); cf. George A. van Hecke, "A Civilian Looks at the Common-Law Lawyer," in *International Contracts: Choice of Law and Language*, ed. Willis L. M. Reese (Dobbs Ferry, N.Y.: Oceana Publications, 1962), p. 8, which indicates that some European practice is closer to that of the Japanese.

2. Dan Fenno Henderson, "Traditional Contract Law in Japan" (Draft for *International Encyclopedia of Comparative Law*, Volume VII on Contracts, 1971).

3. See an unusual recent case between two major Japanese corporations wherein the court enforced an oral sales contract. *Marubeni-Iida K.K.* v. *Ajinomoto K.K.*, 10 Kakyū minshū 594 (Tokyo D. Ct., 26 Mar., 1959).

4. Although the term "Japanese joint-venture corporation" might be applied to corporate ventures in which all the shareholders are nationals of Japan but the activities are elsewhere (or where all or most of the activities of a Japanese corporation are abroad), we use the term here, as it is used in Japanese parlance, to mean a Japanese corporation with operations in Japan and in which the major shareholders include both Japanese and foreign firms. For further general discussions of definitions, see Comment, "International Joint Venture Corporation: Drafting of Control Arrangements," *Duke L.J.* 516 (1963); Wolfgang Friedmann and George Kalmanoff, *Joint International Business Ventures* (Columbia U. Press, 1961), p. 5.

For Japanese literature on joint ventures see: Noritake Kobayashi, *Nihon no gōben gaisha* (Japan's joint-venture companies) (Tokyo: Tōyō keizai shimpōsha, 1967); Michio Matsueda, *Gōben gaisha no hōritsu jitsumu* (Legal practices of joint-venture corporations) (Tokyo: Daiyamondosha, 1969); Tsūshō sangyōshō kigyō-kyoku, ed., *Wagakuni no gōben gaisha no jittai* (Actual conditions of joint-venture corporations) (Tokyo: K.K. Fuji kōhōsha, 1964); Jun'ichi Kawaguchi *et al.*, eds. *Gōben gaisha no setsuritsu yori kessan made* (From establishment to liquidation of a joint-venture corporation) (Tokyo: Kokusai tōshi kenkyūjo, 1970).

5. See *Nihon keizai shimbun* (3 July 1967), p. 5, for recognition that contracts are necessary with foreigners.

6. Sawada, *Subsequent Conduct and Supervening Events*, p. 199, reporting on a survey of contracting practices in thirty-two Japanese firms, says, "Japanese companies now are tending to prepare more forms with detailed clauses."

7. In fact, Sawada says that the increased reliance on more elaborate contracts in domestic dealings was attributed by seven executives interviewed to experiences with international contracts. Ibid. Also see model contracts, Tanikawa Hisashi, *Shōhin no baibai* (Sales of goods) (Tokyo: Yūhikaku, 1964), pp. 24–36.

8. Dan Fenno Henderson and Yasuhiro Fujita, "Cases and Materials on Justiciability in U.S.-Japanese Disputes," University of Washington, School of Law, 1968, mimeo; and Dan Fenno Henderson and Kazuaki Sono, "Kokusai keiyaku ni okeru funsō kaiketsu jōkō—kokusai shihō gensoku no konran to chūsai" (Dispute settlement clauses in international contracts—confusion in conflicts principles and arbitration), 14 *Hōgaku ronshū* 745–65 (Feb. 1965).

9. This chapter hereafter is a revision of my previous article, "Contract Problems in U.S.-Japanese Joint Venture," 39 *Wash. L. Rev.* 459–515 (1964). See also Carl J. Bradshaw, "Joint Ventures in Japan," 38 *Wash. L. Rev.* 58 (1963). For more general treatment of contract drafting problems see Comment, "International Joint Venture Corpo-

ration," *Duke L.J.*, p. 516; for a leading work on U.S. joint ventures generally in various countries see Friedmann and Kalmanoff, *Joint International Business Ventures;* also see A. Harding Boulton, *Business Consortia* (London: Sweet & Maxwell, 1961), pp. 52–62, for a detailed discussion on "documenting the consortium," which coincides rather closely with our problem of drafting joint-venture contracts.

Since joint ventures are usually close corporations, the discussion in F. Hodges O'Neal, *Close Corporations* (Chicago: Callaghan, 1958), 1: 77–81, will be useful; and Symposium, "Close Corporations," *U. of Ill. Law Forum* 1–60, 139–223 (1969).

10. It seems to be an almost unique professional privilege of U.S. lawyers to be consulted by businessmen during the contracting process. For the little use made of lawyers in contract matters in Europe, see van Hecke, "A Civilian," in *International Contracts*, ed. Reese, pp. 5, 8; for England, see G. S. Keeton, "The Future of the Legal Profession in England," 25 *U. Cinc. L. Rev.* 279, 285 (1956); and for Japan see Sawada, *Subsequent Conduct and Supervening Events*, p. 193, for "Role of the Legal Section" (*bunshoka*) staffed by law-trained officers but not lawyers (*bengoshi*); and Takaaki Hattori, "The Legal Profession: Its Historical Development and Present State," in *Law in Japan*, ed. Arthur T. von Mehren (Harvard U. Press, 1963).

11. See Zentarō Kitagawa, "Damages in Contracts for the Sale of Goods," 3 *Law in Japan: An Annual* 43–89 (1969).

12. See Abram Chayes, "Madame Wagner and the Close Corporation," 73 *Harv. L. Rev.* 1532 (1960).

13. Note what a surprise the outcome must have been for the Japanese corporate defendant in a jury trial on an oral contract claim brought against the Japanese corporation by a Nisei broker in the New York federal courts. *Masuda* v. *Kawasaki Dockyard Co.*, 328 F. 2d 662, 664 (2d Cir. 1964).

14. See generally Dan Fenno Henderson, *Conciliation and Japanese Law* (U. of Wash. Press, 1965) 1: 183. The Japanese practice of using extralegal dispute settlement techniques is noted in *Nippon Hodō* v. *United States*, 285 F. 2d 766, 768 (Ct. Cl. 1961).

15. See Kiyoshi Igarashi, *Keiyaku to jijō henkō* (Contracts and changed circumstances) (Tokyo: Yūhikaku, 1969), p. 147, and Kiyoshi Igarashi, "Keiyaku to jijō henkō no gensoku" (Contracts and the principle of change in circumstances) in 1 *Keiyakuhō taikei* (Tokyo: Yūhikaku, 1962), p. 29; and see text, "Frustration and Modification" at notes 125–38 *infra*.

16. See generally Arthur Lenhoff, "The Parties' Choice of a Forum: 'Prorogation Agreements,'" 15 *Rutgers L. Rev.* 414 (1961); Robert C. McCartney, "The Use of Choice-of-Law Clauses in International Commercial Contracts," 6 *Wayne L. Rev.* 340 (1959–60); Carlyle E. Maw, "Conflicts Avoidance in International Contracts," in *International Contracts*, ed. Reese, p. 23.

17. Dan Fenno Henderson, "The Roles of Lawyers in U.S.-Japanese Business Transactions," 38 *Wash. L. Rev.* 1 (1963).

18. But, of course, one or the other can always bring suit elsewhere and at least test the jurisdictional points, and therein lies the basic ambiguity. On matters of jurisdiction and "competence," see Yasuhiro Fujita, "Japanese Rules of Jurisdiction," 4 *Law in Japan: An Annual* 55 (1971); Albert A. Ehrenzweig, Sueo Ikehara, and Norman Jensen, *American-Japanese Private International Law*, Parker School Bilateral Studies in Private International Law, No. 12 (Dobbs Ferry, N.Y.: Oceana Publications, 1964), p. 26.

19. See Zentarō Kitagawa, *Keiyaku sekinin no kenkyū* (Study of contractual liability) (Tokyo: Yūhikaku, 1963); Sakae Wagatsuma, *Mimpō kōgi* (Series of lectures on the civil code) (Tokyo: Iwanami shoten, 1963), 1: 196, on general provisions, including juristic acts, and volumes 4, 5 (1), (2), and (3) (1962) on obligations; *Keiyakuhō taikei* (Compendium [essays] on contract law) (Tokyo: Yūhikaku, 1963), a six-volume memorial collection of essays by many scholars on various contract law topics, dedicated to Professors Saichi Matsuzaka, Nobuo Nishimura, Jun Funabashi, Kaoru Yunoki, and Masao Ishimoto; Toshio Hironaka, *Keiyakuhō no kenkyū* (Studies in contract law) (Tokyo: Yūhikaku, 1958); Zennosuke Nakagawa, etc., ed. *Chūshaku mimpō* (Commen-

taries, civil law) (Tokyo: Yūhikaku, 1965–), Vols. 10–19; Sakae Wagatsuma *et al.*, eds., *Hanrei kommentāru* (Case commentary) (Tokyo: Kommentāru kankōkai, 1963), Vol. 1, is on the general provisions (*sōsoku*) of the Civil Code, and Volume 4 is on the general remarks of obligations (*saiken sōron*) (1965); Fumio Ōno and Isamu Imanishi, *Keiyaku zensho* (Complete collection on contracts) (Tokyo: Seirin shoin shinsha, 1963), is a collection of contract forms plus a commentary.

20. See, generally, Kan'ichi Nishihara, *Shōkōihō* (Law of commercial transactions) 29 *Hōritsugaku zenshū* (Tokyo: Yūhikaku, 1960), pp. 1–2, for the dominant theory that the objects of the Commercial Code are *kigyō*.

21. The definitions of various kinds of commercial transactions are found in Commercial Code, Arts. 501, 502, and 503. For the definition of a trader as mentioned in Art. 503 (1), see Commercial Code, Arts. 4, 52, and 523, and Limited Company Law (*Yūgengaishahō*), Arts. 1 and 2 (Law No. 74, 1938).

22. As a consequence of several provisions (Commercial Code, Arts. 3, 4, 52, 501, 502, 503, 523, and Limited Company Law, Arts. 1 and 2), the Commercial Code applies to any business-related transaction of a company, whether stock-type or not, as long as it is incorporated in accordance with the provisions of the Commercial Code (Book II) or the Limited Company Law. The Commercial Code will always apply to any transactions effected in Japan by a foreign company with a Japanese company, whether it is recognized by Japanese law as a trader or not. This is because, if the Japanese company is a trader and if the transaction is related to his business, as is generally the case (*i.e.*, whenever it is in pursuit of benefit in the broadest sense), the Commercial Code always applies to the other party. Commercial Code, Arts. 3 (1) and 503.

23. Civil Code, Arts. 521–28. Also, on offer and acceptance see Commercial Code, Arts. 507, 508, and 509. Note that in American law fraud, duress, etc., are usually conceived as "formation" problems.

24. These questions are generally covered by Book I (General Provisions) of the Civil Code. The relevant provisions are Arts. 3–20 on Capacity and Arts. 90–137 on Juristic Act (*hōritsu kōi*). See Commercial Code, Art. 504, on representation ("agency"), Wagatsuma, *Mimpō kōgi*, 5 (1): 79. Hiroshi Suekawa, *Keiyakuhō* (Contract law) (Tokyo: Iwanami shoten, 1958), p. 20.

25. Of course, there is no direct Japanese case authority for the proposition that consideration is not required. But see Kōhei Izawa, *Beikoku shōgyō shōkenhō* (U.S. law on commercial papers) (Tokyo: Yūhikaku, 1955), p. 244, and the discussion at note 41 *infra*.

26. There are exceptional contracts regulated by special statutes that specifically require that the contract be in writing. *E.g.*, tenancy contracts, Farm Land Law (*Nōchihō*), Art. 25 (Law No. 229, 1952); contracts for construction work, Construction Industry Law (*Kensetsugyōhō*), Art. 19 (Law No. 100, 1949). Compare share subscriptions (Commercial Code, Art. 175), bond subscriptions (Commercial Code, Art. 301 [1]), and prorogation clauses in domestic suits (Code of Civil Procedure, Art. 25), all of which require written documents related to contracts for regulatory law purposes; but in Japanese legal conception failure to comply with these requirements of writing has only regulatory significance and does not invalidate the respective oral contracts or defeat an action on them for damages.

27. Note that we have a rule derived from agency in some states, however, that mutual bilateral promises alone will not support an irrevocable proxy, *e.g.*, *Johnson* v. *Spartanburg County Fair Ass'n.*, 210 S.C. 56, 41 S.E. 2d 599 (1947). But see notes 96–98 *infra*.

28. The types are: gift (Arts. 549–54); sale (Arts. 555–85); exchange (Art. 586); loan for consumption (Arts. 587–92); loan for use (Arts. 593–600); lease (Arts. 601–22); employment (or service) (Arts. 623–31); contract for work (Arts. 632–42); mandate (Arts. 643–45); bailment (Arts. 657–60); partnership (Arts. 667–88); life annuity (Arts. 689–94); and compromise (Arts. 695–96). Also see discussion at note 31 *infra*.

29. For the Japanese theory of mixed contracts (*kōngo keiyaku*) and atypical contracts (*hitenkei keiyaku*), see Wagatsuma, *Mimpō kōgi*, 5 (3): 883, and for judicial handling of

atypical contracts see *Arimatsu* v. *Furukawa*, 22 Daishin'in minji hanketsuroku (hereafter cited Minroku) 1450 (Gr. Ct. Cass., 16 Sept. 1916) (contract to make a gift of property held to be atypical as distinguished from a gift contract in the Civil Code); *Kawachi Bank* v. *Matsumura*, 10 Kakyū saibansho minji hanreishū (hereafter cited Kakyū minshū) 373 (Osaka Dist. Ct., 23 Feb. 1959) (mixed contract: consuming bailment contract [Civil Code, Art. 666], plus mandate contract [Civil Code, Arts. 643–56]).

30. Early Japanese courts confused the use of *jun'yō* and *ruisui tekiyō*. *Morikawa* v. *Mori*, 22 Minroku 1663 (Gr. Ct. Cass., 22 Aug. 1916), where *mutatis mutandis* (*jun'yō*) is used like the word "analogous" (*ruisui tekiyō*). However, recently scholars and courts have generally agreed that *jun'yō* is a statutory technique and must be provided in the law, whereas *ruisui tekiyō* is a method of legal reasoning employed in decisions by the courts on their own. *Nagamoto and Takeshita* v. *Fukuhisa*, 8 Saikō saibansho minji hanreishū (hereafter cited Minshū) 1505 (Sup. Ct., 20 Aug. 1954). See Wagatsuma, *Mimpō kōgi*, 1: 24.

31. Among the special statutes recognizing atypical contracts are: Law Concerning Fidelity Guaranty (*Mimoto hoshō ni kansuru hōritsu*) (Law No. 42, 1933), in 2 EHS No. 2124; Land Lease Law (*Shakuchihō*) (Law No. 49, 1921), in 2 EHS No. 2131; House Lease Law (*Shakuyahō*) (Law No. 50, 1921) in EHS No. 2131; and Labor Standards Law (*Rōdō kijunhō*), Arts. 13–28 (Law No. 49, 1947), in 8 EHS No. 8040 (as to labor contracts).   The Commercial Code also provides a number of types of contracts of a commercial nature such as contracts of account current (Arts. 529–34), contracts of undisclosed association (Arts. 535–42), etc. The code applies to all contracts of a commercial nature, whether typical or atypical.

32. The phrase *gōben gaisha* (joint-venture company), though popular recently in Japanese parlance, is not a legal term. It does not appear in the statutes, and the question is whether it has not come into use only recently with reference to the precise international problems we are discussing. See Jūkagaku kōgyō tsūshinsha, *Gaikoku*, p. 45.

33. On this point in the United States, see Harry G. Henn, *Corporations* (St. Paul: West Pub. Co., 1961), p. 64: "Generally, joint ventures are governed by some of the principles of partnership law, with some differences resulting from the more limited extent of the business undertaken by the joint venture. The authority of the adventurer to bind the others is more limited, and there is sometimes said to be no general agency."

34. Civil Code, Arts. 667–88.

35. Wagatsuma, *Mimpō kōgi*, 5(3): 772. *Ujiya* v. *Ishizuka*, 4 Kakyū minshū 195, 213 (Osaka Dist. Ct., 17 Feb. 1953), in which the court found a promoter-partnership that was organized at first by seven incorporators in order to incorporate but was later reduced to two partners after the others withdrew and incorporation failed.

36. Commercial Code, Art. 165: "Seven or more promoters [*hokkinin;* "incorporator" is a better equivalent English term] are required for the incorporation of a '*kabushiki kaisha*.' " Seven "promoters" are required only during incorporation. One shareholder only is legal after registration; for example, where the other "promoters" transfer their shares to one person, the prohibition against one shareholder does not apply to a *kabushiki kaisha*. Commercial Code, Arts. 404 and 94.

37. Commercial Code, Arts. 192–94, 196, and 198; *Nakajima* v. *Kondō*, 24 Minroku 1480, 1483 (Gr. Ct. Cass., 10 July 1918); *Hyaku-sanjūhachi Bank* v. *Tōyō Seien Co.*, 16 Minroku 982 (Gr. Ct. Cass., 23 Dec. 1910); and cases cited in 13 (IV) *Hanrei taikei* (Compendium of decisions), 206–9 (Tokyo: Daiichi hōki shuppan K.K., 1960). See Masahiro Kitazawa, "Setsuritsu-chū no kaisha" (Company in the establishment process), 1 *Kabushiki kaishahō kōza* (Lectures on corporation law), 211, 218 (1958); and Teruhisa Ishii, *Shōhō* (Commercial law), 3rd. rev. ed. (Tokyo: Keisō shobō, 1959), 1: 163.

38. Specifically note that transactions by "promoters" before the corporation comes into existence, which go beyond the scope of incorporation and have to do with the commencement of the future companies' business, are not binding on the corporation when it comes into existence, and the promoter may be held personally liable under

Civil Code, Art. 675. *Shinsei Kōgyō K.K.* v. *Shimazaki*, 7 Kakyū minshū 890 (Tokyo Dist. Ct., 9 Apr. 1956) (new corporation not entitled to enforce a lease signed by person *before* he became one of plaintiff's "promoters"; moreover, here the lease was connected with future business, not incorporation). *Tsuji* v. *Daiei Baseball K.K.*, 12 Minshū 3228 (Sup. Ct., 24 Oct. 1958) ("promoter" liable personally to baseball team because his arrangement for a game to celebrate the new company's inauguration was not within the scope of "promoters' " duties re incorporation).

39. Commercial Code, Arts. 186, 192–95, for liability of "promoters." Note that in Japanese law, unless he actually shows that he is signing for someone else, the person whose signature appears on the articles of incorporation is the promoter, regardless of how formalistic his participation may be intended to be by all concerned; *Kasuda* v. *Matsuura Suisan K.K.*, 22 Minroku 1862 (Gr. Ct. Cass., 7 Oct. 1916). For many other cases and a discussion of "promoters' " liability, see Toshio Takeuchi, "Hokkinin no sekinin" (Liability of promoters), 2 *Sōgō hanrei kenkyū shōhō* 147, 152 (Tokyo: Yūhi-kaku, 1961).

40. *E.g.*, *Campbell* v. *Campbell*, 198 Kan. 181, 422 P. 2d 932 (1967), 7 *Washburn L. Rev.* 110–14; *Elsbach* v. *Mulligan*, 58 Cal. App. 2d 354, 136 P. 2d 651 (1943). See note, 44 *Calif. L. Rev.* 590 (1956). *Contra*. *Jackson* v. *Hooper*, 76 N.J. Eq. 592, 75 Atl. 568 (Ct. Err. & App. 1910). See 69 *Harv. L. Rev.* 565 (1956).

Some U.S. authorities say that a joint venture among promoters must terminate upon incorporation because coexistence is inconsistent with the corporate structure. *Weisman* v. *Awnair Corp. of America*, 3 N.Y. 2d 444, 144 N.E. 2d 415 (1957). See, generally, George D. Hornstein, "Judicial Tolerance of the Incorporated Partnership," 18 *Law & Contemp. Prob.* 435, 443 (1953); and Henn, *Corporations*, p. 65.

Another problem is whether a corporation can be a joint venturer in some U.S. jurisdictions in which partnership law is largely applicable to joint ventures and corporations are not allowed to enter a partnership. Usually, however, even in such jurisdictions a corporation is permitted, specifically, to be a joint venturer. *Weisman* v. *Awnair Corp. of America; U.S. Fid. and Guar. Co.* v. *Dawson Produce Co.*, 200 Okla. 540, 197 P. 2d 978 (1948); *Nolan* v. *J. & M. Doyle Co.*, 338 Pa. 398, 13 A. 2d 59 (1940); *Excelsior Motor Mfg. & Supply Co.* v. *Sound Equipment, Inc.*, 73 F. 2d 725 (7th Cir. 1934), cert. denied 294 U.S. 706 (1935). See ABA-ALI Model Bus. Corp. Act. §4(5) (1953).

41. See, for details, Kitazawa, "Setsuritsu-chū," *Kabushiki*, pp. 211, 218, 219.

42. *Ogoshi* v. *Tokyo Tatemono*, 22 Minshū 1845 (Gr. Ct. Cass., 4 Oct. 1916), where, of course, the court did not mention a lack of consideration, there being no such requirement in Japanese law, but the court did enforce a promise to pay more than the original contract called for without any further consideration from the other party. See, for comparison, Arthur T. von Mehren, "Civil Law Analogues to Consideration: An Exercise in Comparative Analysis," 72 *Harv. L. Rev.* 1009 (1959).

43. Commercial Code, Art. 188 (2) (viii), requires that the name of the *daihyō torishimariyaku* be registered at the appropriate public registry and Art. 40 provides for registration of *shihainin* (managers).

44. Commercial Code, Arts. 42, 262; also see Civil Code, Arts. 109, 110, 112.

45. Law Concerning Matters To Be Signed Under the Commercial Code (*Shōhō-chū shomei subeki baai ni kansuru hōritsu*), Art. 1 (Law No. 17, 1900), provides for execution of commercial documents by seal.

46. Commercial Registration Law (*Shōgyō tōkihō*), Art. 12 (Law No. 125, 1963); Commercial Registration Regulations (*Shōgyō tōki kisoku*), Art. 16 (Ministry of Justice, Regulation No. 112, 1951). The Commercial Registration Law was enacted in 1963, and the provisions of the Law of Procedure in Non-Contentious Matters (*Hishō jiken tetsuzukihō*), Arts. 142–205 (Law No. 14, 1898), in 2 EHS No. 2380, which previously regulated this subject, were deleted. The representative's seal is registered at the Commercial Registry, and this particular seal for corporate purposes is usually different from the seal that the same individual files with the municipal offices (in Tokyo the Ward Office [*kuyakusho*]) for his personal use.

47. *E.g.*, see Commercial Registration Regulations (*Shōgyō tōki kisoku*), Art. 38 (Ministry of Justice, Regulation No. 112, 1951), which presupposes the description to be in Japanese. According to the Notary Law, if the articles of incorporation are made as a notarial deed (*kōsei shōsho*), it must be in Japanese. Notary Law (*Kōshōninhō*), Art. 27 (Law No. 53, 1908), in 2 EHS No. 2050.

However, in most cases, the articles of incorporation are drafted as a private deed (*shisei shōsho*) and the notary (*kōshōnin*) can attest any private deed written in a foreign language, except that the statement of attestation must be in Japanese (Notary Law, Art. 27). See Sadahide Miyaji, "Soshō ni kansuru tetsuzuki" (Procedure for acknowledgments), 10 *Jiyū to seigi* (Freedom and justice) (No. 9) 30 (1959).

Of course, the language of the Japanese courts is Japanese. Court Organization Law (*Saibanshohō*), Art. 74 (Law No. 59, 1947), in 2 EHS No. 2010. However, there is no such clear-cut provision for noncontentious matters (*hishō jiken*) such as commercial registrations that are not within the jurisdiction of the court but under the Ministry of Justice. The Law of Procedure in Non-Contentious Matters (*Hishō jiken tetsuzukihō*), Art. 139 (Law No. 14, 1898), in 2 EHS No. 2380. Nevertheless, in Japanese practice the registry will not accept foreign-language documents for commercial registration, such as articles of incorporation. So, even though the articles had been attested by a notary as a private deed, they would not be accepted in a foreign language by the registry office. Note that there is a similar rule against a trade name in English, which states that an English trade name cannot be accepted for registration. Takeo Suzuki, *Kabushiki jitsumu* (Practices relating to shares) (Tokyo: Yūhikaku, 1963), 1: 10.

48. Gaishi dōnyū nenkan henshū iinkai, ed., *Gaishi dōnyū nenkan* (Annual on foreign capital induction) (Tokyo: Shōkōkaikan, 1969), p. 65.

49. See Seiji Tanaka, *Saishin kaishahō shōron* (The latest and detailed explanation of company law) (Tokyo: Keisō shobō, 1967), 1: 128–29, which notes that certain provisions of the Commercial Code seem to presuppose bylaws. *E.g.*, see Art. 282 (2): "Any shareholder or creditor of the company may, at any time during business hours, demand inspection of the documents mentioned in the preceding paragraph and may demand delivery of a copy or an abstract copy of such documents, paying such fees as fixed by the company."

50. Even in some U.S. jurisdictions extraordinary controls over director or shareholder action can only be provided in the articles. Others allow restrictions in the bylaws. See O'Neal, *Close Corporations*, 1: 200–2.

51. The question is whether unregistered "bylaws," providing for abbreviated procedures, etc., would be valid under the corporation law.

52. Definitions of the close corporation vary, but generally the term means a corporation with only a few shareholders wherein ownership and management are coalesced and the shares are not traded on the securities markets. O'Neal, *Close Corporations*, 1: 2–5, discusses various criteria suggested by the writers and courts.

53. Limited Company Law (*Yūgengaishahō*) (Law No. 74, 1938); English: 2 EHS No. 2230. See Eisuke Yoshinaga, "The Medium and Small Enterprises in Japan and Their Forms of Corporation," 1 *Hitotsubashi J. of L. & Politics* 16–29 (1960).

54. See L. C. B. Gower, "The English Private Company," 18 *Law & Contemp. Prob.* 535 (1953); and Colin McFadyean, "The American Close Corporation and Its British Equivalent," 14 *Bus. Law* 215 (1958).

55. Dieter Schneider, "The American Close Corporation and Its German Equivalent," 14 *Bus. Law* 228 (1958).

56. See generally, Seiji Tanaka, Eisuke Yoshinaga, and Chūhei Yamamura, *Saizentei kommentāru kaishahō* (Again completely revised commentary on company law) (Tokyo: Keisō shobō, 1968), pp. 1501–622; Ishii, *Shōhō*, 1: 556; Taku Nomura, *Yūgengaisha setsuritsu annai* (Guide to establishment of a limited company) (Tokyo: Tōeidō, 1962).

57. Limited Company Law (*Yūgengaishahō*), Art. 3 (1) (Law No. 74, 1938).

58. See Ken'ichirō Ōsumi, Kan'ichi Nishihara, and Akinobu Ueda, "Kabushiki kaishahō no komponteki kaisei ni tsuite no kenkyū" (Study on basic revision of the

stock corporation law), *Shōji hōmu kenkyū* (No. 30), 1, 5 (1956). The members (*shain*) are limited to 50, but the size of capital and operations are, of course, not limited. They could conceivably attain great size, for example, like the Ford Motor Company in this country before it went public.

59. O'Neal, *Close Corporations*, 1: 27; Joseph L. Weiner, "Legislative Recognition of the Close Corporation," 27 *Mich. L. Rev.* 273 (1929).

60. Note that the Ill. Bus. Corp. Act, in contrast to New York's pre-amendment law, is said to be flexible enough to accommodate the close corporation reasonably well. William L. Cary, "How Illinois Corporations May Enjoy Partnership Advantages: Planning for the Closely Held Firm," 48 *Nw. U.L. Rev.* 427, 440 (1953). For new legislation addressed to close corporation problems, see O'Neal, *Close Corporations* (1970 Supp.), §1.14 Recent Statutes Designed for Close Corporations. Separate integrated statutes for close corporations are: Pa. State Ann. Tit. 15 §§1371–1386 (1968); Ann. Code Md., Art. 23 §§100–111 (1967); Del. Code Ann. Tit. 8 §§341–356 (1967); Fla. Stats. Ann. §§608.70–608.77 (1963, amended 1967, renumbered from 608.0100–608.0107 in 1969). Note: the 1963 Fla. Act was the first separate Close Corp. Act but was vaguely drawn; improved with 1969 amendments.

New York Business Corporation Law (1961), South Carolina Business Corporation Act (1962), and North Carolina Gen. Stat. §55–1 to 55–175 (1955) all focus on the close corporation with an extensive array of close corporation provisions that are incorporated into the laws without separating them from the provisions for widely held corporations.

61. Both the cases and the periodical literature are exhaustively cited throughout both volumes of O'Neal, *Close Corporations* (1970 Supp.).

62. Commercial Code, Art. 204 (1): "The shares may be transferred to other persons. Provided that, this shall not prejudice to establish the stipulation in the articles of incorporation to the effect that the transfer needs the approval of the board of directors."

This is a 1966 amendment replacing the old Art. 204 (1): "The transfer of a share shall not be prohibited or restricted even by the provisions of the articles of incorporation."

This pre-1966 version was added by an occupation-sponsored amendment (Law No. 167, 1950) that also changed other features of Japanese corporation law relating to shares and shareholders. In English, see Lester N. Salwin, "The New Commercial Code of Japan: Symbol of Gradual Progress toward Democratic Goals," 50 *Georgetown L.J.* 478 (1962).

63. Note that Commercial Code, Art. 204 (1), applies only to *kabushiki kaisha*. There are two other types of juristic entities (besides *yūgengaisha*, text accompanying note 53 *supra*), provided in the Commercial Code, Book II. They are *gōmei kaisha* (Arts. 62–145) and *gōshi kaisha* (Arts. 146–64), both of which resemble in some respects our partnership. Being of unlimited liability, they are normally inappropriate for an international joint venture.

64. See revised Commercial Code, Art. 348.

65. *Tōhoku Kōgyō K.K.* v. *Tōhoku Aen Kōgyō K.K.*, 6 Kakyū minshū 950 (Tokyo Dist. Ct., 9 May 1960), which has been criticized for upholding a transfer condition. Upon failure of the conditions the court denied the transferee's right to the share. The criticism was that this kind of agreement should not affect a third-party transferee and that it should only give rise to a claim for damages between the shareholders. Tanaka, Yoshinaga, and Yamamura, *Saizentei*, p. 471.

For insights on the law before the 1950 amendment to Art. 204, which allowed both contractual and corporate restrictions, see *Ōkura* v. *Iwata*, 1 Kakyū minshū 1697 (Tokyo Dist. Ct., 25 Oct. 1950), where the restriction by contract between shareholders was upheld in an action under Commercial Code, Art. 247, to rescind a resolution the propriety of which depended on whether the transferee had a right to vote.

66. *E.g.*, Jirō Matsuda, *Shin kaishahō gairon* (Treatise on the new stock corporation law) (Tokyo: Iwanami shoten, 1957), pp. 154–55, and Tanaka, Yoshinaga, and Yamamura, *Saizentei*, p. 471, would strike down most corporation-shareholder transfer re-

strictions as violative of Art. 204 (1); but Ishii, *Shōhō*, 1(1): 298, and Takeo Suzuki and Teruhisa Ishii, *Kaisei kabushiki kaishahō kaisetsu* (Commentary on the revised stock corporation law) (Tokyo: Nihon hyōron, 1951), p. 8, would uphold most corporation-shareholder agreements, except those of the adherence type (*i.e.*, subscription forms, etc.).

67. *E.g.*, Ishii, *Shōhō*, 1(1): 299; and Tanaka, Yoshinaga, and Yamamura, *Saizentei*, p. 474.

68. Matsuda, *Shin kaishahō gairon*, p. 155, takes the view, stemming apparently from his individualistic obligation theory (*saikensetsu*) regarding shareholders' rights, that all such contractual restrictions are void.

69. Ken'ichirō Ōsumi, "Kabushiki no jōto" (Transfer of shares), in 2 *Kabushiki kaishahō kōza* (Lectures on corporation law) 639, 648 (1956); Ishii, *Shōhō*, 1(1): 299.

70. Note that the pre-amendment cases uniformly held, with only one exception, that a transfer restriction provided in the articles of incorporation always bars the acquisition of the right by the transferee, whether he was a bona fide transferee or not. See cases cited in 17 (III) *Hanrei taikei* (1958), pp. 508–13. Also, *cf.* discussion of the *Tōhoku Kōgyō* case, note 65 *supra.*, which was decided under the pre-1966 law.

71. The writer witnessed a similar problem in one joint venture when a U.S. firm was bought by another U.S. firm with less interest and concern for foreign operations.

72. *Unreported* v. *Unreported*, 29 *Hanrei taikei* (1956), p. 704 (Osaka Dist. Ct., 6 Sept. 1939). The court dismissed (*kikyaku*) an attack under Code of Civil Procedure, Art. 759, against an injunction ordering the petitioner not to transfer shares.

73. See Hajime Kaneko, *Kyōsei shikkōhō* (Execution law) (Tokyo: Kōbundō, 1951), p. 294; and Daijirō Kitsukawa, *Hanrei hozen shobun* (Provisional disposition decisions) (Kyoto: Hōritsu bunkasha, 1959), p. 200.

74. *Shimomura* v. *Japan*, 18 Minshū 761 (Gr. Ct. Cass., 19 July 1939), supported by scholarly comments in Kitsukawa, *Hanrei hozen shobun*, pp. 197, 200, and in Case No. 53 (Saburō Kurusu's comment), in *Hanrei minjihō, Shōwa jūyonendo* (Judicial review of civil cases, 1939) (Tokyo: Yūhikaku, 1940), Vol. 19.

This holding is explained by the doctrine of relative effect (*sōtaiteki kōryoku*) of injunctions. Since injunctions should bind only parties so included in the action, persons not parties to the action or not actually named in an injunction are free from its effect. In this case, the injunction only prohibited a transfer by the transferor, and, though the telephone company was informed of this injunction, it could not effectively bind the company by prohibiting it to change the registration.

This restrictive use of the so-called "doctrine of relative effect" of injunctions is very important on the practice level, and it also leads to the conclusion that injunctions must be specific as to the parties. *E.g.*, where X obtains an injunction prohibiting Y company from registering a transfer of shares from A to B, X still cannot prevent A's transferring those shares to C, and Y company cannot refuse C's request to register. At the same time an attempt to obtain an injunction against all third parties in general would not be supported, since it would injure some interested third parties then unknown and violate the doctrine of relative effect. See also *Nomura* v. *Fuji Seitetsu*, 10 Kōtō saibansho minji hanreishū (hereafter cited Kōsai minshū) 181 (Tokyo High Ct., 19 Apr. 1957); Hajime Kaneko, "Kabushiki ni taisuru kyōsei shikkō (Execution on shares), in 2 *Kabushiki kaishahō kōza* 765, 774 (1956).

75. *Cf.* Kitsukawa, *Hanrei hozen shobun*, p. 200.

76. Matsuda, *Shin kaishahō gairon*, pp. 154–55.

77. Civil Code, Art. 420:

1. The parties may determine in advance the amount of compensation for damages payable in the event of the nonperformance of an obligation; in such case the Court cannot increase or reduce the amount.

2. The determination in advance of the amount of compensation for damages shall not prejudice the obligee's right to demand performance or rescission.

3. A penalty is presumed to be a determination in advance of the amount of compensation for damages.

78. *Utano* v. *Gyokuzōhō*, 1 Minshū 431 (Gr. Ct. Cass., 26 July 1922) (Liquidated damages granted despite lessee-defendant's claim that the land had been leased again after the breach without any actual loss); *Mitate* v. *Takahashi*, 13 Minroku 36 (Gr. Ct. Cass., 2 Feb. 1907) (Proof of actual loss not required).

79. *Yamamura* v. *Kanzaki*, 23 Minshū 147 (Gr. Ct. Cass., 14 Nov. 1944) (Denied, as against Civil Code, Art. 90, liquidated damages for delay of payment on a note, where the amount was excessive, even though the usury law might not apply to a commercial matter).

80. *E.g.*, N.Y. Bus. Corp. Law §715 (effective 1963) provides that shareholders may be allowed to elect officers. See note 60 *supra* for state statutes most responsive to close corporation needs.

81. See the following for recent discussion: Robert Kessler, "Hooray (?) for the Model Act—the 1969 Revision and the Close Corporation," 38 *Fordham L.R.* 743 (1970); E. J. Bradley, "Comparative Evaluation of the Delaware and Maryland Close Corporation Statutes," 1968 *Duke L.J.* 525 (1968). Also see various articles in "Close Corporations: A Symposium," 1969 *U. Ill. L. Forum* 1–73, 139–223 (1969), including J. A. C. Hetherington, "Special Characteristics, Problems and Needs of the Close Corporation"; B. R. Burrus and J. Casson, "Capitalization and Allocation of Securities"; F. Hodge O'Neal, "Control Distribution Devices"; C. R. Wetzel, "Employment Contracts and Non-Competition Agreements."

Comment, "Failure of the Ohio General Corporation Law to Adequately Provide for Close Corporations—Proposals for Change," 37 *U. Cin. L. Rev.*, 620–34 (1968); Comment, "A Comparison of the Close Corporation Statutes of Delaware, Florida, and New York," 23 *U. Miami L. Rev.* 515–30 (1969); C. Harris, "Separate Treatment for Close Corporations: Lessons from England and Australia," 17 *Am. J. Comp. L.* 194 (1969).

82. FIL (*Gaishi ni kansuru hōritsu*), Art. 11 (Law No. 163, 1950, as amended through 1 April 1968).

83. Ibid.

84. FIL Arts. 26 and 29 provide criminal penalties of up to three years' imprisonment and/or 300,000 yen fine for violation of the law.

85. *Tomita* v. *Inoue*, 19 Minshū 2306 (Sup. Ct., 1965); *Lewin* v. *Greenberg*, 11 Kakyū minshū 2034 (Tokyo D. Ct., 30 Sept. 1960). Both parties in this latter suit for $10,000 were Americans. Defendant was a resident, and plaintiff was a nonresident. Thus, the transaction required a license under the Foreign Exchange and Foreign Trade Control Law (*Gaikoku kawase oyobi gaikoku bōeki kanrihō*), Art. 27 (Law No. 228, 1949) (hereafter cited FECL). Defendant asserted (1) a lack of foreign-exchange license and (2) duress as defenses. Judgment was for defendant, based on duress. But, in so deciding, the court also found that the lack of an FECL license did not invalidate the plaintiff's claim, reasoning that the FECL could not deprive the court of competence to handle suits between residents and nonresidents. The holding has been properly criticized for reaching the right decision for wrong reasons. It would seem that the case has nothing to do with the court's competence; rather, the issue was whether the FECL restrictions invalidated an unapproved contract, and, consistent with Japanese legal concept, the answer is that it would not, because the FECL is a regulatory law with its own purposes (and enforcement measures) going only to means of payment, quite separate from the contract law, which creates private rights. For a critical comment on this case by Kan Nishi, see "Shōgai hanrei kenkyū," *Jurisuto* (No. 241) 127 (1962). See also Kimikuni Namoto, "Gaikoku kawase oyobi gaikoku bōeki kanri hōki to sono shōgai-teki kōryoku ni tsuite" (Concerning the laws and regulations for control of foreign exchange and foreign trade and their external effect), 54 *Kokusaihō gaikō zasshi* (The journal of international law and diplomacy) (No. 4) 47, 79 (1955); *Greenhill Trading Co.* v. *Shiro Trading Corp.*, 13 Kōsai minshū 696 (Tokyo High Ct., 29 Oct. 1960), recognizes an unapproved claim, conditioned on obtaining foreign-exchange approval. The court's decision has been criticized for attaching a condition, *Jurisuto* (No. 229) 82 (1961). *Suzuki* v. *Japan*, 11 Kakyū minshū 779 (Tokyo Dist. Ct., 11 Apr. 1960). *Cf. G. M.*

Casaregi Compania de Navigazione e commerce S.P.A. v. *Nishi Shōji K.K.*, 10 Kakyū minshū 1711 (Tokyo Dist. Ct., 30 Aug. 1959), upholding an unapproved arbitration agreement between resident and nonresident.

86. See, *e.g.*, an analogous issue in the recent antimonopoly case: *Novo Industrials* v. *FTC, Hanrei Taimuzu* (No. 264) (1971), p. 215. See also Wagatsuma, *Mimpō kōgi*, 1: 225.

87. *Tamaki* v. *Nakagawa*, 25 Minshū 1715 (Gr. Ct. Cass., 25 Sept. 1919), unlicensed plaintiff, who maintained a rendezvous (*machiai*) for customers, was not precluded from collecting his fees.

88. What kind of regulatory statutes, if any, in Japan could be enacted to establish a policy strong enough to void a conflicting contract? See *Tomita* v. *Inoue*, 9 Minshū 2306 (Sup. Ct., 1965), Matsuda's dissent, for a persuasive plea for flexibility. It seems that the Japanese concept of separate operative spheres for administrative and private contract law is basically different from the early position of our common law that contracts opposed to acts of Parliament were void. Of course, with increased regulation of all activity, both U.S. and Japanese law are receding from their opposite but inflexible positions and now often contracts are enforced (U.S.) or vice versa (Japan) depending on their relationship in fact to pertinent regulatory statutes, except where the statute expressly prohibits such a contract. *E.g.*, in the U.S. see *Kaiser-Frazer Corp.* v. *Otis & Co.* 195 F. 2d 838 (2d Cir. 1952). See *Restatement, Contract* §580 (1932); 6A Corbin, *Contracts* §1374 (1962), and cases there cited. See *Chapman* v. *Zakzaska*, 273 Wis. 64, 76 N.W. 2d 537 (1956), where the court reasoned, like the Japanese courts, that the regulation had its remedies and that accomplishing its purpose did not require voiding a contrary contract.

89. See text accompanying notes 64 to 68 *supra*.

90. Harris, "Separate Treatment for Close Corporations, *Am. J. Comp. L.*, p. 194; L. C. B. Gower, "Some Contrasts Between British and American Corporation Law," 69 *Harv. L. Rev.* 1369, 1375–76 (1956).

91. See, for example, an older case consistent with this thinking, 17 (II) *Hanrei taikei* (Compendium of decisions) 190, where a provision in the articles to the effect that directors would be liable for the company's obligation was held by a Tokyo Appellate Chamber decision (14 Mar. 1932) not to make directors liable directly to a corporate creditor.

92. *Benitendi* v. *Kenton Hotel, Inc.* 294 N.Y. 112, 60 N.E. 2d 829 (1945); *Sensabaugh* v. *Polson Plywood Co.*, 135 Mont. 562, 342 P. 2d 1064 (1959). In these cases the courts declined to enforce admittedly invalid bylaws as contracts between the parties.

93. Compare, *e.g.*, *Jackson* v. *Hooper*, 76 N.J. Eq. 592, 75 Atl. 568 (Ct. of Err. & App. 1910) and *Loverdos* v. *Vomvouras*, 200 N.Y.S. 2d 921, 923 (1960) (holding against survival of pre-incorporation joint-venture agreements because they are inconsistent with the corporate form) with *De Boy* v. *Harris*, 207 Md. 212, 13 A. 2d 903 (1955), noted 69 *Harv. L. Rev.* 565 (1956) (holding for survival).

94. *E. K. Buck Retail Stores* v. *Harkert*, 157 Neb. 867, 62 N.E. 2d 288 (1954). *Cf. New England Trust Co.* v. *Abbott*, 162 Mass. 148, 38 N.E. 432 (1894); *Barrett* v. *King*, 181 Mass. 476, 63 N.E. 934 (1902). In both of these latter cases, it was argued that the bylaws restricting share transfers were illegal; however, the court enforced the restrictions as contracts, without actually determining whether as bylaws they were illegal. See also *Sensabaugh* v. *Polson Plywood Co.*, 135 Mont. 562, 342 P. 2d 1064 (1959) (dictum), to the effect that denying cumulative voting by contract would be legal, even though the decision was that such a bylaw was against the state constitution.

95. Note that the majority in *Benintendi* v. *Kenton Hotel, Inc.*, 294 N.Y. 112, 60 N.E. 2d 829, 832 (1948), in answering the argument of the dissenters that the illegal bylaws should be enforced as a contract, were "at a loss to understand how any court could entertain a suit, or frame a judgment, to enforce such a compact" (*i.e.*, to compel unanimous voting of shareholders and directors).

96. Commercial Code, Arts. 342 (1) and 343:

> 342 (1). For effecting any alteration of the articles of incorporation, a resolution of the general meeting of shareholders is required.

343. The resolution provided for in paragraph 1 of the preceding Article shall be adopted by two-thirds or more of the votes of the shareholders present who hold shares representing more than one-half of the total number of the issued shares.

See Tanaka, Yoshinaga, and Yamamura, *Saizentei*, p. 1164; Matsueda, *Gōben gaisha*, p. 189.

97. Note that the provision against irrevocable proxies (Commercial Code, Art. 239-4) is not held to prevent appointment of a permanent representative (*jōnin dairinin*) in Japan to act for foreign shareholders. Both the corporate practice and the recent scholarly comment support the proposition that a foreign shareholders' Japan representative, duly appointed, can vote for the shareholder without special proxies at each meeting and can also appoint a sub-proxy. See Suzuki, *Kabushiki jitsumu*, 1: 76–78. See revised Commercial Code, Art. 239–2, allowing a shareholder for the benefit of others (*e.g.*, ADR) to vote each beneficial owner's shares separately.

98. As to the various aspects of the voting trust problem, see Akinobu Ueda, "Giketsuken to sono dairikōshi" (Voting right and its proxy), in *Zoku jitsumu kabushiki kaishahō rokkō* (Six more essays on practical stock corporation law), ed. Shōji hōmu kenkyūkai (Tokyo: Shōji hōmu kenkyūkai, 1960), pp. 155, 164; Ichirō Kawamoto, "Kimei kabuken to furikae kessai seido" (Nonbearer shares and the exchange system by way of pooling shares with a trustee), 13 *Kobe hōgaku zasshi* (Kobe law journal) 18, 72, 74 (1963).

99. Commercial Code, Art. 239 (3) and (4):
   3. A shareholder may exercise his vote by proxy. Such a proxy, however, shall file with the company a document establishing his power of representation.
   4. The conferment of the power of representation mentioned in the preceding paragraph shall be made for each general meeting.

100. Commercial Code, Art. 222. See Suzuki, *Kabushiki jitsumu*, 2: 7–10.

101. Commercial Code, Art. 242 (1) and (2):
   1. In cases where a company issues two or more classes of shares, it may be provided for by the articles of incorporation that with respect to shares of preferred class regarding the distribution of profits, a shareholder shall not be entitled to vote; however, such shareholder shall be entitled to vote from the time when the resolution to the effect that he shall not receive the preferred distribution provided for by the articles of incorporation has been adopted to the time when the resolution to the effect that he shall receive such distribution has been adopted.
   2. The total number of the shares mentioned in the preceding paragraph shall not exceed one-fourth of the total number of the issued shares.

102. Suzuki, *Kabushiki jitsumu*, 1: 4–8; and Seiji Tanaka, *Kaishahō* (Company law) (Tokyo: Chikura shōbō, 1963), p. 100.

103. Tanaka, Yoshinaga, and Yamamura, *Saizentei*, p. 762.

104. *Agetsuma* v. *Kawai*, 8 Kakyū minshū 2139 (Osaka Dist. Ct., 16 Nov. 1957).

105. The procedure and arithmetic of cumulative voting can pose intricate problems, especially when the legal requirements as to how the voting is to be done are not specified. See generally Ichirō Sakai, "Ruiseki tōhyō" (Cumulative voting), in 3 *Kabushiki kaishahō kōza* (Lectures on stock corporation law) 1005–28 (1956). See also Lewis R. Mills, "The Mathematics of Cumulative Voting," 1968 *Duke L.J.* 28–43 (1968).

106. Gaikoku kawase bōeki kenkyūkai, *Gaikokujin no Nippon ni okeru gōben gaisha no setsuritsu keiyaku ni tsuite* (Concerning contracts to establish foreigners' joint-venture companies in Japan) (Gaikoku kawase bōeki kenkyūkai, 1963), p. 14.

107. Commercial Code, Art. 168 (1) (v) and (vi):
   The following matters shall not be effective unless they are stated in the articles of incorporation:
   v. The full names of the persons whose contributions are in the form of property other than money, the property forming the subject-matter of such contributions, the value of such property, and a statement as to whether shares to be

given therefor are those having par value or those without par value, together with their classes and their number;

    vi. Property which has been stipulated to be taken over after the coming into existence of the company, its value and the full name of the transferor.

Note that these items, among others, are known technically as items of abnormal incorporation (*hentai setsuritsu jikō*). See generally Hiroshi Imai, "Hentai setsuritsu jikō" (Items of abnormal incorporation), in 2 *Sōgō hanrei kenkyū soshō shōhō* 94 (1961). Note that the requirement to list these in the articles brings with it the duty of passing a court inspection of the transaction before registration of the articles can be accomplished. Commercial Code, Art. 173 (2), in case of incorporator incorporation (*hokki setsuritsu*); Arts. 181, 185 (1), in case of public offering incorporation (*boshū setsuritsu*).

    108. Commercial Code, Art. 168 (1) (v) and (vi).

    109. *Unreported* v. *Unreported*, 17 (II) *Hanrei taikei* (Compendium of decisions) (Gr. Ct. Cass., 24 Dec. 1932) (constituent meeting not empowered to accept a setoff of property of a subscriber in lieu of his obligation to pay cash for shares). Ishii, *Shōhō*, 1: 188.

    110. Commercial Code, Art. 246:

    The provisions of Article 245 paragraph 1 shall apply *mutatis mutandis* in cases where, within two years after its coming into existence, a company makes an agreement to acquire, for value equivalent to not less than one-twentieth of the capital, property existing prior to its incorporation and intended to be continuously used for purposes of the business.

    111. Commercial Code, Art. 245 (1):

    A resolution as provided for in Article 343 is required for a company to effect the following acts:

    (1) The transfer of the whole or of an important part of the business of the company;

    (2) The making, alteration or rescission of a contract for leasing the whole of the business, for giving a mandate to manage such business, or for sharing with another person the entire profits and losses in relation to the business or of a similar contract;

    (3) The taking over of the whole of the business of any other company.

    112. *Wakō Seizō Kōgyō K.K.* v. *Maruyama*, 7 Minshū 1299 (Sup. Ct., 13 Dec. 1953), holding against new corporation attempting to defend (against seller's claim of rescission) old promoter's contract to buy land because corporation adopted the sale contract by two-thirds vote provided in Commercial Code, Art. 246. The court held that a new sales contract could have been so adopted but not the old one, which was void for failure to list it in the articles. Tanaka, Yoshinaga, and Yamamura, *Saizentei*, p. 332.

    113. Ishii, *Shōhō*, 1: 165; *Fuji Kōsoku Insatsu K.K.* v. *Tomita*, 7 Kakyū minshū 135 (Tokyo Dist. Ct., 30 Jan. 1956); also, *Unreported* v. *Unreported*, 17 *Hanrei taikei* 94 (Gr. Ct. Cass., 24 Nov. 1924).

    114. Commercial Code, Art. 168 (1) (v). Note that only incorporators may contribute property for shares, but this is a restriction on initial share issues at the time of establishment. Property instead of cash may be exchanged for shares in subsequent issues after incorporation by anyone where agreeable to the directors, and no court inspection is required. Commercial Code, Art. 280–2 (1). So the technique of a later share issue, if agreed in a side agreement, would avoid the court inspection procedures but not the FIL scrutiny, of course.

    115. Commercial Code, Art. 185 (1).

    116. Commercial Code, Art. 173 (2).

    117. See note 106 *supra*.

    118. *Shirai K.K.* v. *Daiei Marugumi*, 12 Minshū 2861, 2866 (Gr. Ct. Cass., 18 Dec. 1933).

    119. Civil Code, Art. 537:

    1. Where a party to a contract has agreed therein to effect an act of performance in favor of a third person, such third person is entitled to demand such act of performance directly to the obligor.

2. In the case mentioned in the preceding paragraph, the right of the third person shall come into existence as from the time when he declares to the obligor his intention to accept the benefit of the contract.

120. *Osaka Seiki K.K.* v. *Nakata*, 9 Minroku 299 (Gr. Ct. Cass., 10 Mar. 1903) (enforcing a contract against a third-party beneficiary incorporated after the contract); *Matsuyama* v. *Matsuo*, 24 Minroku 2131 (Gr. Ct. Cass., 5 Nov. 1918) (unborn third-party beneficiary).

121. See *Nagase* v. *Matsuda*, 20 Minroku 313 (Gr. Ct. Cass., 22 Apr. 1914), holding that the contract is binding between the original parties, whether or not the third-party beneficiary elects to accept the contract.

122. See note 111 *supra*. *Wakō Seizō Kōgyō K.K.* v. *Maruyama*, 7 Minshū 1299 (Sup. Ct., 13 Dec. 1953).

123. If on the facts it is to the advantage of the new corporation to accept the benefit of the contract, as was the situation in the *Wakō* case (apparently the value of the land had gone up from 1944 to 1953 far beyond the contract price), then it seems that the court should give effect to the overriding policy of upholding the bargain of the parties. In the *Wakō* case there were, however, added considerations, *e.g.*, the new corporation did not pay the price in time and seller had opted to rescind.

124. See note, "Economic Duress after the Demise of Free Will Theory," 53 *Iowa L. Rev.* 892–924 (1968); and old analysis, Arthur L. Corbin, "Does a Pre-existing Duty Defeat Consideration?" 27 *Yale L. J.* 362, 373–79 (1918); John Dalzell, "Duress by Economic Pressure I," 20 *N.C. L. Rev.* 237 (1942); John P. Dawson, "Economic Duress— An Essay in Perspective," 45 *Mich. L. Rev.* 253 (1947). See, *e.g.*, *United States* v. *L. B. Miller Inc.*, 81 F. 2d 8 (2d Cir. 1936); 1 Corbin, *Contacts* §171 (1950).

125. *E.g.*, *Healy* v. *Brewster*, 30 *Cal. Reptr.* 129, 380 P. 2d 817 (1963); Note, 51 *Cal. L. Rev.* 1001 (1963).

126. See notes 1–8 *supra*. Also Sawada, *Subsequent Conduct and Supervening Events*, pp. 221–24. Note that Europeans also are said to use formal contracts much less than Americans. Van Hecke, "A Civilian," in *International Contracts*, ed. Reese, p. 5.

127. For a behavioral study, see Sawada, *Subsequent Conduct and Supervening Events*, pp. 221–24. There are also occasional journalistic comments in the English literature critical of Japanese attitudes toward contracts with foreigners. *E.g.*, *U.S. News and World Report*, 18 May 1964, p. 104; "Themes and Variations," *Wall Street Journal*, 3 Feb. 1964; Boyce De Mente, *Japanese Manners and Ethics in Business* (Tokyo: East Asia Pub. Co., 1960), p. 41; and Boyce De Mente, *How Business Is Done in Japan—A Personal View* (Japan: Simpson-Doyle Co., 1963), p. 17. Comments in these latter books are sometimes extreme but doubtless express the feeling and misunderstanding of some foreigners dealing with Japan, and they are cited here only for evidence of those attitudes of some foreigners; cf. F. Herbert Glazer, *The International Businessman in Japan: The Japanese Image* (Tokyo: Sophia U. and Charles E. Tuttle, 1968), p. 59.

128. Civil Code, Arts. 513–18. Article 513 reads:

1. If the parties have entered into a contract in which the essential elements of the obligation are modified, such obligation shall be extinguished by novation.

2. The removal, addition, or alteration of conditions shall be deemed to be a modification of the essential elements of the obligation. The same shall apply where a bill of exchange is issued in lieu of the performance.

129. *Ogoshi* v. *Tokyo Tatemono*, 22 Minshū 1845 (Gr. Ct. Cass., 4 Oct. 1916) (no "consideration" but change in rent upheld); *Unreported* v. *Unreported*, Hōritsu shimbun (No. 2055) 17 (Tokyo Appellate Chamber, 21 July 1922); *Unreported* v. *Unreported*, 11 (II) *Hanrei taikei* (1957) 1137; *Hanrei taikei* (No. 30) 34 (1953) (Sup. Ct., 20 Mar. 1953) (no "consideration" but change of price for immovables upheld); see cases cited in 13 (III) *Hanrei taikei* (1960) 312. Note the interesting emphasis of the foregoing cases on novation. The discussion centers around the problem of whether a subsequent promise to pay more without any change in the other's performance was a change in the "essential elements" of the obligation in each case which would extinguish the prior contract by novation (per Art. 513; see note 127 *supra*). In common law such a subsequent "nova-

tion" would doubtless fail for lack of consideration, leaving the original contract the same. See James Barr Ames, "Two Theories of Consideration," 12 *Harv. L. Rev.* 515, 521 (1899). But in the *Ogoshi* case, *supra*, where a surety was defended by arguing that a novation took place without his consent, thus superseding all the old contracts, the court held that the price change was not a change of an "essential element" required for novation, which would extinguish the prior contract; so the court held the surety liable on the subsisting old contract.

For the German and French approach, see Arthur T. von Mehren, "Civil Law Analogies to Consideration: An Exercise in Comparative Analysis," 72 *Harv. L. Rev.* 1009 (1959); William Noel Keyes, "Cause and Consideration in California—A Re-Appraisal," 47 *Cal. L. Rev.* 74 (1959); and J. Denson Smith, "A Refresher Course in Cause," 12 *La. L. Rev.* 2 (1951).

130. For discussion of various aspects of the problem, see Corbin, *Contracts*, and Note, 51 *Cal. L. Rev.* (1963); *cf.* Note, 2 *Houston L. Rev.* 132 (1964).

131. Civil Code, Art. 536:

> 1. Except in the cases mentioned in the preceding two Articles, if the performance of an obligation becomes impossible by any cause for which neither of the parties is responsible, the obligor is not entitled to counter-performance.
>
> 2. If performance becomes impossible by any cause for which the obligee is responsible, the obligor shall not lose his right to demand counter-performance; however, if he has received any benefit through being relieved of his own obligation, he shall return such benefit to the obligee.

The text alone is confusing on the point because it only provides that the obligor is not entitled to counter-performance without saying he is excused from performance (*i.e.*, need not pay damages to the obligee). But the article is interpreted to have the effect attributed to it above. Wagatsuma, *Mimpō kōgi*, 5(1): 99–112. *Unreported* v. *Unreported*, 12 (I) *Hanrei taikei* 482 (1958) (Tokyo Dist. Ct., 8 Dec. 1928), where a seller of a business that was later destroyed in the 1923 earthquake before delivery was held not entitled to the price from the buyer.

132. Civil Code, Arts. 534–36. See criticism of Article 534 in Wagatsuma, *Mimpō kōgi*, 5(1): 85, note 130; for a practical discussion of this problem, see Kikuo Kōriki, Tōru Ichikawa, and Shigeo Satō, "Bōeki to hōritsu" (Trade and law), 352–79 *Bōeki jitsumu kōza* (Lectures on trade practice) (Tokyo: Yūhikaku, 1962).

133. See, generally, Wagatsuma, *Mimpō kōgi*, 5(1): 28, note 130; Toshio Fukuji, "Jijō henkō no gensoku" (Principle of changed circumstances), in 3 *Mimpō enshū* (Seminar on the Civil Code), ed. Tomohei Taniguchi and Ichirō Katō (Tokyo: Yūhikaku, 1958).

This doctrine is similar to frustration in our law. See Kōriki, Ichikawa, and Satō, "Bōeki to hōritsu," *Bōeki jitsumu kōza*, p. 331. Compare Restatement, Contracts §288 (1932). See, generally, Harold J. Berman, "Excuse for Nonperformance in the Light of Contract Practices in International Trade, 63 *Colum. L. Rev.* 1413 (1963); Hans Smit, "Frustration of Contract: A Comparative Attempt at Consolidation," 58 *Colum. L. Rev.* 287 (1958); Arthur Anderson, "Frustration of Contract—A Rejected Doctrine," 3 *De Paul L. Rev.* 1 (1953); Leo M. Drachler, "Frustration of Contract: Comparative Law Aspects of Remedies in Cases of Supervening Illegality," 3 *N.Y. L. F.* 50 (1957).

134. *Iguchi* v. *Ikegami*, 8 Minshū 449, 459 (Sup. Ct., 12 Feb. 1954) (compromise agreement upheld against defense of change of circumstances).

135. Civil Code, Art. 1 (2): "The exercise of rights and performance of duties shall be done in faith and in accordance with the principles of trust."

136. Wagatsuma, *Mimpō kōgi*, 5(1): 27, note 130; Masaaki Katsumoto, *Mimpō kenkyū* (Study of the Civil Code) (Tokyo: Ganshōdō, 1934), p. 41.

137. *Iguchi* v. *Ikegami*, 8 Minshū 448 (Sup. Ct., 12 Feb. 1954); *Taiyō Tochi K.K.* v. *Ōfuruta*, 9 Minshū 2027 (Sup. Ct., 20 Dec. 1955); *Iwanari* v. *Kurihara*, 10 Minshū (Sup. Ct., 5 Apr. 1956); *Masuda* v. *Higuchi*, 10 Minshū 566 (Sup. Ct., 25 May 1956). All four of these cases refused to accept a defense of changed circumstances to excuse performance.

138. Sawada, *Subsequent Conduct and Supervening Events*, p. 197.

CHAPTER IX

1. *E.g.*, Japan Industrial Promotion Association, *A Key to the Japanese Market* (Tokyo: Japan Ind. Pro. Assoc., 1968), 1: 72.

2. See *Zip Mfg. Co.* v. *Pep Mfg. Co.*, 44 F. 2d 184 (D.C. Del. 1930). See also James A. Dobkin, "Arbitrability of Patent Disputes Under the U.S. Arbitration Act," 23 *Arb. J.* 1–17 (1968).

3. Hereafter, this chapter relies heavily on my article published earlier with Prof. Tarō Kawakami, "Arbitration in U.S.-Japanese Sales Disputes," in 42 *Wash. L. Rev.* 541 (1967). Parts of that article have been outdated by the U.S. adoption of the UN Convention (as hereafter discussed) and later legislation, cases, and literature, which have been canvassed thoroughly in updating and rewriting this chapter.

4. Steven Lazarus, John J. Bray, Jr., Larry L. Carter, Kent H. Collins, Bruce A. Giedt, Robert V. Holton, Jr., Phillip D. Matthews, and Gordon C. Willard, *Resolving Business Disputes: The Potential of Commercial Arbitration* (New York: American Management Ass'n., 1965), p. 17: "Characteristically, commercial arbitration derives its vitality and power from the modern arbitration statutes. The most important single influence on commercial arbitration is its complex involvement with the law."

5. Lazarus *et al.*, *Resolving Business Disputes*, pp. 14 ff. See Kiyoshi Morii, *Kokusai shōji chūsai* (International commercial arbitration) (Tokyo: Tōyō keizai shimpōsha, 1970), p. 203.

6. See a new American teaching tool, Merton C. Bernstein, *Private Dispute Settlement* (New York: Free Press, 1968).

7. In Soia Mentschikoff, "The Significance of Arbitration—A Preliminary Inquiry," 17 *Law & Contemp. Prob.* 698 (1952), the author estimates that, excluding personal injury cases, more than 70% of the legal disputes between private persons are decided through arbitration. This was of course only an estimate and it seems high to us, but nevertheless arbitration has long been important, and it is now growing rapidly in both the United States and Japan. See William Carton Jones, "Three Centuries of Commercial Arbitration in New York," 1956 *Wash. U. L. Q.* 193 (1956), where the point is made that American arbitration has been important from the very beginning, especially in New York. See also, Lazarus *et al.*, *Resolving Business Disputes*, p. 20.

8. Soia Mentschikoff, "Commercial Arbitration," 61 *Colum. L. Rev.* 846, 859 (1961): "Personal observation at the Association leads me to the reluctant conclusion that in the great majority of the cases observed, lawyer participation not only failed to facilitate decision but was so inadequate as to materially lengthen and complicate the presentation of the cases. Nonetheless, the Association encourages lawyer participation." For similar comment see Morii, *Kokusai shōji chūsai*, p. 259.

9. See Samuel H. Jaffee, "Battle Report: The Problem of Stenographic Records in Arbitration," 20 *Arb. J.* 97 (1965).

10. *E.g.*, *Burchell* v. *Marsh*, 58 U.S. (17 How.) 344 (1854). See also Martin Domke, *Commercial Arbitration* (Englewood Cliffs, N.J.: Prentice-Hall, 1965), p. 80; Robert Coulson, "Appropriate Procedures for Receiving Proof in Commercial Arbitration, 71 *Dick. L. Rev.* 63 (1966). Compare the English practice, William Henry Gill, *Evidence and Procedure in Arbitration* (London: Sweet & Maxwell, 1965), p. 73.

11. Lawyers show much dissatisfaction with the performance of arbitrators and vice versa. Lazarus *et al.*, *Resolving Business Disputes*, p. 115. Professor Warren L. Shattuck is quoted in ibid., pp. 187–88: "In my estimation a disservice has been done arbitration by the development in some circles of the notion that this is a service which should be free. I would welcome research into this aspect of the subject and would expect the findings to disclose what seems to me to be the fact, namely, that the kind of special skill and competence in arbitrations which are essential to the long-range success of the method for resolving disputes must be paid for." For problems alleged to arise from paid arbitration see Justice Black's dissent in *Prima Paint* v. *Flood & Conklin Mfg. Co.*, 388 U.S. 395, 87 S. Ct. 1801, 1808 (1967).

12. See Domke, *Commercial Arbitration*, p. 91. Only Mississippi requires written reasons in the award. Martin Domke, "Arbitral Awards Without Written Opinions: Comparative Aspects in International Commercial Arbitration," in *20th Century Comparative and Conflicts Law*, ed., Kurt H. Nadelmann *et al.* (Leydon: A. W. Sythoff, 1961), p. 249; Stanley Mosk, "The Lawyer and Commercial Arbitration: The Modern Law," 39 *A.B. A.J.* 193 (1953). In the United States—labor and maritime awards usually include reasoning—some American trade associations provide for reasoned opinions. Lazarus *et al.*, *Resolving Business Disputes*, p. 187. But the general rule in American commercial law is otherwise, and the American Arbitration Association has discouraged them in accordance with commercial arbitration practice. England and Commonwealth countries usually follow this practice of unreasoned awards, but France, the Netherlands, and Japan, among others, require reasoned opinions.

13. The American rule that awards are valid even when based on errors of law goes back at least to *Fudickar* v. *Guardian Mut. Life Ins. Co.*, 62 N.Y. 392, 399 (1875). In England the rule is different and an award can be vacated for errors of law which show on the face of the award. *Czarnikow* v. *Roth, Schmidt & Co.* 2 K.B. 478 (1922). See Note, "Judicial Review of Arbitration Awards on the Merits," 63 *Harv. L. Rev.* 681, 686 (1950).

The American contrast is well shown in *Interinsurance Exch. of Auto Club* v. *Bailes*, 219 Cal. App. 2d 830, 33 Cal. Rptr. 533 (Dis. Ct., App. 1963), where, even though the court reviewing an award recognized that the arbitrator erred, because the holding was not only contrary to law but the point was *res judicata* (contrary earlier decision by the same reviewing court) in the arbitration, the court still upheld the award, saying "a decision of an arbitrator is binding, whether or not correct either in law or in fact." Ibid. at 833, 33 Cal. Rptr. at 536. Other cases upholding awards on errors of law alone are: *In re Compu Dyne Cpr.*, 255 F. Supp. 1004, 1008 (E. D. Pa. 1966); *South East Atl. Shipping Ltd.* v. *Garnac Grain Co.*, 356 F. 2d 189, 192 (2d Cir. 1966); *Raytheon Co.* v. *Rheem Mfg. Co.*, 322 F. 2d 173, 182 (9th Cir. 1963); *Torano* v. *Motor Vehicle Acc. Indemn. Corp.*, 15 N.Y. 2d 882, 206 N.E. 2d 353, 258 N.Y.S. 2d 418 (1965). Pennsylvania is an exception, because there awards may be set aside for errors of law. *Pa. Stat. Ann.*, Tit. 5, §4 (1963); *Gasparini Excavating Corp.* v. *Pennsylvania Turnpike Comm'n.*, 409 Pa. 136, 185 A. 2d 320 (1962).

See Daniel G. Collins, "Arbitration and the Uniform Commercial Code," 41 *N.Y. U. L. Rev.* 736, 752 (1966), suggesting that the entire Uniform Commercial Code may be undermined by the growing practice of arbitrating sales disputes, since the doctrine of the valid erroneous award may mean that the arbitrators cannot be compelled to comply with the code: "In larger perspective, it would be nothing short of scandalous if, by virtue of a common-law rule or a process of statutory harmonization, it were not to be discovered that the great effort that went into creating the Uniform Commercial Code produced a statute that was viable only when a commercial agreement did *not* contain an arbitration clause. Such a discovery would, of course, also have the effect of subverting the Code's stated goal of a uniform commercial law for the United States."

Cf. Merton C. Bernstein, "The Impact of the Uniform Commercial Code Upon Arbitration," 22 *Arb. J.* 65 (1967). And see Mentschikoff, "Commercial Arbitration," *Colum. L. Rev.*, p. 861, for the attitude of arbitrators toward the rules of law.

14. *E.g.*, in American law, 9 U.S.C. §10 (1964); N.Y. Civ. Prac. Law §7511 (b); Wash. Rev. Code §§7.04.170–.180 (1956). Note that no appeal is allowed from an order compelling arbitration under 7.04.040 because such an order is not a "final order." *All-Rite Contracting Co.* v. *Omey*, 27 Wn. 2d 898, 181 P. 2d 636 (1947). See *South East Atl. Shipping Ltd.* v. *Garnac Grain Co.*, 356 F. 2d 189, 192 (2d Cir. 1966); *Orion Shipping & Trading Co.* v. *Eastern States Petroleum Corp. of Panama*, 206 F. Supp. 777 (S.D.N.Y 1962), aff'd. 312 F. 2d 299 (2d Cir.), cert. denied, 373 U.S. 949 (1963); *General Constr. Co.* v. *Hering Realty Co.*, 201 F. Supp. 487 (E.D.S.C. 1962); *Interinsurance Exch. of Auto Club* v. *Bailes*, 219 Cal. App. 2d 830, 33 Cal. Rptr. 533 (Dist. Ct., App. 1963); *Simons* v. *A. C. Israel Commodity Co.*, 37 Misc. 2d 299, 238 N.Y.S. 2d 341 (Supp. Ct.

1962). On Japanese law, see Jun'ichi Nakata, "Japan," in *International Commercial Arbitration: A World Handbook*, ed. Pieter Sanders (The Hague: Martinus Nijhoff, 1965), 3: 93.

15. See Lazare Kopelmanes, "The Settlement of Disputes in International Trade," 61 *Colum. L. Rev.* 384 at 390 (1961); and Lazarus *et al.*, *Resolving Business Disputes*, p. 167. One hundred top American executives engaged in international commerce were sent a questionnaire. Sixty-five percent of those who answered the questionnaire "believed commercial arbitration to be more suitable internationally than domestically. . . . One hundred percent of the responding exporters and importers used the international commercial arbitration clause in their purchase-sale contracts. . . . One hundred percent of the responding traders preferred international commercial arbitration to court litigation." Ibid., p. 168.

16. *Hyōjun kessai hōhō ni kansuru shōrei* (Ministerial ordinance concerning standard method of settlement) (MOF Ordinance No. 62, 1962), *Beppyō* (Schedule) No. 1, in 28 *Genkō hōki* 3426. Payment terms complying with this standard require no MITI approval. See *Yushutsu bōeki kanrirei* (Export trade control order), Art. 1 (1) (iii) (Cabinet Order No. 373, 1949), in 28 *Genkō hōki* 3437.

17. In *Kuchiki Shōji K.K.* v. *Mikami K.K.*, 7 Minshū 848, 861 (Gr. Ct. Cass., 27 Oct. 1928), the court makes it quite clear that arbitrators are not confined by the law in rendering their awards.

18. Note that the American Arbitration Association (AAA) warns its arbitrators *against* compromising; AAA, *A Manual for Commercial Arbitrators* 24 (1964).

19. See *Kuchiki* case, *supra*, note 17; compare *Yamada* v. *Bellini*, 10 Minroku 621 (Gr. Ct. Cass., 9 May 1904); also see Noboru Koyama, "Chūsaihō" (Arbitration law), in 38 *Hōritsugaku zenshū* 88 (1958).

20. Code of Civil Procedure, Arts. 786–805. See English language treatment: Teruo Doi, "International Commercial Arbitration in Japan," in *International Commercial Arbitration: Labor Amicorum for Martin Domke*, ed. Pieter Sanders (The Hague: Martinus Nijhoff, 1967), pp. 65–77; Tokusuke Kitagawa, "Contractual Autonomy in International Commercial Arbitration, Including a Japanese Perspective," in *International Arbitration*, ed. Sanders, pp. 133–42; Kazuromi Ōuchi, "Problems of Competence of International Commercial Arbitral Tribunals," 3 *Philippine Int'l L. J.* 16–132 (1964); Tokusuke Kitagawa, "Commercial Arbitration Law and Practice in Japan," 12 *Japanese Annual of Int'l. Law* 59–70 (1968); Jun'ichi Nakata, "Japan," in *International Commercial Arbitration*, ed. Sanders, 3: 72–97.

Older articles in English on certain phases of Japanese arbitration law are: Teruo Doi, "Recognition and Enforcement of Foreign Judgments and Arbitral Awards" (Pts. 1–2), *Quarterly of J.C.A.A.* (Nos. 13, 14) 1, 5 (1963); Hilliard A. Gardiner, "Japanese Arbitration Law," 8 *Arb. J.* 89 (1953); and Hajime W. Tanaka, "Enforcement of American Arbitration Awards in Japan," 10 *Arb. J.* 88 (1955).

21. Dan Fenno Henderson, *Conciliation and Japanese Law: Tokugawa and Modern* (U. of Tokyo and U. of Wash. Press, 1965) 1: 1–13.

22. Morii, *Kokusai shōji chūsai*, p. 203; and Jun'ichi Nakata, "Shōji chūsai seido no gaiken" (General survey of the commercial arbitration system), *Hōkei gakkai zasshi* (Okayama daigaku) (No. 3) 2 (1952). See also Yasuo Ishimoto, "Meiji-ki ni okeru chūsai saiban no senrei (Pt. 2) (Precedents of international arbitration in the Meiji era), 8 *Hōgaku zasshi* (No. 1) 73–96 (1961).

23. Toshio Sawada, *Subsequent Conduct and Supervening Events* (Tokyo: U. of Tokyo Press, 1967), pp. 192, 196, 199. *Cf.* Jirō Matsuda, "Doitsu shōji chūsai seido no ichi-kōsatsu" (Pt. 2) (An inquiry into the German commercial arbitration system), 9 *Hōsōkai zasshi* (No. 11) 73 (1931); Otto Mathies, "Hamburugu ni okeru jōsetsu chūsai saiban-sho" (The standing arbitration court in Hamburg), 74 *Shihō shiryō* 62 (1925).

Actual examples of incorporation of arbitration provisions in early contract forms in preparation for future disputes in certain Japanese trades are: wool yarn, ship, and crude petroleum sales contracts, joint business (*kyōdō eigyō*) contracts, and wage agreements (*hōshū no torikime*) in the 1911 employment contracts. However, the parties in all these were foreign firms.

24. Kazuo Muramoto, "Wagakuni no chūsai seido no jitsujō" (The actual state of affairs in the Japanese arbitration system), 28 *Shihō kenkyū hōkokusho* (No. 6) 108 (1938).

The types of cases were: shipping, 83 (or 40%); building evacuation (*kaoku akewatashi*) and rent (*yachin*), 42; rice fertilizer transactions, 27; electrical industry, 4; and all others, 53. These figures do not represent the entire number of arbitrations conducted, but we can conclude that arbitration was particularly common in shipping disputes.

25. For example, in connection with the disposition of claims concerning building construction for the American military authorities in Japan, see Taizō Watanabe, *Ukeoi kōji ni okeru funsō to "kuremu"* (Disputes in contract construction and claims) (Tokyo: Kajima kensetsu gijutsu kenkyū shuppanbu, 1954), which is primarily based on materials concerning construction of American Air Force bases in Japan during 1950. The International Commercial Arbitration Committee was established (1 Feb. 1950) in order to manage the affairs in Japan of the Japan-American Arbitration Committee (*Nichibei chūsai iinkai*), established by an agreement dated 25 Nov. 1949, among the Japanese Chamber of Commerce and Industry (*Nihon shōkō kaigisho*), the American Arbitration Association, and the American Chamber of Commerce in Japan (*Zai-nichi Amerika shōkō kaigisho*). The Japan-American Arbitration Committee became an agency for the disposition of claims arising out of Japan-American trade during the occupation; it was reorganized and incorporated (3 Dec. 1953) and became the present-day "Japan Commercial Arbitration Association" (*Kokusai shōji chūsai kyōkai;* literally, International Commercial Arbitration Association; the English title is that used by the JCAA itself.)

26. The generous assistance of Mr. K. Kurata, at that time chief, Arbitration Department, Japan Commercial Arbitration Association in Tokyo, is gratefully acknowledged. Copies of the arbitration agreements with the various countries and information concerning JCAA operations were obtained in Tokyo in the summer of 1966.

27. See Morii, *Kokusai shōji chūsai*, p. 326, for a list, as well as Japanese language versions of pertinent provisions.

28. These figures were kindly supplied to me in early 1973 by the Japan Commercial Arbitration Association in Tokyo.

29. See dissent by Justice Black in *Prima Paint Corp.* v. *Flood & Conklin Mfg. Co.*, 388 U.S. 395, 407; 87 S. Ct. 1801, 1808 (1967).

30. See *Continental Ins. Co.* v. *Furudono*, Hōritsu shimbun (No. 3904) 5 (Tokyo App. Ct., 5 Aug. 1935), where the prewar court deals indirectly with the characterization problem, calling arbitration essentially "substantive" (*i.e.*, contractual). *Accord, Compania de Transportes de ma S.A.* v. *Mataichi K.K.*, 4 Kakyū minshū 502 (Tokyo Dist. Ct., 10 Apr. 1953).

31. See *A. D. Rarande* v. *Oriental Hotel, Ltd.*, 24 Minroku 865, 875 (Gr. Ct. Cass., 15 Apr. 1918). The case seems to permit an arbitration in Japan under foreign law. It also supports a characterization of arbitral agreements as essentially "procedural."

32. 2 Apr. 1953, [1954] 4 U.S.T. & O.I.A. 2063, T.I.A.S. No. 2863.

33. Japanese Constitution, Art. 98 (2): "The treaties concluded by Japan and established laws of nations shall be faithfully observed." See 2 (2) *Chūkai Nihonkoku kempō* (Commentaries on the Japanese Constitution) 1484 (Hōgaku kyōkai ed., 1953), for a view that treaties are superior to even the Constitution in Japan. *Contra*, Shirō Kiyomiya and Toshiyoshi Miyazawa, *Kempō* I (Constitution I), 3 *Hōritsugaku zenshū* (Tokyo: Yūhikaku, 1960), p. 60. Compare Elbert M. Byrd, *Treaties and Executive Agreements in the United States* (The Hague: M. Nijhoff, 1960), p. 83. See *Reid* v. *Covert*, 354 U.S. 1, 17 (1957), for the proposition that the United States Supreme Court "has regularly and uniformly recognized the supremacy of the Constitution over a treaty." See generally Hans Aufricht, "Suppression of Treaties in International Law," 17 *Cornell L.Q.* 655 (1952); Sedgwick W. Green, "The Treaty Making Power and Extraterritorial Effect of the Constitution," 42 *Minn. L. Rev.* 825 (1958); William W. Bishop, Jr., "Unconstitutional Treaties," 42 *Minn. L. Rev.* 773 (1958).

34. Code of Civil Procedure, Arts. 786–805.
35. For citations to all general arbitration statutes in the various states of the United States, see Katherine Seide, ed., *A Dictionary of Arbitration and Its Terms* (Dobbs Ferry, N.Y.: Oceana Publications, 1970), p. 255. Texas and Maryland enacted modern arbitration statutes in 1965, also Alaska (1968), Arkansas (1968), Indiana (1969), Maine (1968), and Virginia (1968), bringing the total to twenty-seven states. But note that the new Texas statute places severe requirements on the conclusion of arbitral agreements; see note 72 *infra*.
36. 9 U.S.C. §§1–14 (1964), enacted 1925; 9 USCA §§200–208 (effective 29 December 1970).
37. *Uniform Commercial Code, 1962, Official Text with Comments.*
38. Convention on the Recognition and Enforcement of Foreign Arbitral Awards (1958). 330 UNTS 38, T.J.A.S. No. 6997 (29 Dec. 1970). A copy of the 1958 UN Convention may also be found along with a convenient group of statutes on arbitration in Seide, ed., *A Dictionary of Arbitration*, p. 314, and copies of the Geneva Protocol on Arbitration Clauses (24 Sept. 1923) and the Geneva Convention on the Execution of Foreign Arbitral Awards (26 Sept. 1927) may be found conveniently in Martin Domke, ed., *International Trade Arbitration* (New York: American Arbitration Association, 1958), pp. 283, 285.
39. 84 Stat. 692 (1 July 1970). One reason the United States had not joined before is that our bilateral treaties were considered adequate by some authorities. Other reasons given were: conflicts between state statutes and the United Nations Convention as well as deficiencies in the federal act; probably a cautious lack of confidence in arbitral tribunals in less-developed countries with little experience with arbitration. See Lazarus *et al.*, *Resolving Business Disputes*, pp. 160–64.
See also John J. Czyak and Charles H. Sullivan, "American Arbitration Law and the U.N. Convention," 13 *Arb. J.* 197 (1958). *Cf.* Clifford J. Hynning and George W. Haight, "International Commercial Arbitration," 48 *A.B.A.J.* 236 (1962), urging accession and amendments to the Federal Arbitration Act as suggested by the American Bar Association resolution recommending United States accession to the United Nations Convention.
40. The Japanese text is found in Morii, *Kokusai shōji chūsai*, p. 269. For a full discussion see Seidō Agawa, "Gaikoku chūsai handan no shōnin oyobi shikkō ni kansuru jōyaku ni tsuite" (Pts. 1–2) (Concerning convention on the recognition and enforcement of foreign arbitral awards), *Jurisuto* (Nos. 231, 232), pp. 18, 42 (1961); Tarō Kawakami, "Gaikoku chūsai handan no shōnin oyobi shikkō ni kansuru kokuren jōyaku to Nipponkoku no ka'nyū" (Convention on the recognition and enforcement of foreign arbitral awards and Japan's accession thereto), 45 *Minshōhō zasshi* (No. 5) 591–620 (1962).
41. For text see Appendix XI.
42. Tarō Kawakami and Keisuke Masakame, "Nihon ni okeru kokusai-teki gijutsu enjo keiyaku funsō shori jōkō no jittai to kokusai shihō mondai" (A survey of dispute-settlement clauses in international technical assistance contracts in Japan and problems of private international law) 16 *Kobe hōgaku zasshi* 570 (1966).
43. See Dan Fenno Henderson, "Business Procedures in Japanese Licensing," 4 *Les Nouvelles* (No. 1) 26 (1969).
44. See Appendix XI. Compare the ICC clause: "All disputes arising in connection with the present contract shall be finally settled under the Rules of Conciliation and Arbitration of the ICC by one or more arbitrators appointed in accordance with the rules." If in a U.S.-Japanese agreement, "contract" is translated "*keiyaku*," *quaere*, whether in my clause suggested at the end of this chapter, Japanese law and American law might not yield different results on the question of arbitrability of the issue of fraud in contract formation, since in Japan a "*keiyaku*" is nonetheless "formed"; the fraud goes only to the effect, not the existence of a "*keiyaku*." But fraud can prevent formation (existence) of a "contract" in the U.S.
45. See E. J. Cohn, "Rules of Arbitration of the International Chamber of Com-

merce," 14 *Int'l & Comp. L. Q.* 132 (1965); and Frederic Eisemann, "Arbitration under the International Chamber of Commerce Rules," 15 *Int'l. & Comp. L. Q.* 726–36 (1966).

46. The new JCAA rules became effective 1 Feb. 1971 and can be found in Japanese: 18 *Bōeki kuremu to chūsai* (No. 162) 3 (1971); in English, JCAA, *Commercial Arbitration Rules* (rev., 1971). This revision is the first major revision since World War II, and for international cases it authorizes English language awards but makes the Japanese version of the rules controlling in cases of differences in interpretation.

47. The AAA rules can be found conveniently: in English, Seide, ed., *A Dictionary of Arbitration*, p. 289; in Japanese, Morii, *Kokusai shōji chūsai*, p. 451.

48. Lazarus *et al.*, *Resolving Business Disputes*, pp. 42, 65, 99, 124.

49. The court held in *Rose Int'l. Corp.* v. *Japan Commercial Arbitration Ass'n.*, 13 Kakyū minshū 338 (Tokyo High Ct., 5 Mar. 1962), that Osaka was a proper place despite the American corporation's contention that it should be in Tokyo.

50. Lazarus *et al.*, *Resolving Business Disputes*, p. 31, notes that 2,522 cases out of a total of 3,858 handled by the AAA were processed in New York City.

51. See Warren Shattuck and Zentarō Kitagawa, "U.S.-Japanese Contracts and Sales Problems," University of Washington School of Law, 1970, mimeo., 3 vols., which analyzes a wide range of issues, where differences in reasoning and/or results occur.

52. See *Batson Yarn & Fabrics Machinery Group, Inc.* v. *Saurer-Allma GmbH-Allgauer Maschinenbau*, 311 F. Supp. 68 (D. Ct. So. Car.)(1970), for an example of a troublesome clause produced by the parties' ineffectual attempt to fix the place of arbitration.

53. Japan Commercial Arbitration Ass'n., *Commercial Arbitration Rules* §17 (rev. 1 Feb. 1971); American Arbitration Ass'n., *Commercial Arbitration Rules of the American Arbitration Association* §16 (as amended 1 June 1964).

54. See the clause in the Mitsui & Co. sales form in *Oregon-Pacific Forest Prods. Corp.* v. *Welsh Panel Co.*, 248 F. Supp. 903, 906 n. 1 (D. Ore. 1965):

> 10. Any claims by Buyer of whatever nature arising under this contract shall be made by cable within thirty (30) days after arrival of the merchandise at the destination specified in the bills of lading. . . . Settlement of such claim or any disputes will be effected by agreement of the parties as promptly as possible, but, failing amicable settlement, will be submitted to two arbitrators, one appointed by each of the parties hereto, and the two arbitrators so chosen shall, if unable to agree, choose a third arbitrator as umpire without unnecessary delay. The decision in writing signed by those assenting thereto of any two of the arbitrators shall be final and binding on the parties hereto. Arbitration under this provision shall be carried out in Japan, and the costs thereof, including compensation to the arbitrators, will be borne by the party against whom the award is made.

55. 9 U.S.C. §5 (1964).

56. Code of Civil Procedure, Art. 789(2).

57. See Takeyoshi Kawashima, "Chōtei to chūsai" (Conciliation and arbitration), 18 *Bōeki kuremu to chūsai* (No. 165) 2 (1971).

58. Recently several useful references for commercial arbitration have appeared: in Japanese, Morii, *Kokusai shōji chūsai;* and in English, *e.g.*, Martin Domke, *The Law and Practice of Commercial Arbitration* (Mundelein, Ill.: Callaghan & Co., 1968); Sanders, ed., *International Arbitration: Labor Amicorum for Martin Domke;* Seide, *A Dictionary of Arbitration.*

59. See Comment (Donald P. Swisher), "International Commercial Arbitration under the United Nations Convention and the Amended Federal Arbitration Statute," 47 *Wash. L. Rev.* 441–488 (1972); John P. McMahon, "Implementation of the United Nations Convention on Foreign Arbitral Awards in the United States," 2 *J. Maritime Law and Commerce* 735 (1971); and Gerald Aksen, "American Arbitration Accession Arrives in the Age of Aquarius: United States Implements United Nations Convention on the Recognition and Enforcement of Foreign Arbitral Awards," 3 *Southwestern U. L. Rev.*, 1–38 (1971).

60. One might argue that, even though patent infringement claims may not be "com-

merce" (see note 2 above), they are "commercial" (appertaining to "commerce"). For legislative history on "commercial" see G. W. Haight, *Convention on the Recognition and Enforcement of Foreign Arbitral Awards: Summary and Analysis of United Nations Conference, May–June 1958* (New York, 1958), p. 7; also Leonard V. Quigley, "Accession by the U.S. to the UN Convention on the Recognition and Enforcement of Foreign Arbitral Awards," 70 *Yale L. J.* 1049 (1961); Paolo Contini, "International Commercial Arbitration: The UN Convention on the Recognition and Enforcement of Foreign Arbitral Awards," 8 *Am. J. of Comp. L.* 283; Allen Sultan, "The UN Arbitration Convention and U.S. Policy," 53 *Am. J. of Int'l. Law* 807 (1959).

61. 9 USCA §203 (Supp. 1971).
62. 9 USCA §204 (Supp. 1971).
63. 9 USCA §205 (Supp. 1971).
64. 9 USCA §206 (Supp. 1971).
65. 9 USCA §207 (Supp. 1971).
66. Charles H. Sullivan, "United States Treaty Policy on Commercial Arbitration—1920–46," in *International Trade Arbitration*, ed. Domke, p. 35; Herman Walker, "Commercial Arbitration in United States Treaties," 11 *Arb. J.* 68–84 (1956); S. A. Bayith, "Treaty Law of Private Arbitration," 10 *Arb. J.* 188, 191 (1955).
67. FCN Treaty, Art. IV (2):

> Contracts entered into between nationals and companies of either Party and nationals and companies of the other Party, that provide for the settlement by arbitration of controversies, shall not be deemed unenforceable within the territories of such other Party merely on the grounds that the place designated for the arbitration proceedings is outside such territories or that the nationality of one or more of the arbitrators is not that of such other Party. Awards duly rendered pursuant to any such contracts, which are final and enforceable under the laws of the place where rendered, shall be deemed conclusive in enforcement proceedings brought before the courts of competent jurisdiction of either Party, and shall be entitled to be declared enforceable by such courts, except where found contrary to public policy. When so declared, such awards shall be entitled to privileges and measures of enforcement appertaining to awards rendered locally. It is understood, however, that awards rendered outside the United States of America shall be entitled in any court in any State thereof only to the same measure of recognition as awards rendered in other States thereof.

68. See, *e.g.*, *Compania de Transportes de ma S.A.* v. *Mataichi K.K.*, 4 Kakyū minshū 502 (Tokyo Dist. Ct., 10 Apr. 1953), where the Japanese court rejected defendant's argument that since the contract was made in New York the United States federal rule (*i.e.*, a suit should only be stayed) should apply. The court followed the Japanese rule and dismissed, holding that the question concerned procedure; so, on the choice-of-law point, the law of the forum applies to the question of what remedy is available to enforce an arbitration clause in case of a violative Japanese suit.
69. See, *e.g.*, *Bank of Pittsburgh* v. *United Elec. Coal Co.*, 16 Del. Ch. 151, 142 Atl. 368, 370 (Ch. Ct. 1928), 6 A.L.R. 2d 910n. The Delaware court refused to enjoin an Illinois suit alleged to be a breach of an arbitration agreement.
70. For United States discussion, see Sol Neil Corbin, "Enforceability of Contractual Agreements for Dispute Settlement Abroad," in *International Trade Arbitration*, ed. Domke, p. 251.
71. An exceptional case is *San Martine Compania de Navegacion, S.A.* v. *Saguenay Terminals, Ltd.*, 293 F. 2d 796 (9th Cir. 1961), where initially the District Court in Hawaii seems to have ordered arbitration in Montreal under 9 USCA §4 (1964), though it may have only stayed the suit (lower court opinion unreported).
72. Compare *Giuffre* v. *The Magdalene Vinnen and North German Lloyd*, 152 F. Supp. 123 (E.D.N.Y. 1957) (action stayed in favor of arbitration in Bremen), with *Chemical Carriers* v. *L. Smit & Co. Internationale S.*, 154 F. Supp. 886 (S.D.N.Y. 1957) (prorogation in favor of District Court, Rotterdam, not enforced). See Annot., "Validity of

Contractual Provisions Limiting Place or Court in Which Action May Be Brought," 56 *A.L.R.* 2d 300, 306 (1957), for cases showing that the weight of authority is against the effectiveness of prorogation clauses to prevent inconsistent suits elsewhere. For recent unenforceable prorogation clauses, see *Huntley* v. *Alejandre*, 139 So. 2d 911 (Fla. 1962), citing an older New York case, *Kent* v. *Universal Film Mfg. Co.*, 200 App. Div. 539, 193 N.Y. Supp. 838 (1922) (decided, however, on a slightly different point); *Kyler* v. *United States Trotting Ass'n.*, 12 App. Div. 874, 210 N.Y.S. 2d 25 (1961); *Arsenis* v. *Atlantic Tankers, Ltd.*, 39 Misc. 2d 124, 240 N.Y.S. 2d 69 (Civ. Ct. 1963); *Carbon Black Export* v. *S.S. Monrosa*, 254 F. 2d 297 (5th Cir. 1958). A prorogation clause was upheld in *W. H. Muller & Co.* v. *Swedish Am. Line, Ltd.*, 224 F. 2d 806 (2d Cir.) *cert. denied*, 350 U.S. 903 (1955); *Takemura* v. *S.S. Tsuneshima Maru*, 197 F. Supp. 909 (S.D.N.Y. 1960).

On the United States preference for foreign arbitral contracts and awards, see Corbin, "Enforceability of Contractual Agreements," in *International Trade Arbitration*, ed. Domke, p. 252; and for reciprocity problems of enforcing United States judgments in Japan, see Albert E. Ehrenzweig, Sueo Ikehara, and Norman Jensen, *American-Japanese Private International Law*, Parker School Bilateral Studies in Private International Law, No. 12 (Dobbs Ferry, N.Y.: Oceana Publications, 1964), p. 31.

On prorogation clauses see Albert A. Ehrenzweig, *A Treatise on the Conflicts of Laws* (St. Paul: West Publ. Co., 1962), pp. 148–53; G. Merle Bergman, "Contractual Restrictions on the Forum," 48 *Cal. L. Rev.* 438 (1960); Willis L. M. Reese, "The Contractual Forum: Situations in the United States," 13 *Am. J. Comp. L.* 187 (1964).

It is quite clear under the Japanese law that no requirement of "mutual guarantee" (reciprocity), as required to enforce a foreign judgment, is needed to enforce an arbitral agreement. See Hajime Kaneko, *Minji soshōhō taikei* (Study of the law of civil procedure) (Tokyo: Sakai shoten, 1958); Akira Mikazuki, "Minji soshōhō" (Law of civil procedure) 254, in 35 *Hōritsugaku zenshū* (1960); Kikuo Kōriki, Tōru Ichikawa, and Shigeo Satō, "Bōeki to hōritsu" (Trade and law) 352–79, in 8 *Bōeki jitsumu kōza* (Tokyo: Yūhikaku, 1962). For the Japanese rule of party autonomy generally, see *Hōrei* (Law concerning the application of laws in general), Art. 7 (Law No. 10, 1898), in 1 EHS No. 1001.

For comparative coverage see Arthur Lenhoff, "The Parties' Choice of a Forum: 'Prorogation Agreements,' " 15 *Rutgers L. Rev.* 414 (1961). This exhaustive study of prorogation in the United States and most European countries unfortunately has no discussion of the Japanese law. It is said that clauses excluding domestic jurisdiction are upheld generally in Austria, Belgium, Brazil, Denmark, France, Germany, Greece, Norway, Poland, Sweden, and Switzerland, and in the Netherlands and Italy they are upheld with some qualifications; while in Spain, Portugal, and Hungary derogations of domestic courts are generally denied enforcement, as they usually are in all but the most progressive courts in the United States (*e.g.*, Second Circuit Court of Appeals, New York and Massachusetts). Ibid., p. 419 ff.

73. See Domke, *Law and Practice of Commercial Arbitration*, p. 20.

Of course, unless only federal law clearly applies, there is no single actually applicable "American" arbitration law until the problem can be limited by an actual case with its "American" terminus fixed in one of the fifty-one American jurisdictions (fifty states plus federal). For the practitioner actual cases are often conveniently narrowed in "American" law by the facts of the transaction. But often he too has to grapple with the multiple possibilities of governing law, because prospectively no one can predict for sure where his multi-state client may sue or be sued on the contract he is drafting. Of course, even the federal jurisdiction in its substantive law aspects is sometimes not a singular unit because of the frequent splits among the circuits as yet unresolved by the Supreme Court. For example, in arbitral law it was not known whether the Second Circuit doctrine of "separability" (see text accompanying notes 113–22 *infra*.) would be upheld, until the Supreme Court so decided. *Prima Paint Corp.* v. *Flood & Conklin Mfg. Co.*, 388 U.S. 395, 87 S. Ct. 1801 (1967). So there are even more than fifty-one potential jurisdictions on certain issues, at least temporarily.

Except for the initial general classifications of the statutes of all of the fifty-one jurisdictions (see notes 63–67 *infra* and accompanying text), we have used the federal law, the restatements, and, where appropriate, citation to the law of several key states (*e.g.*, New York, California, or Washington) as an approximation of "American" law.

74. Though now superseded, the old Restatement, Contracts §550 (1932), reflects the common-law history:

> Bargain for Arbitration.
>
> Except as stated in §558, a bargain to arbitrate either an existing or a possible future dispute is not illegal, unless the agreed terms of arbitration are unfair, but will not be specifically enforced, and only nominal damages are recoverable for its breach. Nor is any bargain to arbitrate a bar to an action on the claim to which the bargain related.

Except as stated in §558, a bargain to arbitrate either an existing or a possible future dispute, without statutory provisions to the contrary, is revocable. The new section corresponding to the old §550 has not yet been released.

75. Besides citations at note 58 above, see, *e.g.*, articles on international arbitration, some dealing with American phases, in Domke, ed., *International Trade Arbitration*. For older law, see Wesley Sturges, *Commercial Arbitrations and Awards* (Kansas City: Vernon Law Book Company, 1930). Corbin, *Contracts* §§1431–1444B (1962) Vol. 6A, with supplements, is a useful recent coverage of the American case law on contractual points. Domke, *Commercial Arbitration*, is a brief up-to-date description mainly for non-lawyers; and Lazarus *et al.*, *Resolving Business Disputes*, is a very well done empirical study of the United States arbitration process, which gives a quantified picture of the uses of arbitration in various contexts (labor, trade, accidents), its efficiency in operation, and attitudes of both businessmen and lawyers toward it.

Some of the more useful articles dealing with commercial arbitration are: Daniel G. Collins, "Arbitration and the Uniform Commercial Code," 41 *N.Y. U. L. Rev.* 736 (1966); Charles Horowitz, "Guides for Resorting to Commercial Arbitration," 8 *Prac. Law.* 67–84 (1962); Heinrich Kronstein, "Arbitration Is Power," 38 *N.Y. U. L. Rev.* 661 (1963); Soia Mentschikoff, "Commercial Arbitration," 61 *Colum. L. Rev.* 846 (1961); Wesley A. Sturges and Richard E. Reckson, "Common-Law and Statutory Arbitration: Problems Arising From Their Coexistence," 46 *Minn. L. Rev.* 819 (1962); Symposium, "Commercial Arbitration," 17 *Law & Contemp. Probl.* 417–710 (1952); Symposium, "Arbitration and the Courts," 58 *Nw. U. L. Rev.* 466–582 (1963); Note, "Judicial Supervision of Commercial Arbitration," 53 *Georgetown L. J.* 1079 (1965).

76. Alabama, Colorado, Delaware, Georgia, Idaho, Iowa, Kansas, Kentucky, Mississippi, Missouri, Montana, Nebraska, New Mexico, North Carolina, North Dakota, Oklahoma, South Carolina, South Dakota, Tennessee, Utah, Vermont, and West Virginia. Recent amendments have improved the following: Alaska (1968); Arkansas (1968); and Indiana (1969); and judicial decisions have enforced arbitration without a modern statute in Colorado and Nevada.

77. Paul L. Sayre, "Development of Commercial Arbitration Law," 37 *Yale L. J.* 595 (1928); Earl S. Wolaver, "The Historical Background of Commercial Arbitation," 83 *U. Pa. L. Rev.* 132 (1934). Before the 1925 statute, federal courts also refused to enforce clauses covering future disputes. *Tatsuma K.K. Kaisha* v. *Prescott*, 4 F. 2d 670 (9th Cir. 1925).

For recent state cases reflecting this common-law doctrine refusing to enforce arbitral clauses see, *e.g.*, *Green* v. *Wolff*, 372 P. 2d 427 (Mont. 1962); *Fenster* v. *Makovsky*, 67 So. 2d 427 (Fla. 1953); *Skinner* v. *Gaither Corp.*, 234 N.C. 385, 67 S.E. 2d 267 (1951); *Boughton* v. *Farmers Ins. Exch.*, 354 P. 2d 1085 (Okla. 1960); *Wilson* v. *Gregg*, 208 Okla. 291, 255 P. 2d 517 (1953); *Barnhart* v. *Civil Serv. Employees Ins. Co.*, 16 Utah 2d 223, 398 P. 2d 873 (1965); *King* v. *Beale*, 198 Va. 802, 96 S.E. 2d 765 (1957).

Note that *Hill* v. *Mercury Record Corp.*, 26 Ill. App. 2d 350, 168 N.E. 2d 461 (1960), and *Huntington Corp.* v. *Inwood Constr. Co.*, 348 S.W. 2d 442 (Tex. Civ. App. 1961), refused enforcement of an arbitral clause, which would be enforced now since the passage of new statutes in 1961 and 1965 respectively.

78. The twenty-eight states include most of those important in U.S.-Japanese business: Alaska (1968); Arkansas (1968); Arizona (1962); California (1925, revised 1961); Connecticut (1958); Florida (1957); Hawaii (1955); Illinois (1961); Indiana (1969); Louisiana (1951); Maine (1968); Maryland (1965); Massachusetts (1961); Michigan (court rules, 1963); Minnesota (1961); Nevada (1969); New Hampshire (1955); New Jersey (1923); New York (1920, revised 1962 and 1963); Ohio (1955); Oregon (1955); Pennsylvania (1926); Rhode Island (1966); Texas (1965); Virginia (1968); Washington (1943); Wisconsin (1938); and Wyoming (1961). Of these, the following have, with varying changes, adopted the Uniform Arbitration Act of 1956 superseding the prior Uniform Act of 1926: Alaska, Arizona, Florida, Illinois, Indiana, Maine, Minnesota, Maryland, Massachusetts, Michigan, Nevada, New York, Texas, and Wyoming.

Two other states, Colorado and Nevada, have made arbitral clauses (including foreign arbitration) enforceable, though not by statute in Colorado yet. Respectively: *Ezell* v. *Rocky Mtn. Bean & Elevator Co.*, 76 Colo. 409, 232 P. 680 (1925); and *United Ass'n. of Journeymen & Apprentices of Plumbing* v. *Stine*, 76 Nev. 189, 351 P. 2d 965 (1960).

79. U.S.C. §§1–14 (1964) and 9 U.S.C. §§200–208. For coverage of the act see Swisher, "International Commercial Arbitration," 47 *Wash. L. Rev.* 457, and Clifford V. Hynning and George W. Haight, "International Commercial Arbitration," 48 *A.B.A.J.* 236 (1962); Wesley A. Sturges and Irving Olds Murphy, "Some Confusing Matters Relating to Arbitration under the U.S. Arbitration Act," 17 *Law & Contemp. Prob.* 580, 586 (1952); Symposium, "Scope of the United States Arbitration Act in Commercial Arbitration: Problems in Federalism," 58 *Nw. U. L. Rev.* 46 (1963).

80. See Maynard E. Pirsig, "Some Comments on Arbitration Legislation and the Uniform Act," 10 *Vand. L. Rev.* 685 (1957).

81. United States Arbitration Act, 9 U.S.C. §3 (1964); *California Lima Bean Growers' Ass'n.* v. *Mankowitz*, 9 N.J. Misc. 362, 154 Atl. 532 (Cir. Ct. 1931); *Amtorg Trading Corp.* v. *Camden Fibre Mills*, 304 N.Y. 519, 109 N.E. 2d 606 (1952); *Nippon Ki-Itō Kaisha* v. *Ewing-Thomas Corp.*, 313 Pa. 442, 170 Atl. 286 (1934); Cf. *James H. Rhodes & Co.* v. *Chausovsky*, 137 *N.J.L.* 459, 60 A. 2d 623 (Sup. Ct. 1948).

82. *The Silverbrook*, 18 F. 2d 144 (E. D. La. 1927), first suggested the interpretation limiting §4 to orders compelling domestic arbitration; the court, on that premise, also denied a stay under §3. Later courts (*e.g.*, *Danielson* v. *Entre Rios Rys.*, 22 F. 2d 326 [D. Md. 1927], distinguished §3 stays of lawsuits pending foreign arbitrations from §4 orders to compel foreign arbitration, thus establishing §4 as an aid to domestic arbitration. Later, heavy reliance has been placed on dicta in *Shanferoke Coal & Supply Corp.* v. *Westchester Service Corp.*, 293 U.S. 449 (1934), a §3 case without foreign elements; see, *e.g.*, *Batson Yarn & Fabrics Machinery Group, Inc.* v. *Saurer-Allma GmbH-Allgauer Maschinenbau*, 311 F. Supp. 68 (D. Ct. So. Car.) (1970). For a rare case where apparently in the background there had been a §4 order compelling foreign arbitration is *San Martine Compania de Navegacion, S.A.* v. *Saguenay Germinals, Ltd.*, 293 F. 2d 796 (9th Cir. 1961), where the court was then asked to enforce the foreign award.

83. 9 USCA §§203 and 205 (Supp. 1971).

84. UN Convention (1958), Art. 1(3); *cf.* 9 U.S.C. §1 (1964).

85. *Prima Paint* v. *Flood & Conklin Mfg. Co.*, 388 U.S. 395, 87 S. Ct. 1801 (1967); also see *Robert Lawrence Co.* v. *Devonshire Fabrics, Inc.*, 271 F. 2d 402 (2d Cir. 1959), *cert. granted*, 362 U.S. 909. *cert. dismissed per stipulation*, 364 U.S. 801 (1960).

86. Even after the *Prima* case there remain questions as to the duty of states to follow it in "commerce" cases. Note that the New York court, *Ludwig Monwinckels Rederi* v. *Dow Chemical Co.*, 297 N.Y.S. 2d 1011 (1969), held that the question of whether the underlying claim to be arbitrated by a clause in a charter party was time barred was not for the court per N.Y.C.P.L.R. 7502(b), but for arbitration as required by the Federal Arbitration Act (9 USCA §4), though Justice Steven dissenting properly pointed out that the U.S. Supreme Court had left the question open as to whether state courts must apply the federal act, citing the concurring opinion of Justice Harlan in *Prima Paint Corp.* v. *Flood and Conklin Mfg. Co.*, 388 U.S. 395, 87 C. Ct. 1801 at 1807 (1967).

For other difficulties with this rule: *Lummus Co.* v. *Commonwealth Oil Refinery Co.*, 280 F. 2d 915 (1st Cir. 1960), *cert. denied*, 364 U.S. 911 (1960), case on the problem of characterizing arbitration; also *Continental Ins. Co.* v. *Furudono*, Hōritsu shimbun (No. 3904) 5 (Tokyo App. Ch., 15 Aug. 1935). For a survey of these problems see Symposium, "Scope of the U.S. Arbitration Act," *Nw. U.L. Rev.*, p. 469.

87. *Bernhardt* v. *Polygraphic Co. of Am.*, 350 U.S. 198 (1956); *Cook* v. *Kuljan Corp.*, 201 F. Supp. 531 (E.D. Pa. 1962).

88. See note 71 *supra*.

89. Note, though, that for all practical purposes Texas still has no modern statute, because of the anomaly of Art. 224 of the new Texas General Arbitration Act requiring that the parties' lawyers sign arbitral agreements before such agreements are enforceable against the parties. Texas Laws 1965, Ch. 689, Art. 224. See Paul Carrington, "The 1965 General Arbitration Statute of Texas," 20 *Sw. L. J.* 21 (1966).

90. *United Ass'n. of Journeymen & Apprentices of Plumbing* v. *Stine*, 76 Nev. 189, 351 P. 2d 965 (1960); *Ezell* v. *Rocky Mt. Bean & Elevator Co.*, 76 Colo. 409, 232 P. 680 (1925); and *Park Constr. Co.* v. *Independent School Dist. No. 32*, 209 Minn. 182, 296 N.W. 475 (1941), 135 A.L.R. 59.

91. Cal. Civ. Pro. Code §§1280–94.2 (West Supp. 1966); N.Y. Civ. Prac. Law §§7501–14 (McKinney 1963). See Eddy S. Feldmann, "Arbitration Modernized—the New California Arbitration Act," 34 *So. Cal. L. Rev.* 413 (1961).

92. For judicial statements to this effect see, *e.g.*, *Necchi* v. *Necchi Sewing Mach. Sales Corp.*, 348 F. 2d 693, 696 (2d Cir. 1965); *Miller* v. *Allstate Ins. Co.*, 238 F. Supp. 565, 567 (W.D. Pa. 1965).

93. See, for prior English language literature, citation at note 20 *supra*. The Japanese code provisions are: Code of Civil Procedure, Arts. 786–805; and see interpretive treatise, Noboru Koyama, "Chōteihō, chūsaihō" (Conciliation law, arbitration law), in 38 *Hōritsugaku zenshū* 51–106 (1958), on Japanese domestic arbitration.

94. *K.K. Kobayashi Shōten* v. *Kenlick Far East K.K.*, 9 Kakyū minshū 111 (Tokyo Dist. Ct., 25 Jan. 1958). Note that only Japanese Supreme Court cases can be cited with something like the authority of American case law. However, since there are so few Japanese Supreme Court cases reported in the field of arbitration, we have cited certain lower court cases that we have found related to points discussed, not because they are binding authority but because they illustrate what the Japanese lower courts have done in a certain concrete instance and because they would probably be followed in the same court. Also they may in some degree be persusaive in future cases in other courts, where they are consulted. See also *Texas Co.* v. *Gōshi Kaisha Taiheiyō Shōkai*, Hōritsu shimbun (No. 2168) 13 (Tokyo App. Ch., 7 Mar. 1923); *Tōwa Kōgyō K.K.* v. *Mitsui Sempaku K.K.*, 1 Kakyū minshū (Yokohama Dist. Ct., Nov. 1950).

95. *Compania de Transportes de ma S.A.* v. *Mataichi K.K.*, 4 Kakyū minshū 502 (Tokyo Dist. Ct., 10 Apr. 1953).

96. *E.g.*, in *K.K. Kobayashi Shōten* v. *Kenlick Far East K.K.*, 9 Kakyū minshū 111 (Tokyo Dist. Ct., 25 Jan. 1958), the court appointed an arbitrator under Code of Civil Procedure, Art. 789 (2), when the defendant failed to do so. Several prior cases also so hold, citing *Hōrei*, Art. 7: *e.g.*, *A. D. Rarande* v. *The Oriental Hotel, Ltd.*, 24 Minroku 865 (Gr. Ct. Cass., 15 Apr. 1918); *Compania de Transportes de ma S.A.* v. *Mataichi K.K.*, 4 Kakyū minshū 502 (Tokyo Dist. Ct., 10 Apr. 1953).

There is no specific rule in Japan covering prorogation such as *Hōrei*, Art. 7, supporting the parties' choice-of-law. However, a party's choice-of-forum among domestic courts is valid (Code of Civil Procedure, Art. 25), and similarly the commentators state that prorogation of a foreign tribunal, judicial or arbitral, is valid. Hajime Kaneko, "Saibanhō" (Law of trials), in 34 *Hōritsugaku zenshū* 17 (1959); Tarō Kawakami, "Kokusai shōji chūsai no shōrai" (The future of international commercial arbitration), 7 *Bōeki kuremu to chūsai* (No. 3) 121–125 (1960).

The only treatment in English seems to be a paragraph in Ehrenzweig, Ikehara, and Jensen, *American-Japanese Private International Law*, p. 29; and Gardiner, "Japanese

Arbitration Law," p. 89. The latter article is outdated, and note that it seems to assume erroneously that the arbitration law of Japan effective from 1891 (Code of Civil Procedure, Arts 786–805) was enacted after World War II.

97. *K.K. Kobayashi Shōten* v. *Kenlick Far East K.K.*, 9 Kakyū minshū 111 (Tokyo Dist. Ct., 25 Jan. 1958).

98. 13 Kakyū minshū 338 (Tokyo High Ct., 5 Mar. 1962).

99. 10 Kakyū minshū 1711 (Tokyo Dist. Ct., 20 Aug. 1959).

100. Compare Yasuhiro Fujita's comment on this case in *Hanrei jihō* (No. 242) 33 (1970).

101. 9 U.S.C. §3 (1964); *Altshul Stern & Co., Inc.* v. *Mitsui Bussan Kaisha, Ltd.*, 385 F. 2d 158 (1967); *Oregon-Pacific Forest Prods. Corp.* v. *Welsh Panel Co.*, 248 F. Supp. 903 (D. Ore. 1965), cited the FCN Treaty also; and, of course, the UN Convention and 9 USCA §206 (Supp. 171) make this remedy more accessible where arbitration is provided for in the U.S. or Japan.

102. See, *e.g.*, *Clogston* v. *Schiff-Lang Co.*, 2 Cal. 2d 414, 41 P. 2d 555 (1935); *In Petition of Uraga Dock Co.*, 6 App. Div. 2d 443, 179 N.Y.S. 2d 474 (1958), *aff'd.* 6 N.Y. 2d 773, 159 N.E. 2d 212, 186 N.Y.S. 2d 669 (1959). But *cf. Vector S. S. Co.* v. *Mitsubishi Bank, Ltd.*, 12 App. Div. 2d 910, 210 N.Y.S. 2d 910 (1961).

See also Wash. Rev. Code Ch. 7.04 (1956); Uniform Arbitration Act §2 (c), which reads: "If an issue referable to arbitration under the alleged agreement is involved in an action or proceeding pending in a court having jurisdiction to hear applications under Subdivision (a) of this Section, the application shall be made therein. Otherwise and subject to Section 18, the application may be made in any court of competent jurisdiction."

This act has been adopted with varying modifications in Arizona, Florida, Illinois, Minnesota, Maryland, Massachusetts, Michigan, New York, Texas, and Wyoming.

103. *Hinode Kagaku Kōgyō K.K.* v. *Sankō Kisen K.K.*, 10 Kakyū minshū 970 (Osaka Dist. Ct., 11 May 1959).

104. *Compania de Transportes de ma S.A.* v. *Mataichi K.K.*, 4 Kakyū minshū 502 (Tokyo Dist. Ct., 10 Apr. 1953). See also domestic dismissal cases: *Utsuro* v. *Sasatani*, 19 Minroku 8 (Gr. Ct. Cass., 23 Jan. 1913); *Yamada* v. *Bellini*, 6 Minroku 142 (Gr. Ct. Cass., 27 Nov. 1900).

But note that the right to arbitrate will not be enforced by dismissal if the defendant fails to assert the arbitration clause as a defense until after nine hearings in the suit. See *K.K. Kyokutō Sekkei Jimusho* v. *Edgar P. Sharp*, 11 Kakyū minshū 2450 (Tokyo Dist. Ct., 7 Dec. 1960); *cf. Hashimoto* v. *Katayama*, Hōritsu shimbun (No. 1140) 28 (Gr. Ct. Cass., 15 May 1916). For a similar United States result, see *American Locomotive Co.* v. *Chemical Research Corp.*, 171 F. 2d 115 (6th Cir., 1948); *Radiator Specialty Co.* v. *Cannon Mills, Inc.*, 97 F. 2d 318 (4th Cir., 1938), 117 A.L.R. 299; *Hill* v. *Mercury Record Corp.*, 26 Ill. App. 2d 350, 168 N.E. 2d 461, 466 (1960) (decided before the changes in the Illinois statute in 1961).

105. *Compania de Transportes de ma S.A.* v. *Mataichi K.K.*, 4 Kakyū minshū 502 (Tokyo Dist. Ct., 10 Apr. 1953).

106. 10 Kakyū minshū 970 (Osaka Dist. Ct., 11 May 1959).

107. *Compania de Transportes de ma S.A.* v. *Mataichi K.K.*, 4 Kakyū minshū 502 (Tokyo Dist. Ct., 10 Apr. 1953).

108. See, *e.g.*, *Boughton* v. *Farmers Ins. Exch.*, 354 P. 2d 1085 (Okla. 1960). See Annot., 135 A.L.R. 79 (1941).

109. *Cf. Restatement* (second), Conflict of Laws §218 (1971), which provides that the law governing the validity of the arbitration contract determines whether a suit can be brought in violation of its terms; but the law of the forum governs the method of enforcement. Ibid., §219.

110. See citations in notes 85 and 86, *supra*.

111. Koyama, "Chōteihō, chūsaihō," *Hōritsugaku zenshū*, p. 93.

112. In *MacDonald, Ltd. & I. H. MacDonald* v. *Tomoi Trade Yūgen Kaisha*, unre-

ported case (Tokyo Dist. Ct., 6 May 1966) (consolidated cases: 1959 [*wa*] No. 9286; 1962 [*wa*] No. 4868; 1964 [*wa*] No. 2386), the court determined, against the challenge of the losing party, that an arbitral contract was created between the parties.

113. See 6A Corbin, *Contracts* §§1444, 1444A (1962).

114. The key case was *Robert Lawrence Co.* v. *Devonshire Fabrics. Inc*, 271 F. 2d 402 (2d Cir. 1959).

115. 388 U.S. 395, 87 S. Ct. 1801 (1967).

116. See Justice Black's dissent in *Prima Paint Corp.* v. *Flood and Conklin Mfg. Co.*, 388 U.S. 407 at 416, 87 S. Ct. 1808 at 1812 (1967).

117. 271 F. 2d 4031 (2d Cir. 1959).

118. Collins, "Arbitration and the Uniform Commercial Code," *N.Y. U. L. Rev.*, p. 736; Note, "Judicial Supervision," *Georgetown L. J.*, p. 1079. For an earlier discussion see Arthur Nussbaum, "The 'Separability Doctrine' in American and Foreign Arbitration," 17 *N.Y. U. L. Rev.* 609 (1940).

119. *Prima Paint Corp.* v. *Flood and Conklin Mfg. Co.*, 388 U.S. 395, 87 S. Ct. 1808 (1967).

120. *El Hoss Eng'r. & Transp. Co.* v. *American Independent Oil Co.*, 287 F. 2d 346, 349 (2d Cir.), *cert. denied*, 368 U.S. 837 (1961).

121. But see Wesley Sturges, "Fraudulent Inducement as a Defense to the Enforcement of Arbitration Contracts," 36 *Yale L. J.* 866, 873 (1927), where it is suggested that the presumption be for separability. This comment is perhaps the earliest source of this questionable doctrine.

122. 6A Corbin, *Contracts* §1444 (1962), criticizes several decisions that fail to observe this point. See *Walker* v. *Maged*, 154 *N.Y. L. J.* (No. 97) 15 Col. 7 (Sup. Ct. 1965), where plaintiffs were compelled to arbitrate because they were found to have affirmed the allegedly fraudulent contract by relying on the existence of the contract, rather than seeking rescission.

123. Note that in *Prima Paint Corp.* v. *Flood and Conklin Mfg. Co.*, 360 F. 2d 315 (2d Cir. 1966), the plaintiff did seek rescission, but the court found the arbitral clause separable and compelled arbitration of the question of fraud in the inducement of the container contract. Though the court noted the importance of rescission of the container contract, still it found the arbitral contract to be separable (not rescinded) because the plaintiff did not allege fraud in the inducement of the arbitral clause as such. Perhaps there was none, but presumably there often would be in such cases, and where there is, it is critical to raise the point properly.

124. Federal Judge Medina recognizes this point in *Robert Lawrence Co.* v. *Devonshire Fabrics, Inc.*, 271 F. 2d 402, 412 (2d Cir. 1959), citing *Wrap-Vertiser Corp.* v. *Plotnick*, 3 N.Y. 2d 17, 143 N.E. 2d 366, 163 N.Y.S. 2d 639 (1957).

125. *Petition of Uraga Dock Co.*, 6 App. Div. 2d 443, 179 N.Y.S. 2d 474 (1958), *aff'd.* 6 N.Y. 2d 773, 159 N.E. 2d 212, 186 N.Y.S. 2d 669 (1959).

126. In the matter of *Evercycle Corp. & Maratta*, 9 N.Y. 2d 339, 174 N.E. 2d 463, 214 N.Y.S. 2d 353 (1961).

127. See the concurring and dissenting opinions in *Exercycle*, *supra* note 126.

128. See *Necchi* v. *Necchi Sewing Mach. Sales Corp.*, 348 F. 2d 693, 696 (2d Cir. 1965), where *United Steelworkers* v. *Warrior & Gulf Nav. Co.*, 363 U.S. 574 (1960), is cited to support dictum that the parties might empower arbitrators to determine the *scope* of the arbitral clause. See Paul R. Hayes, *Labor Arbitration: A Dissenting View* (Yale U. Press, 1966), pp. 9–10, for the view that even in labor the Supreme Court's expansive concept of the role of arbitration as reflected in Justice Douglas's opinions in *United Steelworkers* v. *American Mfg. Co.*, 363 U.S. 564 (1960); *United Steelworkers* v. *Warrior & Gulf Nav. Co.*, 363 U.S. 574 (1960); *United Steelworkers* v. *Enterprise Wheel & Car Corp.* 363 U.S. 593 (1960), is unsound and inconsistent with the major authorities. Whether or not one agrees with Hayes as to labor arbitration, there is surely enough difference between commercial and labor arbitration to counsel care in cross-citing authorities, lest the admitted consensual foundations of commercial arbitration be

undermined. See Archibald Cox, "Reflections Upon Labor Arbitration," 72 *Harv. L. Rev.* 1482, 1490–91 (1959). Ibid., p. 1498: "[T]here was some truth to the saying that arbitration was a substitute not for a lawsuit but for a strike." This itself expresses a major difference (interdependence). In commercial transactions arbitration is largely only a substitute for a lawsuit.

129. This reason is given in the case that originated the separability doctrine, *Robert Lawrence Co.* v. *Devonshire Fabrics, Inc.*, 271 F. 2d 402, 410 (2d Cir. 1959).

130. Matter of *Kinoshita & Co.*, 287 F. 2d 951 (2d Cir. 1961).

131. Petition of *Uraga Dock Co.*, 6 App. Div. 2d 443, 179 N.Y.S. 2d 474 (1958), *aff'd.* 6 N.Y. 2d 773, 159 N.E. 2d 212, 186 N.Y.S. 2d 669 (1959).

132. See Ōuchi, "Problems of Competence," *Phil. Int'l. L. J.*, pp. 16, 66; Nussbaum, "The 'Separability Doctrine,' " *N.Y. U. L. Rev.*, p. 609.

133. See the rather typical exchanges of boiler-plate in *Oregon-Pacific Forest Prods. Corp.* v. *Welsh Panel Co.*, 248 F. Supp. 903 (D. Ore. 1965) (considering Mitsui & Co.'s form, court preliminarily determined that an arbitration clause was a part of the contract); *S. M. Wolff Co.* v. *Tulkoff*, 9 N.Y. 2d 356, 174 N.E. 2d 478, 214 N.Y.S. 2d 374 (1961) (telephone exchange followed by "Bought Note" including arbitral clause); *Matter of Arbitration between Doughboy Indus., Inc. & Pantasote Co.*, 17 App. Div. 2d 216, 233 N.Y.S. 2d 488 (1962) (Appellate Division reversed the New York Supreme Court's denial of a stay of arbitration, finding the arbitration clause in the form last mailed was not a part of the contract). Note the drastic solution to inadvertent agreement found in the Texas statute of 1965. An arbitral clause was only enforceable if "concluded upon the advice of counsel to both parties as evidenced by counsels' signatures thereto"), Texas Laws 1965, Ch. 689, Aft. 224.

134. Domke, *Law and Practice of Commercial Arbitration*, §37.1; Sturges, *Commercial Arbitrations*, p. 520.

135. But see Frances T. Freeman Jalet, "Judicial Review of Arbitration: The Judicial Attitude," 45 *Cornell L. Q.* 519, 532 (1960), stating that although courts "pledge allegiance" to awards, this in practice is often lip service only.

136. See Sturges, *Commercial Arbitration*, pp. 2–17, where he says that nearly all states have both common-law and statutory arbitration systems concurrently. Accord, Sturges and Reckson, "Common-Law and Statutory Arbitration," *Minn. L. Rev.*, p. 819. Note, however, that in Washington statutory arbitration seems to have pre-empted common-law arbitration. *Greyhound Corp.* v. *Division* 1384, 44 Wn. 2d 808, 271 P. 2d 689 (1954). *Cf. In re Arbitration of Puget Sound Bridge & Dredging Co.* v. *Lake Washington Shipyards*, 1 Wn. 2d 401, 96 P. 2d 257 (1939) (construing prior statute); *Dickie Mfg. Co.* v. *Sound Constr. Eng'r. Co.*, 92 Wash. 316, 159 Pac. 129 (1916) (same). But see Wesley A. Sturges and William W. Sturges, "Some Confusing Matters Relating to Arbitration in Washington," 25 *Wash. L. Rev.* 16 (1950).

137. *E.g.*, 9 U.S.C. §9 (1964).

138. Japanese Code of Civil Procedure, Art. 802 (in 2 EHS No. 2300 [1955]):

(1) Execution to be undertaken by virtue of an award shall be made only when an execution judgment has been rendered for the admissibility thereof.

(2) The foregoing judgment shall not be rendered in case there exists a reason under which cancellation of award may be moved.

139. Enforcement of foreign awards has seldom occurred in the United States courts; for a rare example, see *Standard Magnesium Corp.* v. *Fuchs*, 251 F. 2d 455 (10 Cir., 1957). For a general discussion of United States treatment of foreign awards see Martin Domke, "International Arbitration of Commercial Disputes," in *Southwestern Legal Foundation: Proceedings of the Institute on Private Investments Abroad* (Albany: Bender, 1960) pp. 131, 151; Domke, "Enforcement of Foreign Arbitral Awards in the United States," 13 *Arb. J.* 91 (1958); Raymond V. Heilman, "The Enforceability of Foreign Awards in the United States," 3 *Arb. J.* 183 (1939); Ernest G. Lorenzen, "Commercial Arbitration—Enforcement of Foreign Awards," 45 *Yale L. J.* 39 (1935); 1 *Restatement* (Second), *Conflict of Laws*, §220 (1971).

Compare Martin Domke, "On the Enforcement Abroad of American Arbitration Awards," 17 *Law & Contemp. Prob.* 545, 550 (1952); and Domke, "American Arbitral Awards: Enforcement in Foreign Countries," 1965 *U. of Ill. L. F.* 399 (1965).

See, generally, Jalet, "Judicial Review," *Cornell L. Q.*, pp. 519, 532; Note, "Judicial Review of Arbitration Awards on the Merits," 63 *Harv. L. Rev.* 681 (1950).

For enforcement of foreign awards in Japan see Tarō Kawakami, "Gaikoku chūsai handan no kōryoku (The effect of foreign arbitration awards in our country), *Jurisuto* (No. 179) 53–54; Ehrenzweig, Ikehara, and Jensen, *American-Japanese Private International Law*, pp. 32–33; *cf.* Tanaka, "Enforcement of American Arbitration Awards in Japan," *Arb. J.*, p. 88.

140. *American President Lines* v. *C. Subra K.K.*, 10 Kakyū minshū 2232 (Tokyo Dist. Ct., 23 Oct. 1959), English translation in 6 *Japanese Annual of International Law* 203 (1962). Instead of enforcing the United States federal district court's judgment confirming a United States award, the Tokyo court enforced the award and refused to order the Japanese corporation to pay 6% interest (from date of award to payment) included in the judgment, but not in the award. This holding amounted in this special situation to more effect for the award than for the judgment, and it does not treat the award as merged in the judgment.

Note also that, contrary to English law, the doctrine of merger (award into a foreign judgment thereon) is not followed in New York either. Hence, execution was granted in New York on an underlying English award, even where it had already been reduced to a London judgment unenforceable in New York. *Oilcakes & Oilseeds Trading Co.* v. *Sinason Teicher Inter Am. Grain Corp.*, 9 Misc. 2d 651, 170 N.Y.S. 2d 378 (Sup. Ct. 1958), *aff'd. with modification regarding interest on the award*, 7 App. Div. 2d 977, 183 N.Y.S. 2d 838 (1959), *aff'd.* 8 N.Y. 2nd 852, 168 N.E. 2nd 708, 203 N.Y.S. 2d 904 (1960).

See *Ralph A. Fields* v. *K.K. Taiheiyō TV.*, Hanrei jihō (No. 586) 73 (Tokyo D. Ct., 6 Sept. 1969) where a California judgment, based on a California award, was enforced in Japan.

141. German Civil Procedure Code, Art. 1044.

142. Hellan Graff, "Sweden," in *International Commercial Arbitration*, ed. Sanders, 1: 427.

143. Art. IV (2), 2 Apr. 1953 [1954] 4 U.S.T. & O.I.A. 2063, T.I.A.S. No. 2863.

144. Though not Japanese awards, the federal courts enforced foreign awards in the following two cases: *Standard Magnesium Corp.* v. *Fuchs*, 251 F. 2d 255 (10 Cir. 1957); and *San Martine Compania de Navegacion, S.A.* v. *Saguenay Terminals, Ltd.*, 293 F. 2d 796 (9th Cir. 1961). No cases have been found construing similar provisions in other FCN treaties, *e.g.*, the U.S.-Germany Treaty, Art. VI (2), 29 Oct. 1954 [1956] 7 U.S.T. & O.I.A. 1836, T.I.A.S. No. 3593.

145. *Restatement* (Second), *Conflict of Laws*, §220 (1971), provides:

§220. Enforcement of Foreign Arbitration Award

A foreign arbitration award will be enforced in other states provided:

(a) the award is enforceable in the state whose local law governs the award and was rendered by an arbitration tribunal which had personal jurisdiction over the defendant and afforded him reasonable notice of the proceeding and a reasonable opportunity to be heard, and

(b) the forum has judicial jurisdiction over either the defendant or his property and the cause of action on which the award was based is not contrary to the strong public policy of the forum.

146. The leading New York cases enforcing foreign awards are *Gilbert* v. *Burnstine*, 255 N.Y. 348, 174 N.E. 706 (1931) (*ex parte* award enforced), and *Sargant* v. *Monroe*, 268 App. Div. 123, 49 N.Y.S. 2d 546 (1944) (both on English awards). See also *Cerf* v. *La Maison du Paysan du Sud-Ouest*, 202 Misc. 322, 110 N.Y.S. 2d 127 (Sup. Ct. 1952) (London award); *Coudenhove-Kalergi* v. *Dieterle*, 36 N.Y.S. 2d 313 (Sup. Ct. 1942) (German award).

A Norwegian award rendered *ex parte* (even without a court order, see 9 U.S.C. §4) after defendants refused to participate was enforced in Oklahoma. *Standard Magnesium Corp.* v. *Fuchs*, 251 F. 2d 455 (10th Cir. 1957). The general conflicts rule is stated in *Moyer* v. *Van-Dye-Way Corp.*, 126 F. 2d 339, 340 (3d Cir. 1942): "The general authority is to the effect that the validity of an arbitration award is determined by the place of its rendition." For interstate awards see *Restatement* (Second) *Conflict of Laws* §220, (1971).

147. See generally, Tarō Kawakami, "Chūsai" (Arbitration), 3 *Kokusai shihō kōza* 848 (1964); and Tarō Kawakami, "Kokusai shōji chūsai ni kansuru kokusai shihō riron (Theory of private international law concerning international commercial arbitration), 1 *Kobe hōgaku zasshi* (No. 3), 577, 604 (1951).

Also Ernest Mezger, "The Arbitrator and Private International Law," in *International Trade Arbitration*, ed. Domke, p. 229; Barrett J. Foerster, "Arbitration Agreements and the Conflicts of Law," 21 *Arb. J.* 129 (1966); Gabriel M. Wilner, "Determining the Law Governing Performance in International Commercial Arbitration: A Comparative Study," 19 *Rutgers L. Rev.* 646 (1965).

148. This is a difficult question still not fully resolved. Compare *Bernhardt* v. *Polygraphic Co. of Am.*, 350 U.S. 198 (1956), with *Prima Paint Corp.* v. *Flood and Conklin Mfg. Co.*, 388 U.S. 395, and *Robert Lawrence* v. *Devonshire Fabrics, Inc.*, 271 F. 2d 402 (2d Cir. 1959), *cert. denied*, 364 U.S. 801 (1960), and *Lummus Co.* v. *Commonwealth Oil Refinery Co.*, 280 F. 2d 915 (1st Cir. 1950), *cert. denied*, 364 U.S. 911 (1960).

149. *Hōrei*, Art. 7 (2) (in 1 EHS 1001 [1958]): "In case the intention of the parties is uncertain, the law of the place where the act is done shall govern." Ibid., Art. 9 (2): "As regards the formation and effect of a contract, the place from which the notice of the offer is dispatched shall be regarded as the place of the act. In case the recipient of the offer is ignorant, at the time of his acceptance, of the place from which the offer has been dispatched, the place of the offeror's domicile shall be regarded as the place of the act."

Note that, as a preliminary point, in Japan there is a split of authority as to whether arbitration agreements should be characterized as procedural or substantive (contract). If viewed as procedural the law of the forum (place of arbitration) governs. The "contract" characterization is the more authoritative view in Japan. *Compania de Transportes de ma S.A.* v. *Mataichi K.K.*, 4 Kakyū minshū 502 (Tokyo Dist. Ct., 10 Apr. 1953), and *Continental Ins. Co.* v. *Fuji Shōkai*, in *Kokusai shihō jiken hanreishū* (International private law cases) 1728 (Tokyo App. Ch., 5 Aug. 1935), are cases recognizing this indirectly. See Kawakami, "Gaikoku chūsai handan," *Jurisuto*, p. 53.

Compare United States federal problems: *Bernhardt* v. *Polygraphic Co. of Am.*, 350 U.S. 198 (1956). The United States Supreme Court held that under *Erie R.R.* v. *Tompkins*, 304 U.S. 64 (1938), the enforceability of an arbitration contract in a diversity suit is outcome determinative, hence subject to the law of the state where the federal court sits. See generally Wilner, "Determining the Law," *Rutgers L. Rev.*, pp. 646, 648.

150. See Jalet, "Judicial Review," *Cornell L. Q.*, pp. 519, 532, and Note, "Judicial Review of Arbitration Awards on the Merits," *Harv. L. Rev.*, p. 681. for the diverse, actual review policies of several American courts. Generally the courts seem to review awards more than might be expected from the general statements to the effect that awards duly rendered are not subject to review on the law or the facts.

151. 6 Williston, *Contracts* §1929, at 5396 (rev. ed., 1938).

152. See, *e.g.*, *Interinsurance Exch. of Auto Club* v. *Bailes*, 219 Cal. App. 2d 830, 33 Cal. Rptr. 533, 536 (Dist. Ct. App. 1963), where it was held that an award, clearly contrary to the law, was binding. There is an early case involving a Japanese firm in which the court refused to review an award for an error of law. *In the Matter of C. Itoh & Co.* v. *Boyer Oil Co.*, 198 App. Div. 881, 191 N.Y. Supp. 290 (1921). The court said, 191 N.Y. Supp. at 292: "The courts of this state have adhered with great steadiness to the general rule that awards will not be opened for errors of law or fact on the part of arbitrators. . . . The merits of an award cannot be reinvestigated, for otherwise the award instead of being the end of litigation, would simply be a useless step in its progress."

153. See *London* v. *Zackery*, 92 Cal. App. 2d 654, 207 P. 2d 1067 (1949) (award adjudged invalid because rendered under an invalid arbitral contract is no bar to suit).

154. *E.g.*, Ga. Code Ann. §7–219 (1936), *Barnes* v. *Avery*, 192 Ga. 874, 16 S.E. 2d 861 (1961); Ala. Code tit. 7 §843 (1960), *Bell* v. *McKay & Co.*, 196 Ala. 408, 72 So. 83 (1916); Pa. Stat. Ann. tit. 5 §171 (d) (1963); Iowa Code Ann. §679.12 (1950); Neb. Rev. Stat. §25–2115 (1965).

155. Note that the American Arbitration Association, which handles all U.S.-Japanese arbitration in the United States, where its recommended clause has been incorporated into U.S.-Japanese contracts, has advised against stating reasons, or if stated, to state them in a document separate from the award. American Arbitration Association, *A Manual for Commercial Arbitrators* (New York: American Arbitration Association, 1964), p. 23.

156. Code of Civil Procedure, Art. 801:
> (1) Motion for cancellation of an award shall be made in the following cases:
> . . . In case the award is not accompanied by reasons. . . .
> (2) Cancellation of an award shall not be made by the reasons as mentioned . . . in case parties have otherwise agreed.

157. Code of Civil Procedure, Art. 802.

158. Code of Civil Procedure, Art. 801.

159. See, *e.g.*, *Loving & Evans* v. *Black*, 33 Cal. 2d 603, 204 P. 2d 23 (1949) (commercial award vacated on public policy grounds); *Franklin* v. *Nat C. Goldstone Agency*, 33 Cal. 2d 628, 204 P. 2d 37 (1949) (same). *Contra, Grayson-Robinson Stores* v. *Ires Constr. Corp.*, 8 N.Y. 2d 133, 168 N.E. 2d 377, 202 N.Y.S. 2d 303 (1960) (specific performance of construction contract upheld against public policy attack); *Staklinski* v. *Pyramid Elec. Co.*, 6 N.Y. 2d 159, 160 N.E. 2d 78, 188 N.Y.S. 2d 541 (1959) (employment contract). *Cf. Goodman* v. *Lazarus*, App. Div. 2d 530, 222 N.Y.S. 2d 891 (1961) (arbitration permitted despite challenge that underlying award intended to violate United States custom duties on imported watches). See also Henri Battifol, "Public Policy and the Autonomy of the Parties," in *The Conflicts of Law and International Contracts*, ed. Willis Reese (Ann Arbor: U. of Mich. Press, 1951), pp. 68, 78. *Cf.* (labor cases) *Black* v. *Cutter Labs.*, 43 Cal. 2d 788, 278 P. 2d 905, *aff'd.* 351 U.S. 292 (1956) (upheld judgment setting aside award for public policy reasons, *i.e.*, award held to violate public policy because it ordered reinstatement of an alleged communist employee); *Avco Corp.* v. *Preteska*, 22 Conn. Supp. 475, 174 A. 2d 684 (Super. Ct. 1961). See Robert Meiners, "Arbitration Awards and 'Public Policy,' " 17 *Arb. J.* 145 (1962).

160. See, generally, Symposium, "Judicial Review of Arbitration: The Role of Public Policy," 58 *Nw. U. L. Rev.* 445 (1963).

161. Alfred W. Blumrosen, "Public Policy Considerations in Labor Arbitration Cases," 14 *Rutgers L. Rev.* 217 (1960).

162. *MacDonald, Ltd., & I. H. MacDonald* v. *Tomoi Trade Yūgenkaisha*, unreported case (Tokyo Dist. Ct., 6 May 1966) (consolidated cases: 1959 [*wa*] No. 9287; 1962 [*wa*] No. 4868; 1964 [*wa*] No. 2836).

163. 9 U.S.C. §§1–14 (1964).

164. 9 U.S.C. §10 (1964):
> *Same; vacation; grounds; rehearing*
> In either of the following cases the United States court in and for the district wherein the award was made may make an order vacating the award upon the application of any party to the arbitration—
> (a) Where the award was procured by corruption, fraud, or undue means.
> (b) Where there was evident partiality or corruption in the arbitrators, or either of them.
> (c) Where the arbitrators were guilty of misconduct in refusing to postpone the hearing, upon sufficient cause shown, or in refusing to hear evidence pertinent and material to the controversy; or of any other misbehavior by which the rights of any party have been prejudiced.

(d) Where the arbitrators exceed their powers, or so imperfectly executed them that a mutual, final, and definite award upon the subject matter submitted was not made.

(e) Where an award is vacated and the time within which the agreement required the award to be made has not expired the court may, in its discretion, direct a rehearing by the arbitrators.

165. 9 U.S.C. §11 (1964):

Same; modification or correction; grounds; order

In either of the following cases the United States court in and for the district wherein the award was made may make an order modifying or correcting the award upon the application of any party to the arbitration—

(a) Where there was an evident material miscalculation of figures or an evident material mistake in the description of any person, thing, or property referred to in the award.

(b) Where the arbitrators have awarded upon a matter not submitted to them, unless it is a matter not affecting the merits of the decision upon the matter submitted.

(c) Where the award is imperfect in matter of form not affecting the merits of the controversy.

The order may modify and correct the award, so as to effect the intent thereof and promote justice between the parties.

166. 10 Kakyū minshū 2232 (Tokyo Dist. Ct., 23 Oct. 1959), English translation in 6 *Japanese Annual of International Law* 203 (1962).

167. The court's transliteration of the defendant's name from "Soubra" to "Subura" in the Japanese syllabary (*kata-kana*) and erroneously back to "Subra" in English is a good example of one major "minor problem" of U.S.-Japanese litigation requiring the English language charter parties and the like to be translated into Japanese. Note here, though, that the defendant was Subura Kabushiki Kaisha, a Japanese corporation that came into existence only on registration in Japan, which can be done only in the Japanese language. Consequently, the legal name of Soubra's Japanese corporation was Subura (in *kata-kana*) K.K.

168. 10 Kakyū minshū 2232 (Tokyo Dist. Ct., 23 Oct. 1959), English translation in 6 *Japanese Annual of International Law* 203 (1962). The Japanese court seemed uncertain of the legality, in American law, of the interest ordered by the United States judgment, but in any event it chose not to include it in its Japanese judgment, limiting it to the amount of the award, which included interest only prior to the award date. Domke, *Commercial Arbitration*, p. 92, says on this point: "Courts have no authority to add any interest for the time prior to award. This would amount to a review of the award on its merits, which is excluded in the prevailing court practice in the United States." But note that 28 U.S.C. §1961 (1964) authorizes the court to award interest from the judgment to payment in "civil cases." Compare *In the Matter of John J. Kennedy Bldg. Corp.* v. *Longworth, N.Y.L.J.*, 30 Aug. 1929 (City Court, Bronx County Spec. Term), where the court stated: "It was brought to my attention that one of the arbitrators stated orally after the board of arbitrators made their findings that defendants were not to pay any interest. I cannot pay any attention to what an arbitrator said or the interpretation he gave to his report. The award itself must govern the court. The arbitrators would have no right to exclude interest from their award, and even if they did so exclude it the court would add proper interest to the award."

169. *G. M. Casaregi Compagnia di Navigazione e Commèrcio S.P.A.* v. *Nishi Shōji K.K.*, 10 Kakyū minshū 1711 (Tokyo Dist. Ct., 30 Aug. 1959), English translation in 5 *Japanese Annual of International Law* 112 (1961); Tarō Kawakami, "Wagakuni ni okeru Eikoku chūsai handan no shikkō" (Execution of English arbitration awards in Japan), *Jurisuto* (No. 195) 58–60 (1960). See also text accompanying note 99 *supra*.

170. 14 Geo. 6, c. 27 (1950).

171. U.N., "Final Act and Convention on the Recognition and Enforcement of Foreign Arbitral Awards," E/Conf. 26/8 Rev. (1958), Art. IV.

172. Ibid., Art. V.

173. *E.g.*, Sweden and Germany. See notes 141 and 142 *supra*.

174. Code of Civil Procedure, Art. 802 (1): "Execution to be undertaken by virtue of an award shall be made only when an execution judgment has been rendered for the admissibility thereof."

175. *Murray Oil Prods. Co.* v. *Mitsui & Co.*, 146 F. 2d 381 (2d Cir. 1944); Domke, "International Arbitration," in *Southwestern Legal Foundation*, pp. 131, 151.

176. See notes 151–56 *supra* and accompanying text.

177. See Georgia and other statutes cited *supra* note 154.

178. *MacDonald, Ltd. & I. H. MacDonald* v. *Tomoi Trade Yūgenkaisha*, unreported case (Tokyo Dist. Ct., 6 May 1966) consolidated cases: 1959 (*wa*) No. 9287; 1962 (*wa*) No. 4868; 1964 (*wa*) No. 2836.

179. See the discussion in *G. M. Casageri Compagnia di Navigazione e Commèrcio, S.P.A.* v. *Nishi Shōji K.K.*, 10 Kakyū minshū 1711 (Tokyo Dist. Ct., 30 Aug. 1959).

180. See new JCAA Rule 37 (effective 1971), which provides that awards will be in Japanese, unless a party requests an award in English, in which case both Japanese and English versions will be issued of equal force and effect. 18 *Bōeki kurēmu to chūsai* (No. 162) 6 (March 1971).

181. See ICC, Rule 7 (3).

182. While in this chapter I have supported strongly the usefulness of international commercial arbitration, it seems important at the end to stress again the fundamental consensual basis of arbitration, which I believe got lost in the more lyrical writing of other proponents during the "separability" litigation. Besides the very persuasive dissent by Justice Black in *Prima Paint Corp.* v. *Flood and Conklin Mfg. Co.*, 388 U.S. 395, 87 S. Ct. 1808 (1967), the following articles are recommended for balance: Heinrich Kronstein, "Arbitration Is Power," 38 *N.Y. U. L. Rev.* 661–700 (1963); Hayes, *Labor Arbitration;* Karl H. Schwab, "The Legal Foundations and Limitations of Arbitration Procedures in the U.S. and Germany," in *International Commercial Arbitration*, ed. Sanders, pp. 301–12.

Glossary of Japanese Names and Terms

Abe, Hiroshi 阿部 浩
Agawa, Seido 阿川 清道
Ajimura, Osamu 味村 浩
amae 甘え
ama kudari 天下り
Amano, Takeichi 天野 武一
Amaya, Naohiro 天谷 直弘
Araki, Nobuyoshi 荒木 信義
Asahi Shimbunsha 朝日新聞社
Asayama, Toyozō 朝山 豊三
Ashida, [Hitoshi] 芦田 (均)
Azuma, Mitsutoshi 吾妻 光俊
bantō 番頭
bengoshi 弁護士
bengoshikai 弁護士会
benrishi 弁理士
bōeki shinkō-kyoku 貿易振興局
bu 部
bugyō 奉行
bugyōsho 奉行所
chambara チャンバラ

chihō hōmu-kyoku 地方法務局
chikyū minzoku shugi 地球民族主義
chō 長
chōei 長栄
chōsa tōkei-bu 調査統計部
chūkai 註解
chūritsu rōren 中立労連
chūshō kigyō 中小企業
Chūshō Kigyō Kin'yū 中小企業金融公庫
Kōko
chūto saiyō 中途採用
Dai hōtei 大法廷
daihyō 代表取締役
torishimariyaku
daijin kambō 大臣官房
daikan 代官
daimyō 大名
dantai 団体
dantai kōshō 団体交渉
dantai kyōyaku 団体協約
deiri-suji 出入筋

Dejima 出島

dekasegi 出稼ぎ

Doi, Teruo 土井輝生

Dōmei 同盟

doru shokku ドル ショック

Dōyūkai 同友会

Edo 江戸

Fudōsan 不動産

fudōteki mukō 浮動的無効

Fujii, Shin'ichi 藤井新一

Fujimoto, Genzō 藤本巌三

Fujita, Wakao 藤田若雄

Fujita, Yasuhiro 藤田泰弘

Fujiwara, Hirotatsu 藤原弘達

fukoku kyōhei 富国強兵

Fukuda, [Takeo] 福田 (赳夫)

Fukuji, Toshio 福地俊雄

fumie 踏絵

Furukawa, Noboru 古川昇

gaijin 外人

gaikoku shihonka azukeire kanjō 外国資本家預入甚勘定

gaisai 外債

gaishi dōnyū kaisha 外資導入会社

Gaishi kanji-kai 外資幹事会

gaishi-kei kigyō 外資系企業

Gaishi shingi-kai 外資審議会

gakubatsu 学閥

gakusetsu 学説

gampon kaishūkin 元本回収金

gappei 合併

gembutsu shusshi 現物出資

geta 下駄

Giga, Sōichirō 儀我壮一郎

gijutsu dōnyū 技術導入

gijutsu enjo keiyaku 技術援助契約

gijutsu-kei 技術系

gimmi-suji 吟味筋

gōben gaisha 合併会社

Gohara, Hiroshi 郷原弘

Gumma 群馬

gyōsei kikan 行政機関

gyōsei shidō 行政指導

gyōsei shoshi 行政書士

habatsu 派閥

hanjiho 判事補

Hashimoto, Masaharu 橋本正治

hassei 発生

Hatoyama, [Ichirō] 鳩山 (一郎)

Hattori, Eizo 服部栄三

Hattori, Sadao 服部定雄

Hayashi, Shintarō 林信太郎

Hidemura, Senzō 秀村選三

hijiyūka gyōshu 非自由化業種

hijōkin 非常勤

hikyojūsha 非居住者

Hiramatsu, Yoshirō 平松義郎

Hironaka, Toshio 広中俊雄

Hitotsubashi 一ツ橋

hōjin 法人

Hokkaidō 北海道

hokkinin 発起人

honkō 本工

honsha 本社

hōritsu kōi 法律行為

hōritsu ni yoru gyosei 法律による行政

hōritsu no konkyo 法律の根拠

Hoshino, Eiichi 星野 英一

Hoshino, Tōru 星野 通

hōsō ichigenka 法曹一元化

Hozumi, Yatsuka 穂積 八束

hyōken daihyō 表見代表

Ichihashi, Akira 市橋 明

Ichikawa, Susumu 市川 享

Idemitsu, Sazō 出光 佐三

Igarashi, Kiyoshi 五十嵐 清

Iida, Tsuneo 飯田 経夫

iken 意見

Imai, Hiroshi 今井 宏

Imai, Noriyoshi 今井 則義

Imamura, Shigekazu 今村 成和

Imanishi, Isamu 今西 勇

inkan shōmei 印鑑証明

Inoue, Kowashi 井上 毅

ippanhō 一般法

Ishibashi, Shōjirō 石橋 正二郎

Ishida, Shin'ichi 石田 晋一

Ishii, Ryōsuke 石井 良助

Ishii, Teruhisa 石井 照久

Ishikawa, Kichiemon 石川 吉右衛門

Ishimoto, Yasuo 石本 泰雄

Itō, Hirobumi 伊藤 博文

Itō, Miyoji 伊東 巳代治

Iwao, Hirozumi 岩尾 裕純

Iwasaki, Yatarō 岩崎 弥太郎

Iyori, Hiroshi 伊従 寛

Izawa, Kōhei 伊沢 孝平

jankempon ジャンケンポン

Jichichō 自治庁

Jigyōbu-sei 事業部制

Jigyō shokan shō 事業所管省

Jijō henkō no gensoku 事情変更の原則

jimu jikan 事務次官

jimu-kei 事務系

Jinji-in 人事院

jitsuyō shin'an 実用新案

Jiyū minshu-tō 自由民主党

jōkai 条解

jōkin 常勤

jōmu-kai 常務会

jōmu-torishimariyaku 常務取締役

Jōnan Shin'yō Kinko 城南信用金庫

jueki shōken 受益証券

jūkōgyō-kyoku 重工業局

jun gaishi kaisha 準外資会社

jun'yō 準用

jūyaku 重役

ka 課

kabushiki kaisha 株式会社

kachō 課長

Kagaku gijutsu-chō 科学技術庁

kagaku kōgyō-kyoku 科学工業局

kaichō 会長

kaigyō jumbi kōi 開業準備行為

Kaino, Michitaka 戒能 通孝

kaisha 会社

Kaishintō 改進党

kajitsu 果実

kakari 係

Kakinuma, Kōichirō 柿沼 幸一郎

kambatsu 官閥

Kanazawa, Yoshio 金沢 良雄

Kaneda, Heiichirō 金田 平一郎

Kaneko, Hajime 兼子 一

Kaneko, Kentarō 金子 堅太郎

kanji 幹事

kanjikai 幹事会

kankei kanchō 関係官庁

kankoku 勧告

Kanno, Masao 神野 正雄

Kanno, Watarō 菅野 和太郎

kansayaku 監査役

kanshō 勧奨

kanson mimpi 官尊民卑

kashitsukekin saiken 貸付金債権

Katayama, Tetsu 片山 哲

Katō, Ichirō 加藤 一郎

katō kyōsō 過当競争

Katō, Takaaki 加藤 高顕

Katō, Toshihiko 加藤 俊彦

Kawaguchi, Jun'ichi 川口 順一

Kawakami, Tarō 川上 太郎

Kawamoto, Ichirō 河本 一郎

Kawanaka, Nikō 河中 二講

Kawasaki, Hirotarō 川崎 博太郎

Kawashima, 川島 武宜
　Takeyoshi

Kazahaya, Yasoji 風早 八十二

keibatsu 閨閥

Keidanren 経団連

keieiken 経営権

keikoku 警告

Keiō 慶応

keiretsu 系列

keirishi 経理士

keiyaku 契約

Keizai Dantai Rengō- 経済団体連合会（経団連
　kai (Keidanren)

Keizai kyōryoku-bu 経済協力部

Keizai Saiken 経済再建懇談会
　Kondankai (KSK)

kenami 毛並

kigyō 企業

kigyō-betsu kumiai 企業別組合

Mannari, Hiroshi　万成博

Masakame, Keisuke　正亀慶介

Matsuda, Jirō　松田二郎

Matsueda, Michio　松枝迪夫

Matsui, Yasuhiro　松井康浩

Matsumoto, Jōji　松本烝治

Matsumura, [Kenzō]　松村謙三

Matsuo, Kinzō　松尾金蔵

Matsuo, Kunihiko　松尾邦彦

Matsushima, Shizuo　松島静雄

Matsushita, Kōnosuke　松下幸之助

Meiji　明治

meishi　名刺

Michida, Shin'ichirō　道田信一郎

Mikazuki, Akira　三ヶ月章

Miki, [Takeo]　三木(武夫)

Minagawa, Takeshi　皆川洸

Minseitō　民政党

Minshu shakai-tō　民主社会党

Misonō, Hitoshi　御園生等

Miyagawa, Kiyoshi　宮川澄

Miyaji, Sadahide　宮地貞穎

Miyamoto, Mataji　宮本又二

Miyazaki, Giichi　宮崎義一

Miyazawa, Toshiyoshi　宮沢俊義

mochibun　持分

Mon'ya, Nobuo　紋谷暢男

Mori, Gorō　森五郎

Morii, Kiyoshi　森井清

Muramatsu, Toshio　村松俊夫

Muramoto, Kazuo　村本一男

Muraoka, Yoshitaka　村岡好隆

Nagai, Arekisan　長井亜歴山

naiki　内規

Nakada, Kaoru　中田薫

Nakagawa, Zennosuke　中川善之助

Nakamura, Kikuo　中村菊男

Nakamura, Shūichirō　中村秀一郎

Nakamura, Takahide　中村隆英

Nakamura, Yūichi　中村雄一

Nakane, Chie　中根千枝

Nakasone, Yasuhiro　中曽根康弘

Nakata, Jun'ichi　中田淳一

nakōdo　仲人

namban byōbu　南蛮屏風

Namoto, Kimikuni　名本公洲

Narita, Yoriaki　成田頼明

nega risuto　ネガリスト

nenkō joretsu　年功序列

Nichiren　日蓮

Nihon Kaihatsu Ginkō　日本開発銀行

Nihon Keieisha Dantai Remmei (Nikkeiren)　日本経営者団体連盟 (日経連)

Nihon Keizai Dōyūkai (Dōyūkai)　日本経済同友会 (同友会)

Nihon Kyōshokuin 日本教職員組合
Kumiai (Nikkyōso) （日教組）

Nihon no rieki 日本の利益

Nihon Shōkō 日本商工会議所（日商）
Kaigisho (Nisshō)

Nikkeiren 日経連

ninka 認可

Nippon Ginkō 日本銀行

Nippon Kōnin 日本公認会計士協会
Kaikeishi Kyōkai

Nishi, Kan 西 寛

Nishi, Zen'ya 西 善弥

Nishihara, Kan'ichi 西原 寛一

Nishio, Suehiro 西尾 末広

Noda, Kazuo 野田 一夫

Noguchi, Yoshimitsu 野口 良光

Nojima, Atsushi 野島 篤

Nomura, Taku 野村 卓

nōritsu-kyū 能率給

nōryoku 能力

Ōba, Osamu 大庭 脩

Ogawa, Ichirō 雄川 一郎

Ohara, Keiji 小原 敬士

Ohara, Yoshio 小原 喜雄

Ōhira, Zengo 大平 善悟

Ōkōchi, Kazuo 大河内 一夫

Ōkuma, Shigenobu 大隈 重信

Okuno, Hikoroku 奥野 彦六

Ōkura-shō 大蔵省

Okuyama, Keikichi 奥山 恵吉

Ōmori, Tadao 大森 忠夫

Ōnishi, Masao 大西 正雄

Ōno, [Bamboku] 大野 伴睦

Ōno, Fumio 大野 文雄

Ono, Toyoaki 小野 豊明

Osatake, Takeshi 尾佐竹 猛

Ōsumi, Ken'ichirō 大隅 健一郎

Otake, Chikashi 尾竹 親

oyabun 親分

oyabun/kobun 親分子分

Ōyama, Kikuji 大山菊治

pachinko パチンコ

poji risuto ポジ リスト

ringi 稟議

ringisei 稟議制

ringi-sho 稟議書

rōdō kyōyaku 労働協約

rōdō sampō 労働三法

ruiseki tōhyō 累積投票

ruisui tekiyō 類推適用

Saga 佐賀

sagyōsho heisa 作業所閉鎖

saiken 債権

saishin 再審

Saitō, Hideo 斉藤 秀夫

Sakai, Ichirō 境 一郎

Sakuragi, Masayasu 桜木昌靖

Sakurai, Masao 桜井 雅夫

samurai 侍

Sangyō Mondai Kenkyūkai (Sanken) 産業問題研究会（産研）

sanshu no jingi 三種の神器

sashimi 刺身

Satō, Eisaku 佐藤 栄作

Satō, Hideo 佐藤 英夫

Satō, Isao 佐藤 功

Sawa, Eizō 沢 栄三

seimu jikan 政務次官

seiritsuchū no kaisha 成立中の会社

seisan kanri 生産管理

Seiyūkai 政友会

sekitan-bu 石炭部

semmon gakkō 専門学校

Semmon iin 専門委員

semmu-torishimari-yaku 専務取締役

sempai/kōhai 先輩後輩

sen'i zakka-kyoku 繊維雑貨局

Senō, Akira 妹尾 晃

shachō 社長

shachō-shitsu 社長室

shain 社員

shakai chitsujo no keisei 社会秩序の形成

Shakaitō 社会党

shakin 謝金

shakubuku 折伏

shasai 社債

Shibagaki, Kazuo 柴垣 和夫

Shidehara, Kijūrō 幣原 喜重郎

shiharai 支払い

Shihō kenshūjo 司法研修所

Shihō shiken 司法試験

shihō shoshi 司法書士

shiji 指示

Shimizu, Hideo 清水 英夫

Shingikai 審議会

shingi seijitsu no gensoku 信義誠実の原則

shinsangyō chitsujoron 新産業秩序論

Shiraishi, Kenzō 白石 健三

shisan no un'yō 資産の運用

shiwayose 皺寄せ

shizoku 士族

Shōda, Akira 正田 彬

shōgai bengoshi 渉外弁護士

Shogun 将軍

shōgyō tōkibo 商業登記簿

shōkai 詳解

Shōken torihiki-hō 証券取引法

shōkōi 商行為

shokuin 職員

shōnin 商人

Shōshū 正宗

shūgyō kisoku 就業規則

shumu daijin 主務大臣

shuntō 春闘

tokubetsuhō   特別法

Tokugawa   徳川

tomeyaku   留役

Tomizawa, Hiroshi   富沢宏

torisage   取り下げ

torishimari hōki   取締り法規

toro   トロ

Tōyama, Shigeki   遠山茂樹

Toyotomi, Hideyoshi   豊臣秀吉

Tsuchiya, Takao   土屋喬雄

Tsuji, Kiyoaki   辻清明

tsūsetsu   通説

tsūshō-kyoku   通商局

Tsūshō sangyo daijin   通商産業大臣

Tsutsui, Wakamizu   筒井若水

Ueda, Akinobu   上田明信

Uemura, Kōgorō   植村甲午郎

Ujihara, Shōjirō   氏原正治郎

Ukai, Nobushige   鵜飼信成

wa   和

Wagatsuma, Sakae   我妻栄

ware ware Nihonjin   我々日本人

Waseda   早稲田

Watanabe, Taizō   渡辺耐三

yakusha   役者

Yamamura, Chūhei   山村忠平

Yamanaka, Rikimatsu   山中利喜松

Yamauchi, Kazuo   山内一夫

yatō   野党

Yazawa, Makoto   矢沢惇

yen   円

yōbō   要望

yoko suberi   横滑り

Yokoi, Masami   横井正美

Yorashimu-beshi; shirashimu-bekarazu   依らしむべし知らしむべからず

Yoshida, Fujio   吉田富士雄

Yoshida, Jimpū   吉田仁風

Yoshida, Kō   吉田昻

Yoshida, Seigo   吉田斉吾

Yoshida, [Shigeru]   吉田(茂)

Yoshinaga, Eisuke   吉永栄助

Yumoto, Takunaga   湯本宅長

zaibatsu   財閥

zaikai   財界

zeirishi   税理士

Zeirishi-hō   税理士法

zettaiteki kisai jikō   絶対的記載事項

Bibliography

DOCUMENTARY SOURCES

Bureau of Statistics, Office of the Prime Minister. *Nihon tōkei nenkan* (Japan statistical yearbook). Tokyo: Ōkurashō insatsukyoku, 1972. 683 pp.

Chūshō kigyōchō (MITI, Medium and Small Enterprise Agency), ed. *Chūshō kigyō hakusho* (White paper on medium and small enterprises). Tokyo: Ōkurashō insatsukyoku, 1972. 348 pp.

Commission on International Trade and Investment (CITI). *United States International Economic Policy in an Interdependent World*. Washington, D.C.: GPO, 1971. 394 pp.

Committee for Economic Development. *Japan in the Free World Economy*. New York: CED, 1963. 104 pp.

Confederation of British Industries. *Japanese Restrictions on Free Capital Movements*. London: CIB, July 1966. 23 pp.

Connor, John T. "Expanding the Fabric of U.S.-Japanese Economic Relations." 50 *The Department of State Bulletin* (8 Aug. 1966).

Foreign Exchange Study Association. *Japan Laws, Ordinances and Other Regulations Concerning Foreign Exchange and Foreign Trade*. Tokyo: Foreign Exchange Study Association, 1971.

Genshiryoku iinkai (Atomic Power Committee), ed. *Genshiryoku hakusho* (White paper on atomic power). Tokyo: Ōkurashō insatsukyoku, 1971. 194 pp.

Hōmushō (Ministry of Justice). *Gaikokujin tōroku kokuseki-betsu jin'in chōsa geppō* (Monthly report of investigation into the registration of aliens, classified by nationality). Tokyo: Hōmushō, 1970. 46 pp.

International Monetary Fund. *International Monetary Fund*. Washington, D.C.: IMF, 1969. Vol. III.

————. *22nd Annual Report: Exchange Restrictions*. Washington, D.C.: IMF, 1971. 307 pp.

Japan: Statistical Survey of Japan's Economy (1972). Tokyo: Economic Affairs Bureau, Ministry of Foreign Affairs, 1972. 112 pp.

Kagaku gijutsuchō (Science and Technology Agency), ed. *Kagaku gijutsuchō nempō* (Annual report of the Science and Technology Agency). Tokyo: Ōkurashō insatsukyoku, 1971. 226 pp.

———. *Kagaku gijutsu hakusho* (White paper on science and technology). Tokyo: Ōkurashō insatsukyoku, 1972. 354 pp.

———. *Kagaku gijutsu hakusho* (White paper on science and technology). Tokyo: Ōkurashō insatsukyoku, 1971. 314 pp.

———. *Kagaku gijutsu roppō* (Collection of codes on science and technology). Tokyo: Taisei shuppansha, 1971. 812 pp.

———, keikakukyoku (Planning Bureau), ed. *Kagaku gijutsu yōran* (A survey of science and technology). Tokyo: Ōkurashō insatsukyoku, 1971. 233 pp.

Kagaku gijutsu kaigi (Science and Technology Conference), ed. *1970 nendai ni okeru kagaku gijutsu seisaku* (Policy on science and technology during 1970s). Tokyo: Ōkurashō insatsukyoku, 1971. 75 pp.

Keizai kikakuchō (Economic Planning Agency), ed. *Getsurei keizai hōkoku* (Monthly economic report), No. 11. Tokyo: Ōkurashō insatsukyoku, 15 Feb. 1972. 55 pp.

———. *Shin-keizai shakai hatten keikaku* (New plan for economic and social development). Tokyo: Ōkurashō insatsukyoku, 1970. 244 pp.

———, chōsakyoku (Research Bureau), ed. *Nihon keizai no genjō* (Present status of Japanese economy). Tokyo: Ōkurashō insatsukyoku, 1972. 264 pp.

Keizai shingikai kokusai shihon idō kenkyū iinkai (Economic Council International Capital Movement Study Committee), ed. *Shihon jiyūka to kaigai kigyō shinshutsu* (Capital liberalization and the advance of enterprise abroad). Tokyo: Ōkurashō insatsukyoku, 1969. 232 pp.

Kōsei torihiki iinkai (Fair Trade Commission), ed. *Kōsei torihiki iinkai nenji hōkoku—Dokusen hakusho* (Fair Trade Commission annual report—white paper on monopolies). Tokyo: Ōkurashō insatsukyoku, 1971. 365 pp.

Legal Training and Research Institute, Supreme Court of Japan. *The Legal Training and Research Institute of Japan.* Tokyo: Japanese Supreme Court, 1970. 30 pp.

Memorandum of Understanding between the Organization for Economic Cooperation and Development and the Government of Japan Concerning the Assumption by the Government of Japan of the Obligations of Membership of the Organization. Paris: OECD, 1963. 26 pp.

Ministry of Finance (International Finance Bureau) and Bank of Japan (Foreign Department). *Manual of Foreign Investment in Japan.* Tokyo: Ōkurashō insatsukyoku, Nov. 1971. 45 pp.

Nichibei keizai kankei no shomondai (Problems of Japanese-American economic relations). Tokyo: Keizai dantai rengokai (keidanren), 1967. 21 pp.

Nihon ginkō chōsakyoku (Bank of Japan Research Bureau), ed. *Wagakuni no kinyū seido* (Financial system of Japan). Tokyo: Nihon ginkō chōsakyoku, 1971. 399 pp.

OECD, Business and Industry Advisory Committee (BIAC). "The Control of the Inflow of Investment into Japan." Annex to Circular C-438 of 17 March 1967. 25 pp.

OECD. *Liberalisation of International Capital Movements: Japan.* Paris: OECD, 1968. 179 pp.

Ōkurashō insatsukyoku (Ministry of Finance Printing Bureau), ed. *Hakusho no gaiyō* (An outline of white papers for the latter part of 1970). Tokyo: Ōkurashō insatsukyoku, 1971. 290 pp.

Panel on Foreign Investment in Developing Countries, U.N. Economic and Social Council. *Agreed Statement on Private Foreign Investment in the Development Process* (Panel Doc. #17, 20 Feb. 1969). 12 pp.

Report of the Fact Finding and Conciliation Commission on Freedom of Association Concerning Persons Employed in the Public Sector in Japan. Geneva: International Labor Office, 1965. 758 pp.

Rōdō kumiai kihon chōsa (Basic survey of labor unions). Tokyo: Ministry of Labor, 1966. 214 pp.

Rōdōshō (Ministry of Labor), ed. *Rōdō hakusho* (White paper on labor). Tokyo: Ōkurashō insatsukyoku, 1971. 490 pp.

SCAP, Government Section. *Political Reorientation of Japan (1945–1948).* Washington, D.C.: GPO, 1947. 2 vols.

Shihō kenshūjo (Legal Training and Research Institute). *Hōrei hanrei gakusetsu no chōsa ni tsuite* (Concerning investigation of law, judicial precedents, and academic theories). Tokyo: Japanese Supreme Court, 1962. 131 pp.

Shihō tōkei nempō (Annual report of judicial statistics, civil and administrative). Tokyo: Saikō saibanshō, 1967. 412 pp.

Shūgiin, Sangiin (House of Representatives, House of Councilors), ed. *Gikai seido shichijūnen-shi: Kokkai gian kemmeiroku* (70-year history of the legislative system: National Diet registry of bills). Tokyo: Ōkurashō insatsukyoku, 1961. 429 pp.

Sōrifu tōkeikyoku (Bureau of Statistics, Office of the Prime Minister, Japan), ed. *Kagaku gijutsu kenkyū chōsa hōkoku* (Report on the survey of research and development in Japan). Tokyo: K.K. Sangyō tōkei kenkyūsha, 1972. 206 pp.

Supreme Court of Japan. *Outline of Japanese Judicial System.* Tokyo: Japanese Supreme Court, 1961. 21 pp.

Tainai chokusetsu tōshi jiyūka kankei gaishi shingikai tōshin tō oyobi kakugi kettei (Report of the Foreign Investment Council on the liberalization of inward direct investment and [matters] decided upon by the Cabinet). Tokyo: Gaishi shingikai, Sept. 1970. 19 pp.

Tokkyochō (Patent Agency). *Tokkyochō kōhō* (Official bulletin of the Patent Agency). Vol. 23. Tokyo: Hatsumei kyokai, 1971. 257 pp.

Tsūsanshō kōho. *Tokushū—daiyonji shihon jiyūka* (Special issue on the 4th round capital liberalization). Tokyo: Tsūshō sangyōshō, 1971. 7 pp.

Tsūshō sangyō daijin kambō kōhōka (MITI, Minister's Office, Information Section). 7 *Tsūshō sangyō* (Trade and industry), No. 9. Tokyo: Tsūshō sangyō chōsakai, 1972. 24 pp.

Tsūshō sangyōshō (MITI), ed. *Keizai kyōryoku no genjō to mondaiten* (Present condition of economic cooperation and its problems). Tokyo: Maruzen K.K., 1969. 507 pp.

————. *Shigen mondai no tembō* (Outlook of natural resource problems). Tokyo: Tsūshō sangyō chōsakai, 1971. 440 pp.

————. *Tsūshō hakusho* (White paper on trade and industries). Tokyo: Tsūshō sangyō chōsakai, 1972. 2 vols.

Tsūshō sangyōshō, chūshō kigyōchō (MITI, Medium and Small Enterprise Agency). *Chūshō kigyō hakusho* (White paper on medium and small enterprises). Tokyo: Ōkurashō insatsukyoku, 1971. 330 pp.

Tsūshō sangyōshō, daijin kanshō chōsaka (MITI, Research Sec.). *Nihon sangyō to dokusen kinshi-hō* (Japanese industry and the Antimonopoly Law). Tokyo: Tsūshō sangyō kenkyūsha, 1968. 319 pp.

Tsūshō sangyōshō, kigyōkyoku (MITI, Enterprise Bureau), ed. *Gaishi-kei kigyō no dōkō* (Trends of foreign-capital-related enterprises). Tokyo: Ōkurashō insatsukyoku, 1971. 177 pp.

————. *Gaishi-kei kigyō—sono jittai to eikyō* (Foreign-capital-related enterprises—their actual condition and influence). Tokyo: Ōkurashō insatsukyoku, 1969. 376 pp.

————. *Wagakuni no gōben gaisha no jittai* (Actual condition of joint ventures in our country). Tokyo: Fuji kōhōsha, 1964. 319 pp.

Tsūshō sangyōshō, kigyōkyoku, gaishika (MITI, Enterprise Bureau, Foreign Capital Sec.). *Gaikoku gijutsu dōnyū keiyaku* (Contracts introducing foreign technology). Tokyo: Tsūshō sangyō chōsakai, 1970. 186 pp.

————. *Shiryōshū* (Collection of materials). Tokyo: Tsushō sangyōshō, 1 Sept. 1971. 342 pp.

Tsūshō sangyōshō, kōgyō gijutsuin (MITI, Industrial Technology Office), ed. *Gijutsu dōkō chōsa hōkokusho* (Research report on technological trends). Tokyo: K.K. Jitsugyō kōhōsha, 1963. 483 pp.

————. *Gijutsu kakushin to Nihon no kōgyō* (Technological improvements and Japanese industries). Tokyo: Nikkan kōgyō shinbunsha, 1964. 535 pp.

U.S. Department of Commerce. *Japan: The Government-Business Relationship.* Washington, D.C.: GPO, 1971. 158 pp.

————. *The Multinational Corporation.* Washington, D.C.: GPO, 1972. 2 vols.

————. *Statistical Abstract of the U.S.* Washington, D.C.: GPO, 1971. 1008 pp.

————. *Survey of Current Business.* Washington, D.C.: GPO, Oct. 1971.

World Economic Information Services. *Economic Information File, Japan.* Tokyo: World Economic Information Services, 1972. 217 pp. and Supplements, Nos. 1, 2, 3.

JAPANESE LANGUAGE SOURCES: BOOKS

Azuma, Mitsutoshi, ed. *Chūkai rōdō kumiai-hō* (Commentary on the Labor Union Law). 3rd ed. Tokyo: Seirin shoin, 1960. 646 pp.

Bank of Japan. *Keizai tōkei nempō* (Economic statistics annual). Tokyo: Bank of Japan, 1970. 301 pp.

Benrishikai. *Benrishi meibo* (A list of members), 1970. 286 pp.

————, ed. *Benrishikaishi* (History of the patent agent association). Tokyo: Benrishikai, 1959. 373 pp.

Daiyamondosha (staff). *Nihon no "mirai gijutsu"* ("Future technology" of Japan), *Shūkan daiyamondo bessatsu*. Tokyo: Daiyamondosha, 1971. 216 pp.

Dokusen shihon kenkyūkai, ed. *Gendai Nihon no dokusen shihon* (Monopoly capital in contemporary Japan). Tokyo: Nihon hyōron shinsha, 1958. 306 pp.

Fujii, Shin'ichi. *Teikoku kempō to Kaneko-haku* (The imperial constitution and Count Kaneko). Tokyo: Dai Nihon yūbenkai kōdansha, 1942. 774 pp.

Fujimoto, Genzō. *Kokusai shūshi tōkei geppō* (Balance of international payments monthly), No. 65. Tokyo: Nihon ginkō gaikokukyoku, 1971. 72 pp.

Fujita, Wakao. *Rōdō kumiai to rōdō kyōyaku* (Labor unions and collective labor agreements). Tokyo: Hakutō shobō, 1963. 299 pp.

Furukawa, Noboru (Chingin rōmu kanri kenkyūjo shochō), ed. *'72 Chingin kentō shiryō* (Materials with which to study wages). Tokyo: Nihon hōrei yōshiki hambaisho, 1971. 430 pp.

Gaikoku kawase bōeki kenkyūkai. *Gaikokujin no Nippon ni okeru gōbengaisha no setsuritsu keiyaku ni tsuite* (Concerning contracts to establish foreigners' joint-venture companies in Japan). Tokyo: Gaikoku kawase bōeki kenkyūkai, 1963. 241 pp.

Gaishi dōnyū nenkan henshū iinkai, ed. *Gaishi dōnyū nenkan* (Annual on foreign capital induction). Tokyo: Shōkō kaikan, 1969. 228 pp.

Giga, S. *Gendai Nihon no dokusen kigyō* (Contemporary Japanese monopoly enterprise). Kyoto: Mineruba shobō, 1962. 390 pp.

Gōhara, Hiroshi. *Nihon no keiei soshiki* (Organization of Japanese management). Tokyo: Tōyō keizai shimpōsha, 1968. 265 pp.

Gyōsei saibansho gojūnen-shi (History of fifty years of the administrative court). Tokyo: Gyōsei saibansho, 1941. 522 pp.

Hara, Shirō. *Nihon no ginkō* (Japanese banks). Tokyo: Tōeidō, 1972. 260 pp.

Hiramatsu, Yoshirō. *Kinsei keiji soshōhō no kenkyū* (Study of the law of criminal procedure in recent era). Tokyo: Sōbunsha, 1960. 1084 pp.

Hironaka, Toshio. *Keiyakuhō no kenkyū* (Studies in contract law). Tokyo: Yūhikaku, 1958. 188 pp.

Hirozumi, Iwao. *Biggu bijinesu to kaihō taisei* (Liberalization and big business). Tokyo: Nihon hyōronsha, 1970. 346 pp.

Hisashi, Tanikawa. *Shōhin no baibai* (Sales of goods). Tokyo: Yūhikaku, 1964. 322 pp.

Hoshino, Tōru. *Meiji mimpō hensanshi kenkyū* (Study of the history of the Meiji compilation of the civil code). Tokyo: Daiyamondosha, 1943. 545 pp.

————. *Mimpōten ronsōshi* (History of the civil code dispute). Tokyo: Kawade shobō, 1949. 312 pp.

Hosotani, Makoto, ed. *Nihon kigyō no kaigai shinshutsu to kokunai shotetsuzuki* (Advancement of Japanese enterprises abroad and various domestic procedures). Tokyo: Kokusai tōshi kensyūsho, 1971. 177 pp.

Ichihashi, Akira, and Muraoka, Yoshitaka. *Shin tokkyohō no jitsumu kaisetsu*

(Explanations of practices under the new patent law). Tokyo: Nihon keizai shimbunsha, 1971. 296 pp.

Igarashi, Kiyoshi. *Keiyaku to jijō henkō* (Contracts and changed circumstances). Tokyo: Yūhikaku, 1969. 222 pp.

Imai, Noriyoshi. *Gendai Nihon no dokusen shihon: dokusen keitai* (Monopolistic capital in contemporary Japan: monopolistic forms), Vol. I. Tokyo: Shiseidō, 1964. 232 pp.

Ishii, Ryōsuke. *Nihon hōseishi gaisetsu* (General survey of the Japanese legal history). Tokyo: Sōbunsha, 1960. 664 pp.

Ishii, Teruhisa. *Shōhō* (Commercial law). 3rd rev. ed. Tokyo: Keisō shobō, 1959. 628 pp.

Izawa, Kōhei. *Beikoku shōgyō shōkenhō* (U.S. law of commercial paper). Tokyo: Yūhikaku, 1955. p. 244

Jūkagaku kōgyō tsūshinsha, ed. *Kaigai tōshi gijutsu yushutsu yōran* (Survey of overseas investment and exports of technology). Tokyo: Jūkagaku kōgyō tsūshinsha, 1970. 421 pp.

———. *Nihon no kaigai shigen kaihatsu* (Japan's development of overseas resources). Tokyo: Jūkagaku kōgyō tsūshinsha, 1972. 161 pp.

Jurisuto nenkan, No. 425 (1969). 592 pp.

Kaisei shōken torihikihō no kaisetsu (Commentary on the revised securities transactions law). Tokyo: Shōji hōmu kenkyūkai, 1971. 312 pp.

Kanazawa, Yoshio, ed. *Bōeki kankeihō* (Laws related to trade). Hōritsugaku taikei, Vol. 25. Tokyo: Nihon hyōronshinsha, 1956. 384 pp.

Kaneko, Hajime. *Kyōsei shikkōhō* (Execution law). Tokyo: Kōbundō, 1951. 336 pp.

———. *Minji soshōhō taikei* (Study of the law of civil procedure). Tokyo: Sakai shoten, 1958. 523 pp.

———. *Saibanhō* (Law of trials). Hōritsugaku zenshū, Vol. 34. Tokyo: Yūhikaku, 1959. 298 pp.

Kaneko, Kentarō. *Kempō seitei to ōbeijin no hyōron* (Establishment of the constitution and European and American comments). Tokyo: Nihon seinenkan, 1937. 395 pp.

Kanno, Masao (Japan BIAC). *Shihon jiyūka to kokusai kyōsōryoku* (Capital liberalization and international competitiveness). Tokyo: K.K. Shiseidō, 1968. 438 pp.

Kanno, Waterō. *Nihon kaisha kigyō hasseishi no kenkyū* (Studies in the history of development of joint stock companies in Japan). Tokyo: Keizai hyōronsha, 1966. 726 pp.

Kata keizai kenkyijō, ed. *Kaisha keiretsu o saguru* (Search for corporate lineages). Tokyo: Kata keizai kenkyijō, 1972. 768 pp.

Katō, Toshihiko. *Nihon no ginkōka—dai ginkō no seikaku to sono shidhaōs* (Japanese bankers—characters of big banks and leaders thereof). Tokyo: Chūō kōronsha, 1970. 196 pp.

Katsumoto, Masaakira. *Mimpō kenkyū* (Study of the Civil Code). Tokyo: Ganshōdō, 1932–39. 4 vols.

Kawaguchi, Jun'ichi, *et al.*, eds. *Gōben gaisha no setsuritsu yori kessan made* (From establishment to liquidation of a joint-venture corporation). Tokyo: Kokusai tōshi kenkyūjo, 1970. 151 pp.

Kawanaka, Nikō. *Gendai no kanryōsei* (The contemporary bureaucratic system). Tokyo: Chūō daigaku shuppambu, 1962. 166 pp.

Kawashima, Takeyoshi. *Ideorogī to shite no kazoku seido* (The family system as an ideology). Tokyo: Iwanami shoten, 1964. 382 pp.

————. *Nihonjin no hōishiki* (Japanese legal consciousness). Tokyo: Iwanami shoten, 1967. 203 pp.

————. *Nihon shakai no kazokuteki kōsei* (The familial structure of Japanese society). Tokyo: Nihon hyōronsha, 1950. 206 pp.

Kazahaya, Yasoji, ed. *Zenkoku minji kanrei ruishū* (Country-wide classified collection of civil customary practices). Tokyo: Nihon hyōronsha, 1944. 323 pp.

Keidanren, ed. *Nichibei keizai kankei no shomondai* (Problems of Japanese-American economic relations). Tokyo: Keizai dantai rengōkai, 1969. 230 pp.

Keiyakuhō taikei (Compendium [essays] on contract law). Tokyo: Yūhikaku, 1963. 7 vols.

Keizai chōsa kyōkai, ed. *Nempō, keiretsu no kenkyū* (Annual report, studies of *keiretsu*). Tokyo: Keizai chōsa kyōkai, 1962. 605 pp.

Keizai dōyūkai. *Keizai dōyūkai jūgonen-shi* (Fifteen-year history of the Committee on Economic Development). Tokyo: Keizai dōyūkai, 1962. 530 pp.

Keizai dōyūkai, keizai hōsei iinkai. *Keiei no kokusaika ni kanren suru hōsei ni tsuite no ankēto chōsa—chūkan hōkoku* (Research by questionnaire on the legislation related to the internationalization of management—interim report). Tokyo: Keizai dōyūkai, 1971. 53 pp.

Keizai hatten kyōkai. *Wagakuni no kaigai toshi* (Overseas investments of our country). Tokyo: Keizai hatten kyōkai, 1972. 51 pp.

Kigyō kenkyūkai. *Ringi-teki keiei to ringi seido* (*Ringi*-style management and the *ringi* system). Tokyo: Tōyō keizai shimpōsha, 1966. 512 pp.

Kikawada, Kazutaka. *Ningen shugi no keizai shakai* (Humanistic economic society). Tokyo: Yomiuri shimbunsha, 1971. 196 pp.

Kikkawa, Daijirō. *Hanrei hozen shobun* (Provisional disposition decisions). Kyoto: Hōritsu bunkasha, 1959. 719 pp.

Kimoto, Kin'ya. *Gendai shihonshugi to keizaihō* (Contemporary capitalism and economic law). Tokyo: Shin hyōron, 1970. 260 pp.

Kinreikō zenshū (Consideration of Tokugawa regulations, first compilation), Vol. 6. Tokyo: Sōbunsha, 1959. 440 pp.

Kitagawa, Zentarō. *Keiyaku sekinin no kenkyū* (Study of contractual liability). Tokyo: Yūhikaku, 1963. 411 pp.

————. *Nihon hōgaku no rekishi to riron* (Theory and history of Japanese jurisprudence). Tokyo: Nihon hyōronsha, 1968. 422 pp.

Kiyomiya, Shirō. *Kempō* I (Constitution I), rev. ed. Hōritsugaku zenshū, Vol. 3. Tokyo: Yūhikaku, 1971. 472 pp.

Kobayakawa, Kingo. *Kinsei minji soshō seido no kenkyū* (Study of the civil litigation system in the recent era). Tokyo: Nihon hyōronsha, 1957. 754 pp.

————. *Meiji hōseishiron* (Treatise on the legal history of the Meiji era). Tokyo: Ganshōdō, 1940. 2 vols.

————. *Nihon kinsei minji saiban tetsuzukikō kenkyū* (A study of civil trial procedure in the Japanese recent era). Nihon hōri sōsho (Series on Japanese legal theory), Vol. 18. Tokyo: Nihon hōri kenkyūkai, 1942. 141 pp.

Kobayashi, Ken'ichi. *Gendai Nihon no koyō kōzō* (Employment structure in present-day Japan). Tokyo: Iwanami shoten, 1966. 400 pp.

Kobayashi, Noritake. *Intānashonaru bijinesu* (International business). Keieigaku zenshū, Vol. 17. Tokyo: Chikuma shobō, 1972. 270 pp.

————. *Nihon no gōben gaisha* (Japanese joint-venture corporations). Tokyo: Tōyō keizai shimpōsha, 1967. 384 pp.

Kokusai tōshi kenkyūjo, ed. *Zainichi shiten katsudō to shokisei* (Activities of foreign branches in Japan and various regulations). Tokyo: Kokusai tōshi kenkyūjo, 1969. 145 pp.

Kōsei torihiki iinkai (FTC), ed. *Dokusen kinshi seisaku nijūnenshi* (A twenty-year history of antimonopoly policies). Tokyo: Ōkurashō insatsukyoku, 1968. 758 pp.

Koyama, Noboru. *Minji chōteihō gaisetsu* (General survey of the civil conciliation law). Tokyo: Yūhikaku, 1954. 249 pp.

Mannari, Hiroshi. *Za bijinesu erīto, Nihon ni okeru keieisha no jōken* (The business elite, the background of business leaders in Japan). Tokyo: Kōdansha, 1965. 194 pp.

Matsuda, Jirō. *Shin kaishahō gairon* (Treatise on the new stock corporation law). Tokyo: Iwanami shoten, 1957. 469 pp.

Matsueda, Michio. *Gōben gaisha no hōritsu jitsumu* (Legal practices of joint-venture corporations). Tokyo: Daiyamondosha, 1969. 427 pp.

Matsushima, Shizuo. *Rōmu kanri no Nihon-teki tokushitsu to hensen* (Japanese characteristics and fluctuations in labor management). Tokyo: Daiyamondosha, 1962. 480 pp.

Misonō, Hitoshi. *Nihon no dokusen* (Monopoly in Japan). Tokyo: Shiseidō, 1965. 334 pp.

Miyagawa, Kiyoshi. *Kyū-mimpō to Meiji mimpō* (The old civil code and the Meiji civil code). Tokyo: Aoki shoten, 1965. 256 pp.

Miyamoto, Mataji. *Osaka no kenkyū* (Studies of Osaka). Osaka: Seibundō shuppan, 1967–70. 5 vols.

Miyazaki, Giichi. *Gendai Nihon no dokusen shihon: shikin chōtatsu, chikuseki to shin'yo* (Monopolistic capital in contemporary Japan: capital formation, accumulation, and credit). Vol. V. Tokyo: Shiseidō, 1966. 279 pp.

————. *Sengo Nihon no keizai kikō* (Economic structure in postwar Japan). Tokyo: Shin hyoronsha, 1966. 276 pp.

Miyazawa, Toshiyoshi. *Kempō* (Constitution). Tokyo: Yūhikaku, 1949. 401 pp.

————. *Kempō* II (Constitution II). 4 Hōritsugaku zenshū, Vol. 4. Rev. ed. Tokyo: Yūhikaku, 1971. 496 pp.

————. *Nihon koku kempō taikei* (Commentary on the Japanese national constitutions). Tokyo: Yūhikaku, 1955. 612 pp.

Mori, Gorō. *Sengo Nihon no rōmu kanri* (Labor management in postwar Japan). Tokyo: Daiyamondosha, 1961. 222 pp.

Morii, Kiyoshi. *Kokusai shōji chūsai* (International commercial arbitration). Tokyo: Tōyō keizai shimpōsha, 1970. 577 pp.

Nagai, Arekisan, and Noguchi, Yoshimitsu. *Kaitei gijutsu enjo keiyaku no jissai* (Revised: actualities of technological assistance contracts). Tokyo: Nihon kōgyō shimbunsha shuppanbu, 1967. 313 pp.

Nakagawa, Zennosuke, *et al.*, eds. *Chūshaku mimpō* (Commentaries, civil law). Tokyo: Yūhikaku, 1965. Vols. 1–19.

Nakamura, Kikuo. *Kindai Nihon no hōteki keisei* (The legal formation of modern Japan). Tokyo: Tsūshindō, 1956. 393 pp.

Nakamura, Shūichirō; Sugioka, Sekio; Takenaka, Ichirō; and Masamura, Kimishirō. *Nihon sangyō to kasen taisei* (Japanese industry and oligopolistic structure). Tokyo: Shin hyōronsha, 1966. 244 pp.

Nakamura, Yūichi, ed. *Gijutsu dōnyū keiyaku nintei kijun no kaisetsu* (Explanation of validation criteria concerning international contracts introducing technology). Tokyo: Shōji hōmu kenkyūkai, 1968. 153 pp.

Nakane, Chie. *Tate-shakai no ningen kankei* (Human relationship in a vertically [organized] society). Tokyo: Kōdansha, 1967. 189 pp.

Nihon bengoshi rengōkai. *Kaiin meibo* (Japanese Bar Ass'n, membership register). Tokyo: Nihon bengōshi rengōkai, 1971. 849 pp.

———. *Nihon bengoshi enkakushi* (History of the development of the Japanese lawyer). Tokyo: Nihon bengōshi rengōkai, 1959. 434 pp.

Nihon kokusai mondai kenkyūjo. *Kokusai keizaihō no shomondai* (Problems of international economic law), No. 4. Tokyo: Nihon kokusai mondai kenkyūjo, 1962. 270 pp.

Nihon kōshonin kyōkai. *Kaiin meibo* (Japan Notary Public Ass'n, membership register). Tokyo: Nihon kōshonin kyōkai, 1970. 271 pp.

Nihon seisansei hombu. *Chingin hakusho, 1972* (White paper on wages). Tokyo: Nihon seisansei hombu, 1972. 449 pp.

Nihon zeirishikai. *Chōsa-shitsu shiryō*. Tokyo: Nihon zeirishikai, July 1969. 131 pp.

Nihon zeirishi rengōkai. *Zeirishi kaigyō no tebiki* (Guide to opening a tax agent's business). Tokyo: Nihon zeirishi rengōkai, 1962. 35 pp.

Nishi, Zen'ya, ed. *Kaigai shijō hakusho, tenki ni tatsu sekai bōeki* (White paper on overseas market, world trade at its turning point). Tokyo: Nihon bōeki shinkōkai, 1972. 381 pp.

Nishihara, Kan'ichi. *Shōkōihō* (Law of commercial transactions). Hōritsugaku zenshū, Vol. 29. Tokyo: Yūhikaku, 1960. 416 pp.

Noda, Kazuo. *Nihon no jūyaku* (Japan's top executives). Tokyo: Daiyamondosha, 1960. 381 pp.

Nomura, Taku. *Yūgengaisha setsuritsu annai* (Guide to establishment of a limited company). Tokyo: Tōeidō, 1962. 285 pp.

Ōba, Osamu. *Edo jidai ni okeru karabune mochiwatarisho no kenkyū* (Study of books brought over by T'ang [Chinese] ships in the Edo period). Osaka: Kansai University, 1967. 804 pp.

Ogata, Masumi. *Gyōsei soshō seido no rekishi-teki kenkyū* (Historical study of the system of administrative litigation). Kyoto: K.K. Mineruba shobō, 1963. 89 pp.

Ohara, Keiji, ed. *Nichibei bunka kōshō-shi: tsūshō sangyō-hen* (History of Japanese-American cultural exchange: part on commerce and industry), Vol. 2 Tokyo: Yōyōsha, 1954. 537 pp.

Ōkōchi, Kazuo; Ujihara, Shōjirō; and Fujita, Wakao, eds. *Rōdō kumiai no kōzō to kinō* (The structure and function of labor unions). Tokyo: Tokyo daigaku shuppankai, 1959. 633 pp.

Okumura, Hiroshi. *Gaikoku shihon—Nihon ni okeru kōdō to ronri* (Foreign capital—its behavior and rationale in Japan). Tokyo: Tōyō keizai shinpōsha, 1969. 272 pp.

Okuno, Hikoroku. *Kinsei Nihon koyūhō ronkō* (Inquiry into Japanese traditional law of the recent era). Tokyo: Kasahara shoten, 1943. 284 pp.

Ōmori, Tadeo, and Yazawa, Makoto, eds. *Chūshaku kaishahō: Kabushiki* (Annotated commentary on company law: part on stock). Tokyo: Yūhikaku, 1967. 473 pp.

Ōnishi, Akira, ed. *Shin kaigai-tōshi* (New foreign investment). Tokyo: Sangyō shinchōsha, 1972. 219 pp.

Ōnishi, Masao, *et al*. *Nihon kigyō no kaigai shinshutsu to kokunai shotetsuzuki* (Japanese enterprises' advancement abroad and various domestic procedures). Tokyo: Kokusai tōshi kenkyūjo, 1971. 177 pp.

Ōno, Fumio, and Imanishi, Isamu. *Keiyaku zensho* (Complete collection on contracts). Tokyo: Seirin shoin shinsha, 1962. 1302 pp.

Ono, Toyoaki. *Nihon-teki keiei to ringi seido* (The system of *ringi* and Japanese-style management). Tokyo: Daiyamondosha, 1960. 217 pp.

Osatake, Takeshi. *Nihon kenseishi taikō* (Outline of the history of Japanese constitutional government). Tokyo: Nihon hyōronsha, 1939. 2 vols.

Ōsumi, Ken'ichirō. *Kaishahō-ron* (Theory of company law). Tokyo: Yūhikaku, 1962. 2 vols.

Saitō, Gorō, ed. *Nihon ni okeru gaikoku shihon no jittai* (Actual condition of foreign capitals in Japan). Tokyo: Marunouchi risāchi sentā, 1972. 1404 pp.

Saitō, Hideo. *Saibankanron* (Treatise on judges). Tokyo: Ichiryūsha, 1963. 301 pp.

Sakurai, Masao. *Wagakuni no keizai kyōryoku* (Economic cooperation of Japan). Tokyo: Ajia keizai kenkyūjo, 1972. 198 pp.

Sangyō-kōzō shingikai kokusai keizai bukai, ed. *Nihon no taigai keizai seisaku—Shinrai sareru Nihon e no michi* (Japanese foreign economic policy—road to a trustworthy Japan). Tokyo: Daiyamondosha, 1972. 298 pp.

Shibagaki, Kazuo. *Mitsui Mitsubishi no hyakunen—Nihon shihon shugi to zaibatsu* (A hundred years with Mitsui Mitsubishi—Japanese capitalism and *zaibatsu*). Tokyo: Chūō kōronsha, 1968. 208 pp.

Shimizu, Hideo. *Tokyo daigaku hōgaku-bu* (The law department of Tokyo University). Tokyo: Kōdansha, 1965. 217 pp.

Shimomura, Osamu, and Takenaka, Kazuo. *Nihon keizai no tenkaiten* (Turning point of Japanese economy). Tokyo: Tōyō keizai shinpōsha, 1972. 224 pp.

Shōda, Akira. *Dokusen kinshihō* (The antimonopoly law). Tokyo: Nihon hyōronsha, 1966. 1092 pp.

———. *Karuteru to hōritsu* (Cartels and law). Tokyo: Tōyō keizai shimpōsha, 1968. 310 pp.

Shukan Daiyamondo. *Nihon no "mirai gijutsu" besuto 600, bessatsu* ("Future technology" of Japan, best 600, special issue). Tokyo: Daiyamondosha, 1971. 216 pp.

Shunjūsha, ed. *Nihon keizai no kiso kōzō* (The basic structure of Japan's economy). 9th ed. Tokyo: Shunjūsha, 1971. 224 pp.

Suekawa, Hiroshi. *Keiyakuhō* (Contract law). Tokyo: Iwanami shoten, 1958. 179 pp.

Suekawa, Hiroshi, ed. *Shiryō sengo nijūnen-shi* (Materials for a twenty-year post-war history), Vol. 3. Tokyo: Nihon hyōronsha, 1966. 673 pp.

Suzuki, Ken'ichi. *Sumitomo—kigyō gurūpu no dōtai* (*Sumitomo*—movements of enterprise groups). Tokyo: Chūō kōronsha, 1971. 193 pp.

Suzuki, Takeo. *Kabushiki jitsumu* (Practices relating to shares). Vol. 5 on *gappei*. Tokyo: Yūhikaku, 1963. 195 pp.

———, and Ishii, Teruhisa. *Kaisei kabushiki kaishahō kaisetsu* (Commentary on the revised stock corporation law). Tokyo: Nihon hyōronsha, 1950. 428 pp.

Suzuki, Yasuzō. *Kempō seitei to Roesureru* (Establishment of the constitution and Roesler). Tokyo: Tōyō keizai shimpōsha, 1942. 440 pp.

Suzuki, Yukio. *Keizai kanryō; shin-sangyō kokka no purodyūsā* (The economic bureaucracy, producers of the new industrial state). Tokyo: Nihon keizai shimbunsha, 1969. 214 pp.

Tahara, Osamu, ed. *Kibo betsu kigyō keiei bunseki* (Analysis of enterprise management by size). Tokyo: Nihon shinyō chōsa K.K., 1970. 44 pp.

Takagi, Umon. *Bengoshi kara mita saibankan* (Judges as viewed by lawyers). Tokyo: Yūhikaku, 1963. 130 pp.

Takano, Yūichi, and Tsutsui, Wakamizu. *Kokusai keizai soshiki-hō* (The law of international economic organizations). Tokyo: Tokyo daigaku shuppambu, 1965. 333 pp.

Takeyama, Yasuo. *Nihon no keiei: sono fūdo to tembō* (Japanese management: its climate and perspective). Tokyo: Kashima kenkyūjo shuppankai, 1965. 294 pp.

Takezawa, Shin'ichi. *Ningen no kanri* (Management of men). Tokyo: Kōdansha, 1960. 224 pp.

Takigawa, Masajirō. *Kujiyado no kenkyū—Nihon bengoshi zenshi—Kujiyado henjutsu "Hikae" no shōkai* (A study of the suit inns—a pre-history of the Japanese lawyer—an introduction to the "Hikae" compiled by a suit inn). Tokyo: Waseda daigaku hikakuhō kenkyūjo, 1959. 166 pp.

———, *et al. Nijō Jin'ya no kenkyū* (Study of Nijō Jin'ya). Tokyo: Waseda daigaku hikakuhō kenkyūjo, 1962. 294 pp.

Takimoto, Seiichi, ed. "Zenkoku minji kanrei ruishū" (Country-wide classified collection of civil customary practices). In 50 *Nihon keizai taiten.* Tokyo: Hakutōsha, 1932; reprint Tokyo: Meiji bunken, 1971. 390 pp.

———. "Shōji kanrei ruishū" (Classified collection of commercial customary practices). In 49 and 50 *Nihon keizai taiten.* Tokyo: Hakutōsha, 1932; reprint Tokyo: Meiji bunken, 1971.

Tamba, Tsuneo. *Yokohama ukiyoe.* Tokyo: Asahi shimbunsha, 1962. 29 pp. 419 plates.

Tanaka, Jirō. *Gyōseihō kōgi, jō* (Lectures in administrative law, Vol. One). Tokyo: Ryosho fukyukai, 1965. 312 pp.

Tanaka, Seiji. *Kaishahō* (Company law). Tokyo: Chikura shobō, 1963. 477 pp.

———. *Saishin kaishahō shōron* (The latest and detailed explanation of company law). Tokyo: Keisō shobō, 1967. 2 vols.

———, Yoshinaga, Eisuke, and Yamamura, Chūhei. *Saizentei kommentāru kaishahō* (Again completely revised commentary on company law). Tokyo: Keisō shobō, 1968. 1622 pp.

Taniguchi, Tomohei, and Katō, Ichirō, eds. *Mimpō enshū* (Seminar on the Civil Code). Tokyo: Yūhikaku, 1958–59. 5 vols.

Tanigawa, Hisashi. *Shōhin no baibai* (Sales of goods). Tokyo: Yūhikaku, 1964. 322 pp.

Tezuka, Yutaka. *Meiji shoki keihō-shi no kenkyū* (Study of history of early Meiji criminal law). Tokyo: Keiō gijuku daigaku hōgaku kenkyūkai, 1956. 266 pp.

Tokyo daigaku rōdōhō kenkyūkai, ed. *Chūshaku rōdō kumiaihō* (Commentary on the Labor Union Law). Tokyo: Yūhikaku, 1949. 350 pp.

Tokyo ginkō chōsabu, ed. *Gaikoku kawase* (Foreign exchange), *Shin-ginkō jitsumu kōza* (New essays on bank practice), Vol. 8. Tokyo: Yūhikaku, 1967. 403 pp.

Tokyo shōken torihikijo. *Jōjō shinsa kijun* (Listing screening standards). Tokyo: Shōken torihikijo, 1971. 25 pp.

Tsuji, Kiyoaki. *Nihon kanryōsei no kenkyū* (Study of the Japanese bureaucracy). Tokyo: Tokyo daigaku shuppankai, 1969. 343 pp.

Tsuchiya, Takao. *Nihon no keieisha seishin* (Managerial mentality in Japan). Tokyo: Keizai ōraisha, 1963. 318 pp.

Unabara, Kimiteru, ed. *Gōben gaisha no setsuritsu yori kessan made* (From incorporation to liquidation of joint-venture corporations). Tokyo: Kokusai tōshi kenkyūjo, 1964. 147 pp.

Wagakuni no kaigai tōshi—genjō to kankyō (Investment abroad of our country—present status and environment). Tokyo: Keizai hatten kyōkai, 1972. 51 pp.

Wagatsuma, Sakae. *Mimpō kōgi* (Series of lectures on the Civil Code). Tokyo: Iwanami shoten, 1965–67. 3 vols.

———, et al., eds. *Hanrei kommentāru* (Case commentary). Tokyo: Kommentāru kankōkai, 1963–66. 8 vols.

Watanabe, Taizō. *Ukeoi kōji ni okeru funsō to "kurēmu"* (Disputes in contract construction and claims). Tokyo: Kajima kensetsu gijutsu kenkyū shuppanbu, 1954. 149 pp.

Yazawa, Makoto, ed. *Kigyō kaikei kisokushū* (Collection of regulations in enterprise accounting). Tokyo: Yūhikaku, 1961. 136 pp.

Yomiuri shimbunsha. *Sōri daijin* (Prime minister). Tokyo: Yomiuri shimbunsha, 1971. 333 pp.

Yoshida, Fujio. *Shihon jiyūka to gaishi-hō* (Capital liberalization and the FIL). Tokyo: K.K. Zaisei keizai kōhō-sha, 1967. 635 pp.

Yoshida, Jimpū. *Nihon no karuteru* (Japanese cartels). Tokyo: Tōyō keizai shimpōsha, 1964. 219 pp.

Yoshida, Seigo. '*71 Nikkan keizai kyōryoku no genjō to mondaiten* (Present status of Japan-Korea economic cooperation and the problems thereof). Tokyo: Kōgyō jiji tsūshinsha, 1971. 202 pp.

Zaisei kin'yū hōki kenkyū iinkai. *Zaisei kin'yū hōki kaisetsu zenshū, bōeki kawase-hen* (Series on the explanations of financial and monetary laws and ordinances, part on trade and exchange). Tokyo: Taisei shuppansha, 1969. 2758 pp.

Zenkoku shōken torihikijo, comp. *Kabushiki bumpu jōkyō chōsa* (Research on the situation of stock distribution). Tokyo: Zenkoku shōken torihikijo, 1971. 91 pp.

JAPANESE LANGUAGE SOURCES: ARTICLES

Abe, Hiroshi. "Hōritsuka no yōsei" (Training of jurists). 14 *Hōsō jihō* 1–35 (1962).

Agawa, Seidō. "Gaikoku chūsai handan no shōnin oyobi shikkō ni kansuru jōyaku ni tsuite" (Pts. 1–2) (Concerning convention on the recognition and enforcement of foreign arbitral awards). *Jurisuto* (Nos. 231, 232) 18, 42 (1961).

Ajimura, O. "Jūgyōin mochikabu seido" (Employee shareholding system). *Shōji hōmu kenkyū* (No. 430) 3 (15 Nov. 1967).

" 'Amae' no kokusai kankaku" ("Indulgence" in the international sense). *Gekkan ekonomisuto* 44 (Oct. 1971).

"Amae tōranu jitsuryoku" (Actual power warrants no more indulgence). *Asahi Shimbun* (24 April 1969).

Amano, Takeichi. "Hōsō jinkō" (Lawyer population). *Jurisuto* (No. 249) 40–63 (1962).

Amaya, Naohiro (MITI). "Shihon jiyūka to nashonaru intaresuto" (Capital liberalization and national interest). *Tōyō keizai* 4 (31 July 1969).

Araki, Nobuyoshi. "Shihon yushutsu no hitsuyō takamaru kongo no Nihon keizai" (The Japanese economy hereafter as the need to export capital increases). *Tōyō keizai* 35 (13 July 1969).

Asayama, T. "Shihon jiyūka to kabushiki kaishime no hōteki kōsa" (A legal analysis of capital liberalization and buying-up shares). *Jiyū to seigi* 39 (Jan. 1968).

"Bengoshi no daitoshi shūchū tō ni kansuru sankō shiryō" (Reference materials regarding the concentration of lawyers in large cities, etc.). 13 *Jiyū to seigi* (No. 3) 45–47 (1962).

Benrishikai. "Tokkyo jimu hyōjungakuhyō" (List of standard sums for patent service). Ass'n order (*kairei*) No. 8 (1972).

"Bibliography." *Hōgaku annai* (Guide to legal studies). In *Jurisuto* (Extra Issue) July 1967.

"Dai-yonji shihon jiyūka tōshin" (FIC report on the 4th round capital liberalization). *Zaisei keizai kōhō* (No. 1422) 3 (16 Aug. 1971).

Editors. "Towareru seifu no shihon jiyūka seisaku" (Government capital liberalization policy questioned). 48 *Ekonomisuto* (No. 30) 7–8 (21 July 1970).

Fujita, Yasuhiro. "Gaishi kisei wa jōyaku ni ihan suru ka" (Do Japan's controls of foreign capital violate treaties?). *Jurisuto* (No. 426) 124 (1969); in English, 3 *Law in Japan* 162 (1969).

Fukuji, Toshio. "Jijō henkō no gensoku" (Principle of changed circumstances). In 3 *Mimpō enshū* (Seminar on the Civil Code), edited by Tomohei Taniguchi and Ichirō Katō. Tokyo: Yūhikaku, 1958.

"Gaikoku shōken gyōsha ni kansuru hōritsu-an" (Draft of law concerning foreign securities dealers). *Zaisei keizai kōhō* (No. 1396) 9 (15 Feb. 1971).

"Gaishi no shinsenryaku o tenken suru" (Reviewing the new battle strategies of foreign capital). *Tōyō keizai* (No. 3585) 44 (13 Mar. 1971).

"Gaishi shingikai semmon iinkai hōkoku" (Report of the expert committee of the FIC). *Shōji hōmu kenkyū* (No. 415) 4 (5 June 1967).

"Gaishi tokushū" (Special symposium on foreign capital). *Tōyō keizai* 3 (31 July 1969).

"Gyōshu dake de wa fujūbun" (By industrial types only is not enough). *Asahi Shimbun*, 22 Aug. 1970.

Hashimoto, Masaharu, *et al.* "Gyōsei shoshihō kaisei ni tsuite no seigansho" (A petition concerning the amendment of the administrative scriveners' law). *Kaihō* (Ass'n report) (No. 3) (1962).

Hattori, Eiichi. "Teikan ni yoru gaikokujin yakuin no senshutsu seigen ni tsuite" (Concerning restrictions on election of foreign directors by articles of incorporation). *Shōji hōmu kenkyū* (No. 421) 2 (25 July 1967).

Hattori, Sadao. "Kōnin kaikeishi to bengoshi to no kengyō tō ni tsuite" (Concerning the overlap of CPA and lawyer business, etc.). 10 *Jiyū to seigi* (No. 3) 16 (1959).

Hayashi, Shintarō (MITI). "Shihon jiyūka to keiki chōsei-saku" (Capital liberalization and counter-cyclical measures). *Bōeki to kanzei* 10–11 (Jan. 1967).

Hedburg, Hakan; Adachi, James; and VanZandt, Howard. "Zainichi gaijin wa chūkoku suru" (Advice from foreigners living in Japan). *Gekkan ekonomisuto* 44–50 (Oct. 1971).

Henderson, Dan Fenno, and, Sono, Kazuaki. "Kokusai keiyaku ni okeru funsō kaiketsu jōkō—kokusai shihō gensoku no konran to chūsai" (Dispute settlement clauses in international contracts—confusion in conflicts principles and arbitration). 14 *Hōgaku ronshū* 745–65 (Feb. 1965).

Hidemura, Sanzō. "Meiji shonen Zōheiryō ni okeru o-yatoi gaikokujin no koyō mondai" (The problems of terminating employment of hired foreigners in the early Meiji Mint). In *Osaka no kenkyū* (Studies of Osaka), edited by Mataji Miyamoto. Osaka: Seibundo shuppan, 1968. Vol. 2.

Hoshino, Eiichi. "Gendai ni okeru keiyaku" (Contemporary contract). 8 *Gendaihō* 206–70 (1966).

Hoshino, Tōru. "San hakushi to mimpō seitei" (The three doctors and the enactment of the civil code). 49 *Hōgaku shirin* 33–55 (1951).

"Hōshū kitei kijun'an" (Draft standards for computing compensation [for the Tokyo judicial scriveners' association]). *Nihon shihō shoshikai rengōkai kaihō* (No. 67) 58 (Sept. 1962).

Hozumi, Yatsuka. "Mimpō idete, chūkō horobu" (The civil code emerges: loyalty and piety collapse). In Tōru Hoshino, *Meiji mimpō hensanshi kenkyū* (Study of the history of the Meiji compilation of the civil code). Tokyo: Daiyamondosha, 1943. 545 pp.

Igarashi, Kiyoshi. "Keiyaku to jijō henkō no gensoku" (Contracts and the principle of change in circumstances). 1 *Keiyakuhō taikei* 29. Tokyo: Yūhikaku, 1962.

Iida, Tsuneo. "Kokueki-ron ni hisomu Nihonjin no higaisha ishiki" (Japanese injured feelings concealed in the national-interest theory). *Tōyō keizai* (No. 3486) 14 (31 July 1969).

Imai, Hiroshi. "Hentai setsuritsu jikō" (Items of abnormal incorporation). 2 *Sōgō hanrei kenkyū soshō shōhō* 94 (1961).

———. "Shihaiken kakuho no tame no jiko kabushiki shutoku" (Acquisition of own shares in order to preserve the power to control). *Shōji hōmu kenkyū* (No. 547) 2 (25 Jan. 1971).

Imamura, Shigekazu. "Dokusen kinshi-hō" (The antimonopoly law). 52 *Hōritsugaku zenshū*. Tokyo: Yūhikaku, 1961.

Ishida, Shin'ichi. "Benrishi hōshū o meguru shomondai" (Various problems concerning the compensation of patent agents). 14 *Patento* (No. 11) 39–44 (1961).

Ishikawa, Kichiemon. "Futō rōdō-kōi no shinsa sokushin ni tsuite" (Proposals for expediting examinations of unfair labor practices). *Saiban to hō* (Law and trials). Tokyo: Yūhikaku, 1967; in English, 4 *Law in Japan* 17 (1970).

Ishikawa, Kichiemon. "Rokumihō to kempō 28-jō to no kankei" (The relationship between LUL and Const. Art. 28). 87 *Hōgaku kyōkai zasshi* 1–14 (1970).

Ishimoto, Yasuo. "Meiji-ki ni okeru chūsai saiban no senrei" (Pt. 2) (Precedents of international arbitration in the Meiji era). 8 *Hōgaku zasshi* (No. 1) 73–96 (1961).

Iyori, Hiroshi. "Dokusen kinshi-hō to gyōsei shidō" (Administrative guidance and the AML). *Jurisuto* (No. 342) 59 (1966).

"Jugyōin mochikabu seido no saiyō ni tsuite" (Concerning adoption of an employee shareholding system [Kawasaki Seitetsu's]). *Shōji hōmu kenkyū* (No. 536) 5 (25 Sept. 1970).

Kainō, Michitaka. "Nihon no bengoshi" (Japan's lawyers). 32 *Hōritsu jihō* 432 (1960).

Kakinuma, K. (FTC). "Shihon jiyūka to dokusen kinshihō" (Capital liberalization and antimonopoly law). *Shōji hōmu kenkyū* (No. 552) 19 (15 Mar. 1971).

Kanazawa, Yoshio. "Keizaihō" (Economic law). 52 *Hōritsugaku zenshū*. Tokyo: Yūhikaku, 1961.

Kaneda, Heiichirō. "Tokugawa jidai ni okeru soshōjō no wakai" (Compromise in litigation in Tokugawa period). 1 *Shien* (No. 2) 64–88; (No. 3) 44–53 (1928).

———. "Tokugawa jidai no tokubetsu minji soshōhō—kanekuji no kenkyū" (Special civil procedural law of the Tokugawa period—study of money suits). 42 *Kokka gakkai zasshi* 1934–84, 1136–64, 1423–45 (1929).

Kaneko, Hajime. "Kabushiki ni taisuru kyōsei shikkō" (Execution on shares). 2 *Kabushiki kaishahō kōza* 765, 774 (1956).

———. "Saibanhō" (Law of trials). 34 *Hōritsugaku zenshū* 71 (1959).

Kawakami, Tarō. "Chusai" (Arbitration). 3 *Kokusai shihō kōza* 848 (1964).

———. "Gaikoku chūsai handan no kōryoku" (The effect of foreign arbitration awards in our country). *Jurisuto* (No. 179) 53–54 (1959).

———. "Gaikoku chūsai handan no shōnin shikkō ni kansuru kokuren jōyaku to Nipponkoku no ka'nyū" (Convention on the recognition and enforcement of foreign arbitral awards and Japan's accession thereto). 45 *Minshō-hō zasshi* (No. 5) 291–620 (1962).

———. "Kokusai shōji chūsai ni kansuru kokusai shihō riron" (Theory of private international law concerning international commercial arbitration). 1 *Kobe hōgaku zasshi* (No. 3) 577, 604 (1951).

———. "Kokusai shōji chūsai no shōrai" (The future of international commercial arbitration). 7 *Bōeki kurēmu to chūsai* (No. 3) 121–25 (1960).

———. "Wagakuni ni okeru Eikoku chūsai handan no shikkō" (Execution of English arbitration awards in Japan). *Jurisuto* (No. 195) 58–60 (1960).

———, and Masakame, Keisuke. "Nihon ni okeru kokusai-teki gijutsu enjo keiyaku funsō shori jōkō no jittai to kokusai shihō mondai" (A survey of dispute settlement clauses in international technical assistance contracts in Japan and problems of private international law). 16 *Kobe hōgaku zasshi* 550 (1966).

Kawamoto, Ichirō. "Jiko kabushiki no shutoku kinshi kanwa ron no haikei to sono konkyō" (Background and basis of argument for relaxing acquisition of own shares). *Shōji hōmu kenkyū* (No. 535) 3 (15 Sept. 1970).

———. "Jōto seigen-tsuki kimei kabushiki to jōjō seido" (Listing system and transfer-restricted shares). *Shōji hōmu kenkyū* (No. 423) 144 (25 Aug. 1967).

———. "Kimei kabuken to furikae kessai seido" (Nonbearer shares and the exchange system by way of pooling shares with a trustee). 13 *Kobe hōgaku zasshi* 18 (1963).

Kawasaki, Hirotarō. "Gyōsei shidō no jittai—saikin no mittsu no kēsu ni miru" (Actualities of administrative guidance—as seen in three recent cases). *Jurisuto* (No. 342) 51 (1966).

Kawashima, Takeyoshi. "Chōtei to chūsai" (Conciliation and arbitration). 18 *Bōeki kurēmu to chūsai* (No. 165) 2 (1971).

"Keiei mondai" (Management problems). *Chūō kōron: bessatsu* 51 (Fall 1967).

"Kigyō kaikei gensoku" (General principles for enterprise accounting). In *Kigyō kaikei kisokushū* (Collection of regulations in enterprise accounting), edited by Makoto Yazawa. Tokyo: Yūhikaku, 1961.

"Kigyōnai hōritsu gyōmu ni kansuru jittai chōsa" (Survey of legal work within the enterprises). *Shōji hōmu kenkyū* (No. 360) 7 (1963).

Kiribuchi, Toshihiro. "Daiyonji shihon jiyūka no mondaiten" (The problems of the 4th round capital liberalization). *Zaisei keizai kōhō* (No. 1423) 1–3 (23 Aug. 1971).

Kitazawa, Masahiro. "Setsuritsu-chū no kaisha" (Company under establishment process). 1 *Kabushiki kaishahō kōza* (Lectures on corporation law) 211, 218 (1958).

Kobayakawa, Kingo. "Kinsei minji saiban no gainen to tokushitsu" (General concepts and special characteristics of civil litigation of the recent era). 5 *Hōgaku ronsō* 372–492 (1921).

———. "Kinsei no saiban soshiki to shinkyū oyobi kankatsu ni kansuru jakkan no kōsatsu" (Some considerations of the organization, appeals, and jurisdiction of the courts of the recent era). 31 *Hōgaku ronsō* 994–1020 (1934); 32 *Hōgaku ronsō* 100–21, 801–44 (1935).

Koide, Yoshio. "Osadamegaki hyakkajō hensan no jijō ni tsuite" (Concerning the conditions of the compilation of the Osadamegaki Hyakkajō). *Shichō* (No. 3) 112–37 (1934).

"Kokusai-teki gijutsu dōnyū keiyaku ni kansuru nintei kijun" (Validation criteria concerning international contracts introducing technology). In *Gijutsu dōnyū keiyaku nintei kijun no kaisetsu*, edited by Yūichi Nakamura. Tokyo: Shōji hōmu kenkyukai, 1968.

Komiya, Ryūtarō. "Shihon jiyūka no keizaigaku" (The economics of capital liberalization). *Ekonomisuto* 4 (25 July 1967).

Kōriki, Kikuo; Ichikawa, Tōru; and Satō, Shigeo. "Bōeki to hōritsu" (Trade and law). 8 *Bōeki jitsumu kōza* (Lectures on trade practice) 352–79. Tokyo: Yūhikaku, 1962.

Koshikawa, Junkichi. "Nihon shōgai minji soshōhō no juritsu" (Establishment of a Japanese liaison civil procedure law). *Hōkei ronshū* (No. 28) 205 (1959); (No. 30) 65 (1960).

Koyama, Noboru. "Chūsaihō" (Arbitration law). 38 *Hōritsugaku zenshū* 88 (1958).

———. "Chōteihō, chūsaihō" (Conciliation law, arbitration law). 38 *Hōritsugaku zenshū* 51–106 (1958).

Kozeki, Toshimasa. "Saibankan yori bengoshi e no chūmon" (A request from a judge to lawyers). 12 *Jiyū to seigi* (No. 8) 2–6 (1961).

Kumekawa, Isao. "Benrishi no shokumu han'i ni tsuite" (Concerning the scope of the patent agents' services). 11 *Patento* (No. 12) 7–8 (1958).

Kurimoto, Ichirō. "Saikin no shomondai" (Recent problems). *Nihon shihō shoshikai rengōkaihō* (No. 4) 1–4 (1 Nov. 1962).

Kuwabara, T. "Saikeikoku jōkō no seigen ni kansuru shomondai" (Various problems relating to limitations on the most-favored-nation clause). In Nihon kokusai mondai kenkyūjo, *Kokusai keizaihō no shomondai* (Problems of international economic law) (No. 3) 124 (1961).

Maekawa, Kōzō (MOF). "Kōkai kaitsuke no todokeide seido ni tsuite" (Concerning the filing system for public take-over bids). 23 *Kigyō kaikei* (No. 11) 99 (Sept. 1971).

Maki, Kenji. "Kinsei bukehō no wakai oyobi chōtei" (Conciliation and compromise in the law of the military houses of the recent era). *Saitō hakushi kanreki kinen, hō to saiban* 201 (1942). Tokyo: Yūhikaku, 1942. 720 pp.

Mathies, Otto. "Hamburugu ni okeru jōsetsu chūsai saibansho" (The standing arbitration court in Hamburg). 74 *Shihō shiryō* 62 (1925).

Matsuda, Jirō. "Doitsu shōji chūsai seido no ichikōsatsu" (Pt. 2) (An inquiry into the German commercial arbitration system). 9 *Hōsōkai zasshi* (No. 11) 73 (1931).

Matsui, Yasuhiro, *et al.* "Bengoshi no seikatsu to ishiki" (Life and thought of lawyers). 32 *Hōritsu jihō* 458 (1960).

Matsumoto, Jōji, *et al.* "Ume Kenjirō hakushi no omoide" (Memories of Dr. Kenjirō Ume). 49 *Hōgaku shirin* 88–104 (1951).

Matsuo, Kunihiko. "Benrishi no gyōmu han'i o kakudai" (The extension of the patent agents' business). *Toki no hōrei* (No. 352) 10–15 (1960).

Matsushita, Chū. "Bengoshi no chii kōjō to shokuiki kakujū" (Advancement of the lawyers' social status and expansion of their scope of services). *Nihon hōritsu shimbun* (No. 81) 3 (1963).

Michida, Shin'ichirō. "Jōyaku mondai to shite no shihon jiyūka to gaishi-kōbō no senryaku" (Capital liberalization as a treaty question and offensive and defensive strategies concerning foreign capital). *Jurisuto* (No. 364) 48 (1967); in English, 2 *Law in Japan: An Annual* 1 (1968).

Mikazuki, Akira. "Minji soshōhō" (Law of civil procedure). 35 *Hōritsugaku zenshū* 254 (1960).

Minagawa, T. "ILO kenshō no shuyō mondai" (Major problems regarding the ILO chapter). In Nihon kokusai mondai kenkyūjo, *Kokusai keizaihō no shomondai* (Problems of international economic law) (No. 4) 1–35 (1962).

Miyaji, Sadahide. "Soshō ni kansuru tetsuzuki" (Procedure for acknowledgments). 10 *Jiyū to seigi* (No. 9) 30 (1959).

Miyazawa, Toshiyoshi. "Minobe sensei no gyōseki" (Accomplishments of teacher Minobe). 62 *Kokka gakkai zasshi* 327–36 (1948).

Mon'ya, N. "Gijutsu dōnyū no jiyūka to tokkyohō" (Liberalization of induction of technology and the patent law). *Keizaihō* (No. 11) 16 (1968).

Muramatsu, Toshio. "Shihō shoshi to shitei dairinin" (Judicial scriveners and appointed attorneys). 29 *Hōritsu jihō* (No. 9) 50–51 (1957).

Muramoto, Kazuo. "Wagakuni chūsai seido no jitsujō" (The actual state of affairs in the Japanese arbitration system). 28 *Shihō kenkyū hōkokusho* (No. 6) 108 (1938).

Nakada, Kaoru. "Tokugawa jidai no minji saiban jitsuroku" (Actual records of civil trial in the Tokugawa period). 3 *Hōseishi ronshū* 756–85 (1943).

Nakamura, Kikuo. "Mimpōten ronsō no keika to mondaiten." 29 *Hōgaku kenkyū* 473–97, 753–71, 853–75 (1956).

Nakata, Jun'ichi. "Shōji chūsai seido no gaiken" (General survey of the commercial arbitration system). *Hōkei gakkai zasshi* (Okayama daigaku) (No. 3) 2 (1952).

Namoto, Kimikuni. "Gaikoku kawase oyobi gaikoku bōeki kanri hōki to sono shōgai-teki kōryoku ni tsuite" (Concerning the laws and regulations for control of foreign exchange and foreign trade and their external effect). 54 *Kokusaihō zasshi* (The journal of international law and diplomacy) (No. 4) 47, 79 (1955).

Narita, Yoriaki. "Gyōsei shidō" (Administrative guidance). *Gendaihō*, Vol. 4. Tokyo: Iwanami shoten, 1966; in English, 2 *Law in Japan: An Annual* 45 (1968).

Nihon shihō shoshikai rengōkai. "Dai-nijūikkai teiji sōkai shiryō" (Materials on the 21st regular general meeting) 181 (June 1968).

Nihon zeirishi rengōkai. "Zeirishihō chikujō kaisetsu" (Article-by-article commentary on the Tax Agents Law) 2–8. Tokyo: Nihon zeirishi rengōkai, 1958.

Nisan-ki shūshūsei yūshi. "Shinjin bengoshi no keizaiteki jittai" (Economic status of newly born lawyers). 43 *Hōritsu jihō* 83 (1971).

Nishi, Kan. "Shōgai hanrei kenkyū." *Jurisuto* (No. 241) 127 (1962).

Nojima, Atsushi. "Gaikokujin no bengonin wa Nihon no hōtei ni tateru ka" (Can foreign lawyers appear in Japanese courts?). 10 *Hōritsu no hiroba* (No. 9) 14 (1957).

Ogawa, Ichirō. "Gendai ni okeru gyōsei to hō" (Law and contemporary administration). 4 *Gendaihō* (Contemporary law). Tokyo: Iwanami shoten, 1966.

———, Kanazawa, Yoshio; Narita, Yoriaki; Matsuo, Kinzō; Yazawa, Makoto; and Yamauchi, Kazuo (Symposium). "Gyōsei shidō no kompon mondai" (Basic problems of administrative guidance). *Jurisuto* (No. 342) 21 (1966).

Ohara, Yoshio (FTC). "Shihon jiyūka no kokusai jōyaku-jō no mondaiten" (Problem points of capital liberalization from the standpoint of international treaties). *Keizaihō* (No. 11) 2 (1968).

Ōhira, Zengo. "Kokusai tōshihō no josetsu" (An introduction to international investment law). In *Kokusai keizaihō no shomondai* (No. 3) 214–30 (1961).

"Ōkurashō—Rikō tokei ni chōsei todokeide shohōkokusho no teishutsu o meirei" (Ministry of finance order against Rikō watch to submit revised submissions and reports). *Shōji hōmu kenkyū* (No. 283) 25 (1963).

Okuyama, Keikichi. "Benrishi no chii kōjō" (Improvement of the patent agents' status). 14 *Patento* (No. 10) 3 (1961).

"¼ jiyūka ni suginu" (Not more than ¼ liberalization). *Asahi Shimbun*, 30 July 1971.

"Opinion (*ikensho*) of the chairman (Ataru Kobayashi) of the FIC to Minister of Finance Mikio Mizuta July 29, 1971." *Zaisei keizai kōhō* (No. 1422) 4 (16 Aug. 1971).

"Osadamegaki," Second Book, Art. 71, Para. 44 (1742). *Shihō shiryō bessatsu* (No. 17). *Nihon kindai keiji hōreishū (jō)*. Tokyo: Shihōshō, 1942.

Ōsumi, Ken'ichirō. "Kabushiki no jōto" (Transfer of shares). 2 *Kabushiki kaishahō kōza* (Lectures on corporation law) 639, 648 (1956).

————, Nishihara, Kan'ichi, and Ueda, Akinobu. "Kabushiki kaishahō no komponteki kaisei ni tsuite no kenkyū" (Study on basic revision of the stock corporation law). *Shōji hōmu kenkyū* (No. 30) 1, 5 (1956).

Ōyama, Kikuji. "Hōsō ichigen seido" (The system of unification of the legal profession). 14 *Jiyū to seigi* (No. 2) 1–21 (1963).

Saitō, Hideo. "Wagakuni no saibankan no tokushoku" (Special characteristics of judges in our country). *Jurisuto* (No. 239) 89 (1961); (No. 245) 451 (1962).

Sakai, Ichirō. "Ruiseki tōhyō" (Cumulative voting). 3 *Kabushiki kaishahō kōza* (Lectures on stock corporation law) 1005–28 (1956).

————. "Ruiseki tōhyō seido no kaiseian ni tsuite" (Concerning the draft revision of the cumulative voting system). *Shōji hōmu kenkyū* (No. 549) 2 (15 Nov. 1970).

Sakuragi, Masayasu. "Shihon no jiyūka to hōritsu mondai" (Capital liberalization and legal problems). 24 *Hōritsu no hiroba* (No. 12) 18 (1971).

Sawa, Eizō. "Soshō chien to hōsō jinkō" (Delay of lawsuits and lawyer population). *Shōji hōmu kenkyū* (No. 94) 2 (1958).

"Sengo hōsei no hensen" (Changes in the postwar legal system). *Jurisuto* (No. 100) 2–189 (1956).

Senō, Akira. "Zainichi beijin bengoshi no gyōmu seigen mondai" (The problem of limiting the practice of American lawyers resident in Japan). 5 *Jiyū to seigi* (No. 1) 12 (1954).

"Shihō shoshi hōshū kitei kijun" (Standard fees for judicial scriveners). *Nihon shihō shoshi rengōkai kaihō* (No. 67) 48 (1970).

Shiraishi, Kenzō. "Gyōsei jiken soshō no arikata" (A model for administrative case litigation). *Hanrei jihō* (No. 428) 3 (1966).

Shōda, Akira. "Keizaihō" (Economic law). 7 *Gendaihō* 200 (1966).

"Shōken torihikihō kaisei ni tomanau jūyō jikō no kaisetsu" (Commentary on the chief items relating to the revision of the securities exchange law). 23 *Kigyō kaikei* (Enterprise accounting) (No. 11) 2–69 (Sept. 1971).

Special Symposium. "Fukuro dataki no Nippon" (Japan in a bag). *Gekkan ekonomisuto* 16–61 (Oct. 1971).

Sugii, S. "Paakusu hinan ronsō" (The dispute over Parkes's criticism). 38 *Shirin* (No. 4).

Suzuki, Saizō, *et al.* "Hōsō ichigen no airo" (Bottleneck in unification of the legal profession). 13 *Jiyū to seigi* (No. 11) 1–17 (1962).

Suzuki, Takeo. "Shihon jiyūka no seido-teki taisaku" (Systematic counter-measures for capital liberalization). *Shōji hōmu kenkyū* (No. 415) 8 (5 June 1967); English summary, 4 *Journal ACCJ* (No. 7) 20 (5 July 1967).

————. "Shōgaihō no kenkyū o suishin shitai" (We want to promote studies of liaison law). *Shōji hōmu kenkyū* (No. 192) 2 (1960).

"Tainai chokusetsu tōshi to no jiyūka ni tsuite" (Concerning liberalization of inward direct investments, etc.). In *Shihon jiyūka to gaishi-hō* (Capital liberalization and the FIL), edited by Fujio Yoshida. Tokyo: K.K. Zaisei keizai kōhō-sha, 1967.

Takanashi, Katsuyoshi. "Kōsei shōsho" (Notarial deeds). *Jurisuto* (207) 59–66 (1060).

Takayanagi, Shinzō. "Wakaishugi ni tatsu saiban" (Trials based on the principle of compromise). 56 *Chūō kōron* (No. 4) 139 (1941).

Takeuchi, Toshio. "Hokkinin no sekinin" (Liability of promoters). 2 *Sōgō hanrei kenkyū soshō, shōhō*. Tokyo: Yūhikaku, 1961.

Takiuchi, Reisaku, *et al.* "Hōtei gijutsu no kentō" (Review of technique in court). 33 *Hōritsu jihō* (No. 12) 4–19 (1961).

Tanabe, Akira. "Shōhō no ichibu kaisei hōritsuan yōkōan tsuika kōmoku no kaisetsu" (Commentary on supplemental items to the draft of a partial revision of the Commercial Code). *Shōji hōmu kenkyū* (No. 540) 28 (15 Nov. 1970).

Tateishi, Setsuo. "Hōshū kitei no chūkai" (Comments on the compensation regulations). *Nihon shihō shoshikai rengōkai kaihō* (No. 4) 13 (11 Nov. 1962).

Terada, Kumao. "Bengoshi gyōmu no hatten hōsoku" (A plan for the development of the lawyer's business). 10 *Jiyū to seigi* (No. 3) 21 (1959).

"Tokushū: Gyōsei jiken soshōhō goshūnen" (Special symposium: five years under the administrative case litigation law). *Jurisuto* (No. 383) 22–75 (1967).

"Tokyo shōkō kaigisho ruiseki tōhyō seido, jiko kabushiki shutoku seigen ni kansuru iken chōsa kekka o happyō" (Publication of Tokyo Chamber of Commerce results of opinion poll concerning cumulative voting and restrictions on acquiring own shares). *Shōji hōmu kenkyū* (No. 552) 18 (15 Mar. 1971).

Tomizawa, Hiroshi. "Daiyonji shihon jiyūka ni tsuite" (Concerning the 4th round of capital liberalization). *Toki no hōrei* (No. 761) 28 (1971).

Tōyama, Shigeki. "Mimpōten ronsō no seijishiteki kōsatsu" (Historical political considerations of the civil code dispute). 40 *Hōgaku shirin* 56–87 (1951).

Ueda, Akinobu. "Giketsuken to sono dairikōshi" (Voting right and its proxy). *Zoku jitsumu kabushiki kaishahō rokkō* (Six more essays on practical stock corporation law). Tokyo: Shōji hōmu kenkyūkai, 1960.

Ukai, Nobushige. "Minobe hakase no shisō to gakusetsu—sono rekishiteki igi" (Theory and thought of Dr. Minobe—its historical meaning). 20 *Hōritsu jihō* 381–85 (1948).

Yamanaka, Rikimatsu. "Shihō shoshi to soshō kōi—Muramatsu hanji no shoron ni kotau" (Judicial scriveners and acting in litigation—in response to Judge Muramatsu's argument). 20 *Hōritsu jihō* (No. 11) 87 (1957).

Yazawa, Makoto. "Gijutsu dōnyū no jiyūka ni kansuru hōteki taisaku" (Legal countermeasures concerning liberalization of the induction of technology). *Shōji hōmu kenkyū* (No. 450) 2–12 (25 Mar. 1968).

Yokoi, M. "Gātto no kitei to sono un'yō" (The provisions of GATT and their application). 32 *Hōritsu jihō* 630 (1960).

Yoshida, Kō. "Kansayaku kansa to kōnin kaikeishi no kansa" (Audit by auditors and audits by CPAs). 28 *Hōritsu jihō* (No. 6) 22–31 (1956).

Yumoto, Takunaga. "Shihō shoshi no shokuiki kakuritsu ni tsuite" (Concerning the marking out of a field of competence for the judicial scrivener). *Nihon shihō shoshikai rengōkai kaihō* (Report of the Japanese federation of judicial scriveners' association) (No. 1) 6–7 (1959).

Zadankai. "Shōken torihikihō kaisei no mondaiten" (Problem points in the revision of the securities exchange law). *Jurisuto* (No. 483) 82 and (No. 485) 83 (1 Aug. 1971).

"Zeirishi no jittai chōsa" (Empirical investigation of tax agents). *Chōsa-shitsu shiryō*, July 1969, p. 44-2.

"Zeirishi no oitachi" (The growth of tax agents). *Zeirishikai* (Tax agents world), 18 Dec. 1962, p. 7.

"Zen jōjō kaisha no keiretsu seimitsu chōsa" (A detailed investigation of the *keiretsu* of all listed companies). *Tōyō keizai* (Special issue, 15 Nov. 1967).

"Zōshi hakusho" (White paper on capital increase). *Shōji hōmu kenkyū* (No. 577) 12–13 (20 Apr. 1971).

ENGLISH LANGUAGE SOURCES: BOOKS

Abe, Makoto. *A Monetary Model of the Japanese Economy.* Ann Arbor: University Microfilms, 1969. 430 pp.

Abegglen, James C. *The Japanese Factory: Aspects of Its Social Organization.* Glencoe, Ill.: Free Press, 1958. 41 pp.

————. *Management and Labor: The Japanese Solution.* Tokyo: Kōdansha International, Ltd., 1973. 200 pp.

————, ed. *Business Strategies for Japan.* Tokyo: Sophia University, 1970. 217 pp.

Ackerman, Edward A. *Japan's Natural Resources and Their Relation to Japan's Economic Future.* Chicago: University of Chicago Press, 1953. 655 pp.

Adams, Louis Jerold. "Theory, Law and Policy of Contemporary Japanese Treaties." Ph.D. dissertation, University of Washington, 1972. 303 pp.

Adams, T. F. M., and Hoshii, Iwao. *A Financial History of the New Japan.* Tokyo: Kōdansha International, Ltd., 1972. 547 pp.

Adams, T. F. M., and Kobayashi, Noritake. *The World of Japanese Business.* Tokyo: Kōdansha International, Ltd., 1969. 326 pp.

Akita, George. *Foundations of Constitutional Government in Modern Japan, 1868–1900.* Cambridge: Harvard University Press, 1967. 292 pp.

Allen, G. C., and Donnithorne, Audrey. *Western Enterprises in Far Eastern Development: China and Japan.* London: George Allen & Unwin, Ltd., 1954. 199 pp.

Allison, Richard C., ed. *Current Legal Aspects of Doing Business in the Far East.* Chicago: American Bar Association, 1972. 208 pp.

American Association for the Advancement of Science. *Science in Japan: A Symposium Presented at the Cleveland Meeting of the American Association for the Advancement of Science, 26–31 December 1963.* Edited by Arthur H. Livermore. Baltimore: Horn-Shafer, 1965. 486 pp.

American Bar Foundation. *The 1971 Lawyer Statistical Report.* Chicago: American Bar Association, 1972. 142 pp.

American Chamber of Commerce in Japan. *Digest of Japanese Court Decisions in Patentability and Patent Infringement Cases, 1964–1965.* Tokyo: The American Chamber of Commerce in Japan, 1968. 93 pp.

————. *Digest of Japanese Court Decisions in Patent Infringement Cases, 1955–1963.* Tokyo: The American Chamber of Commerce in Japan, 1965. 102 pp.

Annual Report of PICA (Private Investment Company for Asia). Tokyo: PICA, 1970. 31 pp.

Arai, Shunzō. *An Intersection of East and West.* Tokyo: Rikugei Publishing House, 1971. 212 pp.

Asahi Shimbun Staff. *The Pacific Rivals: A Japanese View of Japanese-American Relations.* Tokyo and New York: Weatherhill-Asahi, 1972. 431 pp.

Aubrey, Henry G. *Atlantic Economic Cooperation: The Case of the OECD.* New York: Praeger, 1967. 214 pp.

Aufricht, Hans. *International Monetary Fund: Legal Bases, Structure, Functions.* Washington, D.C.: IMF, 1964. 250 pp.

Ayusawa, Iwao F. *A History of Labor in Modern Japan.* Honolulu: East-West Center Press, 1966. 406 pp.

Azumi, Kōya. *Higher Education and Business Recruitment in Japan.* New York: Columbia University, Teachers College Press, 1969. 126 pp.

Baerwald, Hans. *The Purge of Japanese Leaders Under the Occupation.* Berkeley: University of California Press, 1959. 111 pp.

Bakke, E. Wight. *Revolutionary Democracy: Challenge and Testing in Japan.* Hamden, Conn.: Archon Books, 1968. 343 pp.

Ballon, Robert J., ed. *Doing Business in Japan.* Tokyo: Sophia University and Charles E. Tuttle Co., 1968. 221 pp.

————. *The Japanese Employee.* Tokyo: Sophia University and Charles E. Tuttle Co., 1969. 317 pp.

————. *Japan's Market and Foreign Business.* Tokyo: Sophia University, 1971. 304 pp.

————. *Joint Ventures and Japan.* Tokyo: Sophia University and Charles E. Tuttle Co., 1967. 138 pp.

————, and Lee, Eugene H., eds. *Foreign Investment and Japan.* Tokyo: Sophia University, 1972. 340 pp.

Bank of Japan. *The Bank of Japan: Its Function and Organization.* Tokyo: Bank of Japan, 1962. 126 pp.

————. *Manual of Foreign Investment in Japan.* Tokyo: Bank of Japan, Nov. 1971. 34 pp.

Beckmann, George. *The Making of the Meiji Constitution.* Lawrence, Kansas: University of Kansas Press, 1957. 158 pp.

————, and Ōkubo, Genji. *The Japanese Communist Party, 1922–1945.* Stanford: Stanford University Press, 1969. 453 pp.

Behrman, Jack N. *Some Patterns in the Rise of the Multinational Enterprise.* University of North Carolina School of Business Administration Research Paper, No. 18, 1969. 180 pp.

Bellah, Robert. *Tokugawa Religion.* Glencoe, Ill.: Free Press, 1957. 249 pp.

Bernstein, Merton C. *Private Dispute Settlement.* New York: Free Press, 1968. 741 pp.

BIAC. *The Control of the Inflow of Investments in Japan* (Annexed to Circular C–438 of 17 Mar. 1967). 21 pp.

Bisson, T. A. *Zaibatsu Dissolution in Japan.* Berkeley: University of California Press, 1954. 314 pp.

Black, John R. *Young Japan: Yokohama and Yedo, 1858–79.* London: Oxford Press (1st printed 1883), 1968. 2 vols.

Blumenthal, Tuvia. *Savings in Postwar Japan.* Cambridge: Harvard University Press, 1970. 117 pp.

Boissonade de Fontarabie, Emile Gustave. *Les Anciennes Coutumes du Japon et le Nouveau Code Civil.* Tokyo: Hakubunsha, 1894.

Boulton, A. Harding. *Business Consortia.* London: Sweet & Maxwell, 1961.

Boxer, C. R. *The Christian Century in Japan, 1549–1650.* Berkeley: University of California Press, 1951. 535 pp.

———. *The Great Ship from Amacon: Annals of Macao and the Old Japan Trade, 1555–1640.* 2d ed. Lisbon: Centro de Estudos Historicos Ultramarinos, 1963. 359 pp.

Broadbridge, Seymour. *Industrial Dualism in Japan.* Chicago: Aldine Publishing Co., 1966. 103 pp.

Burks, Ardath V. *The Government of Japan.* New York: Crowell, 1961. 269 pp.

Byrd, Elbert M. *Treaties and Executive Agreements in the United States.* The Hague: M. Nijhoff, 1960. 276 pp.

Cocks, R. *Diary of Richard Cocks, Cape-merchant in the English Factory in Japan, 1615–1622.* Edited by N. Murakami. Tokyo: Sankūsha, 1899. 2 vols.

Cole, Allen B. "Political Tendencies of Japanese in Small Enterprise." New York: Institute of Pacific Relations, 1959. Mimeographed. 155 pp.

———; Totten, George O.; and Uyehara, Cecil H. *Socialist Parties in Postwar Japan.* New Haven: Yale University Press, 1966. 490 pp.

Cole, Robert E. *Japanese Blue Collar: The Changing Tradition.* Berkeley: University of California Press, 1971. 300 pp.

Coleman, Rex. "An Index to Japanese Law (1867–1961)." Preliminary Draft, 1961. Mimeographed. 181 pp.

Continuing Education of the Bar [Cal.], *Functions of Corporate Legal Departments.* San Francisco: California Bar Association, 1961. 233 pp.

Cook, Alice H. *An Introduction to Japanese Trade Unionism.* Ithaca, N.Y.: Cornell University Press, 1966. 216 pp.

Cooper, M. *They Came to Japan.* Berkeley: University of California Press, 1965. 439 pp.

Corbin, Arthur L. *Corbin on Contracts.* St. Paul, Minn.: West Publishing Co., 1962. Vols. 1–6A.

Cosenza, Mario, ed. *The Complete Journal of Townsend Harris.* Rev. ed. Tokyo: Charles E. Tuttle Co., 1959. 578 pp.

Crowley, James, ed. *Modern East Asia: Essays in Interpretation.* New York: Harcourt Brace Jovanovich, 1970. 385 pp.

Curtis, Gerald L. *Election Campaigning Japanese Style.* New York: Columbia University Press, 1971. 275 pp.

Dandō, Shigemitsu. *Japanese Criminal Procedure.* Translated by B. J. George, Jr. South Hackensack, N.J.: Fred B. Rothman & Co., 1965. 663 pp.

Dator, James A. *Sōka Gakkai: Builders of the Third Civilization.* Seattle: University of Washington Press, 1969. 171 pp.

De Mente, Boye. *How Business Is Done in Japan—A Personal View.* Tokyo: Sampson-Doyle Co., 1963.

————. *Japanese Manners and Ethics in Business.* Tokyo: East Asia Publishing Co., 1960. 179 pp.

————, and Perry, Fred. *The Japanese as Consumers.* Tokyo: Walker-Weatherhill, 1968. 256 pp.

Dicey, Albert V. *Introduction to the Study of the Law of the Constitution.* 10th ed. London: Macmillan, 1959. 535 pp.

Dimock, Marshall E. *The Japanese Technocracy.* Tokyo: Walker-Weatherhill, 1968. 197 pp.

Domke, Martin. *Commercial Arbitration.* Englewood Cliffs, N.J.: Prentice-Hall, 1965. 116 pp.

————. *The Law and Practice of Commercial Arbitration.* Mundelein, Ill.: Callagahan & Co., 1968. 469 pp.

————, ed. *International Trade Arbitration.* New York: American Arbitration Association, 1958. 311 pp.

Dore, Ronald P. *City Life in Japan.* Berkeley: University of California Press, 1960. 472 pp.

————. *Land Reforms in Japan.* London: Oxford University Press, 1959. 510 pp.

————, ed. *Aspects of Social Change in Modern Japan.* Princeton: Princeton University Press, 1967. 474 pp.

Duus, Peter. *Party Rivalry and Political Change in Taishō Japan.* Cambridge: Harvard University Press, 1968. 317 pp.

Economic Planning Agency, Government of Japan. *New Economic and Social Development Plan, 1970–1975.* Printing Bureau, Ministry of Finance, 1970. 185 pp.

Economic Research Department, Bank of Japan. *The Japanese Financial System.* Tokyo: Bank of Japan, July 1970. 86 pp.

Ehrenzweig, Albert A. *A Treatise on the Conflicts of Laws.* St. Paul, Minn.: West Publishing Co., 1962. 824 pp.

————; Ikehara, Sueo; and Jensen, Norman. *American-Japanese Private International Law.* Parker School Bilateral Studies in Private International Law, No. 12. Dobbs Ferry, N.Y.: Oceana Publications, 1964. 172 pp.

Evans, Robert, Jr. *The Labor Economics of Japan and the United States.* New York: Praeger, 1971. 276 pp.

Fairbank, John. *A History of East Asian Civilization—East Asia: The Great Tradition.* Boston: Houghton Mifflin, 1960. 739 pp.

Foreign Capital Affiliated Enterprises in Japan. Tokyo: Business Intercommunications Incorporated, 1972. 204 pp.

Foster, Richard, and Ono, Masao, trans. *The Patent and Trademark Laws of Japan.* Tokyo: Asahi Evening News, 1970. 121 pp.

Friedmann, Wolfgang, and Kalmanoff, George. *Joint International Business Ventures.* New York: Columbia University Press, 1961. 558 pp.

Fuji Bank, Ltd. *Banking in Modern Japan.* 2d ed. Tokyo: The Fuji Bank, Ltd., 1967. 299 pp.

Fujii, Shin'ichi. *The Essentials of Japanese Constitutional Law.* Tokyo: Yūhikaku, 1940. 463 pp.

Fujiwara, Hirotatsu. *I Denounce Sōka Gakkai.* Tokyo: Nihon Hodo Co., 1970. 287 pp.

Fukui, Haruhiro. *Party in Power: The Japanese Liberal Democrats and Policy-making.* Canberra: Australian National University Press, 1970. 301 pp.

Fukutake, Tadashi. *Man and Society in Japan.* Tokyo: University of Tokyo Press, 1962. 241 pp.

General Agreement on Tariffs and Trade (GATT). *Japan's Economic Expansion and Foreign Trade, 1955-1970.* Geneva: GATT Studies in International Trade, No. 2, 1971. 52 pp.

Gill, William Henry. *Evidence and Procedure in Arbitration.* London: Sweet & Maxwell, 1965. 200 pp.

Glazer, F. Herbert. *The International Businessman in Japan: The Japanese Image.* Tokyo: Sophia University, 1968. 115 pp.

Gold, Joseph. *Stand-by Arrangements.* Washington, D.C.: International Monetary Fund, 1970. 295 pp.

Gould. Rowland. *The Matsushita Phenomenon.* Tokyo: Diamondosha, 1970. 224 pp.

Hadley, Eleanor. *Antitrust in Japan.* Princeton: Princeton University Press, 1970. 528 pp.

Haight, G. W. *Convention on the Recognition and Enforcement of Foreign Arbitral Awards: Summary and Analysis of United Nations Conference, May/June 1958* New York: United Nations, 1958. 108 pp.

Hayashi, Shintarō. "Japan's Trade and Industrial Policy." 5 Oct. 1971. Mimeographed. 28 pp.

————. "Present Picture of Japanese Economy—Centering on Comparison of Japanese and American Economies." Oct. 1971. Mimeographed. 39 pp.

Hayashi, Viscount. *For His People.* London: Harper & Brothers, 1903. 227 pp.

Hayes, Paul R. *Labor Arbitration: A Dissenting View.* New Haven: Yale University Press, 1966. 125 pp.

Hellman, Donald C. *Japan and East Asia: The New International Order.* New York: Praeger, 1972. 243 pp.

Henderson, Dan Fenno. *Conciliation and Japanese Law: Tokugawa and Modern.* Seattle: University of Washington Press, 1965; Tokyo: University of Tokyo Press, 1965. 2 vols.

————, ed. *The Constitution of Japan: Its First Twenty Years, 1947–1967.* Seattle: University of Washington Press, 1968. 323 pp.

————, and Fujita, Yasuhiro. "Cases and Materials on Justifiability in U.S.-

Japanese Disputes." School of Law, University of Washington, 1968. Mimeographed. 3 vols.

Henn, Harry G. *Corporations.* St. Paul, Minn.: West Publishing Co., 1961. 956 pp.

Higa, Mikio. "The Role of Bureaucracy in Contemporary Japanese Politics." Ph.D. dissertation, University of California, University Microfilms #69–3612, 1968. 392 pp.

Hirschmeier, Johannes. *The Origins of Entrepreneurship in Meiji Japan.* Cambridge: Harvard University Press, 1964. 354 pp.

Ho, Alfred K. *The Far East in World Trade.* New York: Praeger, 1967. 388 pp.

Hollerman, Leon. *Japan's Dependence on the World Economy.* Princeton: Princeton University Press, 1967. 293 pp.

Hoshii, Iwao. *The Dynamics of Japan's Business Evolution.* Tokyo and Philadelphia: Orient-West Publishers, 1966. 164 pp.

———. *Japan's Business Concentration.* Philadelphia: Orient-West Publishers, 1969. 235 pp.

Hozumi, Nobushige. *The New Japanese Civil Code as Material for the Study of Comparative Jurisprudence.* Tokyo: Maruzen, 1912. 166 pp.

Huh, Kyung-Mo. *Japan's Trade in Asia.* New York: Praeger, 1966. 282 pp.

Ike, Nobutaka, trans. *The Beginning of Political Democracy in Japan.* Baltimore: Johns Hopkins University Press, 1950. 246 pp.

Institute of Foreign Exchange and Trade Research. *Japan: Foreign Exchange and Trade Control Handbook.* Tokyo: Institute of Foreign Exchange and Trade Research, 1971.

Institute of International Investment. *Setting Up in Japan.* Tokyo: Institute of International Investment, 1972. 81 pp.

International Law Association of Japan. *The Japanese Annual of International Law*, No. 15. Tokyo: Japan Times, Ltd., 1971. 391 pp.

Ishida, Takeshi. *Japanese Society.* New York: Random House, 1971. 145 pp.

Ishii, Ryōsuke. *Japanese Legislation in the Meiji Era.* Translated by William J. Chambliss. Tokyo: Pan-Pacific Press, 1958. 741 pp.

Itō, Hirobumi. *Commentaries on the Constitution of the Empire of Japan.* 3d ed. Tokyo: Chūō daigaku, 1931. 300 pp.

Iyori, Hiroshi. *Antimonopoly Legislation in Japan.* New York: Federal Legal Publications, 1969. 265 pp.

Jansen, Marius B., ed. *Changing Japanese Attitudes Toward Modernization.* Princeton: Princeton University Press, 1967. 546 pp.

Japan Economic Research Center. *18 Month Forecast of Japan's Economy.* Tokyo: JERC, May 1971. 113 pp.

———. *Japan's Economy in 1975.* Tokyo: JERC, March 1970. 48 pp.

———. *Japan's Economy in 1985: The Outlook for a Trillion Dollar Economy.* Tokyo: JERC, 1971. 98 pp.

———. *Quarterly Forecast*, No. 19. Tokyo: JERC, Dec. 1971. 103 pp.

Japanese Institute of CPAs. *CPAs in Japan.* Tokyo: Japanese Institute of CPAs, 1962.

Japan Industrial Promotion Association. *The Key to the Japanese Market: Its Possibilities and Prospects.* Tokyo: Japan Industrial Promotion Association, 1968. 2 vols.

Jennings, Sir William Ivor. *The Law and the Constitution.* 5th ed. London: University of London Press, 1959. 354 pp.

Jones, F. C. *Extraterritoriality in Japan.* New Haven: Yale University Press, 1931. 237 pp.

Jones, Hazel. "The Meiji Government and Foreign Employees, 1868–1900." Ph.D. dissertation, University of Michigan, 1967. 436 pp.

Kaempfer, E. *The History of Japan.* Glasgow: James Maclehose & Sons, 1906. (Written 1690–92.) 3 vols.

Kahn, Herman. *The Emerging Japanese Superstate: Challenge and Response.* Englewood Cliffs, N.J.: Prentice-Hall, 1970. 274 pp.

Kawasaki, Ichirō. *Japan Unmasked.* Rutland, Vt.: Charles E. Tuttle Co., 1969. 231 pp.

Kelsall, R. K. *Higher Civil Service in Britain from 1870 to the Present Day.* London: Routledge & Kegan Paul, 1955. 233 pp.

Kerr, Clark; Dunlop, John T.; Harbison, Frederick H.; and Myers, Charles A. *Industrialism and Industrial Man: The Problems of Labor and Management in Economic Growth.* Cambridge: Harvard University Press, 1960. 263 pp.

Kindleberger, Charles P., ed. *The International Corporation—A Symposium.* Cambridge: The MIT Press, 1970. 415 pp.

Kiyooka, Eiichi, trans. *The Autobiography of Fukuzawa Yukichi.* Tokyo: Hokuseidō, 1960. 401 pp.

Kojima, Kiyoshi. *Nontariff Barriers to Japan's Trade.* Tokyo: JERC, 1971. 93 pp.

Komiya, Ryūtarō, ed. *Postwar Economic Growth in Japan.* Translated by Robert Osaki. Berkeley: University of California Press, 1966. 260 pp.

Kubota, Akira. *Higher Civil Servants in Postwar Japan.* Princeton: Princeton University Press, 1969. 197 pp.

Lazarus, Steven; Bray, John J., Jr.; Carter, Larry L.; Collins, Kent H.; Giedt, Bruce A.; Holton, Robert V., Jr.; Matthews, Phillip D.; and Willard, Gordon C. *Resolving Business Disputes: The Potential of Commercial Arbitration.* New York: American Management Association, 1965. 208 pp.

Lee, Luke T. *Consular Law and Practice.* New York: Praeger, 1961. 431 pp.

Levine, Solomon B. *Industrial Relations in Postwar Japan.* Urbana: University of Illinois Press, 1958. 200 pp.

Litkac, Isaiah A., and Maule, J. Christopher, eds. *Foreign Investment: The Experience of Host Countries.* New York: Praeger, 1970. 406 pp.

Livermore, Arthur J., ed. *Science in Japan.* Washington: American Association for the Advancement of Science, 1965. 486 pp.

Lockwood, William W. *The Economic Development of Japan: Growth and Structural Change, 1868–1938.* Princeton: Princeton University Press, 1954. 603 pp.

————, ed. *The State and Economic Enterprise in Japan.* Princeton: Princeton University Press, 1965. 753 pp.

Lynch, John. *Toward an Orderly Market: An Intensive Study of Japan's Voluntary Quota in Cotton Textile Exports.* Tokyo: Sophia University and Charles E. Tuttle Co., 1968. 215 pp.

Machlup, Fritz. *Remaking the International Monetary System.* Baltimore: Johns Hopkins Press, 1968. 161 pp.

Maddison, Angus. *Economic Growth in Japan and the USSR.* London: George Allen and Unwin, Ltd., 1969. 174 pp.

Mainichi Daily News. *Mitsubishi Group—A Century of Progress—A Bigger Century to Come.* Tokyo: Mainichi Newspapers, 1971. 56 pp.

———. *"Sōgō Shōsha"—General Trading Firms in Japan—A Unique Economic Setup.* Tokyo: Mainichi Daily News, 1969. 56 pp.

Maki, John M. *Court and Constitution in Japan: Selected Supreme Court Decisions (1948–1960).* Seattle: University of Washington Press, 1964. 445 pp.

Maruyama, Masao. *Thought and Behavior in Modern Japanese Politics.* Edited by Ivan Morris. New York: Oxford University Press, 1963. 344 pp.

Marshall, Byron K. *Capitalism and Nationalism in Prewar Japan: The Ideology of the Business Elite, 1868–1941.* Stanford: Stanford University Press, 1967. 163 pp.

Matsukata, Masayoshi. *Report on the Adoption of the Gold Standard in Japan.* Tokyo: Japanese Government Press, 1899. 389 pp.

Matsunami, Niichirō. *The Constitution of Japan.* Tokyo: Maruzen & Co., 1930. 358 pp.

McNelly, Theodore H. "Domestic and International Influences on Constitutional Revision in Japan, 1945–46." Ph.D. dissertation, Columbia University, 1952. 444 pp.

Minear, Richard H. *Japanese Tradition and Western Law.* Cambridge: Harvard University Press, 1970. 244 pp.

Mizoguchi, Toshiyuki. *Personal Savings and Consumption in Postwar Japan.* Tokyo: Kinokuniya Bookstore, 1970. 301 pp.

Mody, N. *A Collection of Nagasaki Color Prints and Paintings.* Tokyo: Charles E. Tuttle Co., 1969. 32 pp. and 250 plates.

Moore, Charles A., ed. *The Japanese Mind.* Honolulu: East-West Center Press, 1968. 357 pp.

———. *The Status of the Individual in East and West.* Honolulu: East-West Center Press, 1968. 606 pp.

Morgan Guaranty Trust Co. *The Financing of Business in Japan.* Tokyo: Morgan Guaranty Trust Co., 1965. 33 pp.

Moulton, H. G. *Japan, An Economic and Financial Appraisal.* Washington, D.C.: Brookings Institution, 1931. 495 pp.

Mueller, Gerhard G., and Yoshida, Hiroshi. *Accounting Practices in Japan.* Seattle: Graduate School of Business Administration, University of Washington, 1968. 78 pp.

Nadelmann, Kurt H., et al., eds. *20th Century Comparative and Conflicts Law.* Leyden: A. W. Sythoff, 1961. 249 pp.

Najita, Tetsuo. *Hara Kei in the Politics of Compromise (1905–1915)*. Cambridge: Harvard University Press, 1967. 185 pp.

Nakamura, Hajime. *Ways of Thinking of Eastern Peoples: India, China, Tibet and Japan*. Honolulu: East-West Center Press, 1964. 712 pp.

Nakane, Chie. *Japanese Society*. Berkeley: University of California Press, 1970. 157 pp.

———. *Kinship and Economic Organization in Rural Japan*. New York: Humanities Press, Inc., 1967. 203 pp.

Nitobe, Inazō. *Japanese Traits and Foreign Influences*. London: Kegan & Co., 1927. 216 pp.

Nivison, David S., and Wright, Arthur F., eds. *Confucianism in Action*. Stanford: Stanford University Press, 1959.

Noma, S. *Arts of Japan*, Vol. II. Translated by Glen Webb. Palo Alto: Kōdansha International, 1967.

Norman, E. H. *Japan's Emergence as a Modern State*. New York: Institute of Pacific Relations, 1938. 248 pp.

Northrop, F. S. C. *The Meeting of East and West*. New York: Macmillan Co., 1946. 531 pp.

Nukazawa, Kazu. *Japan's Foreign Economic Policy: Options for the Seventies*. Washington, D.C.: U.S.–Japan Trade Council, Inc., 1970. 24 pp.

OECD. *Japan* (OECD Economic Surveys). Paris: OECD, June 1971. 82 pp.

———. *Liberalisation of International Capital Movements: Japan*. Paris: OECD, 1968. 179 pp.

Ōkuma, Shigenobu, ed. *Fifty Years of New Japan*. London: Smith & Elder Co., 1909. 2 vols.

O'Neal, F. Hodges. *Close Corporations*. Chicago: Callaghan, 1958. 2 vols.

Orchard, John E. *Japan's Economic Position*. New York: McGraw-Hill, 1930. 504 pp.

Ozaki, Robert S. *The Control of Import and Foreign Capital in Japan*. New York: Praeger, 1972. 309 pp.

Passin, Herbert. *Society and Education in Japan*. New York: Teachers College, Columbia University and East Asian Institute, 1965. 347 pp.

Patrick, Hugh T. *Monetary Policy and Central Banking in Contemporary Japan*. Bombay: University of Bombay, 1962. 219 pp.

Peterson, Peter G. *The United States in the Changing World Economy*. Washington, D.C.: GPO, 1972. 2 vols.

President Directory 1973. Tokyo: Diamond-Time Co., Ltd., 1972. 128 pp.

Quigley, Leonard V., and Turner, John E. *The New Japan*. Minneapolis: University of Minnesota Press, 1956. 456 pp.

Reese, Willis L. M., ed. *International Contracts: Choice of Law and Language*. Dobbs Ferry, N.Y.: Oceana Publications, 1962. 76 pp.

Research Division, The Fuji Bank, Ltd. *Banking in Modern Japan*. 2nd ed. Tokyo: The Fuji Bank, Ltd., 1967. 299 pp.

Rolfe, Sydney E. *The International Corporation*. Paris: International Chamber of Commerce, 1969. 202 pp.

Rosovsky, Henry. *Capital Formation in Japan, 1868–1940.* Glencoe, Ill.: Free Press, 1961. 358 pp.

Sanders, Pieter, ed. *International Arbitration: Liber Amicorum for Martin Domke.* The Hague: Martinus Nijhoff, 1967. 357 pp.

———. *International Commercial Arbitration: A World Handbook.* The Hague. Martinus Nijhoff, 1965. 3 vols.

Sansom, George. *The Western World and Japan.* New York: Alfred A. Knopf, 1950. 504 pp.

Sarasas, Phra. *Money and Banking in Japan.* London: Heath Cranston, Ltd., 1940. 544 pp.

Sawada, Toshio. *Subsequent Conduct and Supervening Events.* Tokyo: University of Tokyo Press, 1967. 233 pp.

Scalapino, Robert A. *American-Japanese Relations in a Changing Era.* New York: The Library Press, 1972. 127 pp.

———. *Democracy and the Party Movement in Prewar Japan: The Failure of the First Attempt.* Berkeley: University of California Press, 1953. 471 pp.

———. *The Japanese Communist Movement, 1922–1966.* Berkeley: University of California Press, 1967. 412 pp.

———, and Masumi, Junnosuke. *Parties and Politics in Contemporary Japan.* Berkeley: University of California Press, 1962. 190 pp.

Schiffer, Hubert F. *The Modern Japanese Banking System.* New York: University Publishing Inc., 1962. 240 pp.

Schmitthoff, Clive M., ed. *The Sources of the Law of International Trade.* New York: Praeger, 1964. 292 pp.

Schumpeter, E. B., ed. *The Industrialization of Japan and Manchukuo, 1930–1940.* New York: Macmillan Company, 1940. 944 pp.

Scidmore, G. H. *United States Courts in Japan.* Tokyo: Igitisu hōritsu gakkō, 1887. 210 pp.

Seide, Katherine. *A Dictionary of Arbitration and Its Terms.* Dobbs Ferry, N.Y.: Oceana Publications, 1970. 334 pp.

Shattuck, Warren, and Kitawaga, Zentarō. "U.S.-Japanese Contract and Sales Problems." Seattle: School of Law, University of Washington, 1970. Mimeographed. 3 vols.

Shinohara, Miyohei. *Structural Changes in Japan's Economic Development.* Economic Research Series, No. 11. Tokyo: Hitotsubashi University, 1970. 445 pp.

Shroeder, F. *Notes on the Civil Code of Japan.* 1898.

Shultz, George P., and Aliber, Robert Z., eds. *Guidelines, Informal Contracts and the Market Place.* Chicago: University of Chicago Press, 1966. 357 pp.

Siemes, Johannes. *Herman Roesler and the Making of the Meiji State.* Tokyo: Sophia University and Charles E. Tuttle Co., 1968. 252 pp.

Smith, Robert J., and Beardsley, Richard K., eds. *Japanese Culture: Its Development and Characteristics.* Chicago: Aldine Publishing Co., 1962. 248 pp.

Smith, Thomas C. *Political Change and Industrial Development in Japan: Government Enterprise, 1868–1880.* Stanford: Stanford University Press, 1955. 126 pp.

Spaulding, Robert M., Jr. *Imperial Japan's Higher Civil Service Examinations.* Princeton: Princeton University Press, 1967. 416 pp.

Steiner, Kurt. *Local Government in Japan.* Stanford: Stanford University Press, 1965. 564 pp.

Stockwin, J. A. A. *The Japanese Socialist Party and Neutralism.* Melbourne, Australia: University of Melbourne Press, 1969. 197 pp.

Sturges, Wesley A. *Commercial Arbitrations and Awards.* Kansas City: Vernon Law Book Company, 1930. 504 pp.

Taira, Kōji, *Economic Development and the Labor Market in Japan.* New York: Columbia University Press, 1970. 282 pp.

Tajima, Yoshihiro. *How Goods Are Distributed in Japan.* Translated by Jack Seward. Tokyo: Walton-Ridgeway & Co., 1971. 128 pp.

Takayanagi, Kenzō. *Reception and Influence of Occidental Legal Ideas in Japan.* Western Influence in Modern Japan, No. 4. Tokyo: Japan Council of the Institute of Pacific Relations, 1929. 21 pp.

Takekoshi, Yosaburō. *The Economic Aspects of the History of the Civilization of Japan.* London: Dawson of Pall Mall, 1930. 3 vols.

Tatsuta, Misao. *Securities Regulation in Japan.* Tokyo: University of Tokyo Press, 1970. 127 pp.

————, and Henderson, Dan Fenno. *Cases and Materials on Japanese Business Corporation Law.* School of Law, University of Washington, 1967. Mimeographed. 3 vols.

Thayer, Nathaniel B. *How the Conservatives Rule Japan.* Princeton: Princeton University Press, 1969. 349 pp.

Tokyo Stock Exchange. *Tokyo Stock Exchange History, Organization, Operation.* Tokyo: Tokyo Stock Exchange, 1972. 28 pp.

————. *Listing of Securities; Regulations of the Tokyo Stock Exchange.* Tokyo: Tokyo Stock Exchange, March 1970. 26 pp. and forms.

Trade Bulletin Corporation. "Problems of the Liberalizing Operation of the Recognition Standards for International Contract of Introduction of Technology," Books I & II. Tokyo: Trade Bulletin Corporation, 1968–69. Mimeographed. 80 pp.

————. "Social and Economic Laws of Japan." Tokyo: Trade Bulletin Corporation, 1969. Mimeographed.

Tsurumi, Kazuko. *Social Change and the Individual: Japan Before and After Defeat in World War II.* Princeton: Princeton University Press, 1970. 441 pp.

Tuge, Hideomi. *Historical Development of Science and Technology in Japan.* Rev. ed. Tokyo: Kokusai bunka shinkōkai, 1968. 200 pp.

Uemura, Kōgorō (Pres. of Keidanren). *Challenge for Responsible Partnership.* Washington, D.C.: U.S.-Japanese Trade Council, 15 June 1971. 18 pp.

Valignamo, Alessandro. *Historia del Principio y Progresso de la Campania de Jesus en las Indias Orientales, 1542–1564.* Edited by Josef Wicki, S.J. Rome, 1944.

Vogel, Ezra. *Japan's New Middle Class.* Berkeley: University of California Press, 1963. 299 pp.

Von Mehren, Arthur T., ed. *Law in Japan: The Legal Order in a Changing Society.* Cambridge: Harvard University Press, 1963. 706 pp.

Ward, Robert E., ed. *Political Development in Modern Japan.* Princeton: Princeton University Press, 1968. 637 pp.

Walworth, Arthur. *Black Ships Off Japan.* Hamden, Conn.: Archon Books, 1946. 278 pp.

Warner, Reinhard W. Lloyd; Van Piper, Paul P.; Martin, Norman H.; and Collins, Orvis F. *The American Federal Executive: A Study of Social and Personal Characteristics of the Civilian and Military Leaders of the U.S. Federal Government.* New Haven: Yale University Press, 1963. 373 pp.

Whitehall, Arthur M., Jr., and Takezawa, Shin'ichi. *The Other Worker: A Comparative Study of Industrial Relations in the U.S. and Japan.* Honolulu: East-West Press, 1968. 481 pp.

Wilkinson, Thomas O. *The Urbanization of Japanese Labor, 1868–1955.* Amherst: University of Massachusetts Press, 1965. 243 pp.

Yamamura, Kōzō. *Economic Policy in Postwar Japan.* Berkeley: University of California Press, 1967. 226 pp.

Yamanaka, Tokutarō, ed. *Small Business in Japan's Economic Progress.* Tokyo: Asahi Evening News, 1971. 145 pp.

Yamasaki, Y., trans. *Digest of Japanese Court Decisions in Patentability and Patent Infringement Cases, 1966–1968.* Tokyo: The American Chamber of Commerce in Japan, 1970. 180 pp.

Yanaga, Chitoshi. *Big Business in Japanese Politics.* New Haven: Yale University Press, 1968. 371 pp.

———. *Japan Since Perry.* New York: McGraw-Hill, 1949. 721 pp.

Yoshino, M. Y. *The Japanese Marketing System: Adaptations and Innovations.* Cambridge: The MIT Press, 1971. 319 pp.

———. *Japan's Managerial System: Tradition and Innovation.* Cambridge: The MIT Press, 1968. 292 pp.

ENGLISH LANGUAGE SOURCES: ARTICLES

Abe, Hakaru. "Education of the Legal Profession in Japan." In *Law in Japan: The Legal Order in a Changing Society,* edited by Arthur T. Von Mehren. Cambridge: Harvard University Press, 1963.

Aksen, Gerald. "American Arbitration Accession Arrives in the Age of Aquarius: United States Implements United Nations Convention on the Recognition and Enforcement of Foreign Arbitral Awards." 2 *Southwestern U. L. Rev.* 1–38 (1971).

Ames, James Barr. "Two Theories of Consideration." 12 *Harv. L. Rev.* 515, 521 (1899).

Anderson, Arthur. "Frustration of Contract—A Rejected Doctrine." 3 *De Paul L. Rev.* 1 (1953).

Anderson, Joseph V. "The Tax Practice Controversy in Historical Perspective." 1 *Wm. & Mary L. Rev.* 18 (1957).

Annotation. "Validity of Contractual Provisions Limiting Place or Court in Which Action May Be Brought." 56 *A.L.R.* 2d 300, 306 (1957).

Anthony, Robert A. "The American Response to Dumping from Capitalist and Socialist Economies—Substantive Premises and Restructured Procedures after the 1967 GATT Code." 54 *Cornell L. Rev.* 159 (1969).

Appleton, Richard B. "Reforms in Japanese Criminal Procedure under the Allied Occupation." 24 *Wash. L. Rev.* 401 (1949).

Ariga, Michiko. "The Antimonopoly Law." In *Joint Ventures and Japan*, edited by Robert J. Ballon. Tokyo: Sophia University and Charles E. Tuttle Co., 1967.

Ariga, M., and Rieke, L. "The Antimonopoly Law of Japan and Its Enforcement." 39 *Wash. L. Rev.* 437 (1964).

Aufricht, Hans. "Exchange Restrictions under the Fund Agreement." 2 *J. of World Trade Law* 297–323 (1968).

———. "Suppression of Treaties in International Law." 37 *Cornell L. Q.* 655 (1952).

Bairy, Maurice. "Japanese Ways." In *Doing Business in Japan*, edited by Robert J. Ballon. Tokyo: Sophia University and Charles E. Tuttle Co., 1968.

———. "Motivational Forces in Japanese Life." In *The Japanese Employee*, edited by Robert J. Ballon. Tokyo: Sophia University and Charles E. Tuttle Co., 1969.

Ball, George W. "The Role of the Lawyer in International Investment Fields." 11 *Virginia Law Weekly—Dicta* 1 (1959).

Ballon, Robert J. "The Japanese Dimension of Industrial Enterprises." In *The Japanese Employee*, edited by Robert J. Ballon. Tokyo: Sophia University and Charles E. Tuttle Co., 1969.

———. "Lifelong Remuneration System." In *The Japanese Employee*, edited by Robert J. Ballon. Tokyo: Sophia University and Charles E. Tuttle Co., 1969.

———. "Participative Employment." In *The Japanese Employee*, edited by Robert J. Ballon. Tokyo: Sophia University and Charles E. Tuttle Co., 1969.

Battifol, Henri. "Public Policy and the Autonomy of the Parties." In *The Conflicts of Law and International Contracts*. Ann Arbor: University of Michigan Press, 1951.

Bayith, S. A. "Treaty Law of Private Arbitration." 10 *Arb. J.* 188 (1955).

Beer, Lawrence W. "The Public Welfare Standard and Freedom of Expression in Japan." In *The Constitution of Japan: Its First Twenty Years, 1947–67*, edited by Dan Fenno Henderson. Seattle: University of Washington Press, 1968.

Bennett, John W. "Japanese Economic Growth: Background for Social Change." In *Aspects of Social Change in Modern Japan*, edited by Ronald P. Dore. Princeton: Princeton University Press, 1967.

Bergman, G. Merle. "Contractual Restrictions on the Forum." 48 *Cal. L. Rev.* 438 (1960).

Berman, Harold J. "Excuse for Nonperformance in the Light of Contract Practices in International Trade." 63 *Colum. L. Rev.* 1413 (1963).

Bernstein, Merton C. "The Impact of the Uniform Commercial Code upon Arbitration," 22 *Arb. J.* 65 (1967).

Bishop, William W., Jr. "Unconstitutional Treaties." 42 *Minn. L. Rev.* 773 (1958).

Blakemore, Thomas, and Yazawa, Makoto. "Japanese Commercial Code Revisions." 2 *Am. J. Comp. L.* 12–24 (1953).

Blunrosen, Alfred W. "Public Policy Considerations in Labor Arbitration Cases." 14 *Rutgers L. Rev.* 217 (1960).

Bradley, E. J. "Comparative Evaluation of the Delaware and Maryland Close Corporation Statutes." 1968 *Duke L. J.* 525 (1968).

Bradshaw, Carl J. "Joint Ventures in Japan." 38 *Wash. L. Rev.* 58 (1963).

Brewster, Kingman. "Legal Aspects of the Foreignness of Foreign Investment." 17 *Ohio St. L. J.* 267 (1956).

Brundno, Walter W. "Basic Questions in Foreign Trade and Investment—A Lawyer's Check-List." 3 *Institute of Private Investment Abroad* 5 (1961).

Burrus, B. R., and Casson, J. "Capitalization and Allocation of Securities," in "Close Corporations: A Symposium." 1969 *U. Ill. L. Forum* 30 (1969).

Capistrano, Francisco. "Mistakes and Inaccuracies in Fisher's Translation of the Spanish Civil Code." 9 *Philippine L. J.* 89 (1929).

Carrington, Paul. "The 1965 General Arbitration Statute of Texas." 20 *Sw. L. J.* 21 (1966).

Caves, Richard. "Industrial Economics of Foreign Investment: The Case of the International Corporation." 5 *Journal of World Trade Law* 303 (1971).

Chao, Kang. "Labor Institutions in Japan and Her Economic Growth." 28 *J. of Asian Studies* 5–17 (1968).

Chayes, Abram. "Madame Wagner and the Close Corporation." 73 *Harv. L. Rev.* 1532 (1960).

Cohn, E. J. "Rules of Arbitration of the International Chamber of Commerce." 14 *Int'l & Comp. L. Q.* 132 (1965).

Collins, Daniel G. "Arbitration and the Uniform Commercial Code." 41 *N.Y. U. L. Rev.* 736 (1966).

Comment. "A Comparison of the Close Corporation Statutes of Delaware, Florida, and New York." 23 *U. Miami L. Rev.* 515–30 (1969).

———. "Executive Authority and Antitrust Considerations in Voluntary Limits on Steel Imports." 118 *U. of Penn. L. Rev.* 105 (1969).

———. "Failure of the Ohio General Corporation Law to Adequately Provide for Close Corporations—Proposals for Change." 37 *U. Cin. L. Rev.* 620–34 (1968).

———. "International Joint Venture Corporation: Drafting of Control Arrangements." 1963 *Duke L. J.* 516 (1963).

Contini, Paolo. "International Commercial Arbitration: The UN Convention on the Recognition and Enforcement of Foreign Arbitral Awards." 8 *Am. J. of Comp. L.* 283 (1959).

Corbin, Arthur L. "Does a Pre-existing Duty Defeat Consideration?" 27 *Yale L. J.* 362 (1918).

Corbin, Sol Neil. "Enforceability of Contractual Agreements for Dispute Settlement Abroad." In *International Trade Arbitration*, edited by Martin Domke. New York: American Arbitration Association, 1958.

Coulson, Robert. "Appropriate Procedures for Receiving Proof in Commercial Arbitration." 71 *Dick. L. Rev.* 63 (1966).

Cox, Archibald. "Reflections Upon Labor Arbitration." 72 *Harv. L. Rev.* 1483 (1959).

Curtis, Gerald D. "The Kōenkai and the Liberal Democratic Party." 6 *Japan Interpreter* 206 (1970).

Czyak, John J., and Sullivan, Charles H. "American Arbitration Law and the U.N. Convention." 13 *Arb. J.* 197 (1958).

Dalzell, John. "Duress by Economic Pressure I." 20 *N.C. L. Rev.* 237 (1942).

Dambach, James. "Corporations: Survival of Joint Agreement after Incorporation." 3 *U.C.L.A. L. Rev.* 94 (1955).

Dawson, John P. "Economic Duress—An Essay in Perspective." 45 *Mich L. Rev.* 253 (1947).

Dean, Arthur. "The Role of International Law in a Metropolitan Practice." 103 *U. Pa. L. Rev.* 886 (1955).

"Decontrol of Computers Will Be 3 Years Hence." *Japan Economic Journal*, 27 July 1971, p. 1.

Dobkin, James A. "Arbitrability of Patent Disputes Under the U.S. Arbitration Act." 23 *Arb. J.* 1–17 (1968).

Dodd, E. Merrick. "For Whom Are Corporate Managers Trustees?" 45 *Harv. L. Rev.* 1145 (1932).

Doi, L. Takeo. "*Amae:* A Key Concept for Understanding Japanese Personality Structure." In *Japanese Culture: Its Development and Characteristics*, edited by Robert J. Smith and Richard K. Beardsley. Chicago: Aldine Publishing Co., 1962.

Doi, Teruo. "International Commercial Arbitration in Japan." In *International Commercial Arbitration: Liber Amicorum for Martin Domke*, edited by Pieter Sanders. The Hague: Maritinus Nijhoff, 1967.

————."Recognition and Enforcement of Foreign Judgments and Arbitral Awards," (Pts. 1–2). *Quarterly of J.C.A.A.* (Nos. 13, 14) 1, 5 (1963).

————. "The Validity of Contracts Made in Violation of Forum's Exchange Controls." 2 *Law in Japan* 180–93 (1968).

Domke, Martin. "American Arbitral Awards: Enforcement in Foreign Countries." 1965 *U. of Ill. L. F.* 399 (1965).

————. "Arbitral Awards Without Written Opinions: Comparative Aspects in International Commercial Arbitration." In *20th Century Comparative and Conflicts Law*, edited by Kurt H. Nadelmann et al. Leyden: A. W. Sythoff, 1961.

————. "Enforcement of Foreign Arbitral Awards in the United States." 13 *Arb. J.* 14 (1958).

————. "International Arbitration of Commercial Disputes." In *Southwestern Legal Foundation: Proceedings of the Institute on Private Investments Abroad.* Albany: Bender, 1960.

————. "On the Enforcement Abroad of American Arbitration Awards." 17 *Law & Contemp. Prob.* 545 (1952).

Dore, Ronald P. "The Future of Japan's Meritocracy." *Bulletin of the Int'l House of Japan* (No. 26) 30 (1970).

Drachler, Leo M. "Frustration of Contract: Comparative Law Aspects of Remedies in Cases of Supervening Illegality." 3 *N.Y. L. F.* 50 (1957).

"Economic Duress after the Demise of Free Will Theory." 53 *Iowa L. Rev.* 892–924 (1968).

Editorial, *Fortune*, Oct. 1967, p. 25.

Editorial, "Liberalization." 7 *Journal ACCJ* 5 (1970).

Editorial, *Wall Street Journal*, 9 Mar. 1971, p. 14.

Edmunds, Lester E. "Japan's Present Foreign Capital Liberalization: Woefully Short of International Standards." 7 *Journal ACCJ* 35 (1970).

Edwards, Corwin. "The Internationality of Economic Interests." 111 *U. Pa. L. Rev.* 183 (1962).

Eisemann, Frederic. "Arbitration under the International Chamber of Commerce Rules." 15 *Int'l & Comp. L. Q.* 726–36 (1966).

Epp, Robert. "The Challenge from Tradition: Attempts to Compile A Civil Code in Japan, 1866–78." 22 *Monumenta Nipponica* 15–48 (1967).

Etō, Jun. "Japan and the U.S.: A Personal Reflection." *Bulletin of the Int'l House of Japan* (No. 28) 2 (1971).

Fayerweather, John. "Lawyers, Foreign Governments and Business Abroad." 44 *Va. L. Rev.* 185 (1958).

Feldmann, Eddy S. "Arbitration Modernized—The New California Arbitration Act." 34 *So. Cal. L. Rev.* 413 (1961).

FIC, Committee of Experts. "Domestic Rules Recommended for Investment Liberalization." 4 *Journal of ACCJ* (No. 7) (Special Supplement) 20–23 (1967).

Foerster, Barrett J. "Arbitration Agreements and the Conflicts of Law." 21 *Arb. J.* 129 (1966).

Fujita, Yasuhiro. "Japanese Regulation of Foreign Transactions and Private Law Consequences." 18 *New York Law Forum* 1 (1972).

————. "Japanese Rules of Jurisdiction." 4 *Law in Japan* 55 (1971).

Fukuda, Takeo. "Statement." *The President Directory*. Tokyo: Diamond-Time Co., 1971.

Fukui, Haruhiro. "Liberal Democratic Party and Constitutional Revision." In *Papers on Modern Japan*, edited by David Sissons. Canberra: Australian National University Press, 1968.

————. "Twenty Years of Revision." In *The Constitution of Japan: Its First Twenty Years, 1947–67*, edited by Dan Fenno Henderson. Seattle: Universit⟨ of Washington Press, 1968.

Gardiner, Hilliard A. "Japanese Arbitration Law." 8 *Arb. J.* 89 (1953).

Gary, William L. "How Illinois Corporations May Enjoy Partnership Advantages: Planning for the Closely Held Firm." 48 *Nw. U. L. Rev.* 427 (1953).

Gibney, Frank. "The View from Japan." 50 *Foreign Affairs* 102 (1971).

Glazer, F. Herbert. "The Japanese Executive." In *The Japanese Employee*, edited by Robert J. Ballon. Tokyo: Sophia University and Charles E. Tuttle Co., 1969.

Gleason, Alan. "Economic Growth and Consumption in Japan." In *The State and Economic Enterprise in Japan*, edited by William W. Lockwood. Princeton: Princeton University Press, 1965.

Gower, L. C. B. "The English Private Company." 18 *Law & Contemp. Prob.* 535 (1953).

———. "Some Contrasts Between British and American Corporation Law." 69 *Harv. L. Rev.* 1369 (1956).

Graaf, Hellan. "Sweden." In *International Commercial Arbitration: A World Handbook*, Vol. 1, edited by Pieter Sanders. Paris: Dalloz et Sirey, 1956.

Green, Sedgwick W. "The Treaty Making Power and Extraterritorial Effect of the Constitution." 42 *Minn. L. Rev.* 825 (1958).

Hadley, Eleanor. "Trust Busting in Japan." 26 *Harvard Bus. Rev.* 425–40 (1948).

Hall, John C. "The Tokugawa Legislation (Part IV)." 41 *Transactions of the Asiatic Society of Japan* (TASJ) (Part V) 683 (1913).

Hall, John W. "Changing Conceptions of the Modernization of Japan." In *Changing Japanese Attitudes Toward Modernization*, edited by Marius B. Jansen. Princeton: Princeton University Press, 1967.

———. "The Confucian Teacher in Tokugawa Japan." In *Confucianism in Action*, edited by David S. Nivison and Arthur F. Wright. Stanford: Stanford University Press, 1959.

Hara, Yoshi, and Yano, Masakazu. "Changes in Education in Postwar Japan: A Graphic Explanation." 7 *Developing Economies* 640 (1969).

Harris, C. "Separate Treatment for Close Corporations: Lessons from England and Australia." 17 *Am. J. Comp. L.* 194 (1969).

Hartley, William D. "Eating Humble Pie: In Trading with China, Japan Sometimes Gets More Abuse Than Goods." *Wall Street Journal*, 11 Nov. 1970.

Hashimoto, Kiminobu. "The Rule of Law: Some Aspects of Judicial Review of Administrative Action." In *Law in Japan: The Legal Order in a Changing Society*, edited by Arthur T. Von Mehren. Cambridge: Harvard University Press, 1963.

Hatoyama, K. "Japanese Personal Legislation." In *Fifty Years of New Japan*, edited by Shigenobu Ōkuma. London: Smith & Elder Co., 1909.

Hattori, Ichirō. "Management Practices." In *Doing Business in Japan*, edited by Robert J. Ballon. Tokyo: Sophia University and Charles E. Tuttle Co., 1968.

Hattori, Takaaki. "The Legal Profession in Japan: Its Historical Development and Present State." In *Law in Japan: The Legal Order in a Changing Society*, edited by Arthur T. Von Mehren. Cambridge: Harvard University Press, 1963.

Hattori, Y. "The Foreign Commerce of Japan Since the Restoration, 1869–1900." *Studies in Historical and Political Science: Social and Industrial History*, Vol. 22. Baltimore: Johns Hopkins Press, 1904.

Heilman, Raymond V. "The Enforceability of Foreign Awards in the United States." 3 *Arb. J.* 183 (1939).

Henderson, Dan Fenno. "Business Procedures in Japanese Licensing." 4 *Les Nouvelles* (No. 1) 25 (1969).

————. "Contract Problems in U.S.-Japanese Joint Venture." 39 *Wash. L. Rev.* 459–515 (1964).

————. "Japanese Judicial Review of Legislation." In *The Constitution of Japan: Its First Twenty Years, 1947–1967*, edited by Dan Fenno Henderson. Seattle: University of Washington Press, 1968.

————. "Japanese Legal History of the Tokugawa Period: Scholars and Sources." *U. of Mich. Center of Japanese Studies, Occasional Paper* (No. 7) 100–21 (1957).

————. "Law and Political Modernization in Japan." In *Political Development in Modern Japan*, edited by Robert E. Ward. Princeton: Princeton University Press, 1968.

————. "Perspectives on the Japanese Constitution after Twenty Years." In *The Constitution of Japan: Its First Twenty Years, 1947–1967*, edited by Dan Fenno Henderson. Seattle: University of Washington Press, 1968.

————. "Promulgation of Tokugawa Statutes." 1 *Journal of Asian and African Statutes* 9 (1967).

————. "Review." 11 *Harv. J. of Int'l Law* 287–93 (1970).

————. "Review: Von Mehren, *Law in Japan*." 16 *Stanford L. Rev.* 1129 (1964).

————. "The Roles of Lawyers in U.S.-Japanese Business Transactions." 38 *Wash. L. Rev.* 1–21 (1963).

————. "Some Aspects of Tokugawa Law." 27 *Wash. L. Rev.* 85–109 (1952).

————. "Traditional Contract Law in Japan." (Draft for International Encyclopedia of Comparative Law) Vol. VII on Contracts (1971).

————, and Matsuo, Tasuku. "Japan's Trade Experience with the People's Republic of China." Mimeographed, 1971.

Hetherington, J. A. C. "Special Characteristics, Problems and Needs of the Close Corporation," in "Close Corporation: A Symposium." 1969 *U. Ill. L. Forum* 1–73, 139–223 (1969).

Hirano, Ryūichi. "Some Aspects of Criminal Law." In *Law in Japan: The Legal Order in a Changing Society*, edited by Arthur T. Von Mehren. Cambridge: Harvard University Press, 1963.

Hirono, Ryokichi. "Personnel Management in Foreign Corporations." In *The Japanese Employee*, edited by Robert J. Ballon. Tokyo: Sophia University and Charles E. Tuttle Co., 1969.

Hollerman, Leon. "Liberalization and Japanese Trade in the 1970s." 10 *Asian Survey* 27–37 (1970).

————. "Recent Difficulties in Japan's Economic Development." *Banca Nazionale del Lavoro Quarterly Review*, No. 88. (March 1969).

Horie, Y. "Foreign Capital and the Japanese Capitalism after World War I." 20 *Kyoto U. Econ. Rev.* 38–59 (1950).

Hornstein, George D. "Judicial Tolerance of the Incorporated Partnership." 18 *Law & Contemp. Prob.* 435 (1953).

Horowitz, Charles. "Guides for Resorting to Commercial Arbitration." 8 *Prac. Law* 67–84 (1962).

Hoshii, Iwao. "Japan and European Economic Community." 7 *Orient-West* (No. 11) 11 (1962).

Hoshino, Eiichi. "The Contemporary Contract." 5 *Law in Japan: An Annual* 1 (1972).

"How the Japanese Mount the Export Blitz." *Fortune*, Sept. 1970, p. 126.

Hynning, Clifford J., and Haight, George W. "International Commercial Arbitration." 48 *A.B.A.J.* 236 (1962).

Ishida, Takeshi. "The Development of Interest Groups and the Pattern of Political Modernization in Japan." In *Political Development in Modern Japan*, edited by Robert E. Ward. Princeton: Princeton University Press, 1968.

Ishikawa, Kichiemon. "The Regulation of the Employer-Employee Relationship: Japanese Labor-Relations Law." In *Law in Japan: The Legal Order in a Changing Society*, edited by Arthur T. Von Mehren. Cambridge: Harvard University Press, 1963.

Itō, Hirobumi. "Some Reminiscences of the Grant of the New Constitution." In *Fifty Years of New Japan*, edited by Shigenobu Ōkuma. London: Smith & Elder Co., 1909.

Itō, Masami. "The Rule of Law: Constitutional Development." In *Law in Japan: The Legal Order in a Changing Society*, edited by Arthur T. Von Mehren. Cambridge: Harvard University Press, 1963.

Jaffee, Samuel H. "Battle Report: The Problem of Stenographic Records in Arbitration." 20 *Arb. J.* 97 (1965).

Jalet, Frances T. Freeman. "Judicial Review of Arbitration: The Judicial Attitude." 45 *Cornell L. Q.* 519, 532 (1960).

Jan, George P. "Japan's Trade with Communist China." 9 *Asian Survey* 900–18 (1969).

"Japan's Remarkable Industrial Machine." *Business Week*, 7 Mar. 1970.

Javits, Jacob K. "A Senator Looks at U.S.–Japan Relations." 18 *Am. Jap. Soc'y. Bull.* 8 (November 1969–January 1970).

Jones, Hazel. "The Formulation of Meiji Policy toward the Employment of Foreigners." 23 *Monumenta Nipponica* 9–30 (1968).

Jones, William Carton. "Three Centuries of Commercial Arbitration in New York." 1956 *Wash. U. L. Q.* 193 (1956).

Kanazawa, Yoshio. "The Regulation of Corporate Enterprise." In *Law in Japan: The Legal Order in a Changing Society*, edited by Arthur T. Von Mehren. Cambridge: Harvard University Press, 1963.

Kaneda, Hiromitsu. "Long Term Changes in Food Consumption Patterns in Japan." In *Agriculture and Economic Growth: Japan's Experience*, edited by Kazushi Ohkawa, Bruce F. Johnston, and Hiromitsu Kaneda. Princeton: Princeton University Press and Tokyo: University of Tokyo Press, 1970.

Katō, Hidetoshi. "Sanken: A Power above Government." 7 *The Japan Interpreter* 36 (1971).

Katz, Milton. "The International Role of Law and Lawyers." In *Proceedings of the International Association of Law Libraries for 1961.* Ann Arbor, Mich.: International Association of Law Libraries, 1961. 58 pp.

Kawakami, Tarō, and Henderson, Dan Fenno. "Arbitration in U.S.-Japanese Sales Disputes." 42 *Wash. L. Rev.* 541 (1967).

Keeton, G. W. "The Future of the Legal Profession in England." 25 *U. Cinc. L. Rev.* 279 (1956).

Kelso, Robert C. "Check List of Legal Problems in Considering Foreign Investment." 1959 *U. Ill. L. J.* 416 (1959).

Kessler, Robert. "Hooray (?) for the Model Act—The 1969 Revision and the Close Corporation." 38 *Fordham L. R.* 743 (1970).

Keyes, William Noel. "Cause and Consideration in California—A Re-Appraisal." 47 *Cal. L. Rev.* 74 (1959).

Kitagawa, Tokusuke. "Commercial Arbitration Law and Practice in Japan." 12 *Japanese Annual of Int'l. Law* 59–70 (1968).

———. "Contractual Autonomy in International Commercial Arbitration, Including a Japanese Perspective." In *International Arbitration: Liber Amicorum for Martin Domke*, edited by Pieter Sanders. The Hague: Martinus Nijhoff, 1967.

Kitagawa, Zentarō. "Damages in Contracts for the Sale of Goods." 3 *Law in Japan: An Annual* 43–89 (1969).

Kobayashi, Ken'ichi. "The Employment and Wage System in Postwar Japan." 7 *Developing Economies* 187 (1969).

Kobayashi, Noritake. "Management Differences." In *The World of Japanese Business*, by T. F. M. Adams and Noritake Kobayashi. Tokho: Kōdansha International, Ltd., 1969.

Komiya, Ryūtarō. "The Supply of Personal Savings." In *Postwar Economic Growth in Japan*, edited by Ryūtarō Komiya, translated by Robert Ozaki. Berkeley: University of California Press, 1966.

Kopelmanes, Lazare. "The Settlement of Disputes in International Trade." 61 *Colum. L. Rev.* 384 (1961).

Kronstein, Heinrich. "Arbitration Is Power." 38 *N. Y. U. L. Rev.* 661–700 (1963).

Kubota, Akira, and Ward, Robert E. "Family Influence and Political Socialization in Japan." *Comparative Political Studies* 3, No. 2 (July 1970): 140–75.

Langdon, Frank. "Big Business Lobbying in Japan: The Case of Central Bank Reform." 55 *Am. Pol. Sci. Rev.* 538 (1961).

———. "Organized Interests in Japan and Their Influence on Political Parties." 34 *Pacific Affairs* 271–78 (1961).

———. "The Political Contributions of Big Business in Japan." 3 *Asian Survey* 465–73 (1963).

Lee, Chae-Jin. "The Politics of Sino-Japanese Trade Relations, 1963–68." 42 *Pacific Affairs* 129–44 (1969).

Lee, Jooinn. "Kōmeitō Sōkagakkai-ism in Japanese Politics." 10 *Asian Survey* 501 (1970).

Leiserson, Michael. "Factions and Coalitions in One-Party Japan." 62 *Am. Pol. Sci. Rev.* 770 (1968).

Lenhoff, Arthur. "The Parties' Choice of a Forum: 'Prorogation Agreements.' " 15 *Rutgers L. Rev.* 414 (1961).

Levine, Solomon B. "Labor Markets and Collective Bargaining in Japan." In *The State and Economic Enterprise in Japan*, edited by William W. Lockwood. Princeton: Princeton University Press, 1965.

―――. "Postwar Trade Unionism, Collective Bargaining, and Japanese Social Structure." In *Aspects of Social Change in Modern Japan*, edited by Ronald P. Dore. Princeton: Princeton University Press, 1967.

Lorenzen, Ernest G. "Commercial Arbitration—Enforcement of Foreign Awards." 45 *Yale L. J.* 29 (1935).

Massel, Mark S. "The Lawyer's Role in International Trade." In *Legal Problems in International Trade and Investment*, edited by Crawford Shaw. New Haven: World Community Association, Yale Law School, 1962.

Maw, Caryle E. "Conflicts Avoidance in International Contracts." In *International Contracts: Choice of Law and Language*, edited by Willis L. M. Reese. Dobbs Ferry, N.Y.: Oceana Publications, 1962.

McCartney, Robert C. "The Use of Choice-of-Law Clauses in International Commercial Contracts." 6 *Wayne L. Rev.* 340 (1959–60).

McFadyean, Colin. "The American Close Corporation and Its British Equivalent." 14 *Bus. Law* 215 (1958).

McMahon, John P. "Implementation of the United Nations Convention of Foreign Arbitral Awards in the United States." 2 *J. Maritime Law and Commerce* 735 (1971).

Meiners, Robert. "Arbitration Awards and 'Public Policy.' " 17 *Arb. J.* 145 (1962).

Mentschikoff, Soia. "Commercial Arbitration." 61 *Colum. L. Rev.* 846 (1961).

―――. "The Significance of Arbitration—A Preliminary Inquiry." 17 *Law & Contemp. Prob.* 698 (1952).

Meyers, Howard. "Revisions of the Criminal Code of Japan During the Occupation." 25 *Wash. L. Rev.* 104 (1950).

Mezger, Ernest. "The Arbitrator and Private International Law." In *International Trade Arbitration*, edited by Martin Domke. New York: American Arbitration Association, 1958.

Michida, Shin'ichirō. "Capital Liberalization as a Treaty Question and Offensive and Defensive Strategies Concerning Foreign Capital." 2 *Law in Japan: An Annual* 1 (1968).

Mills, Lewis R. "The Mathematics of Cumulative Voting." 1968 *Duke L. J.* 28–43 (1958).

"MITI Studies Criteria on Conduct of Foreign Companies." *Japan Economic Journal*, 27 July 1971, p. 2.

Miyamoto, Shōson; Yukawa, Hideki; Hori, Ichirō; and Moore, Charles A.

"Editor's Supplement: The Enigmatic Japanese Mind." In *The Japanese Mind*, edited by Charles A. Moore. Honolulu: East-West Center Press, 1968.

Morley, James. "Growth for What? The Issues of the Seventies." In *Japanese-American Relations in the 1970's*, edited by Gerald L. Curtis. Washington, D.C.: Columbia Books, 1970.

Moses, Fritz. "International Legal Practice." 4 *Fordham L. Rev.* 244 (1935).

Mosk, Stanley. "The Lawyer and Commercial Arbitration: The Modern Law." 39 *A.B.A.J.* 193 (1953).

Mukai, Ken, and Toshitani, Nobuyoshi. "The Progress and Problems of Compiling the Civil Code in the Early Meiji Era." Translated by Dan Fenno Henderson. 1 *Law in Japan: An Annual* 25–59 (1967).

Nagai, Michio. "Social Change in Postwar Japan." 7 *Developing Economies* 395 (1969).

———. "University Problems in Japan." 23 *Bulletin of the Int'l House of Japan* 1–25 (1969).

Nagashima, A. "The Accused and Society: The Administration of Criminal Justice in Japan." In *Law in Japan: The Legal Order in a Changing Society*, edited by Arthur T. Von Mehren. Cambridge: Harvard University Press, 1963.

Nakamura, Hajime. "Consciousness of the Individual and the Universal among the Japanese." In *The Status of the Individual in East and West*, edited by Charles A. Moore. Honolulu: East-West Center Press, 1968.

———; Furukawa, Tesshi; Kōsaka, Masaaki; and Kawashima, Takeyoshi. "Statements." In *The Status of the Individual in East and West*, edited by Charles A. Moore. Honolulu: East-West Center Press, 1968.

Nakamura, James I. "Growth of Japanese Agriculture, 1875–1920." In *The State and Economic Enterprise in Japan*, edited by William W. Lockwood. Princeton: Princeton University Press, 1965.

Nakamura, Kikuo. "Japan's Role in the United Nations." 3 *Japanese Annual of International Law* 92–102 (1959).

Nakanishi, Naomichi. "Changes in Living Patterns Brought about by Television." 7 *Developing Economies* 572 (1969).

Nakata, Jun'ichi. "Japan." In *International Commercial Arbitration: A World Handbook*, Vol. 3, edited by Pieter Sanders. The Hague: Martinus Nijhoff, 1965.

Narutomi, Nobuo. "Collective Action in Industrial Disputes." 58 *Law Society's Gazette* 15–20 (1961).

———. "From the Rule of Force to the Rule of Law in Labor-Management Relations." 15 *Bus. Lawyer* 607–32 (1960).

Nathanson, Nathaniel L. "Constitutional Adjudication in Japan." 7 *Am. J. of Comp.* 195 (1958).

———, and Fujita, Yasuhiro. "The Right to Fair Hearing in Japanese Administrative Law." 45 *Wash. Law Rev.* 273 (1970).

"Negative List is Revised to Screening." *Japan Economic Journal*, 27 July 1971, p. 1.

Nehmer, Stanley. "Japan's Trade and Investment Policies." 8 *Journal ACCJ* (No. 6) 49 (1971).

"Nipponese Naderism." *Wall Street Journal*, 29 Jan. 1971, p. 1.

Note. "Courts: Contracts: Maritime Law: Forum Non Conveneins: Stipulations of Exclusive Jurisdiction: Bill of Lading: Carbon Black Export, Inc. v. The Monrosa." 45 *Cornell L. Q.* 364 (1960).

Note. "Judicial Review of Arbitration Awards on the Merits." 63 *Harv. L. Rev.* 681 (1950).

Note. "Judicial Supervision of Commercial Arbitration." 53 *Georgetown L. J.* 1079 (1965).

Note. "Arbitration and Award—Commercial Law—An Agreement to Submit an Existing or Future Dispute to Arbitration is Valid and Enforceable. Texas General Arbitration Act, Texas Laws, 1965." 44 *Texas L. Rev.* 372 (1966).

Nussbaum, Arthur. "The 'Separability Doctrine' in American and Foreign Arbitration." 17 *N.Y. U. L. Rev.* 609 (1940).

Ogawa, Ichirō. "Judicial Review of Administrative Action in Japan." In *The Constitution of Japan: Its First Twenty Years, 1947–1967*, edited by Dan Fenno Henderson. Seattle: University of Washington Press, 1969.

Ōhira, Kaname, and Stevens, George. "Admission to the Bar, Disbarment and Disqualification of Lawyers in Japan and the United States—A Comparative Study." 38 *Wash. L. Rev.* 22–57 (1963).

Ohkawa, Kazushi. "Agriculture and Turning Points." 3 *Developing Economies* 471 (1965).

———. "Phases of Agricultural Development and Economic Growth." In *Agricultural and Economic Growth: Japan's Experience*, edited by Kazushi Ohkawa, Bruce F. Johnston, and Hiromitsu Kaneda. Princeton: Princeton University Press and Tokyo: University of Tokyo Press, 1970.

———, and Rosovsky, Henry. "A Century of Japanese Economic Growth." In *The State and Economic Enterprise in Japan*, edited by William W. Lockwood. Princeton: Princeton University Press, 1965.

Okada, Tadao. "The Unchanging Bureaucracy." 12 *Japan Quarterly* (No. 2) 168 (1965).

Okano, Mitsuya. "The Role of Foreign Technology and Government Policies for Economic Development in Post-War Japan." *Les Nouvelles* (June 1972), pp. 23–28.

O'Meara, Arthur C. "Organizational Structure, Operation, and Administration for Large Corporate Law Departments" (25 or more lawyers). 17 *Bus. Law* 584 (1962).

O'Neal, F. Hodges. "Control Distribution Devices," in "Close Corporation: A Symposium." 1969 *U. Ill. L. Forum* 48 (1969).

Onuma, Tōru *et al.* "Current Developments in Antitrust and Trade Practice Laws and Policy in Japan and the Relation thereto of Industrial Property Rights." 7 *Patent, TM, and Copyright Journal of Research and Education* [Georgetown] 25–44 (1963).

Oppler, Alfred. "Japan's Courts and Law in Transition." 21 *Contemporary Japan* (Nos. 1–3) 1–37 (1952).
———. "The Reform of Japan's Legal and Judicial System under Allied Occupation." 24 *Wash. L. Rev.* 290–324 (1949).
Ōtsuka, Hisao. "The Formation of Modern Man: The Popular Base for Democratization." 6 *The Japan Interpreter* 1 (1970).
———. "Modernization Reconsidered." 3 *The Developing Economies* 387–403 (1965).
Ōuchi, Kazuomi. "Problems of Competence of International Commercial Arbitral Tribunals." 3 *Philippine Int'l L. J.* 16–132 (1964).
Ozaki, Robert S. "Japanese Views on Foreign Capital." 11 *Asian Survey* 1071–83 (1971).
———. "Japanese Views on Industrial Organization." 10 *Asian Survey* 872–89 (1970).
Patrick, Hugh. "Japan's Interest Rates and the Grey Financial Market." 38 *Pacific Affairs* 326–344 (1965–66).
———. "The Phoenix Risen from the Ashes: Postwar Japan." In *Modern East Asia: Essays in Interpretation*, edited by James Crowley. New York: Harcourt Brace Jovanovich, Inc., 1970.
Pearl, Allan R. "Liberalization of Capital in Japan." 13 *Harvard Inter. L. J.* 59, 245 (1972).
"Perspective: Concept toward Decontrol of Capital is Changing." *Japan Economic Journal*, 9 Mar. 1971, p. 3.
Pirsig, Maynard E. "Some Comments on Arbitration Legislation and the Uniform Act." 10 *Vand. L. Rev.* 685 (1957).
"Preface." In *The Japanese Mind*, edited by Charles A. Moore. Honolulu: East-West Center Press, 1968.
Pyle, Kenneth B. "Some Recent Approaches to Japanese Nationalism." 31 *J. of Asian Studies* 5 (1971).
Quigley, Leonard V. "Accession by the U.S. to the UN Convention on the Recognition and Enforcement of Foreign Arbitral Awards." 70 *Yale L. J.* 1049 (1961).
Rabinowitz, Richard. "The Historical Development of the Japanese Bar." 70 *Harv. L. Rev.* 61–81 (1956).
Reese, Willis L. M. "The Contractual Forum: Situations in the United States." 13 *Am. J. Comp. L.* 187 (1964).
Riess, Ludwig. "History of the English Factory at Hirado (1613–1622)." *Transactions of the Asiatic Society of Japan*, Vol. 26. Tokyo: Asiatic Society of Japan, 1898; reprint, 1964.
Rosovsky, Henry, and Ohkawa, Kazushi. "The Indigenous Components in the Modern Japanese Economy." 9 *Econ. Dev. and Cultural Change* 476 (1961).
Sakita, Saburō. "Japanese Economic Cooperation in Asia in the 1970's." In *Japanese-American Relations in the 1970's*, edited by Gerald L. Curtis. Washington, D.C.: Columbia Books, 1970.
Sakurabayashi, Makoto. "Enterprise Unionism and Wage Increases." In *The*

Japanese Employee, edited by Robert J. Ballon. Tokyo: Sophia University and Charles E. Tuttle Co., 1969.

Salwin, Lester N. "The New Commercial Code of Japan: Symbol of Gradual Progress toward Democratic Goals." 50 *Georgetown L. J.* 478–512 (1962).

Satō, Isao. "Treaties and the Constitution." In *The Constitution of Japan: Its First Twenty Years, 1947–1967*. Seattle: University of Washington Press, 1969.

Sayre, Paul L. "Development of Commercial Arbitration Law." 37 *Yale L. J.* 595 (1928).

Scalapino, Robert A. "Labor and Politics in Postwar Japan." In *The State and Economic Enterprise in Japan*, edited by William W. Lockwood. Princeton: Princeton University Press, 1965.

Scher, V. Alexander. "What Foreign Patent Attorneys Think of American Patent Practice." 44 *J. Pat. Off. Soc'y* 544 (1962).

Schneider, Dieter. "The American Close Corporation and Its German Equivalent." 14 *Bus. Law* 228 (1958).

Schwab, Karl H. "The Legal Foundations and Limitations of Arbitration Procedures in the U.S. and Germany." In *International Arbitration: Liber Amicorum for Martin Domke*, edited by Pieter Sanders. The Hague: Martinus Nijhoff, 1967.

Shannon, Thomas, and Marx, William. "The International Anti-Dumping Code and United States Anti-Dumping Law—An Appraisal." 7 *Columbia J. of Transnational Law* 171–202 (1968).

"The Sharp Side of the Rising Sun," *Business Week*, 6 Sept. 1969, p. 124.

Shaw, John F. "Valedictory Remarks of a Commercial Counselor." 20 *Am. Jap. Soc'y Bull.* (No. 2) 6 (Aug.-Oct. 1971).

———. "What Prompted President Nixon's Economic Program?" 8 *Journal ACCJ* (No. 10) 7 (5 Oct. 1971).

Shigehisa, Tokutarō. "Foreigners in Early Meiji." *Japan Advertiser* (28 Oct. 1939).

Silberman, Bernard S. "The Bureaucracy and Economic Development in Japan." 5 *Asian Survey* 529–37 (1965).

Sissons, David C. S. "Dissolution of the Japanese Lower House." In *Papers on Modern Japan*, edited by David C. S. Sissons. Canberra: Australian National U. Press, 1968.

Smethurst, Richard J. "The Origin and the Politics of the Japan Teachers' Union 1945–56." In Center of Japanese Studies, University of Michigan, *Occasional Papers*, No. 10. Ann Arbor: University of Michigan Press, 1967.

Smit, Hans. "Frustration of Contract: A Comparative Attempt at Consolidation." 58 *Colum. L. Rev.* 287 (1958).

Smith, J. Denson. "A Refresher Course in *Cause*." 12 *La. L. Rev.* 2 (1951).

Soukup, James R. "Business Political Participation in Japan: Continuity and Change." *Studies on Asia* 163–78 (1965).

———. "Comparative Studies in Political Finance: Japan." 25 *J. of Politics* 727–56 (1963).

Steiner, Kurt. "Postwar Changes in the Japanese Civil Code." 25 *Wash. L. Rev.* 286 (1950).

————. "The Revision of the Civil Code of Japan: Provisions Affecting the Family." 9 *Far East Q.* 169 (1950).

Sturges, Wesley A. "Fraudulent Inducement as a Defense to the Enforcement of Arbitration Contracts." 36 *Yale L. J.* 866, 873 (1927).

————, and Murphy, Irving Olds. "Some Confusing Matters Relating to Arbitration under the U.S. Arbitration Act." 17 *Law & Contemp. Prob.* 580 (1952).

————, and Reckson, Richard E. "Common-Law and Statutory Arbitration: Problems Arising From Their Coexistence." 46 *Minn. L. Rev.* 819 (1962).

————, and Sturges, William W. "Some Confusing Matters Relating to Arbitration in Washington." 25 *Wash. L. Rev.* 16 (1950).

Sullivan, Charles H. "United States Treaty Policy on Commercial Arbitration—1920–46." In *International Trade Arbitration*, edited by Martin Domke. New York: American Arbitration Association, 1958.

Sultan, Allen. "The UN Arbitration Convention and U.S. Policy." 53 *Am. J. of Int'l. Law* 807 (1959).

Susato, Shigeru. "The White Collar Strata in Postwar Japan." 7 *Developing Economies* 451 (1969).

Surrey, Walter. "American Investments Abroad—Foreign Legal Aspects for American Lawyers." 7 *Prac. Law* (No. 8) Pt. I (1961); Pt. II (1962).

Swisher, Donald P. "International Commercial Arbitration and the Federal Courts: Judicial Review by Advice and Consent of Congress." 46 *Wash. L. Rev.* 441–88 (1972).

Symposium. "Arbitration and the Courts." 58 *Nw. U. L. Rev.* 466–582 (1963).

————. "Commercial Arbitration." 17 *Law & Contemp. Probl.* 471–710 (1952).

————. "Close Corporations." 1969 *U. of Ill. Law Forum* 1–60, 139–223 (1969).

————. "Judicial Review of Arbitration: The Role of Public Policy." 58 *Nw. U. L. Rev.* 545 (1963).

————. "Scope of the United States Arbitration Act in Commercial Arbitration: Problems in Federalism." 58 *Nw. U. L. Rev.* 46 (1963).

Szladits, Charles. "Illegality of Prohibited Contracts: Comparative Aspects." In *XXth Century Comparative and Conflicts Law: Legal Essays in Honor of Hessel E. Yntema*, edited by Kurt H. Nadelmann, Arthur T. Von Mehren, and John N. Hazard. Leyden: A. W. Sythoff, 1961.

Tachi, Minoru, and Okazaki, Yōichi. "Japan's Postwar Population and Labor Force." 7 *Developing Economies* 170 (1969).

Takamiya, Susumu. "Business Organization." In *Doing Business in Japan*, edited by Robert J. Ballon. Tokyo: Sophia University and Charles E. Tuttle Co., 1968.

Takano, Y. "Japan and the International Organizations." 1 *Japanese Annual of International Law* (JAIL) 38–42 (1957).

Takayanagi, Kenzō. "A Century of Innovation: The Development of Japanese Law, 1868–1961." In *Law in Japan: The Legal Order in a Changing Society*, edited by Arthur T. Von Mehren. Cambridge: Harvard University Press, 1963.

————. "Common and Civil Law in Japan." 4 *Am. J. Comp. L.* 60 (1955).

Tanabe, Kōji. "The Process of Litigation: An Experiment with the Adversary

System." In *Law in Japan: The Legal Order in a Changing Society*, edited by Arthur T. Von Mehren. Cambridge: Harvard University Press, 1963.

Tanaka, Hajime W. "Enforcement of American Arbitration Awards in Japan." 10 *Arb. J.* 88 (1955).

Taniguchi, Tomohei. "Comment on *Tomita* v. *Inoue*." 2 *Law in Japan: An Annual* 194–97 (1968).

Teraoka, T. W. M. "Accounting Practice." In *Doing Business in Japan*, edited by Robert J. Ballon. Tokyo: Sophia University and Charles E. Tuttle Co., 1968.

Thayer, Nathaniel B. "The Election of a Japanese Prime Minister." 9 *Asian Survey* 477 (1969).

"Themes and Variations." *Wall Street Journal*, 3 Feb. 1964.

Tominaga, Ken'ichi. "Trend Analysis of Social Stratification and Social Mobility in Contemporary Japan." 7 *Developing Economies* 471 (1969).

Trade Bulletin Corporation. "Rules of Employment: How to Prepare Them, Together with Sample Text of Collective Labor Agreement." *Social and Economic Laws of Japan*, Vol. V, Book 2. Tokyo: Trade Bulletin Corporation, 1969. Mimeographed.

Trezise, Philip H. "The Realities of Japan-U.S. Economic Relations." 1 *Pacific Community* 353 (1970).

Tsuji, Kiyoaki. "Decision Making in the Japanese Government: A Study of *Ringisei*." In *Political Development in Modern Japan*, edited by Robert E. Ward. Princeton: Princeton University Press, 1968.

Uemura, Kōgorō. "New Challenge for Japan's Foreign Economic Policy." 8 *Journal of ACCJ* 40 (1971).

Ukai, Nobushige. "The Individual and the Rule of Law under the New Constitution." 51 *Nw. U. L. Rev.* 733–37 (1956–57).

"U.S. Companies Aren't Excited by Easing of Japanese Investment Rules, Poll Finds." *Wall Street Journal*, 22 Sept. 1970.

"U.S. Hits Japan T.V. Sets." *New York Times*, 29 Aug. 1970.

Vagts, Detlev. "The Multinational Enterprise." 83 *Harv. L. Rev.* 739 (1970).

Van Hecke, George A. "A Civilian Looks at the Common-Law Lawyer." In *International Contracts: Choice of Law and Language*, edited by Willis L. M. Reese. Dobbs Ferry, N.Y.: Oceana Publications, 1962.

Van Zandt, Howard. "The Japanese Culture and the Business Boom." 48 *Foreign Affairs* 344 (1970).

Vernon, Raymond. "The Role of U.S. Enterprise Abroad." *Daedalus* 11 (Winter 1969), p. 218.

Vogel, Ezra. "Beyond Salary: Mamachi Revisited." 6 *Japan Interpreter* 105 (1970).

Von Mehren, Arthur T. "Civil Law Analogues to Consideration: An Exercise in Comparative Analysis." 72 *Harv. L. Rev.* 1009 (1959).

Wagatsuma, Sakae. "Democratization of the Family Relations in Japan." 23 *Wash. L. Rev.* 405 (1950).

Walker, Herman. "Commercial Arbitration in United States Treaties." 11 *Arb. J.* 68–84 (1956).

Ward, Robert E. "The Commission on the Constitution and Prospects for Constitutional Changes in Japan." 24 *J. Asian Studies* 401–29 (1965).

Watanabe, Yōzō. "The Family and Law: The Individualistic Premise and Modern Japanese Family Law." In *Law in Japan: The Legal Order in a Changing Society*, edited by Arthur T. Von Mehren. Cambridge: Harvard University Press, 1963.

Weiner, Joseph L. "Legislative Recognition of the Close Corporation." 27 *Mich. L. Rev.* 273 (1929).

Wetzel, C. R. "Employment Contracts and Non-competition Agreements," in "Close Corporations: A Symposium." 1969 *U. Ill. L. Forum* 61 (1969).

Wigmore, J. H. "New Codes and Old Customs." *Japan Mail*, 29 Oct. 1892.

———. "The Legal System of Old Japan." 4 *Green Bag* 403–11, 478–84 (1892).

Wilner, Gabriel M. "Determining the Law Governing Performance in International Commercial Arbitration: A Comparative Study." 19 *Rutgers L. Rev.* 646 (1965).

Wolaver, Earl S. "The Historical Background of Commercial Arbitration." 83 *U. Pa. L, Rev.* 132 (1934).

Woodruff, Judson S. "The Japanese Lawyer." 35 *Neb. L. Rev.* 429–457 (1956).

Yazawa, Makoto. "The Legal Structure for Corporate Enterprise: Shareholder-Management Relations under Japanese Law." In *Law in Japan: The Legal Order in a Changing Society*, edited by Arthur T. Von Mehren. Cambridge: Harvard University Press, 1963.

"Yen Revaluation Comes as a Relief in Japan after Uncertainty." *Wall Street Journal*, 22 Dec. 1971.

Yoshinaga, Eisuke. "The Medium and Small Enterprises in Japan and Thier Form of Corporation." 1 *Hitotsubashi J. of L. & Politics* 16–29 (1960).

TABLE OF LAWS AND ORDINANCES (JAPANESE)

Bengoshihō (Lawyers' law), Law No. 205, 10 June 1949.

Benrishihō (Patent agents' law), Law No. 100, 30 Apr. 1922.

Benrishihō shikōrei (Order for enforcement of the patent agents' law), Imperial Ordinance No. 466, 16 Dec. 1921.

Bōeki kankei bōeki-gai torihiki no kanri ni kansuru shōrei (Ministerial ordinance concerning control of invisible transactions relating to foreign trade), Attached List No. 9; Form 12–2 (MITI Ord. No. 49, 1 Apr. 1963, as amended); English: EHS *Law Bulletin Service*, No. 5222.

Branch Reporting Ordinance (MOF and MITI joint ministerial ordinance, No. 1, 1 July 1963).

Chihō kōeki kigyō rōdō kankei-hō (Local public enterprise labor relations law), Law No. 289, 31 July 1952; English: 8 EHS *Law Bulletin Service*, No. 8030.

Chūshō kigyō dantai no soshiki ni kansuru hōritsu (Law concerning the organization of medium and small enterprise association), Law No. 185, 25 Nov. 1957.

Denki jigyō oyobi sekitan kōgyō ni okeru sōgi kōi no hōhō no kisei ni kansurū hōritsu (Law covering the regulations of the methods of acts of dispute in the electricity business and the coal industry), Law No. 171, 7 Aug. 1953.

Futō keihinrui oyobi futō hyōji bōshi-hō (Law to prevent unfair prizes and false marking), Law No. 134, 15 May 1962.

Gaikoku kawase ginkō-hō (Foreign-exchange bank law), Law No. 67, 10 Apr. 1954; English: EHS *Law Bulletin Service*, No. 5045.

Gaikoku kawase kanrirei (Cabinet order for control of foreign exchange), Cabinet Order No. 203, 27 June 1950, as amended.

Gaikoku kawase oyobi gaikoku bōeki kanrihō (Foreign exchange and foreign trade control law [FECL]), Law No. 228, 1 Dec. 1949; English: EHS *Law Bulletin Service*, No. 5010.

Gaikoku shōken gyōsha ni kansuru hōritsu (Law concerning foreign securities dealers), Law No. 5, 3 Mar. 1971.

Gaikoku tōshika yokin kanjō ni kansuru seirei (Cabinet order concerning foreign investors' deposit accounts), Cab. Order 427, 30 Sept. 1952; English: EHS *Law Bulletin Service*, No. 5460.

Gaishi dōnyū ni kansuru shinsa tetsuzuki kanso-ka sochi (Provisions concerning expedition of screening procedures covering capital induction).

Gaishi ni kansuru hōritsu (Foreign investment law [FIL]), Law No. 163, 10 May 1950; English: 5 EHS *Law Bulletin Service*, No. 5410.

Gaishi ni kansuru hōritsu no kitei ni motozuku ninka no kijun no tokurei-tō ni kansuru seirei (Cabinet order concerning exception to standards of validation, etc., based on the FIL), Cabinet Order No. 221, 1 July 1950, as amended to 1967; English: EHS *Law Bulletin Service*, No. 5470.

Gaishi ni kansuru hōritsu shikō kisoku (Regulations for enforcement of the FIL), FIC Regulation No. 2, 28 June 1950, as amended; English: EHS *Law Bulletin Service*, No. 5430.

Gaishi ni kansuru hōritsu no kitei ni yori Nihon Ginkō ni toriatsukawaseru jimu no han'i o kimeru seirei (Cabinet order fixing business scope to be handled by the Bank of Japan under provisions of the FIL), Cab. Order No. 412, 11 Sept. 1952, as amended; English: EHS *Law Bulletin Service*, No. 5488.

Gaishi shingikai-rei (Foreign investment council order), Cab. Order No. 309, 31 July 1952, as amended; English: EHS *Law Bulletin Service*, No. 5475.

Gijutsu dōnyū no jiyūka ni tsuite (Concerning liberalization of induction of technology), Cab. Decision, 10 May 1968.

Gyōsei shoshihō (Administrative scriveners law), Law No. 4, 22 Feb. 1951.

Gyōsei shoshihō shikō saisoku (Rules for enforcement of the administrative scriveners law), Tokyo City Reg. No. 61, 7 Apr. 1951, amended to 1 Aug. 1970.

Hishō jiken tetsuzukihō (Law of procedure in noncontentious matters), Law No. 14, 21 June 1898; English: 2 EHS *Law Bulletin Service*, No. 2380.

Hōrei ("Law concerning the application of laws in general"), Law No. 10, 21 June 1898.

Hyōjun kessai hōhō ni kansuru shōrei (Ministerial ordinance concerning standard method of settlement) (MOF Ordinance No. 62, 1962, *Beppyō* [Schedule] No. 1). 28 *Genkō hōki* 3426.

Hyōjun kessai hōhō ni yori hikyojū-sha kara shiharai no jun'yō o suru koto ga dekinai baai no shitei (Designating cases where receipt of payment from exchange nonresidents under the standard methods of settlement is not allowed). MOF Notification, No. 191, 1 July 1963.

Kempō (Constitution), 3 Nov. 1946.

Kensetsugyōhō (Construction industry law), Law No. 100, 24 May 1949.

Kogitte-hō (Laws of checks), Law No. 57, 29 July 1933.

Kokka kōmuin-hō (National public servants law), Law No. 120, 21 Oct. 1946.

Kokusai kaijō buppin unsōhō (International carriage of goods by sea act), Law No. 172, 13 June 1957.

Kōkyō kigyō-tai tō rōdō kankei-hō (Public enterprise, etc. labor relations law), Law No. 257, 20 Dec. 1948; English: 8 EHS *Law Bulletin Serivce*, No. 8020.

Kōnin kaikeishi-hō (Certified public accountants law), Law No. 103, 6 July 1948.

Kōshonin-hō (Notary law), Law No. 53, 14 Apr. 1908.

Mimoto hoshō ni kansuru hōritsu (Law concerning fidelity guaranty), Law No. 42, 1 Apr. 1933; English: 2 EHS *Law Bulletin Service*, No. 2124.

Minji soshōhō (Code of civil procedure), Law No. 89, 27 Apr. 1896.

Nōchihō (Farm land law), Law No. 229, 15 July 1952.

Rōdō kankei chōsei-hō (Labor relations adjustment law), Law No. 25, 27 Sept. 1946; English: 8 EHS *Law Bulletin Service*, No. 8010.

Rōdō kijun-hō (Labor standards law), Law No. 49, 7 Apr. 1947; English: 8 EHS *Law Bulletin Service*, No. 8040.

Rōdō kumiai-hō (Labor union law), Law No. 174, 1 June 1949; English: 8 EHS *Law Bulletin Service*, No. 8000.

Saibansho-hō (Law of courts or "court organization law"), Law No. 59, 16 Apr. 1947; English: 2 EHS *Law Bulletin Service*, No. 2010.

Shakuchihō (Land lease law), Law No. 49, 8 Apr. 1921; English: 2 EHS *Law Bulletin Service*, No. 21301.

Shakuyahō (House lease law), Law No. 50, 8 Apr. 1921; English: EHS *Law Bulletin Service*, No. 2131.

Shihō shoshihō (Judicial scrivener law of 1950), Law No. 197, 22 May 1950.

Shiteki dokusen no kinshi oyobi kōsei torihiki no kakuho ni kansuru hōritsu (Law concerning the prohibition of private monopoly and the maintenance of fair trade), Law No. 54, 1947, as amended.

Shōgyō tōkihō (Commercial registration law), Law No. 125, 9 July 1963.

Shōgyō tōki kisoku (Commercial registration regulations), Ministry of Justice Reg. No. 23, 11 March 1964.

Shōhō-chū shomei subeki baai ni kansuru hōritsu (Law concerning cases where signing is required within Commercial Code), Law No. 17, 26 Feb. 1900.

Shōken torihikihō (Securities exchange law), Law No. 25, 13 Apr. 1948, as amended effective 1 July 1971.

"*Shōken torihikihō no ichibu o kaisei suru hōritsu o koko ni kōfu suru*" (Herein promulgating the law revising a part of the securities exchange law), *Hōrei zensho* 1 (March 1971).

Tainai chokusetsu tōshi tō no jiyūka ni tsuite (Concerning liberalization of inward direct investment, etc.), Cab. Decision, 6 June 1967, as amended; English: *Japan: Regulations*, p. D–138.

Tegata-hō (Bills of exchange), Law No. 20, 15 July 1932.

Tokkyohō (Patent law), Law No. 121, 13 Apr. 1959; English: EHS *Law Bulletin Service*, 6850A.

Yūgengaishahō (Limited company law), Law No. 74, 5 Apr. 1938.

Yūka shōken no kōkai kaitsuke no todokeide tō ni kansuru shōrei (Ministerial ordinance concerning filings for public take-over bids for securities), Ministry of Finance Ordinance No. 38, 9 June 1971.

Zeirishihō (Tax agents' law), Law No. 237, 15 June 1951.

TABLE OF CASES

JAPANESE CASES:

A. D. Rarande v. *Oriental Hotel, Ltd.*, 24 Minroku 865 (Gr. Ct. Cass., 15 Apr. 1918).

Agetsuma v. *Kawai*, 8 Kakyū minshū 2139 (Osaka Dist. Ct., 16 Nov. 1957).

Akita v. *Dai Nippon Kōgyō K.K. Hatsumori Kōgyōjo Rōdō Kumiai*, 11 Rōminshū 1801 (Akita Dist. Ct., 29 Sept. 1960).

American President Lines v. *C. Subura K.K.*, 10 Kakyū minshū 2232 (Tokyo Dist. Ct., 23 Oct. 1959).

Arimatsu v. *Furukawa*, 22 Daishin'in minji hanketsuroku 1450 (Gr. Ct. Cass., 16 Sept. 1916).

Arita v. *Kajima et al.* (Yawata Steel Case), 14 Kakyū minshū 657 (Tokyo Dist. Ct., 5 Apr. 1963).

Asahi Shimbun case, 8 Kōsai minshū (No. 2) 177 (1953).

Compania de Transportes de ma S.A. v. *Mataichi K.K.*, 4 Kakyū minshū 502 (Tokyo Dist. Ct., 10 Apr. 1953).

Continental Ins. Co. v. *Furudono*, Hōritsu shimbun (No. 3904) 5 (Tokyo App. Ch., 5 Aug. 1935).

Daikō denki case, Rōkeisoku (No. 644) (Utsunomiya Dist. Ct., 29 Feb. 1968).

Domex International Co. v. *Yokohama Tsūshō K.K. et al.*, Hanrei jihō (No. 430) 17 (1966) (Tokyo Dist. Ct., 6th Dept., 28 Oct. 1965).

Fuji Kōsoku Insatsu K.K. v. *Tomita*, 7 Kakyū minshū 135 (Tokyo Dist. Ct., 30 Jan. 1956).

G. M. Casaregi Compagnia di Navigazione e Commèrcio S.P.A. v. *Nishi Shōji K.K.*, 10 Kakyū minshū 1711 (Tokyo Dist. Ct., 20 Aug. 1959).

Greenhill Trading Co. v. *Shiro Trading Corp.*, 13 Kōsai minshū 696 (Tokyo High Ct., 29 Oct. 1960).

Hashimoto v. *Katayama*, Hōritsu shimbun (No. 1140) 28 (Gr. Ct. Cass., 15 May 1916).

Hinode Kagaku Kōgyō K.K. v. *Sankō Kisen K.K.*, 10 Kakyū minshū 970 (Osaka Dist. Ct., 11 May 1959).

Hyaku-sanjūhachi Bank v. *Tōyō Seien Co.*, 16 Minroku 982 (Gr. Ct. Cass., 23 Dec. 1910).

Iguchi v. *Ikegami*, 8 Minshū 449 (Sup. Ct., 12 Feb. 1954).

International Union Lines, Ltd. v. *Banno Brothers*, 12 Kakyū minshū 1552 (Osaka Dist. Ct., 30 June 1961).

Iwanari v. *Kurihara*, 10 Minshū 342 (Sup. Ct., 5 Apr. 1956).

Japan v. *Hirata*, 10 Keishū 1605 (Sup. Ct., 11 Dec. 1956).

Japan v. *Sakata* (the *Sunagawa* case), 13 Keishū 3225 (Sup. Ct., G.B., 16 Dec. 1959); English translation in John M. Maki, *Court and Constitution in Japan: Selected Supreme Court Decisions (1948–1960)* (Seattle: University of Washington Press, 1964), p. 305.

Kasuda v. *Matsuura Suisan K.K.*, 22 Minroku 1862 (Gr. Ct. Cass., 7 Oct. 1916).

Kawachi Bank v. *Matsumura*, 10 Kakyū minshū 373 (Osaka Dist. Ct., 23 Feb. 1959).

K.K. Greenhill-Katō Shōkai v. *Shirō Trading Corp.*, 13 Kōsai minshū 696 (Tokyo H. Ct., 29 Oct. 1960).

K.K. Kobayashi Shōten v. *Kenlick Far East K.K.*, 9 Kakyū minshū 111 (Tokyo Dist. Ct., 25 Jan. 1958).

K.K. Kyukutō Sekkei Jimusho v. *Edgar P. Sharp*, 11 Kakyū minshū 2450 (Tokyo Dist. Ct., 7 Dec. 1960).

K.K. Meguro Seisakujo v. *Sōhyō*, 12 Rōminshū 161 (Tokyo D. Ct., 28 Mar. 1961).

Kuchiki Shōji K.K. v. *Mikami K.K.*, 7 Minshū 848, 861 (Gr. Ct. Cass., 27 Oct. 1928).

Lewin v. *Greenberg*, 11 Kakyū minshū 2034 (Tokyo D. Ct., 30 Sept. 1960).

MacDonald, Ltd. & I. H. MacDonald v. *Tomoi Trade Yūgen Kaisha*, unreported case (Tokyo Dist. Ct., 6 May 1966).

Marubeni-Iida K.K. v. *Ajinomoto K.K.*, 10 Kakyū minshū 594 (Tokyo D. Ct., 26 Mar. 1959).

Masuda v. *Higuchi*, 10 Minshū 566 (Sup. Ct., 25 May 1956).

Matsuyama v. *Matsuo*, 24 Minroku 2131 (Gr. Ct. Cass., 5 Nov. 1918).

Mitate v. *Takahashi*, 13 Minroku 36 (Gr. Ct. Cass., 2 Feb. 1907).

Morikawa v. *Mori*, 22 Minroku 1663 (Gr. Ct. Cass., 33 Aug. 1916).

Nagamoto and Takeshita v. *Fukuhisa*, 8 Minshū 1505 (Sup. Ct., 20 Aug. 1954).

Nagase v. *Matsuda*, 20 Minroku 313 (Gr. Ct. Cass., 22 Apr. 1914).

Nakajima v. *Kondō*, 24 Minroku (Gr. Ct. Cass., 10 July 1918).

Nakamura v. *Japan*, 16 Keishū 1953 (Sup. Ct. G. B., 28 Nov. 1962).

Nomura v. *Suzuki*, 14 Minshū 1657 (Sup. Ct. G. B., 6 July 1970).

Oba v. *Toyota* (Nagoya D. Ct., 30 Apr. 1971), reported in *Shōji hōmu kenkyū* (No. 560) 16 (25 May 1967).

Odaka v. *Japan*, 4 Keishū 2257 (Sec. G.B., 15 Nov. 1950).

Ogoshi v. *Tokyo Tatemono*, 22 Minshū 1845 (Gr. Ct. Cass., 4 Oct. 1916).

Ōkura v. *Iwata*, 1 Kakyū minshū 1697 (Tokyo Dist. Ct., 25 Oct. 1950).

Osaka Seiki K.K. v. *Nakata*, 9 Minroku 299 (Gr. Ct. Cass., 10 Mar. 1903).

Ralph A. Fields v. *K.K. Taiheiyō TV*, *Hanrei jihō* (No. 586) 73 (Tokyo Dist. Ct., 6 Sept. 1969).

Ryūkyū Bank v. *Tōkai Denki-Kōji K.K.*, *Hanrei jihō* (No. 602) 90 (Nagoya Dist. Ct., 31 Jan. 1970).

Sakagami v. *Japan*, 7 Minshū 1562 (Sup. Ct. G.B., 8 Oct. 1953).

San'yō Denki case, Rōjun (No. 682) (Yamaguchi Dist. Ct., 29 Mar. 1968).

Shimomura v. *Japan*, 18 Minshū 761 (Gr. Ct. Cass., 19 July 1939).

Shinsei Kōgyō K.K. v. *Shimazaki*, 7 Kakyū minshū 890 (Tokyo Dist. Ct., 9 Apr. 1956).

Shirai K.K. v. *Daiei Marugumi*, 12 Minshū 2861, 2866 (Gr. Ct. Cass., 18 Dec. 1933).

Suzuki v. *Ishigaki*, 10 Minshū 1355 (Sup. Ct. G.B., 1956), *Jurisuto* (No. 209) 44 (1960).

Suzuki v. *Japan*, 6 Minshū 783 (Sup. Ct., G.B., 8 Oct. 1952); English translation in John M. Maki, *Court and Constitution in Japan: Selected Supreme Court Decisions (1948–1960)* (Seattle: University of Washington Press, 1964), p. 364

Taiyō Tochi K.K. v. *Ofuruta*, 9 Minshū 2027 (Sup. Ct., 20 Dec. 1955).

Tamaki v. *Nakagawa*, 25 Minshū 1715 (Gr. Ct. Cass., 25 Sept. 1919).

Texas Co. v. *Gōshi Kaisha Taiheiyō Shōkai*, Hōritsu shimbun (No. 2168) 13 (Tokyo App. Ch., 7 Mar. 1923).

Tōhoku Kōgyō K.K. v. *Tōhoku Aen Kōgyō K.K.*, 6 Kakyū minshū 950 (Tokyo Dist. Ct., 9 May 1960).

Tokiyasu v. *Japan*, 12 Keishū 1694 (Sup. Ct. G.B., 28 May 1958).

Tokyo Rikuunkyoku v. *Kawakami*, 25 Minshū 482 (Sup. Ct., 28 Oct. 1971).

Tomabechi v. *Japan*, 14 Minshū 1206 (Sup. Ct., G.B., 8 June 1960).

Tomita v. *Inoue*, 19 Minshū 2306 (Sup. Ct., 23 Dec. 1965).

Tōwa Kōgyō v. *Mitsui Sempaku K.K.*, 1 Kakyū minshū (Yokohama Dist. Ct., Nov. 1950).

Tsuji v. *Daiei Baseball K.K.*, 12 Minshū 3228 (Sup. Ct., 24 Oct. 1958).

Ujiya v. *Ishizuka*, 4 Kakyū minshū (Osaka Dist. Ct., 17 Feb. 1953).

Unreported v. *Unreported*, 12 (I) *Hanrei taikei* 482 (Tokyo Dist. Ct., 8 Dec. 1928).

Unreported v. *Unreported*, 17 *Hanrei taikei* 94 (Gr. Ct. Cass., 24 Nov. 1924).

Unreported v. *Unreported*, 17 (II) *Hanrei taikei* (Gr. Ct. Cass., 24 Dec. 1932).

Unreported v. *Unreported*, 29 *Hanrei taikei* 704 (Osaka Dist. Ct., 6 Sept. 1939).

Unreported v. *Unreported*, 11 (II) *Hanrei taikei* 1137.

Unreported v. *Unreported*, Hōritsu shimbun (No. 2055) 17 (Tokyo Appellate Chamber, 21 July 1922).

Utano v. *Gyokuzōhō*, 1 Minshū 431 (Gr. Ct. Cass., 26 July 1922).

Utsuro v. *Sasatani*, 19 Minroku 8 (Gr. Ct. Cass., 23 Jan. 1913).

Wakō Seizō Kōgyō K.K. v. *Maruyama*, 7 Minshū 1299 (Sup. Ct., 13 Dec. 1953).

Yamada v. *Bellini*, 10 Minroku 621 (Gr. Ct. Cass., 9 May 1904).

Yamamura v. *Kanzaki*, 23 Minshū 147 (Gr. Ct. Cass., 14 Nov. 1944).

U.S. CASES:

All-Rite Contracting Co. v. *Omey*, 27 Wn. 2d 898, 181 P. 2d 636 (1947).

Altshul Stern & Co., Inc. v. *Mitsui Bussan Kaisha, Ltd.*, 385 F. 2d 158 (1967).

American Locomotive Co. v. *Chemical Research Corp.*, 171 F. 2d 115 (6th Cir., 1948).

Amtorg Trading Corp. v. *Camden Fibre Mills*, 304 N.Y. 519, 109 N.E. 2d 606 (1952).

Arsenis v. *Atlantic Tankers, Ltd.*, 39 Misc. 2d 124, 240 N.Y.S. 2d 69 (Civ. Ct. 1963).

Avco Corp. v. *Preteska*, 22 Conn. Supp. 475, 174 A. 2d 684 (Super. Ct., 1961).

Bank of Pittsburgh v. *United Elec. Coal Co.*, 16 Del. Ch. 151, 142 Atl. 368 (Ch. Ct. 1928), 6 A.L.R. 2d 910n.

Barnhart v. *Civil Serv. Employees Ins. Co.*, 16 Utah 2d 223, 398 P. 2d 873 (1965).

Barnes v. *Avery*, 192 Ga. 874, 16 S. E. 2d 861 (1961).

Barrett v. *King*, 181 Mass. 476, 63 N.E. 934 (1902).

Batson Yarn & Fabrics Machinery Group, Inc. v. *Saurer-Allma GmbH-Allgauer Maschinenbau*, 311 F. Supp. 68 (D. Ct. So. Car. 1970).

Bell v. *McKay & Co.*, 196 Ala. 408, 72 So. 83 (1916).

Benitendi v. *Kenton Hotel, Inc.*, 294 N.Y. 112, 60 N.E. 2d 829 (1945).

Bernhardt v. *Polygraphic Co. of Am.*, 350 U.S. 198 (1956).

Black v. *Cutter Labs.*, 43 Cal. 2d 788, 278 P. 2d 905, aff'd. 351 U.S. 292 (1956).

Boughton v. *Farmers Ins. Exch.*, 354 P. 2d 1085 (Okla. 1960).

Burchell v. *Marsh*, 58 U.S. (17 How.) 344 (1854).

California Lima Bean Growers' Ass'n. v. *Mankowitz*, 9 N.J. Misc. 362, 154 Atl. 532 (Cir. Ct. 1931).

Campbell v. *Campbell*, 198 Kan. 181, 422 P. 2d 932 (1967), 7 *Washburn L. Rev.* 110–14.

Carbon Black Export v. *S.S. Monrosa*, 254 F. 2d 297 (5th Cir. 1958).

Chapman v. *Zakzaska*, 273 Wis. 64, 76 N.W. 2d 437 (1956).

Chemical Carriers v. *L. Smit & Co. Internationale S.*, 154 F. Supp. 886 (S.D.N.Y. 1957).

Clogston v. *Schiff-Lang Co.*, 2 Cal. 2d 414, 41 P. 2d 555 (1935).

Cook v. *Kuljan Corp.*, 201 F. Supp. 531 (E.D. Pa. 1962).

Czarnikow v. *Roth, Schmidt & Co.*, 2 K.B. 478 (1922).

Danielson v. *Entre Rios Rys.*, 22 F. 2d 326 (D. Md. 1927).

DeBoy v. *Harris*, 207 Md. 212, 13 A. 2d 903 (1955).

Dred Scott v. *Sanford*, 60 U.S. (19 How.) 404 (1857).

E. K. Buck Retail Stores v. *Harkert*, 157 Neb. 867, 62 N.W. 2d 288 (1954).

El Hoss Eng'r. & Transp. Co. v. *American Independent Oil Co.*, 287 F. 2d 346 (2d Cir.), *cert. denied*, 368 U.S. 837 (1961).

Elsbach v. *Mulligan*, 58 Cal. App. 2d 354, 136 P. 2d 651 (1943).

Erie R.R. v. *Tompkins*, 304 U.S. 64 (1938).

Excelsior Motor Mfg. & Supply Co. v. *Sound Equipment, Inc.*, 73 F. 2d 725 (7th Cir. 1934).

Ezell v. *Rocky Mtn. Bean & Elevator Co.*, 76 Colo. 409, 232 P. 680 (1925).

Fenster v. *Makovsky*, 67 So. 2d 427 (Fla. 1953).

Franklin v. *Nat C. Goldstone Agency*, 33 Cal. 2d 628, 204 P. 2d 37 (1949).

Fudickar v. *Guardian Mut. Life Ins. Co.*, 62 N.Y. 392 (1875).

Gasparini Excavating Corp. v. *Pennsylvania Turnpike Comm'n.*, 409 Pa. 136, 185 A. 2d 320 (1962).

General Constr. Co. v. *Hering Realty Co.*, 201 F. Supp. 487 (E.D.S.C. 1962).

Giuffre v. *The Magdalene Vinnen and North German Lloyd*, 152 F. Supp. 123 (E.D.N.Y. 1957).

Goodman v. *Lazarus*, App. Div. 2d 530, 222 N.Y.S. 2d 891 (1961).

Grayson-Robinson Stores v. *Ires Constr. Corp.*, 8 N.Y. 2d 133, 168 N.E. 2d 377, 202 N.Y.S. 2d 303 (1960).

Green v. *Wolff*, 372 P. 2d 427 (Mont. 1962).

Greyhound Corp. v. *Division 1384*, 44 Wn. 2d 808, 271 P. 24 689 (1954).

Healy v. *Brewster*, 30 *Cal. Reptr.* 129, 380 P. 2d 817 (1963).

Hill v. *Mercury Record Corp.*, 26 Ill. App. 2d 350, 168 N.E. 2d 461 (1960).

Huntington Corp. v. *Inwood Constr. Co.*, 348 S.W. 2d 442 (Tex. Civ. App. 1961).

Huntley v. *Alejandre*, 139 So. 2d 911 (Fla. 1962).

Interinsurance Exch. of Auto Club v. *Bailes*, 219 Cal. App. 2d 830, 33 *Cal. Rptr.* 533 (Dis. Ct., App. 1963).

Jackson v. *Hooper*, 76 N.J. Eq. 592, 75 Atl. 568 (Ct. Err. & App. 1910).

James H. Rhodes & Co. v. *Chausovky*, 137 N.J.L. 459, 60 A. 2d 623 (Sup. Ct. 1948).

Johnson v. *Spartanburg County Fair Ass'n.*, 210 S.C. 56, 41 S.E. 2d 599 (1947).

Kaiser-Frazer Corp. v. *Otis & Co.*, 195 F. 2d 838 (2d Cir. 1952).

Kent v. *Universal Film Mfg. Co.*, 200 App. Div. 539, 193 N.Y. Supp. 838 (1922).

King v. *Beale*, 198 Va. 802, 96 S.E. 2d 765 (1957).

Kyler v. *United States Trotting Ass'n.*, 12 App. Div. 874, 210 N.Y.S. 2d 25 (1961).

London v. *Zachery*, 92 Cal. App. 2d 654, 207 P. 2d 1067 (1949).

Loverdos v. *Vomvouras*, 200 N.Y.S. 2d 921 (1960).

Loving & Evans v. *Black*, 33 Cal. 2d 603, 204 P. 2d 23 (1949).

Ludwig Monwinckels Rederi v. *Dow Chemical Co.*, 297 N.Y.S. 2d 1011 (1969).

Lummus Co. v. *Commonwealth Oil Refinery Co.*, 280 F. 2d 915 (1st Cir. 1960), *cert. denied* 364 U.S. 911 (1960).

Marbury v. *Madison*, 5 U.S. (1 Cranch) 137 (1803).

Miller v. *Allstate Ins. Co.*, 238 F. Supp. 565 (W.D. Pa. 1965).

Moyer v. *Van-Dye-Way Corp.*, 126 F. 2d 339 (3d Cir., 1942).

Murray Oil Prods. Co. v. *Mitsui & Co.*, 146 F. 2d 381 (2d Cir., 1944).

Necchi v. *Necchi Sewing Mach. Sales Corp.*, 348 F. 2d 693 (2d Cir. 1965).

New England Trust Co. v. *Abbott*, 162 Mass. 148, 38 N.E. 432 (1894).

Nippon Hodō v. *United States*, 285 F. 2d 766 (Ct. Cl. 1961).

Nippon Ki-Itō Kaisha v. *Ewing-Thomas Corp.*, 313 Pa. 442, 170 Atl. 286 (1934).

Nolan v. *J. & M. Doyle Co.*, 338 Pa. 398, 13 A. 2d 59 (1940).

Oilcakes & Oilseeds Trading Co. v. *Sinason Teicher Inter-Am. Grain Corp.*, 9 Misc. 2d 651, 170 N.Y.S. 2d 378 (Sup. Ct., 1958).

Oregon-Pacific Forest Prods. Corp. v. *Welsh Panel Co.*, 248 F. Supp. 903 (D. Ore. 1965).

Orion Shipping & Trading Co. v. *Eastern States Petroleum Corp. of Panama*, 206 F. Supp. 777 (S.D.N.Y. 1962), aff'd. 312 F. 2d 299 (2d Cir.), *cert. denied*, 373 U.S. 949 (1963).

Park Constr. Co. v. *Independent School Dist., No. 32*, 209 Minn. 182, 296 N.W. 475 (1941).

Prima Paint Corp. v. *Flood and Conklin Mfg. Co.*, 388 U.S. 395, 87 S. Ct. 1801 (1967).

Radiator Specialty Co. v. *Cannon Mills, Inc.*, 97 F. 2d 318 (4th Cir., 1938).

Raytheon Co. v. *Rheem Mfg. Co.*, 322 F. 2d 173 (9th Cir. 1963).

Reid v. *Covert*, 354 U.S. 1 (1957).

Robert Lawrence Co. v. *Devonshire Fabrics, Inc.*, 271 F. 2d 402 (2d Cir. 1959), *cert. granted*, 362 U.S. 909, *cert. dismissed per stipulation*, 364 U.S. 801 (1960).

San Martine Compania de Navegacion, S.A. v. *Saguenay Terminals, Ltd.*, 293 F. 2d 796 (9th Cir. 1961).

Sargant v. *Monroe*, 268 App. Div. 123, 49 N.Y.S. 2d 546 (1944).

Sensabaugh v. *Polson Plywood Co.*, 135 Mont. 562, 342 P. 2d 1064 (1959).

Shanferoke Coal & Supply Corp. v. *Westchester Service Corp.*, 293 U.S. 449 (1934).

Simons v. *A. C. Israel Commodity Co.*, 37 Misc. 2d 299, 238 N.Y.S. 2d 341 (Sup. Ct. 1962).

Skinner v. *Gaither Corp.*, 234 N.C. 385, 67 S.E. 2d 267 (1951).

S. M. Wolff Co. v. *Tulkoff*, 9 N.Y. 2d 356, 174 N.E. 2d 478, 214 N.Y.S. 2d 374 (1961).

South East Atl. Shipping Ltd. v. *Garnac Grain Co.*, 356 F. 2d 189 (2d Cir. 1966).

Stalinski v. *Pyramid Elec. Co.*, 6 N.Y. 2d 159, 160 N.E. 2d 78, 188 N.Y.S. 541 (1959).

Standard Magnesium Corp. v. *Fuchs*, 251 F. 2d 455 (10 Cir., 1957).

Takemura v. *S.S. Tsuneshima Maru*, 197 F. Supp. 909 (S.D.N.Y. 1960).

Tatsuuma K.K. Kaisha v. *Prescott*, 4 F. 2d 670 (9th Cir. 1925).

Torano v. *Motor Vehicle Acc. Indemn. Corp.*, 15 N.Y. 2d 882, 206 N.E. 2d 353, 258 N.Y.S. 2d 418 (1965).

United Ass'n of Journeymen & Apprentices of Plumbing v. *Stine*, 76 Nev. 189, 351 P. 2d 965 (1960).

United States v. *L. B. Miller Inc.*, 81 F. 2d 8 (2d. Cir. 1936).

United Steelworkers v. *American Mfg. Co.*, 363 U.S. 564 (1960).

United Steelworkers v. *Enterprise Wheel & Car Corp.*, 363 U.S. 593 (1960).

United Steelworkers v. *Warrior & Gulf Nav. Co.*, 363 U.S. 574 (1960).

U.S. v. *Aluminum Co. of America*, 748 F. 2d 416 (2d Cir. 1945).

U.S. v. *Lerner Co.*, 215 F. Supp. 603 (1963).

U.S. Fid. and Guar. Co. v. *Dawson Produce Co.*, 200 Okla. 540, 197 P. 2d 978 (1948).

Vector S.S. Co. v. *Mitsubishi Bank, Ltd.*, 12 App. Div. 2d 910, 210 N.Y.S. 2d 910 (1961).

Weisman v. *Awnair Corp. of America*, 3 N.Y. 2d 444, 144 N.E. 2d 415 (1957).

W. H. Muller & Co. v. *Swedish Am. Line, Ltd.*, 224 F. 2d 806 (2d Cir.) *cert. denied*, 350 U.S. 903 (1955).

Wilson v. *Gregg*, 208 Okla. 291, 255 P. 2d 517 (1953).

Zip Mfg. Co. v. *Pep Mfg. Co.*, 44 F. 2d 184 (D.C. Del. 1930).

Index